The Dialogues of Plato in Five Volumes

Vol II:
Containing Meno, Euthyphro, Apology, Crito, Phaedo, Gorgias, Appendix I - Lesser, Hippias, Alcibiades I, Menexenus, Appendix II - Alcibiades II, Eryxias

Translated with Anlyses and Introductions by
B. Jowett, M.A.

Edited by
Paul A. Böer, Sr.

VERITATIS SPLENDOR PUBLICATIONS

et cognoscetis veritatem et veritas liberabit vos (Jn 8:32)

MMXII

The Dialogues of Plato

This is a re-publication of a work found in:

The Dialogues of Plato, vol. 2, translated into English with Analyses and Introductions by B. Jowett, M.A. in Five Volumes. 3rd edition revised and corrected (Oxford University Press, 1892).

The contents of which is in the public domain.

However, this edition is copyrighted.

ALL RIGHTS RESERVED.

This publication may not be reproduced, stored in a retrieval system, or transmitted in any form or by any means, in whole or in part, without written permission from the Publisher, except as permitted by United States and International copyright law.

Copyright © 2012. Veritatis Splendor Publications.

AD MAJOREM DEI GLORIAM

The Dialogues of Plato

TABLE OF CONTENTS

INTRODUCTION TO MENO. 7
On the Ideas of Plato. 14
MENO. 25
INTRODUCTION TO EUTHYPHRO. 96
EUTHYPHRO. 101
INTRODUCTION TO APOLOGY. 133
APOLOGY. 142
INTRODUCTION TO CRITO. 164
CRITO. 167
INTRODUCTION TO PHAEDO. 185
PHAEDO. 212
INTRODUCTION TO GORGIAS. 286
The Myths of Plato. 321
GORGIAS. 328
APPENDIX I. 484
INTRODUCTION TO LESSER HIPPIAS. 489
LESSER HIPPIAS. 492
INTRODUCTION TO ALCIBIADES I. 523
ALCIBIADES I. 526
INTRODUCTION TO MENEXENUS. 628
MENEXENUS. 631
APPENDIX II. ALCIBIADES II. ERYXIAS. 646
INTRODUCTION TO ALCIBIADES II. 648
INTRODUCTION TO ERYXIAS. 673
ERYXIAS. 674

The Dialogues of Plato

INTRODUCTION TO MENO.

Meno. Analysis.

70This Dialogue begins abruptly with a question of Meno, who asks 'whether virtue can be taught.' Socrates replies that he 71does not as yet know what virtue is, and has never known any one who did. 'Then he cannot have met Gorgias when he was at Athens.' Yes, Socrates had met him, but he has a bad memory, and has forgotten what Gorgias said. Will Meno tell him his own notion, which is probably not very different from 72that of Gorgias? 'O yes—nothing easier: there is the virtue of a man, of a woman, of an old man, and of a child; there is a virtue of every age and state of life, all of which may be easily described.'

73Socrates reminds Meno that this is only an enumeration of the virtues and not a definition of the notion which is common to them all. In a second attempt Meno defines virtue to be 'the power of command.' But to this, again, exceptions are taken. For there must be a virtue of those who obey, as well as of those who command; and the power of command must be justly or not unjustly exercised. Meno is very ready to admit that justice is virtue: 'Would you say virtue or a virtue, for there are other 74virtues, such as courage, temperance, and the like; just as round is a figure, and black and white are colours, and yet there are other figures and other colours. Let Meno take the examples of figure and colour, and try to define them.' Meno confesses his inability, and after a process of interrogation, in which Socrates 75explains to him the nature of a 'simile in multis,' Socrates himself defines figure as 'the accompaniment of colour.' But some one may object that he does not know the meaning of the word 'colour;' and if he is a candid friend, and not a mere disputant, Socrates is willing to furnish him with a simpler and more philosophical definition, into which no disputed word is allowed to intrude: 'Figure is the limit of form.' Meno imperiously 76insists that he must still have a definition of colour. Some raillery follows; and at length Socrates is induced to reply, 'that colour is the effluence of form, sensible, and in due proportion to the sight.' This definition is exactly suited to the taste of Meno, who welcomes the familiar language of Gorgias and Empedocles. Socrates is of opinion that the more abstract or dialectical definition of figure is far better.

Now that Meno has been made to understand the nature of a general definition, he answers in the spirit of a Greek gentleman, and in the words of a poet, 'that virtue is to delight in 77things honourable, and to have the power of getting them.' This is a nearer approximation than he has yet made to a complete definition, and, regarded as a piece of proverbial or popular morality, is not far from the truth. But the objection is urged, 'that the honourable is the good,' and as every one equally desires the good, the point of the definition is contained in the words, 78'the power of getting them.' 'And they must be got justly or with justice.' The definition will then stand thus: 'Virtue is the power of getting good with justice.' But justice is a part of 79virtue, and therefore virtue is the getting of good with a part of virtue. The definition repeats the word defined.

Meno complains that the conversation of Socrates has the effect 80of a torpedo's shock upon him. When he talks with other persons he has plenty to say about virtue; in the presence of Socrates, his thoughts desert him. Socrates replies that he is only the cause of perplexity in others, because he is himself perplexed. He proposes to continue the enquiry. But how, asks Meno, can he enquire either into what he knows or into what he does not know? This is a sophistical puzzle, which, 81as Socrates remarks, saves a great deal of trouble to him who accepts it. But the puzzle has a real difficulty latent under it, to which Socrates will endeavour to find a reply. The difficulty is the origin of knowledge:—

He has heard from priests and priestesses, and from the poet Pindar, of an immortal soul which is born again and again in successive periods of existence, returning into this world when she has paid the penalty of ancient crime, and, having wandered over all places of the upper and under world, and seen and known all things at one time or other, is by association out of one thing capable of recovering all. For nature is of one kindred; and 82every soul has a seed or germ which may be developed into all knowledge. The existence of this latent knowledge is further proved by the interrogation of one of Meno's slaves, who, in the skilful hands of Socrates, is made to acknowledge some elementary relations of geometrical figures. The theorem that 83the square of the diagonal is double the square of the side—that famous discovery of primitive mathematics, in honour of which the legendary Pythagoras is said to have sacrificed a hecatomb—is elicited from him. The first step in the process of teaching has made him conscious of his own ignorance. He has had the 'torpedo's shock' given him, and is the better for the operation. 86But whence had the uneducated man this knowledge? He had never learnt geometry in this world; nor was it born with him; he must therefore have had it when he was not a man. And as he always either was or was not a man, he must have always had it. (Cp. Phaedo, 73 B.)

After Socrates has given this specimen of the true nature of teaching, the original question of the teachableness of virtue is renewed. Again he professes a desire to know 'what virtue is' 87first. But he is willing to argue the question, as mathematicians say, under an hypothesis. He will assume that if virtue is knowledge, 88then virtue can be taught. (This was the stage of the argument at which the Protagoras concluded.)

Socrates has no difficulty in showing that virtue is a good, and that goods, whether of body or mind, must be under the direction of knowledge. Upon the assumption just made, then, 89virtue is teachable. But where are the teachers? There are none to be found. This is extremely discouraging. Virtue is no sooner discovered to be teachable, than the discovery follows that it is not taught. Virtue, therefore, is and is not teachable.

90In this dilemma an appeal is made to Anytus, a respectable and well-to-do citizen of the old school, and a family friend of Meno, 91who happens to be present. He is asked 'whether Meno shall 92go to the Sophists and be taught.' The suggestion throws him into 93a rage. 'To whom, then, shall Meno go?' asks Socrates. To any Athenian gentleman—to the great Athenian statesmen of past times. Socrates replies here, as elsewhere (Laches, 179 C foll.; Prot. 319 foll.), that Themistocles, Pericles, and other great men, 94had sons to whom they would surely, if they could have done so, have imparted their own political wisdom; but no one ever heard that these sons of theirs were remarkable for anything except riding and wrestling and similar accomplishments. Anytus is angry at the imputation which is cast on his favourite statesmen, and on a class to which he supposes himself to belong (cp. 95 A); he breaks off with a significant hint. The mention of 95another opportunity of talking with him (99 E), and the suggestion that Meno may do the Athenian people a service by pacifying him (100), are evident allusions to the trial of Socrates.

Socrates returns to the consideration of the question 'whether virtue is teachable,' which was denied on the ground that there are no teachers of it: (for the Sophists are bad teachers, and the 96rest of the world do not profess to teach). But there is another point which we failed to observe, and in which Gorgias has never instructed Meno, nor Prodicus Socrates. This is the nature of right opinion. For virtue may be under the guidance of right 97opinion as well as of knowledge; and right opinion is for practical purposes as good as knowledge, but is incapable of being taught, and is also liable, like the images of Daedalus, to 'walk off,' 98because not bound by the tie of the cause. This is the sort of instinct which is possessed by statesmen, who are not wise or knowing persons, but only inspired or divine. The higher virtue, 99which is identical with knowledge, is an ideal only. If the statesman had this knowledge, and could teach what he knew, he would be like Tiresias in the world below,—'he alone has wisdom, 100but the rest flit like shadows.'

Introduction.

This Dialogue is an attempt to answer the question, Can virtue be taught? No one would either ask or answer such a question in modern times. But in the age of Socrates it was only by an effort that the mind could rise to a general notion of virtue as distinct from the particular virtues of courage, liberality, and the like. And when a hazy conception of this ideal was attained, it was only by a further effort that the question of the teachableness of virtue could be resolved.

The answer which is given by Plato is paradoxical enough, and seems rather intended to stimulate than to satisfy enquiry. Virtue is knowledge, and therefore virtue can be taught. But virtue is not taught, and therefore in this higher and ideal sense there is no virtue and no knowledge. The teaching of the Sophists is confessedly inadequate, and Meno, who is their pupil, is ignorant of the very nature of general terms. He can only produce out of their armoury the sophism, 'that you can neither enquire into what you know nor into what you do not know;' to which Socrates replies by his theory of reminiscence.

To the doctrine that virtue is knowledge, Plato has been constantly tending in the previous Dialogues. But the new truth is no sooner found than it vanishes away. 'If there is knowledge, there must be teachers; and where are the teachers?' There is no knowledge in the higher sense of systematic, connected, reasoned knowledge, such as may one day be attained, and such as Plato himself seems to see in some far off vision of a single science. And there are no teachers in the higher sense of the word; that is to say, no real teachers who will arouse the spirit of enquiry in their pupils, and not merely instruct them in rhetoric or impart to them ready-made information for a fee of 'one' or of 'fifty drachms.' Plato is desirous of deepening the notion of education, and therefore he asserts the paradox that there are no educators. This paradox, though different in form, is not really different from the remark which is often made in modern times by those who would depreciate either the methods of education commonly employed, or the standard attained—that 'there is no true education among us.'

There remains still a possibility which must not be overlooked. Even if there be no true knowledge, as is proved by 'the wretched state of education,' there may be right opinion, which is a sort of guessing or divination resting on no knowledge of causes, and incommunicable to others. This is the gift which our statesmen have, as is proved by the circumstance that they are unable to impart their knowledge to their sons. Those who are possessed of it cannot be said to be men of science or philosophers, but they are inspired and divine.

There may be some trace of irony in this curious passage, which forms the concluding portion of the Dialogue. But Plato certainly does not mean to intimate that the supernatural or divine is the true basis of human life. To him knowledge, if only attainable in this world, is of all things the most divine. Yet, like other philosophers, he is willing to admit that 'probability is the guide. of life ;' and he is at the same time desirous of contrasting the wisdom which governs the world with a higher wisdom. There are many instincts, judgments, and anticipations of the human mind which cannot be reduced to rule, and of which the grounds cannot always be given in words. A person may have some skill or latent experience which he is able to use himself and is yet unable to teach others, because he has no principles, and is incapable of collecting or arranging his ideas. He has practice, but not theory; art, but not science. This is a true fact of psychology, which is recognized by Plato in this passage. But he is far from saying, as some have imagined, that inspiration or divine grace is to be regarded as higher than knowledge. He would not have preferred the poet or man of action to the philosopher, or the virtue of custom to the virtue based upon ideas.

Also here, as in the Ion and Phaedrus, Plato appears to acknowledge an unreasoning element in the higher nature of man. The philosopher only has knowledge, and yet the statesman and the poet are inspired. There may be a sort of irony in regarding in this way the gifts of genius. But there is no reason to suppose that he is deriding them, any more than he is deriding the phenomena of love or of enthusiasm in the Symposium, or of oracles in the Apology, or of divine intimations when he is speaking of the daemonium of Socrates. He recognizes the lower form of right opinion, as well as the higher one of science, in the spirit of one who desires to include in his philosophy every aspect of human life; just as he recognizes the existence of popular opinion as a fact, and the Sophists as the expression of it.

This Dialogue contains the first intimation of the doctrine of reminiscence and of the immortality of the soul. The proof is very slight, even slighter than in the Phaedo and Republic. Because men had abstract ideas in a previous state, they must have always had them, and their souls therefore must have always existed (86 A). For they must always have been either men or not men. The fallacy of the latter words is transparent. And Socrates himself appears to be conscious of their weakness; for he adds immediately afterwards, 'I have said some things of which I am not altogether confident.' (Cp. Phaedo 114 D, 115 D.) It may be observed, however, that the fanciful notion of pre-existence is combined with a true but partial view of the origin and unity of knowledge, and of the association of ideas. Knowledge is prior to any particular knowledge, and exists not in the previous state of the individual, but of the race. It is potential, not actual, and can only be appropriated by strenuous exertion.

The idealism of Plato is here presented in a less developed form than in the Phaedo and Phaedrus. Nothing is said of the pre-existence of ideas of justice, temperance, and the like. Nor is Socrates positive of anything but the duty of enquiry (86 B). The doctrine of reminiscence too is explained more in accordance with fact and experience as arising out of the affinities of nature (ἅτε τῆς φύσεως ὅλης συγγενοῦς οὔσης). Modern philosophy says that all things in nature are dependent on one another; the ancient philosopher had the same truth latent in his mind when he affirmed that out of one thing all the rest may be recovered. The subjective was converted by him into an objective; the mental phenomenon of the association of ideas (cp. Phaedo 73 foll.) became a real chain of existences. The germs of two valuable principles of education may also be gathered from the 'words of priests and priestesses:' (1) that true knowledge is a knowledge of causes (cp. Aristotle's theory of ἐπιστήμη); and (2) that the process of learning consists not in what is brought to the learner, but in what is drawn out of him.

Some lesser points of the dialogue may be noted, such as (1) the acute observation that Meno prefers the familiar definition, which is embellished with poetical language, to the better and truer one (76 D); or (2) the shrewd reflection, which may admit of an application to modern as well as to ancient teachers, that the Sophists having made large fortunes; this must surely be a criterion of their powers of teaching, for that no man could get a living by shoemaking who was not a good shoemaker (91 C); or (3) the remark conveyed, almost in a word, that the verbal sceptic is saved the labour of thought and enquiry (οὐδεν δει τω τοιούτῳ ζητήσεως, 80 E). Characteristic also of the temper of the Socratic enquiry is, (4) the proposal to discuss the teachableness of virtue under an hypothesis, after the manner of the mathematicians (87 A); and (5) the repetition of the favourite doctrine which occurs so frequently in the earlier and more Socratic Dialogues, and gives a colour to all of them—that mankind only desire evil through ignorance (77, 78 foll.); (6) the experiment of eliciting from the slave-boy the mathematical truth which is latent in him, and (7) the remark (84 B) that he is all the better for knowing his ignorance.

The character of Meno, like that of Critias, has no relation to the actual circumstances of his life. Plato is silent about his treachery to the ten thousand Greeks, which Xenophon has recorded, as he is also silent about the crimes of Critias. He is a Thessalian Alcibiades, rich and luxurious—a spoilt child of fortune, and is described as the hereditary friend of the great king. Like Alcibiades he is inspired with an ardent desire of knowledge, and is equally willing to learn of Socrates and of the Sophists. He may be regarded as standing in the same relation to Gorgias as Hippocrates in the Protagoras to the other great Sophist. He is the sophisticated youth on whom Socrates tries his cross-examining powers, just as in the Charmides, the Lysis, and the Euthydemus, ingenuous boyhood is made the subject of a similar experiment. He is treated by Socrates in a half-playful manner suited to his character; at the same time he appears not quite to understand the process to which he is being subjected. For he is exhibited as ignorant of the very elements of dialectics, in which the Sophists have failed to instruct their disciple. His definition of virtue as 'the power and desire of attaining things honourable,' like the first definition of justice in the Republic, is taken from a poet. His answers have a sophistical ring, and at the same time show the sophistical incapacity to grasp a general notion.

Anytus is the type of the narrow-minded man of the world, who is indignant at innovation, and equally detests the popular teacher and the true philosopher. He seems, like Aristophanes, to regard the new opinions, whether of Socrates or the Sophists, as fatal to Athenian greatness. He is of the same class as Callicles in the Gorgias, but of a different variety; the immoral and sophistical doctrines of Callicles are not attributed to him. The moderation with which he is described is remarkable, if he be the accuser of Socrates, as is apparently indicated by his parting words. Perhaps Plato may have been desirous of showing that the accusation of Socrates was not to be attributed to badness or malevolence, but rather to a tendency in men's minds. Or he may have been regardless of the historical truth of the characters of his dialogue, as in the case of Meno and Critias. Like Chaerephon (Apol. 21) the real Anytus was a democrat, and had joined Thrasybulus in the conflict with the thirty.

The Protagoras arrived at a sort of hypothetical conclusion, that if 'virtue is knowledge, it can be taught.' In the Euthydemus, Socrates himself offered an example of the manner in which the true teacher may draw out the mind of youth; this was in contrast to the quibbling follies of the Sophists. In the Meno the subject is more developed; the foundations of the enquiry are laid deeper, and the nature of knowledge is more distinctly explained. There is a progression by antagonism of two opposite aspects of philosophy. But at the moment when we approach nearest, the truth doubles upon us and passes out of our reach. We seem to find that the ideal of knowledge is irreconcilable with experience. In human life there is indeed the profession of knowledge, but right opinion is our actual guide. There is another sort of progress from the general notions of Socrates, who asked simply, 'what is friendship?' 'what is temperance?' 'what is courage?' as in the Lysis, Charmides, Laches, to the transcendentalism of Plato, who, in the second stage of his philosophy, sought to find the nature of knowledge in a prior and future state of existence.

The difficulty in framing general notions which has appeared in this and in all the previous Dialogues recurs in the Gorgias and Theaetetus as well as in the Republic. In the Gorgias too the statesmen reappear, but in stronger opposition to the philosopher. They are no longer allowed to have a divine insight, but, though acknowledged to have been clever men and good speakers, are denounced as 'blind leaders of the blind.' The doctrine of the immortality of the soul is also carried further, being made the foundation not only of a theory of knowledge, but of a doctrine of rewards and punishments. In the Republic the relation of knowledge to virtue is described in a manner more consistent with modern distinctions. The existence of the virtues without the possession of knowledge in the higher or philosophical sense is admitted to be possible. Right opinion is again introduced in the Theaetetus as an account of knowledge, but is rejected on the ground that it is irrational (as here, because it is not bound by the tie of the cause), and also because the conception of false opinion is given up as hopeless. The doctrines of Plato are necessarily different at different times of his life, as new distinctions are realized, or new stages of thought attained by him. We are not therefore justified, in order to take away the appearance of inconsistency, in attributing to him hidden meanings or remote allusions.

There are no external criteria by which we can determine the date of the Meno. There is no reason to suppose that any of the Dialogues of Plato were written before the death of Socrates; the Meno, which appears to be one of the earliest of them, is proved to have been of a later date by the allusion of Anytus (94 E, 95 A. Cp. also 80 B, 100 B).

We cannot argue that Plato was more likely to have written, as he has done, of Meno before than after his miserable death; for we have already seen, in the examples of Charmides and Critias, that the characters in Plato are very far from resembling the same characters in history. The repulsive picture which is given of him in the Anabasis of Xenophon (ii. 6), where he also appears as the friend of Aristippus 'and a fair youth having lovers,' has no other trait of likeness to the Meno of Plato.

The place of the Meno in the series is doubtfully indicated by internal evidence. The main character of the Dialogue is Socrates; but to the 'general definitions' of Socrates is added the Platonic doctrine of reminiscence. The problems of virtue and knowledge have been discussed in the Lysis, Laches, Charmides, and Protagoras; the puzzle about knowing and learning has already appeared in the Euthydemus. The doctrines of immortality and pre-existence are carried further in the Phaedrus and Phaedo; the distinction between opinion and knowledge is more fully developed in the Theaetetus. The lessons of Prodicus, whom he facetiously calls his master, are still running in the mind of Socrates. Unlike the later Platonic Dialogues, the Meno arrives at no conclusion. Hence we are led to place the Dialogue at some point of time later than the Protagoras, and earlier than the Phaedrus and Gorgias. The place which is assigned to it in this work is due mainly to the desire to bring together in a single volume all the Dialogues which contain allusions to the trial and death of Socrates.

On the Ideas of Plato.

Plato's doctrine of ideas has attained an imaginary clearness and definiteness which is not to be found in his own writings. The popular account of them is partly derived from one or two passages in his Dialogues interpreted without regard to their poetical environment. It is due also to the misunderstanding of him by the Aristotelian school; and the erroneous notion has been further narrowed and has become fixed by the realism of the schoolmen. This popular view of the Platonic ideas may be summed up in some such formula as the following: 'Truth consists not in particulars, but in universals, which have a place in the mind of God, or in some far-off heaven. These were revealed to men in a former state of existence, and are recovered by reminiscence (ἀνάμνησις) or association from sensible things. The sensible things are not realities, but shadows only, in relation to the truth.' These unmeaning propositions are hardly suspected to be a caricature of a great theory of knowledge, which Plato in various ways and under many figures of speech is seeking to unfold. Poetry has been converted into dogma; and it is not remarked that the Platonic ideas are to be found only in about a third of Plato's writings and are not confined to him. The forms which they assume are numerous, and if taken literally, inconsistent with one another. At one time we are in the clouds of mythology, at another among the abstractions of mathematics or metaphysics; we pass imperceptibly from one to the other. Reason and fancy are mingled in the same passage. The ideas are sometimes described as many, coextensive with the universals of sense and also with the first principles of ethics; or again they are absorbed into the single idea of good, and subordinated to it. They are not more certain than facts, but they are equally certain (Phaedo 100 A). They are both personal and impersonal. They are abstract terms: they are also the causes of things; and they are even transformed into the demons or spirits by whose help God made the world. And the idea of good (Rep. vi. 505 ff.) may without violence be converted into the Supreme Being, who 'because He was good' created all things (Tim. 29 E).

It would be a mistake to try and reconcile these differing modes of thought. They are not to be regarded seriously as having a distinct meaning. They are parables, prophecies, myths, symbols, revelations, aspirations after an unknown world. They derive their origin from a deep religious and contemplative feeling, and also from an observation of curious mental phenomena. They gather up the elements of the previous philosophies, which they put together in a new form. Their great diversity shows the tentative character of early endeavours to think. They have not yet settled down into a single system. Plato uses them, though he also criticises them; he acknowledges that both he and others are always talking about them, especially about the Idea of Good; and that they are not peculiar to himself (Phaedo 100 B; Rep. vi. 505; Soph. 248 ff.). But in his later writings he seems to have laid aside the old forms of them. As he proceeds he makes for himself new modes of expression more akin to the Aristotelian logic.

Yet amid all these varieties and incongruities, there is a common meaning or spirit which pervades his writings, both those in which he treats of the ideas and those in which he is silent about them. This is the spirit of idealism, which in the history of philosophy has had many names and taken many forms, and has in a measure influenced those who seemed to be most averse to it. It has often been charged with inconsistency and fancifulness, and yet has had an elevating effect on human nature, and has exercised a wonderful charm and interest over a few spirits who have been lost in the thought of it. It has been banished again and again, but has always returned. It has attempted to leave the earth and soar heavenwards, but soon has found that only in experience could any solid foundation of knowledge be laid. It has degenerated into pantheism, but has again emerged. No other knowledge has given an equal stimulus to the mind. It is the science of sciences, which are also ideas, and under either aspect require to be defined. They can only be thought of in due proportion when conceived in relation to one another. They are the glasses through which the kingdoms of science are seen, but at a distance. All the greatest minds, except when living in an age of reaction against them, have unconsciously fallen under their power.

The account of the Platonic ideas in the Meno is the simplest and clearest, and we shall best illustrate their nature by giving this first and then comparing the manner in which they are described elsewhere, e.g. in the Phaedrus, Phaedo, Republic; to which may be added the criticism of them in the Parmenides, the personal form which is attributed to them in the Timaeus, the logical character which they assume in the Sophist and Philebus, and the allusion to them in the Laws (xii. 964). In the Cratylus they dawn upon him with the freshness of a newly-discovered thought (439).

The Meno (81 ff.) goes back to a former state of existence, in which men did and suffered good and evil, and received the reward or punishment of them until their sin was purged away and they were allowed to return to earth. This is a tradition of the olden time, to which priests and poets bear witness. The souls of men returning to earth bring back a latent memory of ideas, which were known to them in a former state. The recollection is awakened into life and consciousness by the sight of the things which resemble them on earth. The soul evidently possesses such innate ideas before she has had time to acquire them. This is proved by an experiment tried on one of Meno's slaves, from whom Socrates elicits truths of arithmetic and geometry, which he had never learned in this world. He must therefore have brought them with him from another.

The notion of a previous state of existence is found in the verses of Empedocles and in the fragments of Heracleitus. It was the natural answer to two questions, 'Whence came the soul? What is the origin of evil?' and prevailed far and wide in the East. It found its way into Hellas probably through the medium of Orphic and Pythagorean rites and mysteries. It was easier to think of a former than of a future life, because such a life has really existed for the race though not for the individual, and all men come into the world, if not 'trailing clouds of glory,' at any rate able to enter into the inheritance of the past. In the Phaedrus (245 ff.), as well as in the Meno, it is this former rather than a future life on which Plato is disposed to dwell. There the Gods, and men following in their train, go forth to contemplate the heavens, and are borne round in the revolutions of them. There they see the divine forms of justice, temperance, and the like, in their unchangeable beauty, but not without an effort more than human. The soul of man is likened to a charioteer and two steeds, one mortal, the other immortal. The charioteer and the mortal steed are in fierce conflict; at length the animal principle is finally overpowered, though not extinguished, by the combined energies of the passionate and rational elements. This is one of those passages in Plato which, partaking both of a philosophical and poetical character, is necessarily indistinct and inconsistent. The magnificent figure under which the nature of the soul is described has not much to do with the popular doctrine of the ideas. Yet there is one little trait in the description which shows that they are present to Plato's mind, namely, the remark that the soul, which had seen truths in the form of the universal (248 C, 249 C), cannot again return to the nature of an animal.

In the Phaedo, as in the Meno, the origin of ideas is sought for in a previous state of existence. There was no time when they could have been acquired in this life, and therefore they must have been recovered from another. The process of recovery is no other than the ordinary law of association, by which in daily life the sight of one thing or person recalls another to our minds, and by which in scientific enquiry from any part of knowledge we may be led on to infer the whole. It is also argued that ideas, or rather ideals, must be derived from a previous state of existence because they are more perfect than the sensible forms of them which are given by experience (74 ff.). But in the Phaedo the doctrine of ideas is subordinate to the proof of the immortality of the soul. 'If the soul existed in a previous state, then it will exist in a future state, for a law of alternation pervades all things.' And, 'If the ideas exist, then the soul exists; if not, not.' It is to be observed, both in the Meno and the Phaedo, that Socrates expresses himself with diffidence. He speaks in the Phaedo (114 D, 115 D) of the words with which he has comforted himself and his friends, and will not be too confident that the description which he has given of the soul and her mansions is exactly true, but he 'ventures to think that something of the kind is true.' And in the Meno, after dwelling upon the immortality of the soul, he adds, 'Of some things which I have said I am not altogether confident' (cp. 86 C, and Apology, pp. 40 ff.; Gorgias 527 B). From this class of uncertainties he exempts the difference between truth and appearance, of which he is absolutely convinced (98 B).

In the Republic the ideas are spoken of in two ways, which though not contradictory are different. In the tenth book (596 ff.) they are represented as the genera or general ideas under which individuals having a common name are contained. For example, there is the bed which the carpenter makes, the picture of the bed which is drawn by the painter, the bed existing in nature of which God is the author. Of the latter all visible beds are only the shadows or reflections. This and similar illustrations or explanations are put forth, not for their own sake, or as an exposition of Plato's theory of ideas, but with a view of showing that poetry and the mimetic arts are concerned with an inferior part of the soul and a lower kind of knowledge. On the other hand, in the 6th and 7th books of the Republic we reach the highest and most perfect conception, which Plato is able to attain, of the nature of knowledge. The ideas are now finally seen to be one as well as many, causes as well as ideas, and to have a unity which is the idea of good and the cause of all the rest. They seem, however, to have lost their first aspect of universals under which individuals are contained, and to have been converted into forms of another kind, which are inconsistently regarded from the one side as images or ideals of justice, temperance, holiness and the like; from the other as hypotheses, or mathematical truths or principles.

In the Timaeus, which in the series of Plato's works immediately follows the Republic, though probably written some time afterwards, no mention occurs of the doctrine of ideas. Geometrical forms and arithmetical ratios furnish the laws according to which the world is created. But though the conception of the ideas as genera or species is forgotten or laid aside, the distinction of the visible and intellectual is as firmly maintained as ever (30, 37). The *idea* of good likewise disappears and is superseded by the conception of a personal God, who works according to a final cause or principle of goodness which he himself is. No doubt is expressed by Plato, either in the Timaeus or in any other dialogue, of the truths which he conceives to be the first and highest. It is not the existence of God or the idea of good which he approaches in a tentative or hesitating manner, but the investigations of physiology. These he regards, not seriously, as a part of philosophy, but as an innocent recreation (Tim. 59 D).

Passing on to the Parmenides (128–136), we find in that dialogue not an exposition or defence of the doctrine of ideas, but an assault upon them, which is put into the mouth of the veteran Parmenides, and might be ascribed to Aristotle himself, or to one of his disciples. The doctrine which is assailed takes two or three forms, but fails in any of them to escape the dialectical difficulties which are urged against it. It is admitted that there are ideas of all things, but the manner in which individuals partake of them, whether of the whole or of the part, and in which they become like them, or how ideas can be either within or without the sphere of human knowledge, or how the human and divine can have any relation to each other, is held to be incapable of explanation. And yet, if there are no universal ideas, what becomes of philosophy? (Parmenides 130–135). In the Sophist the theory of ideas is spoken of as a doctrine held not by Plato, but by another sect of philosophers, called 'the Friends of Ideas,' probably the Megarians, who were very distinct from him, if not opposed to him (Sophist 242 ff.). Nor in what may be termed Plato's abridgement of the history of philosophy (Soph. 241 ff.), is any mention made such as we find in the first book of Aristotle's Metaphysics, of the derivation of such a theory or of any part of it from the Pythagoreans, the Eleatics, the Heracleiteans, or even from Socrates. In the Philebus, probably one of the latest of the Platonic Dialogues, the conception of a personal or semi-personal deity expressed under the figure of mind, the king of all, who is also the cause, is retained. The one and many of the Phaedrus and Theaetetus is still working in the mind of Plato, and the correlation of ideas, not of 'all with all,' but of 'some with some,' is asserted and explained. But they are spoken of in a different manner, and are not supposed to be recovered from a former state of existence. The metaphysical conception of truth passes into a psychological one, which is continued in the Laws, and is the final form of the Platonic philosophy, so far as can be gathered from his own writings (see especially Laws v. 727 ff.). In the Laws he harps once more on the old string, and returns to general notions:—these he acknowledges to be many, and yet he insists that they are also one. The guardian must be made to recognize the truth, for which he has contended long ago in the Protagoras, that the virtues are four, but they are also in some sense one (Laws xii. pp. 965–966; cp. Protagoras 329.).

So various, and if regarded on the surface only, inconsistent, are the statements of Plato respecting the doctrine of ideas. If we attempted to harmonize or to combine them, we should make out of them, not a system, but the caricature of a system. They are the ever-varying expression of Plato's Idealism. The terms used in them are in their substance and general meaning the same, although they seem to be different. They pass from the subject to the object, from earth (diesseits) to heaven (jenseits) without regard to the gulf which later theology and philosophy have made between them. They are also intended to supplement or explain each other. They relate to a subject of which Plato himself would have said that 'he was not confident of the precise form of his own statements, but was strong in the belief that something of the kind was true.' It is the spirit, not the letter, in which they agree—the spirit which places the divine above the human, the spiritual above the material, the one above the many, the mind before the body.

The stream of ancient philosophy in the Alexandrian and Roman times widens into a lake or sea, and then disappears underground to reappear after many ages in a distant land. It begins to flow again under new conditions, at first confined between high and narrow banks, but finally spreading over the continent of Europe. It is and is not the same with ancient philosophy. There is a great deal in modern philosophy which is inspired by ancient. There is much in ancient philosophy which was 'born out of due time' and before men were capable of understanding it. To the fathers of modern philosophy, their own thoughts appeared to be new and original, but they carried with them an echo or shadow of the past, coming back by recollection from an elder world. Of this the enquirers of the seventeenth century, who to themselves appeared to be working out independently the enquiry into all truth, were unconscious. They stood in a new relation to theology and natural philosophy, and for a time maintained towards both an attitude of reserve and separation. Yet the similarities between modern and ancient thought are greater far than the differences. All philosophy, even that part of it which is said to be based upon experience, is really ideal; and ideas are not only derived from facts, but they are also prior to them and extend far beyond them, just as the mind is prior to the senses.

Early Greek speculation culminates in the ideas of Plato, or rather in the single idea of good. His followers, and perhaps he himself, having arrived at this elevation, instead of going forwards went backwards from philosophy to psychology, from ideas to numbers. But what we perceive to be the real meaning of them, an explanation of the nature and origin of knowledge, will always continue to be one of the first problems of philosophy.

Plato also left behind him a most potent instrument, the forms of logic—arms ready for use, but not yet taken out of their armoury. They were the late birth of the early Greek philosophy, and were the only part of it which has had an uninterrupted hold on the mind of Europe. Philosophies come and go; but the detection of fallacies, the framing of definitions, the invention of methods still continue to be the main elements of the reasoning process.

Modern philosophy, like ancient, begins with very simple conceptions. It is almost wholly a reflection on self. It might be described as a quickening into life of old words and notions latent in the semi-barbarous Latin, and putting a new meaning into them. Unlike ancient philosophy, it has been unaffected by impressions derived from outward nature: it arose within the limits of the mind itself. From the time of Descartes to Hume and Kant it has had little or nothing to do with facts of science. On the other hand, the ancient and mediaeval logic retained a continuous influence over it, and a form like that of mathematics was easily impressed upon it; the principle of ancient philosophy which is most apparent in it is scepticism; we must doubt nearly every traditional or received notion, that we may hold fast one or two. The being of God in a personal or impersonal form was a mental necessity to the first thinkers of modern times: from this alone all other ideas could be deduced. There had been an obscure presentiment of 'cogito, ergo sum' more than 2000 years previously. The Eleatic notion that being and thought were the same was revived in a new form by Descartes. But now it gave birth to consciousness and self-reflection: it awakened the 'ego' in human nature. The mind naked and abstract has no other certainty but the conviction of its own existence. 'I think, therefore I am;' and this thought is God thinking in me, who has also communicated to the reason of man his own attributes of thought and extension—these are truly imparted to him because God is true (cp. Rep. ii. 382 ff.). It has been often remarked that Descartes, having begun by dismissing all presuppositions, introduces several: he passes almost at once from scepticism to dogmatism. It is more important for the illustration of Plato to observe that he, like Plato, insists that God is true and incapable of deception (Rep. ii. 382)—that he proceeds from general ideas, that many elements of mathematics may be found in him. A certain influence of mathematics both on the form and substance of their philosophy is discernible in both of them. After making the greatest opposition between thought and extension, Descartes, like Plato, supposes them to be reunited for a time, not in their own nature but by a special divine act (cp. Phaedrus 246 C), and he also supposes all the parts of the human body to meet in the pineal gland, that alone affording a principle of unity in the material frame of man. It is characteristic of the first period of modern philosophy, that having begun (like the Presocratics) with a few general notions, Des Cartes first falls absolutely under their influence, and then quickly discards them. At the same time he is less able to observe facts, because they are too much magnified by the glasses through which they are seen. The common logic says 'the greater the extension, the less the comprehension,' and we may put the same thought in another way and say of abstract or general ideas, that the greater the abstraction of them, the less are they capable of being applied to particular and concrete natures.

Not very different from Descartes in his relation to ancient philosophy is his successor Spinoza, who lived in the following generation. The system of Spinoza is less personal and also less dualistic than that of Descartes. In this respect the difference between them is like that between Xenophanes and Parmenides. The teaching of Spinoza might be described generally as the Jewish religion reduced to an abstraction and taking the form of the Eleatic philosophy. Like Parmenides, he is overpowered and intoxicated with the idea of Being or God. The greatness of both philosophies consists in the immensity of a thought which excludes all other thoughts; their weakness is the necessary separation of this thought from actual existence and from practical life. In neither of them is there any clear opposition between the inward and outward world. The substance of Spinoza has two attributes, which alone are cognizable by man, thought and extension; these are in extreme opposition to one another, and also in inseparable identity. They may be regarded as the two aspects or expressions under which God or substance is unfolded to man. Here a step is made beyond the limits of the Eleatic philosophy. The famous theorem of Spinoza, 'Omnis determinatio est negatio,' is already contained in the 'negation is relation' of Plato's Sophist. The grand description of the philosopher in Republic vi, as the spectator of all time and all existence, may be paralleled with another famous expression of Spinoza, 'Contemplatio rerum sub specie eternitatis.' According to Spinoza finite objects are unreal, for they are conditioned by what is alien to them, and by one another. Human beings are included in the number of them. Hence there is no reality in human action and no place for right and wrong. Individuality is accident. The boasted freedom of the will is only a consciousness of necessity. Truth, he says, is the direction of the reason towards the infinite, in which all things repose; and herein lies the secret of man's well-being. In the exaltation of the reason or intellect, in the denial of the voluntariness of evil (Timaeus 86 C, D; Laws, ix. 860) Spinoza approaches nearer to Plato than in his conception of an infinite substance. As Socrates said that virtue is knowledge, so Spinoza would have maintained that knowledge alone is good and what contributes to knowledge useful. Both are equally far from any real experience or observation of nature. And the same difficulty is found in both when we seek to apply their ideas to life and practice. There is a gulf fixed between the infinite substance and finite objects or individuals of Spinoza, just as there is between the ideas of Plato and the world of sense.

Removed from Spinoza by less than a generation is the philosopher Leibnitz, who after deepening and intensifying the opposition between mind and matter, reunites them by his preconcerted harmony (cp. again Phaedrus 246 C). To him all the particles of matter are living beings which reflect on one another, and in the least of them the whole is contained. Here we catch a reminiscence both of the ὁμοιομερη or similar particles of Anaxagoras, and of the world-animal of the Timaeus.

In Bacon and Locke we have another development in which the mind of man is supposed to receive knowledge by a new method and to work by observation and experience. But we may remark that it is the idea of experience, rather than experience itself, with which the mind is filled. It is a symbol of knowledge rather than the reality which is vouchsafed to us. The Organon of Bacon is not much nearer to actual facts than the Organon of Aristotle or the Platonic idea of good. Many of the old rags and ribbons which defaced the garment of philosophy have been stripped off, but some of them still adhere. A crude conception of the ideas of Plato survives in the 'forms' of Bacon. And on the other hand, there are many passages of Plato in which the importance of the investigation of facts is as much insisted upon as by Bacon. Both are almost equally superior to the illusions of language, and are constantly crying out against them, as against other idols.

Locke cannot be truly regarded as the author of sensationalism any more than of idealism. His system is based upon experience, but with him experience includes reflection as well as sense. His analysis and construction of ideas has no foundation in fact; it is only the dialectic of the mind 'talking to herself.' The philosophy of Berkeley is but the transposition of two words. For objects of sense he would substitute sensations. He imagines himself to have changed the relation of the human mind towards God and nature; they remain the same as before, though he has drawn the imaginary line by which they are divided at a different point. He has annihilated the outward world, but it instantly reappears governed by the same laws and described under the same names.

A like remark applies to David Hume, of whose philosophy the central principle is the denial of the relation of cause and effect. He would deprive men of a familiar term which they can ill afford to lose; but he seems not to have observed that this alteration is merely verbal and does not in any degree affect the nature of things. Still less did he remark that he was arguing from the necessary imperfection of language against the most certain facts. And here, again, we may find a parallel with the ancients. He goes beyond facts in his scepticism, as they did in their idealism. Like the ancient Sophists, he relegates the more important principles of ethics to custom and probability. But crude and unmeaning as this philosophy is, it exercised a great influence on his successors, not unlike that which Locke exercised upon Berkeley and Berkeley upon Hume himself. All three were both sceptical and ideal in almost equal degrees. Neither they nor their predecessors had any true conception of language or of the history of philosophy. Hume's paradox has been forgotten by the world, and did not any more than the scepticism of the ancients require to be seriously refuted.

Like some other philosophical paradoxes, it would have been better left to die out. It certainly could not be refuted by a philosophy such as Kant's, in which, no less than in the previously mentioned systems, the history of the human mind and the nature of language are almost wholly ignored, and the certainty of objective knowledge is transferred to the subject; while absolute truth is reduced to a figment, more abstract and narrow than Plato's ideas, of 'thing in itself,' to which, if we reason strictly, no predicate can be applied.

The question which Plato has raised respecting the origin and nature of ideas belongs to the infancy of philosophy; in modern times it would no longer be asked. Their origin is only their history, so far as we know it; there can be no other. We may trace them in language, in philosophy, in mythology, in poetry, but we cannot argue *à priori* about them. We may attempt to shake them off, but they are always returning, and in every sphere of science and human action are tending to go beyond facts. They are thought to be innate, because they have been familiar to us all our lives, and we can no longer dismiss them from our mind. Many of them express relations of terms to which nothing exactly or nothing at all *in rerum naturâ* corresponds. We are not such free agents in the use of them as we sometimes imagine. Fixed ideas have taken the most complete possession of some thinkers who have been most determined to renounce them, and have been vehemently affirmed when they could be least explained and were incapable of proof. The world has often been led away by a word to which no distinct meaning could be attached. Abstractions such as 'authority,' 'equality,' 'utility,' 'liberty,' 'pleasure,' 'experience,' 'consciousness,' 'chance,' 'substance,' 'matter,' 'atom,' and a heap of other metaphysical and theological terms, are the source of quite as much error and illusion and have as little relation to actual facts as the ideas of Plato. Few students of theology or philosophy have sufficiently reflected how quickly the bloom of a philosophy passes away; or how hard it is for one age to understand the writings of another; or how nice a judgment is required of those who are seeking to express the philosophy of one age in the terms of another. The 'eternal truths' of which metaphysicians speak have hardly ever lasted more than a generation. In our own day schools or systems of philosophy which have once been famous have died before the founders of them. We are still, as in Plato's age, groping about for a new method more comprehensive than any of those which now prevail; and also more permanent. And we seem to see at a distance the promise of such a method, which can hardly be any other than the method of idealized experience, having roots which strike far down into the history of philosophy. It is a method which does not divorce the present from the past, or the part from the whole, or the abstract from the concrete, or theory from fact, or the divine from the human, or one science from another, but labours to connect them. Along such a road we have proceeded a few steps, sufficient, perhaps, to make us reflect on the want of method which prevails in our own day. In another age, all the branches of knowledge, whether relating to God or man or nature, will become the knowledge of 'the revelation of a single science' (Symp. 210, 211), and all things, like the stars in heaven, will shed their light upon one another.

MENO.

PERSONS OF THE DIALOGUE.

Meno.

Socrates.

A Slave of Meno.

Anytus.

Meno.

*Meno.*Socrates, Meno.

Can you tell me, Socrates, whether virtue is acquired by teaching or by practice; or if neither by teaching nor by practice, then whether it comes to man by nature, or in what other way?

Socrates.

Meno asks Socrates 'How virtue can be acquired?' Before giving an answer Socrates must enquire 'What is virtue?'

O Meno, there was a time when the Thessalians were famous among the other Hellenes only for their riches and their riding; but now, if I am not mistaken, they are equally famous for their wisdom, especially at Larisa, which is the native city of your friend Aristippus. And this is Gorgias' doing; for when he came there, the flower of the Aleuadae, among them your admirer Aristippus, and the other chiefs of the Thessalians, fell in love with his wisdom. And he has taught you the habit of answering questions in a grand and bold style, which becomes those who know, and is the style in which he himself answers all comers; and any 71Hellene who likes may ask him anything. How different is our lot! my dear Meno. Here at Athens there is a dearth of the commodity, and all wisdom seems to have emigrated from us to you. I am certain that if you were to ask any Athenian whether virtue was natural or acquired, he would laugh in your face, and say: 'Stranger, you have far too good an opinion of me, if you think that I can answer your question. For I literally do not know what virtue is, and much less whether it is acquired by teaching or not.' And I myself, Meno, living as I do in this region of poverty, am as poor as the rest of the world; and I confess with shame that I know literally nothing about virtue; and when I do not know the 'quid' of anything how can I know the 'quale'? How, if I knew nothing at all of Meno, could I tell if he was fair, or the opposite of fair; rich and noble, or the reverse of rich and noble? Do you think that I could?

Men.

No, indeed. But are you in earnest, Socrates, in saying that you do not know what virtue is? And am I to carry back this report of you to Thessaly?

Soc.

He does not know, and never met with any one who did.

Not only that, my dear boy, but you may say further that I have never known of any one else who did, in my judgment.

Men.

Then you have never met Gorgias when he was at Athens?

Soc.

Yes, I have.

Men.

And did you not think that he knew?

Soc.

I have not a good memory, Meno, and therefore I cannot now tell what I thought of him at the time. And I dare say that he did know, and that you know what he said: please, therefore, to remind me of what he said; or, if you would rather, tell me your own view; for I suspect that you and he think much alike.

Men.

Very true.

Soc.

Then as he is not here, never mind him, and do you tell me: By the gods, Meno, be generous, and tell me what you say that virtue is; for I shall be truly delighted to find that I have been mistaken, and that you and Gorgias do really have this knowledge; although I have been just saying that I have never found anybody who had.

Men.

Meno describes the different kinds of virtue, but is unable to give a common notion of them.

There will be no difficulty, Socrates, in answering your question. Let us take first the virtue of a man—he should know how to administer the state, and in the administration of it to benefit his friends and harm his enemies; and he must also be careful not to suffer harm himself. A woman's virtue, if you wish to know about that, may also be easily described: her duty is to order her house, and keep what is indoors, and obey her husband. Every age, every condition of life, young or old, male or female, bond or free, has a different virtue: there are virtues numberless, 72and no lack of definitions of them; for virtue is relative to the actions and ages of each of us in all that we do. And the same may be said of vice, Socrates .

Soc.

Meno, not without difficulty and by help of many illustrations, is made to understand the nature of common notions.

How fortunate I am, Meno! When I ask you for one virtue, you present me with a swarm of them which are in your keeping. Suppose that I carry on the figure of the swarm, and ask of you, What is the nature of the bee? and you answer that there are many kinds of bees, and I reply: But do bees differ as bees, because there are many and different kinds of them; or are they not rather to be distinguished by some other quality, as for example beauty, size, or shape? How would you answer me?

Men.

I should answer that bees do not differ from one another, as bees.

Soc.

And if I went on to say: That is what I desire to know, Meno; tell me what is the quality in which they do not differ, but are all alike; would you be able to answer?

Men.

I should.

Soc.

And so of the virtues, however many and different they may be, they have all a common nature which makes them virtues; and on this he who would answer the question, 'What is virtue?' would do well to have his eye fixed: Do you understand?

Men.

I am beginning to understand; but I do not as yet take hold of the question as I could wish.

Soc.

When you say, Meno, that there is one virtue of a man, another of a woman, another of a child, and so on, does this apply only to virtue, or would you say the same of health, and size, and strength? Or is the nature of health always the same, whether in man or woman?

Men.

I should say that health is the same, both in man and woman.

Soc.

Health and strength, and virtue and temperance and justice are the same both in men and women.

And is not this true of size and strength? If a woman is strong, she will be strong by reason of the same form and of the same strength subsisting in her which there is in the man. I mean to say that strength, as strength, whether of man or woman, is the same. Is there any difference?

Men.

I think not.

Soc.

And will not virtue, as virtue, be the same, whether 73in a child or in a grown-up person, in a woman or in an man?

Men.

I cannot help feeling, Socrates, that this case is different from the others.

Soc.

But why? Were you not saying that the virtue of a man was to order a state, and the virtue of a woman was to order a house?

Men.

I did say so.

Soc.

And can either house or state or anything be well ordered without temperance and without justice?

Men.

Certainly not.

Soc.

Then they who order a state or a house temperately or justly order them with temperance and justice?

Men.

Certainly.

Soc.

Then both men and women, if they are to be good men and women, must have the same virtues of temperance and justice?

Men.

True.

Soc.

And can either a young man or an elder one be good, if they are intemperate and unjust?

Men.

They cannot.

Soc.

They must be temperate and just?

Men.

Yes.

Soc.

Then all men are good in the same way, and by participation in the same virtues?

Men.

Such is the inference.

Soc.

And they surely would not have been good in the same way, unless their virtue had been the same?

Men.

They would not.

Soc.

Then what is virtue? Gorgias and Meno reply, 'The power of governing mankind.'

Then now that the sameness of all virtue has been proven, try and remember what you and Gorgias say that virtue is.

Men.

Will you have one definition of them all?

Soc.

That is what I am seeking.

Men.

If you want to have one definition of them all, I know not what to say, but that virtue is the power of governing mankind.

Soc.

And does this definition of virtue include all virtue? Is virtue the same in a child and in a slave, Meno? Can the child govern his father, or the slave his master; and would he who governed be any longer a slave?

Men.

But this cannot apply to all persons.

I think not, Socrates.

Soc.

No, indeed; there would be small reason in that. Yet once more, fair friend; according to you, virtue is 'the power of governing;' but do you not add 'justly and not unjustly'?

Men.

Yes, Socrates; I agree there; for justice is virtue.

Soc.

Would you say 'virtue,' Meno, or 'a virtue'?

Men.

What do you mean?

Soc.

I mean as I might say about anything; that a round, for example, is 'a figure' and not simply 'figure,' and I should adopt this mode of speaking, because there are other figures.

Men.

Quite right; and that is just what I am saying about virtue—that there are other virtues as well as justice.

Soc.

What are they? tell me the names of them, as I would tell you the names of the other figures if you asked me.

Men.

Meno names the virtues, but is unable to get at the common notion of them.

Courage and temperance and wisdom and magnanimity are virtues; and there are many others.

Soc.

Yes, Meno; and again we are in the same case: in searching after one virtue we have found many, though not in the same way as before; but we have been unable to find the common virtue which runs through them all.

Men.

Why, Socrates, even now I am not able to follow you in the attempt to get at one common notion of virtue as of other things.

Soc.

No wonder; but I will try to get nearer if I can, for you know that all things have a common notion. Suppose now that some one asked you the question which I asked before: Meno, he would say, what is figure? And if you answered 'roundness,' he would reply to you, in my way of speaking, by asking whether you would say that roundness is 'figure' or 'a figure;' and you would answer 'a figure.'

Men.

Certainly.

Soc.

And for this reason—that there are other figures?

Men.

Yes.

Soc.

And if he proceeded to ask, What other figures are there? you would have told him.

Men.

I should.

Soc.

And if he similarly asked what colour is, and you answered whiteness, and the questioner rejoined, Would you say that whiteness is colour or a colour? you would reply, A colour, because there are other colours as well.

Men.

I should.

Soc.

And if he had said, Tell me what they are?—you would have told him of other colours which are colours just as much as whiteness.

Men.

Yes.

Soc.

He has a similar difficulty about the nature of Figure.

And suppose that he were to pursue the matter in my way, he would say: Ever and anon we are landed in particulars, but this is not what I want; tell me then, since you call them by a common name, and say that they are all figures, even when opposed to one another, what is that common nature which you designate as figure—which contains straight as well as round, and is no more one than the other—that would be your mode of speaking?

Men.

Yes.

Soc.

And in speaking thus, you do not mean to say that the round is round any more than straight, or the straight any more straight than round?

Men.

Certainly not.

Soc.

You only assert that the round figure is not more a figure than the straight, or the straight than the round?

Men.

Very true.

Soc.

To what then do we give the name of figure? Try and answer. Suppose that when a person asked you this question either about figure or colour, you were to reply, Man, I do not understand what you want, or know what you are saying; he would look rather astonished and say: Do you not understand that I am looking for the 'simile in multis'? And then he might put the question in another form: Meno, he might say, what is that 'simile in multis' which you call figure, and which includes not only round and straight figures, but all? Could you not answer that question, Meno? I wish that you would try; the attempt will be good practice with a view to the answer about virtue.

Men.

I would rather that you should answer, Socrates.

Soc.

Shall I indulge you?

Men.

By all means.

Soc.

And then you will tell me about virtue?

Men.

I will.

Soc.

Then I must do my best, for there is a prize to be won.

Men.

Certainly.

Soc.

Figure is defined by Socrates to be that which always follows colour.

Well, I will try and explain to you what figure is. What do you say to this answer?—Figure is the only thing which always follows colour. Will you be satisfied with it, as I am sure that I should be, if you would let me have a similar definition of virtue?

Men.

But, Socrates, it is such a simple answer.

Soc.

Why simple?

Men.

Because, according to you, figure is that which always follows colour.

(*Soc.* Granted).

Men.

But if a person were to say that he does not know what colour is, any more than what figure is—what sort of answer would you have given him?

Soc.

I should have told him the truth. And if he were a philosopher of the eristic and antagonistic sort, I should say to him: You have my answer, and if I am wrong, your business is to take up the argument and refute me. But if we were friends, and were talking as you and I are now, I should reply in a milder strain and more in the dialectician's vein; that is to say, I should not only speak the truth, but I should make use of premisses which the person interrogated would be willing to admit. And this is the way in which I shall endeavour to approach you. You will acknowledge, will you not, that there is such a thing as an end, or termination, or extremity?—all which words I use in the same sense, although I am aware that Prodicus might draw distinctions about them: but still you, I am sure, would speak of a thing as ended or terminated—that is all which I am saying—not anything very difficult.

Men.

Yes, I should; and I believe that I understand your meaning.

Soc.

76And you would speak of a surface and also of a solid, as for example in geometry.

Men.

Yes.

Soc.

Well then, you are now in a condition to understand my definition of figure. I define figure to be that in which the solid ends; or, more concisely, the limit of solid.

Men.

And now, Socrates, what is colour?

Soc.

And now, what is colour?

You are outrageous, Meno, in thus plaguing a poor old man to give you an answer, when you will not take the trouble of remembering what is Gorgias' definition of virtue.

Men.

When you have told me what I ask, I will tell you, Socrates.

Soc.

A man who was blindfolded has only to hear you talking, and he would know that you are a fair creature and have still many lovers.

Men.

Why do you think so?

Soc.

Why, because you always speak in imperatives: like all beauties when they are in their prime, you are tyrannical; and also, as I suspect, you have found out that I have a weakness for the fair, and therefore to humour you I must answer.

Men.

Please do.

Soc.

Would you like me to answer you after the manner of Gorgias, which is familiar to you?

Men.

I should like nothing better.

Soc.

Meno, Gorgias, and Empedocles are all agreed that colour is an effluence of existence, proportioned to certain passages.

Do not he and you and Empedocles say that there are certain effluences of existence?

Men.

Certainly.

Soc.

And passages into which and through which the effluences pass?

Men.

Exactly.

Soc.

And some of the effluences fit into the passages, and some of them are too small or too large?

Men.

True.

Soc.

And there is such a thing as sight?

Men.

Yes.

Soc.

And now, as Pindar says, 'read my meaning:'—colour is an effluence of form, commensurate with sight, and palpable to sense.

Men.

That, Socrates, appears to me to be an admirable answer.

Soc.

Why, yes, because it happens to be one which you have been in the habit of hearing: and your wit will have discovered, I suspect, that you may explain in the same way the nature of sound and smell, and of many other similar phenomena.

Men.

Quite true.

Soc.

The answer, Meno, was in the orthodox solemn vein, and therefore was more acceptable to you than the other answer about figure.

Men.

Yes.

Soc.

And yet, O son of Alexidemus, I cannot help thinking that the other was the better; and I am sure that you would be of the same opinion, if you would only stay and be initiated, and were not compelled, as you said yesterday, to go away before the mysteries.

Men.

But I will stay, Socrates if you will give me many 77such answers.

Soc.

Virtue, according to Meno, is the desire of the honourable and the good. His definition is analysed by Socrates.

Well then, for my own sake as well as for yours, I will do my very best; but I am afraid that I shall not be able to give you very many as good: and now, in your turn, you are to fulfil your promise, and tell me what virtue is in the universal; and do not make a singular into a plural, as the facetious say of those who break a thing, but deliver virtue to me whole and sound, and not broken into a number of pieces: I have given you the pattern.

Men.

Well then, Socrates, virtue, as I take it, is when he, who desires the honourable, is able to provide it for himself; so the poet says, and I say too—

- 'Virtue is the desire of things honourable and the power of attaining them.'

Soc.

And does he who desires the honourable also desire the good.

Men.

Certainly.

Soc.

Then are there some who desire the evil and others who desire the good? Do not all men, my dear sir, desire good?

Men.

I think not.

Soc.

There are some who desire evil?

Men.

Yes.

Soc.

Do you mean that they think the evils which they desire, to be good; or do they know that they are evil and yet desire them?

Men.

Both, I think.

Soc.

And do you really imagine, Meno, that a man knows evils to be evils and desires them notwithstanding?

Men.

Certainly I do.

Soc.

And desire is of possession?

Men.

Yes, of possession.

Soc.

Men desire evil, but not what they think to be evil.

And does he think that the evils will do good to him who possesses them, or does he know that they will do him harm?

Men.

There are some who think that the evils will do them good, and others who know that they will do them harm.

Soc.

And, in your opinion, do those who think that they will do them good know that they are evils?

Men.

Certainly not.

Soc.

Is it not obvious that those who are ignorant of their nature do not desire them; but they desire what they suppose to be goods although they are really evils; and if they are mistaken and suppose the evils to be goods they really desire goods?

Men.

Yes, in that case.

Soc.

Well, and do those who, as you say, desire evils, and think that evils are hurtful to the possessor of them, know that they will be hurt by them?

Men.

They must know it.

Soc.

And must they not suppose that those who are hurt 78are miserable in proportion to the hurt which is inflicted upon them?

Men.

How can it be otherwise?

Soc.

But are not the miserable ill-fated?

Men.

Yes, indeed.

Soc.

And does any one desire to be miserable and ill-fated?

Men.

I should say not, Socrates.

Soc.

But if there is no one who desires to be miserable, there is no one, Meno, who desires evil; for what is misery but the desire and possession of evil?

Men.

That appears to be the truth, Socrates, and I admit that nobody desires evil.

Soc.

And yet, were you not saying just now that virtue is the desire and power of attaining good?

Men.

Yes, I did say so.

Soc.

But if this be affirmed, then the desire of good is common to all, and one man is no better than another in that respect?

Men.

The desire of good is really common to all of them.

True.

Soc.

And if one man is not better than another in desiring good, he must be better in the power of attaining it?

Men.

Exactly.

Soc.

Virtue is the power of attaining good with justice.

Then, according to your definition, virtue would appear to be the power of attaining good?

Men.

I entirely approve, Socrates, of the manner in which you now view this matter.

Soc.

Then let us see whether what you say is true from another point of view; for very likely you may be right:—You affirm virtue to be the power of attaining goods?

Men.

Yes.

Soc.

And the goods which you mean are such as health and wealth and the possession of gold and silver, and having office and honour in the state—those are what you would call goods?

Men.

Yes, I should include all those.

Soc.

Then, according to Meno, who is the hereditary friend of the great king, virtue is the power of getting silver and gold; and would you add that they must be gained piously, justly, or do you deem this to be of no consequence? And is any mode of acquisition, even if unjust or dishonest, equally to be deemed virtue?

Men.

Not virtue, Socrates, but vice.

Soc.

Then justice or temperance or holiness, or some other part of virtue, as would appear, must accompany the acquisition, and without them the mere acquisition of good will not be virtue.

Men.

Why, how can there be virtue without these?

Soc.

And the non-acquisition of gold and silver in a dishonest manner for oneself or another, or in other words the want of them, may be equally virtue?

Men.

True.

Soc.

Then the acquisition of such goods is no more virtue than the non-acquisition and want of them, but whatever is accompanied by justice or honesty is virtue, and whatever 79is devoid of justice is vice.

Men.

It cannot be otherwise, in my judgment.

Soc.

And were we not saying just now that justice, temperance, and the like, were each of them a part of virtue?

Men.

But this definition repeats the thing defined:—virtue=the power of attaining good with a part of virtue.

Yes.

Soc.

And so, Meno, this is the way in which you mock me.

Men.

Why do you say that, Socrates?

Soc.

Why, because I asked you to deliver virtue into my hands whole and unbroken, and I gave you a pattern according to which you were to frame your answer; and you have forgotten already, and tell me that virtue is the power of attaining good justly, or with justice; and justice you acknowledge to be a part of virtue.

Men.

Yes.

Soc.

Then it follows from your own admissions, that virtue is doing what you do with a part of virtue; for justice and the like are said by you to be parts of virtue.

Men.

What of that?

Soc.

But if we do not know the nature of virtue as a whole, how can we know what a part of virtue is?

What of that! Why, did not I ask you to tell me the nature of virtue as a whole? And you are very far from telling me this; but declare every action to be virtue which is done with a part of virtue; as though you had told me and I must already know the whole of virtue, and this too when frittered away into little pieces. And, therefore, my dear Meno, I fear that I must begin again and repeat the same question: What is virtue? for otherwise, I can only say, that every action done with a part of virtue is virtue; what else is the meaning of saying that every action done with justice is virtue? Ought I not to ask the question over again; for can any one who does not know virtue know a part of virtue?

Men.

No; I do not say that he can.

Soc.

Do you remember how, in the example of figure, we rejected any answer given in terms which were as yet unexplained or unadmitted?

Men.

Yes, Socrates; and we were quite right in doing so.

Soc.

But then, my friend, do not suppose that we can explain to any one the nature of virtue as a whole through some unexplained portion of virtue, or anything at all in that fashion; we should only have to ask over again the old question, What is virtue? Am I not right?

Men.

I believe that you are.

Soc.

Then begin again, and answer me, What, according to you and your friend Gorgias, is the definition of virtue?

Men.

Meno compares Socrates to a torpedo whose touch has taken away his sense and speech.

O Socrates, I used to be told, before I knew you, that 80you were always doubting yourself and making others doubt; and now you are casting your spells over me, and I am simply getting bewitched and enchanted, and am at my wits' end. And if I may venture to make a jest upon you, you seem to me both in your appearance and in your power over others to be very like the flat torpedo fish, who torpifies those who come near him and touch him, as you have now torpified me, I think. For my soul and my tongue are really torpid, and I do not know how to answer you; and though I have been delivered of an infinite variety of speeches about virtue before now, and to many persons—and very good ones they were, as I thought—at this moment I cannot even say what virtue is. And I think that you are very wise in not voyaging and going away from home, for if you did in other places as you do in Athens, you would be cast into prison as a magician.

Soc.

You are a rogue, Meno, and had all but caught me.

Men.

What do you mean, Socrates?

Soc.

I can tell why you made a simile about me.

Men.

Why?

Soc.

Socrates is the cause of dulness in others because he is himself dull.

In order that I might make another simile about you. For I know that all pretty young gentlemen like to have pretty similes made about them—as well they may—but I shall not return the compliment. As to my being a torpedo, if the torpedo is torpid as well as the cause of torpidity in others, then indeed I am a torpedo, but not otherwise; for I perplex others, not because I am clear, but because I am utterly perplexed myself. And now I know not what virtue is, and you seem to be in the same case, although you did once perhaps know before you touched me. However, I have no objection to join with you in the enquiry.

Men.

And how will you enquire, Socrates, into that which you do not know? What will you put forth as the subject of enquiry? And if you find what you want, how will you ever know that this is the thing which you did not know?

Soc.

How can you enquire about what you do not know, and if you know why should you enquire?

I know, Meno, what you mean; but just see what a tiresome dispute you are introducing. You argue that a man cannot enquire either about that which he knows, or about that which he does not know; for if he knows, he has no need to enquire;

and if not, he cannot; for he does not know the very subject about which he is to enquire .

Men.

Well, Socrates, and is not the argument sound? 81

Soc.

I think not.

Men.

Why not?

Soc.

I will tell you why: I have heard from certain wise men and women who spoke of things divine that—

Men.

What did they say?

Soc.

They spoke of a glorious truth, as I conceive.

Men.

What was it? and who were they?

Soc.

The ancient poets tell us that the soul of man is immortal and has a recollection of all that she has ever known in former states of being.Socrates, Meno, Meno's Slave.

Some of them were priests and priestesses, who had studied how they might be able to give a reason of their profession: there have been poets also, who spoke of these things by inspiration, like Pindar, and many others who were inspired. And they say—mark, now, and see whether their words are true—they say that the soul of man is immortal, and at one time has an end, which is termed dying, and at another time is born again, but is never destroyed. And the moral is, that a man ought to live always in perfect holiness. *'For in the ninth year Persephone sends the souls of those from whom she has received the penalty of ancient crime back again from beneath into the light of the sun above, and these are they who become noble kings and mighty men and great in wisdom and are called saintly heroes in after ages.'* The soul, then, as being immortal, and having been born again many times, and having seen all things that exist, whether in this world or in the world below, has knowledge of them all; and it is no wonder that she should be able to call to remembrance all that she ever knew about virtue, and about everything; for as all nature is akin, and the soul has learned all things, there is no difficulty in her eliciting or as men say learning, out of a single recollection all the rest, if a man is strenuous and does not faint; for all enquiry and all learning is but recollection. And therefore we ought not to listen to this sophistical argument about the impossibility of enquiry: for it will make us idle, and is sweet only to the sluggard; but the other saying will make us active and inquisitive. In that confiding, I will gladly enquire with you into the nature of virtue.

Men.

Yes, Socrates; but what do you mean by saying that we do not learn, and that what we call learning is only a process of recollection? Can you teach me how this is?

Soc.

I told you, Meno, just now that you were a rogue, and now you ask whether I can teach you, when I am saying that 82there is no teaching, but only recollection; and thus you imagine that you will involve me in a contradiction.

Men.

Indeed, Socrates, I protest that I had no such intention. I only asked the question from habit; but if you can prove to me that what you say is true, I wish that you would.

Soc.

A Greek slave is introduced, from whom certain mathematical conclusions which he has never learned are elicited by Socrates.

It will be no easy matter, but I will try to please you to the utmost of my power. Suppose that you call one of your numerous attendants, that I may demonstrate on him.

Men.

Certainly. Come hither, boy.

Soc.

He is Greek, and speaks Greek, does he not?

Men.

Yes, indeed; he was born in the house.

Soc.

Attend now to the questions which I ask him, and observe whether he learns of me or only remembers.

Men.

I will.

Soc.

Tell me, boy, do you know that a figure like this is a square?

Boy.

I do.

Soc.

And you know that a square figure has these four lines equal?

Boy.

Certainly.

Soc.

And these lines which I have drawn through the middle of the square are also equal?

Boy.

Yes.

Soc.

A square may be of any size?

Boy.

Certainly.

Soc.

And if one side of the figure be of two feet, and the other side be of two feet, how much will the whole be? Let me explain: if in one direction the space was of two feet, and in the other direction of one foot, the whole would be of two feet taken once?

Boy.

Yes.

Soc.

But since this side is also of two feet, there are twice two feet?

Boy.

There are.

Soc.

Then the square is of twice two feet?

Boy.

Yes.

Soc.

And how many are twice two feet? count and tell me.

Boy.

Four, Socrates.

Soc.

And might there not be another square twice as large as this, and having like this the lines equal?

Boy.

Yes.

Soc.

And of how many feet will that be?

Boy.

Of eight feet.

Soc.

And now try and tell me the length of the line which forms the side of that double square: this is two feet—what will that be?

Boy.

Clearly, Socrates, it will be double.

Soc.

He is partly guessing.

Do you observe, Meno, that I am not teaching the boy anything, but only asking him questions; and now he fancies that he knows how long a line is necessary in order to produce a figure of eight square feet; does he not?

Men.

Yes.

Soc.

And does he really know?

Men.

Certainly not.

Soc.

He only guesses that because the square is double, the line is double.

Men.

True.

Soc.

Observe him while he recalls the steps in regular order. (*To the Boy.*) Tell me, boy, do you assert that a double space comes from a double line? Remember that I am not speaking of an oblong, but of a figure equal every way, and twice the size of this—that is to say of eight feet; and I want to know whether you still say that a double square comes from a double line?

Boy.

Yes.

Soc.

But does not this line become doubled if we add another such line here?

Boy.

Certainly.

Soc.

And four such lines will make a space containing eight feet?

Boy.

Yes.

Soc.

Socrates, Meno's Slave.

Let us describe such a figure: Would you not say that this is the figure of eight feet?

Boy.

Yes.

Soc.

And are there not these four divisions in the figure, each of which is equal to the figure of four feet?

Boy.

True.

Soc.

And is not that four times four?

Boy.

Certainly.

Soc.

And four times is not double?

Boy.

No, indeed.

Soc.

But how much?

Boy.

Four times as much.

Soc.

Therefore the double line, boy, has given a space, not twice, but four times as much.

Boy.

True.

Soc.

Four times four are sixteen—are they not?

Boy.

Yes.

Soc.

What line would give you a space of eight feet, as this gives one of sixteen feet;—do you see?

Boy.

Yes.

Soc.

And the space of four feet is made from this half line?

Boy.

Yes.

Soc.

Good; and is not a space of eight feet twice the size of this, and half the size of the other?

Boy.

Certainly.

Soc.

Such a space, then, will be made out of a line greater than this one, and less than that one?

Boy.

Yes; I think so.

Soc.

Very good; I like to hear you say what you think. And now tell me, is not this a line of two feet and that of four?

Boy.

Yes.

Soc.

He has now learned to realize his own ignorance, and therefore will endeavour to remedy it.

Then the line which forms the side of eight feet ought to be more than this line of two feet, and less than the other of four feet?

Boy.

It ought.

Soc.

Try and see if you can tell me how much it will be.

Boy.

Three feet.

Soc.

Socrates, Meno, Meno's Slave.

Then if we add a half to this line of two, that will be the line of three. Here are two and there is one; and on the other side, here are two also and there is one: and that makes the figure of which you speak?

Boy.

Yes.

Soc.

But if there are three feet this way and three feet that way, the whole space will be three times three feet?

Boy.

That is evident.

Soc.

And how much are three times three feet?

Boy.

Nine.

Soc.

And how much is the double of four?

Boy.

Eight.

Soc.

Then the figure of eight is not made out of a line of three?

Boy.

No.

Soc.

But from what line?—tell me exactly; and if you 84would rather not reckon, try and show me the line.

Boy.

Indeed, Socrates, I do not know.

Soc.

Do you see, Meno, what advances he has made in his power of recollection? He did not know at first, and he does not know now, what is the side of a figure of eight feet: but then he thought that he knew, and answered confidently as if he knew, and had no difficulty; now he has a difficulty, and neither knows nor fancies that he knows.

Men.

True.

Soc.

Is he not better off in knowing his ignorance?

Men.

I think that he is.

Soc.

If we have made him doubt, and given him the 'torpedo's shock,' have we done him any harm?

Men.

I think not.

Soc.

We have certainly, as would seem, assisted him in some degree to the discovery of the truth; and now he will wish to remedy his ignorance, but then he would have been ready to tell all the world again and again that the double space should have a double side.

Men.

True.

Soc.

But do you suppose that he would ever have enquired into or learned what he fancied that he knew, though he was really ignorant of it, until he had fallen into perplexity under the idea that he did not know, and had desired to know?

Men.

I think not, Socrates.

Soc.

Then he was the better for the torpedo's touch?

Men.

I think so.

Soc.

The boy arrives at another true conclusion:

Mark now the farther development. I shall only ask him, and not teach him, and he shall share the enquiry with me: and do you watch and see if you find me telling or explaining anything to him, instead of eliciting his opinion. Tell me, boy, is not this a square of four feet which I have drawn?

Boy.

Yes.

Soc.

And now I add another square equal to the former one?

Boy.

Yes.

Soc.

And a third, which is equal to either of them?

Boy.

Yes.

Soc.

Suppose that we fill up the vacant corner?

Boy.

Very good.

Soc.

Here, then, there are four equal spaces?

Boy.

Yes.

Soc.

which is, that the square of the diagonal is double the square of the side.

And how many times larger is this space than this other?

Boy.

Four times.

Soc.

But it ought to have been twice only, as you will remember.

Boy.

True.

Soc.

And does not this line, reaching from corner to corner, 85bisect each of these spaces?

Boy.

Yes.

Soc.

And are there not here four equal lines which contain this space?

Boy.

There are.

Soc.

Look and see how much this space is.

Boy.

I do not understand.

Soc.

Has not each interior line cut off half of the four spaces?

Boy.

Yes.

Soc.

And how many such spaces are there in this section?

Boy.

Four.

Soc.

And how many in this?

Boy.

Two.

Soc.

And four is how many times two?

Boy.

Twice.

Soc.

And this space is of how many feet?

Boy.

Of eight feet.

Soc.

And from what line do you get this figure?

Boy.

From this.

Soc.

That is, from the line which extends from corner to corner of the figure of four feet?

Boy.

Yes.

Soc.

And that is the line which the learned call the diagonal. And if this is the proper name, then you, Meno's slave, are prepared to affirm that the double space is the square of the diagonal?

Boy.

Certainly, Socrates.

Soc.

What do you say of him, Meno? Were not all these answers given out of his own head?

Men.

Yes, they were all his own.

Soc.

And yet, as we were just now saying, he did not know?

Men.

True.

Soc.

But still he had in him those notions of his—had he not?

Men.

Yes.

Soc.

Then he who does not know may still have true notions of that which he does not know?

Men.

He has.

Soc.

At present he is in a dream; he will soon grow clearer.

And at present these notions have just been stirred up in him, as in a dream; but if he were frequently asked the same questions, in different forms, he would know as well as any one at last?

Men.

I dare say.

Soc.

Without any one teaching him he will recover his knowledge for himself, if he is only asked questions?

Men.

Yes.

Soc.

And this spontaneous recovery of knowledge in him is recollection?

Men.

True.

Soc.

And this knowledge which he now has must he not either have acquired or always possessed?

Men.

Yes.

Soc.

Socrates, Meno.Either this knowledge was acquired by him in a former state of existence, or was always known to him.

But if he always possessed this knowledge he would always have known; or if he has acquired the knowledge he could not have acquired it in this life, unless he has been taught geometry; for he may be made to do the same with all geometry and every other branch of knowledge. Now, has any one ever taught him all this? You must know about him, if, as you say, he was born and bred in your house.

Men.

And I am certain that no one ever did teach him.

Soc.

And yet he has the knowledge?

Men.

The fact, Socrates, is undeniable.

Soc.

But if he did not acquire the knowledge in this life, 86then he must have had and learned it at some other time?

Men.

Clearly he must.

Soc.

Which must have been the time when he was not a man?

Men.

Yes.

Soc.

And if there have been always true thoughts in him, both at the time when he was and was not a man, which only need to be awakened into knowledge by putting questions to him, his soul must have always possessed this knowledge, for he always either was or was not a man?

Men.

Obviously.

Soc.

And if the truth of all things always existed in the soul, then the soul is immortal. Wherefore be of good cheer, and try to recollect what you do not know, or rather what you do not remember.

Men.

I feel, somehow, that I like what you are saying.

Soc.

Better to enquire than to fancy that there is no such thing as enquiry and no use in it.

And I, Meno, like what I am saying. Some things I have said of which I am not altogether confident. But that we shall be better and braver and less helpless if we think that we ought to enquire, than we should have been if we indulged in the idle fancy that there was no knowing and no use in seeking to know what we do not know;—that is a theme upon which I am ready to fight, in word and deed, to the utmost of my power.

Men.

There again, Socrates, your words seem to me excellent.

Soc.

Then, as we are agreed that a man should enquire about that which he does not know, shall you and I make an effort to enquire together into the nature of virtue?

Men.

By all means, Socrates. And yet I would much rather return to my original question, Whether in seeking to acquire virtue we should regard it as a thing to be taught, or as a gift of nature, or as coming to men in some other way?

Soc.

Socrates cannot enquire whether virtue can be taught until he knows what virtue is, except upon an hypothesis, such as geometricians sometimes employ: e. g. can a triangle of given area be inscribed in a given circle, if when the side of it is produced this or that consequence follows? [The hypothesis appears to be rather trivial and to have no mathematical value.] Upon the hypothesis 'that virtue is knowledge,' can it be taught?

Had I the command of you as well as of myself, Meno, I would not have enquired whether virtue is given by instruction or not, until we had first ascertained 'what it is.' But as you think only of controlling me who am your slave, and never of controlling yourself,—such being your notion of freedom, I must yield to you, for you are irresistible. And therefore I have now to enquire into the qualities of a thing of which I do not as yet know the nature. At any rate, will you condescend a little, and allow the question 'Whether virtue is given by instruction, or in any other way,' to be argued upon hypothesis? As the geometrician, when he is asked whether 87a a certain triangle is capable of being inscribed in a certain circle, will reply: 'I cannot tell you as yet; but I will offer a hypothesis which may assist us in forming a conclusion: If the figure be such that when you have produced a given side of it, the given area of the triangle falls short by an area corresponding to the part produced, then one consequence follows, and if this is impossible then some other; and therefore I wish to assume a hypothesis before I tell you whether this triangle is capable of being inscribed in the circle:'—that is a geometrical hypothesis. And we too, as we know not the nature and qualities of virtue, must ask, whether virtue is or is not taught, under a hypothesis: as thus, if virtue is of such a class of mental goods, will it be taught or not? Let the first hypothesis be that virtue is or is not knowledge,—in that case will it be taught or not? or, as we were just now saying, 'remembered'? For there is no use in disputing about the name. But is virtue taught or not? or rather, does not every one see that knowledge alone is taught?

Men.

I agree.

Soc.

Then if virtue is knowledge, virtue will be taught?

Men.

Certainly.

Soc.

Then now we have made a quick end of this question: if virtue is of such a nature, it will be taught; and if not, not?

Men.

Certainly.

Soc.

Of course.

The next question is, whether virtue is knowledge or of another species?

Men.

Yes, that appears to be the question which comes next in order.

Soc.

But is virtue knowledge?

Do we not say that virtue is a good?—This is a hypothesis which is not set aside.

Men.

Certainly.

Soc.

Virtue is a good, and profitable: and all profitable things are either profitable or the reverse according as they are or are not under the guidance of knowledge.

Now, if there be any sort of good which is distinct from knowledge, virtue may be that good; but if knowledge embraces all good, then we shall be right in thinking that virtue is knowledge?

Men.

True.

Soc.

And virtue makes us good?

Men.

Yes.

Soc.

And if we are good, then we are profitable; for all good things are profitable?

Men.

Yes.

Soc.

Then virtue is profitable?

Men.

That is the only inference.

Soc.

Then now let us see what are the things which severally profit us. Health and strength, and beauty and wealth—these, and the like of these, we call profitable?

Men.

True.

Soc.

88And yet these things may also sometimes do us harm: would you not think so?

Men.

Yes.

Soc.

And what is the guiding principle which makes them profitable or the reverse? Are they not profitable when they are rightly used, and hurtful when they are not rightly used?

Men.

Certainly.

Soc.

Next, let us consider the goods of the soul: they are temperance, justice, courage, quickness of apprehension, memory, magnanimity, and the like?

Men.

Surely.

Soc.

And such of these as are not knowledge, but of another sort, are sometimes profitable and sometimes hurtful; as, for example, courage wanting prudence, which is only a sort of confidence? When a man has no sense he is harmed by courage, but when he has sense he is profited?

Men.

True.

Soc.

And the same may be said of temperance and quickness of apprehension; whatever things are learned or done with sense are profitable, but when done without sense they are hurtful?

Men.

Very true.

Soc.

And in general, all that the soul attempts or endures, when under the guidance of wisdom, ends in happiness; but when she is under the guidance of folly, in the opposite?

Men.

That appears to be true.

Soc.

And so all virtue must be a sort of wisdom or knowledge.

If then virtue is a quality of the soul, and is admitted to be profitable, it must be wisdom or prudence, since none of the things of the soul are either profitable or hurtful in themselves, but they are all made profitable or hurtful by the addition of wisdom or of folly; and therefore if virtue is profitable, virtue must be a sort of wisdom or prudence?

Men.

I quite agree.

Soc.

And the other goods, such as wealth and the like, of which we were just now saying that they are sometimes good and sometimes evil, do not they also become profitable or hurtful, accordingly as the soul guides and uses them rightly or wrongly; just as the things of the soul herself are benefited when under the guidance of wisdom and harmed by folly?

Men.

True.

Soc.

And the wise soul guides them rightly, and the foolish soul wrongly?

Men.

Yes.

Soc.

And is not this universally true of human nature? All other things hang upon the soul, and the things of the soul herself hang upon wisdom, if they are to be good; and 89so wisdom is inferred to be that which profits—and virtue, as we say, is profitable?

Men.

Certainly.

Soc.

Virtue is either wholly or partly wisdom.

And thus we arrive at the conclusion that virtue is either wholly or partly wisdom?

Men.

I think that what you are saying, Socrates, is very true.

Soc.

But if this is true, then the good are not by nature good?

Men.

I think not.

Soc.

If this is true, virtue must be taught; but then where are the teachers?

If they had been, there would assuredly have been discerners of characters among us who would have known our future great men; and on their showing we should have adopted them, and when we had got them, we should have kept them in the citadel out of the way of harm, and set a stamp upon them far rather than upon a piece of gold, in order that no one might tamper with them; and when they grew up they would have been useful to the state?

Men.

Yes, Socrates, that would have been the right way.

Soc.

But if the good are not by nature good, are they made good by instruction?

Men.

There appears to be no other alternative, Socrates. On the supposition that virtue is knowledge, there can be no doubt that virtue is taught.

Soc.

Yes, indeed; but what if the supposition is erroneous?

Men.

I certainly thought just now that we were right.

Soc.

Yes, Meno; but a principle which has any soundness should stand firm not only just now, but always.

Men.

Well; and why are you so slow of heart to believe that knowledge is virtue?

Soc.

I will try and tell you why, Meno. I do not retract the assertion that if virtue is knowledge it may be taught; but I fear that I have some reason in doubting whether virtue is knowledge: for consider now and say whether virtue, and not only virtue but anything that is taught, must not have teachers and disciples?

Men.

Surely.

Soc.

And conversely, may not the art of which neither teachers nor disciples exist be assumed to be incapable of being taught?

Men.

True; but do you think that there are no teachers of virtue?

Soc.

Can Anytus tell us who they are?

I have certainly often enquired whether there were any, and taken great pains to find them, and have never succeeded; and many have assisted me in the search, and they were the persons whom I thought the most likely to know. 90Here at the moment when he is wanted we fortunately have sitting by us Anytus, the very person of whom we should make enquiry; to him then let us repair. In the first place, he is the son of a wealthy and wise father, Anthemion, who acquired his wealth, not by accident or gift, like Ismenias the Theban (who has recently made himself as rich as Polycrates), but by his own skill and industry, and who is a well-conditioned, modest man, not insolent, or overbearing, or annoying; moreover, this son of his has received a good education, as the Athenian people certainly appear to think, for they choose him to fill the highest offices. And these are the sort of men from whom you are likely to learn whether there are any teachers of virtue, and who they are. Please, Anytus, to help me and your friend Meno in answering our question, Who are the teachers? Consider the matter thus: If we wanted Meno to be a good physician, to whom should we send him? Should we not send him to the physicians?

Any.

Certainly.

Soc.

Or if we wanted him to be a good cobbler, should we not send him to the cobblers?

Any.

Yes.

Soc.

And so forth?

Any.

Yes.

Soc.

The arts are taught by the professors of them. And have we not heard of those who profess to teach virtue at a fixed price?

Let me trouble you with one more question. When we say that we should be right in sending him to the physicians if we wanted him to be a physician, do we mean that we should be right in sending him to those who profess the art, rather than to those who do not, and to those who demand payment for teaching the art, and profess to teach it to any one who will come and learn? And if these were our reasons, should we not be right in sending him?

Any.

Yes.

Soc.

And might not the same be said of flute-playing, and of the other arts? Would a man who wanted to make another a flute-player refuse to send him to those who profess to teach the art for money, and be plaguing other persons to give him instruction, who are not professed teachers and who never had a single disciple in that branch of knowledge which he wishes him to acquire—would not such conduct be the height of folly?

Any.

Yes, by Zeus, and of ignorance too.

Soc.

Very good. And now you are in a position to advise with me about my friend Meno. He has been telling me, Anytus, that he desires to attain that kind of wisdom and virtue by which men order the state or the house, and honour their parents, and know when to receive and when to send away citizens and strangers, as a good man should. Now, to whom should he go in order that he may learn this virtue? Does not the previous argument imply clearly that we should send him to those who profess and avouch that they are the common teachers of all Hellas, and are ready to impart instruction to any one who likes, at a fixed price?

Any.

Whom do you mean, Socrates?

Soc.

You surely know, do you not, Anytus, that these are the people whom mankind call Sophists?

Any.

Anytus inveighs against the corrupting influence of the Sophists.

By Heracles, Socrates, forbear! I only hope that no friend or kinsman or acquaintance of mine, whether citizen or stranger, will ever be so mad as to allow himself to be corrupted by them; for they are a manifest pest and corrupting influence to those who have to do with them.

Soc.

Why surely they cannot really be corrupters? See what fortunes they make, and what an excellent reputation many of them bear!

What, Anytus? Of all the people who profess that they know how to do men good, do you mean to say that these are the only ones who not only do them no good, but positively corrupt those who are entrusted to them, and in return for this disservice have the face to demand money? Indeed, I cannot believe you; for I know of a single man, Protagoras, who made more out of his craft than the illustrious Pheidias, who created such noble works, or any ten other statuaries. How could that be? A mender of old shoes, or patcher up of clothes, who made the shoes or clothes worse than he received them, could not have remained thirty days undetected, and would very soon have starved; whereas during more than forty years, Protagoras was corrupting all Hellas, and sending his disciples from him worse than he received them, and he was never found out. For, if I am not mistaken, he was about seventy years old at his death, forty of which were spent in the practice of his profession; and during all that time he had a good reputation, which to this day he retains: and not only Protagoras, but many others are well spoken of; some who lived before him, and others who are still living. Now, when you say that they deceived and 92corrupted the youth, are they to be supposed to have corrupted them consciously or unconsciously? Can those who were deemed by many to be the wisest men of Hellas have been out of their minds?

Any.

The wisest men in Hellas could not have been out of their minds? No:—the people who gave their money to them were out of their minds.

Out of their minds! No, Socrates; the young men who gave their money to them were out of their minds, and their relations and guardians who entrusted their youth to the care of these men were still more out of their minds, and most of all, the cities who allowed them to come in, and did not drive them out, citizen and stranger alike.

Soc.

Has any of the Sophists wronged you, Anytus? What makes you so angry with them?

Any.

No, indeed, neither I nor any of my belongings has ever had, nor would I suffer them to have, anything to do with them.

Soc.

Then you are entirely unacquainted with them?

Any.

And I have no wish to be acquainted.

Soc.

How can Anytus know that they are bad, if he does not know them at all?

Then, my dear friend, how can you know whether a thing is good or bad of which you are wholly ignorant?

Any.

Quite well; I am sure that I know what manner of men these are, whether I am acquainted with them or not.

Soc.

Then who will teach Meno virtue?

You must be a diviner, Anytus, for I really cannot make out, judging from your own words, how, if you are not acquainted with them, you know about them. But I am not enquiring of you who are the teachers who will corrupt Meno (let them be, if you please, the Sophists); I only ask you to tell him who there is in this great city who will teach him how to become eminent in the virtues which I was just now describing. He is the friend of your family, and you will oblige him.

Any.

Why do you not tell him yourself?

Soc.

I have told him whom I supposed to be the teachers of these things; but I learn from you that I am utterly at fault, and I dare say that you are right. And now I wish that you, on your part, would tell me to whom among the Athenians he should go. Whom would you name?

Any.

Any Athenian gentleman who has learned of a previous generation of gentlemen.

Why single out individuals? Any Athenian gentleman, taken at random, if he will mind him, will do far more good to him than the Sophists.

Soc.

And did those gentlemen grow of themselves, and without having been taught by any one, were they nevertheless 93able to teach others that which they had never learned themselves?

Any.

I imagine that they learned of the previous generation of gentlemen. Have there not been many good men in this city?

Soc.

Yes, certainly, Anytus; and many good statesmen also there always have been and there are still, in the city of Athens. But the question is whether they were also good teachers of their own virtue;—not whether there are, or have been, good men in this part of the world, but whether virtue can be taught, is the question which we have been discussing. Now, do we mean to say that the good men of our own and of other times knew how to impart to others that virtue which they had themselves; or is virtue a thing incapable of being communicated or imparted by one man to another? That is the question which I and Meno have been arguing. Look at the matter in your own way: Would you not admit that Themistocles was a good man?

Any.

Certainly; no man better.

Soc.

Good men may not have been good teachers. There never was a better man than Themistocles; but he did not make much of his own son.

And must not he then have been a good teacher, if any man ever was a good teacher, of his own virtue?

Any.

Yes, certainly,—if he wanted to be so.

Soc.

But would he not have wanted? He would, at any rate, have desired to make his own son a good man and a gentleman; he could not have been jealous of him, or have intentionally abstained from imparting to him his own virtue. Did you never hear that he made his son Cleophantus a famous horseman; and had him taught to stand upright on horseback and hurl a javelin, and to do many other marvellous things; and in anything which could be learned from a master he was well trained? Have you not heard from our elders of him?

Any.

I have.

Soc.

Then no one could say that his son showed any want of capacity?

Any.

Very likely not.

Soc.

But did any one, old or young, ever say in your hearing that Cleophantus, son of Themistocles, was a wise or good man, as his father was?

Any.

I have certainly never heard any one say so.

Soc.

He had him taught accomplishments because there was no one to teach virtue.

And if virtue could have been taught, would his father Themistocles have sought to train him in these minor accomplishments, and allowed him who, as you must remember, was his own son, to be no better than his neighbours in those qualities in which he himself excelled?

Any.

Indeed, indeed, I think not.

Soc.

Here was a teacher of virtue whom you admit to be among the best men of the past. Let us take another,—Aristides, 94the son of Lysimachus: would you not acknowledge that he was a good man?

Any.

To be sure I should.

Soc.

Aristides was also a good man, and Pericles and Thucydides:—they made their sons good horsemen, and wrestlers, and the like, but they did not have them taught to be good, because virtue cannot be taught.

And did not he train his son Lysimachus better than any other Athenian in all that could be done for him by the help of masters? But what has been the result? Is he a bit better than any other mortal? He is an acquaintance of yours, and you see what he is like. There is Pericles, again, magnificent in his wisdom; and he, as you are aware, had two sons, Paralus and Xanthippus.

Any.

I know.

Soc.

And you know, also, that he taught them to be unrivalled horsemen, and had them trained in music and gymnastics and all sorts of arts—in these respects they were on a level with the best—and had he no wish to make good men of them? Nay, he must have wished it. But virtue, as I suspect, could not be taught. And that you may not suppose the incompetent teachers to be only the meaner sort of Athenians and few in number, remember again that Thucydides had two sons, Melesias and Stephanus, whom, besides giving them a good education in other things, he trained in wrestling, and they were the best wrestlers in Athens: one of them he committed to the care of Xanthias, and the other of Eudorus, who had the reputation of being the most celebrated wrestlers of that day. Do you remember them?

Any.

I have heard of them.

Soc.

Socrates, Anytus, Meno.

Now, can there be a doubt that Thucydides, whose children were taught things for which he had to spend money, would have taught them to be good men, which would have cost him nothing, if virtue could have been taught? Will you reply that he was a mean man, and had not many friends among the Athenians and allies? Nay, but he was of a great family, and a man of influence at Athens and in all Hellas, and, if virtue could have been taught, he would have found out some Athenian or foreigner who would have made good men of his sons, if he could not himself spare the time from cares of state. Once more, I suspect, friend Anytus, that virtue is not a thing which can be taught?

Any.

Anytus gives an angry warning to Socrates.

Socrates, I think that you are too ready to speak evil of men: and, if you will take my advice, I would recommend you to be careful. Perhaps there is no city in which it is not easier to do men harm than to do them good, and this is certainly the case at Athens, as I believe that you know.

Soc.

O Meno, I think that Anytus is in a rage. And he may well be in a rage, for he thinks, in the first place, that I am defaming these gentlemen; and in the second place, he is of opinion that he is one of them himself. But some day he will know what is the meaning of defamation, and if he ever does, he will forgive me. Meanwhile I will return to you, Meno; for I suppose that there are gentlemen in your region too?

Men.

Certainly there are.

Soc.

And are they willing to teach the young? and do they profess to be teachers? and do they agree that virtue is taught?

Men.

The Thessalian gentry are not agreed about the possibility of teaching virtue.

No indeed, Socrates, they are anything but agreed; you may hear them saying at one time that virtue can be taught, and then again the reverse.

Soc.

Can we call those teachers who do not acknowledge the possibility of their own vocation?

Men.

I think not, Socrates.

Soc.

And what do you think of these Sophists, who are the only professors? Do they seem to you to be teachers of virtue?

Men.

Gorgias professes to teach rhetoric, but laughs at those who pretend to teach virtue.

I often wonder, Socrates, that Gorgias is never heard promising to teach virtue: and when he hears others promising he only laughs at them; but he thinks that men should be taught to speak.

Soc.

Then do you not think that the Sophists are teachers?

Men.

Socrates, Meno.

I cannot tell you, Socrates; like the rest of the world, I am in doubt, and sometimes I think that they are teachers and sometimes not.

Soc.

And are you aware that not you only and other politicians have doubts whether virtue can be taught or not, but that Theognis the poet says the very same thing?

Men.

Where does he say so?

Soc.

In these elegiac verses :—

Theognis implies in one passage that virtue can, and in another that it cannot, be taught.

'Eat and drink and sit with the mighty, and make yourself agreeable to them; for from the good you will learn what is good, but if you mix with the bad you will lose the intelligence which you already have.'

Do you observe that here he seems to imply that virtue can be taught?

Men.

Clearly.

Soc.

But in some other verses he shifts about and says :—

'If understanding could be created and put into a man, then they' [who were able to perform this feat] 'would have obtained great rewards.'

And again:—

'Never would a bad son have sprung from a good sire, for he would have 96heard the voice of instruction; but not by teaching will you ever make a bad man into a good one.'

And this, as you may remark, is a contradiction of the other.

Men.

Clearly.

Soc.

How can they be teachers who are so inconsistent with themselves?

And is there anything else of which the professors are affirmed not only not to be teachers of others, but to be ignorant themselves, and bad at the knowledge of that which they are professing to teach? or is there anything about which even the acknowledged 'gentlemen' are sometimes saying that 'this thing can be taught,' and sometimes the opposite? Can you say that they are teachers in any true sense whose ideas are in such confusion?

Men.

I should say, certainly not.

Soc.

But if neither the Sophists nor the gentlemen are teachers, clearly there can be no other teachers?

Men.

No.

Soc.

And if there are no teachers, neither are there disciples?

Men.

Agreed.

Soc.

And we have admitted that a thing cannot be taught of which there are neither teachers nor disciples?

Men.

We have.

Soc.

If there are no teachers and no scholars, virtue cannot be taught.

And there are no teachers of virtue to be found anywhere?

Men.

There are not.

Soc.

And if there are no teachers, neither are there scholars?

Men.

That, I think, is true.

Soc.

Then virtue cannot be taught?

Men.

Not if we are right in our view. But I cannot believe, Socrates, that there are no good men: And if there are, how did they come into existence?

Soc.

But were we not mistaken in our view? There may be another guide to good action as well as knowledge,

I am afraid, Meno, that you and I are not good for much, and that Gorgias has been as poor an educator of you as Prodicus has been of me. Certainly we shall have to look to ourselves, and try to find some one who will help in some way or other to improve us. This I say, because I observe that in the previous discussion none of us remarked that right and good action is possible to man under other guidance than that of knowledge (ἐπιστήμη);—and indeed if this be denied, there is no seeing how there can be any good men at all.

Men.

How do you mean, Socrates?

Soc.

I mean that good men are necessarily useful or 97profitable. Were we not right in admitting this? It must be so.

Men.

Yes.

Soc.

And in supposing that they will be useful only if they are true guides to us of action— there we were also right?

Men.

Yes.

Soc.

But when we said that a man cannot be a good guide unless he have knowledge (φρόνησις), in this we were wrong.

Men.

What do you mean by the word 'right'?

Soc.

I will explain. If a man knew the way to Larisa, or anywhere else, and went to the place and led others thither, would he not be a right and good guide?

Men.

Certainly.

Soc.

And a person who had a right opinion about the way, but had never been and did not know, might be a good guide also, might he not?

Men.

Certainly.

Soc.

And while he has true opinion about that which the other knows, he will be just as good a guide if he thinks the truth, as he who knows the truth?

Men.

Exactly.

Soc.

Right opinion is as good a guide to action as knowledge.

Then true opinion is as good a guide to correct action as knowledge; and that was the point which we omitted in our speculation about the nature of virtue, when we said that knowledge only is the guide of right action; whereas there is also right opinion.

Men.

True.

Soc.

Then right opinion is not less useful than knowledge?

Men.

The difference, Socrates, is only that he who has knowledge will always be right; but he who has right opinion will sometimes be right, and sometimes not.

Soc.

What do you mean? Can he be wrong who has right opinion, so long as he has right opinion?

Men.

I admit the cogency of your argument, and therefore, Socrates, I wonder that knowledge should be preferred to right opinion—or why they should ever differ.

Soc.

And shall I explain this wonder to you?

Men.

Do tell me.

Soc.

You would not wonder if you had ever observed the images of Daedalus ; but perhaps you have not got them in your country?

Men.

What have they to do with the question?

Soc.

Because they require to be fastened in order to keep them, and if they are not fastened they will play truant and run away.

Men.

Well, what of that?

Soc.

But right opinions are apt to walk away, like the images of Daedalus.

I mean to say that they are not very valuable possessions if they are at liberty, for they will walk off like runaway slaves; but when fastened, they are of great value, for they are really beautiful works of art. Now this is an illustration of the nature of true opinions: while they abide 98with us they are beautiful and fruitful, but they run away out of the human soul, and do not remain long, and therefore they are not of much value until they are fastened by the tie of the cause; and this fastening of them, friend Meno, is recollection, as you and I have agreed to call it. But when they are bound, in the first place, they have the nature of knowledge; and, in the second place, they are abiding. And this is why knowledge is more honourable and excellent than true opinion, because fastened by a chain.

Men.

What you are saying, Socrates, seems to be very like the truth.

Soc.

I too speak rather in ignorance; I only conjecture. And yet that knowledge differs from true opinion is no matter of conjecture with me. There are not many things which I profess to know, but this is most certainly one of them.

Men.

Yes, Socrates; and you are quite right in saying so.

Soc.

And am I not also right in saying that true opinion leading the way perfects action quite as well as knowledge?

Men.

There again, Socrates, I think that you are right.

Soc.

Then right opinion is not a whit inferior to knowledge, or less useful in action; nor is the man who has right opinion inferior to him who has knowledge?

Men.

True.

Soc.

And surely the good man has been acknowledged by us to be useful?

Men.

Yes.

Soc.

Seeing then that men become good and useful to states, not only because they have knowledge, but because they have right opinion, and that neither knowledge nor right opinion is given to man by nature or acquired by him—(do you imagine either of them to be given by nature?

Men.

Not I.)

Soc.

Then if they are not given by nature, neither are the good by nature good?

Men.

Certainly not.

Soc.

And nature being excluded, then came the question whether virtue is acquired by teaching?

Men.

Yes.

Soc.

If virtue was wisdom [or knowledge], then, as we thought, it was taught?

Men.

Yes.

Soc.

And if it was taught it was wisdom?

Men.

Certainly.

Soc.

And if there were teachers, it might be taught; and if there were no teachers, not?

Men.

True.

Soc.

But surely we acknowledged that there were no teachers of virtue?

Men.

Yes.

Soc.

Then we acknowledged that it was not taught, and was not wisdom?

Men.

Certainly.

Soc.

And yet we admitted that it was a good?

Men.

Yes.

Soc.

And the right guide is useful and good? 99

Men.

Certainly.

Soc.

If virtue and knowledge cannot be taught, the only right guides of men are true opinions.

And the only right guides are knowledge and true opinion—these are the guides of man; for things which happen by chance are not under the guidance of man: but the guides of man are true opinion and knowledge.

Men.

I think so too.

Soc.

But if virtue is not taught, neither is virtue knowledge.

Men.

Clearly not.

Soc.

Then of two good and useful things, one, which is knowledge, has been set aside, and cannot be supposed to be our guide in political life.

Men.

I think not.

Soc.

And therefore not by any wisdom, and not because they were wise, did Themistocles and those others of whom Anytus spoke govern states. This was the reason why they were unable to make others like themselves—because their virtue was not grounded on knowledge.

Men.

That is probably true, Socrates.

Soc.

Right opinion is in politics what divination is in religion; diviners, prophets, poets, statesmen, may all be truly called 'divine men.

But if not by knowledge, the only alternative which remains is that statesmen must have guided states by right opinion, which is in politics what divination is in religion; for diviners and also prophets say many things truly, but they know not what they say.

Men.

So I believe.

Soc.

And may we not, Meno, truly call those men 'divine' who, having no understanding, yet succeed in many a grand deed and word?

Men.

Certainly.

Soc.

Then we shall also be right in calling divine those whom we were just now speaking of as diviners and prophets, including the whole tribe of poets. Yes, and statesmen above all may be said to be divine and illumined, being inspired and possessed of God, in which condition they say many grand things, not knowing what they say.

Men.

Yes.

Soc.

And the women too, Meno, call good men divine—do they not? and the Spartans, when they praise a good man, say 'that he is a divine man.'

Men.

And I think, Socrates, that they are right; although very likely our friend Anytus may take offence at the word.

Soc.

I do not care; as for Anytus, there will be another opportunity of talking with him. To sum up our enquiry—the result seems to be, if we are at all right in our view, that virtue is neither natural nor acquired, but an instinct given 100by God to the virtuous. Nor is the instinct accompanied by reason, unless there may be supposed to be among statesmen some one who is capable of educating statesmen. And if there be such an one, he may be said to be among the living what Homer says that Tiresias was among the dead, 'he alone has understanding; but the rest are flitting shades;' and he and his virtue in like manner will be a reality among shadows.

Men.

That is excellent, Socrates.

Soc.

Virtue comes by the gift of God.

Then, Meno, the conclusion is that virtue comes to the virtuous by the gift of God. But we shall never know the certain truth until, before asking how virtue is given, we enquire into the actual nature of virtue. I fear that I must go away, but do you, now that you are persuaded yourself, persuade our friend Anytus. And do not let him be so exasperated; if you can conciliate him, you will have done good service to the Athenian people.

INTRODUCTION TO EUTHYPHRO.

*Euthyphro.*Introduction.

In the Meno, Anytus had parted from Socrates with the significant words: 'That in any city, and particularly in the city of Athens, it is easier to do men harm than to do them good' (94 E); and Socrates was anticipating another opportunity of talking with him (99 E). In the Euthyphro, Socrates is awaiting his trial for impiety. But before the trial begins, Plato would like to put the world on their trial, and convince them of ignorance in that very matter touching which Socrates is accused. An incident which may perhaps really have occurred in the family of Euthyphro, a learned Athenian diviner and soothsayer, furnishes the occasion of the discussion.

Analysis.

This Euthyphro and Socrates are represented as meeting in the 2porch of the King Archon. (Cp. Theaet. sub fin.) Both have legal business in hand. Socrates is defendant in a suit for impiety 3which Meletus has brought against him (it is remarked by the way that he is not a likely man himself to have brought a suit against another); and Euthyphro too is plaintiff in an action for 4murder, which he has brought against his own father. The latter has originated in the following manner:—A poor dependant of the family had slain one of their domestic slaves in Naxos. The guilty person was bound and thrown into a ditch by the command of Euthyphro's father, who sent to the interpreters of religion at Athens to ask what should be done with him. Before the messenger came back the criminal had died from hunger and exposure.

This is the origin of the charge of murder which Euthyphro brings against his father. Socrates is confident that before he could have undertaken the responsibility of such a prosecution, he must have been perfectly informed of the nature of piety and 5impiety; and as he is going to be tried for impiety himself, he thinks that he cannot do better than learn of Euthyphro (who will be admitted by everybody, including the judges, to be an unimpeachable authority) what piety is, and what is impiety. What then is piety?

Euthyphro, who, in the abundance of his knowledge, is very willing to undertake all the responsibility, replies: That piety is doing as I do, prosecuting your father (if he is guilty) on a charge of murder; doing as the gods do—as Zeus did to Cronos, and Cronos to Uranus.

Socrates has a dislike to these tales of mythology, and he fancies 6that this dislike of his may be the reason why he is charged with impiety. 'Are they really true?' 'Yes, they are;' and Euthyphro will gladly tell Socrates some more of them. But Socrates would like first of all to have a more satisfactory answer to the question, 'What is piety?' 'Doing as I do, charging a father with murder,' may be a single instance of piety, but can hardly be regarded as a general definition.

Euthyphro replies, that 'Piety is what is dear to the gods, 7and impiety is what is not dear to them.' But may there not be differences of opinion, as among men, so also among the gods? Especially, about good and evil, which have no fixed rule; and these are precisely the sort of differences which give rise to quarrels. And therefore what may be dear to one 8god may not be dear to another, and the same action may be both pious and impious; e. g. your chastisement of your father, Euthyphro, may be dear or pleasing to Zeus (who inflicted a similar chastisement on his own father), but not equally pleasing to Cronos or Uranus (who suffered at the hands of their sons).

Euthyphro answers that there is no difference of opinion, either among gods or men, as to the propriety of punishing a murderer. Yes, rejoins Socrates, when they know him to be a murderer; but you are assuming the point at issue. If all the circumstances of the case are considered, are you able to show that your father 9was guilty of murder, or that all the gods are agreed in approving of our prosecution of him? And must you not allow that what is hated by one god may be liked by another? Waiving this last, however, Socrates proposes to amend the definition, and say that 'what all the gods love is pious, and what they all hate is impious.' To this Euthyphro agrees.

10Socrates proceeds to analyze the new form of the definition. He shows that in other cases the act precedes the state; e.g. the act of being carried, loved, &c. precedes the state of being carried, loved, &c., and therefore that which is dear to the gods is dear to the gods because it is first loved of them, not loved of them because it is dear to them. But the pious or holy is loved by the gods because it is pious or holy, which is equivalent to saying, that it is loved by them because it is dear to them. Here 11then appears to be a contradiction,—Euthyphro has been giving an attribute or accident of piety only, and not the essence. Euthyphro acknowledges himself that his explanations seem to walk away or go round in a circle, like the moving figures of Daedalus, the ancestor of Socrates, who has communicated his art to his descendants.

12Socrates, who is desirous of stimulating the indolent intelligence of Euthyphro, raises the question in another manner: 'Is all the pious just?' 'Yes.' 'Is all the just pious?' 'No.' 'Then what part of justice is piety?' Euthyphro replies that piety is that part of justice which 'attends' to the gods, as there is another 13part of justice which 'attends' to men. But what is the meaning of 'attending' to the gods? The word 'attending,' when applied to dogs, horses, and men, implies that in some way they are made better. But how do pious or holy acts make the gods any better? Euthyphro explains that he means by pious acts, acts of service or ministration. Yes; but the ministrations of the husbandman, the physician, and the builder have an end. To what end do 14we serve the gods, and what do we help them to accomplish? Euthyphro replies, that all these difficult questions cannot be resolved in a short time; and he would rather say simply that piety is knowing how to please the gods in word and deed, by prayers and sacrifices. In other words, says Socrates, piety is 'a 15science of asking and giving'—asking what we want and giving what they want; in short, a mode of doing business between gods and men. But although they are the givers of all good, how can we give them any good in return? 'Nay, but we give them honour.' Then we give them not what is beneficial, but what is pleasing or dear to them; and this is the point which has been already disproved.

Socrates, although weary of the subterfuges and evasions of Euthyphro, remains unshaken in his conviction that he must know the nature of piety, or he would never have prosecuted his old father. He is still hoping that he will condescend to instruct him. But Euthyphro is in a hurry and cannot stay. And Socrates' last 16hope of knowing the nature of piety before he is prosecuted for impiety has disappeared. As in the Euthydemus the irony is carried on to the end.

Introduction.

The Euthyphro is manifestly designed to contrast the real nature of piety and impiety with the popular conceptions of them. But when the popular conceptions of them have been overthrown, Socrates does not offer any definition of his own: as in the Laches and Lysis, he prepares the way for an answer to the question which he has raised; but true to his own character, refuses to answer himself.

Euthyphro is a religionist, and is elsewhere spoken of, if he be the same person, as the author of a philosophy of names, by whose 'prancing steeds' Socrates in the Cratylus is carried away (p. 396). He has the conceit and self-confidence of a Sophist; no doubt that he is right in prosecuting his father has ever entered into his mind. Like a Sophist too, he is incapable either of framing a general definition or of following the course of an argument. His wrong-headedness, one-sidedness, narrowness, positiveness, are characteristic of his priestly office. His failure to apprehend an argument may be compared to a similar defect which is observable in the rhapsode Ion. But he is not a bad man, and he is friendly to Socrates, whose familiar sign he recognizes with interest. Though unable to follow him he is very willing to be led by him, and eagerly catches at any suggestion which saves him from the trouble of thinking. Moreover he is the enemy of Meletus, who, as he says, is availing himself of the popular dislike to innovations in religion in order to injure Socrates; at the same time he is amusingly confident that he has weapons in his own armoury which would be more than a match for him. He is quite sincere in his prosecution of his father, who has accidentally been guilty of homicide, and is not wholly free from blame. To purge away the crime appears to him in the light of a duty, whoever may be the criminal.

Thus begins the contrast between the religion of the letter, or of the narrow and unenlightened conscience, and the higher notion of religion which Socrates vainly endeavours to elicit from him. 'Piety is doing as I do' is the idea of religion which first occurs to him, and to many others who do not say what they think with equal frankness. For men are not easily persuaded that any other religion is better than their own; or that other nations, e. g. the Greeks in the time of Socrates, were equally serious in their religious beliefs and difficulties. The chief difference between us and them is, that they were slowly learning what we are in process of forgetting. Greek mythology hardly admitted of the distinction between accidental homicide and murder: that the pollution of blood was the same in both cases is also the feeling of the Athenian diviner. He had not as yet learned the lesson, which philosophy was teaching, that Homer and Hesiod, if not banished from the state, or whipped out of the assembly, as Heracleitus more rudely proposed, at any rate were not to be appealed to as authorities in religion; and he is ready to defend his conduct by the examples of the gods. These are the very tales which Socrates cannot abide; and his dislike of them, as he suspects, has branded him with the reputation of impiety. Here is one answer to the question, 'Why Socrates was put to death,' suggested by the way. Another is conveyed in the words, 'The Athenians do not care about any man being thought wise until he begins to make other men wise; and then for some reason or other they are angry:' which may be said to be the rule of popular toleration in most other countries, and not at Athens only. In the course of the argument (7 A, B) Socrates remarks that the controversial nature of morals and religion arises out of the difficulty of verifying them. There is no measure or standard to which they can be referred.

The next definition, 'Piety is that which is loved of the gods,' is shipwrecked on a refined distinction between the state and the act, corresponding respectively to the adjective (φίλον) and the participle (φιλούμενον), or rather perhaps to the participle and the verb (φιλούμενον and φιλεῖται). The act is prior to the state (as in Aristotle the ἐνέργεια precedes the δύναμις); and the state of being loved is preceded by the act of being loved. But piety or holiness is preceded by the act of being pious, not by the act of being loved; and therefore piety and the state of being loved are different. Through such subtleties of dialectic Socrates is working his way into a deeper region of thought and feeling. He means to say that the words 'loved of the gods' express an attribute only, and not the essence of piety.

Then follows the third and last definition, 'Piety is a part of justice.' Thus far Socrates has proceeded in placing religion on a moral foundation. He is seeking to realize the harmony of religion and morality, which the great poets Æschylus, Sophocles, and

Pindar had unconsciously anticipated, and which is the universal want of all men. To this the soothsayer adds the ceremonial element, 'attending upon the gods.' When further interrogated by Socrates as to the nature of this 'attention to the gods,' he replies, that piety is an affair of business, a science of giving and asking, and the like. Socrates points out the anthropomorphism of these notions. (Cp. Symp. 202 E; Rep. ii. 365 E; Politicus 290 C, D.) But when we expect him to go on and show that the true service of the gods is the service of the spirit and the co-operation with them in all things true and good, he stops short; this was a lesson which the soothsayer could not have been made to understand, and which every one must learn for himself.

There seem to be altogether three aims or interests in this little Dialogue: (1) the dialectical development of the idea of piety; (2) the antithesis of true and false religion, which is carried to a certain extent only; (3) the defence of Socrates.

The subtle connection with the Apology and the Crito; the holding back of the conclusion, as in the Charmides, Lysis, Laches, Protagoras, and other Dialogues; the deep insight into the religious world; the dramatic power and play of the two characters; the inimitable irony, are reasons for believing that the Euthyphro is a genuine Platonic writing. The spirit in which the popular representations of mythology are denounced recalls Republic II (378 ff.) The virtue of piety has been already mentioned as one of five in the Protagoras, but is not reckoned among the four cardinal virtues of Republic IV (428 ff.). The figure of Daedalus (15 C) has occurred in the Meno (97 D); that of Proteus (15 D) in the Euthydemus (288 B) and Io (541 E). The kingly science has already appeared in the Euthydemus, and will reappear in the Republic and Statesman. But neither from these nor any other indications of similarity or difference, and still less from arguments respecting the suitableness of this little work to aid Socrates at the time of his trial or the reverse, can any evidence of the date be obtained.

EUTHYPHRO.

PERSONS OF THE DIALOGUE.

Socrates.

Euthyphro.

Scene:—The Porch of the King Archon.

Euthyphro.

*Euthyphro.*Socrates, Euthyphro.Euthyphro and Socrates meet at the Porch of the King Archon. Both have legal business on hand.

2Why have you left the Lyceum, Socrates? and what are you doing in the Porch of the King Archon? Surely you cannot be concerned in a suit before the King, like myself?

Socrates.

Not in a suit, Euthyphro; impeachment is the word which the Athenians use.

Euth.

What! I suppose that some one has been prosecuting you, for I cannot believe that you are the prosecutor of another.

Soc.

Certainly not.

Euth.

Then some one else has been prosecuting you?

Soc.

Yes.

Euth.

And who is he?

Soc.

A young man who is little known, Euthyphro; and I hardly know him: his name is Meletus, and he is of the deme of Pitthis. Perhaps you may remember his appearance; he has a beak, and long straight hair, and a beard which is ill grown.

Euth.

No, I do not remember him, Socrates. But what is the charge which he brings against you?

Soc.

Meletus has brought a charge against Socrates.

What is the charge? Well, a very serious charge, which shows a good deal of character in the young man, and for which he is certainly not to be despised. He says he knows how the youth are corrupted and who are their corruptors. I fancy that he must be a wise man, and seeing that I am the reverse of a wise man, he has found me out, and is going to accuse me of corrupting his young friends. And of this our mother the state is to be the judge. Of all our political men he is the only one who seems to me to begin in the right way, with the cultivation of virtue in youth; like a good husbandman, he makes the young shoots his first 3care, and clears away us who are the destroyers of them. This is only the first step; he will afterwards attend to the elder branches; and if he goes on as he has begun, he will be a very great public benefactor.

Euth.

I hope that he may; but I rather fear, Socrates, that the opposite will turn out to be the truth. My opinion is that in attacking you he is simply aiming a blow at the foundation of the state. But in what way does he say that you corrupt the young?

Soc.

The nature of the charge against Socrates.

He brings a wonderful accusation against me, which at first hearing excites surprise: he says that I am a poet or maker of gods, and that I invent new gods and deny the existence of old ones; this is the ground of his indictment.

Euth.

I understand, Socrates; he means to attack you about the familiar sign which occasionally, as you say, comes to you. He thinks that you are a neologian, and he is going to have you up before the court for this. He knows that such a charge is readily received by the world, as I myself know too well; for when I speak in the assembly about divine things, and foretell the future to them, they laugh at me and think me a madman. Yet every word that I say is true. But they are jealous of us all; and we must be brave and go at them.

Soc.

Their laughter, friend Euthyphro, is not a matter of much consequence. For a man may be thought wise; but the Athenians, I suspect, do not much trouble themselves about him until he begins to impart his wisdom to others; and then for some reason or other, perhaps, as you say, from jealousy, they are angry.

Euth.

I am never likely to try their temper in this way.

Soc.

I dare say not, for you are reserved in your behaviour, and seldom impart your wisdom. But I have a benevolent habit of pouring out myself to everybody, and would even pay for a listener, and I am afraid that the Athenians may think me too talkative. Now if, as I was saying, they would only laugh at me, as you say that they laugh at you, the time might pass gaily enough in the court; but perhaps they may be in earnest, and then what the end will be you soothsayers only can predict.

Euth.

I dare say that the affair will end in nothing, Socrates, and that you will win your cause; and I think that I shall win my own.

Soc.

And what is your suit, Euthyphro? are you the pursuer or the defendant?

Euth.

I am the pursuer.

Soc.

Of whom?

Euth.

You will think me mad when I tell you.

Soc.

Why, has the fugitive wings?

Euth.

Nay, he is not very volatile at his time of life.

Soc.

Who is he?

Euth.

My father.

Soc.

Your father! my good man?

Euth.

Yes.

Soc.

And of what is he accused?

Euth.

Of murder, Socrates.

Soc.

The irony of Socrates.

By the powers, Euthyphro! how little does the common herd know of the nature of right and truth. A man must be an extraordinary man, and have made great strides in wisdom, before he could have seen his way to bring such an action.

Euth.

Indeed, Socrates, he must.

Soc.

Euthyphro is under a sacred obligation to prosecute a homicide, even if he be his own father.

I suppose that the man whom your father murdered was one of your relatives—clearly he was; for if he had been a stranger you would never have thought of prosecuting him.

Euth.

I am amused, Socrates, at your making a distinction between one who is a relation and one who is not a relation; for surely the pollution is the same in either case, if you knowingly associate with the murderer when you ought to clear yourself and him by proceeding against him. The real question is whether the murdered man has been justly slain. If justly, then your duty is to let the matter alone; but if unjustly, then even if the murderer lives under the same roof with you and eats at the same table, proceed against him. Now the man who is dead was a poor dependant of mine who worked for us as a field labourer on our farm in Naxos, and one day in a fit of drunken passion he got into a quarrel with one of our domestic servants and slew him. My father bound him hand and foot and threw him into a ditch, and then sent to Athens to ask of a diviner what he should do with him. Meanwhile he never attended to him and took no care about him, for he regarded him as a murderer; and thought that no great harm would be done even if he did die. Now this was just what happened. For such was the effect of cold and hunger and chains upon him, that before the messenger returned from the diviner, he was dead. And my father and family are angry with me for taking the part of the murderer and prosecuting my father. They say that he did not kill him, and that if he did, the dead man was but a murderer, and I ought not to take any notice, for that a son is impious who prosecutes a father. Which shows, Socrates, how little they know what the gods think about piety and impiety.

Soc.

Good heavens, Euthyphro! and is your knowledge of religion and of things pious and impious so very exact, that, supposing the circumstances to be as you state them, you are not afraid lest you too may be doing an impious thing in bringing an action against your father?

Euth.

The best of Euthyphro, and that which distinguishes him, Socrates, from other men, is his exact knowledge of all 5such matters. What should I be good for without it?

Soc.

Socrates, who is accused of false theology, thinks that he cannot do better than become the disciple of so great a theologian as Euthyphro.

Rare friend! I think that I cannot do better than be your disciple. Then before the trial with Meletus comes on I shall challenge him, and say that I have always had a great interest in religious questions, and now, as he charges me with rash imaginations and innovations in religion, I have become your disciple. You, Meletus, as I shall say to him, acknowledge Euthyphro to be a great theologian, and sound in his opinions; and if you approve of him you ought to approve of me, and not have me into court; but if you disapprove, you should begin by indicting him who is my teacher, and who will be the ruin, not of the young, but of the old; that is to say, of myself whom he instructs, and of his old father whom he admonishes and chastises. And if Meletus refuses to listen to me, but will go on, and will not shift the indictment from me to you, I cannot do better than repeat this challenge in the court.

Euth.

Yes, indeed, Socrates; and if he attempts to indict me I am mistaken if I do not find a flaw in him; the court shall have a great deal more to say to him than to me.

Soc.

He asks, 'What is piety?'

And I, my dear friend, knowing this, am desirous of becoming your disciple. For I observe that no one appears to notice you—not even this Meletus; but his sharp eyes have found me out at once, and he has indicted me for impiety. And therefore, I adjure you to tell me the nature of piety and impiety, which you said that you knew so well, and of murder, and of other offences against the gods. What are they? Is not piety in every action always the same? and impiety, again—is it not always the opposite of piety, and also the same with itself, having, as impiety, one notion which includes whatever is impious?

Euth.

To be sure, Socrates.

Soc.

And what is piety, and what is impiety?

Euth.

Piety is doing as I am doing;—like Zeus, I am proceeding against my father.

Piety is doing as I am doing; that is to say, prosecuting any one who is guilty of murder, sacrilege, or of any similar crime—whether he be your father or mother, or whoever he may be—that makes no difference; and not to prosecute them is impiety. And please to consider, Socrates, what a notable proof I will give you of the truth of my words, a proof which I have already given to others:—of the principle, I mean, that the impious, whoever he may be, ought not to go unpunished. For do not men regard 6Zeus as the best and most righteous of the gods? and yet they admit that he bound his father (Cronos) because he wickedly devoured his sons, and that he too had punished his own father (Uranus) for a similar reason, in a nameless manner. And yet when I proceed against my father, they are angry with me. So inconsistent are they in their way of talking when the gods are concerned, and when I am concerned.

Soc.

Does Euthyphro believe these amazing stories about the gods?

May not this be the reason, Euthyphro, why I am charged with impiety—that I cannot away with these stories about the gods? and therefore I suppose that people think me wrong. But, as you who are well informed about them approve of them, I cannot do better than assent to your superior wisdom. What else can I say, confessing as I do, that I know nothing about them? Tell me, for the love of Zeus, whether you really believe that they are true.

Euth.

Yes, Socrates; and things more wonderful still, of which the world is in ignorance.

Soc.

And do you really believe that the gods fought with one another, and had dire quarrels, battles, and the like, as the poets say, and as you may see represented in the works of great artists? The temples are full of them; and notably the robe of Athene, which is carried up to the Acropolis at the great Panathenaea, is embroidered with them. Are all these tales of the gods true, Euthyphro?

Euth.

Yes, and things more amazing still.

Yes, Socrates; and, as I was saying, I can tell you, if you would like to hear them, many other things about the gods which would quite amaze you.

Soc.

I dare say; and you shall tell me them at some other time when I have leisure. But just at present I would rather hear from you a more precise answer, which you have not as yet given, my friend, to the question, What is 'piety'? When asked, you only replied, Doing as you do, charging your father with murder.

Euth.

And what I said was true, Socrates.

Soc.

No doubt, Euthyphro; but you would admit that there are many other pious acts?

Euth.

There are.

Soc.

Remember that I did not ask you to give me two or three examples of piety, but to explain the general idea which makes all pious things to be pious. Do you not recollect that there was one idea which made the impious impious, and the pious pious?

Euth.

I remember.

Soc.

Tell me what is the nature of this idea, and then I shall have a standard to which I may look, and by which I may measure actions, whether yours or those of any one else, and then I shall be able to say that such and such an action is pious, such another impious.

Euth.

A more correct definition:—Piety is that which is dear to the gods.

I will tell you, if you like.

Soc.

I should very much like.

Euth.

Piety, then, is that which is dear to the gods, and impiety is that which is not dear to them.

Soc.

Very good, Euthyphro; you have now given me the 7 sort of answer which I wanted. But whether what you say is true or not I cannot as yet tell, although I make no doubt that you will prove the truth of your words.

Euth.

Of course.

Soc.

Come, then, and let us examine what we are saying. That thing or person which is dear to the gods is pious, and that thing or person which is hateful to the gods is impious, these two being the extreme opposites of one another. Was not that said?

Euth.

It was.

Soc.

And well said?

Euth.

Yes, Socrates, I thought so; it was certainly said.

Soc.

And further, Euthyphro, the gods were admitted to have enmities and hatreds and differences?

Euth.

Yes, that was also said.

Soc.

Differences about numbers and figures create no ill-will because they can be settled by a sum or by a weighing machine, but enmities about the just and unjust are the occasions of quarrels, both among gods and men.

And what sort of difference creates enmity and anger? Suppose for example that you and I, my good friend, differ about a number; do differences of this sort make us enemies and set us at variance with one another? Do we not go at once to arithmetic, and put an end to them by a sum?

Euth.

True.

Soc.

Or suppose that we differ about magnitudes, do we not quickly end the difference by measuring?

Euth.

Very true.

Soc.

And we end a controversy about heavy and light by resorting to a weighing machine?

Euth.

To be sure.

Soc.

But what differences are there which cannot be thus decided, and which therefore make us angry and set us at enmity with one another? I dare say the answer does not occur to you at the moment, and therefore I will suggest that these enmities arise when the matters of difference are the just and unjust, good and evil, honourable and dishonourable. Are not these the points about which men differ, and about which when we are unable satisfactorily to decide our differences, you and I and all of us quarrel, when we do quarrel?

Euth.

Yes, Socrates, the nature of the differences about which we quarrel is such as you describe.

Soc.

And the quarrels of the gods, noble Euthyphro, when they occur, are of a like nature?

Euth.

Certainly they are.

Soc.

They have differences of opinion, as you say, about good and evil, just and unjust, honourable and dishonourable: there would have been no quarrels among them, if there had been no such differences—would there now?

Euth.

You are quite right.

Soc.

Men and gods alike love the things which they deem noble and just, but they are not agreed what these are.

Does not every man love that which he deems noble and just and good, and hate the opposite of them?

Euth.

Very true.

Soc.

But, as you say, people regard the same things, some as just and others as unjust,—about these they dispute; and so there arise wars and fightings among them. 8

Euth.

Very true.

Soc.

Then the same things are hated by the gods and loved by the gods, and are both hateful and dear to them?

Euth.

True.

Soc.

And upon this view the same things, Euthyphro, will be pious and also impious?

Euth.

So I should suppose.

Soc.

Then, my friend, I remark with surprise that you have not answered the question which I asked. For I certainly did not ask you to tell me what action is both pious and impious: but now it would seem that what is loved by the gods is also hated by them. And therefore, Euthyphro, in thus chastising your father you may very likely be doing what is agreeable to Zeus but disagreeable to Cronos or Uranus, and what is acceptable to Hephaestus but unacceptable to Herè, and there may be other gods who have similar differences of opinion.

Euth.

But I believe, Socrates, that all the gods would be agreed as to the propriety of punishing a murderer: there would be no difference of opinion about that.

Soc.

Well, but speaking of men, Euthyphro, did you ever hear any one arguing that a murderer or any sort of evil-doer ought to be let off?

Euth.

I should rather say that these are the questions which they are always arguing, especially in courts of law: they commit all sorts of crimes, and there is nothing which they will not do or say in their own defence.

Soc.

But do they admit their guilt, Euthyphro, and yet say that they ought not to be punished?

Euth.

No; they do not.

Soc.

Then there are some things which they do not venture to say and do: for they do not venture to argue that the guilty are to be unpunished, but they deny their guilt, do they not?

Euth.

Yes.

Soc.

Then they do not argue that the evil-doer should not be punished, but they argue about the fact of who the evil-doer is, and what he did and when?

Euth.

True.

Soc.

Neither God nor man will say that the doer of evil is not to be punished, but they are doubtful about particular acts. What proof is there that all the gods approve of the prosecution of your father?

And the gods are in the same case, if as you assert they quarrel about just and unjust, and some of them say while others deny that injustice is done among them. For surely neither God nor man will ever venture to say that the doer of injustice is not to be punished?

Euth.

That is true, Socrates, in the main.

Soc.

But they join issue about the particulars—gods and men alike; and, if they dispute at all, they dispute about some act which is called in question, and which by some is affirmed to be just, by others to be unjust. Is not that true?

Euth.

Quite true.

Soc.

9Well then, my dear friend Euthyphro, do tell me, for my better instruction and information, what proof have you that in the opinion of all the gods a servant who is guilty of murder, and is put in chains by the master of the dead man, and dies because he is put in chains before he who bound him can learn from the interpreters of the gods what he ought to do with him, dies unjustly; and that on behalf of such an one a son ought to proceed against his father and accuse him of murder. How would you show that all the gods absolutely agree in approving of his act? Prove to me that they do, and I will applaud your wisdom as long as I live.

Euth.

It will be a difficult task; but I could make the matter very clear indeed to you.

Soc.

I understand; you mean to say that I am not so quick of apprehension as the judges: for to them you will be sure to prove that the act is unjust, and hateful to the gods.

Euth.

Yes indeed, Socrates; at least if they will listen to me.

Soc.

Let us say then that what all the gods approve is pious and holy.

But they will be sure to listen if they find that you are a good speaker. There was a notion that came into my mind while you were speaking; I said to myself: 'Well, and what if Euthyphro does prove to me that all the gods regarded the death of the serf as unjust, how do I know anything more of the nature of piety and impiety? for granting that this action may be hateful to the gods, still piety and impiety are not adequately defined by these distinctions, for that which is hateful to the gods has been shown to be also pleasing and dear to them.' And therefore, Euthyphro, I do not ask you to prove this; I will suppose, if you like, that all the gods condemn and abominate such an action. But I will amend the definition so far as to say that what all the gods hate is impious, and what they love pious or holy; and what some of them love and others hate is both or neither. Shall this be our definition of piety and impiety?

Euth.

Why not, Socrates?

Soc.

Why not! certainly, as far as I am concerned, Euthyphro, there is no reason why not. But whether this admission will greatly assist you in the task of instructing me as you promised, is a matter for you to consider.

Euth.

Yes, I should say that what all the gods love is pious and holy, and the opposite which they all hate, impious.

Soc.

Ought we to enquire into the truth of this, Euthyphro, or simply to accept the mere statement on our own authority and that of others? What do you say?

Euth.

We should enquire; and I believe that the statement will stand the test of enquiry.

Soc.

But does the state follow the act, or the act the state?

We shall know better, my good friend, in a little while. The point which I should first wish to understand is whether the pious or holy is beloved by the gods because it 10is holy, or holy because it is beloved of the gods.

Euth.

I do not understand your meaning, Socrates.

Soc.

I will endeavour to explain: we speak of carrying and we speak of being carried, of leading and being led, seeing and being seen. You know that in all such cases there is a difference, and you know also in what the difference lies?

Euth.

I think that I understand.

Soc.

And is not that which is beloved distinct from that which loves?

Euth.

Certainly.

Soc.

Well; and now tell me, is that which is carried in this state of carrying because it is carried, or for some other reason?

Euth.

No; that is the reason.

Soc.

And the same is true of what is led and of what is seen?

Euth.

True.

Soc.

And a thing is not seen because it is visible, but conversely, visible because it is seen; nor is a thing led because it is in the state of being led, or carried because it is in the state of being carried, but the converse of this. And now I think, Euthyphro, that my meaning will be intelligible; and my meaning is, that any state of action or passion implies previous action or passion. It does not become because it is becoming, but it is in a state of becoming because it becomes; neither does it suffer because it is in a state of suffering, but it is in a state of suffering because it suffers. Do you not agree?

Euth.

Yes.

Soc.

Is not that which is loved in some state either of becoming or suffering?

Euth.

Yes.

Soc.

The latter is the truer account, and therefore we can only say that what is loved by all the gods is in a state to be loved by them; but holiness has a wider meaning than this.

And the same holds as in the previous instances; the state of being loved follows the act of being loved, and not the act the state.

Euth.

Certainly.

Soc.

And what do you say of piety, Euthyphro: is not piety, according to your definition, loved by all the gods?

Euth.

Yes.

Soc.

Because it is pious or holy, or for some other reason?

Euth.

No, that is the reason.

Soc.

It is loved because it is holy, not holy because it is loved?

Euth.

Yes.

Soc.

And that which is dear to the gods is loved by them, and is in a state to be loved of them because it is loved of them?

Euth.

Certainly.

Soc.

Then that which is dear to the gods, Euthyphro, is not holy, nor is that which is holy loved of God, as you affirm; but they are two different things.

Euth.

How do you mean, Socrates?

Soc.

I mean to say that the holy has been acknowledged by us to be loved of God because it is holy, not to be holy because it is loved.

Euth.

Yes.

Soc.

But that which is dear to the gods is dear to them because it is loved by them, not loved by them because it is dear to them.

Euth.

True.

Soc.

What is the essential meaning of holiness or piety?

But, friend Euthyphro, if that which is holy is the same with that which is dear to God, and is loved because it is holy, then that which is dear to God would have been

11loved as being dear to God; but if that which is dear to God is dear to him because loved by him, then that which is holy would have been holy because loved by him. But now you see that the reverse is the case, and that they are quite different from one another. For one (θεοφιλες) is of a kind to be loved because it is loved, and the other (Ὅσιον) is loved because it is of a kind to be loved. Thus you appear to me, Euthyphro, when I ask you what is the essence of holiness, to offer an attribute only, and not the essence—the attribute of being loved by all the gods. But you still refuse to explain to me the nature of holiness. And therefore, if you please, I will ask you not to hide your treasure, but to tell me once more what holiness or piety really is, whether dear to the gods or not (for that is a matter about which we will not quarrel); and what is impiety?

Euth.

I really do not know, Socrates, how to express what I mean. For somehow or other our arguments, on whatever ground we rest them, seem to turn round and walk away from us.

Soc.

Your words, Euthyphro, are like the handiwork of my ancestor Daedalus; and if I were the sayer or propounder of them, you might say that my arguments walk away and will not remain fixed where they are placed because I am a descendant of his. But now, since these notions are your own, you must find some other gibe, for they certainly, as you yourself allow, show an inclination to be on the move.

Euth.

Nay, Socrates, I shall still say that you are the Daedalus who sets arguments in motion; not I, certainly, but you make them move or go round, for they would never have stirred, as far as I am concerned.

Soc.

Then I must be a greater than Daedalus: for whereas he only made his own inventions to move, I move those of other people as well. And the beauty of it is, that I would rather not. For I would give the wisdom of Daedalus, and the wealth of Tantalus, to be able to detain them and keep them fixed. But enough of this. As I perceive that you are lazy, I will myself endeavour to show you how you might instruct me in the nature of piety; and I hope that you will not grudge your labour. Tell me, then,—Is not that which is pious necessarily just?

Euth.

Yes.

Soc.

All which is pious is just:—is therefore all which is just pious?

And is, then, all which is just pious? or, is that which is pious all just, but that which is just, only in part and not all, pious?

Euth.

I do not understand you, Socrates.

Soc.

And yet I know that you are as much wiser than I am, as you are younger. But, as I was saying, revered friend, the abundance of your wisdom makes you lazy. Please to exert yourself, for there is no real difficulty in understanding me. What I mean I may explain by an illustration of what I do not mean. The poet (Stasinus) sings—

- 'Of Zeus, the author and creator of all these things,
- You will not tell: for where there is fear there is also reverence.'

Now I disagree with this poet. Shall I tell you in what respect?

Euth.

By all means.

Soc.

We may say, e.g., that wherever there is reverence there will be fear, but not that wherever there is fear there will be reverence.

I should not say that where there is fear there is also reverence; for I am sure that many persons fear poverty and disease, and the like evils, but I do not perceive that they reverence the objects of their fear.

Euth.

Very true.

Soc.

But where reverence is, there is fear; for he who has a feeling of reverence and shame about the commission of any action, fears and is afraid of an ill reputation.

Euth.

No doubt.

Soc.

Then we are wrong in saying that where there is fear there is also reverence; and we should say, where there is reverence there is also fear. But there is not always reverence where there is fear; for fear is a more extended notion, and reverence is a part of fear, just as the odd is a part of number, and number is a more extended notion than the odd. I suppose that you follow me now?

Euth.

Quite well.

Soc.

That was the sort of question which I meant to raise when I asked whether the just is always the pious, or the pious always the just; and whether there may not be justice where there is not piety; for justice is the more extended notion of which piety is only a part. Do you dissent?

Euth.

No, I think that you are quite right.

Soc.

Then, if piety is a part of justice, I suppose that we should enquire what part? If you had pursued the enquiry in the previous cases; for instance, if you had asked me what is an even number, and what part of number the even is, I should have had no difficulty in replying, a number which represents a figure having two equal sides. Do you not agree?

Euth.

Yes, I quite agree.

Soc.

Piety or holiness is that part of justice which attends upon the gods.

In like manner, I want you to tell me what part of justice is piety or holiness, that I may be able to tell Meletus not to do me injustice, or indict me for impiety, as I am now adequately instructed by you in the nature of piety or holiness, and their opposites.

Euth.

Piety or holiness, Socrates, appears to me to be that part of justice which attends to the gods, as there is the other part of justice which attends to men.

Soc.

That is good, Euthyphro; yet still there is a little 13point about which I should like to have further information, What is the meaning of 'attention'? For attention can hardly be used in the same sense when applied to the gods as when applied to other things. For instance, horses are said to require attention, and not every person is able to attend to them, but only a person skilled in horsemanship. Is it not so?

Euth.

Certainly.

Soc.

I should suppose that the art of horsemanship is the art of attending to horses?

Euth.

Yes.

Soc.

Nor is every one qualified to attend to dogs, but only the huntsman?

Euth.

True.

Soc.

And I should also conceive that the art of the huntsman is the art of attending to dogs?

Euth.

Yes.

Soc.

As the art of the oxherd is the art of attending to oxen?

Euth.

Very true.

Soc.

In like manner holiness or piety is the art of attending to the gods?—that would be your meaning, Euthyphro?

Euth.

Yes.

Soc.

Attention to others is designed to benefit and improve them. But how are the gods benefited or improved by the holy acts of men?

And is not attention always designed for the good or benefit of that to which the attention is given? As in the case of horses, you may observe that when attended to by the horseman's art they are benefited and improved, are they not?

Euth.

True.

Soc.

As the dogs are benefited by the huntsman's art, and the oxen by the art of the oxherd, and all other things are tended or attended for their good and not for their hurt?

Euth.

Certainly, not for their hurt.

Soc.

But for their good?

Euth.

Of course.

Soc.

And does piety or holiness, which has been defined to be the art of attending to the gods, benefit or improve them? Would you say that when you do a holy act you make any of the gods better?

Euth.

No, no; that was certainly not what I meant.

Soc.

And I, Euthyphro, never supposed that you did. I asked you the question about the nature of the attention, because I thought that you did not.

Euth.

You do me justice, Socrates; that is not the sort of attention which I mean.

Soc.

The attention to the gods called piety is such as servants show their masters.

Good: but I must still ask what is this attention to the gods which is called piety?

Euth.

It is such, Socrates, as servants show to their masters.

Soc.

I understand—a sort of ministration to the gods.

Euth.

Exactly.

Soc.

Medicine is also a sort of ministration or service, having in view the attainment of some object—would you not say of health?

Euth.

I should.

Soc.

Again, there is an art which ministers to the ship-builder with a view to the attainment of some result?

Euth.

Yes, Socrates, with a view to the building of a ship.

Soc.

As there is an art which ministers to the house-builder with a view to the building of a house?

Euth.

Yes.

Soc.

But in what way do men help the work of God?

And now tell me, my good friend, about the art which ministers to the gods: what work does that help to accomplish? For you must surely know if, as you say, you are of all men living the one who is best instructed in religion.

Euth.

And I speak the truth, Socrates.

Soc.

Tell me then, oh tell me—what is that fair work which the gods do by the help of our ministrations?

Euth.

Many and fair, Socrates, are the works which they do.

Soc.

Why, my friend, and so are those of a general. But 14the chief of them is easily told. Would you not say that victory in war is the chief of them?

Euth.

Certainly.

Soc.

Many and fair, too, are the works of the husbandman, if I am not mistaken; but his chief work is the production of food from the earth?

Euth.

Exactly.

Soc.

And of the many and fair things done by the gods, which is the chief or principal one?

Euth.

I have told you already, Socrates, that to learn all these things accurately will be very tiresome. Let me simply say that piety or holiness is learning how to please the gods in word and deed, by prayers and sacrifices. Such piety is the salvation of families and states, just as the impious, which is unpleasing to the gods, is their ruin and destruction.

Soc.

I think that you could have answered in much fewer words the chief question which I asked, Euthyphro, if you had chosen. But I see plainly that you are not disposed to instruct me—clearly not: else why, when we reached the point, did you turn aside? Had you only answered me I should have truly learned of you by this time the nature of piety. Now, as the asker of a question is necessarily dependent on the answerer, whither he leads I must follow; and can only ask again, what is the pious, and what is piety? Do you mean that they are a sort of science of praying and sacrificing?

Euth.

Yes, I do.

Soc.

And sacrificing is giving to the gods, and prayer is asking of the gods?

Euth.

Yes, Socrates.

Soc.

Upon this view, then, piety is a science of asking and giving?

Euth.

You understand me capitally, Socrates.

Soc.

Yes, my friend; the reason is that I am a votary of your science, and give my mind to it, and therefore nothing which you say will be thrown away upon me. Please then to tell me, what is the nature of this service to the gods? Do you mean that we prefer requests and give gifts to them?

Euth.

Yes, I do.

Soc.

Is not the right way of asking to ask of them what we want?

Euth.

Certainly.

Soc.

Men give to the gods, and the gods give to men; they do business with one another.

And the right way of giving is to give to them in return what they want of us. There would be no meaning in an art which gives to any one that which he does not want.

Euth.

Very true, Socrates.

Soc.

Then piety, Euthyphro, is an art which gods and men have of doing business with one another?

Euth.

That is an expression which you may use, if you like.

Soc.

But I have no particular liking for anything but the truth. I wish, however, that you would tell me what benefit accrues to the gods from our gifts. There is no doubt about 15what they give to us; for there is no good thing which they do not give; but how we can give any good thing to them in return is far from being equally clear. If they give everything and we give nothing, that must be an affair of business in which we have very greatly the advantage of them.

Euth.

And do you imagine, Socrates, that any benefit accrues to the gods from our gifts?

Soc.

But if not, Euthyphro, what is the meaning of gifts which are conferred by us upon the gods?

Euth.

What else, but tributes of honour; and, as I was just now saying, what pleases them?

Soc.

Piety, then, is pleasing to the gods, but not beneficial or dear to them?

Euth.

I should say that nothing could be dearer.

Soc.

Then once more the assertion is repeated that piety is dear to the gods?

Euth.

Certainly.

Soc.

Again, the argument walks away.

And when you say this, can you wonder at your words not standing firm, but walking away? Will you accuse me of being the Daedalus who makes them walk away, not perceiving that there is another and far greater artist than Daedalus who makes them go round in a circle, and he is yourself; for the argument, as you will perceive, comes round to the same point. Were we not saying that the holy or pious was not the same with that which is loved of the gods? Have you forgotten?

Euth.

I quite remember.

Soc.

And are you not saying that what is loved of the gods is holy; and is not this the same as what is dear to them—do you see?

Euth.

True.

Soc.

Then either we were wrong in our former assertion; or, if we were right then, we are wrong now.

Euth.

One of the two must be true.

Soc.

Nevertheless, Socrates is confident that Euthyphro knows the truth, but will not tell him.

Then we must begin again and ask, What is piety? That is an enquiry which I shall never be weary of pursuing as far as in me lies; and I entreat you not to scorn me, but to apply your mind to the utmost, and tell me the truth. For, if any man knows, you are he; and therefore I must detain you, like Proteus, until you tell. If you had not certainly known the nature of piety and impiety, I am confident that you would never, on behalf of a serf, have charged your aged father with murder. You would not have run such a risk of doing wrong in the sight of the gods, and you would have had too much respect for the opinions of men. I am sure, therefore, that you know the nature of piety and impiety. Speak out then, my dear Euthyphro, and do not hide your knowledge.

Euth.

Euthyphro is in a hurry to depart, and finally leaves Socrates to his fate.

Another time, Socrates; for I am in a hurry, and must go now.

Soc.

Alas! my companion, and will you leave me in despair? I was hoping that you would instruct me in the nature of piety and impiety; and then I might have cleared myself of Meletus and his indictment. I would have told 16him that I had been enlightened by Euthyphro, and had given up rash innovations and speculations, in which I indulged only through ignorance, and that now I am about to lead a better life.

INTRODUCTION TO APOLOGY.

Apology. Introduction.

In what relation the Apology of Plato stands to the real defence of Socrates, there are no means of determining. It certainly agrees in tone and character with the description of Xenophon, who says in the Memorabilia (iv. 4, 4) that Socrates might have been acquitted 'if in any moderate degree he would have conciliated the favour of the dicasts;' and who informs us in another passage (iv. 8, 4), on the testimony of Hermogenes, the friend of Socrates, that he had no wish to live; and that the divine sign refused to allow him to prepare a defence, and also that Socrates himself declared this to be unnecessary, on the ground that all his life long he had been preparing against that hour. For the speech breathes throughout a spirit of defiance, 'ut non supplex aut reus sed magister aut dominus videretur esse judicum' (Cic. de Orat. i. 54); and the loose and desultory style is an imitation of the 'accustomed manner' in which Socrates spoke in 'the agora and among the tables of the money-changers.' The allusion in the Crito (45 B) may, perhaps, be adduced as a further evidence of the literal accuracy of some parts (37 C, D). But in the main it must be regarded as the ideal of Socrates, according to Plato's conception of him, appearing in the greatest and most public scene of his life, and in the height of his triumph, when he is weakest, and yet his mastery over mankind is greatest, and his habitual irony acquires a new meaning and a sort of tragic pathos in the face of death. The facts of his life are summed up, and the features of his character are brought out as if by accident in the course of the defence. The conversational manner, the seeming want of arrangement, the ironical simplicity, are found to result in a perfect work of art, which is the portrait of Socrates.

Yet some of the topics may have been actually used by Socrates; and the recollection of his very words may have rung in the ears of his disciple. The Apology of Plato may be compared generally with those speeches of Thucydides in which he has embodied his conception of the lofty character and policy of the great Pericles, and which at the same time furnish a commentary on the situation of affairs from the point of view of the historian. So in the Apology there is an ideal rather than a literal truth; much is said which was not said, and is only Plato's view of the situation. Plato was not, like Xenophon, a chronicler of facts; he does not appear in any of his writings to have aimed at literal accuracy. He is not therefore to be supplemented from the Memorabilia and Symposium of Xenophon, who belongs to an entirely different class of writers. The Apology of Plato is not the report of what Socrates said, but an elaborate composition, quite as much so in fact as one of the Dialogues. And we may perhaps even indulge in the fancy that the actual defence of Socrates was as much greater than the Platonic defence as the master was greater than the disciple. But in any case, some of the words used by him must have been remembered, and some of the facts recorded must have actually occurred. It is significant that Plato is said to have been present at the defence (Apol. 38 B), as he is also said to have been absent at the last scene in the Phaedo (59 B). Is it fanciful to suppose that he meant to give the stamp of authenticity to the one and not to the other?—especially when we consider that these two passages are the only ones in which Plato makes mention of himself. The circumstance that Plato was to be one of his sureties for the payment of the fine which he proposed has the appearance of truth. More suspicious is the statement that Socrates received the first impulse to his favourite calling of cross-examining the world from the Oracle of Delphi; for he must already have been famous before Chaerephon went to consult the Oracle (Riddell, i. p. xvi), and the story is of a kind which is very likely to have been invented. On the whole we arrive at the conclusion that the Apology is true to the character of Socrates, but we cannot show that any single sentence in it was actually spoken by him. It breathes the spirit of Socrates, but has been cast anew in the mould of Plato.

There is not much in the other Dialogues which can be compared with the Apology. The same recollection of his master may have been present to the mind of Plato when depicting the sufferings of the Just in the Republic (ii. 361 foll., vi. 500 A). The Crito may also be regarded as a sort of appendage to the Apology, in which Socrates, who has defied the judges, is nevertheless represented as scrupulously obedient to the laws. The idealization of the sufferer is carried still further in the Gorgias (476 foll.), in which the thesis is maintained, that 'to suffer is better than to do evil;' and the art of rhetoric is described as only useful for the purpose of self-accusation. The parallelisms which occur in the so-called Apology of Xenophon are not worth noticing, because the writing in which they are contained is manifestly spurious. The statements of the Memorabilia (i. 2; iv. 8) respecting the trial and death of Socrates agree generally with Plato; but they have lost the flavour of Socratic irony in the narrative of Xenophon.

The Apology or Platonic defence of Socrates is divided into three parts: 1st. The defence properly so called; 2nd. The shorter address in mitigation of the penalty; 3rd. The last words of prophetic rebuke and exhortation.

Analysis.

17The first part commences with an apology for his colloquial style; he is, as he has always been, the enemy of rhetoric, and knows of no rhetoric but truth; he will not falsify his character by 18making a speech. Then he proceeds to divide his accusers into two classes; first, there is the nameless accuser—public opinion. All the world from their earliest years had heard that he was a corrupter of youth, and had seen him caricatured in the Clouds of Aristophanes. Secondly, there are the professed accusers, who are but the mouth-piece of the others. The accusations of both might be summed up in a formula. The first say, 'Socrates is an evil-doer and a curious person, searching into things under the earth and above the heaven; and making the worse appear the better cause, and teaching all this to others.' The second, 'Socrates is an evil-doer and corrupter of the youth, who does not receive the gods whom the state receives, but introduces other new divinities.' These last words appear to have been the actual indictment (cp. Xen. Mem. i. 1); and the previous formula, which is a summary of public opinion, assumes the same legal style.

19The answer begins by clearing up a confusion. In the representations of the Comic poets, and in the opinion of the multitude, he had been identified with the teachers of physical science and with the Sophists. But this was an error. For both of them he professes a respect in the open court, which contrasts with his manner of speaking about them in other places. (Cp. for Anaxagoras, Phaedo 98 B, Laws xii. 967; for the Sophists, Meno 95 D, Rep. vi. 492, Tim. 19 E, Theaet. 154 E, Soph. 265 foll., etc.) But at the same time he shows that he is not one of them. Of natural philosophy he knows nothing; not that he despises such pursuits, but the fact is that he is ignorant of them, and never says a word about them. Nor is he paid for giving instruction— that is another mistaken notion:—he has nothing to teach. But he commends 20Evenus for teaching virtue at such a 'moderate' rate as five minae. Something of the 'accustomed irony,' which may perhaps be expected to sleep in the ear of the multitude, is lurking here.

He then goes on to explain the reason why he is in such an evil name. That had arisen out of a peculiar mission which he had taken upon himself. The enthusiastic Chaerephon (probably in 21anticipation of the answer which he received) had gone to Delphi and asked the oracle if there was any man wiser than Socrates; and the answer was, that there was no man wiser. What could be the meaning of this—that he who knew nothing, and knew that he knew nothing, should be declared by the oracle to be the wisest of men? Reflecting upon the answer, he determined to refute it by finding 'a wiser;' and first he went to the politicians, and then to the poets, and then to the craftsmen, but 22always with the same result—he found that they knew nothing, or hardly anything more than himself; and that the little advantage which in some cases they possessed was more than counterbalanced by their conceit of knowledge. He knew nothing, and knew that he knew nothing: they knew little or nothing, and imagined that they knew all things. Thus he had passed his 23life as a sort of missionary in detecting the pretended wisdom of mankind; and this occupation had quite absorbed him and taken him away both from public and private affairs. Young men of the richer sort had made a pastime of the same pursuit, 'which was not unamusing.' And hence bitter enmities had arisen; the professors of knowledge had revenged themselves by calling him a villainous corrupter of youth, and by repeating the commonplaces about atheism and materialism and sophistry,

24which are the stock-accusations against all philosophers when there is nothing else to be said of them.

The second accusation he meets by interrogating Meletus, who is present and can be interrogated. 'If he is the corrupter, who is the improver of the citizens?' (Cp. Meno 91 C.) 'All men 25everywhere.' But how absurd, how contrary to analogy is this! How inconceivable too, that he should make the citizens worse when he has to live with them. This surely cannot be intentional; 26and if unintentional, he ought to have been instructed by Meletus, and not accused in the court.

But there is another part of the indictment which says that he teaches men not to receive the gods whom the city receives, and has other new gods. 'Is that the way in which he is supposed to corrupt the youth?' 'Yes, it is.' 'Has he only new gods, or none at all?' 'None at all.' 'What, not even the sun and moon?' 'No; why, he says that the sun is a stone, and the moon earth.' That, replies Socrates, is the old confusion about Anaxagoras; the Athenian people are not so ignorant as to attribute to the influence of Socrates notions which have found their way into the drama, and may be learned at the theatre. Socrates undertakes 27to show that Meletus (rather unjustifiably) has been compounding a riddle in this part of the indictment: 'There are no gods, but Socrates believes in the existence of the sons of gods, which is absurd.'

28Leaving Meletus, who has had enough words spent upon him, he returns to the original accusation. The question may be asked, Why will he persist in following a profession which leads him to death? Why?—because he must remain at his post where the god has placed him, as he remained at Potidaea, and Amphipolis, 29and Delium, where the generals placed him. Besides, he is not so overwise as to imagine that he knows whether death is a good or an evil; and he is certain that desertion of his duty 30is an evil. Anytus is quite right in saying that they should never have indicted him if they meant to let him go. For he will certainly obey God rather than man; and will continue to preach to all men of all ages the necessity of virtue and improvement; and if they refuse to listen to him he will still persevere and reprove them. This is his way of corrupting the youth, which he will not cease to follow in obedience to the god, even if a thousand deaths await him.

He is desirous that they should let him live—not for his own sake, but for theirs; because he is their heaven-sent friend (and 31they will never have such another), or, as he may be ludicrously described, he is the gadfly who stirs the generous steed into motion. Why then has he never taken part in public affairs? Because the familiar divine voice has hindered him; if he had been a public man, and had fought for the right, as he would certainly have fought against the many, he would not have lived, and could therefore have done no good. Twice in public matters 32he has risked his life for the sake of justice—once at the trial of the generals; and again in resistance to the tyrannical commands of the Thirty.

But, though not a public man, he has passed his days in instructing the citizens without fee or reward—this was his mission. Whether his disciples have turned out well or ill, he cannot justly be charged with the result, for he never promised to teach them 33anything. They might come if they liked, and they might stay away if they liked: and they did come, because they found an amusement in hearing the pretenders to wisdom detected. If they have been corrupted, their elder relatives (if not themselves) might surely come into court and witness against him, and there is an opportunity still for them to appear. But their fathers 34and brothers all appear in court (including 'this' Plato), to witness on his behalf; and if their relatives are corrupted, at least they are uncorrupted; 'and they are my witnesses. For they know that I am speaking the truth, and that Meletus is lying.'

This is about all that he has to say. He will not entreat the judges to spare his life; neither will he present a spectacle of weeping children, although he, too, is not made of 'rock or oak.' 35Some of the judges themselves may have complied with this practice on similar occasions, and he trusts that they will not be angry with him for not following their example. But he feels that such conduct brings discredit on the name of Athens: he feels, too, that the judge has sworn not to give away justice; and he cannot be guilty of the impiety of asking the judge to break his oath, when he is himself being tried for impiety.

36As he expected, and probably intended, he is convicted. And now the tone of the speech, instead of being more conciliatory, becomes more lofty and commanding. Anytus proposes death as the penalty: and what counter-proposition shall he make? He, the benefactor of the Athenian people, whose whole life has been spent in doing them good, should at least have the Olympic 37victor's reward of maintenance in the Prytaneum. Or why should he propose any counter-penalty when he does not know whether death, which Anytus proposes, is a good or an evil? and he is certain that imprisonment is an evil, exile is an evil. Loss of money might be no evil, but then he has none to give; 38perhaps he can make up a mina. Let that be the penalty, or, if his friends wish, thirty minae; for which they will be excellent securities.

[*He is condemned to death.*]

He is an old man already, and the Athenians will gain nothing but disgrace by depriving him of a few years of life. Perhaps he could have escaped, if he had chosen to throw down his arms and entreat for his life. But he does not at all repent of the manner of his defence; he would rather die in his own fashion than live 39in theirs. For the penalty of unrighteousness is swifter than death; that penalty has already overtaken his accusers as death will soon overtake him.

And now, as one who is about to die, he will prophesy to them. They have put him to death in order to escape the necessity of giving an account of their lives. But his death 'will be the seed' of many disciples who will convince them of their evil ways, and will come forth to reprove them in harsher terms, because they are younger and more inconsiderate.

40He would like to say a few words, while there is time, to those who would have acquitted him. He wishes them to know that the divine sign never interrupted him in the course of his defence; the reason of which, as he conjectures, is that the death to which he is going is a good and not an evil. For either death is a long sleep, the best of sleeps, or a journey to another world in which the souls of the dead are gathered together, and in which 41there may be a hope of seeing the heroes of old—in which, too, there are just judges; and as all are immortal, there can be no fear of any one suffering death for his opinions.

Nothing evil can happen to the good man either in life or death, and his own death has been permitted by the gods, because it was better for him to depart; and therefore he forgives his judges because they have done him no harm, although they never meant to do him any good.

He has a last request to make to them—that they will trouble 42his sons as he has troubled them, if they appear to prefer riches to virtue, or to think themselves something when they are nothing.

Introduction.

'Few persons will be found to wish that Socrates should have defended himself otherwise,'—if, as we must add, his defence was that with which Plato has provided him. But leaving this question, which does not admit of a precise solution, we may go on to ask what was the impression which Plato in the Apology intended to give of the character and conduct of his master in the last great scene? Did he intend to represent him (1) as employing sophistries; (2) as designedly irritating the judges? Or are these sophistries to be regarded as belonging to the age in which he lived and to his personal character, and this apparent haughtiness as flowing from the natural elevation of his position?

For example, when he says that it is absurd to suppose that one man is the corrupter and all the rest of the world the improvers of the youth; or, when he argues that he never could have corrupted the men with whom he had to live; or, when he proves his belief in the gods because he believes in the sons of gods, is he serious or jesting? It may be observed that these sophisms all occur in his cross-examination of Meletus, who is easily foiled and mastered in the hands of the great dialectician. Perhaps he regarded these answers as good enough for his accuser, of whom he makes very light. Also there is a touch of irony in them, which takes them out of the category of sophistry. (Cp. Euthyph. 2.)

That the manner in which he defends himself about the lives of his disciples is not satisfactory, can hardly be denied. Fresh in the memory of the Athenians, and detestable as they deserved to be to the newly restored democracy, were the names of Alcibiades, Critias, Charmides. It is obviously not a sufficient answer that Socrates had never professed to teach them anything, and is therefore not justly chargeable with their crimes. Yet the defence, when taken out of this ironical form, is doubtless sound: that his teaching had nothing to do with their evil lives. Here, then, the sophistry is rather in form than in substance, though we might desire that to such a serious charge Socrates had given a more serious answer.

Truly characteristic of Socrates is another point in his answer, which may also be regarded as sophistical. He says that 'if he has corrupted the youth, he must have corrupted them involuntarily.' But if, as Socrates argues, all evil is involuntary, then all criminals ought to be admonished and not punished. In these words the Socratic doctrine of the involuntariness of evil is clearly intended to be conveyed. Here again, as in the former instance, the defence of Socrates is untrue practically, but may be true in some ideal or transcendental sense. The commonplace reply, that if he had been guilty of corrupting the youth their relations would surely have witnessed against him, with which he concludes this part of his defence, is more satisfactory.

Again, when Socrates argues that he must believe in the gods because he believes in the sons of gods, we must remember that this is a refutation not of the original indictment, which is consistent enough—'Socrates does not receive the gods whom the city receives, and has other new divinities'—but of the interpretation put upon the words by Meletus, who has affirmed that he is a downright atheist. To this Socrates fairly answers, in accordance with the ideas of the time, that a downright atheist cannot believe in the sons of gods or in divine things. The notion that demons or lesser divinities are the sons of gods is not to be regarded as ironical or sceptical. He is arguing 'ad hominem' according to the notions of mythology current in his age. Yet he abstains from saying that he believed in the gods whom the State approved. He does not defend himself, as Xenophon has defended him, by appealing to his practice of religion. Probably he neither wholly believed, nor disbelieved, in the existence of the popular gods; he had no means of knowing about them. According to Plato (cp. Phaedo 118 B; Symp. 220 D), as well as Xenophon (Memor. i. 1, 30), he was punctual in the performance of the least religious duties; and he must have believed in his own oracular sign, of which he seemed to have an internal witness. But the existence of Apollo or Zeus, or the other gods whom the State approves, would have appeared to him both uncertain and unimportant in comparison of the duty of self-examination, and of those principles of truth and right which he deemed to be the foundation of religion. (Cp. Phaedr. 230; Euthyph. 6, 7; Rep. ii. 373 ff.).

The second question, whether Plato meant to represent Socrates as braving or irritating his judges, must also be answered in the negative. His irony, his superiority, his audacity, 'regarding not the person of man,' necessarily flow out of the loftiness of his situation. He is not acting a part upon a great occasion, but he is what he has been all his life long, 'a king of men.' He would rather not appear insolent, if he could avoid it (οὐχ ὡς αὐθαδιζόμενος τουτο λέγω). Neither is he desirous of hastening his own end, for life and death are simply indifferent to him. But such a defence as would be acceptable to his judges and might procure an acquittal, it is not in his nature to make. He will not say or do anything that might pervert the course of justice; he cannot have his tongue bound even 'in the throat of death.' With his accusers he will only fence and play, as he had fenced with other 'improvers of youth,' answering the Sophist according to his sophistry all his life long. He is serious when he is speaking of his own mission, which seems to distinguish him from all other reformers of mankind, and originates in an accident. The dedication of himself to the improvement of his fellow-citizens is not so remarkable as the ironical spirit in which he goes about doing good only in vindication of the credit of the oracle, and in the vain hope of finding a wiser man than himself. Yet this singular and almost accidental character of his mission agrees with the divine sign which, according to our notions, is equally accidental and irrational, and is nevertheless accepted by him as the guiding principle of his life. Socrates is nowhere represented to us as a freethinker or sceptic. There is no reason to doubt his sincerity when he speculates on the possibility of seeing and knowing the heroes of the Trojan war in another world. On the other hand, his hope of immortality is uncertain;—he also conceives of death as a long sleep (in this respect differing from the Phaedo), and at last falls back on resignation to the divine will, and the certainty that no evil can happen to the good man either in life or death. His absolute truthfulness seems to hinder him from asserting positively more than this; and he makes no attempt to veil his ignorance in mythology and figures of speech. The gentleness of the first part of the speech contrasts with the aggravated, almost threatening, tone of the conclusion. He characteristically remarks that he will not speak as a rhetorician, that is to say, he will not make a regular defence such as Lysias or one of the orators might have composed for him, or, according to some accounts, did compose for him. But he first procures himself a hearing by conciliatory words. He does not attack the Sophists; for they were open to the same charges as himself; they were equally ridiculed by the Comic poets, and almost equally hateful to Anytus and Meletus. Yet incidentally the antagonism between Socrates and the Sophists is allowed to appear. He is poor and they are rich; his profession that he teaches nothing is opposed to their readiness to teach all things; his talking in the marketplace to their private instructions; his tarry-at-home life to their wandering from city to city. The tone which he assumes towards them is one of real friendliness, but also of concealed irony. Towards Anaxagoras, who had disappointed him in his hopes of learning about mind and nature, he shows a less kindly feeling, which is also the feeling of Plato in other passages (Laws xii. 967 B). But Anaxagoras had been dead thirty years, and was beyond the reach of persecution.

It has been remarked that the prophecy of a new generation of teachers who would rebuke and exhort the Athenian people in harsher and more violent terms was, as far as we know, never fulfilled. No inference can be drawn from this circumstances as to the probability of the words attributed to him having been actually uttered. They express the aspiration of the first martyr of philosophy, that he would leave behind him many followers, accompanied by the not unnatural feeling that they would be fiercer and more inconsiderate in their words when emancipated from his control.

The above remarks must be understood as applying with any degree of certainty to the Platonic Socrates only. For, although these or similar words may have been spoken by Socrates himself, we cannot exclude the possibility, that like so much else, *e.g.* the wisdom of Critias, the poem of Solon, the virtues of Charmides, they may have been due only to the imagination of Plato. The arguments of those who maintain that the Apology was composed during the process, resting on no evidence, do not require a serious refutation. Nor are the reasonings of Schleiermacher, who argues that the Platonic defence is an exact or nearly exact reproduction of the words of Socrates, partly because Plato would not have been guilty of the impiety of altering them, and also because many points of the defence might have been improved and strengthened, at all more conclusive. (See English Translation, p. 137.) What effect the death of Socrates produced on the mind of Plato, we cannot certainly determine; nor can we say how he would or must have written under the circumstances. We observe that the enmity of Aristophanes to Socrates does not prevent Plato from introducing them together in the Symposium engaged in friendly intercourse. Nor is there any trace in the Dialogues of an attempt to make Anytus or Meletus personally odious in the eyes of the Athenian public.

APOLOGY.

Apology.Socrates.Socrates begs to be allowed to speak in his accustomed manner.The judges must excuse Socrates if he defends himself in his own fashion.

17How you, O Athenians, have been affected by my accusers, I cannot tell; but I know that they almost made me forget who I was—so persuasively did they speak; and yet they have hardly uttered a word of truth. But of the many falsehoods told by them, there was one which quite amazed me;—I mean when they said that you should be upon your guard and not allow yourselves to be deceived by the force of my eloquence. To say this, when they were certain to be detected as soon as I opened my lips and proved myself to be anything but a great speaker, did indeed appear to me most shameless—unless by the force of eloquence they mean the force of truth; for if such is their meaning, I admit that I am eloquent. But in how different a way from theirs! Well, as I was saying, they have scarcely spoken the truth at all; but from me you shall hear the whole truth: not, however, delivered after their manner in a set oration duly ornamented with words and phrases. No, by heaven! but I shall use the words and arguments which occur to me at the moment; for I am confident in the justice of my cause : at my time of life I ought not to be appearing before you, O men of Athens, in the character of a juvenile orator—let no one expect it of me. And I must beg of you to grant me a favour:—If I defend myself in my accustomed manner, and you hear me using the words which I have been in the habit of using in the agora, at the tables of the money-changers, or anywhere else, I would ask you not to be surprised, and not to interrupt me on this account. For I am more than seventy years of age, and appearing now for the first time in a court of law, I am quite a stranger to the language of the place; and therefore I would have you regard me as if I were really a stranger, whom you would excuse if 18he spoke in his native tongue, and after the fashion of his country:—Am I making an unfair request of you? Never mind the manner, which may or may not be good; but think only of the truth of my words, and give heed to that: let the speaker speak truly and the judge decide justly.

He has to meet two sorts of accusers.

And first, I have to reply to the older charges and to my first accusers, and then I will go on to the later ones. For of old I have had many accusers, who have accused me falsely to you during many years; and I am more afraid of them than of Anytus and his associates, who are dangerous, too, in their own way. But far more dangerous are the others, who began when you were children, and took possession of your minds with their falsehoods, telling of one Socrates, a wise man, who speculated about the heaven above, and searched into the earth beneath, and made the worse appear the better cause. The disseminators of this tale are the accusers whom I dread; for their hearers are apt to fancy that such enquirers do not believe in the existence of the gods. And they are many, and their charges against me are of ancient date, and they were made by them in the days when you were more impressible than you are now—in childhood, or it may have been in youth—and the cause when heard went by default, for there was none to answer. And hardest of all, I do not know and cannot tell the names of my accusers; unless in the chance case of a Comic poet. All who from envy and malice have persuaded you—some of them having first convinced themselves—all this class of men are most difficult to deal with; for I cannot have them up here, and cross-examine them, and therefore I must simply fight with shadows in my own defence, and argue when there is no one who answers. I will ask you then to assume with me, as I was saying, that my opponents are of two kinds; one recent, the other ancient: and I hope that you will see the propriety of my answering the latter first, for these accusations you heard long before the others, and much oftener.

Well, then, I must make my defence, and endeavour to clear 19away in a short time, a slander which has lasted a long time. May I succeed, if to succeed be for my good and yours, or likely to avail me in my cause! The task is not an easy one; I quite understand the nature of it. And so leaving the event with God, in obedience to the law I will now make my defence.

There is the accusation of the theatres; which declares that he is a student of natural philosophy.

I will begin at the beginning, and ask what is the accusation which has given rise to the slander of me, and in fact has encouraged Meletus to prefer this charge against me. Well, what do the slanderers say? They shall be my prosecutors, and I will sum up their words in an affidavit: 'Socrates is an evil-doer, and a curious person, who searches into things under the earth and in heaven, and he makes the worse appear the better cause; and he teaches the aforesaid doctrines to others.' Such is the nature of the accusation: it is just what you have yourselves seen in the comedy of Aristophanes , who has introduced a man whom he calls Socrates, going about and saying that he walks in air, and talking a deal of nonsense concerning matters of which I do not pretend to know either much or little—not that I mean to speak disparagingly of any one who is a student of natural philosophy. I should be very sorry if Meletus could bring so grave a charge against me. But the simple truth is, O Athenians, that I have nothing to do with physical speculations. Very many of those here present are witnesses to the truth of this, and to them I appeal. Speak then, you who have heard me, and tell your neighbours whether any of you have ever known me hold forth in few words or in many upon such matters. . . . You hear their answer. And from what they say of this part of the charge you will be able to judge of the truth of the rest.

There is the report that he is a Sophist who receives money. The ironical question which Socrates put to Callias.

As little foundation is there for the report that I am a teacher, and take money; this accusation has no more truth in it than the other. Although, if a man were really able to instruct mankind, to receive money for giving instruction would, in my opinion, be an honour to him. There is Gorgias of Leontium, and Prodicus of Ceos, and Hippias of Elis, who go the round of the cities, and are able to persuade the young men to leave their own citizens by whom 20they might be taught for nothing, and come to them whom they not only pay, but are thankful if they may be allowed to pay them. There is at this time a Parian philosopher residing in Athens, of whom I have heard; and I came to hear of him in this way:—I came across a man who has spent a world of money on the Sophists, Callias, the son of Hipponicus, and knowing that he had sons, I asked him: 'Callias,' I said, 'if your two sons were foals or calves, there would be no difficulty in finding some one to put over them; we should hire a trainer of horses, or a farmer probably, who would improve and perfect them in their own proper virtue and excellence; but as they are human beings, whom are you thinking of placing over them? Is there any one who understands human and political virtue? You must have thought about the matter, for you have sons; is there any one?' 'There is,' he said. 'Who is he?' said I; 'and of what country? and what does he charge?' 'Evenus the Parian,' he replied; 'he is the man, and his charge is five minae.' Happy is Evenus, I said to myself, if he really has this wisdom, and teaches at such a moderate charge. Had I the same, I should have been very proud and conceited; but the truth is that I have no knowledge of the kind.

The accusations against me have arisen out of a sort of wisdom which I practise. My practice of it arose out of a declaration of the Delphian Oracle that I was the wisest of men.

I dare say, Athenians, that some one among you will reply, 'Yes, Socrates, but what is the origin of these accusations which are brought against you; there must have been something strange which you have been doing? All these rumours and this talk about you would never have arisen if you had been like other men: tell us, then, what is the cause of them, for we should be sorry to judge hastily of you.' Now I regard this as a fair challenge, and I will endeavour to explain to you the reason why I am called wise and have such an evil fame. Please to attend then. And although some of you may think that I am joking, I declare that I will tell you the entire truth. Men of Athens, this reputation of mine has come of a certain sort of wisdom which I possess. If you ask me what kind of wisdom, I reply, wisdom such as may perhaps be attained by man, for to that extent I am inclined to believe that I am wise; whereas the persons of whom I was speaking have a superhuman wisdom, which I may fail to describe, because I have it not myself; and he who says that I have, speaks falsely, and is taking away my character. And here, O men of Athens, I must beg you not to interrupt me, even if I seem to say something extravagant. For the word which I will speak is not mine. I will refer you to a witness who is worthy of credit; that witness shall be the God of Delphi—he will tell you about my wisdom, if I have any, and of what sort it is. You must have known Chaerephon; he was early 21a friend of mine, and also a friend of yours, for he shared in the recent exile of the people, and returned with you. Well, Chaerephon, as you know, was very impetuous in all his doings, and he went to Delphi and boldly asked the oracle to tell him whether—as I was saying, I must beg you not to interrupt—he asked the oracle to tell him whether any one was wiser than I was, and the Pythian prophetess answered, that there was no man wiser. Chaerephon is dead himself; but his brother, who is in court, will confirm the truth of what I am saying.

I went about searching after a man who was wiser than myself: at first among the politicians; then among the philosophers; and found that I had an advantage over them, because I had no conceit of knowledge.

Why do I mention this? Because I am going to explain to you why I have such an evil name. When I heard the answer, I said to myself, What can the god mean? and what is the interpretation of his riddle? for I know that I have no wisdom, small or great. What then can he mean when he says that I am the wisest of men? And yet he is a god, and cannot lie; that would be against his nature. After long consideration, I thought of a method of trying the question. I reflected that if I could only find a man wiser than myself, then I might go to the god with a refutation in my hand. I should say to him, 'Here is a man who is wiser than I am; but you said that I was the wisest.' Accordingly I went to one who had the reputation of wisdom, and observed him—his name I need not mention; he was a politician whom I selected for examination—and the result was as follows: When I began to talk with him, I could not help thinking that he was not really wise, although he was thought wise by many, and still wiser by himself; and thereupon I tried to explain to him that he thought himself wise, but was not really wise; and the consequence was that he hated me, and his enmity was shared by several who were present and heard me. So I left him, saying to myself, as I went away: Well, although I do not suppose that either of us knows anything really beautiful and good. I am better off than he is,—for he knows nothing, and thinks that he knows; I neither know nor think that I know. In this latter particular, then, I seem to have slightly the advantage of him. Then I went to another who had still higher pretensions to wisdom, and my conclusion was exactly the same. Whereupon I made another enemy of him, and of many others besides him.

I found that the poets were the worst possible interpreters of their own writings.

Then I went to one man after another, being not unconscious of the enmity which I provoked, and I lamented and feared this: but necessity was laid upon me,—the word of God, I thought, ought to be considered first. And I said to myself, Go I must to all who appear to know, and find out the meaning of the oracle. And I swear to you, Athenians, 22by the dog I swear!—for I must tell you the truth—the result of my mission was just this: I found that the men most in repute were all but the most foolish; and that others less esteemed were really wiser and better. I will tell you the tale of my wanderings and of the 'Herculean' labours, as I may call them, which I endured only to find at last the oracle irrefutable. After the politicians, I went to the poets; tragic, dithyrambic, and all sorts. And there, I said to myself, you will be instantly detected; now you will find out that you are more ignorant than they are. Accordingly, I took them some of the most elaborate passages in their own writings, and asked what was the meaning of them—thinking that they would teach me something. Will you believe me? I am almost ashamed to confess the truth, but I must say that there is hardly a person present who would not have talked better about their poetry than they did themselves. Then I knew that not by wisdom do poets write poetry, but by a sort of genius and inspiration; they are like diviners or soothsayers who also say many fine things, but do not understand the meaning of them. The poets appeared to me to be much in the same case; and I further observed that upon the strength of their poetry they believed themselves to be the wisest of men in other things in which they were not wise. So I departed, conceiving myself to be superior to them for the same reason that I was superior to the politicians.

The artisans had some real knowledge, but they had also a conceit that they knew things which were beyond them.

At last I went to the artisans, for I was conscious that I knew nothing at all, as I may say, and I was sure that they knew many fine things; and here I was not mistaken, for they did know many things of which I was ignorant, and in this they certainly were wiser than I was. But I observed that even the good artisans fell into the same error as the poets;—because they were good workmen they thought that they also knew all sorts of high matters, and this defect in them overshadowed their wisdom; and therefore I asked myself on behalf of the oracle, whether I would like to be as I was, neither having their knowledge nor their ignorance, or like them in both; and I made answer to myself and to the oracle that I was better off as I was.

The oracle was intended to apply, not to Socrates, but to all men who know that their wisdom is worth nothing.

This inquisition has led to my having many enemies of 23the worst and most dangerous kind, and has given occasion also to many calumnies. And I am called wise, for my hearers always imagine that I myself possess the wisdom which I find wanting in others: but the truth is, O men of Athens, that God only is wise; and by his answer he intends to show that the wisdom of men is worth little or nothing; he is not speaking of Socrates, he is only using my name by way of illustration, as if he said, He, O men, is the wisest, who, like Socrates, knows that his wisdom is in truth worth nothing. And so I go about the world, obedient to the god, and search and make enquiry into the wisdom of any one, whether citizen or stranger, who appears to be wise; and if he is not wise, then in vindication of the oracle I show him that he is not wise; and my occupation quite absorbs me, and I have no time to give either to any public matter of interest or to any concern of my own, but I am in utter poverty by reason of my devotion to the god.

There are my imitators who go about detecting pretenders, and the enmity which they arouse falls upon me.Socrates, Meletus.

There is another thing:—young men of the richer classes, who have not much to do, come about me of their own accord; they like to hear the pretenders examined, and they often imitate me, and proceed to examine others; there are plenty of persons, as they quickly discover, who think that they know something, but really know little or nothing; and then those who are examined by them instead of being angry with themselves are angry with me: This confounded Socrates, they say; this villainous misleader of youth!—and then if somebody asks them, Why, what evil does he practise or teach? they do not know, and cannot tell; but in order that they may not appear to be at a loss, they repeat the ready-made charges which are used against all philosophers about teaching things up in the clouds and under the earth, and having no gods, and making the worse appear the better cause; for they do not like to confess that their pretence of knowledge has been detected—which is the truth; and as they are numerous and ambitious and energetic, and are drawn up in battle array and have persuasive tongues, they have filled your ears with their loud and inveterate calumnies. And this is the reason why my three accusers, Meletus and Anytus and Lycon, have set upon me; Meletus, who has a quarrel with me on behalf of the poets; Anytus, on behalf of the craftsmen and politicians; Lycon, on behalf of the rhetoricians: and as I said 24at the beginning, I cannot expect to get rid of such a mass of calumny all in a moment. And this, O men of Athens, is the truth and the whole truth; I have concealed nothing, I have dissembled nothing. And yet, I know that my plainness of speech makes them hate me, and what is their hatred but a proof that I am speaking the truth? Hence has arisen the prejudice against me; and this is the reason of it, as you will find out either in this or in any future enquiry.

The second class of accusers.

I have said enough in my defence against the first class of my accusers; I turn to the second class. They are headed by Meletus, that good man and true lover of his country, as he calls himself. Against these, too, I must try to make a defence:—Let their affidavit be read: it contains something of this kind: It says that Socrates is a doer of evil, who corrupts the youth; and who does not believe in the gods of the state, but has other new divinities of his own. Such is the charge; and now let us examine the particular counts. He says that I am a doer of evil, and corrupt the youth;

but I say, O men of Athens, that Meletus is a doer of evil, in that he pretends to be in earnest when he is only in jest, and is so eager to bring men to trial from a pretended zeal and interest about matters in which he really never had the smallest interest. And the truth of this I will endeavour to prove to you.

Come hither, Meletus, and let me ask a question of you. You think a great deal about the improvement of youth?

Yes, I do.

All men are discovered to be improvers of youth with the single exception of Socrates.

Tell the judges, then, who is their improver; for you must know, as you have taken the pains to discover their corrupter, and are citing and accusing me before them. Speak, then, and tell the judges who their improver is.—Observe, Meletus, that you are silent, and have nothing to say. But is not this rather disgraceful, and a very considerable proof of what I was saying, that you have no interest in the matter? Speak up, friend, and tell us who their improver is.

The laws.

But that, my good sir, is not my meaning. I want to know who the person is, who, in the first place, knows the laws.

The judges, Socrates, who are present in court.

What, do you mean to say, Meletus, that they are able to instruct and improve youth?

Certainly they are.

What, all of them, or some only and not others?

All of them.

By the goddess Herè, that is good news! There are plenty of improvers, then. And what do you say of the 25audience,—do they improve them?

Yes, they do.

And the senators?

Yes, the senators improve them.

But perhaps the members of the assembly corrupt them?—or do they too improve them?

They improve them.

Then every Athenian improves and elevates them; all with the exception of myself; and I alone am their corrupter? Is that what you affirm?

That is what I stoutly affirm.

But this rather unfortunate fact does not accord with the analogy of the animals.

I am very unfortunate if you are right. But suppose I ask you a question: How about horses? Does one man do them harm and all the world good? Is not the exact opposite the truth? One man is able to do them good, or at least not many;—the trainer of horses, that is to say, does them good, and others who have to do with them rather injure them? Is not that true, Meletus, of horses, or of any other animals? Most assuredly it is; whether you and Anytus say yes or no. Happy indeed would be the condition of youth if they had one corrupter only, and all the rest of the world were their improvers. But you, Meletus, have sufficiently shown that you never had a thought about the young: your carelessness is seen in your not caring about the very things which you bring against me.

And now, Meletus, I will ask you another question—by Zeus I will: Which is better, to live among bad citizens, or among good ones? Answer, friend, I say; the question is one which may be easily answered. Do not the good do their neighbours good, and the bad do them evil?

Certainly.

And is there any one who would rather be injured than benefited by those who live with him? Answer, my good friend, the law requires you to answer—does any one like to be injured?

Certainly not.

When I do harm to my neighbour I must do harm to myself: and therefore I cannot be supposed to injure them intentionally.

And when you accuse me of corrupting and deteriorating the youth, do you allege that I corrupt them intentionally or unintentionally?

Intentionally, I say.

But you have just admitted that the good do their neighbours good, and the evil do them evil. Now, is that a truth which your superior wisdom has recognized thus early in life, and am I, at my age, in such darkness and ignorance as not to know that if a man with whom I have to live is corrupted by me, I am very likely to be harmed by him; and yet I corrupt him, and intentionally, too—so you say, although neither I nor any other human being is ever likely to be convinced by you. But either I do not corrupt them, or 26I corrupt them unintentionally; and on either view of the case you lie. If my offence is unintentional, the law has no cognizance of unintentional offences: you ought to have taken me privately, and warned and admonished me; for if I had been better advised, I should have left off doing what I only did unintentionally—no doubt I should; but you would have nothing to say to me and refused to teach me. And now you bring me up in this court, which is a place not of instruction, but of punishment.

It will be very clear to you, Athenians, as I was saying, that Meletus has no care at all, great or small, about the matter. But still I should like to know, Meletus, in what I am affirmed to corrupt the young. I suppose you mean, as I infer from your indictment, that I teach them not to acknowledge the gods which the state acknowledges, but some other new divinities or spiritual agencies in their stead. These are the lessons by which I corrupt the youth, as you say.

Yes, that I say emphatically.

Socrates is declared by Meletus to be an atheist and to corrupt the religion of the young.

Then, by the gods, Meletus, of whom we are speaking, tell me and the court, in somewhat plainer terms, what you mean! for I do not as yet understand whether you affirm that I teach other men to acknowledge some gods, and therefore that I do believe in gods, and am not an entire atheist—this you do not lay to my charge,—but only you say that they are not the same gods which the city recognizes—the charge is that they are different gods. Or, do you mean that I am an atheist simply, and a teacher of atheism?

I mean the latter—that you are a complete atheist.

What an extraordinary statement! Why do you think so, Meletus? Do you mean that I do not believe in the godhead of the sun or moon, like other men?

I assure you, judges, that he does not: for he says that the sun is stone, and the moon earth.

Meletus has confounded Socrates with Anaxagoras;

Friend Meletus, you think that you are accusing Anaxagoras: and you have but a bad opinion of the judges, if you fancy them illiterate to such a degree as not to know that these doctrines are found in the books of Anaxagoras the Clazomenian, which are full of them. And so, forsooth, the youth are said to be taught them by Socrates, when there are not unfrequently exhibitions of them at the theatre (price of admission one drachma at the most); and they might pay their money, and laugh at Socrates if he pretends to father these extraordinary views. And so, Meletus, you really think that I do not believe in any god?

and he has contradicted himself in the indictment.

I swear by Zeus that you believe absolutely in none at all.

Nobody will believe you, Meletus, and I am pretty sure that you do not believe yourself. I cannot help thinking, men of Athens, that Meletus is reckless and impudent, and that he has written this indictment in a spirit of mere wantonness and youthful bravado. Has he not compounded a 27riddle, thinking to try me? He said to himself:—I shall see whether the wise Socrates will discover my facetious contradiction, or whether I shall be able to deceive him and the rest of them. For he certainly does appear to me to contradict himself in the indictment as much as if he said that Socrates is guilty of not believing in the gods, and yet of believing in them—but this is not like a person who is in earnest.

I should like you, O men of Athens, to join me in examining what I conceive to be his inconsistency; and do you, Meletus, answer. And I must remind the audience of my request that they would not make a disturbance if I speak in my accustomed manner:

How can Socrates believe in divine agencies and not believe in gods?

Did ever man, Meletus, believe in the existence of human things, and not of human beings? . . . I wish, men of Athens, that he would answer, and not be always trying to get up an interruption. Did ever any man believe in horsemanship, and not in horses? or in flute-playing, and not in flute-players? No, my friend; I will answer to you and to the court, as you refuse to answer for yourself. There is no man who ever did. But now please to answer the next question: Can a man believe in spiritual and divine agencies, and not in spirits or demigods?

He cannot.

How lucky I am to have extracted that answer, by the assistance of the court! But then you swear in the indictment that I teach and believe in divine or spiritual agencies (new or old, no matter for that); at any rate, I believe in spiritual agencies,—so you say and swear in the affidavit; and yet if I believe in divine beings, how can I help believing in spirits or demigods;—must I not? To be sure I must; and therefore I may assume that your silence gives consent. Now what are spirits or demigods? are they not either gods or the sons of gods?

Certainly they are.

Apology. Socrates.

But this is what I call the facetious riddle invented by you: the demigods or spirits are gods, and you say first that I do not believe in gods, and then again that I do believe in gods; that is, if I believe in demigods. For if the demigods are the illegitimate sons of gods, whether by the nymphs or by any other mothers, of whom they are said to be the sons—what human being will ever believe that there are no gods if they are the sons of gods? You might as well affirm the existence of mules, and deny that of horses and asses. Such nonsense, Meletus, could only have been intended by you to make trial of me. You have put this into the indictment because you had nothing real of which to accuse me. But no one who has a particle of understanding will ever be convinced by you that the same men can believe in divine and superhuman things, and yet not believe that there are gods and demigods and heroes.

I have said enough in answer to the charge of Meletus: any elaborate defence is unnecessary; but I know only too well how many are the enmities which I have incurred, and this is what will be my destruction if I am destroyed;—not Meletus, nor yet Anytus, but the envy and detraction of the world, which has been the death of many good men, and will probably be the death of many more; there is no danger of my being the last of them.

Let no man fear death or fear anything but disgrace.

Some one will say: And are you not ashamed, Socrates, of a course of life which is likely to bring you to an untimely end? To him I may fairly answer: There you are mistaken: a man who is good for anything ought not to calculate the chance of living or dying; he ought only to consider whether in doing anything he is doing right or wrong—acting the part of a good man or of a bad. Whereas, upon your view, the heroes who fell at Troy were not good for much, and the son of Thetis above all, who altogether despised danger in comparison with disgrace; and when he was so eager to slay Hector, his goddess mother said to him, that if he avenged his companion Patroclus, and slew Hector, he would die himself—'Fate,' she said, in these or the like words, 'waits for you next after Hector;' he, receiving this warning, utterly despised danger and death, and instead of fearing them, feared rather to live in dishonour, and not to avenge his friend. 'Let me die forthwith,' he replies, 'and be avenged of my enemy, rather than abide here by the beaked ships, a laughing-stock and a burden of the earth.' Had Achilles any thought of death and danger? For wherever a man's place is, whether the place which he has chosen or that in which he has been placed by a commander, there he ought to remain in the hour of danger; he should not think of death or of anything but of disgrace. And this, O men of Athens, is a true saying.

Socrates, who has often faced death in battle, will not make any condition in order to save his own life; for he does not know whether death is a good or an evil. He must always be a preacher of philosophy. 'Necessity is laid upon me:' 'I must obey God rather than man.'

Strange, indeed, would be my conduct, O men of Athens, if I who, when I was ordered by the generals whom you chose to command me at Potidaea and Amphipolis and Delium, remained where they placed me, like any other man, facing death—if now, when, as I conceive and imagine, God orders me to fulfil the philosopher's mission of searching into myself and other men, I were to desert my post through fear 29of death, or any other fear; that would indeed be strange, and I might justly be arraigned in court for denying the existence of the gods, if I disobeyed the oracle because I was afraid of death, fancying that I was wise when I was not wise. For the fear of death is indeed the pretence of wisdom, and not real wisdom, being a pretence of knowing the unknown; and no one knows whether death, which men in their fear apprehend to be the greatest evil, may not be the greatest good. Is not this ignorance of a disgraceful sort, the ignorance which is the conceit that a man knows what he does not know? And in this respect only I believe myself to differ from men in general, and may perhaps claim to be wiser than they are:—that whereas I know but little of the world below, I do not suppose that I know: but I do know that injustice and disobedience to a better, whether God or man, is evil and dishonourable, and I will never fear or avoid a possible good rather than a certain evil. And therefore if you let me go now, and are not convinced by Anytus, who said that since I had been prosecuted I must be put to death; (or if not that I ought never to have been prosecuted at all); and that if I escape now, your sons will all be utterly ruined by listening to my words—if you say to me, Socrates, this time we will not mind Anytus, and you shall be let off, but upon one condition, that you are not to enquire and speculate in this way any more, and that if you are caught doing so again you shall die;—if this was the condition on which you let me go, I should reply: Men of Athens, I honour and love you; but I shall obey God rather than you, and while I have life and strength I shall never cease from the practice and teaching of philosophy, exhorting any one whom I meet and saying to him after my manner:

You, my friend,—a citizen of the great and mighty and wise city of Athens,—are you not ashamed of heaping up the greatest amount of money and honour and reputation, and caring so little about wisdom and truth and the greatest improvement of the soul, which you never regard or heed at all? And if the person with whom I am arguing, says: Yes, but I do care; then I do not leave him or let him go at once; but I proceed to interrogate and examine and cross-examine him, and if I think that he has no virtue in him, but only says that he has, I reproach him with undervaluing the greater, and overvaluing the less. And I shall repeat the same words to every one whom I meet, young and old, citizen and alien, but especially to the citizens, inasmuch as they are my brethren. For know that this is the command of God; and I believe that no greater good has ever happened in the state than my service to the God. For I do nothing but go about persuading you all, old and young alike, not to take thought for your persons or your properties, but first and chiefly to care about the greatest improvement of the soul. I tell you that virtue is not given by money, but that from virtue comes money and every other good of man, public as well as private. This is my teaching, and if this is the doctrine which corrupts the youth, I am a mischievous person. But if any one says that this is not my teaching, he is speaking an untruth. Wherefore, O men of Athens, I say to you, do as Anytus bids or not as Anytus bids, and either acquit me or not; but whichever you do, understand that I shall never alter my ways, not even if I have to die many times.

Neither you nor Meletus can ever injure me.

Men of Athens, do not interrupt, but hear me; there was an understanding between us that you should hear me to the end: I have something more to say, at which you may be inclined to cry out; but I believe that to hear me will be good for you, and therefore I beg that you will not cry out. I would have you know, that if you kill such an one as I am, you will injure yourselves more than you will injure me. Nothing will injure me, not Meletus nor yet Anytus—they cannot, for a bad man is not permitted to injure a better than himself. I do not deny that Anytus may, perhaps, kill him, or drive him into exile, or deprive him of civil rights; and he may imagine, and others may imagine, that he is inflicting a great injury upon him: but there I do not agree. For the evil of doing as he is doing—the evil of unjustly taking away the life of another—is greater far.

I am the gadfly of the Athenian people, given to them by God, and they will never have another, if they kill me.

And now, Athenians, I am not going to argue for my own sake, as you may think, but for yours, that you may not sin against the God by condemning me, who am his gift to you. For if you kill me you will not easily find a successor to me, who, if I may use such a ludicrous figure of speech, am a sort of gadfly, given to the state by God; and the state is a great and noble steed who is tardy in his motions owing to his very size, and requires to be stirred into life. I am that gadfly which God has attached to the state, and all day long 31and in all places am always fastening upon you, arousing and persuading and reproaching you. You will not easily find another like me, and therefore I would advise you to spare me. I dare say that you may feel out of temper (like a person who is suddenly awakened from sleep), and you think that you might easily strike me dead as Anytus advises, and then you would sleep on for the remainder of your lives, unless God in his care of you sent you another gadfly. When I say that I am given to you by God, the proof of my mission is this:—if I had been like other men, I should not have neglected all my own concerns or patiently seen the neglect of them during all these years, and have been doing yours, coming to you individually like a father or elder brother, exhorting you to regard virtue; such conduct, I say, would be unlike human nature. If I had gained anything, or if my exhortations had been paid, there would have been some sense in my doing so; but now, as you will perceive, not even the impudence of my accusers dares to say that I have ever exacted or sought pay of any one; of that they have no witness. And I have a sufficient witness to the truth of what I say—my poverty.

The internal sign always forbade him to engage in politics; and if he had done so, he would have perished long ago.

Some one may wonder why I go about in private giving advice and busying myself with the concerns of others, but do not venture to come forward in public and advise the state. I will tell you why. You have heard me speak at sundry times and in divers places of an oracle or sign which comes to me, and is the divinity which Meletus ridicules in the indictment. This sign, which is a kind of voice, first began to come to me when I was a child; it always forbids but never commands me to do anything which I am going to do. This is what deters me from being a politician. And rightly, as I think. For I am certain, O men of Athens, that if I had engaged in politics, I should have perished long ago, and done no good either to you or to myself. And do not be offended at my telling you the truth: for the truth is, that no man who goes to war with you or any other multitude, honestly striving against the many lawless and unrighteous 32deeds which are done in a state, will save his life; he who will fight for the right, if he would live even for a brief space, must have a private station and not a public one.

He had shown that he would sooner die than commit injustice at the trial of the generals and under the tyranny of the Thirty.

I can give you convincing evidence of what I say, not words only, but what you value far more—actions. Let me relate to you a passage of my own life which will prove to you that I should never have yielded to injustice from any fear of death, and that 'as I should have refused to yield' I must have died at once. I will tell you a tale of the courts, not very interesting perhaps, but nevertheless true. The only office of state which I ever held, O men of Athens, was that of senator: the tribe Antiochis, which is my tribe, had the presidency at the trial of the generals who had not taken up the bodies of the slain after the battle of Arginusae; and you proposed to try them in a body, contrary to law, as you all thought afterwards; but at the time I was the only one of the Prytanes who was opposed to the illegality, and I gave my vote against you; and when the orators threatened to impeach and arrest me, and you called and shouted, I made up my mind that I would run the risk, having law and justice with me, rather than take part in your injustice because I feared imprisonment and death. This happened in the days of the democracy. But when the oligarchy of the Thirty was in power, they sent for me and four others into the rotunda, and bade us bring Leon the Salaminian from Salamis, as they wanted to put him to death. This was a specimen of the sort of commands which they were always giving with the view of implicating as many as possible in their crimes; and then I showed, not in word only but in deed, that, if I may be allowed to use such an expression, I cared not a straw for death, and that my great and only care was lest I should do an unrighteous or unholy thing. For the strong arm of that oppressive power did not frighten me into doing wrong; and when we came out of the rotunda the other four went to Salamis and fetched Leon, but I went quietly home. For which I might have lost my life, had not the power of the Thirty shortly afterwards come to an end. And many will witness to my words.

He is always talking to the citizens, but he teaches nothing; he takes no pay and has no secrets.

Now do you really imagine that I could have survived all these years, if I had led a public life, supposing that like a good man I had always maintained the right and had made justice, as I ought, the first thing? No indeed, men of Athens, neither I nor any other man. But I have been 33always the same in all my actions, public as well as private, and never have I yielded any base compliance to those who are slanderously termed my disciples, or to any other. Not that I have any regular disciples. But if any one likes to come and hear me while I am pursuing my mission, whether he be young or old, he is not excluded. Nor do I converse only with those who pay; but any one, whether he be rich or poor, may ask and answer me and listen to my words; and whether he turns out to be a bad man or a good one, neither result can be justly imputed to me; for I never taught or professed to teach him anything. And if any one says that he has ever learned or heard anything from me in private which all the world has not heard, let me tell you that he is lying.

The parents and kinsmen of those whom he is supposed to have corrupted do not come forward and testify against him.

But I shall be asked, Why do people delight in continually conversing with you? I have told you already, Athenians, the whole truth about this matter: they like to hear the cross-examination of the pretenders to wisdom; there is amusement in it. Now this duty of cross-examining other men has been imposed upon me by God; and has been signified to me by oracles, visions, and in every way in which the will of divine power was ever intimated to any one. This is true, O Athenians; or, if not true, would be soon refuted. If I am or have been corrupting the youth, those of them who are now grown up and have become sensible that I gave them bad advice in the days of their youth should come forward as accusers, and take their revenge; or if they do not like to come themselves, some of their relatives, fathers, brothers, or other kinsmen, should say what evil their families have suffered at my hands. Now is their time. Many of them I see in the court. There is Crito, who is of the same age and of the same deme with myself, and there is Critobulus his son, whom I also see. Then again there is Lysanias of Sphettus, who is the father of Aeschines—he is present; and also there is Antiphon of Cephisus, who is the father of Epigenes; and there are the brothers of several who have associated with me. There is Nicostratus the son of Theosdotides, and the brother of Theodotus (now Theodotus himself is dead, and therefore he, at any rate, will not seek to stop him); and there is Paralus the son of Demodocus, who had a brother Theages; 34and Adeimantus the son of Ariston, whose brother Plato is present; and Aeantodorus, who is the brother of Apollodorus, whom I also see. I might mention a great many others, some of whom Meletus should have produced as witnesses in the course of his speech; and let him still produce them, if he has forgotten—I will make way for him. And let him say, if he has any testimony of the sort which he can produce. Nay, Athenians, the very opposite is the truth. For all these are ready to witness on behalf of the corrupter, of the injurer of their kindred, as Meletus and Anytus call me; not the corrupted youth only—there might have been a motive for that—but their uncorrupted elder relatives. Why should they too support me with their testimony? Why, indeed, except for the sake of truth and justice, and because they know that I am speaking the truth, and that Meletus is a liar.

He is flesh and blood, but he will not appeal to the pity of his judges: or make a scene in the court such as he has often witnessed.

Well, Athenians, this and the like of this is all the defence which I have to offer. Yet a word more. Perhaps there may be some one who is offended at me, when he calls to mind how he himself on a similar, or even a less serious occasion, prayed and entreated the judges with many tears, and how he produced his children in court, which was a moving spectacle, together with a host of relations and friends; whereas I, who am probably in danger of my life, will do none of these things. The contrast may occur to his mind, and he may be set against me, and vote in anger because he is displeased at me on this account. Now if there be such a person among you,—mind, I do not say that there is,—to him I may fairly reply: My friend, I am a man, and like other men, a creature of flesh and blood, and not 'of wood or stone,' as Homer says; and I have a family, yes, and sons, O Athenians, three in number, one almost a man, and two others who are still young; and yet I will not bring any of them hither in order to petition you for an acquittal. And why not? Not from any self-assertion or want of respect for you. Whether I am or am not afraid of death is another question, of which I will not now speak. But, having regard to public opinion, I feel that such conduct would be discreditable to myself, and to you, and to the whole state. One who has reached my years, and who has a name for wisdom, ought not to demean himself. Whether this opinion of me be deserved or not, at any rate the world has decided that Socrates is in some way superior to other men. And if those 35among you who are said to be superior in wisdom and courage, and any other virtue, demean themselves in this way, how shameful is their conduct! I have seen men of reputation, when they have been condemned, behaving in the strangest manner: they seemed to fancy that they were going to suffer something dreadful if they died, and that they could be immortal if you only allowed them to live; and I think that such are a dishonour to the state, and that any stranger coming in would have said of them that the most eminent men of Athens, to whom the Athenians themselves give honour and command, are no better than women. And I say that these things ought not to be done by those of us who have a reputation; and if they are done, you ought not to permit them; you ought rather to show that you are far more disposed to condemn the man who gets up a doleful scene and makes the city ridiculous, than him who holds his peace.

The judge should not be influenced by his feelings, but convinced by reason.

But, setting aside the question of public opinion, there seems to be something wrong in asking a favour of a judge, and thus procuring an acquittal, instead of informing and convincing him. For his duty is, not to make a present of justice, but to give judgment; and he has sworn that he will judge according to the laws, and not according to his own good pleasure; and we ought not to encourage you, nor should you allow yourselves to be encouraged, in this habit of perjury—there can be no piety in that. Do not then require me to do what I consider dishonourable and impious and wrong, especially now, when I am being tried for impiety on the indictment of Meletus. For if, O men of Athens, by force of persuasion and entreaty I could overpower your oaths, then I should be teaching you to believe that there are no gods, and in defending should simply convict myself of the charge of not believing in them. But that is not so—far otherwise. For I do believe that there are gods, and in a sense higher than that in which any of my accusers believe in them. And to you and to God I commit my cause, to be determined by you as is best for you and me.

There are many reasons why I am not grieved, O men of 36Athens, at the vote of condemnation. I expected it, and am only surprised that the votes are so nearly equal; for I had thought that the majority against me would have been far larger; but now, had thirty votes gone over to the other side, I should have been acquitted. And I may say, I think, that I have escaped Meletus. I may say more; for without the assistance of Anytus and Lycon, any one may see that he would not have had a fifth part of the votes, as the law requires, in which case he would have incurred a fine of a thousand drachmae.

Socrates all his life long has been seeking to do the greatest good to the Athenians. Should he not be rewarded with maintenance in the Prytaneum?

And so he proposes death as the penalty. And what shall I propose on my part, O men of Athens? Clearly that which is my due. And what is my due? What return shall be made to the man who has never had the wit to be idle during his whole life; but has been careless of what the many care for—wealth, and family interests, and military offices, and speaking in the assembly, and magistracies, and plots, and parties. Reflecting that I was really too honest a man to be a politician and live, I did not go where I could do no good to you or to myself; but where I could do the greatest good privately to every one of you, thither I went, and sought to persuade every man among you that he must look to himself, and seek virtue and wisdom before he looks to his private interests, and look to the state before he looks to the interests of the state; and that this should be the order which he observes in all his actions. What shall be done to such an one? Doubtless some good thing, O men of Athens, if he has his reward; and the good should be of a kind suitable to him. What would be a reward suitable to a poor man who is your benefactor, and who desires leisure that he may instruct you? There can be no reward so fitting as maintenance in the Prytaneum, O men of Athens, a reward which he deserves far more than the citizen who has won the prize at Olympia in the horse or chariot race, whether the chariots were drawn by two horses or by many. For I am in want, and he has enough; and he only gives you the appearance of happiness, and I give you the reality. And if I am to estimate the penalty fairly, I should say that maintenance in the Prytaneum 37is the just return.

The consciousness of innocence gives him confidence. No alternative in his own judgment preferable to death.

Perhaps you think that I am braving you in what I am saying now, as in what I said before about the tears and prayers. But this is not so. I speak rather because I am convinced that I never intentionally wronged any one, although I cannot convince you—the time has been too short; if there were a law at Athens, as there is in other cities, that a capital cause should not be decided in one day, then I believe that I should have convinced you. But I cannot in a moment refute great slanders; and, as I am convinced that I never wronged another, I will assuredly not wrong myself. I will not say of myself that I deserve any evil, or propose any penalty. Why should I? Because I am afraid of the penalty of death which Meletus proposes? When I do not know whether death is a good or an evil, why should I propose a penalty which would certainly be an evil? Shall I say imprisonment? And why should I live in prison, and be the slave of the magistrates of the year—of the Eleven? Or shall the penalty be a fine, and imprisonment until the fine is paid? There is the same objection. I should have to lie in prison, for money I have none, and cannot pay. And if I say exile (and this may possibly be the penalty which you will affix), I must indeed be blinded by the love of life, if I am so irrational as to expect that when you, who are my own citizens, cannot endure my discourses and words, and have found them so grievous and odious that you will have no more of them, others are likely to endure me. No indeed, men of Athens, that is not very likely. And what a life should I lead, at my age, wandering from city to city, ever changing my place of exile, and always being driven out! For I am quite sure that wherever I go, there, as here, the young men will flock to me; and if I drive them away, their elders will drive me out at their request; and if I let them come, their fathers and friends will drive me out for their sakes.

For wherever he goes he must speak out.

Some one will say: Yes, Socrates, but cannot you hold your tongue, and then you may go into a foreign city, and no one will interfere with you? Now I have great difficulty in making you understand my answer to this. For if I tell you that to do as you say would be a disobedience to the God, and therefore that I cannot hold my tongue, you will not 38believe that I am serious; and if I say again that daily to discourse about virtue, and of those other things about which you hear me examining myself and others, is the greatest good of man, and that the unexamined life is not worth living, you are still less likely to believe me. Yet I say what is true, although a thing of which it is hard for me to persuade you. Also, I have never been accustomed to think that I deserve to suffer any harm. Had I money I might have estimated the offence at what I was able to pay, and not have been much the worse. But I have none, and therefore I must ask you to proportion the fine to my means. Well, perhaps I could afford a mina, and therefore I propose that penalty: Plato, Crito, Critobulus, and Apollodorus, my friends here, bid me say thirty minae, and they will be the sureties. Let thirty minae be the penalty; for which sum they will be ample security to you.

They will be accused of killing a wise man. Why could they not wait a few years?

Not much time will be gained, O Athenians, in return for the evil name which you will get from the detractors of the city, who will say that you killed Socrates, a wise man; for they will call me wise, even although I am not wise, when they want to reproach you. If you had waited a little while, your desire would have been fulfilled in the course of nature. For I am far advanced in years, as you may perceive, and not far from death. I am speaking now not to all of you, but only to those who have condemned me to death. And I have another thing to say to them: You think that I was convicted because I had no words of the sort which would have procured my acquittal—I mean, if I had thought fit to leave nothing undone or unsaid. Not so; the deficiency which led to my conviction was not of words—certainly not. But I had not the boldness or impudence or inclination to address you as you would have liked me to do, weeping and wailing and lamenting, and saying and doing many things which you have been accustomed to hear from others, and which, as I maintain, are unworthy of me. I thought at the time that I ought not to do anything common or mean when in danger: nor do I now repent of the style of my defence; I would rather die having spoken after my manner, than speak in your manner and live. For neither in war nor yet at law ought I or any man to use every way of escaping death. 39Often in battle there can be no doubt that if a man will throw away his arms, and fall on his knees before his pursuers, he may escape death; and in other dangers there are other ways of escaping death, if a man is willing to say and do anything. The difficulty, my friends, is not to avoid death, but to avoid unrighteousness; for that runs faster than death. I am old and move slowly, and the slower runner has overtaken me, and my accusers are keen and quick, and the faster runner, who is unrighteousness, has overtaken them. And now I depart hence condemned by you to suffer the penalty of death,—they too go their ways condemned by the truth to suffer the penalty of villainy and wrong; and I must abide by my award—let them abide by theirs. I suppose that these things may be regarded as fated,—and I think that they are well.

They are about to slay Socrates because he has been their accuser: other accusers will rise up and denounce them more vehemently.

And now, O men who have condemned me, I would fain prophesy to you; for I am about to die, and in the hour of death men are gifted with prophetic power. And I prophesy to you who are my murderers, that immediately after my departure punishment far heavier than you have inflicted on me will surely await you. Me you have killed because you wanted to escape the accuser, and not to give an account of your lives. But that will not be as you suppose: far otherwise. For I say that there will be more accusers of you than there are now; accusers whom hitherto I have restrained: and as they are younger they will be more inconsiderate with you, and you will be more offended at them. If you think that by killing men you can prevent some one from censuring your evil lives, you are mistaken; that is not a way of escape which is either possible or honourable; the easiest and the noblest way is not to be disabling others, but to be improving yourselves. This is the prophecy which I utter before my departure to the judges who have condemned me.

He believes that what is happening to him will be good, because the internal oracle gives no sign of opposition.

Friends, who would have acquitted me, I would like also to talk with you about the thing which has come to pass, while the magistrates are busy, and before I go to the place at which I must die. Stay then a little, for we may as well talk 40with one another while there is time. You are my friends, and I should like to show you the meaning of this event which has happened to me. O my judges—for you I may truly call judges—I should like to tell you of a wonderful circumstance. Hitherto the divine faculty of which the internal oracle is the source has constantly been in the habit of opposing me even about trifles, if I was going to make a slip or error in any matter; and now as you see there has come upon me that which may be thought, and is generally believed to be, the last and worst evil. But the oracle made no sign of opposition, either when I was leaving my house in the morning, or when I was on my way to the court, or while I was speaking, at anything which I was going to say; and yet I have often been stopped in the middle of a speech, but now in nothing I either said or did touching the matter in hand has the oracle opposed me. What do I take to be the explanation of this silence? I will tell you. It is an intimation that what has happened to me is a good, and that those of us who think that death is an evil are in error. For the customary sign would surely have opposed me had I been going to evil and not to good.

Death either a good or nothing:=a profound sleep.How blessed to have a just judgment passed on us; to converse with Homer and Hesiod; to see the heroes of Troy, and to continue the search after knowledge in another world!

Let us reflect in another way, and we shall see that there is great reason to hope that death is a good; for one of two things—either death is a state of nothingness and utter unconsciousness, or, as men say, there is a change and migration of the soul from this world to another. Now if you suppose that there is no consciousness, but a sleep like the sleep of him who is undisturbed even by dreams, death will be an unspeakable gain. For if a person were to select the night in which his sleep was undisturbed even by dreams, and were to compare with this the other days and nights of his life, and then were to tell us how many days and nights he had passed in the course of his life better and more pleasantly than this one, I think that any man, I will not say a private man, but even the great king will not find many such days or nights, when compared with the others. Now if death be of such a nature, I say that to die is gain; for eternity is then only a single night. But if death is the journey to another place, and there, as men say, all the dead abide, what good, O my friends and judges, can be greater than this? If indeed when the pilgrim arrives in the world below, he is delivered from the professors 41of justice in this world, and finds the true judges who are said to give judgment there, Minos and Rhadamanthus and Aeacus and Triptolemus, and other sons of God who were righteous in their own life, that pilgrimage will be worth making. What would not a man give if he might converse with Orpheus and Musaeus and Hesiod and Homer? Nay, if this be true, let me die again and again. I myself, too, shall have a wonderful interest in there meeting and conversing with Palamedes, and Ajax the son of Telamon, and any other ancient hero who has suffered death through an unjust judgment; and there will be no small pleasure, as I think, in comparing my own sufferings with theirs. Above all, I shall then be able to continue my search into true and false knowledge; as in this world, so also in the next; and I shall find out who is wise, and who pretends to be wise, and is not. What would not a man give, O judges, to be able to examine the leader of the great Trojan expedition; or Odysseus or Sisyphus, or numberless others, men and women too! What infinite delight would there be in conversing with them and asking them questions! In another world they do not put a man to death for asking questions: assuredly not. For besides being happier than we are, they will be immortal, if what is said is true.

Wherefore, O judges, be of good cheer about death, and know of a certainty, that no evil can happen to a good man, either in life or after death. He and his are not neglected by the gods; nor has my own approaching end happened by mere chance. But I see clearly that the time had arrived when it was better for me to die and be released from trouble; wherefore the oracle gave no sign. For which reason, also, I am not angry with my condemners, or with my accusers; they have done me no harm, although they did not mean to do me any good; and for this I may gently blame them.

Do to my sons as I have done to you.

Still I have a favour to ask of them. When my sons are grown up, I would ask you, O my friends, to punish them; and I would have you trouble them, as I have troubled you, if they seem to care about riches, or anything, more than about virtue; or if they pretend to be something when they are really nothing,—then reprove them, as I have reproved you, for not caring about that for which they ought to care, and thinking that they are something when they are really 42nothing. And if you do this, both I and my sons will have received justice at your hands.

The hour of departure has arrived, and we go our ways—I to die, and you to live. Which is better God only knows.

INTRODUCTION TO CRITO.

Crito. Introduction.

The Crito seems intended to exhibit the character of Socrates in one light only, not as the philosopher, fulfilling a divine mission and trusting in the will of heaven, but simply as the good citizen, who having been unjustly condemned is willing to give up his life in obedience to the laws of the state. . . . .

Analysis.

43 The days of Socrates are drawing to a close; the fatal ship has been seen off Sunium, as he is informed by his aged friend and contemporary Crito, who visits him before the dawn has broken; he himself has been warned in a dream that on the 44 third day he must depart. Time is precious, and Crito has come early in order to gain his consent to a plan of escape. This can be easily accomplished by his friends, who will incur no 45 danger in making the attempt to save him, but will be disgraced for ever if they allow him to perish. He should think of his duty to his children, and not play into the hands of his enemies. Money is already provided by Crito as well as by Simmias and 46 others, and he will have no difficulty in finding friends in Thessaly and other places.

Socrates is afraid that Crito is but pressing upon him the opinions of the many: whereas, all his life long he has followed the dictates of reason only and the opinion of the one wise or skilled man. There was a time when Crito himself had allowed the propriety of this. And although some one will say 'the many can kill us,' that makes no difference; but a good life, in other words, a just and honourable life, is alone to be valued. All considerations of loss of reputation or injury to his children should be dismissed: the only question is whether he would be right in attempting to escape. Crito, who is a disinterested 47 person not having the fear of death before his eyes, shall answer this for him. Before he was condemned they had often held discussions, in which they agreed that no man should either do evil, 48 or return evil for evil, or betray the right. Are these principles to be altered because the circumstances of Socrates are altered? Crito admits that they remain the same. Then is his escape consistent 49 with the maintenance of them? To this Crito is unable or unwilling to reply.

Socrates proceeds:—Suppose the Laws of Athens to come 50 and remonstrate with him: they will ask 'Why does he seek to overturn them?' and if he replies, 'they have injured him,' will not the Laws answer, 'Yes, but was that the agreement? Has he any objection to make to them which would justify him in 51overturning them? Was he not brought into the world and educated by their help, and are they not his parents? He might 52have left Athens and gone where he pleased, but he has lived there for seventy years more constantly than any other citizen.' Thus he has clearly shown that he acknowledged the agreement, which he cannot now break without dishonour to himself and danger to his friends. Even in the course of the trial he might have proposed exile as the penalty, but then he declared that he preferred death to exile. And whither will he direct his footsteps? In any well-ordered state the Laws will consider him as 53an enemy. Possibly in a land of misrule like Thessaly he may be welcomed at first, and the unseemly narrative of his escape will be regarded by the inhabitants as an amusing tale. But if he offends them he will have to learn another sort of lesson. Will he continue to give lectures in virtue? That would hardly be decent. And how will his children be the gainers if he takes them into Thessaly, and deprives them of Athenian citizenship? 54Or if he leaves them behind, does he expect that they will be better taken care of by his friends because he is in Thessaly? Will not true friends care for them equally whether he is alive or dead?

Finally, they exhort him to think of justice first, and of life and children afterwards. He may now depart in peace and innocence, a sufferer and not a doer of evil. But if he breaks agreements, and returns evil for evil, they will be angry with him while he lives; and their brethren the Laws of the world below will receive him as an enemy. Such is the mystic voice which is always murmuring in his ears.

Introduction.

That Socrates was not a good citizen was a charge made against him during his lifetime, which has been often repeated in later ages. The crimes of Alcibiades, Critias, and Charmides, who had been his pupils, were still recent in the memory of the now restored democracy. The fact that he had been neutral in the death-struggle of Athens was not likely to conciliate popular good-will. Plato, writing probably in the next generation, undertakes the defence of his friend and master in this particular, not to the Athenians of his day, but to posterity and the world at large.

Whether such an incident ever really occurred as the visit of Crito and the proposal of escape is uncertain: Plato could easily have invented far more than that (Phaedr. 275 B); and in the selection of Crito, the aged friend, as the fittest person to make the proposal to Socrates, we seem to recognize the hand of the artist. Whether any one who has been subjected by the laws of his country to an unjust judgment is right in attempting to escape, is a thesis about which casuists might disagree. Shelley (Prose Works, p. 78) is of opinion that Socrates 'did well to die,' but not for the 'sophistical' reasons which Plato has put into his mouth. And there would be no difficulty in arguing that Socrates should have lived and preferred to a glorious death the good which he might still be able to perform. 'A rhetorician would have had much to say upon that point' (50 B). It may be observed however that Plato never intended to answer the question of casuistry, but only to exhibit the ideal of patient virtue which refuses to do the least evil in order to avoid the greatest, and to show his master maintaining in death the opinions which he had professed in his life. Not 'the world,' but the 'one wise man,' is still the paradox of Socrates in his last hours. He must be guided by reason, although her conclusions may be fatal to him. The remarkable sentiment that the wicked can do neither good nor evil is true, if taken in the sense, which he means, of moral evil; in his own words, 'they cannot make a man wise or foolish.'

This little dialogue is a perfect piece of dialectic, in which granting the 'common principle' (49 D), there is no escaping from the conclusion. It is anticipated at the beginning by the dream of Socrates and the parody of Homer. The personification of the Laws, and of their brethren the Laws in the world below, is one of the noblest and boldest figures of speech which occur in Plato.

CRITO.

PERSONS OF THE DIALOGUE.

Socrates.

Crito.

Scene:—The Prison of Socrates.

Socrates.

Crito. Socrates, Crito.

43 Why have you come at this hour, Crito? it must be quite early?

Crito.

Yes, certainly.

Soc.

Crito appears at break of dawn in the prison of Socrates, whom he finds asleep.

What is the exact time?

Cr.

The dawn is breaking.

Soc.

I wonder that the keeper of the prison would let you in.

Cr.

He knows me, because I often come, Socrates; moreover, I have done him a kindness.

Soc.

And are you only just arrived?

Cr.

No, I came some time ago.

Soc.

Then why did you sit and say nothing, instead of at once awakening me?

Cr.

I should not have liked myself, Socrates, to be in such great trouble and unrest as you are—indeed I should not: I have been watching with amazement your peaceful slumbers; and for that reason I did not awake you, because I wished to minimize the pain. I have always thought you to be of a happy disposition; but never did I see anything like the easy, tranquil manner in which you bear this calamity.

Soc.

Why, Crito, when a man has reached my age he ought not to be repining at the approach of death.

Cr.

And yet other old men find themselves in similar misfortunes, and age does not prevent them from repining.

Soc.

That is true. But you have not told me why you come at this early hour.

Cr.

The ship from Delos is expected.

I come to bring you a message which is sad and painful; not, as I believe, to yourself, but to all of us who are your friends, and saddest of all to me.

Soc.

What? Has the ship come from Delos, on the arrival of which I am to die?

Cr.

No, the ship has not actually arrived, but she will probably be here to-day, as persons who have come from Sunium tell me that they left her there; and therefore to-morrow, Socrates, will be the last day of your life.

Soc.

Very well, Crito; if such is the will of God, I am willing; but my belief is that there will be a delay of a day.

Cr.

Why do you think so? 44

Soc.

I will tell you. I am to die on the day after the arrival of the ship.

Cr.

Yes; that is what the authorities say.

Soc.

A vision of a fair woman who prophesies in the language of Homer that Socrates will die on the third day.

But I do not think that the ship will be here until to-morrow; this I infer from a vision which I had last night, or rather only just now, when you fortunately allowed me to sleep.

Cr.

And what was the nature of the vision?

Soc.

There appeared to me the likeness of a woman, fair and comely, clothed in bright raiment, who called to me and said: O Socrates,

'The third day hence to fertile Phthia shalt thou go .'

Cr.

What a singular dream, Socrates!

Soc.

There can be no doubt about the meaning, Crito, I think.

Cr.

Yes; the meaning is only too clear. But, oh! my beloved Socrates, let me entreat you once more to take my advice and escape. For if you die I shall not only lose a friend who can never be replaced, but there is another evil: people who do not know you and me will believe that I might have saved you if I had been willing to give money, but that I did not care. Now, can there be a worse disgrace than this—that I should be thought to value money more than the life of a friend? For the many will not be persuaded that I wanted you to escape, and that you refused.

Soc.

But why, my dear Crito, should we care about the opinion of the many? Good men, and they are the only persons who are worth considering, will think of these things truly as they occurred.

Cr.

Crito by a variety of arguments tries to induce Socrates to make his escape. The means will be easily provided and without danger to any one.

But you see, Socrates, that the opinion of the many must be regarded, for what is now happening shows that they can do the greatest evil to any one who has lost their good opinion.

Soc.

I only wish it were so, Crito; and that the many could do the greatest evil; for then they would also be able to do the greatest good—and what a fine thing this would be! But in reality they can do neither; for they cannot make a man either wise or foolish; and whatever they do is the result of chance.

Cr.

Well, I will not dispute with you; but please to tell me, Socrates, whether you are not acting out of regard to me and your other friends: are you not afraid that if you escape from prison we may get into trouble with the informers for having stolen you away, and lose either the whole or a great part of our property; or that even a worse evil may happen to us? Now, if you fear on our account, be at ease; for in order to save you, we ought surely to run this, or even a greater risk; be persuaded, then, and do as I say.

Soc.

Yes, Crito, that is one fear which you mention, but by no means the only one.

Cr.

He is not justified in throwing away his life; he will be deserting his children, and will bring the reproach of cowardice on his friends.

Fear not—there are persons who are willing to get you out of prison at no great cost; and as for the informers, they are far from being exorbitant in their demands—a little money will satisfy them. My means, which are certainly ample, are at your service, and if you have a scruple about spending all mine, here are strangers who will give you the use of theirs; and one of them, Simmias the Theban, has brought a large sum of money for this very purpose; and Cebes and many others are prepared to spend their money in helping you to escape. I say, therefore, do not hesitate on our account, and do not say, as you did in the court, that you will have a difficulty in knowing what to do with yourself anywhere else. For men will love you in other places to which you may go, and not in Athens only; there are friends of mine in Thessaly, if you like to go to them, who will value and protect you, and no Thessalian will give you any trouble. Nor can I think that you are at all justified, Socrates, in betraying your own life when you might be saved; in acting thus you are playing into the hands of your enemies, who are hurrying on your destruction. And further I should say that you are deserting your own children; for you might bring them up and educate them; instead of which you go away and leave them, and they will have to take their chance; and if they do not meet with the usual fate of orphans, there will be small thanks to you. No man should bring children into the world who is unwilling to persevere to the end in their nurture and education. But you appear to be choosing the easier part, not the better and manlier, which would have been more becoming in one who professes to care for virtue in all his actions, like yourself. And indeed, I am ashamed not only of you, but of us who are your friends, when I reflect that the whole business will be attributed entirely to our want of courage. The trial need never have come on, or might have been managed differently; and this last act, or crowning folly, will seem to have occurred through our negligence and cowardice, who might have saved you, if we had been good for anything; and you might have saved yourself, for there was no difficulty at all. See now, Socrates, how sad and discreditable are the consequences, both to us and you. Make up your mind then, or rather have your mind already made up, for the time of deliberation is over, and there is only one thing to be done, which must be done this very night, and if we delay at all will be no longer practicable or possible; I beseech you therefore, Socrates, be persuaded by me, and do as I say.

Soc.

Socrates is one of those who must be guided by reason. Ought he to follow the opinion of the many or of the few, of the wise or of the unwise?

Dear Crito, your zeal is invaluable, if a right one; but if wrong, the greater the zeal the greater the danger; and therefore we ought to consider whether I shall or shall not do as you say. For I am and always have been one of those natures who must be guided by reason, whatever the reason may be which upon reflection appears to me to be the best; and now that this chance has befallen me, I cannot repudiate my own words: the principles which I have hitherto honoured and revered I still honour, and unless we can at once find other and better principles, I am certain not to agree with you; no, not even if the power of the multitude could inflict many more imprisonments, confiscations, deaths, frightening us like children with hobgoblin terrors . What will be the fairest way of considering the question? Shall I return to your old argument about the opinions of men?—we were saying that some of them are to be regarded, and others not. Now were we right in maintaining this before I was condemned? And has the argument which was once good now proved to be talk for the sake of talking—mere childish nonsense? That is what I want to consider with your help, Crito:—whether, under my present circumstances, the argument appears to be in any way different or not; and is to be allowed by me or disallowed. That argument, which, as I believe, is maintained by many persons of authority, was to the effect, as I was saying, that the opinions of some men are to be regarded, and of other men not to be regarded. Now 47you, Crito, are not going to die to-morrow—at least, there is no human probability of this—and therefore you are disinterested and not liable to be deceived by the circumstances in which you are placed. Tell me then, whether I am right in saying that some opinions, and the opinions of some men only, are to be valued, and that other opinions, and the opinions of other men, are not to be valued. I ask you whether I was right in maintaining this?

Cr.

Certainly.

Soc.

The good are to be regarded, and not the bad?

Cr.

Yes.

Soc.

And the opinions of the wise are good, and the opinions of the unwise are evil?

Cr.

Certainly.

Soc.

And what was said about another matter? Is the pupil who devotes himself to the practice of gymnastics supposed to attend to the praise and blame and opinion of every man, or of one man only—his physician or trainer, whoever he may be?

Cr.

Of one man only.

Soc.

And he ought to fear the censure and welcome the praise of that one only, and not of the many?

Cr.

Clearly so.

Soc.

And he ought to act and train, and eat and drink in the way which seems good to his single master who has understanding, rather than according to the opinion of all other men put together?

Cr.

True.

Soc.

And if he disobeys and disregards the opinion and approval of the one, and regards the opinion of the many who have no understanding, will he not suffer evil?

Cr.

Certainly he will.

Soc.

And what will the evil be, whither tending and what affecting, in the disobedient person?

Cr.

Clearly, affecting the body; that is what is destroyed by the evil.

Soc.

The opinion of the one wise man is to be followed.

Very good; and is not this true, Crito, of other things which we need not separately enumerate? In questions of just and unjust, fair and foul, good and evil, which are the subjects of our present consultation, ought we to follow the opinion of the many and to fear them; or the opinion of the one man who has understanding? ought we not to fear and reverence him more than all the rest of the world: and if we desert him shall we not destroy and injure that principle in us which may be assumed to be improved by justice and deteriorated by injustice;—there is such a principle?

Cr.

Certainly there is, Socrates.

Soc.

Take a parallel instance:—if, acting under the advice of those who have no understanding, we destroy that which is improved by health and is deteriorated by disease, would life be worth having? And that which has been destroyed is—the body?

Cr.

Yes.

Soc.

Could we live, having an evil and corrupted body?

Cr.

Certainly not.

Soc.

And will life be worth having, if that higher part of man be destroyed, which is improved by justice and depraved by injustice? Do we suppose that principle, whatever it 48may be in man, which has to do with justice and injustice, to be inferior to the body?

Cr.

Certainly not.

Soc.

More honourable than the body?

Cr.

Far more.

Soc.

No matter what the many say of us.

Then, my friend, we must not regard what the many say of us: but what he, the one man who has understanding of just and unjust, will say, and what the truth will say. And therefore you begin in error when you advise that we should regard the opinion of the many about just and unjust, good and evil, honourable and dishonourable. — 'Well,' some one will say, 'but the many can kill us.'

Cr.

Yes, Socrates; that will clearly be the answer.

Soc.

Not life, but a good life, to be chiefly valued.

And it is true: but still I find with surprise that the old argument is unshaken as ever. And I should like to know whether I may say the same of another proposition—that not life, but a good life, is to be chiefly valued?

Cr.

Yes, that also remains unshaken.

Soc.

And a good life is equivalent to a just and honourable one—that holds also?

Cr.

Yes, it does.

Soc.

Admitting these principles, ought I to try and escape or not?

From these premisses I proceed to argue the question whether I ought or ought not to try and escape without the consent of the Athenians: and if I am clearly right in escaping, then I will make the attempt; but if not, I will abstain. The other considerations which you mention, of money and loss of character and the duty of educating one's children, are, I fear, only the doctrines of the multitude, who would be as ready to restore people to life, if they were able, as they are to put them to death—and with as little reason. But now, since the argument has thus far prevailed, the only question which remains to be considered is, whether we shall do rightly either in escaping or in suffering others to aid in our escape and paying them in money and thanks, or whether in reality we shall not do rightly; and if the latter, then death or any other calamity which may ensue on my remaining here must not be allowed to enter into the calculation.

Cr.

I think that you are right, Socrates; how then shall we proceed?

Soc.

Let us consider the matter together, and do you either refute me if you can, and I will be convinced; or else cease, my dear friend, from repeating to me that I ought to escape against the wishes of the Athenians: for I highly value your attempts to persuade me to do so, but I may not be persuaded against my own better judgement. And now please to consider my first position, and try how you can 49best answer me.

Cr.

I will.

Soc.

May we sometimes do evil that good may come?

Are we to say that we are never intentionally to do wrong, or that in one way we ought and in another way we ought not to do wrong, or is doing wrong always evil and dishonourable, as I was just now saying, and as has been already acknowledged by us? Are all our former admissions which were made within a few days to be thrown away? And have we, at our age, been earnestly discoursing with one another all our life long only to discover that we are no better than children? Or, in spite of the opinion of the many, and in spite of consequences whether better or worse, shall we insist on the truth of what was then said, that injustice is always an evil and dishonour to him who acts unjustly? Shall we say so or not?

Cr.

Yes.

Soc.

Then we must do no wrong?

Cr.

Certainly not.

Soc.

Nor when injured injure in return, as the many imagine; for we must injure no one at all ?

Cr.

Clearly not.

Soc.

Again, Crito, may we do evil?

Cr.

Surely not, Socrates.

Soc.

May we render evil for evil?

And what of doing evil in return for evil, which is the morality of the many—is that just or not?

Cr.

Not just.

Soc.

For doing evil to another is the same as injuring him?

Cr.

Very true.

Soc.

Or is evil always to be deemed evil? Are you of the same mind as formerly about all this?

Then we ought not to retaliate or render evil for evil to any one, whatever evil we may have suffered from him. But I would have you consider, Crito, whether you really mean what you are saying. For this opinion has never been held, and never will be held, by any considerable number of persons; and those who are agreed and those who are not agreed upon this point have no common ground, and can only despise one another when they see how widely they differ. Tell me, then, whether you agree with and assent to my first principle, that neither injury nor retaliation nor warding off evil by evil is ever right. And shall that be the premiss of our argument? Or do you decline and dissent from this? For so I have ever thought, and continue to think; but, if you are of another opinion, let me hear what you have to say. If, however, you remain of the same mind as formerly, I will proceed to the next step.

Cr.

Crito assents.

You may proceed, for I have not changed my mind.

Soc.

Then ought Socrates to desert or not?

Then I will go on to the next point, which may be put in the form of a question:—Ought a man to do what he admits to be right, or ought he to betray the right?

Cr.

He ought to do what he thinks right.

Soc.

But if this is true, what is the application? In 50leaving the prison against the will of the Athenians, do I wrong any? or rather do I not wrong those whom I ought least to wrong? Do I not desert the principles which were acknowledged by us to be just—what do you say?

Cr.

I cannot tell, Socrates; for I do not know.

Soc.

The Laws come and argue with him.—Can a State exist in which law is set aside?

Then consider the matter in this way:—Imagine that I am about to play truant (you may call the proceeding by any name which you like), and the laws and the government come and interrogate me: 'Tell us, Socrates,' they say; 'what are you about? are you not going by an act of yours to overturn us—the laws, and the whole state, as far as in you lies? Do you imagine that a state can subsist and not be overthrown, in which the decisions of law have no power, but are set aside and trampled upon by individuals?' What will be our answer, Crito, to these and the like words? Any one, and especially a rhetorician, will have a good deal to say on behalf of the law which requires a sentence to be carried out. He will argue that this law should not be set aside; and shall we reply, 'Yes; but the state has injured us and given an unjust sentence.' Suppose I say that?

Cr.

Very good, Socrates.

Soc.

Has he any fault to find with them?No man has any right to strike a blow at his country any more than at his father or mother.

'And was that our agreement with you?' the law would answer; 'or were you to abide by the sentence of the state?' And if I were to express my astonishment at their words, the law would probably add: 'Answer, Socrates, instead of opening your eyes—you are in the habit of asking and answering questions. Tell us,—What complaint have you to make against us which justifies you in attempting to destroy us and the state? In the first place did we not bring you into existence? Your father married your mother by our aid and begat you. Say whether you have any objection to urge against those of us who regulate marriage?' None, I should reply. 'Or against those of us who after birth regulate the nurture and education of children, in which you also were trained? Were not the laws, which have the charge of education, right in commanding your father to train you in music and gymnastic?' Right, I should reply. 'Well then, since you were brought into the world and nurtured and educated by us, can you deny in the first place that you are our child and slave, as your fathers were before you? And if this is true you are not on equal terms with us; nor can you think that you have a right to do to us what we are doing to you. Would you have any right to strike or revile or do any other evil to your father or your master, if you had one, because you have been struck or reviled by him, or received some other evil at his hands?—you would not say this? And because we think right to 51destroy you, do you think that you have any right to destroy us in return, and your country as far as in you lies? Will you, O professor of true virtue, pretend that you are justified in this? Has a philosopher like you failed to discover that our country is more to be valued and higher and holier far than mother or father or any ancestor, and more to be regarded in the eyes of the gods and of men of understanding? also to be soothed, and gently and reverently entreated when angry, even more than a father, and either to be persuaded, or if not persuaded, to be obeyed? And when we are punished by her, whether with imprisonment or stripes, the punishment is to be endured in silence; and if she lead us to wounds or death in battle, thither we follow as is right; neither may any one yield or retreat or leave his rank, but whether in battle or in a court of law, or in any other place, he must do what his city and his country order him; or he must change their view of what is just: and if he may do no violence to his father or mother, much less may he do violence to his country.' What answer shall we make to this, Crito? Do the laws speak truly, or do they not?

Cr.

I think that they do.

Soc.

The Laws argue that he has made an implied agreement with them which he is not at liberty to break at his pleasure.

Then the laws will say: 'Consider, Socrates, if we are speaking truly that in your present attempt you are going to do us an injury. For, having brought you into the world, and nurtured and educated you, and given you and every other citizen a share in every good which we had to give, we further proclaim to any Athenian by the liberty which we allow him, that if he does not like us when he has become of age and has seen the ways of the city, and made our acquaintance, he may go where he pleases and take his goods with him. None of us laws will forbid him or interfere with him. Any one who does not like us and the city, and who wants to emigrate to a colony or to any other city, may go where he likes, retaining his property. But he who has experience of the manner in which we order justice and administer the state, and still remains, has entered into an implied contract that he will do as we command him. And he who disobeys us is, as we maintain, thrice wrong; first, because in disobeying us he is disobeying his parents; secondly, because we are the authors of his education; thirdly, because he has made an agreement with us that he 52will duly obey our commands; and he neither obeys them nor convinces us that our commands are unjust; and we do not rudely impose them, but give him the alternative of obeying or convincing us:—that is what we offer, and he does neither.

'These are the sort of accusations to which, as we were saying, you, Socrates, will be exposed if you accomplish your intentions; you, above all other Athenians.' Suppose now I ask, why I rather than anybody else? they will justly retort upon me that I above all other men have acknowledged the agreement. 'There is clear proof,' they will say, 'Socrates, that we and the city were not displeasing to you. Of all Athenians you have been the most constant resident in the city, which, as you never leave, you may be supposed to love . For you never went out of the city either to see the games, except once when you went to the Isthmus, or to any other place unless when you were on military service; nor did you travel as other men do. Nor had you any curiosity to know other states or their laws: your affections did not go beyond us and our state; we were your special favourites, and you acquiesced in our government of you; and here in this city you begat your children, which is a proof of your satisfaction. Moreover, you might in the course of the trial, if you had liked, have fixed the penalty at banishment; the state which refuses to let you go now would have let you go then. But you pretended that you preferred death to exile , and that you were not unwilling to die. And now you have forgotten these fine sentiments, and pay no respect to us the laws, of whom you are the destroyer; and are doing what only a miserable slave would do, running away and turning your back upon the compacts and agreements which you made as a citizen. And first of all answer this very question: Are we right in saying that you agreed to be governed according to us in deed, and not in word only? Is that true or not?' How shall we answer, Crito? Must we not assent?

Cr.

We cannot help it, Socrates.

Soc.

This agreement he is now going to break.

Then will they not say: 'You, Socrates, are breaking the covenants and agreements which you made with us at your leisure, not in any haste or under any compulsion or deception, but after you have had seventy years to think of them, during which time you were at liberty to leave the city, if we were not to your mind, or if our covenants appeared to you to be unfair. You had your choice, and might have gone either to Lacedaemon or Crete, both which states are often praised by you for their good government, or to some other Hellenic or foreign state. Whereas you, 53above all other Athenians, seemed to be so fond of the state, or, in other words, of us her laws (and who would care about a state which has no laws?), that you never stirred out of her; the halt, the blind, the maimed were not more stationary in her than you were. And now you run away and forsake your agreements. Not so, Socrates, if you will take our advice; do not make yourself ridiculous by escaping out of the city.

If he does he will injure his friends and will disgrace himself.

'For just consider, if you transgress and err in this sort of way, what good will you do either to yourself or to your friends? That your friends will be driven into exile and deprived of citizenship, or will lose their property, is tolerably certain; and you yourself, if you fly to one of the neighbouring cities, as, for example, Thebes or Megara, both of which are well governed, will come to them as an enemy, Socrates, and their government will be against you, and all patriotic citizens will cast an evil eye upon you as a subverter of the laws, and you will confirm in the minds of the judges the justice of their own condemnation of you. For he who is a corrupter of the laws is more than likely to be a corrupter of the young and foolish portion of mankind. Will you then flee from well-ordered cities and virtuous men? and is existence worth having on these terms? Or will you go to them without shame, and talk to them, Socrates? And what will you say to them? What you say here about virtue and justice and institutions and laws being the best things among men? Would that be decent of you? Surely not. But if you go away from well-governed states to Crito's friends in Thessaly, where there is great disorder and licence, they will be charmed to hear the tale of your escape from prison, set off with ludicrous particulars of the manner in which you were wrapped in a goatskin or some other disguise, and metamorphosed as the manner is of runaways; but will there be no one to remind you that in your old age you were not ashamed to violate the most sacred laws from a miserable desire of a little more life? Perhaps not, if you keep them in a good temper; but if they are out of temper you will hear many degrading things; you will live, but how?—as the flatterer of all men, and the servant of all men; and doing what?—eating and drinking in Thessaly, having gone abroad in order that you may get a dinner. And where will be your fine sentiments 54about justice and virtue? Say that you wish to live for the sake of your children—you want to bring them up and educate them—will you take them into Thessaly and deprive them of Athenian citizenship? Is this the benefit which you will confer upon them? Or are you under the impression that they will be better cared for and educated here if you are still alive, although absent from them; for your friends will take care of them? Do you fancy that if you are an inhabitant of Thessaly they will take care of them, and if you are an inhabitant of the other world that they will not take care of them? Nay; but if they who call themselves friends are good for anything, they will—to be sure they will.

Let him think of justice first, and of life and children afterwards.

'Listen, then, Socrates, to us who have brought you up. Think not of life and children first, and of justice afterwards, but of justice first, that you may be justified before the princes of the world below. For neither will you nor any that belong to you be happier or holier or juster in this life, or happier in another, if you do as Crito bids. Now you depart in innocence, a sufferer and not a doer of evil; a victim, not of the laws but of men. But if you go forth, returning evil for evil, and injury for injury, breaking the covenants and agreements which you have made with us, and wronging those whom you ought least of all to wrong, that is to say, yourself, your friends, your country, and us, we shall be angry with you while you live, and our brethren, the laws in the world below, will receive you as an enemy; for they will know that you have done your best to destroy us. Listen, then, to us and not to Crito.'

The mystic voice.

This, dear Crito, is the voice which I seem to hear murmuring in my ears, like the sound of the flute in the ears of the mystic; that voice, I say, is humming in my ears, and prevents me from hearing any other. And I know that anything more which you may say will be vain. Yet speak, if you have anything to say.

Cr.

I have nothing to say, Socrates.

Soc.

Leave me then, Crito, to fulfil the will of God, and to follow whither he leads.

INTRODUCTION TO PHAEDO.

Phaedo. Analysis.

After an interval of some months or years, and at Phlius, a town of Peloponnesus, the tale of the last hours of Socrates is narrated to Echecrates and other Phliasians by Phaedo the 'beloved disciple.' The Dialogue necessarily takes the form of a narrative, because Socrates has to be described acting as well as speaking. The minutest particulars of the event are interesting to distant friends, and the narrator has an equal interest in them.

During the voyage of the sacred ship to and from Delos, which has occupied thirty days, the execution of Socrates has been deferred. (Cp. Xen. Mem. iv. 8. 2.) The time has been passed by him in conversation with a select company of disciples. But now the holy season is over, and the disciples meet earlier than usual in order that they may converse with Socrates for the last time. Those who were present, and those who might have been expected to be present, are mentioned by name. There are Simmias and Cebes (Crito 45 B), two disciples of Philolaus whom Socrates 'by his enchantments has attracted from Thebes' (Mem. iii. 11. 17), Crito the aged friend, the attendant of the prison, who is as good as a friend—these take part in the conversation. There are present also, Hermogenes, from whom Xenophon derived his information about the trial of Socrates (Mem. iv. 8. 4), the 'madman' Apollodorus (Symp. 173 D), Euclid and Terpsion from Megara (cp. Theaet. sub init.), Ctesippus, Antisthenes, Menexenus, and some other less-known members of the Socratic circle, all of whom are silent auditors. Aristippus, Cleombrotus, and Plato are noted as absent. Almost as soon as the friends of Socrates enter the prison Xanthippè and her children are sent home in the care of one of Crito's servants. Socrates himself has just been released from chains, and is led by this circumstance to make the natural remark that 'pleasure follows pain.' (Observe that Plato is preparing the way for his doctrine of the alternation of opposites.) 'Aesop would have represented them in a fable as a two-headed creature of the gods.' The mention of Aesop reminds Cebes of a question which had been asked by Evenus the poet (cp. Apol. 20 A): 'Why Socrates, who was not a poet, while in prison had been putting Aesop into verse?'—'Because several times in his life he had been warned in dreams that he should practise music; and as he was about to die and was not certain of what was meant, he wished to fulfil the admonition in the letter as well as in the spirit, by writing verses as well as by cultivating philosophy. Tell this to Evenus; and say that I would have him follow me in death.' 'He is not at all the sort of man to comply with your request, Socrates.' 'Why, is he not a philosopher?' 'Yes.' 'Then he will be willing to die, although he will not take his own life, for that is held to be unlawful.'

Cebes asks why suicide is thought not to be right, if death is to 62be accounted a good? Well, (1) according to one explanation, because man is a prisoner, who must not open the door of his prison and run away—this is the truth in a 'mystery.' Or (2) rather, because he is not his own property, but a possession of the gods, and has no right to make away with that which does not belong to him. But why, asks Cebes, if he is a possession of the gods, should he wish to die and leave them? for he is under their protection; and surely he cannot take better care of himself than they take of him. Simmias explains that Cebes is really 63referring to Socrates, whom they think too unmoved at the prospect of leaving the gods and his friends. Socrates answers that he is going to other gods who are wise and good, and perhaps to better friends; and he professes that he is ready to defend himself against the charge of Cebes. The company shall be his judges, and he hopes that he will be more successful in convincing them than he had been in convincing the court.

The philosopher desires death—which the wicked world will 64insinuate that he also deserves: and perhaps he does, but not in any sense which they are capable of understanding. Enough of them: the real question is, What is the nature of that death which he desires? Death is the separation of soul and body—and the philosopher desires such a separation. He would like to be freed from the dominion of bodily pleasures and of the senses, 65which are always perturbing his mental vision. He wants to get rid of eyes and ears, and with the light of the mind only to behold the light of truth. All the evils and impurities and necessities 66of men come from the body. And death separates him from these corruptions, which in life he cannot wholly lay aside. Why 67then should he repine when the hour of separation arrives? Why, if he is dead while he lives, should he fear that other death, 68through which alone he can behold wisdom in her purity?

Besides, the philosopher has notions of good and evil unlike those of other men. For they are courageous because they are 69afraid of greater dangers, and temperate because they desire greater pleasures. But he disdains this balancing of pleasures and pains, which is the exchange of commerce and not of virtue. All the virtues, including wisdom, are regarded by him only as purifications of the soul. And this was the meaning of the founders of the mysteries when they said, 'Many are the wandbearers but few are the mystics.' (Cp. Matt. xxii. 14: 'Many are called, but few are chosen.') And in the hope that he is one of these mystics, Socrates is now departing. This is his answer to any one who charges him with indifference at the prospect of leaving the gods and his friends.

70Still, a fear is expressed that the soul upon leaving the body may vanish away like smoke or air. Socrates in answer appeals first of all to the old Orphic tradition that the souls of the dead are in the world below, and that the living come from them. This he attempts to found on a philosophical assumption that 71all opposites—e.g. less, greater; weaker, stronger; sleeping, waking; life, death—are generated out of each other. Nor can the process of generation be only a passage from living to dying, 72for then all would end in death. The perpetual sleeper (Endymion) would be no longer distinguished from the rest of mankind. The circle of nature is not complete unless the living come from the dead as well as pass to them.

The Platonic doctrine of reminiscence is then adduced as a confirmation of the pre-existence of the soul. Some proofs of 73this doctrine are demanded. One proof given is the same as that of the Meno (82 foll.), and is derived from the latent knowledge of mathematics, which may be elicited from an unlearned person when a diagram is presented to him. Again, there is a power of association, which from seeing Simmias may remember Cebes, or from seeing a picture of Simmias may remember Simmias. The 74lyre may recall the player of the lyre, and equal pieces of wood or stone may be associated with the higher notion of absolute equality. But here observe that material equalities fall short of the conception of absolute equality with which they are compared, and which is the measure of them. And the measure or standard must be prior to that which is measured, the idea of 75equality prior to the visible equals. And if prior to them, then prior also to the perceptions of the senses which recall them, and therefore either given before birth or at birth. But all men have 76not this knowledge, nor have any without a process of reminiscence; which is a proof that it is not innate or given at birth, unless indeed it was given and taken away at the same instant. But if not given to men in birth, it must have been given before birth—this is the only alternative which remains. And if we had ideas in a former state, then our souls must have existed and must have had intelligence in a former state. The pre-existence 77of the soul stands or falls with the doctrine of ideas.

It is objected by Simmias and Cebes that these arguments only prove a former and not a future existence. Socrates answers this objection by recalling the previous argument, in which he had shown that the living come from the dead. But the fear that the soul at departing may vanish into air (especially if there is a wind blowing at the time) has not yet been charmed away. He proceeds: 78When we fear that the soul will vanish away, let us ask ourselves what is that which we suppose to be liable to dissolution? Is it the simple or the compound, the unchanging or the changing, the invisible idea or the visible object of sense? Clearly the latter and not the former; and therefore not the soul, 79which in her own pure thought is unchangeable, and only when using the senses descends into the region of change. Again, the soul commands, the body serves: in this respect too the soul is 80akin to the divine, and the body to the mortal. And in every point of view the soul is the image of divinity and immortality, and the body of the human and mortal. And whereas the body is liable to speedy dissolution, the soul is almost if not quite indissoluble. (Cp. Tim. 41 A.) Yet even the body may be preserved for ages by the embalmer's art: how unlikely, then, that the soul will perish and be dissipated into air while on her way to the good and wise God! She has been gathered into herself, holding 81aloof from the body, and practising death all her life long, and she is now finally released from the errors and follies and passions of men, and for ever dwells in the company of the gods.

But the soul which is polluted and engrossed by the corporeal, and has no eye except that of the senses, and is weighed down by the bodily appetites, cannot attain to this abstraction. In her fear of the world below she lingers about the sepulchre, loath to leave the body which she loved, a ghostly apparition, saturated with sense, and therefore visible. At length entering into some 82animal of a nature congenial to her former life of sensuality or violence, she takes the form of an ass, a wolf or a kite. And of these earthly souls the happiest are those who have practised virtue without philosophy; they are allowed to pass into gentle and social natures, such as bees and ants. (Cp. Rep. x. 619 C, Meno 100 A.) But only the philosopher who departs pure is permitted to enter the company of the gods. (Cp. Phaedrus 249.) This is the reason why he abstains from fleshly lusts, and not because he fears loss or disgrace, which is the motive of other 83men. He too has been a captive, and the willing agent of his own captivity. But philosophy has spoken to him, and he has heard her voice; she has gently entreated him, and brought him out of the 'miry clay,' and purged away the mists of passion and the illusions of sense which envelope him; his soul has escaped from the influence of pleasures and pains, which are like nails 84fastening her to the body. To that prison-house she will not return; and therefore she abstains from bodily pleasures—not from a desire of having more or greater ones, but because she knows that only when calm and free from the dominion of the body can she behold the light of truth.

Simmias and Cebes remain in doubt; but they are unwilling to raise objections at such a time. Socrates wonders at their reluctance. Let them regard him rather as the swan, who, 85having sung the praises of Apollo all his life long, sings at his death more lustily than ever. (Cp. 60 D.) Simmias acknowledges that there is cowardice in not probing truth to the bottom. 'And if truth divine and inspired is not to be had, then let a man take the best of human notions, and upon this frail bark let him sail through life.' He proceeds to state his difficulty: It has 86been argued that the soul is invisible and incorporeal, and therefore immortal, and prior to the body. But is not the soul acknowledged to be a harmony, and has she not the same relation to the body, as the harmony—which like her is invisible—has to the lyre? And yet the harmony does not survive the lyre. Cebes has also an objection, which like Simmias he expresses in a figure. He is willing to admit that the soul is more lasting than the body. But the more lasting nature of the soul 87does not prove her immortality; for after having worn out many bodies in a single life, and many more in successive births and deaths, she may at last perish, or, as Socrates afterwards restates the objection, the very act of birth may be the beginning of her death, and her last body may survive her, just as the coat of an old weaver is left behind him after he is dead, although a man is 88more lasting than his coat. And he who would prove the immortality of the soul, must prove not only that the soul outlives one or many bodies, but that she outlives them all.

The audience, like the chorus in a play, for a moment interpret the feelings of the actors; there is a temporary depression, and 89then the enquiry is resumed. It is a melancholy reflection that arguments, like men, are apt to be deceivers; and those who have been often deceived become distrustful both of arguments and of friends. But this unfortunate experience should not make us either haters of men or haters of arguments. The want of 90health and truth is not in the argument, but in ourselves. Socrates, who is about to die, is sensible of his own weakness; 91he desires to be impartial, but he cannot help feeling that he has too great an interest in the truth of the argument. And therefore he would have his friends examine and refute him, if they think that he is in error.

At his request Simmias and Cebes repeat their objections. They do not go to the length of denying the pre-existence of 92ideas. Simmias is of opinion that the soul is a harmony of the body. But the admission of the pre-existence of ideas, and therefore of the soul, is at variance with this. (Cp. a parallel difficulty in Theaet. 203, 204.) For a harmony is an effect, 93whereas the soul is not an effect, but a cause; a harmony follows, but the soul leads; a harmony admits of degrees, and the soul has no degrees. Again, upon the supposition that the soul is a harmony, why is one soul better than another? Are they more or less harmonized, or is there one harmony within another? 94But the soul does not admit of degrees, and cannot therefore be more or less harmonized. Further, the soul is often engaged in resisting the affections of the body, as Homer describes Odysseus 95'rebuking his heart.' Could he have written this under the idea that the soul is a harmony of the body? Nay rather, are we not contradicting Homer and ourselves in affirming anything of the sort?

The goddess Harmonia, as Socrates playfully terms the argument of Simmias, has been happily disposed of; and now an answer has to be given to the Theban Cadmus. Socrates recapitulates 96the argument of Cebes, which, as he remarks, involves the whole question of natural growth or causation; about this he proposes to narrate his own mental experience. When he was young he had puzzled himself with physics: he had enquired into the growth and decay of animals, and the origin of thought, until at last he began to doubt the self-evident fact that growth is the result of eating and drinking; and so he arrived at the conclusion that he was not meant for such enquiries. Nor was he less perplexed with notions of comparison and number. At first he had imagined himself to understand differences of greater and less, and to know that ten is two more than eight, and the like. But now those very notions appeared to him to contain a 97contradiction. For how can one be divided into two? or two be compounded into one? These are difficulties which Socrates cannot answer. Of generation and destruction he knows nothing. But he has a confused notion of another method in which matters of this sort are to be investigated. (Cp. Rep. iv. 435 D; vii. 533 A; Charm. 170 foll.)

Then he heard some one reading out of a book of Anaxagoras, that mind is the cause of all things. And he said to himself: If mind is the cause of all things, surely mind must dispose them all 98for the best. The new teacher will show me this 'order of the best' in man and nature. How great had been his hopes and how great his disappointment! For he found that his new friend was anything but consistent in his use of mind as a cause, and that he soon introduced winds, waters, and other eccentric notions. (Cp. Arist. Metaph. i. 4, 5.) It was as if a person had said that Socrates is sitting here because he is made up of bones and muscles, 99instead of telling the true reason—that he is here because the Athenians have thought good to sentence him to death, and he has thought good to await his sentence. Had his bones and muscles been left by him to their own ideas of right, they would long ago have taken themselves off. But surely there is a great confusion of the cause and condition in all this. And this confusion also leads people into all sorts of erroneous theories about the position and motions of the earth. None of them know how much stronger than any Atlas is the power of the best. But this 'best' is still undiscovered; and in enquiring after the cause, we can only hope to attain the second best.

Now there is a danger in the contemplation of the nature of things, as there is a danger in looking at the sun during an eclipse, 100unless the precaution is taken of looking only at the image reflected in the water, or in a glass. (Cp. Laws x. 897 D; Rep. vii. 516 foll.) 'I was afraid,' says Socrates, 'that I might injure the eye of the soul. I thought that I had better return to the old and safe method of ideas. Though I do not mean to say that he who contemplates existence through the medium of ideas sees only through a glass darkly, any more than he who contemplates actual effects.'

If the existence of ideas is granted to him, Socrates is of opinion that he will then have no difficulty in proving the immortality of the soul. He will only ask for a further admission:—that beauty is the cause of the beautiful, greatness the cause of the great, smallness of the small, and so on of other things. This is a safe 101and simple answer, which escapes the contradictions of greater and less (greater by reason of that which is smaller!), of addition and subtraction, and the other difficulties of relation. These subtleties he is for leaving to wiser heads than his own; he prefers to test ideas by the consistency of their consequences, and, if asked to give an account of them, goes back to some higher idea or hypothesis which appears to him to be the best, until at last he arrives at a resting-place. (Rep. vi. 510 foll.; Phil. 16 foll.)

The doctrine of ideas, which has long ago received the assent of 102the Socratic circle, is now affirmed by the Phliasian auditor to command the assent of any man of sense. The narrative is continued; Socrates is desirous of explaining how opposite ideas may appear to co-exist but do not really co-exist in the same thing or person. For example, Simmias may be said to have greatness and also smallness, because he is greater than Socrates and less than Phaedo. And yet Simmias is not really great and also small, but only when compared to Phaedo and Socrates. I use the illustration, says Socrates, because I want to show you not only that ideal opposites exclude one another, but also the opposites in us. I, for example, having the attribute of smallness remain small, and cannot become great: the smallness which is in me drives out 103greatness.

One of the company here remarked that this was inconsistent with the old assertion that opposites generated opposites. But that, replies Socrates, was affirmed, not of opposite ideas either in us or in nature, but of opposition in the concrete—not of life and death, but of individuals living and dying. When this objection has been removed, Socrates proceeds: This doctrine of the mutual exclusion of opposites is not only true of the opposites themselves, but of things which are inseparable from them. For example, cold and heat are opposed; and fire, which is inseparable from heat, cannot co-exist with cold, or snow, which is inseparable from cold, with heat. Again, the number three excludes the 104number four, because three is an odd number and four is an even number, and the odd is opposed to the even. Thus we are able to proceed a step beyond 'the safe and simple answer.' We may say, not only that the odd excludes the even, but that the number 105three, which participates in oddness, excludes the even. And in like manner, not only does life exclude death, but the soul, of which life is the inseparable attribute, also excludes death. And that of which life is the inseparable attribute is by the force of the 106terms imperishable. If the odd principle were imperishable, then the number three would not perish but remove, on the approach of the even principle. But the immortal is imperishable; and therefore the soul on the approach of death does not perish but removes.

107Thus all objections appear to be finally silenced. And now the application has to be made: If the soul is immortal, 'what manner of persons ought we to be?' having regard not only to time but to eternity. For death is not the end of all, and the wicked is not released from his evil by death, but every one carries with him into the world below that which he is or has become, and that only.

For after death the soul is carried away to judgment, and when she has received her punishment returns to earth in the course of ages. The wise soul is conscious of her situation, and follows the 108attendant angel who guides her through the windings of the world below; but the impure soul wanders hither and thither without companion or guide, and is carried at last to her own place, as the pure soul is also carried away to hers. 'In order that you may understand this, I must first describe to you the nature and conformation of the earth.'

Now the whole earth is a globe placed in the centre of the heavens, and is maintained there by the perfection of balance. 109That which we call the earth is only one of many small hollows, wherein collect the mists and waters and the thick lower air; but the true earth is above, and is in a finer and subtler element. And if, like birds, we could fly to the surface of the air, in the same manner that fishes come to the top of the sea, then we should behold the true earth and the true heaven and the true stars. Our 110earth is everywhere corrupted and corroded; and even the land which is fairer than the sea, for that is a mere chaos or waste of water and mud and sand, has nothing to show in comparison of the other world. But the heavenly earth is of divers colours, sparkling with jewels brighter than gold and whiter than any snow, having flowers and fruits innumerable. And the inhabitants 111dwell some on the shore of the sea of air, others in 'islets of the blest,' and they hold converse with the gods, and behold the sun, moon and stars as they truly are, and their other blessedness is of a piece with this.

The hollows on the surface of the globe vary in size and shape from that which we inhabit: but all are connected by passages and perforations in the interior of the earth. And there is one huge chasm or opening called Tartarus, into which streams of fire and water and liquid mud are ever flowing; of these small portions find their way to the surface and form seas and rivers and 112volcanoes. There is a perpetual inhalation and exhalation of the air rising and falling as the waters pass into the depths of the earth and return again, in their course forming lakes and rivers, but never descending below the centre of the earth; for on either side the rivers flowing either way are stopped by a precipice. These rivers are many and mighty, and there are four principal ones, Oceanus, Acheron, Pyriphlegethon, and Cocytus. Oceanus is the river which encircles the earth; Acheron takes an opposite direction, and after flowing under the earth through desert places, 113at last reaches the Acherusian lake,—this is the river at which the souls of the dead await their return to earth. Pyriphlegethon is a stream of fire, which coils round the earth and flows into the depths of Tartarus. The fourth river, Cocytus, is that which is called by the poets the Stygian river, and passes into and forms the lake Styx, from the waters of which it gains new and strange powers. This river, too, falls into Tartarus.

The dead are first of all judged according to their deeds, and those who are incurable are thrust into Tartarus, from which they never come out. Those who have only committed venial sins are first purified of them, and then rewarded for the good which they 114have done. Those who have committed crimes, great indeed, but not unpardonable, are thrust into Tartarus, but are cast forth at the end of a year by way of Pyriphlegethon or Cocytus, and these carry them as far as the Acherusian lake, where they call upon their victims to let them come out of the rivers into the lake. And if they prevail, then they are let out and their sufferings cease: if not, they are borne unceasingly into Tartarus and back again, until they at last obtain mercy. The pure souls also receive their reward, and have their abode in the upper earth, and a select few in still fairer 'mansions.'

Socrates is not prepared to insist on the literal accuracy of this description, but he is confident that something of the kind is true. He who has sought after the pleasures of knowledge and rejected the pleasures of the body, has reason to be of good hope at the approach of death; whose voice is already speaking to him, and who will one day be heard calling all men.

115 The hour has come at which he must drink the poison, and not much remains to be done. How shall they bury him? That is a question which he refuses to entertain, for they are burying, not 116 him, but his dead body. His friends had once been sureties that he would remain, and they shall now be sureties that he has run away. Yet he would not die without the customary ceremonies of washing and burial. Shall he make a libation of the poison? In 117 the spirit he will, but not in the letter. One request he utters in the very act of death, which has been a puzzle to after ages. With a sort of irony he remembers that a trifling religious duty is still 118 unfulfilled, just as above (60 E) he desires before he departs to compose a few verses in order to satisfy a scruple about a dream—unless, indeed, we suppose him to mean, that he was now restored to health, and made the customary offering to Asclepius in token of his recovery.

Introduction.

1. The doctrine of the immortality of the soul has sunk deep into the heart of the human race; and men are apt to rebel against any examination of the nature or grounds of their belief. They do not like to acknowledge that this, as well as the other 'eternal ideas' of man, has a history in time, which may be traced in Greek poetry or philosophy, and also in the Hebrew Scriptures. They convert feeling into reasoning, and throw a network of dialectics over that which is really a deeply-rooted instinct. In the same temper which Socrates reproves in himself (91 B) they are disposed to think that even fallacies will do no harm, for they will die with them, and while they live they will gain by the delusion. And when they consider the numberless bad arguments which have been pressed into the service of theology, they say, like the companions of Socrates, 'What argument can we ever trust again?' But there is a better and higher spirit to be gathered from the Phaedo, as well as from the other writings of Plato, which says that first principles should be most constantly reviewed (Phaedo 107 B, and Crat. 436), and that the highest subjects demand of us the greatest accuracy (Rep. vi. 504 E); also that we must not become misologists because arguments are apt to be deceivers.

2. In former ages there was a customary rather than a reasoned belief in the immortality of the soul. It was based on the authority of the Church, on the necessity of such a belief to morality and the order of society, on the evidence of an historical fact, and also on analogies and figures of speech which filled up the void or gave an expression in words to a cherished instinct. The mass of mankind went on their way busy with the affairs of this life, hardly stopping to think about another. But in our own day the question has been reopened, and it is doubtful whether the belief which in the first ages of Christianity was the strongest motive of action can survive the

conflict with a scientific age in which the rules of evidence are stricter and the mind has become more sensitive to criticism. It has faded into the distance by a natural process as it was removed further and further from the historical fact on which it has been supposed to rest. Arguments derived from material things such as the seed and the ear of corn or transitions in the life of animals from one state of being to another (the chrysalis and the butterfly) are not 'in pari materia' with arguments from the visible to the invisible, and are therefore felt to be no longer applicable. The evidence to the historical fact seems to be weaker than was once supposed: it is not consistent with itself, and is based upon documents which are of unknown origin. The immortality of man must be proved by other arguments than these if it is again to become a living belief. We must ask ourselves afresh why we still maintain it, and seek to discover a foundation for it in the nature of God and in the first principles of morality.

3. At the outset of the discussion we may clear away a confusion. We certainly do not mean by the immortality of the soul the immortality of fame, which whether worth having or not can only be ascribed to a very select class of the whole race of mankind, and even the interest in these few is comparatively shortlived. To have been a benefactor to the world, whether in a higher or a lower sphere of life and thought, is a great thing: to have the reputation of being one, when men have passed out of the sphere of earthly praise or blame, is hardly worthy of consideration. The memory of a great man, so far from being immortal, is really limited to his own generation:— so long as his friends or his disciples are alive, so long as his books continue to be read, so long as his political or military successes fill a page in the history of his country. The praises which are bestowed upon him at his death hardly last longer than the flowers which are strewed upon his coffin or the 'immortelles' which are laid upon his tomb. Literature makes the most of its heroes, but the true man is well aware that far from enjoying an immortality of fame, in a generation or two, or even in a much shorter time, he will be forgotten and the world will get on without him.

4. Modern philosophy is perplexed at this whole question, which is sometimes fairly given up and handed over to the realm of faith. The perplexity should not be forgotten by us when we attempt to submit the Phaedo of Plato to the requirements of logic. For what idea can we form of the soul when separated from the body? Or how can the soul be united with the body and still be independent? Is the soul related to the body as the ideal to the real, or as the whole to the parts, or as the subject to the object, or as the cause to the effect, or as the end to the means? Shall we say with Aristotle, that the soul is the entelechy or form of an organized living body? or with Plato, that she has a life of her own? Is the Pythagorean image of the harmony, or that of the monad, the truer expression? Is the soul related to the body as sight to the eye, or as the boatman to his boat? (Arist. de Anim. ii. 1, 11, 12.) And in another state of being is the soul to be conceived of as vanishing into infinity, hardly possessing an existence which she can call her own, as in the pantheistic system of Spinoza? or as

an individual informing another body and entering into new relations, but retaining her own character? (Cp. Gorgias, 524 B, C.) Or is the opposition of soul and body a mere illusion, and the true self neither soul nor body, but the union of the two in the 'I' which is above them? And is death the assertion of this individuality in the higher nature, and the falling away into nothingness of the lower? Or are we vainly attempting to pass the boundaries of human thought? The body and the soul seem to be inseparable, not only in fact, but in our conceptions of them; and any philosophy which too closely unites them, or too widely separates them, either in this life or in another, disturbs the balance of human nature. No thinker has perfectly adjusted them, or been entirely consistent with himself in describing their relation to one another. Nor can we wonder that Plato in the infancy of human thought should have confused mythology and philosophy, or have mistaken verbal arguments for real ones.

5. Again, believing in the immortality of the soul, we must still ask the question of Socrates, 'What is that which we suppose to be immortal?' Is it the personal and individual element in us, or the spiritual and universal? Is it the principle of knowledge or of goodness, or the union of the two? Is it the mere force of life which is determined to be, or the consciousness of self which cannot be got rid of, or the fire of genius which refuses to be extinguished? Or is there a hidden being which is allied to the Author of all existence, who is because he is perfect, and to whom our ideas of perfection give us a title to belong? Whatever answer is given by us to these questions, there still remains the necessity of allowing the permanence of evil, if not for ever, at any rate for a time, in order that the wicked 'may not have too good a bargain.' For the annihilation of evil at death, or the eternal duration of it, seem to involve equal difficulties in the moral government of the universe. Sometimes we are led by our feelings, rather than by our reason, to think of the good and wise only as existing in another life. Why should the mean, the weak, the idiot, the infant, the herd of men who have never in any proper sense the use of reason, reappear with blinking eyes in the light of another world? But our second thought is that the hope of humanity is a common one, and that all or none will be partakers of immortality. Reason does not allow us to suppose that we have any greater claims than others, and experience may often reveal to us unexpected flashes of the higher nature in those whom we had despised. Why should the wicked suffer any more than ourselves? had we been placed in their circumstances should we have been any better than they? The worst of men are objects of pity rather than of anger to the philanthropist; must they not be equally such to divine benevolence? Even more than the good they have need of another life; not that they may be punished, but that they may be educated. These are a few of the reflections which arise in our minds when we attempt to assign any form to our conceptions of a future state.

There are some other questions which are disturbing to us because we have no answer to them. What is to become of the animals in a future state? Have we not seen dogs more faithful and intelligent than men, and men who are more stupid and brutal than any animals? Does their life cease at death, or is there some 'better thing reserved' also for them? They may be said to have a shadow or imitation of morality, and imperfect moral claims upon the benevolence of man and upon the justice of God. We cannot think of the least or lowest of them, the insect, the bird, the inhabitants of the sea or the desert, as having any place in a future world, and if not all, why should those who are specially attached to man be deemed worthy of any exceptional privilege? When we reason about such a subject, almost at once we degenerate into nonsense. It is a passing thought which has no real hold on the mind. We may argue for the existence of animals in a future state from the attributes of God, or from texts of Scripture ('Are not two sparrows sold for one farthing?'&c.), but the truth is that we are only filling up the void of another world with our own fancies. Again, we often talk about the origin of evil, that great bugbear of theologians, by which they frighten us into believing any superstition. What answer can be made to the old commonplace, 'Is not God the author of evil, if he knowingly permitted, but could have prevented it?' Even if we assume that the inequalities of this life are rectified by some transposition of human beings in another, still the existence of the very least evil if it could have been avoided, seems to be at variance with the love and justice of God. And so we arrive at the conclusion that we are carrying logic too far, and that the attempt to frame the world according to a rule of divine perfection is opposed to experience and had better be given up. The case of the animals is our own. We must admit that the Divine Being, although perfect himself, has placed us in a state of life in which we may work together with him for good, but we are very far from having attained to it.

6. Again, ideas must be given through something; and we are always prone to argue about the soul from analogies of outward things which may serve to embody our thoughts, but are also partly delusive. For we cannot reason from the natural to the spiritual, or from the outward to the inward. The progress of physiological science, without bringing us nearer to the great secret, has tended to remove some erroneous notions respecting the relations of body and mind, and in this we have the advantage of the ancients. But no one imagines that any seed of immortality is to be discerned in our mortal frames. Most people have been content to rest their belief in another life on the agreement of the more enlightened part of mankind, and on the inseparable connection of such a doctrine with the existence of a God—also in a less degree on the impossibility of doubting about the continued existence of those whom we love and reverence in this world. And after all has been said, the figure, the analogy, the argument, are felt to be only approximations in different forms to an expression of the common sentiment of the human heart. That we shall live again is far more certain than that we shall take any particular form of life.

7. When we speak of the immortality of the soul, we must ask further what we mean by the word immortality. For of the duration of a living being in countless ages we

can form no conception; far less than a three years' old child of the whole of life. The naked eye might as well try to see the furthest star in the infinity of heaven. Whether time and space really exist when we take away the limits of them may be doubted; at any rate the thought of them when unlimited is so overwhelming to us as to lose all distinctness. Philosophers have spoken of them as forms of the human mind, but what is the mind without them? As then infinite time, or an existence out of time, which are the only possible explanations of eternal duration, are equally inconceivable to us, let us substitute for them a hundred or a thousand years after death, and ask not what will be our employment in eternity, but what will happen to us in that definite portion of time; or what is now happening to those who passed out of life a hundred or a thousand years ago. Do we imagine that the wicked are suffering torments, or that the good are singing the praises of God, during a period longer than that of a whole life, or of ten lives of men? Is the suffering physical or mental? And does the worship of God consist only of praise, or of many forms of service? Who are the wicked, and who are the good, whom we venture to divide by a hard and fast line; and in which of the two classes should we place ourselves and our friends? May we not suspect that we are making differences of kind, because we are unable to imagine differences of degree?—putting the whole human race into heaven or hell for the greater convenience of logical division? Are we not at the same time describing them both in superlatives, only that we may satisfy the demands of rhetoric? What is that pain which does not become deadened after a thousand years? or what is the nature of that pleasure or happiness which never wearies by monotony? Earthly pleasures and pains are short in proportion as they are keen; of any others which are both intense and lasting we have no experience, and can form no idea. The words or figures of speech which we use are not consistent with themselves. For are we not imagining Heaven under the similitude of a church, and Hell as a prison, or perhaps a madhouse or chamber of horrors? And yet to beings constituted as we are, the monotony of singing psalms would be as great an infliction as the pains of hell, and might be even pleasantly interrupted by them. Where are the actions worthy of rewards greater than those which are conferred on the greatest benefactors of mankind? And where are the crimes which according to Plato's merciful reckoning,—more merciful, at any rate, than the eternal damnation of so-called Christian teachers,—for every ten years in this life deserve a hundred of punishment in the life to come? We should be ready to die of pity if we could see the least of the sufferings which the writers of Infernos and Purgatorios have attributed to the damned. Yet these joys and terrors seem hardly to exercise an appreciable influence over the lives of men. The wicked man when old, is not, as Plato supposes (Rep. i. 330 D, E), more agitated by the terrors of another world when he is nearer to them, nor the good in an ecstasy at the joys of which he is soon to be the partaker. Age numbs the sense of both worlds; and the habit of life is strongest in death. Even the dying mother is dreaming of her lost children as they were forty or fifty years before, 'pattering over the boards,' not of reunion with them in another state of being. Most persons when the last hour comes are resigned to the order of nature and the will of God. They are not thinking of Dante's Inferno or Paradiso, or of the Pilgrim's Progress. Heaven and hell are not realities to them, but words or ideas; the outward symbols of some great mystery, they hardly know what. Many noble poems and pictures have been suggested by the traditional representations of them, which have been fixed in forms of art and can no longer be altered. Many sermons have been filled with descriptions of celestial or infernal mansions. But hardly even in childhood did the thought of heaven and hell supply the motives of our actions, or at any time seriously affect the substance of our belief.

8. Another life must be described, if at all, in forms of thought and not of sense. To draw pictures of heaven and hell, whether in the language of Scripture or any other, adds nothing to our real knowledge, but may perhaps disguise our ignorance. The truest conception which we can form of a future life is a state of progress or education—a progress from evil to good, from ignorance to knowledge. To this we are led by the analogy of the present life, in which we see different races and nations of men, and different men and women of the same nation, in various states or stages of cultivation; some more and some less developed, and all of them capable of improvement under favourable circumstances. There are punishments too of children when they are growing up inflicted by their parents, of elder offenders which are imposed by the law of the land, of all men at all times of life, which are attached by the laws of nature to the performance of certain actions. All these punishments are really educational; that is to say, they are not intended to retaliate on the offender, but to teach him a lesson. Also there is an element of chance in them, which is another name for our ignorance of the laws of nature. There is evil too inseparable from good (cp. Lysis 220 E); not always punished here, as good is not always rewarded. It is capable of being indefinitely diminished; and as knowledge increases, the element of chance may more and more disappear.

For we do not argue merely from the analogy of the present state of this world to another, but from the analogy of a probable future to which we are tending. The greatest changes of which we have had experience as yet are due to our increasing knowledge of history and of nature. They have been produced by a few minds appearing in three or four favoured nations, in a comparatively short period of time. May we be allowed to imagine the minds of men everywhere working together during many ages for the completion of our knowledge? May not the science of physiology transform the world? Again, the majority of mankind have really experienced some moral improvement; almost every one feels that he has tendencies to good, and is capable of becoming better. And these germs of good are often found to be developed by new circumstances, like stunted trees when transplanted to a better soil. The differences between the savage and the civilized man, or between the civilized man in old and new countries, may be indefinitely increased. The first difference is the effect of a few thousand, the second of a few hundred years. We congratulate ourselves that slavery has become industry; that law and constitutional government have superseded despotism and violence; that an ethical religion has taken the place of Fetichism. There may yet come a time when the many may be as well off as the few; when no one will be weighed down by excessive toil; when the necessity of providing for the body will not interfere with mental improvement; when the physical frame may be strengthened and developed; and the religion of all men may become a reasonable service.

Nothing therefore, either in the present state of man or in the tendencies of the future, as far as we can entertain conjecture of them, would lead us to suppose that God governs us vindictively in this world, and therefore we have no reason to infer that he will govern us vindictively in another. The true argument from analogy is not, 'This life is a mixed state of justice and injustice, of great waste, of sudden casualties, of disproportionate punishments, and therefore the like inconsistencies, irregularities, injustices are to be expected in another;' but 'This life is subject to law, and is in a state of progress, and therefore law and progress may be believed to be the governing principles of another.' All the analogies of this world would be against unmeaning punishments inflicted a hundred or a thousand years after an offence had been committed. Suffering there might be as a part of education, but not hopeless or protracted; as there might be a retrogression of individuals or of bodies of men, yet not such as to interfere with a plan for the improvement of the whole (cp. Laws, x. 903).

9. But some one will say: That we cannot reason from the seen to the unseen, and that we are creating another world after the image of this, just as men in former ages have created gods in their own likeness. And we, like the companions of Socrates, may feel discouraged at hearing our favourite 'argument from analogy' thus summarily disposed of. Like himself, too, we may adduce other arguments in which he seems to have anticipated us, though he expresses them in different language. For we feel that the soul partakes of the ideal and invisible; and can never fall into the error of confusing the external circumstances of man with his higher self; or his origin with his nature. It is as repugnant to us as it was to him to imagine that our moral ideas are to be attributed only to cerebral forces. The value of a human soul, like the value of a man's life to himself, is inestimable, and cannot be reckoned in earthly or material things. The human being alone has the consciousness of truth and justice and love, which is the consciousness of God. And the soul becoming more conscious of these, becomes more conscious of her own immortality.

10. The last ground of our belief in immortality, and the strongest, is the perfection of the divine nature. The mere fact of the existence of God does not tend to show the continued existence of man. An evil God or an indifferent God might have had the power, but not the will, to preserve us. He might have regarded us as fitted to minister to his service by a succession of existences,—like the animals, without attributing to each soul an incomparable value. But if he is perfect, he must will that

all rational beings should partake of that perfection which he himself is. In the words of the Timaeus, he is good, and therefore he desires that all other things should be as like himself as possible. And the manner in which he accomplishes this is by permitting evil, or rather degrees of good, which are otherwise called evil. For all progress is good relatively to the past, and yet may be comparatively evil when regarded in the light of the future. Good and evil are relative terms, and degrees of evil are merely the negative aspect of degrees of good. Of the absolute goodness of any finite nature we can form no conception; we are all of us in process of transition from one degree of good or evil to another. The difficulties which are urged about the origin or existence of evil are mere dialectical puzzles, standing in the same relation to Christian philosophy as the puzzles of the Cynics and Megarians to the philosophy of Plato. They arise out of the tendency of the human mind to regard good and evil both as relative and absolute; just as the riddles about motion are to be explained by the double conception of space or matter, which the human mind has the power of regarding either as continuous or discrete.

In speaking of divine perfection, we mean to say that God is just and true and loving, the author of order and not of disorder, of good and not of evil. Or rather, that he is justice, that he is truth, that he is love, that he is order, that he is the very progress of which we were speaking; and that wherever these qualities are present, whether in the human soul or in the order of nature, there is God. We might still see him everywhere, if we had not been mistakenly seeking for him apart from us, instead of in us; away from the laws of nature, instead of in them. And we become united to him not by mystical absorption, but by partaking, whether consciously or unconsciously, of that truth and justice and love which he himself is.

Thus the belief in the immortality of the soul rests at last on the belief in God. If there is a good and wise God, then there is a progress of mankind towards perfection; and if there is no progress of men towards perfection, then there is no good and wise God. We cannot suppose that the moral government of God of which we see the beginnings in the world and in ourselves will cease when we pass out of life.

11. Considering the 'feebleness of the human faculties and the uncertainty of the subject,' we are inclined to believe that the fewer our words the better. At the approach of death there is not much said; good men are too honest to go out of the world professing more than they know. There is perhaps no important subject about which, at any time, even religious people speak so little to one another. In the fulness of life the thought of death is mostly awakened by the sight or recollection of the death of others rather than by the prospect of our own. We must also acknowledge that there are degrees of the belief in immortality, and many forms in which it presents itself to the mind. Some persons will say no more than that they trust in God, and that they leave all to Him. It is a great part of true religion not to pretend to know more than we do. Others when they quit this world are comforted with the

hope 'That they will see and know their friends in heaven.' But it is better to leave them in the hands of God and to be assured that 'no evil shall touch them.' There are others again to whom the belief in a divine personality has ceased to have any longer a meaning; yet they are satisfied that the end of all is not here, but that something still remains to us, 'and some better thing for the good than for the evil.' They are persuaded, in spite of their theological nihilism, that the ideas of justice and truth and holiness and love are realities. They cherish an enthusiastic devotion to the first principles of morality. Through these they see, or seem to see, darkly, and in a figure, that the soul is immortal.

But besides differences of theological opinion which must ever prevail about things unseen, the hope of immortaility is weaker or stronger in men at one time of life than at another; it even varies from day to day. It comes and goes; the mind, like the sky, is apt to be overclouded. Other generations of men may have sometimes lived under an 'eclipse of faith,' to us the total disappearance of it might be compared to the 'sun falling from heaven.' And we may sometimes have to begin again and acquire the belief for ourselves; or to win it back again when it is lost. It is really weakest in the hour of death. For Nature, like a kind mother or nurse, lays us to sleep without frightening us; physicians, who are the witnesses of such scenes, say that under ordinary circumstances there is no fear of the future. Often, as Plato tells us, death is accompanied 'with pleasure.' (Tim. 81 D.) When the end is still uncertain, the cry of many a one has been, 'Pray, that I may be taken.' The last thoughts even of the best men depend chiefly on the accidents of their bodily state. Pain soon overpowers the desire of life; old age, like the child, is laid to sleep almost in a moment. The long experience of life will often destroy the interest which mankind have in it. So various are the feelings with which different persons draw near to death; and still more various the forms in which imagination clothes it. For this alternation of feeling cp. the Old Testament,—Psalm vi. 5, xvi. 10, xc; Isaiah xxxviii. 18; Eccles. viii. 8 ff., iii. 19, iv. 2.

12. When we think of God and of man in his relation to God; of the imperfection of our present state and yet of the progress which is observable in the history of the world and of the human mind; of the depth and power of our moral ideas which seem to partake of the very nature of God Himself; when we consider the contrast between the physical laws to which we are subject and the higher law which raises us above them and is yet a part of them; when we reflect on our capacity of becoming the 'spectators of all time and all existence,' and of framing in our own minds the ideal of a perfect Being; when we see how the human mind in all the higher religions of the world, including Buddhism, notwithstanding some aberrations, has tended towards such a belief—we have reason to think that our destiny is different from that of animals; and though we cannot altogether shut out the childish fear that the soul upon leaving the body may 'vanish into thin air,' we have still, so far as the nature of the subject admits, a hope of immortality with which we comfort ourselves on

sufficient grounds. The denial of the belief takes the heart out of human life; it lowers men to the level of the material. As Goethe also says, 'He is dead even in this world who has no belief in another.'

13. It is well also that we should sometimes think of the forms of thought under which the idea of immortality is most naturally presented to us. It is clear that to our minds the risen soul can no longer be described, as in a picture, by the symbol of a creature half bird, half-human, nor in any other form of sense. The multitude of angels, as in Milton, singing the Almighty's praises, are a noble image, and may furnish a theme for the poet or the painter, but they are no longer an adequate expression of the kingdom of God which is within us. Neither is there any mansion, in this world or another, in which the departed can be imagined to dwell and carry on their occupations. When this earthly tabernacle is dissolved, no other habitation or building can take them in: it is in the language of ideas only that we speak of them.

First of all there is the thought of rest and freedom from pain; they have gone home, as the common saying is, and the cares of this world touch them no more. Secondly, we may imagine them as they were at their best and brightest, humbly fulfilling their daily round of duties—selfless, childlike, unaffected by the world; when the eye was single and the whole body seemed to be full of light; when the mind was clear and saw into the purposes of God. Thirdly, we may think of them as possessed by a great love of God and man, working out His will at a further stage in the heavenly pilgrimage. And yet we acknowledge that these are the things which eye hath not seen nor ear heard and therefore it hath not entered into the heart of man in any sensible manner to conceive them. Fourthly, there may have been some moments in our own lives when we have risen above ourselves, or been conscious of our truer selves, in which the will of God has superseded our wills, and we have entered into communion with Him, and been partakers for a brief season of the Divine truth and love, in which like Christ we have been inspired to utter the prayer, 'I in them, and thou in me, that we may be all made perfect in one.' These precious moments, if we have ever known them, are the nearest approach which we can make to the idea of immortality.

14. Returning now to the earlier stage of human thought which is represented by the writings of Plato, we find that many of the same questions have already arisen: there is the same tendency to materialism; the same inconsistency in the application of the idea of mind; the same doubt whether the soul is to be regarded as a cause or as an effect; the same falling back on moral convictions. In the Phaedo the soul is conscious of her divine nature, and the separation from the body which has been commenced in this life is perfected in another. Beginning in mystery, Socrates, in the intermediate part of the Dialogue, attempts to bring the doctrine of a future life into connection with his theory of knowledge. In proportion as he succeeds in this, the individual seems to disappear in a more general notion of the soul; the contemplation

of ideas 'under the form of eternity' takes the place of past and future states of existence. His language may be compared to that of some modern philosophers, who speak of eternity, not in the sense of perpetual duration of time, but as an ever-present quality of the soul. Yet at the conclusion of the Dialogue, having 'arrived at the end of the intellectual world' (Rep. vii. 532 B), he replaces the veil of mythology, and describes the soul and her attendant genius in the language of the mysteries or of a disciple of Zoroaster. Nor can we fairly demand of Plato a consistency which is wanting among ourselves, who acknowledge that another world is beyond the range of human thought, and yet are always seeking to represent the mansions of heaven or hell in the colours of the painter, or in the descriptions of the poet or rhetorician.

15. The doctrine of the immortality of the soul was not new to the Greeks in the age of Socrates, but, like the unity of God, had a foundation in the popular belief. The old Homeric notion of a gibbering ghost flitting away to Hades; or of a few illustrious heroes enjoying the isles of the blest; or of an existence divided between the two; or the Hesiodic, of righteous spirits, who become guardian angels,—had given place in the mysteries and the Orphic poets to representations, partly fanciful, of a future state of rewards and punishments. (Laws ix. 870.) The reticence of the Greeks on public occasions and in some part of their literature respecting this 'underground' religion, is not to be taken as a measure of the diffusion of such beliefs. If Pericles in the funeral oration is silent on the consolations of immortality, the poet Pindar and the tragedians on the other hand constantly assume the continued existence of the dead in an upper or under world. Darius and Laius are still alive; Antigone will be dear to her brethren after death; the way to the palace of Cronos is found by those who 'have thrice departed from evil.' The tragedy of the Greeks is not 'rounded' by this life, but is deeply set in decrees of fate and mysterious workings of powers beneath the earth. In the caricature of Aristophanes there is also a witness to the common sentiment. The Ionian and Pythagorean philosophies arose, and some new elements were added to the popular belief. The individual must find an expression as well as the world. Either the soul was supposed to exist in the form of a magnet, or of a particle of fire, or of light, or air, or water; or of a number or of a harmony of number; or to be or have, like the stars, a principle of motion (Arist. de Anim. i. 1, 2, 3). At length Anaxagoras, hardly distinguishing between life and mind, or between mind human and divine, attained the pure abstraction; and this, like the other abstractions of Greek philosophy, sank deep into the human intelligence. The opposition of the intelligible and the sensible, and of God to the world, supplied an analogy which assisted in the separation of soul and body. If ideas were separable from phenomena, mind was also separable from matter; if the ideas were eternal, the mind that conceived them was eternal too. As the unity of God was more distinctly acknowledged, the conception of the human soul became more developed. The succession, or alternation of life and death, had occurred to Heracleitus. The Eleatic Parmenides had stumbled upon the modern thesis, that 'thought and being are the same.' The Eastern belief in transmigration defined the sense of individuality; and

some, like Empedocles, fancied that the blood which they had shed in another state of being was crying against them, and that for thirty thousand years they were to be 'fugitives and vagabonds upon the earth.' The desire of recognizing a lost mother or love or friend in the world below (Phaedo 68) was a natural feeling which, in that age as well as in every other, has given distinctness to the hope of immortality. Nor were ethical considerations wanting, partly derived from the necessity of punishing the greater sort of criminals, whom no avenging power of this world could reach. The voice of conscience, too, was heard reminding the good man that he was not altogether innocent. (Rep. i. 330.) To these indistinct longings and fears an expression was given in the mysteries and Orphic poets: a 'heap of books' (Rep. ii. 364 E), passing under the names of Musaeus and Orpheus in Plato's time, were filled with notions of an under-world.

16. Yet after all the belief in the individuality of the soul after death had but a feeble hold on the Greek mind. Like the personality of God, the personality of man in a future state was not inseparably bound up with the reality of his existence. For the distinction between the personal and impersonal, and also between the divine and human, was far less marked to the Greek than to ourselves. And as Plato readily passes from the notion of the good to that of God, he also passes almost imperceptibly to himself and his reader from the future life of the individual soul to the eternal being of the absolute soul. There has been a clearer statement and a clearer denial of the belief in modern times than is found in early Greek philosophy, and hence the comparative silence on the whole subject which is often remarked in ancient writers, and particularly in Aristotle. For Plato and Aristotle are not further removed in their teaching about the immortality of the soul than they are in their theory of knowledge.

17. Living in an age when logic was beginning to mould human thought, Plato naturally cast his belief in immortality into a logical form. And when we consider how much the doctrine of ideas was also one of words, it is not surprising that he should have fallen into verbal fallacies: early logic is always mistaking the truth of the form for the truth of the matter. It is easy to see that the alternation of opposites is not the same as the generation of them out of each other; and that the generation of them out of each other, which is the first argument in the Phaedo, is at variance with their mutual exclusion of each other, whether in themselves or in us, which is the last. For even if we admit the distinction which he draws at p. 103, between the opposites and the things which have the opposites, still individuals fall under the latter class; and we have to pass out of the region of human hopes and fears to a conception of an abstract soul which is the impersonation of the ideas. Such a conception, which in Plato himself is but half expressed, is unmeaning to us, and relative only to a particular stage in the history of thought. The doctrine of reminiscence is also a fragment of a former world, which has no place in the philosophy of modern times. But Plato had the wonders of psychology just opening to him, and he had not the

explanation of them which is supplied by the analysis of language and the history of the human mind. The question, 'Whence come our abstract ideas?' he could only answer by an imaginary hypothesis. Nor is it difficult to see that his crowning argument is purely verbal, and is but the expression of an instinctive confidence put into a logical form:—'The soul is immortal because it contains a principle of imperishableness.' Nor does he himself seem at all to be aware that nothing is added to human knowledge by his 'safe and simple answer,' that beauty is the cause of the beautiful; and that he is merely reasserting the Eleatic being 'divided by the Pythagorean numbers,' against the Heracleitean doctrine of perpetual generation. The answer to the 'very serious question' of generation and destruction is really the denial of them. For this he would substitute, as in the Republic, a system of ideas, tested, not by experience, but by their consequences, and not explained by actual causes, but by a higher, that is, a more general notion. Consistency with themselves is the only test which is to be applied to them. (Rep. vi. 510 foll., and Phaedo 101 foll.)

18. To deal fairly with such arguments, they should be translated as far as possible into their modern equivalents. 'If the ideas of men are eternal, their souls are eternal, and if not the ideas, then not the souls.' Such an argument stands nearly in the same relation to Plato and his age, as the argument from the existence of God to immortality among ourselves. 'If God exists, then the soul exists after death; and if there is no God, there is no existence of the soul after death.' For the ideas are to his mind the reality, the truth, the principle of permanence, as well as of intelligence and order in the world. When Simmias and Cebes say that they are more strongly persuaded of the existence of ideas than they are of the immortality of the soul, they represent fairly enough the order of thought in Greek philosophy. And we might say in the same way that we are more certain of the existence of God than we are of the immortality of the soul, and are led by the belief in the one to a belief in the other. The parallel, as Socrates would say, is not perfect, but agrees in as far as the mind in either case is regarded as dependent on something above and beyond herself. The analogy may even be pressed a step further: 'We are more certain of our ideas of truth and right than we are of the existence of God, and are led on in the order of thought from one to the other.' Or more correctly: 'The existence of right and truth is the existence of God, and can never for a moment be separated from Him.'

19. The main argument of the Phaedo is derived from the existence of eternal ideas of which the soul is a partaker; the other argument of the alternation of opposites is replaced by this. And there have not been wanting philosophers of the idealist school who have imagined that the doctrine of the immortality of the soul is a theory of knowledge, and that in what has preceded Plato is accommodating himself to the popular belief. Such a view can only be elicited from the Phaedo by what may be termed the transcendental method of interpretation, and is obviously inconsistent with the Gorgias and the Republic. Those who maintain it are immediately compelled to renounce the shadow which they have grasped, as a play of words only. But the

truth is, that Plato in his argument for the immortality of the soul has collected many elements of proof or persuasion, ethical and mythological as well as dialectical, which are not easily to be reconciled with one another; and he is as much in earnest about his doctrine of retribution, which is repeated in all his more ethical writings, as about his theory of knowledge. And while we may fairly translate the dialectical into the language of Hegel, and the religious and mythological into the language of Dante or Bunyan, the ethical speaks to us still in the same voice, and appeals to a common feeling.

20. Two arguments of this ethical character occur in the Phaedo. The first may be described as the aspiration of the soul after another state of being. Like the Oriental or Christian mystic, the philosopher is seeking to withdraw from impurities of sense, to leave the world and the things of the world, and to find his higher self. Plato recognizes in these aspirations the foretaste of immortality; as Butler and Addison in modern times have argued, the one from the moral tendencies of mankind, the other from the progress of the soul towards perfection. In using this argument Plato has certainly confused the soul which has left the body, with the soul of the good and wise. (Cp. Rep. x. 611 C.) Such a confusion was natural, and arose partly out of the antithesis of soul and body. The soul in her own essence, and the soul 'clothed upon' with virtues and graces, were easily interchanged with one another, because on a subject which passes expression the distinctions of language can hardly be maintained.

21. The other ethical proof of the immortality of the soul is derived from the necessity of retribution. The wicked would be too well off if their evil deeds came to an end. It is not to be supposed that an Ardiaeus, an Archelaus, an Ismenias could ever have suffered the penalty of their crimes in this world. The manner in which this retribution is accomplished Plato represents under the figures of mythology. Doubtless he felt that it was easier to improve than to invent, and that in religion especially the traditional form was required in order to give verisimilitude to the myth. The myth too is far more probable to that age than to ours, and may fairly be regarded as 'one guess among many' about the nature of the earth, which he cleverly supports by the indications of geology. Not that he insists on the absolute truth of his own particular notions: 'no man of sense will be confident in such matters; but he will be confident that something of the kind is true' (114 D). As in other passages (Gorg. 527 A, Tim. 29 D; cp. Crito, 107 B), he wins belief for his fictions by the moderation of his statements; he does not, like Dante or Swedenborg, allow himself to be deceived by his own creations.

The Dialogue must be read in the light of the situation. And first of all we are struck by the calmness of the scene. Like the spectators at the time, we cannot pity Socrates; his mien and his language are so noble and fearless. He is the same that he ever was, but milder and gentler, and he has in no degree lost his interest in dialectics; he will not forego the delight of an argument in compliance with the jailer's intimation that he should not heat himself with talking. At such a time he naturally expresses the hope of his life, that he has been a true mystic and not a mere routineer or wand-bearer: and he refers to passages of his personal history. To his old enemies the Comic poets, and to the proceedings on the trial, he alludes playfully; but he vividly remembers the disappointment which he felt in reading the books of Anaxagoras. The return of Xanthippe and his children indicates that the philosopher is not 'made of oak or rock.' Some other traits of his character may be noted; for example, the courteous manner in which he inclines his head to the last objector, or the ironical touch, 'Me already, as the tragic poet would say, the voice of fate calls;' or the depreciation of the arguments with which 'he comforted himself and them;' or his fear of 'misology;' or his references to Homer; or the playful smile with which he 'talks like a book' about greater and less; or the allusion to the possibility of finding another teacher among barbarous races (cp. Polit. 262 D); or the mysterious reference to another science (mathematics?) of generation and destruction for which he is vainly feeling. There is no change in him; only now he is invested with a sort of sacred character, as the prophet or priest of Apollo the God of the festival, in whose honour he first of all composes a hymn, and then like the swan pours forth his dying lay. Perhaps the extreme elevation of Socrates above his own situation, and the ordinary interests of life (compare his *jeu d'esprit* about his burial, in which for a moment he puts on the 'Silenus mask'), create in the mind of the reader an impression stronger than could be derived from arguments that such a one has in him 'a principle which does not admit of death.'

The other persons of the Dialogue may be considered under two heads: (1) private friends; (2) the respondents in the argument.

First there is Crito, who has been already introduced to us in the Euthydemus and the Crito; he is the equal in years of Socrates, and stands in quite a different relation to him from his younger disciples. He is a man of the world who is rich and prosperous (cp. the jest in the Euthydemus, 304 C), the best friend of Socrates, who wants to know his commands, in whose presence he talks to his family, and who performs the last duty of closing his eyes. It is observable too that, as in the Euthydemus, Crito shows no aptitude for philosophical discussions. Nor among the friends of Socrates must the jailer be forgotten, who seems to have been introduced by Plato in order to show the impression made by the extraordinary man on the common. The gentle nature of the man is indicated by his weeping at the announcement of his errand and then turning away, and also by the words of Socrates to his disciples: 'How charming the man is! since I have been in prison he has been always coming to me, and is as good as could be to me.' We are reminded too that he has retained this gentle nature amid scenes of death and violence by the contrasts which he draws between the behaviour of Socrates and of others when about to die.

Another person who takes no part in the philosophical discussion is the excitable Apollodorus, the same who, in the Symposium, of which he is the narrator, is called 'the madman,' and who testifies his grief by the most violent emotions. Phaedo is also present, the 'beloved disciple' as he may be termed, who is described, if not 'leaning on his bosom,' as seated next to Socrates, who is playing with his hair. He too, like Apollodorus, takes no part in the discussion, but he loves above all things to hear and speak of Socrates after his death. The calmness of his behaviour, veiling his face when he can no longer restrain his tears, contrasts with the passionate outcries of the other. At a particular point the argument is described as falling before the attack of Simmias. A sort of despair is introduced in the minds of the company. The effect of this is heightened by the description of Phaedo, who has been the eye-witness of the scene, and by the sympathy of his Phliasian auditors who are beginning to think 'that they too can never trust an argument again.' And the intense interest of the company is communicated not only to the first auditors, but to us who in a distant country read the narrative of their emotions after more than two thousand years have passed away.

The two principal interlocutors are Simmias and Cebes, the disciples of Philolaus the Pythagorean philosopher of Thebes. Simmias is described in the Phaedrus (242 B) as fonder of an argument than any man living; and Cebes, although finally persuaded by Socrates, is said to be the most incredulous of human beings. It is Cebes who at the commencement of the Dialogue asks why 'suicide is held to be unlawful,' and who first supplies the doctrine of recollection in confirmation of the pre-existence of the soul. It is Cebes who urges that the pre-existence does not necessarily involve the future existence of the soul, as is shown by the illustration of the weaver and his coat. Simmias, on the other hand, raises the question about harmony and the lyre, which is naturally put into the mouth of a Pythagorean disciple. It is Simmias, too, who first remarks on the uncertainty of human knowledge, and only at last concedes to the argument such a qualified approval as is consistent with the feebleness of the human faculties. Cebes is the deeper and more consecutive thinker, Simmias more superficial and rhetorical; they are distinguished in much the same manner as Adeimantus and Glaucon in the Republic.

Other persons, Menexenus, Ctesippus, Lysis, are old friends; Evenus has been already satirized in the Apology; Aeschines and Epigenes were present at the trial; Euclid and Terpsion will reappear in the Introduction to the Theaetetus, Hermogenes has already appeared in the Cratylus. No inference can fairly be drawn from the absence of Aristippus, nor from the omission of Xenophon, who at the time of Socrates' death was in Asia. The mention of Plato's own absence seems like an expression of sorrow, and may, perhaps, be an indication that the report of the conversation is not to be taken literally.

The place of the Dialogue in the series is doubtful. The doctrine of ideas is certainly carried beyond the Socratic point of view; in no other of the writings of Plato is the theory of them so completely developed. Whether the belief in immortality can be attributed to Socrates or not is uncertain; the silence of the Memorabilia, and of the earlier Dialogues of Plato, is an argument to the contrary. Yet in the Cyropaedia Xenophon (viii. 7, 19 foll.) has put language into the mouth of the dying Cyrus which recalls the Phaedo, and may have been derived from the teaching of Socrates. It may be fairly urged that the greatest religious interest of mankind could not have been wholly ignored by one who passed his life in fulfilling the commands of an oracle, and who recognized a Divine plan in man and nature. (Xen. Mem. 1, 4.) And the language of the Apology and of the Crito confirms this view.

The Phaedo is not one of the Socratic Dialogues of Plato; nor, on the other hand, can it be assigned to that later stage of the Platonic writings at which the doctrine of ideas appears to be forgotten. It belongs rather to the intermediate period of the Platonic philosophy, which roughly corresponds to the Phaedrus, Gorgias, Republic, Theaetetus. Without pretending to determine the real time of their composition, the Symposium, Meno, Euthyphro, Apology, Phaedo may be conveniently read by us in this order as illustrative of the life of Socrates. Another chain may be formed of the Meno, Phaedrus, Phaedo, in which the immortality of the soul is connected with the doctrine of ideas. In the Meno the theory of ideas is based on the ancient belief in transmigration, which reappears again in the Phaedrus as well as in the Republic and Timaeus, and in all of them is connected with a doctrine of retribution. In the Phaedrus the immortality of the soul is supposed to rest on the conception of the soul as a principle of motion, whereas in the Republic the argument turns on the natural continuance of the soul, which, if not destroyed by her own proper evil, can hardly be destroyed by any other. The soul of man in the Timaeus (42 foll.) is derived from the Supreme Creator, and either returns after death to her kindred star, or descends into the lower life of an animal. The Apology expresses the same view as the Phaedo, but with less confidence; there the probability of death being a long sleep is not excluded. The Theaetetus also describes, in a digression, the desire of the soul to fly away and be with God—'and to fly to him is to be like him' (176 B). The Symposium may be observed to resemble as well as to differ from the Phaedo. While the first notion of immortality is only in the way of natural procreation or of posthumous fame and glory, the higher revelation of beauty, like the good in the Republic, is the vision of the eternal idea. So deeply rooted in Plato's mind is the belief in immortality; so various are the forms of expression which he employs.

As in several other Dialogues, there is more of system in the Phaedo than appears at first sight. The succession of arguments is based on previous philosophies; beginning with the mysteries and the Heracleitean alternation of opposites, and proceeding to the Pythagorean harmony and transmigration; making a step by the aid of Platonic reminiscence, and a further step by the help of the νο[Editor: illegible character]ς of Anaxagoras; until at last we rest in the conviction that the soul is inseparable from the ideas, and belongs to the world of the invisible and unknown. Then, as in the Gorgias or Republic, the curtain falls, and the veil of mythology descends upon the argument. After the confession of Socrates that he is an interested party, and the acknowledgment that no man of sense will think the details of his narrative true, but that something of the kind is true, we return from speculation to practice. He is himself more confident of immortality than he is of his own arguments; and the confidence which he expresses is less strong than that which his cheerfulness and composure in death inspire in us.

Difficulties of two kinds occur in the Phaedo—one kind to be explained out of contemporary philosophy, the other not admitting of an entire solution. (1) The difficulty which Socrates says that he experienced in explaining generation and corruption; the assumption of hypotheses which proceed from the less general to the more general, and are tested by their consequences; the puzzle about greater and less; the resort to the method of ideas, which to us appear only abstract terms,—these are to be explained out of the position of Socrates and Plato in the history of philosophy. They were living in a twilight between the sensible and the intellectual world, and saw no way of connecting them. They could neither explain the relation of ideas to phenomena, nor their correlation to one another. The very idea of relation or comparison was embarrassing to them. Yet in this intellectual uncertainty they had a conception of a proof from results, and of a moral truth, which remained unshaken amid the questionings of philosophy. (2) The other is a difficulty which is touched upon in the Republic as well as in the Phaedo, and is common to modern and ancient philosophy. Plato is not altogether satisfied with his safe and simple method of ideas. He wants to have proved to him by facts that all things are for the best, and that there is one mind or design which pervades them all. But this 'power of the best' he is unable to explain; and therefore takes refuge in universal ideas. And are not we at this day seeking to discover that which Socrates in a glass darkly foresaw?

Some resemblances to the Greek drama may be noted in all the Dialogues of Plato. The Phaedo is the tragedy of which Socrates is the protagonist and Simmias and Cebes the secondary performers, standing to them in the same relation as to Glaucon and Adeimantus in the Republic. No Dialogue has a greater unity of subject and feeling. Plato has certainly fulfilled the condition of Greek, or rather of all art, which requires that scenes of death and suffering should be clothed in beauty. The gathering of the friends at the commencement of the Dialogue, the dismissal of Xanthippè, whose presence would have been out of place at a philosophical discussion, but who returns again with her children to take a final farewell, the dejection of the audience at the temporary overthrow of the argument, the picture of Socrates playing with the hair of Phaedo, the final scene in which Socrates alone retains his composure—are masterpieces of art. And the chorus at the end might have interpreted the feeling of the play: 'There can no evil happen to a good man in life or death.'

'The art of concealing art' is nowhere more perfect than in those writings of Plato which describe the trial and death of Socrates. Their charm is their simplicity, which gives them verisimilitude; and yet they touch, as if incidentally, and because they were suitable to the occasion, on some of the deepest truths of philosophy. There is nothing in any tragedy, ancient or modern, nothing in poetry or history (with one exception), like the last hours of Socrates in Plato. The master could not be more fitly occupied at such a time than in discoursing of immortality; nor the disciples more divinely consoled. The arguments, taken in the spirit and not in the letter, are our arguments; and Socrates by anticipation may be even thought to refute some 'eccentric notions' current in our own age. For there are philosophers among ourselves who do not seem to understand how much stronger is the power of intelligence, or of the best, than of Atlas, or mechanical force. How far the words attributed to Socrates were actually uttered by him we forbear to ask; for no answer can be given to this question. And it is better to resign ourselves to the feeling of a great work, than to linger among critical uncertainties.

PHAEDO.

PERSONS OF THE DIALOGUE.

Phaedo, *who is the narrator of the Dialogue to*

Echecrates of Phlius.

Socrates.

Attendant of the Prison.

Apollodorus.

Simmias.

Cebes.

Crito.

Scene:—The Prison of Socrates.

Place of the Narration:—Phlius.

Echecrates.

Phaedo. Echecrates, Phaedo.

57Were you yourself, Phaedo, in the prison with Socrates on the day when he drank the poison?

Phaedo.

Yes, Echecrates, I was.

Ech.

I should so like to hear about his death. What did he say in his last hours? We were informed that he died by taking poison, but no one knew anything more; for no

Phliasian ever goes to Athens now, and it is a long time since any stranger from Athens has found his way hither; so that we had no clear account.

Phaed.

58Did you not hear of the proceedings at the trial?

Ech.

Yes; some one told us about the trial, and we could not understand why, having been condemned, he should have been put to death, not at the time, but long afterwards. What was the reason of this?

Phaed.

The death of Socrates was deferred by the holy season of the mission to Delos.

An accident, Echecrates: the stern of the ship which the Athenians send to Delos happened to have been crowned on the day before he was tried.

Ech.

What is this ship?

Phaed.

It is the ship in which, according to Athenian tradition, Theseus went to Crete when he took with him the fourteen youths, and was the saviour of them and of himself. And they are said to have vowed to Apollo at the time, that if they were saved they would send a yearly mission to Delos. Now this custom still continues, and the whole period of the voyage to and from Delos, beginning when the priest of Apollo crowns the stern of the ship, is a holy season, during which the city is not allowed to be polluted by public executions; and when the vessel is detained by contrary winds, the time spent in going and returning is very considerable. As I was saying, the ship was crowned on the day before the trial, and this was the reason why Socrates lay in prison and was not put to death until long after he was condemned.

Ech.

What was the manner of his death, Phaedo? What was said or done? And which of his friends were with him? Or did the authorities forbid them to be present—so that he had no friends near him when he died?

Phaed.

No; there were several of them with him.

Ech.

Phaedo is requested by Echecrates to give an account of the death of Socrates.

If you have nothing to do, I wish that you would tell me what passed, as exactly as you can.

Phaed.

I have nothing at all to do, and will try to gratify your wish. To be reminded of Socrates is always the greatest delight to me, whether I speak myself or hear another speak of him.

Ech.

You will have listeners who are of the same mind with you, and I hope that you will be as exact as you can.

Phaed.

He describes his noble and fearless demeanour.

I had a singular feeling at being in his company. For I could hardly believe that I was present at the death of a friend, and therefore I did not pity him, Echecrates; he died so fearlessly, and his words and bearing were so noble and gracious, that to me he appeared blessed. I thought that in going to the other world he could not be without a divine call, and that he would be happy, if any man ever 59was, when he arrived there; and therefore I did not pity him as might have seemed natural at such an hour. But I had not the pleasure which I usually feel in philosophical discourse (for philosophy was the theme of which we spoke). I was pleased, but in the pleasure there was also a strange admixture of pain; for I reflected that he was soon to die, and this double feeling was shared by us all; we were laughing and weeping by turns, especially the excitable Apollodorus—you know the sort of man?

Ech.

Yes.

Phaed.

He was quite beside himself; and I and all of us were greatly moved.

Ech.

Who were present?

Phaed.

The Socratic circle:—the absence of Plato is noted.

Of native Athenians there were, besides Apollodorus, Critobulus and his father Crito, Hermogenes, Epigenes, Aeschines, Antisthenes; likewise Ctesippus of the deme of Paeania, Menexenus, and some others; Plato, if I am not mistaken, was ill.

Ech.

Were there any strangers?

Phaed.

Yes, there were; Simmias the Theban, and Cebes, and Phaedondes; Euclid and Terpsion, who came from Megara.

Ech.

And was Aristippus there, and Cleombrotus?

Phaed.

No, they were said to be in Aegina.

Ech.

Any one else?

Phaed.

I think that these were nearly all.

Ech.

Well, and what did you talk about?

Phaed.

The meeting at the prison. The friends are denied admission while the Eleven are with Socrates. Socrates, Cebes. Socrates, whose chains have now been taken off, is led by the feeling of relief to remark on the curious manner in which pleasure and pain are always conjoined.

I will begin at the beginning, and endeavour to repeat the entire conversation. On the previous days we had been in the habit of assembling early in the morning at the court in which the trial took place, and which is not far from the prison. There we used to wait talking with one another until the opening of the doors (for they were not opened very early); then we went in and generally passed the day with Socrates. On the last morning we assembled sooner than usual, having heard on the day before when we quitted the prison in the evening that the sacred ship had come from Delos; and so we arranged to meet very early at the accustomed place. On our arrival the jailer who answered the door, instead of admitting us, came out and told us to stay until he called us. 'For the Eleven,' he said, 'are now with Socrates; they are taking off his chains, and giving orders that he is to die to-day.' He soon returned 60and said that we might come in. On entering we found Socrates just released from chains, and Xanthippè, whom you know, sitting by him, and holding his child in her arms. When she saw us she uttered a cry and said, as women will: 'O Socrates, this is the last time that either you will converse with your friends, or they with you.' Socrates turned to Crito and said: 'Crito, let some one take her home.' Some of Crito's people accordingly led her away, crying out and beating herself. And when she was gone, Socrates, sitting up on the couch, bent and rubbed his leg, saying, as he was rubbing: How singular is the thing called pleasure, and how curiously related to pain, which might be thought to be the opposite of it; for they are never present to a man at the same instant, and yet he who pursues either is generally compelled to take the other; their bodies are two, but they are joined by a single head. And I cannot help thinking that if Aesop had remembered them, he would have made a fable about God trying to reconcile their strife, and how, when he could not, he fastened their heads together; and this is the reason why when one comes the other follows: as I know by my own experience now, when after the pain in my leg which was caused by the chain pleasure appears to succeed.

Upon this Cebes said: I am glad, Socrates, that you have mentioned the name of Aesop. For it reminds me of a question which has been asked by many, and was asked of me only the day before yesterday by Evenus the poet—he will be sure to ask it again, and therefore if you would like me to have an answer ready for him, you may as well tell me what I should say to him:—he wanted to know why you, who never before wrote a line of poetry, now that you are in prison are turning Aesop's fables into verse, and also composing that hymn in honour of Apollo.

Having been told in a dream that he should compose music, in order to satisfy a scruple about the meaning of the dream he has been writing verses while he was in prison.Socrates, Simmias, Cebes.Evenus the poet had been curious about the meaning of this behaviour of his, and Socrates gives him the explanation of it, bidding him be of good cheer, and come after him. 'But he will not come.'

Tell him, Cebes, he replied, what is the truth—that I had no idea of rivalling him or his poems; to do so, as I knew, would be no easy task. But I wanted to see whether I could purge away a scruple which I felt about the meaning of certain dreams. In the course of my life I have often had intimations in dreams 'that I should compose music.' The same dream came to me sometimes in one form, and sometimes in another, but always saying the same or nearly the same words: 'Cultivate and make music,' said the dream. And hitherto I had imagined that this was only intended to exhort and encourage me in the study of philosophy, which 61has been the pursuit of my life, and is the noblest and best of music. The dream was bidding me do what I was already doing, in the same way that the competitor in a race is bidden by the spectators to run when he is already running. But I was not certain of this; for the dream might have meant music in the popular sense of the word, and being under sentence of death, and the festival giving me a respite, I thought that it would be safer for me to satisfy the scruple, and, in obedience to the dream, to compose a few verses before I departed. And first I made a hymn in honour of the god of the festival, and then considering that a poet, if he is really to be a poet, should not only put together words, but should invent stories, and that I have no invention, I took some fables of Aesop, which I had ready at hand and which I knew—they were the first I came upon—and turned them into verse. Tell this to Evenus, Cebes, and bid him be of good cheer; say that I would have him come after me if he be a wise man, and not tarry; and that to-day I am likely to be going, for the Athenians say that I must.

Simmias said: What a message for such a man! having been a frequent companion of his I should say that, as far as I know him, he will never take your advice unless he is obliged.

Why, said Socrates,—is not Evenus a philosopher?

I think that he is, said Simmias.

Then he, or any man who has the spirit of philosophy, will be willing to die; but he will not take his own life, for that is held to be unlawful.

Here he changed his position, and put his legs off the couch on to the ground, and during the rest of the conversation he remained sitting.

Why do you say, enquired Cebes, that a man ought not to take his own life, but that the philosopher will be ready to follow the dying?

Socrates replies that a philosopher like Evenus should be ready to die, though he must not take his own life.

Socrates replied: And have you, Cebes and Simmias, who are the disciples of Philolaus, never heard him speak of this?

Yes, but his language was obscure, Socrates.

My words, too, are only an echo; but there is no reason why I should not repeat what I have heard: and indeed, as I am going to another place, it is very meet for me to be thinking and talking of the nature of the pilgrimage which I am about to make. What can I do better in the interval between this and the setting of the sun?

Then tell me, Socrates, why is suicide held to be unlawful? as I have certainly heard Philolaus, about whom you were just now asking, affirm when he was staying with us at Thebes; and there are others who say the same, although I have never understood what was meant by any of them.

This incidental remark leads to a discussion on suicide.

Do not lose heart, replied Socrates, and the day may come 62when you will understand. I suppose that you wonder why, when other things which are evil may be good at certain times and to certain persons, death is to be the only exception, and why, when a man is better dead, he is not permitted to be his own benefactor, but must wait for the hand of another.

Fery true, said Cebes, laughing gently and speaking in his native Boeotian.

Man is a prisoner who has no right to run away; and he is also a possession of the gods and must not rob his masters.

I admit the appearance of inconsistency in what I am saying; but there may not be any real inconsistency after all. There is a doctrine whispered in secret that man is a prisoner who has no right to open the door and run away; this is a great mystery which I do not quite understand. Yet I too believe that the gods are our guardians, and that we men are a possession of theirs. Do you not agree?

Yes, I quite agree, said Cebes.

And if one of your own possessions, an ox or an ass, for example, took the liberty of putting himself out of the way when you had given no intimation of your wish that he should die, would you not be angry with him, and would you not punish him if you could?

Certainly, replied Cebes.

Then, if we look at the matter thus, there may be reason in saying that a man should wait, and not take his own life until God summons him, as he is now summoning me.

And why should he wish to leave the best of services?

Yes, Socrates, said Cebes, there seems to be truth in what you say. And yet how can you reconcile this seemingly true belief that God is our guardian and we his possessions, with the willingness to die which you were just now attributing to the philosopher? That the wisest of men should be willing to leave a service in which they are ruled by the gods who are the best of rulers, is not reasonable; for surely no wise man thinks that when set at liberty he can take better care of himself than the gods take of him. A fool may perhaps think so—he may argue that he had better run away from his master, not considering that his duty is to remain to the end, and not to run away from the good, and that there would be no sense in his running away. The wise man will want to be ever with him who is better than himself. Now this, Socrates, is the reverse of what was just now said; for upon this view the wise man should sorrow and the fool rejoice at passing out of life.

63The earnestness of Cebes seemed to please Socrates. Here, said he, turning to us, is a man who is always enquiring, and is not so easily convinced by the first thing which he hears.

You yourself, Socrates, are too ready to run away.

And certainly, added Simmias, the objection which he is now making does appear to me to have some force. For what can be the meaning of a truly wise man wanting to fly away and lightly leave a master who is better than himself? And I rather imagine that Cebes is referring to you; he thinks that you are too ready to leave us, and too ready to leave the gods whom you acknowledge to be our good masters.

Yes, replied Socrates; there is reason in what you say. And so you think that I ought to answer your indictment as if I were in a court?

We should like you to do so, said Simmias.

Socrates replies that he is going to other gods who are wise and good.

Then I must try to make a more successful defence before you than I did before the judges. For I am quite ready to admit, Simmias and Cebes, that I ought to be grieved at death, if I were not persuaded in the first place that I am going to other gods who are wise and good (of which I am as certain as I can be of any such matters), and secondly (though I am not so sure of this last) to men departed, better than those whom I leave behind; and therefore I do not grieve as I might have done, for I have good hope that there is yet something remaining for the dead, and as has been said of old, some far better thing for the good than for the evil.

But do you mean to take away your thoughts with you, Socrates? said Simmias. Will you not impart them to us?—for they are a benefit in which we too are entitled to share. Moreover, if you succeed in convincing us, that will be an answer to the charge against yourself.

I will do my best, replied Socrates. But you must first let me hear what Crito wants; he has long been wishing to say something to me.

Only this, Socrates, replied Crito:—the attendant who is to give you the poison has been telling me, and he wants me to tell you, that you are not to talk much; talking, he says, increases heat, and this is apt to interfere with the action of the poison; persons who excite themselves are sometimes obliged to take a second or even a third dose.

Then, said Socrates, let him mind his business and be prepared to give the poison twice or even thrice if necessary; that is all.

I knew quite well what you would say, replied Crito; but I was obliged to satisfy him.

Never mind him, he said.

The true philosopher is always dying:—why then should he avoid the death which he desires?

And now, O my judges, I desire to prove to you that the real philosopher has reason to be of good cheer when he is about to die, and that after death he may hope to obtain the 64greatest good in the other world. And how this may be, Simmias and Cebes, I will endeavour to explain. For I deem that the true votary of philosophy is likely to be misunderstood by other men; they do not perceive that he is always pursuing death and dying; and if this be so, and he has had the desire of death all his life long, why when his time comes should he repine at that which he has been always pursuing and desiring?

'How the world will laugh when they hear this!'

Simmias said laughingly: Though not in a laughing humour, you have made me laugh, Socrates; for I cannot help thinking that the many when they hear your words will say how truly you have described philosophers, and our people at home will likewise say that the life which philosophers desire is in reality death, and that they have found them out to be deserving of the death which they desire.

Yes, they do not understand the nature of death, or why the philosopher desires or deserves it.Socrates, Simmias.

And they are right, Simmias, in thinking so, with the exception of the words 'they have found them out;' for they have not found out either what is the nature of that death which the true philosopher deserves, or how he deserves or desires death. But enough of them:—let us discuss the matter among ourselves. Do we believe that there is such a thing as death?

To be sure, replied Simmias.

Is it not the separation of soul and body? And to be dead is the completion of this; when the soul exists in herself, and is released from the body and the body is released from the soul, what is this but death?

Just so, he replied.

Life is best when the soul is most freed from the concerns of the body, and is alone and by herself.

There is another question, which will probably throw light on our present enquiry if you and I can agree about it:—Ought the philosopher to care about the pleasures—if they are to be called pleasures—of eating and drinking?

Certainly not, answered Simmias.

And what about the pleasures of love—should he care for them?

By no means.

And will he think much of the other ways of indulging the body, for example, the acquisition of costly raiment, or sandals, or other adornments of the body? Instead of caring about them, does he not rather despise anything more than nature needs? What do you say?

I should say that the true philosopher would despise them.

Would you not say that he is entirely concerned with the soul and not with the body? He would like, as far as he can, to get away from the body and to turn to the soul.

Quite true.

In matters of this sort philosophers, above all other men, 65may be observed in every sort of way to dissever the soul from the communion of the body.

Very true.

Whereas, Simmias, the rest of the world are of opinion that to him who has no sense of pleasure and no part in bodily pleasure, life is not worth having; and that he who is indifferent about them is as good as dead.

That is also true.

The senses are untrustworthy guides: they mislead the soul in the search for truth.

What again shall we say of the actual acquirement of knowledge?—is the body, if invited to share in the enquiry, a hinderer or a helper? I mean to say, have sight and hearing any truth in them? Are they not, as the poets are always telling us, inaccurate witnesses? and yet, if even they are inaccurate and indistinct, what is to be said of the other senses?—for you will allow that they are the best of them?

Certainly, he replied.

Then when does the soul attain truth?—for in attempting to consider anything in company with the body she is obviously deceived.

True.

Then must not true existence be revealed to her in thought, if at all?

Yes.

And thought is best when the mind is gathered into herself and none of these things trouble her—neither sounds nor sights nor pain nor any pleasure,—when she takes leave of the body, and has as little as possible to do with it, when she has no bodily sense or desire, but is aspiring after true being?

Certainly.

And therefore the philosopher runs away from the body.

And in this the philosopher dishonours the body; his soul runs away from his body and desires to be alone and by herself?

That is true.

Another argument. The absolute truth of justice, beauty, and other ideas is not perceived by the senses, which only introduce a disturbing element.

Well, but there is another thing, Simmias: Is there or is there not an absolute justice?

Assuredly there is.

And an absolute beauty and absolute good?

Of course.

But did you ever behold any of them with your eyes?

Certainly not.

Or did you ever reach them with any other bodily sense?—and I speak not of these alone, but of absolute greatness, and health, and strength, and of the essence or true nature of everything. Has the reality of them ever been perceived by you through the bodily organs? or rather, is not the nearest approach to the knowledge of their several natures made by him who so orders his intellectual vision as to have the most exact conception of the essence of each thing which he considers?

Certainly.

And he attains to the purest knowledge of them who goes to each with the mind alone, not introducing or intruding in the act of thought sight or any other sense together with 66reason, but with the very light of the mind in her own clearness searches into the very truth of each; he who has got rid, as far as he can, of eyes and ears and, so to speak, of the whole body, these being in his opinion distracting elements which when they infect the soul hinder her from acquiring truth and knowledge—who, if not he, is likely to attain to the knowledge of true being?

What you say has a wonderful truth in it, Socrates, replied Simmias.

The soul in herself must perceive things in themselves.

And when real philosophers consider all these things, will they not be led to make a reflection which they will express in words something like the following? 'Have we not found,' they will say, 'a path of thought which seems to bring us and our argument to the conclusion, that while we are in the body, and while the soul is infected with the evils of the body, our desire will not be satisfied? and our desire is of the truth. For the body is a source of endless trouble to us by reason of the mere requirement of food; and is liable also to diseases which overtake and impede us in the search after true being: it fills us full of loves, and lusts, and fears, and fancies of all kinds, and endless foolery, and in fact, as men say, takes away from us the power of thinking at all. Whence come wars, and fightings, and factions? whence but from the body and the lusts of the body? Wars are occasioned by the love of money, and money has to be acquired for the sake and in the service of the body; and by reason of all these impediments we have no time to give to philosophy; and, last and worst of all, even if we are at leisure and betake ourselves to some speculation, the body is always breaking in upon us, causing turmoil and confusion in our enquiries, and so amazing us that we are prevented from seeing the truth. It has been proved to us by experience that if we would have pure knowledge of anything we must be quit of the body—the soul in herself must behold things in themselves: and then we shall attain the wisdom which we desire, and of which we say that we are lovers; not while we live, but after death; for if while in company with the body, the soul cannot have pure knowledge, one of two things follows—either knowledge is not to be attained at all, or, if at all, after death. For then, and not till then, the soul will be parted 67from the body and exist in herself alone. In this present life, I reckon that we make the nearest approach to knowledge when we have the least possible intercourse or communion with the body, and are not surfeited with the bodily nature, but keep ourselves pure until the hour when God himself is pleased to release us. And thus having got rid of the foolishness of the body we shall be pure and hold converse with the pure, and know of ourselves the clear light everywhere, which is no other than the light of truth.' For the impure are not permitted to approach the pure. These are the sort of words, Simmias, which the true lovers of knowledge cannot help saying to one another, and thinking. You would agree; would you not?

Undoubtedly, Socrates.

But, O my friend, if this be true, there is great reason to hope that, going whither I go, when I have come to the end of my journey, I shall attain that which has been the pursuit of my life. And therefore I go on my way rejoicing, and not I only, but every other man who believes that his mind has been made ready and that he is in a manner purified.

Certainly, replied Simmias.

Purification is the separation of the soul from the body.

And what is purification but the separation of the soul from the body, as I was saying before; the habit of the soul gathering and collecting herself into herself from all sides out of the body; the dwelling in her own place alone, as in another life, so also in this, as far as she can;—the release of the soul from the chains of the body?

Very true, he said.

And this separation and release of the soul from the body is termed death?

To be sure, he said.

And the true philosophers, and they only, are ever seeking to release the soul. Is not the separation and release of the soul from the body their especial study?

That is true.

And, as I was saying at first, there would be a ridiculous contradiction in men studying to live as nearly as they can in a state of death, and yet repining when it comes upon them.

Clearly.

And therefore the true philosopher who has been always trying to disengage himself from the body will rejoice in death.

And the true philosophers, Simmias, are always occupied in the practice of dying, wherefore also to them least of all men is death terrible. Look at the matter thus:—if they have been in every way the enemies of the body, and are wanting to be alone with the soul, when this desire of theirs is granted, how inconsistent would they be if they trembled and repined, instead of rejoicing at their departure to that place where, when they arrive, they hope to gain that which 68in life they desired—and this was wisdom—and at the same time to be rid of the company of their enemy. Many a man has been willing to go to the world below animated by the hope of seeing there an earthly love, or wife, or son, and conversing with them. And will he who is a true lover of wisdom, and is strongly persuaded in like manner that only in the world below he can worthily enjoy her, still repine at death? Will he not depart with joy? Surely he will, O my friend, if he be a true philosopher. For he will have a firm conviction that there, and there only, he can find wisdom in her purity. And if this be true, he would be very absurd, as I was saying, if he were afraid of death.

He would indeed, replied Simmias.

And when you see a man who is repining at the approach of death, is not his reluctance a sufficient proof that he is not a lover of wisdom, but a lover of the body, and probably at the same time a lover of either money or power, or both?

Quite so, he replied.

And is not courage, Simmias, a quality which is specially characteristic of the philosopher?

Certainly.

He alone possesses the true secret of virtue, which in ordinary men is merely based on a calculation of lesser and greater evils.

There is temperance again, which even by the vulgar is supposed to consist in the control and regulation of the passions, and in the sense of superiority to them—is not temperance a virtue belonging to those only who despise the body, and who pass their lives in philosophy?

Most assuredly.

For the courage and temperance of other men, if you will consider them, are really a contradiction.

How so?

Well, he said, you are aware that death is regarded by men in general as a great evil.

Very true, he said.

And do not courageous men face death because they are afraid of yet greater evils?

That is quite true.

Ordinary men are courageous only from cowardice; temperate from intemperance.

Then all but the philosophers are courageous only from fear, and because they are afraid; and yet that a man should be courageous from fear, and because he is a coward, is surely a strange thing.

Very true.

And are not the temperate exactly in the same case? They are temperate because they are intemperate—which might seem to be a contradiction, but is nevertheless the sort of thing which happens with this foolish temperance. For there are pleasures which they are afraid of losing; and in their desire to keep them, they abstain from some pleasures, because they are overcome by others; and although to be conquered by pleasure is called by men intemperance, to 69them the conquest of pleasure consists in being conquered by pleasure. And that is what I mean by saying that, in a sense, they are made temperate through intemperance.

Such appears to be the case.

True virtue is inseparable from wisdom.Socrates, Cebes.The thyrsus-bearers and the mystics.

Yet the exchange of one fear or pleasure or pain for another fear or pleasure or pain, and of the greater for the less, as if they were coins, is not the exchange of virtue. O my blessed Simmias, is there not one true coin for which all things ought to be exchanged?—and that is wisdom; and only in exchange for this, and in company with this, is anything truly bought or sold, whether courage or temperance or justice. And is not all true virtue the companion of wisdom, no matter what fears or pleasures or other similar goods or evils may or may not attend her? But the virtue which is made up of these goods, when they are severed from wisdom and exchanged with one another, is a shadow of virtue only, nor is there any freedom or health or truth in her; but in the true exchange there is a purging away of all these things, and temperance, and justice, and courage, and wisdom herself are the purgation of them. The founders of the mysteries would appear to have had a real meaning, and were not talking nonsense when they intimated in a figure long ago that he who passes unsanctified and uninitiated into the world below will lie in a slough, but that he who arrives there after initiation and purification will dwell with the gods. For 'many,' as they say in the mysteries, 'are the thyrsus-bearers, but few are the mystics,'—meaning, as I interpret the words, 'the true philosophers.' In the number of whom, during my whole life, I have been seeking, according to my ability, to find a place;—whether I have sought in a right way or not, and whether I have succeeded or not, I shall truly know in a little while, if God will, when I myself arrive in the other world—such is my belief. And therefore I maintain that I am right, Simmias and Cebes, in not grieving or repining at parting from you and my masters in this world, for I believe that I shall equally find good masters and friends in another world. But most men do not believe this saying; if then I succeed in convincing you by my defence better than I did the Athenian judges, it will be well.

Fears are entertained lest the soul when she dies should be scattered to the winds.

Cebes answered: I agree, Socrates, in the greater part of 70what you say. But in what concerns the soul, men are apt to be incredulous; they fear that when she has left the body her place may be nowhere, and that on the very day of death she may perish and come to an end—immediately on her release from the body, issuing forth dispersed like smoke or air and in her flight vanishing away into nothingness. If she could only be collected into herself after she has obtained release from the evils of which you were speaking, there would be good reason to hope, Socrates, that what you say is true. But surely it requires a great deal of argument and many proofs to show that when the man is dead his soul yet exists, and has any force or intelligence.

True, Cebes, said Socrates; and shall I suggest that we converse a little of the probabilities of these things?

I am sure, said Cebes, that I should greatly like to know your opinion about them.

The discussion suited to the occasion.

I reckon, said Socrates, that no one who heard me now, not even if he were one of my old enemies, the Comic poets, could accuse me of idle talking about matters in which I have no concern:—If you please, then, we will proceed with the enquiry.

Suppose we consider the question whether the souls of men after death are or are not in the world below. There comes into my mind an ancient doctrine which affirms that they go from hence into the other world, and returning hither, are born again from the dead. Now if it be true that the living come from the dead, then our souls must exist in the other world, for if not, how could they have been born again? And this would be conclusive, if there were any real evidence that the living are only born from the dead; but if this is not so, then other arguments will have to be adduced.

Very true, replied Cebes.

All things which have opposites are generated out of opposites.

Then let us consider the whole question, not in relation to man only, but in relation to animals generally, and to plants, and to everything of which there is generation, and the proof will be easier. Are not all things which have opposites generated out of their opposites? I mean such things as good and evil, just and unjust—and there are innumerable other opposites which are generated out of opposites. And I want to show that in all opposites there is of necessity a similar alternation; I mean to say, for example, that anything which becomes greater must become greater after being less.

True.

And that which becomes less must have been once greater and then have become less. 71

Yes.

And the weaker is generated from the stronger, and the swifter from the slower.

Very true.

And the worse is from the better, and the more just is from the more unjust.

Of course.

And is this true of all opposites? and are we convinced that all of them are generated out of opposites?

Yes.

And there are intermediate processes or passages into and out of one another, such as increase and diminution, division and composition, and the like.

And in this universal opposition of all things, are there not also two intermediate processes which are ever going on, from one to the other opposite, and back again; where there is a greater and a less there is also an intermediate process of increase and diminution, and that which grows is said to wax, and that which decays to wane?

Yes, he said.

And there are many other processes, such as division and composition, cooling and heating, which equally involve a passage into and out of one another. And this necessarily holds of all opposites, even though not always expressed in words—they are really generated out of one another, and there is a passing or process from one to the other of them?

Very true, he replied.

Well, and is there not an opposite of life, as sleep is the opposite of waking?

True, he said.

And what is it?

Death, he answered.

And these, if they are opposites, are generated the one from the other, and have their two intermediate processes also?

Of course.

Now, said Socrates, I will analyze one of the two pairs of opposites which I have mentioned to you, and also its intermediate processes, and you shall analyze the other to me. One of them I term sleep, the other waking. The state of sleep is opposed to the state of waking, and out of sleeping waking is generated, and out of waking, sleeping; and the process of generation is in the one case falling asleep, and in the other waking up. Do you agree?

I entirely agree.

Life is opposed to death, as waking is to sleeping, and in like manner they are generated from one another.

Then, suppose that you analyze life and death to me in the same manner. Is not death opposed to life?

Yes.

And they are generated one from the other?

Yes.

What is generated from the living?

The dead.

And what from the dead?

I can only say in answer—the living.

Then the living, whether things or persons, Cebes, are generated from the dead?

That is clear, he replied.

Then the inference is that our souls exist in the world below?

That is true.

And one of the two processes or generations is visible—for surely the act of dying is visible?

Surely, he said.

What then is to be the result? Shall we exclude the opposite process? and shall we suppose nature to walk on one leg only? Must we not rather assign to death some corresponding process of generation?

Certainly, he replied.

And what is that process?

Return to life.

And return to life, if there be such a thing, is the birth of the dead into the world of the living? 72

Quite true.

Then here is a new way by which we arrive at the conclusion that the living come from the dead, just as the dead come from the living; and this, if true, affords a most certain proof that the souls of the dead exist in some place out of which they come again.

Yes, Socrates, he said; the conclusion seems to flow necessarily out of our previous admissions.

If there were no compensation or return in nature, all things would pass into the state of death.

And that these admissions were not unfair, Cebes, he said, may be shown, I think, as follows: If generation were in a straight line only, and there were no compensation or circle in nature, no turn or return of elements into their opposites, then you know that all things would at last have the same form and pass into the same state, and there would be no more generation of them.

What do you mean? he said.

The sleeping Endymion would be unmeaning in a world of sleepers.Socrates, Cebes, Simmias.

A simple thing enough, which I will illustrate by the case of sleep, he replied. You know that if there were no alternation of sleeping and waking, the tale of the sleeping Endymion would in the end have no meaning, because all other things would be asleep too, and he would not be distinguishable from the rest. Or if there were composition only, and no division of substances, then the chaos of Anaxagoras would come again. And in like manner, my dear Cebes, if all things which partook of life were to die, and after they were dead remained in the form of death, and did not come to life again, all would at last die, and nothing would be alive—what other result could there be? For if the living spring from any other things, and they too die, must not all things at last be swallowed up in death?

There is no escape, Socrates, said Cebes; and to me your argument seems to be absolutely true.

Yes, he said, Cebes, it is and must be so, in my opinion; and we have not been deluded in making these admissions; but I am confident that there truly is such a thing as living again, and that the living spring from the dead, and that the souls of the dead are in existence, and that the good souls have a better portion than the evil.

The doctrine of recollection implies a previous existence.

Cebes added: Your favourite doctrine, Socrates, that knowledge is simply recollection, if true, also necessarily implies a previous time in which we have learned that which we now recollect. But this would be impossible unless our 73soul had been in some place before existing in the form of man; here then is another proof of the soul's immortality.

But tell me, Cebes, said Simmias, interposing, what arguments are urged in favour of this doctrine of recollection. I am not very sure at the moment that I remember them.

You put a question to a person, and he answers out of his own mind.

One excellent proof, said Cebes, is afforded by questions. If you put a question to a person in a right way, he will give a true answer of himself, but how could he do this unless there were knowledge and right reason already in him? And this is most clearly shown when he is taken to a diagram or to anything of that sort.

But if, said Socrates, you are still incredulous, Simmias, I would ask you whether you may not agree with me when you look at the matter in another way;—I mean, if you are still incredulous as to whether knowledge is recollection?

Incredulous I am not, said Simmias; but I want to have this doctrine of recollection brought to my own recollection, and, from what Cebes has said, I am beginning to recollect and be convinced: but I should still like to hear what you were going to say.

Socrates, Simmias.

This is what I would say, he replied:—We should agree, if I am not mistaken, that what a man recollects he must have known at some previous time.

Very true.

A person may recollect what he has never seen together with what he has seen. How is this?

And what is the nature of this knowledge or recollection? I mean to ask, Whether a person who, having seen or heard or in any way perceived anything, knows not only that, but has a conception of something else which is the subject, not of the same but of some other kind of knowledge, may not be fairly said to recollect that of which he has the conception?

What do you mean?

I mean what I may illustrate by the following instance:—The knowledge of a lyre is not the same as the knowledge of a man?

True.

Recollection is the knowledge of some person or thing derived from some other person or thing which may be either like or unlike them.

And yet what is the feeling of lovers when they recognize a lyre, or a garment, or anything else which the beloved has been in the habit of using? Do not they, from knowing the lyre, form in the mind's eye an image of the youth to whom the lyre belongs? And this is recollection. In like manner any one who sees Simmias may remember Cebes; and there are endless examples of the same thing.

Endless, indeed, replied Simmias.

And recollection is most commonly a process of recovering that which has been already forgotten through time and inattention.

Very true, he said.

Well; and may you not also from seeing the picture of a horse or a lyre remember a man? and from the picture of Simmias, you may be led to remember Cebes;

True.

Or you may also be led to the recollection of Simmias himself?

Quite so. 74

And in all these cases, the recollection may be derived from things either like or unlike?

It may be.

And when the recollection is derived from like things, then another consideration is sure to arise, which is—whether the likeness in any degree falls short or not of that which is recollected?

Very true, he said.

The imperfect equality of pieces of wood or stone suggests the perfect idea of equality.

And shall we proceed a step further, and affirm that there is such a thing as equality, not of one piece of wood or stone with another, but that, over and above this, there is absolute equality? Shall we say so?

Say so, yes, replied Simmias, and swear to it, with all the confidence in life.

And do we know the nature of this absolute essence?

To be sure, he said.

And whence did we obtain our knowledge? Did we not see equalities of material things, such as pieces of wood and stones, and gather from them the idea of an equality which is different from them? For you will acknowledge that there is a difference. Or look at the matter in another way:—Do not the same pieces of wood or stone appear at one time equal, and at another time unequal?

That is certain.

But are real equals ever unequal? or is the idea of equality the same as of inequality?

Impossible, Socrates.

Then these (so-called) equals are not the same with the idea of equality?

I should say, clearly not, Socrates.

And yet from these equals, although differing from the idea of equality, you conceived and attained that idea?

Very true, he said.

Which might be like, or might be unlike them?

Yes.

But that makes no difference: whenever from seeing one thing you conceived another, whether like or unlike, there must surely have been an act of recollection?

Very true.

But what would you say of equal portions of wood and stone, or other material equals? and what is the impression produced by them? Are they equals in the same sense in which absolute equality is equal? or do they fall short of this perfect equality in a measure?

Yes, he said, in a very great measure too.

But if the material equals when compared to the ideal equality fall short of it, the ideal equality with which they are compared must be prior to them, though only known through the medium of them.

And must we not allow, that when I or any one, looking at any object, observes that the thing which he sees aims at being some other thing, but falls short of, and cannot be, that other thing, but is inferior, he who makes this observation must have had a previous knowledge of that to which the other, although similar, was inferior?

Certainly.

And has not this been our own case in the matter of equals and of absolute equality?

Precisely.

Then we must have known equality previously to the time when we first saw the material equals, and reflected that all these apparent equals strive to attain absolute equality, but fall short of it?

Very true.

And we recognize also that this absolute equality has only been known, and can only be known, through the medium of sight or touch, or of some other of the senses, which are all alike in this respect?

Yes, Socrates, as far as the argument is concerned, one of them is the same as the other.

From the senses then is derived the knowledge that all sensible things aim at an absolute equality of which they fall short?

Yes.

Then before we began to see or hear or perceive in any way, we must have had a knowledge of absolute equality, or we could not have referred to that standard the equals which are derived from the senses?—for to that they all aspire, and of that they fall short.

No other inference can be drawn from the previous statements.

And did we not see and hear and have the use of our other senses as soon as we were born?

Certainly.

That higher sense of equality must have been known to us before we were born, was forgotten at birth, and was recovered by the use of the senses.

Then we must have acquired the knowledge of equality at some previous time?

Yes.

That is to say, before we were born, I suppose?

True.

And if we acquired this knowledge before we were born, and were born having the use of it, then we also knew before we were born and at the instant of birth not only the equal or the greater or the less, but all other ideas; for we are not speaking only of equality, but of beauty, goodness, justice, holiness, and of all which we stamp with the name of essence in the dialectical process, both when we ask and when we answer questions. Of all this we may certainly affirm that we acquired the knowledge before birth?

We may.

But if, after having acquired, we have not forgotten what in each case we acquired, then we must always have come into life having knowledge, and shall always continue to know as long as life lasts—for knowing is the acquiring and retaining knowledge and not forgetting. Is not forgetting, Simmias, just the losing of knowledge?

Quite true, Socrates.

What is called learning therefore is only a recollection of ideas which we possessed in a previous state.

But if the knowledge which we acquired before birth was lost by us at birth, and if afterwards by the use of the senses we recovered what we previously knew, will not the process which we call learning be a recovering of the knowledge which is natural to us, and may not this be rightly termed recollection?

Very true.

76So much is clear—that when we perceive something, either by the help of sight, or hearing, or some other sense, from that perception we are able to obtain a notion of some other thing like or unlike which is associated with it but has been forgotten. Whence, as I was saying, one of two alternatives follows:—either we had this knowledge at birth, and continued to know through life; or, after birth, those who are said to learn only remember, and learning is simply recollection.

Yes, that is quite true, Socrates.

And which alternative, Simmias, do you prefer? Had we the knowledge at our birth, or did we recollect the things which we knew previously to our birth?

I cannot decide at the moment.

At any rate you can decide whether he who has knowledge will or will not be able to render an account of his knowledge? What do you say?

Certainly, he will.

But do you think that every man is able to give an account of these very matters about which we are speaking?

Would that they could, Socrates, but I rather fear that to-morrow, at this time, there will no longer be any one alive who is able to give an account of them such as ought to be given.

Then you are not of opinion, Simmias, that all men know these things?

Certainly not.

They are in process of recollecting that which they learned before?

Certainly.

But when did our souls acquire this knowledge?—not since we were born as men?

Certainly not.

And therefore, previously?

Yes.

But if so, our souls must have existed before they were in the form of man; or if not the souls, then not the ideas.

Then, Simmias, our souls must also have existed without bodies before they were in the form of man, and must have had intelligence.

Unless indeed you suppose, Socrates, that these notions are given us at the very moment of birth; for this is the only time which remains.

Yes, my friend, but if so, when do we lose them? for they are not in us when we are born—that is admitted. Do we lose them at the moment of receiving them, or if not at what other time?

No, Socrates, I perceive that I was unconsciously talking nonsense.

Then may we not say, Simmias, that if, as we are always repeating, there is an absolute beauty, and goodness, and an absolute essence of all things; and if to this, which is now discovered to have existed in our former state, we refer all our sensations, and with this compare them, finding these ideas to be pre-existent and our inborn possession—then our souls must have had a prior existence, but if not, there would be no force in the argument? There is the same proof that these ideas must have existed before we were born, as that our souls existed before we were born; and if not the ideas, then not the souls.

Socrates, Simmias, Cebes.

Yes, Socrates; I am convinced that there is precisely the same necessity for the one as for the other; and the argument 77retreats successfully to the position that the existence of the soul before birth cannot be separated from the existence of the essence of which you speak. For there is nothing which to my mind is so patent as that beauty, goodness, and the other notions of which you were just now speaking, have a most real and absolute existence; and I am satisfied with the proof.

Well, but is Cebes equally satisfied? for I must convince him too.

Simmias and Cebes are agreed in thinking that the previous existence of the soul is sufficiently proved, but not the future existence.

I think, said Simmias, that Cebes is satisfied: although he is the most incredulous of mortals, yet I believe that he is sufficiently convinced of the existence of the soul before birth. But that after death the soul will continue to exist is not yet proven even to my own satisfaction. I cannot get rid of the feeling of the many to which Cebes was referring—the feeling that when the man dies the soul will be dispersed, and that this may be the extinction of her. For admitting that she may have been born elsewhere, and framed out of other elements, and was in existence before entering the human body, why after having entered in and gone out again may she not herself be destroyed and come to an end?

Very true, Simmias, said Cebes; about half of what was required has been proven; to wit, that our souls existed before we were born:—that the soul will exist after death as well as before birth is the other half of which the proof is still wanting, and has to be supplied; when that is given the demonstration will be complete.

But if the soul passes from death to birth, she must exist after death as well as before birth.Socrates, Cebes.

But that proof, Simmias and Cebes, has been already given, said Socrates, if you put the two arguments together—I mean this and the former one, in which we admitted that everything living is born of the dead. For if the soul exists before birth, and in coming to life and being born can be born only from death and dying, must she not after death continue to exist, since she has to be born again?—Surely the proof which you desire has been already furnished. Still I suspect that you and Simmias would be glad to probe the argument further. Like children, you are haunted with a fear that when the soul leaves the body, the wind may really blow her away and scatter her; especially if a man should happen to die in a great storm and not when the sky is calm.

Cebes answered with a smile: Then, Socrates, you must argue us out of our fears—and yet, strictly speaking, they are not our fears, but there is a child within us to whom death is a sort of hobgoblin: him too we must persuade not to be afraid when he is alone in the dark.

The fear that the soul will vanish into air must be charmed away.

Socrates said: Let the voice of the charmer be applied daily until you have charmed away the fear.

And where shall we find a good charmer of our fears, 78Socrates, when you are gone?

Hellas, he replied, is a large place, Cebes, and has many good men, and there are barbarous races not a few: seek for him among them all, far and wide, sparing neither pains nor money; for there is no better way of spending your money. And you must seek among yourselves too; for you will not find others better able to make the search.

The search, replied Cebes, shall certainly be made. And now, if you please, let us return to the point of the argument at which we digressed.

By all means, replied Socrates; what else should I please?

Very good.

What is the element which is liable to be scattered?—Not the simple and unchangeable, but the composite and changing.

Must we not, said Socrates, ask ourselves what that is which, as we imagine, is liable to be scattered, and about which we fear? and what again is that about which we have no fear? And then we may proceed further to enquire whether that which suffers dispersion is or is not of the nature of soul—our hopes and fears as to our own souls will turn upon the answers to these questions.

Very true, he said.

Now the compound or composite may be supposed to be naturally capable, as of being compounded, so also of being dissolved; but that which is uncompounded, and that only, must be, if anything is, indissoluble.

Yes; I should imagine so, said Cebes.

And the uncompounded may be assumed to be the same and unchanging, whereas the compound is always changing and never the same.

I agree, he said.

The soul and the ideas belong to the class of the unchanging, which is also the unseen.

Then now let us return to the previous discussion. Is that idea or essence, which in the dialectical process we define as essence or true existence—whether essence of equality, beauty, or anything else—are these essences, I say, liable at times to some degree of change? or are they each of them always what they are, having the same simple self-existent and unchanging forms, not admitting of variation at all, or in any way, or at any time?

They must be always the same, Socrates, replied Cebes.

And what would you say of the many beautiful—whether men or horses or garments or any other things which are named by the same names and may be called equal or beautiful,—are they all unchanging and the same always, or quite the reverse? May they not rather be described as almost always changing and hardly ever the same, either with themselves or with one another?

The latter, replied Cebes; they are always in a state of change.

And these you can touch and see and perceive with the senses, but the unchanging things you can only perceive with the mind—they are invisible and are not seen?

That is very true, he said.

Well then, added Socrates, let us suppose that there are two sorts of existences—one seen, the other unseen.

Let us suppose them.

The seen is the changing, and the unseen is the unchanging?

That may be also supposed.

And, further, is not one part of us body, another part soul?

To be sure.

And to which class is the body more alike and akin?

Clearly to the seen—no one can doubt that.

And is the soul seen or not seen?

Not by man, Socrates.

And what we mean by 'seen' and 'not seen' is that which is or is not visible to the eye of man?

Yes, to the eye of man.

And is the soul seen or not seen?

Not seen.

Unseen then?

Yes.

Then the soul is more like to the unseen, and the body to the seen?

That follows necessarily, Socrates.

The soul which is unseen, when she makes use of the bodily senses, is dragged down into the region of the changeable, and must return into herself before she can attain to true wisdom.

And were we not saying long ago that the soul when using the body as an instrument of perception, that is to say, when using the sense of sight or hearing or some other sense (for the meaning of perceiving through the body is perceiving through the senses)—were we not saying that the soul too is then dragged by the body into the region of the changeable, and wanders and is confused; the world spins round her, and she is like a drunkard, when she touches change?

Very true.

But when returning into herself she reflects, then she passes into the other world, the region of purity, and eternity, and immortality, and unchangeableness, which are her kindred, and with them she ever lives, when she is by herself and is not let or hindered; then she ceases from her erring ways, and being in communion with the unchanging is unchanging. And this state of the soul is called wisdom?

That is well and truly said, Socrates, he replied.

And to which class is the soul more nearly alike and akin, as far as may be inferred from this argument, as well as from the preceding one?

The soul is of the nature of the unchangeable, the body of the changing; the soul rules, the body serves; the soul is in the likeness of the divine, the body of the mortal.

I think, Socrates, that, in the opinion of every one who follows the argument, the soul will be infinitely more like the unchangeable—even the most stupid person will not deny that.

And the body is more like the changing?

Yes.

Yet once more consider the matter in another light: When the soul and the body are united, then nature orders 80the soul to rule and govern, and the body to obey and serve. Now which of these two functions is akin to the divine? and which to the mortal? Does not the divine appear to you to be that which naturally orders and rules, and the mortal to be that which is subject and servant?

True.

And which does the soul resemble?

The soul resembles the divine, and the body the mortal—there can be no doubt of that, Socrates.

Then reflect, Cebes: of all which has been said is not this the conclusion?—that the soul is in the very likeness of the divine, and immortal, and intellectual, and uniform, and indissoluble, and unchangeable; and that the body is in the very likeness of the human, and mortal, and unintellectual, and multiform, and dissoluble, and changeable. Can this, my dear Cebes, be denied?

It cannot.

But if it be true, then is not the body liable to speedy dissolution? and is not the soul almost or altogether indissoluble?

Certainly.

Even from the body something may be learned about the soul; for the corpse of a man lasts for some time, and when embalmed, in a manner for ever.

And do you further observe, that after a man is dead, the body, or visible part of him, which is lying in the visible world, and is called a corpse, and would naturally be dissolved and decomposed and dissipated, is not dissolved or decomposed at once, but may remain for some time, nay even for a long time, if the constitution be sound at the time of death, and the season of the year favourable? For the body when shrunk and embalmed, as the manner is in Egypt, may remain almost entire through infinite ages; and even in decay, there are still some portions, such as the bones and ligaments, which are practically indestructible:—Do you agree?

Yes.

How unlikely then that the soul should at once pass away!

And is it likely that the soul, which is invisible, in passing to the place of the true Hades, which like her is invisible, and pure, and noble, and on her way to the good and wise God, whither, if God will, my soul is also soon to go,—that the soul, I repeat, if this be her nature and origin, will be blown away and destroyed immediately on quitting the body, as the many say? That can never be, my dear Simmias and Cebes. The truth rather is, that the soul which is pure at departing and draws after her no bodily taint, having never voluntarily during life had connection with the body, which she is ever avoiding, herself gathered into herself;—and making such abstraction her perpetual study—which means that she has been a true disciple of philosophy; 81and therefore has in fact been always engaged in the practice of dying? For is not philosophy the study of death?—

Certainly—

Rather when free from bodily impurity she departs to the seats of the blessed.

That soul, I say, herself invisible, departs to the invisible world—to the divine and immortal and rational: thither arriving, she is secure of bliss and is released from the error and folly of men, their fears and wild passions and all other human ills, and for ever dwells, as they say of the initiated, in company with the gods . Is not this true, Cebes?

Yes, said Cebes, beyond a doubt.

But the soul which has been polluted, and is impure at the time of her departure, and is the companion and servant of the body always, and is in love with and fascinated by the body and by the desires and pleasures of the body, until she is led to believe that the truth only exists in a bodily form, which a man may touch and see and taste, and use for the purposes of his lusts,—the soul, I mean, accustomed to hate and fear and avoid the intellectual principle, which to the bodily eye is dark and invisible, and can be attained only by philosophy;—do you suppose that such a soul will depart pure and unalloyed?

Impossible, he replied.

She is held fast by the corporeal, which the continual association and constant care of the body have wrought into her nature.

Very true.

But the souls of the wicked are dragged down by the corporeal element.

And this corporeal element, my friend, is heavy and weighty and earthy, and is that element of sight by which a soul is depressed and dragged down again into the visible world, because she is afraid of the invisible and of the world below—prowling about tombs and sepulchres, near which, as they tell us, are seen certain ghostly apparitions of souls which have not departed pure, but are cloyed with sight and therefore visible.

That is very likely, Socrates.

Yes, that is very likely, Cebes; and these must be the souls, not of the good, but of the evil, which are compelled to wander about such places in payment of the penalty of their former evil way of life; and they continue to wander until through the craving after the corporeal which never leaves them, they are imprisoned finally in another body. And they may be supposed to find their prisons in the same natures which they have had in their former lives.

What natures do you mean, Socrates?

They wander into the bodies of the animals or of birds which are of a like nature with themselves.

What I mean is that men who have followed after gluttony, and wantonness, and drunkenness, and have had no thought of avoiding them, would pass into asses and animals of that 82sort. What do you think?

I think such an opinion to be exceedingly probable.

And those who have chosen the portion of injustice, and tyranny, and violence, will pass into wolves, or into hawks and kites;—whither else can we suppose them to go?

Yes, said Cebes; with such natures, beyond question.

And there is no difficulty, he said, in assigning to all of them places answering to their several natures and propensities?

There is not, he said.

Some are happier than others; and the happiest both in themselves and in the place to which they go are those who have practised the civil and social virtues which are called temperance and justice, and are acquired by habit and attention without philosophy and mind .

Why are they the happiest?

Because they may be expected to pass into some gentle and social kind which is like their own, such as bees or wasps or ants, or back again into the form of man, and just and moderate men may be supposed to spring from them.

Very likely.

No one who has not studied philosophy and who is not entirely pure at the time of his departure is allowed to enter the company of the Gods, but the lover of knowledge only. And this is the reason, Simmias and Cebes, why the true votaries of philosophy abstain from all fleshly lusts, and hold out against them and refuse to give themselves up to them,—not because they fear poverty or the ruin of their families, like the lovers of money, and the world in general; nor like the lovers of power and honour, because they dread the dishonour or disgrace of evil deeds.

No, Socrates, that would not become them, said Cebes.

No indeed, he replied; and therefore they who have any care of their own souls, and do not merely live moulding and fashioning the body, say farewell to all this; they will not walk in the ways of the blind: and when philosophy offers them purification and release from evil, they feel that they ought not to resist her influence, and whither she leads they turn and follow.

What do you mean, Socrates?

The new consciousness which is awakened by philosophy. The philosopher considers not only the consequences of pleasures and pains, but, what is far worse, the false lights in which they show objects.

I will tell you, he said. The lovers of knowledge are conscious that the soul was simply fastened and glued to the body—until philosophy received her, she could only view real existence through the bars of a prison, not in and through herself; she was wallowing in the mire of every sort of ignorance, and by reason of lust had become the principal accomplice in her own captivity. This was her original state; and then, as I was saying, and as the lovers of knowledge are well aware, philosophy, seeing how terrible was her confinement, of which she was to herself the cause, received and gently comforted her and sought to release her, pointing out that the eye and the ear and the other senses are full of deception, and persuading her to retire from them, and abstain from all but the necessary use of them, and be gathered up and collected into herself, bidding her trust in herself and her own pure apprehension of pure existence, and to mistrust whatever comes to her through other channels and is subject to variation; for such things are visible and tangible, but what she sees in her own nature is intelligible and invisible. And the soul of the true philosopher thinks that she ought not to resist this deliverance, and therefore abstains from pleasures and desires and pains and fears, as far as she is able; reflecting that when a man has great joys or sorrows or fears or desires, he suffers from them, not merely the sort of evil which might be anticipated—as for example, the loss of his health or property which he has sacrificed to his lusts—but an evil greater far, which is the greatest and worst of all evils, and one of which he never thinks.

What is it, Socrates? said Cebes.

The evil is that when the feeling of pleasure or pain is most intense, every soul of man imagines the objects of this intense feeling to be then plainest and truest: but this is not so, they are really the things of sight.

Very true.

And is not this the state in which the soul is most enthralled by the body?

How so?

Why, because each pleasure and pain is a sort of nail which nails and rivets the soul to the body, until she becomes like the body, and believes that to be true which the body affirms to be true; and from agreeing with the body and having the same delights she is obliged to have the same habits and haunts, and is not likely ever to be pure at her departure to the world below, but is always infected by the body; and so she sinks into another body and there germinates and grows, and has therefore no part in the communion of the divine and pure and simple.

Most true, Socrates, answered Cebes.

And this, Cebes, is the reason why the true lovers of knowledge are temperate and brave; and not for the reason which the world gives.

84Certainly not.

Socrates, Cebes, Simmias.The soul which has been emancipated from pleasures and pains will not be blown away at death.

Certainly not! The soul of a philosopher will reason in quite another way; she will not ask philosophy to release her in order that when released she may deliver herself up again to the thraldom of pleasures and pains, doing a work only to be undone again, weaving instead of unweaving her Penelope's web. But she will calm passion, and follow reason, and dwell in the contemplation of her, beholding the true and divine (which is not matter of opinion), and thence deriving nourishment. Thus she seeks to live while she lives, and after death she hopes to go to her own kindred and to that which is like her, and to be freed from human ills. Never fear, Simmias and Cebes, that a soul which has been thus nurtured and has had these pursuits, will at her departure from the body be scattered and blown away by the winds and be nowhere and nothing.

Simmias and Cebes have their doubts, but think that this is not the time to express them.

When Socrates had done speaking, for a considerable time there was silence; he himself appeared to be meditating, as most of us were, on what had been said; only Cebes and Simmias spoke a few words to one another. And Socrates observing them asked what they thought of the argument, and whether there was anything wanting? For, said he, there are many points still open to suspicion and attack, if any one were disposed to sift the matter thoroughly. Should you be considering some other matter I say no more, but if you are still in doubt do not hesitate to say exactly what you think, and let us have anything better which you can suggest; and if you think that I can be of any use, allow me to help you.

Simmias said: I must confess, Socrates, that doubts did arise in our minds, and each of us was urging and inciting the other to put the question which we wanted to have answered but which neither of us liked to ask, fearing that our importunity might be troublesome at such a time.

Socrates rebukes their want of confidence in him. What is the meaning of the swans' singing? They do not lament, as men suppose, at their approaching death; but they rejoice because they are going to the God, whose servants they are. Socrates, who is their fellow-servant, will not leave the world less cheerily.

Socrates replied with a smile: O Simmias, what are you saying? I am not very likely to persuade other men that I do not regard my present situation as a misfortune, if I cannot even persuade you that I am no worse off now than at any other time in my life. Will you not allow that I have as much of the spirit of prophecy in me as the swans? For they, when they perceive that they must die, having sung all their life long, do then sing more lustily than ever, rejoicing 85in the thought that they are about to go away to the god whose ministers they are. But men, because they are themselves afraid of death, slanderously affirm of the swans that they sing a lament at the last, not considering that no bird sings when cold, or hungry, or in pain, not even the nightingale, nor the swallow, nor yet the hoopoe; which are said indeed to tune a lay of sorrow, although I do not believe this to be true of them any more than of the swans. But because they are sacred to Apollo, they have the gift of prophecy, and anticipate the good things of another world; wherefore they sing and rejoice in that day more than ever they did before. And I too, believing myself to be the consecrated servant of the same God, and the fellow-servant of the swans, and thinking that I have received from my master gifts of prophecy which are not inferior to theirs, would not go out of life less merrily than the swans. Never mind then, if this be your only objection, but speak and ask anything which you like, while the eleven magistrates of Athens allow.

Simmias insists that they must probe truth to the bottom.

Very good, Socrates, said Simmias; then I will tell you my difficulty, and Cebes will tell you his. I feel myself (and I daresay that you have the same feeling), how hard or rather impossible is the attainment of any certainty about questions such as these in the present life. And yet I should deem him a coward who did not prove what is said about them to the uttermost, or whose heart failed him before he had examined them on every side. For he should persevere until he has achieved one of two things: either he should discover, or be taught the truth about them; or, if this be impossible, I would have him take the best and most irrefragable of human theories, and let this be the raft upon which he sails through life—not without risk, as I admit, if he cannot find some word of God which will more surely and safely carry him. And now, as you bid me, I will venture to question you, and then I shall not have to reproach myself hereafter with not having said at the time what I think. For when I consider the matter, either alone or with Cebes, the argument does certainly appear to me, Socrates, to be not sufficient.

Socrates, Simmias.

Socrates answered: I dare say, my friend, that you may be right, but I should like to know in what respect the argument is insufficient.

The harmony does not survive the lyre; how then can the soul, which is also a harmony, survive the body?

In this respect, replied Simmias:—Suppose a person to use the same argument about harmony and the lyre—might he not say that harmony is a thing invisible, incorporeal, perfect, divine, existing in the lyre which is harmonized, but 86that the lyre and the strings are matter and material, composite, earthy, and akin to mortality? And when some one breaks the lyre, or cuts and rends the strings, then he who takes this view would argue as you do, and on the same analogy, that the harmony survives and has not perished—you cannot imagine, he would say, that the lyre without the strings, and the broken strings themselves which are mortal remain, and yet that the harmony, which is of heavenly and immortal nature and kindred, has perished—perished before the mortal. The harmony must still be somewhere, and the wood and strings will decay before anything can happen to that. The thought, Socrates, must have occurred to your own mind that such is our conception of the soul; and that when the body is in a manner strung and held together by the elements of hot and cold, wet and dry, then the soul is the harmony or due proportionate admixture of them. But if so, whenever the strings of the body are unduly loosened or overstrained through disease or other injury, then the soul, though most divine, like other harmonies of music or of works of art, of course perishes at once; although the material remains of the body may last for a considerable time, until they are either decayed or burnt. And if any one maintains that the soul, being the harmony of the elements of the body, is first to perish in that which is called death, how shall we answer him?

Socrates looked fixedly at us as his manner was, and said with a smile: Simmias has reason on his side; and why does not some one of you who is better able than myself answer him? for there is force in his attack upon me. But perhaps, before we answer him, we had better also hear what Cebes has to say that we may gain time for reflection, and when they have both spoken, we may either assent to them, if there is truth in what they say, or if not, we will maintain our position. Please to tell me then, Cebes, he said, what was the difficulty which troubled you?

A weaver may outlive many coats and himself be outlived by the last:so the soul which has passed through many bodies may in the end be worn out.Socrates, Cebes, Echecrates.

Cebes said: I will tell you. My feeling is that the argument is where it was, and open to the same objections which 87were urged before; for I am ready to admit that the existence of the soul before entering into the bodily form has been very ingeniously, and, if I may say so, quite sufficiently proven; but the existence of the soul after death is still, in my judgment, unproven. Now my objection is not the same as that of Simmias; for I am not disposed to deny that the soul is stronger and more lasting than the body, being of opinion that in all such respects the soul very far excels the body. Well then, says the argument to me, why do you remain unconvinced?—When you see that the weaker continues in existence after the man is dead, will you not admit that the more lasting must also survive during the same period of time? Now I will ask you to consider whether the objection, which, like Simmias, I will express in a figure, is of any weight. The analogy which I will adduce is that of an old weaver, who dies, and after his death somebody says:—He is not dead, he must be alive;—see, there is the coat which he himself wove and wore, and which remains whole and undecayed. And then he proceeds to ask of some one who is incredulous, whether a man lasts longer, or the coat which is in use and wear; and when he is answered that a man lasts far longer, thinks that he has thus certainly demonstrated the survival of the man, who is the more lasting, because the less lasting remains. But that, Simmias, as I would beg you to remark, is a mistake; any one can see that he who talks thus is talking nonsense. For the truth is, that the weaver aforesaid, having woven and worn many such coats, outlived several of them; and was outlived by the last; but a man is not therefore proved to be slighter and weaker than a coat. Now the relation of the body to the soul may be expressed in a similar figure; and any one may very fairly say in like manner that the soul is lasting, and the body weak and shortlived in comparison. He may argue in like manner that every soul wears out many bodies, especially if a man live many years. While he is alive the body deliquesces and decays, and the soul always weaves another garment and repairs the waste. But of course, whenever the soul perishes, she must have on her last garment, and this will survive her; and then at length, when the soul is dead, the body will show its native weakness, and quickly decompose and pass away. I would therefore rather not rely on the argument from superior strength to prove the continued existence of the soul after death. For granting 88even more than you affirm to be possible, and acknowledging not only that the soul existed before birth, but also that the souls of some exist, and will continue to exist after death, and will be born and die again and again, and that there is a natural strength in the soul which will hold out and be born many times— nevertheless, we may be still inclined to think that she will weary in the labours of successive births, and may at last succumb in one of her deaths and utterly perish; and this death and dissolution of the body which brings destruction to the soul may be unknown to any of us, for no one of us can have had any experience of it: and if so, then I maintain that he who is confident about death has but a foolish confidence, unless he is able to prove that the soul is altogether immortal and imperishable. But if he cannot prove the soul's immortality, he who is about to die will always have reason to fear that when the body is disunited, the soul also may utterly perish.

The despair of the audience at hearing the overthrow of the argument.

All of us, as we afterwards remarked to one another, had an unpleasant feeling at hearing what they said. When we had been so firmly convinced before, now to have our faith shaken seemed to introduce a confusion and uncertainty, not only into the previous argument, but into any future one; either we were incapable of forming a judgment, or there were no grounds of belief.

Ech.

There I feel with you—by heaven I do, Phaedo, and when you were speaking, I was beginning to ask myself the same question: What argument can I ever trust again? For what could be more convincing than the argument of Socrates, which has now fallen into discredit? That the soul is a harmony is a doctrine which has always had a wonderful attraction for me, and, when mentioned, came back to me at once, as my own original conviction. And now I must begin again and find another argument which will assure me that when the man is dead the soul survives. Tell me, I implore you, how did Socrates proceed? Did he appear to share the unpleasant feeling which you mention? or did he calmly meet the attack? And did he answer forcibly or feebly? Narrate what passed as exactly as you can.

Phaed.

The wonderful manner in which Socrates soothes his disappointed hearers and rehabilitates the argument.

Often, Echecrates, I have wondered at Socrates, 89but never more than on that occasion. That he should be able to answer was nothing, but what astonished me was, first, the gentle and pleasant and approving manner in which he received the words of the young men, and then his quick sense of the wound which had been inflicted by the argument, and the readiness with which he healed it. He might be compared to a general rallying his defeated and broken army, urging them to accompany him and return to the field of argument.

Ech.

What followed?

Phaed.

You shall hear, for I was close to him on his right hand, seated on a sort of stool, and he on a couch which was a good deal higher. He stroked my head, and pressed the hair upon my neck—he had a way of playing with my hair; and then he said: To-morrow, Phaedo, I suppose that these fair locks of yours will be severed.

Yes, Socrates, I suppose that they will, I replied.

Not so, if you will take my advice.

What shall I do with them? I said.

To-day, he replied, and not to-morrow, if this argument dies and we cannot bring it to life again, you and I will both shave our locks: and if I were you, and the argument got away from me, and I could not hold my ground against Simmias and Cebes, I would myself take an oath, like the Argives, not to wear hair any more until I had renewed the conflict and defeated them.

Yes, I said; but Heracles himself is said not to be a match for two.

Summon me then, he said, and I will be your Iolaus until the sun goes down.

I summon you rather, I rejoined, not as Heracles summoning Iolaus, but as Iolaus might summon Heracles.

That will do as well, he said. But first let us take care that we avoid a danger.

Of what nature? I said.

Socrates, Phaedo. The danger of becoming haters of ideas greater than of becoming haters of men.

Lest we become misologists, he replied: no worse thing can happen to a man than this. For as there are misanthropists or haters of men, there are also misologists or haters of ideas, and both spring from the same cause, which is ignorance of the world. Misanthropy arises out of the too great confidence of inexperience;—you trust a man and think him altogether true and sound and faithful, and then in a little while he turns out to be false and knavish; and then another and another, and when this has happened several times to a man, especially when it happens among those whom he deems to be his own most trusted and familiar friends, and he has often quarrelled with them, he at last hates all men, and believes that no one has any good in him at all. You must have observed this trait of character?

I have.

There are few very bad or very good men; (although bad arguments may be more numerous than bad men); the main point is that he who has been often deceived by either is apt to lose faith in them.

And is not the feeling discreditable? Is it not obvious that such an one having to deal with other men, was clearly without any experience of human nature; for experience would have taught him the true state of the case, that few are the good and few the evil, and that the great majority are in 90the interval between them.

What do you mean? I said.

I mean, he replied, as you might say of the very large and very small—that nothing is more uncommon than a very large or very small man; and this applies generally to all extremes, whether of great and small, or swift and slow, or fair and foul, or black and white: and whether the instances you select be men or dogs or anything else, few are the extremes, but many are in the mean between them. Did you never observe this?

Yes, I said, I have.

And do you not imagine, he said, that if there were a competition in evil, the worst would be found to be very few?

Yes, that is very likely, I said.

Yes, that is very likely, he replied; although in this respect arguments are unlike men—there I was led on by you to say more than I had intended; but the point of comparison was, that when a simple man who has no skill in dialectics believes an argument to be true which he afterwards imagines to be false, whether really false or not, and then another and another, he has no longer any faith left, and great disputers, as you know, come to think at last that they have grown to be the wisest of mankind; for they alone perceive the utter unsoundness and instability of all arguments, or indeed, of all things, which, like the currents in the Euripus, are going up and down in never-ceasing ebb and flow.

That is quite true, I said.

Yes, Phaedo, he replied, and how melancholy, if there be such a thing as truth or certainty or possibility of knowledge—that a man should have lighted upon some argument or other which at first seemed true and then turned out to be false, and instead of blaming himself and his own want of wit, because he is annoyed, should at last be too glad to transfer the blame from himself to arguments in general: and for ever afterwards should hate and revile them, and lose truth and the knowledge of realities.

Yes, indeed, I said; that is very melancholy.

Socrates, who is soon to die, has too much at stake on the argument to be a fair judge. Simmias and Cebes must help him to consider the matter impartially.Socrates, Cebes, Simmias.

Let us then, in the first place, he said, be careful of allowing or of admitting into our souls the notion that there is no health or soundness in any arguments at all. Rather say that we have not yet attained to soundness in ourselves, and that we must struggle manfully and do our best to gain health of mind—you and all other men having regard to the whole of your future life, and I myself in the prospect of death. For 91at this moment I am sensible that I have not the temper of a philosopher; like the vulgar, I am only a partisan. Now the partisan, when he is engaged in a dispute, cares nothing about the rights of the question, but is anxious only to convince his hearers of his own assertions. And the difference between him and me at the present moment is merely this—that whereas he seeks to convince his hearers that what he says is true, I am rather seeking to convince myself; to convince my hearers is a secondary matter with me. And do but see how much I gain by the argument. For if what I say is true, then I do well to be persuaded of the truth; but if there be nothing after death, still, during the short time that remains, I shall not distress my friends with lamentations, and my ignorance will not last, but will die with me, and therefore no harm will be done. This is the state of mind, Simmias and Cebes, in which I approach the argument. And I would ask you to be thinking of the truth and not of Socrates: agree with me, if I seem to you to be speaking the truth; or if not, withstand me might and main, that I may not deceive you as well as myself in my enthusiasm, and like the bee, leave my sting in you before I die.

Simmias and Cebes are inclined to fear that the soul may perish before the body, but they still hold to the doctrine of reminiscence.

And now let us proceed, he said. And first of all let me be sure that I have in my mind what you were saying. Simmias, if I remember rightly, has fears and misgivings whether the soul, although a fairer and diviner thing than the body, being as she is in the form of harmony, may not perish first. On the other hand, Cebes appeared to grant that the soul was more lasting than the body, but he said that no one could know whether the soul, after having worn out many bodies, might not perish herself and leave her last body behind her; and that this is death, which is the destruction not of the body but of the soul, for in the body the work of destruction is ever going on. Are not these, Simmias and Cebes, the points which we have to consider?

They both agreed to this statement of them.

He proceeded: And did you deny the force of the whole preceding argument, or of a part only?

Of a part only, they replied.

And what did you think, he said, of that part of the argument in which we said that knowledge was recollection, and hence inferred that the soul must have previously existed somewhere else before she was enclosed in the 92body?

Cebes said that he had been wonderfully impressed by that part of the argument, and that his conviction remained absolutely unshaken. Simmias agreed, and added that he himself could hardly imagine the possibility of his ever thinking differently.

The elements of harmony are prior to harmony, but the body is not prior to the soul.

But, rejoined Socrates, you will have to think differently, my Theban friend, if you still maintain that harmony is a compound, and that the soul is a harmony which is made out of strings set in the frame of the body; for you will surely never allow yourself to say that a harmony is prior to the elements which compose it.

Never, Socrates.

Socrates, Simmias.

But do you not see that this is what you imply when you say that the soul existed before she took the form and body of man, and was made up of elements which as yet had no existence? For harmony is not like the soul, as you suppose; but first the lyre, and the strings, and the sounds exist in a state of discord, and then harmony is made last of all, and perishes first. And how can such a notion of the soul as this agree with the other?

Not at all, replied Simmias.

And yet, he said, there surely ought to be harmony in a discourse of which harmony is the theme?

There ought, replied Simmias.

But there is no harmony, he said, in the two propositions that knowledge is recollection, and that the soul is a harmony. Which of them will you retain?

Simmias acknowledges that his argument does not harmonize with the proposition that knowledge is recollection.

I think, he replied, that I have a much stronger faith, Socrates, in the first of the two, which has been fully demonstrated to me, than in the latter, which has not been demonstrated at all, but rests only on probable and plausible grounds; and is therefore believed by the many. I know too well that these arguments from probabilities are impostors, and unless great caution is observed in the use of them, they are apt to be deceptive—in geometry, and in other things too. But the doctrine of knowledge and recollection has been proven to me on trustworthy grounds: and the proof was that the soul must have existed before she came into the body, because to her belongs the essence of which the very name implies existence. Having, as I am convinced, rightly accepted this conclusion, and on sufficient grounds, I must, as I suppose, cease to argue or allow others to argue that the soul is a harmony.

Let me put the matter, Simmias, he said, in another point 93of view: Do you imagine that a harmony or any other composition can be in a state other than that of the elements, out of which it is compounded?

Certainly not.

Or do or suffer anything other than they do or suffer?

He agreed.

Then a harmony does not, properly speaking, lead the parts or elements which make up the harmony, but only follows them.

He assented.

For harmony cannot possibly have any motion, or sound, or other quality which is opposed to its parts.

That would be impossible, he replied.

And does not the nature of every harmony depend upon the manner in which the elements are harmonized?

I do not understand you, he said.

Harmony admits of degrees, but in the soul there are no degrees;

I mean to say that a harmony admits of degrees, and is more of a harmony, and more completely a harmony, when more truly and fully harmonized, to any extent which is possible; and less of a harmony, and less completely a harmony, when less truly and fully harmonized.

True.

But does the soul admit of degrees? or is one soul in the very least degree more or less, or more or less completely, a soul than another?

Not in the least.

Yet surely of two souls, one is said to have intelligence and virtue, and to be good, and the other to have folly and vice, and to be an evil soul: and this is said truly?

Yes, truly.

and therefore there cannot be a soul or harmony within a soul.

But what will those who maintain the soul to be a harmony say of this presence of virtue and vice in the soul?—will they say that here is another harmony, and another discord, and that the virtuous soul is harmonized, and herself being a harmony has another harmony within her, and that the vicious soul is inharmonical and has no harmony within her?

I cannot tell, replied Simmias; but I suppose that something of the sort would be asserted by those who say that the soul is a harmony.

And we have already admitted that no soul is more a soul than another; which is equivalent to admitting that harmony is not more or less harmony, or more or less completely a harmony?

Quite true.

And that which is not more or less a harmony is not more or less harmonized?

True.

And that which is not more or less harmonized cannot have more or less of harmony, but only an equal harmony?

Yes, an equal harmony.

Then one soul not being more or less absolutely a soul than another, is not more or less harmonized?

Exactly.

And therefore has neither more nor less of discord, nor yet of harmony?

She has not.

And having neither more nor less of harmony or of discord, one soul has no more vice or virtue than another, if vice be discord and virtue harmony?

Not at all more.

94Or speaking more correctly, Simmias, the soul, if she is a harmony, will never have any vice; because a harmony, being absolutely a harmony, has no part in the inharmonical.

No.

If the soul is a harmony, all souls must be equally good.

And therefore a soul which is absolutely a soul has no vice?

How can she have, if the previous argument holds?

Then, if all souls are equally by their nature souls, all souls of all living creatures will be equally good?

I agree with you, Socrates, he said.

And can all this be true, think you? he said; for these are the consequences which seem to follow from the assumption that the soul is a harmony?

It cannot be true.

Once more, he said, what ruler is there of the elements of human nature other than the soul, and especially the wise soul? Do you know of any?

Indeed, I do not.

And is the soul in agreement with the affections of the body? or is she at variance with them? For example, when the body is hot and thirsty, does not the soul incline us against drinking? and when the body is hungry, against eating? And this is only one instance out of ten thousand of the opposition of the soul to the things of the body.

Very true.

Socrates, Simmias, Cebes.

But we have already acknowledged that the soul, being a harmony, can never utter a note at variance with the tensions and relaxations and vibrations and other affections of the strings out of which she is composed; she can only follow, she cannot lead them?

It must be so, he replied.

The soul leads and does not follow. She constrains and reprimands the passions.

And yet do we not now discover the soul to be doing the exact opposite—leading the elements of which she is believed to be composed; almost always opposing and coercing them in all sorts of ways throughout life, sometimes more violently with the pains of medicine and gymnastic; then again more gently; now threatening, now admonishing the desires, passions, fears, as if talking to a thing which is not herself, as Homer in the Odyssee represents Odysseus doing in the words—

- 'He beat his breast, and thus reproached his heart:
- Endure, my heart; far worse hast thou endured!'

Do you think that Homer wrote this under the idea that the soul is a harmony capable of being led by the affections of the body, and not rather of a nature which should lead and master them—herself a far diviner thing than any harmony?

Yes, Socrates, I quite think so.

Then, my friend, we can never be right in saying that the soul is a harmony, for we should contradict the divine 95Homer, and contradict ourselves.

True, he said.

Thus much, said Socrates, of Harmonia, your Theban goddess, who has graciously yielded to us; but what shall I say, Cebes, to her husband Cadmus, and how shall I make peace with him?

I think that you will discover a way of propitiating him, said Cebes; I am sure that you have put the argument with Harmonia in a manner that I could never have expected. For when Simmias was mentioning his difficulty, I quite imagined that no answer could be given to him, and therefore I was surprised at finding that his argument could not sustain the first onset of yours, and not impossibly the other, whom you call Cadmus, may share a similar fate.

Socrates, Cebes.Recapitulation of the argument of Cebes.

Nay, my good friend, said Socrates, let us not boast, lest some evil eye should put to flight the word which I am about to speak. That, however, may be left in the hands of those above; while I draw near in Homeric fashion, and try the mettle of your words. Here lies the point:—You want to have it proven to you that the soul is imperishable and immortal, and the philosopher who is confident in death appears to you to have but a vain and foolish confidence, if he believes that he will fare better in the world below than one who has led another sort of life, unless he can prove this: and you say that the demonstration of the strength and divinity of the soul, and of her existence prior to our becoming men, does not necessarily imply her immortality. Admitting the soul to be longlived, and to have known and done much in a former state, still she is not on that account immortal; and her entrance into the human form may be a sort of disease which is the beginning of dissolution, and may at last, after the toils of life are over, end in that which is called death. And whether the soul enters into the body once only or many times, does not, as you say, make any difference in the fears of individuals. For any man, who is not devoid of sense, must fear, if he has no knowledge and can give no account of the soul's immortality. This, or something like this, I suspect to be your notion, Cebes; and I designedly recur to it in order that nothing may escape us, and that you may, if you wish, add or subtract anything.

But, said Cebes, as far as I see at present, I have nothing to add or subtract: I mean what you say that I mean.

Socrates paused awhile, and seemed to be absorbed in reflection. At length he said: You are raising a tremendous question, Cebes, involving the whole nature of generation and corruption, about which, if you like, I will give you my own experience; and if anything which I say is likely to avail towards the solution of your difficulty you may make use of it.

I should very much like, said Cebes, to hear what you have to say.

The speculations of Socrates about physics made him forget the commonest things.

Then I will tell you, said Socrates. When I was young, Cebes, I had a prodigious desire to know that department of philosophy which is called the investigation of nature; to know the causes of things, and why a thing is and is created or destroyed appeared to me to be a lofty profession; and I was always agitating myself with the consideration of questions such as these:—Is the growth of animals the result of some decay which the hot and cold principle contracts, as some have said? Is the blood the element with which we think, or the air, or the fire? or perhaps nothing of the kind—but the brain may be the originating power of the perceptions of hearing and sight and smell, and memory and opinion may come from them, and science may be based on memory and opinion when they have attained fixity. And then I went on to examine the corruption of them, and then to the things of heaven and earth, and at last I concluded myself to be utterly and absolutely incapable of these enquiries, as I will satisfactorily prove to you. For I was fascinated by them to such a degree that my eyes grew blind to things which I had seemed to myself, and also to others, to know quite well; I forgot what I had before thought self-evident truths; e.g. such a fact as that the growth of man is the result of eating and drinking; for when by the digestion of food flesh is added to flesh and bone to bone, and whenever there is an aggregation of congenial elements, the lesser bulk becomes larger and the small man great. Was not that a reasonable notion?

Yes, said Cebes, I think so.

Difficulty of explaining relative notions.

Well; but let me tell you something more. There was a time when I thought that I understood the meaning of greater and less pretty well; and when I saw a great man standing by a little one, I fancied that one was taller than the other by a head; or one horse would appear to be greater than another horse: and still more clearly did I seem to perceive that ten is two more than eight, and that two cubits are more than one, because two is the double of one.

And what is now your notion of such matters? said Cebes.

Socrates.

I should be far enough from imagining, he replied, that I knew the cause of any of them, by heaven I should; for I cannot satisfy myself that, when one is added to one, the one to which the addition is made becomes two, or that the two 97units added together make two by reason of the addition. I cannot understand how, when separated from the other, each of them was one and not two, and now, when they are brought together, the mere juxtaposition or meeting of them should be the cause of their becoming two: neither can I understand how the division of one is the way to make two; for then a different cause would produce the same effect,—as in the former instance the addition and juxtaposition of one to one was the cause of two, in this the separation and subtraction of one from the other would be the cause. Nor am I any longer satisfied that I understand the reason why one or anything else is either generated or destroyed or is at all, but I have in my mind some confused notion of a new method, and can never admit the other.

The great expectations which Socrates had from the doctrine of Anaxagoras, that all was Mind.

Then I heard some one reading, as he said, from a book of Anaxagoras, that mind was the disposer and cause of all, and I was delighted at this notion, which appeared quite admirable, and I said to myself: If mind is the disposer, mind will dispose all for the best, and put each particular in the best place; and I argued that if any one desired to find out the cause of the generation or destruction or existence of anything, he must find out what state of being or doing or suffering was best for that thing, and therefore a man had only to consider the best for himself and others, and then he would also know the worse, since the same science comprehended both. And I rejoiced to think that I had found in Anaxagoras a teacher of the causes of existence such as I desired, and I imagined that he would tell me first whether the earth is flat or round; and whichever was true, he would proceed to explain the cause and the necessity of this being so, and then he would teach me the nature of the best and show that this was best; and if he said that the earth was in the centre, he would further explain that this position was the best, and I should be satisfied with the explanation 98given, and not want any other sort of cause. And I thought that I would then go on and ask him about the sun and moon and stars, and that he would explain to me their comparative swiftness, and their returnings and various states, active and passive, and how all of them were for the best. For I could not imagine that when he spoke of mind as the disposer of them, he would give any other account of their being as they are, except that this was best; and I thought that when he had explained to me in detail the cause of each and the cause of all, he would go on to explain to me what was best for each and what was good for all. These hopes I would not have sold for a large sum of money, and I seized the books and read them as fast as I could in my eagerness to know the better and the worse.

The greatness of his disappointment.Socrates, Cebes.

What expectations I had formed, and how grievously was I disappointed! As I proceeded, I found my philosopher altogether forsaking mind or any other principle of order, but having recourse to air, and ether, and water, and other eccentricities. I might compare him to a person who began by maintaining generally that mind is the cause of the actions of Socrates, but who, when he endeavoured to explain the causes of my several actions in detail, went on to show that I sit here because my body is made up of bones and muscles; and the bones, as he would say, are hard and have joints which divide them, and the muscles are elastic, and they cover the bones, which have also a covering or environment of flesh and skin which contains them; and as the bones are lifted at their joints by the contraction or relaxation of the museles, I am able to bend my limbs, and this is why I am sitting here in a curved posture—that is what he would say; and he would have a similar explanation of my talking to you, which he would attribute to sound, and air, and hearing, and he would assign ten thousand other causes of the same sort, forgetting to mention the true cause, which is, that the Athenians have thought fit to condemn me, and accordingly I have thought it better and more right to remain here and undergo my sentence; for I am inclined to think that these muscles and bones of mine would have gone 99off long ago to Megara or Boeotia—by the dog they would, if they had been moved only by their own idea of what was best, and if I had not chosen the better and nobler part, instead of playing truant and running away, of enduring any punishment which the state inflicts. There is surely a strange confusion of causes and conditions in all this. It may be said, indeed, that without bones and muscles and the other parts of the body I cannot execute my purposes. But to say that I do as I do because of them, and that this is the way in which mind acts, and not from the choice of the best, is a very careless and idle mode of speaking. I wonder that they cannot distinguish the cause from the condition, which the many, feeling about in the dark, are always mistaking and misnaming. And thus one man makes a vortex all round and steadies the earth by the heaven; another gives the air as a support to the earth, which is a sort of broad trough. Any power which in arranging them as they are arranges them for the best never enters into their minds; and instead of finding any superior strength in it, they rather expect to discover another Atlas of the world who is stronger and more everlasting and more containing than the good;—of the obligatory and containing power of the good they think nothing; and yet this is the principle which I would fain learn if any one would teach me. But as I have failed either to discover myself, or to learn of any one else, the nature of the best, I will exhibit to you, if you like, what I have found to be the second best mode of enquiring into the cause.

I should very much like to hear, he replied.

The eye of the soul. The abstract as plain or plainer than the concrete.

Socrates proceeded:—I thought that as I had failed in the contemplation of true existence, I ought to be careful that I did not lose the eye of my soul; as people may injure their bodily eye by observing and gazing on the sun during an eclipse, unless they take the precaution of only looking at the image reflected in the water, or in some similar medium. So in my own case, I was afraid that my soul might be blinded altogether if I looked at things with my eyes or tried to apprehend them by the help of the senses. And I thought that I had better have recourse to the world of mind and seek there the truth of existence. I dare say that the simile is not perfect—for I am very far from admitting that he who contemplates existences through the medium of thought, sees them only 'through a glass darkly,' any more than he who considers them in action and operation. However, this was the method which I adopted: I first assumed some principle which I judged to be the strongest, and then I affirmed as true whatever seemed to agree with this, whether relating to the cause or to anything else; and that which disagreed I regarded as untrue. But I should like to explain my meaning more clearly, as I do not think that you as yet understand me.

No indeed, replied Cebes, not very well.

If the ideas have an absolute existence the soul is immortal.

There is nothing new, he said, in what I am about to tell you; but only what I have been always and everywhere repeating in the previous discussion and on other occasions: I want to show you the nature of that cause which has occupied my thoughts. I shall have to go back to those familiar words which are in the mouth of every one, and first of all assume that there is an absolute beauty and goodness and greatness, and the like; grant me this, and I hope to be able to show you the nature of the cause, and to prove the immortality of the soul.

Cebes said: You may proceed at once with the proof, for I grant you this.

Well, he said, then I should like to know whether you agree with me in the next step; for I cannot help thinking, if there be anything beautiful other than absolute beauty should there be such, that it can be beautiful only in so far as it partakes of absolute beauty—and I should say the same of everything. Do you agree in this notion of the cause?

Yes, he said, I agree.

All things exist by participation in general ideas.

He proceeded: I know nothing and can understand nothing of any other of those wise causes which are alleged; and if a person says to me that the bloom of colour, or form, or any such thing is a source of beauty, I leave all that, which is only confusing to me, and simply and singly, and perhaps foolishly, hold and am assured in my own mind that nothing makes a thing beautiful but the presence and participation of beauty in whatever way or manner obtained; for as to the manner I am uncertain, but I stoutly contend that by beauty all beautiful things become beautiful. This appears to me to be the safest answer which I can give, either to myself or to another, and to this I cling, in the persuasion that this principle will never be overthrown, and that to myself or to any one who asks the question, I may safely reply, That by beauty beautiful things become beautiful. Do you not agree with me?

I do.

And that by greatness only great things become great and greater greater, and by smallness the less become less?

True.

We thus escape certain contradictions of relation.

Then if a person were to remark that A is taller by a head than B, and B less by a head than A, you would refuse to admit his statement, and would stoutly contend that what you mean is only that the greater is greater by, and by reason of, greatness, and the less is less only by, and by reason of, smallness; and thus you would avoid the danger of saying that the greater is greater and the less less by the measure of the head, which is the same in both, and would also avoid the monstrous absurdity of supposing that the greater man is greater by reason of the head, which is small. You would be afraid to draw such an inference, would you not?

Indeed, I should, said Cebes, laughing.

In like manner you would be afraid to say that ten exceeded eight by, and by reason of, two; but would say by, and by reason of, number; or you would say that two cubits exceed one cubit not by a half, but by magnitude?—for there is the same liability to error in all these cases.

Very true, he said.

Socrates, Simmias, Cebes, Echecrates, Phaedo.

Again, would you not be cautious of affirming that the addition of one to one, or the division of one, is the cause of two? And you would loudly asseverate that you know of no way in which anything comes into existence except by participation in its own proper essence, and consequently, as far as you know, the only cause of two is the participation in duality—this is the way to make two, and the participation in one is the way to make one. You would say: I will let alone puzzles of division and addition—wiser heads than mine may answer them; inexperienced as I am, and ready to start, as the proverb says, at my own shadow, I cannot afford to give up the sure ground of a principle. And if any one assails you there, you would not mind him, or answer him, until you had seen whether the consequences which follow agree with one another or not, and when you are further required to give an explanation of this principle, you would go on to assume a higher principle, and a higher, until you found a resting-place in the best of the higher; but you would not confuse the principle and the consequences in your reasoning, like the Eristics—at least if you wanted to discover real existence. Not that this confusion signifies to them, who never care or think about the matter at all, for they have the wit to be well pleased with themselves however great may be the turmoil of their ideas. But you, if you are 102a philosopher, will certainly do as I say.

What you say is most true, said Simmias and Cebes, both speaking at once.

Ech.

Yes, Phaedo; and I do not wonder at their assenting. Any one who has the least sense will acknowledge the wonderful clearness of Socrates' reasoning.

Phaed.

Certainly, Echecrates; and such was the feeling of the whole company at the time.

Ech.

Yes, and equally of ourselves, who were not of the company, and are now listening to your recital. But what followed?

Phaed.

After all this had been admitted, and they had agreed that ideas exist, and that other things participate in them and derive their names from them, Socrates, if I remember rightly, said:—

There may still remain the contradiction of the same person being both greater and less, but this is only because he has greatness or smallness relatively to another person.

This is your way of speaking; and yet when you say that Simmias is greater than Socrates and less than Phaedo, do you not predicate of Simmias both greatness and smallness?

Yes, I do.

But still you allow that Simmias does not really exceed Socrates, as the words may seem to imply, because he is Simmias, but by reason of the size which he has; just as Simmias does not exceed Socrates because he is Simmias, any more than because Socrates is Socrates, but because he has smallness when compared with the greatness of Simmias?

True.

And if Phaedo exceeds him in size, this is not because Phaedo is Phaedo, but because Phaedo has greatness relatively to Simmias, who is comparatively smaller?

That is true.

And therefore Simmias is said to be great, and is also said to be small, because he is in a mean between them, exceeding the smallness of the one by his greatness, and allowing the greatness of the other to exceed his smallness. He added, laughing, I am speaking like a book, but I believe that what I am saying is true.

Simmias assented.

Socrates, Cebes. The idea of greatness can never be small; and the greatness in us drives out smallness.

I speak as I do because I want you to agree with me in thinking, not only that absolute greatness will never be great and also small, but that greatness in us or in the concrete will never admit the small or admit of being exceeded: instead of this, one of two things will happen, either the greater will fly or retire before the opposite, which is the less, or at the approach of the less has already ceased to exist; but will not, if allowing or admitting of smallness, be changed by that; even as I, having received and admitted smallness when compared with Simmias, remain just as I was, and am the same small person. And as the idea of greatness cannot condescend ever to be or become small, in like manner the smallness in us cannot be or become great; nor can any other opposite which remains the same ever 103be of become its own opposite, but either passes away or perishes in the change.

That, replied Cebes, is quite my notion.

Yet the greater comes from the less, and the less from the greater.

Hereupon one of the company, though I do not exactly remember which of them, said: In heaven's name, is not this the direct contrary of what was admitted before—that out of the greater came the less and out of the less the greater, and that opposites were simply generated from opposites; but now this principle seems to be utterly denied.

Distinguish:—The things in which the opposites inhere generate into and out of one another: never the opposites themselves.

Socrates inclined his head to the speaker and listened. I like your courage, he said, in reminding us of this. But you do not observe that there is a difference in the two cases. For then we were speaking of opposites in the concrete, and now of the essential opposite which, as is affirmed, neither in us nor in nature can ever be at variance with itself: then, my friend, we were speaking of things in which opposites are inherent and which are called after them, but now about the opposites which are inherent in them and which give their name to them; and these essential opposites will never, as we maintain, admit of generation into or out of one another. At the same time, turning to Cebes, he said: Are you at all disconcerted, Cebes, at our friend's objection?

No, I do not feel so, said Cebes; and yet I cannot deny that I am often disturbed by objections.

Then we are agreed after all, said Socrates, that the opposite will never in any case be opposed to itself?

To that we are quite agreed, he replied.

Snow may be converted into water at the approach of heat, but not cold into heat.

Yet once more let me ask you to consider the question from another point of view, and see whether you agree with me:—There is a thing which you term heat, and another thing which you term cold?

Certainly.

But are they the same as fire and snow?

Most assuredly not.

Heat is a thing different from fire, and cold is not the same with snow?

Yes.

And yet you will surely admit, that when snow, as was before said, is under the influence of heat, they will not remain snow and heat; but at the advance of the heat, the snow will either retire or perish?

Very true, he replied.

And the fire too at the advance of the cold will either retire or perish; and when the fire is under the influence of the cold, they will not remain as before, fire and cold.

That is true, he said.

And in some cases the name of the idea is not only attached to the idea in an eternal connection, but anything else which, not being the idea, exists only in the form of the idea, may also lay claim to it. I will try to make this clearer by an example:—The odd number is always called by the name of odd?

Very true.

But is this the only thing which is called odd? Are there not other things which have their own name, and yet are called odd, because, although not the same as oddness, they are never without oddness?—that is what I mean to ask—whether numbers such as the number three are not of the class of odd. And there are many other examples: would you not say, for example, that three may be called by its proper name, and also be called odd, which is not the same with three? and this may be said not only of three but also of five, and of every alternate number—each of them without being oddness is odd; and in the same way two and four, and the other series of alternate numbers, has every number even, without being evenness. Do you agree?

Of course.

Not only essential opposites, but some concrete things which contain opposites, exclude each other.

Then now mark the point at which I am aiming:—not only do essential opposites exclude one another, but also concrete things, which, although not in themselves opposed, contain opposites; these, I say, likewise reject the idea which is opposed to that which is contained in them, and when it approaches them they either perish or withdraw. For example; Will not the number three endure annihilation or anything sooner than be converted into an even number, while remaining three?

Very true, said Cebes.

And yet, he said, the number two is certainly not opposed to the number three?

It is not.

Then not only do opposite ideas repel the advance of one another, but also there are other natures which repel the approach of opposites.

Very true, he said.

Suppose, he said, that we endeavour, if possible, to determine what these are.

By all means.

That is to say the opposites which give an impress to other things.

Are they not, Cebes, such as compel the things of which they have possession, not only to take their own form, but also the form of some opposite?

What do you mean?

I mean, as I was just now saying, and as I am sure that you know, that those things which are possessed by the number three must not only be three in number, but must also be odd.

Quite true.

And on this oddness, of which the number three has the impress, the opposite idea will never intrude?

No.

And this impress was given by the odd principle?

Yes.

And to the odd is opposed the even?

True.

Then the idea of the even number will never arrive at three?

No.

Then three has no part in the even?

None.

Then the triad or number three is uneven?

Very true.

Natures may not be opposed, and yet may not admit of opposites; e. g. three is not opposed to two, and yet does not admit the even any more than two admits of the odd.

To return then to my distinction of natures which are not opposed, and yet do not admit opposites—as, in the instance given, three, although not opposed to the even, does not any the more admit of the even, but always brings the opposite into play on the other side; or as two does not receive the odd, or fire the cold—from these examples (and 105there are many more of them) perhaps you may be able to arrive at the general conclusion, that not only opposites will not receive opposites, but also that nothing which brings the opposite will admit the opposite of that which it brings, in that to which it is brought. And here let me recapitulate—for there is no harm in repetition. The number five will not admit the nature of the even, any more than ten, which is the double of five, will admit the nature of the odd. The double has another opposite, and is not strictly opposed to the odd, but nevertheless rejects the odd altogether. Nor again will parts in the ratio 3:2, nor any fraction in which there is a half, nor again in which there is a third, admit the notion of the whole, although they are not opposed to the whole: You will agree?

Yes, he said, I entirely agree and go along with you in that.

The merely verbal truth may be replaced by a higher one.

And now, he said, let us begin again; and do not you answer my question in the words in which I ask it: let me have not the old safe answer of which I spoke at first, but another equally safe, of which the truth will be inferred by you from what has been just said. I mean that if any one asks you 'what that is, of which the inherence makes the body hot,' you will reply not heat (this is what I call the safe and stupid answer), but fire, a far superior answer, which we are now in a condition to give. Or if any one asks you 'why a body is diseased,' you will not say from disease, but from fever; and instead of saying that oddness is the cause of odd numbers, you will say that the monad is the cause of them: and so of things in general, as I dare say that you will understand sufficiently without my adducing any further examples.

Yes, he said, I quite understand you.

Tell me, then, what is that of which the inherence will render the body alive?

We may now say, not life makes alive, but the soul makes alive; and the soul has a life-giving power which does not admit of death and is therefore immortal.

The soul, he replied.

And is this always the case?

Yes, he said, of course.

Then whatever the soul possesses, to that she comes bearing life?

Yes, certainly.

And is there any opposite to life?

There is, he said.

And what is that?

Death.

Then the soul, as has been acknowledged, will never receive the opposite of what she brings.

Impossible, replied Cebes.

And now, he said, what did we just now call that principle which repels the even?

The odd.

And that principle which repels the musical or the just?

The unmusical, he said, and the unjust.

And what do we call that principle which does not admit of death?

The immortal, he said.

And does the soul admit of death?

No.

Then the soul is immortal?

Yes, he said.

And may we say that this has been proven?

Yes, abundantly proven, Socrates, he replied.

Illustrations.

106Supposing that the odd were imperishable, must not three be imperishable?

Of course.

And if that which is cold were imperishable, when the warm principle came attacking the snow, must not the snow have retired whole and unmelted—for it could never have perished, nor could it have remained and admitted the heat?

True, he said.

Again, if the uncooling or warm principle were imperishable, the fire when assailed by cold would not have perished or have been extinguished, but would have gone away unaffected?

Certainly, he said.

And the same may be said of the immortal: if the immortal is also imperishable, the soul when attacked by death cannot perish; for the preceding argument shows that the soul will not admit of death, or ever be dead, any more than three or the odd number will admit of the even, or fire, or the heat in the fire, of the cold. Yet a person may say: 'But although the odd will not become even at the approach of the even, why may not the odd perish and the even take the place of the odd?' Now to him who makes this objection, we cannot answer that the odd principle is imperishable; for this has not been acknowledged, but if this had been acknowledged, there would have been no difficulty in contending that at the approach of the even the odd principle and the number three took their departure; and the same argument would have held good of fire and heat and any other thing.

Very true.

The immortal is imperishable, and therefore the soul is imperishable.

And the same may be said of the immortal: if the immortal is also imperishable, then the soul will be imperishable as well as immortal; but if not, some other proof of her imperishableness will have to be given.

No other proof is needed, he said; for if the immortal, being eternal, is liable to perish, then nothing is imperishable.

Yes, replied Socrates, and yet all men will agree that God, and the essential form of life, and the immortal in general, will never perish.

Yes, all men, he said—that is true; and what is more, gods, if I am not mistaken, as well as men.

Seeing then that the immortal is indestructible, must not the soul, if she is immortal, be also imperishable?

Most certainly.

Then when death attacks a man, the mortal portion of him may be supposed to die, but the immortal retires at the approach of death and is preserved safe and sound?

True.

At death the soul retires into another world.

Then, Cebes, beyond question, the soul is immortal and imperishable, and our souls will truly exist in another 107world!

Socrates, Cebes, Simmias.

I am convinced, Socrates, said Cebes, and have nothing more to object; but if my friend Simmias, or any one else, has any further objection to make, he had better speak out, and not keep silence, since I do not know to what other season he can defer the discussion, if there is anything which he wants to say or to have said.

But I have nothing more to say, replied Simmias; nor can I see any reason for doubt after what has been said. But I still feel and cannot help feeling uncertain in my own mind, when I think of the greatness of the subject and the feebleness of man.

Yes, Simmias, replied Socrates, that is well said: and I may add that first principles, even if they appear certain, should be carefully considered; and when they are satisfactorily ascertained, then, with a sort of hesitating confidence in human reason, you may, I think, follow the course of the argument; and if that be plain and clear, there will be no need for any further enquiry.

Very true.

'Wherefore, seeing all these things, what manner of persons ought we to be?'

But then, O my friends, he said, if the soul is really immortal, what care should be taken of her, not only in respect of the portion of time which is called life, but of eternity! And the danger of neglecting her from this point of view does indeed appear to be awful. If death had only been the end of all, the wicked would have had a good bargain in dying, for they would have been happily quit not only of their body, but of their own evil together with their souls. But now, inasmuch as the soul is manifestly immortal, there is no release or salvation from evil except the attainment of the highest virtue and wisdom. For the soul when on her progress to the world below takes nothing with her but nurture and education; and these are said greatly to benefit or greatly to injure the departed, at the very beginning of his journey thither.

The attendant genius of each brings him after death to the judgmentSocrates, Simmias.The different destinies of pure and impure souls.

For after death, as they say, the genius of each individual, to whom he belonged in life, leads him to a certain place in which the dead are gathered together, whence after judgment has been given they pass into the world below, following the guide, who is appointed to conduct them from this world to the other: and when they have there received their due and remained their time, another guide brings them back again after many revolutions of ages. Now this way to the other world is not, as Aeschylus says in the Telephus, a 108single and straight path—if that were so no guide would be needed, for no one could miss it; but there are many partings of the road, and windings, as I infer from the rites and sacrifices which are offered to the gods below in places where three ways meet on earth. The wise and orderly soul follows in the straight path and is conscious of her surroundings; but the soul which desires the body, and which, as I was relating before, has long been fluttering about the lifeless frame and the world of sight, is after many struggles and many sufferings hardly and with violence carried away by her attendant genius; and when she arrives at the place where the other souls are gathered, if she be impure and have done impure deeds, whether foul murders or other crimes which are the brothers of these, and the works of brothers in crime—from that soul every one flees and turns away; no one will be her companion, no one her guide, but alone she wanders in extremity of evil until certain times are fulfilled, and when they are fulfilled, she is borne irresistibly to her own fitting habitation; as every pure and just soul which has passed through life in the company and under the guidance of the gods has also her own proper home.

Description of the divers regions of earth.

Now the earth has divers wonderful regions, and is indeed in nature and extent very unlike the notions of geographers, as I believe on the authority of one who shall be nameless.

What do you mean, Socrates? said Simmias. I have myself heard many descriptions of the earth, but I do not know, and I should very much like to know, in which of these you put faith.

And I, Simmias, replied Socrates, if I had the art of Glaucus would tell you; although I know not that the art of Glaucus could prove the truth of my tale, which I myself should never be able to prove, and even if I could, I fear, Simmias, that my life would come to an end before the argument was completed. I may describe to you, however, the form and regions of the earth according to my conception of them.

That, said Simmias, will be enough.

The earth is a round body kept in her place by equipoise and the equability of the surrounding element.

Well then, he said, my conviction is, that the earth is a round body in the centre of the heavens, and therefore has 109no need of air or of any similar force to be a support, but is kept there and hindered from falling or inclining any way by the equability of the surrounding heaven and by her own equipoise. For that which, being in equipoise, is in the centre of that which is equably diffused, will not incline any way in any degree, but will always remain in the same state and not deviate. And this is my first notion.

Which is surely a correct one, said Simmias.

Mankind lives only in a small portion of the earth at a distance from the surface. If, like fishes who now and then put their heads out of the water, we could rise to the top of the atmosphere, we should behold the true heaven and the true earth.

Also I believe that the earth is very vast, and that we who dwell in the region extending from the river Phasis to the Pillars of Heracles inhabit a small portion only about the sea, like ants or frogs about a marsh, and that there are other inhabitants of many other like places; for everywhere on the face of the earth there are hollows of various forms and sizes, into which the water and the mist and the lower air collect. But the true earth is pure and situated in the pure heaven—there are the stars also; and it is the heaven which is commonly spoken of by us as the ether, and of which our own earth is the sediment gathering in the hollows beneath. But we who live in these hollows are deceived into the notion that we are dwelling above on the surface of the earth; which is just as if a creature who was at the bottom of the sea were to fancy that he was on the surface of the water, and that the sea was the heaven through which he saw the sun and the other stars, he having never come to the surface by reason of his feebleness and sluggishness, and having never lifted up his head and seen, nor ever heard from one who had seen, how much purer and fairer the world above is than his own. And such is exactly our case: for we are dwelling in a hollow of the earth, and fancy that we are on the surface; and the air we call the heaven, in which we imagine that the stars move. But the fact is, that owing to our feebleness and sluggishness we are prevented from reaching the surface of the air: for if any man could arrive at the exterior limit, or take the wings of a bird and come to the top, then like a fish who puts his head out of the water and sees this world, he would see a world beyond; and, if the nature of man could sustain the sight, he would acknowledge that this other world was the place of the true heaven and the true light and the true earth. For our earth, and the stones, and the entire region which 110surrounds us, are spolit and corroded, as in the sea all things are corroded by the brine, neither is there any noble or perfect growth, but caverns only, and sand, and an endless slough of mud; and even the shore is not to be compared to the fairer sights of this world. And still less is this our world to be compared with the other. Of that upper earth which is under the heaven, I can tell you a charming tale, Simmias, which is well worth hearing.

And we, Socrates, replied Simmias, shall be charmed to listen to you.

The upper earth is in every respect far fairer than the lower. There is gold and purple, and pure light, and trees and flowers lovelier far than our own, and all the stones are more precious than our precious stones.Socrates.The blessed gods dwell there and hold converse with the inhabitants.

The tale, my friend, he said, is as follows:—In the first place, the earth, when looked at from above, is in appearance streaked like one of those balls which have leather coverings in twelve pieces, and is decked with various colours, of which the colours used by painters on earth are in a manner samples. But there the whole earth is made up of them, and they are brighter far and clearer than ours; there is a purple of wonderful lustre, also the radiance of gold, and the white which is in the earth is whiter than any chalk or snow. Of these and other colours the earth is made up, and they are more in number and fairer than the eye of man has ever seen; the very hollows (of which I was speaking) filled with air and water have a colour of their own, and are seen like light gleaming amid the diversity of the other colours, so that the whole presents a single and continuous appearance of variety in unity. And in this fair region everything that grows—trees, and flowers, and fruits—are in a like degree fairer than any here; and there are hills, having stones in them in a like degree smoother, and more transparent, and fairer in colour than our highly-valued emeralds and sardonyxes and jaspers, and other gems, which are but minute fragments of them: for there all the stones are like our precious stones, and fairer still . The reason is, that they are pure, and not, like our precious stones, infected or corroded by the corrupt briny elements which coagulate among us, and which breed foulness and disease both in earth and stones, as well as in animals and plants. They are the jewels of the upper earth, which also 111shines with gold and silver and the like, and they are set in the light of day and are large and abundant and in all places, making the earth a sight to gladden the beholder's eye. And there are animals and men, some in a middle region, others dwelling about the air as we dwell about the sea; others in islands which the air flows round, near the continent; and in a word, the air is used by them as the water and the sea are by us, and the ether is to them what the air is to us. Moreover, the temperament of their seasons is such that they have no disease, and live much longer than we do, and have sight and hearing and smell, and all the other senses, in far greater perfection, in the same proportion that air is purer than water or the ether than air. Also they have temples and sacred places in which the gods really dwell, and they hear their voices and receive their answers, and are conscious of them and hold converse with them; and they see the sun, moon, and stars as they truly are, and their other blessedness is of a piece with this.

Description of the interior of the earth and of the subterranean seas and rivers.

Such is the nature of the whole earth, and of the things which are around the earth; and there are divers regions in the hollows on the face of the globe everywhere, some of them deeper and more extended than that which we inhabit, others deeper but with a narrower opening than ours, and some are shallower and also wider. All have numerous perforations, and there are passages broad and narrow in the interior of the earth, connecting them with one another; and there flows out of and into them, as into basins, a vast tide of water, and huge subterranean streams of perennial rivers, and springs hot and cold, and a great fire, and great rivers of fire, and streams of liquid mud, thin or thick (like the rivers of mud in Sicily, and the lava streams which follow them), and the regions about which they happen to flow are filled up with them. And there is a swinging or see-saw in the interior of the earth which moves all this up and down, and is due to the following cause:—There is a chasm which is the vastest of them all, and pierces right through the whole earth; this is that chasm which Homer describes in the words,—

'Far off, where is the inmost depth beneath the earth;'

and which he in other places, and many other poets, have called Tartarus. And the see-saw is caused by the streams flowing into and out of this chasm, and they each have the nature of the soil through which they flow. And the reason why the streams are always flowing in and out, is that the watery element has no bed or bottom, but is swinging and surging up and down, and the surrounding wind and air do the same; they follow the water up and down, hither and thither, over the earth—just as in the act of respiration the air is always in process of inhalation and exhalation;—and the wind swinging with the water in and out produces fearful and irresistible blasts: when the waters retire with a rush into the lower parts of the earth, as they are called, they flow through the earth in those regions, and fill them up like water raised by a pump, and then when they leave those regions and rush back hither, they again fill the hollows here, and when these are filled, flow through subterranean channels and find their way to their several places, forming seas, and lakes, and rivers, and springs. Thence they again enter the earth, some of them making a long circuit into many lands, others going to a few places and not so distant; and again fall into Tartarus, some at a point a good deal lower than that at which they rose, and others not much lower, but all in some degree lower than the point from which they came. And some burst forth again on the opposite side, and some on the same side, and some wind round the earth with one or many folds like the coils of a serpent, and descend as far as they can, but always return and fall into the chasm. The rivers flowing in either direction can descend only to the centre and no further, for opposite to the rivers is a precipice.

Oceanus, Acheron, Pyriphlegethon, and Styx (or Cocytus).

Now these rivers are many, and mighty, and diverse, and there are four principal ones, of which the greatest and outermost is that called Oceanus, which flows round the earth in a circle; and in the opposite direction flows Acheron, which passes under the earth through desert places into the 113Acherusian lake: this is the lake to the shores of which the souls of the many go when they are dead, and after waiting an appointed time, which is to some a longer and to some a shorter time, they are sent back to be born again as animals. The third river passes out between the two, and near the place of outlet pours into a vast region of fire, and forms a lake larger than the Mediterranean Sea, boiling with water and mud; and proceeding muddy and turbid, and winding about the earth, comes, among other places, to the extremities of the Acherusian lake, but mingles not with the waters of the lake, and after making many coils about the earth plunges into Tartarus at a deeper level. This is that Pyriphlegethon, as the stream is called, which throws up jets of fire in different parts of the earth. The fourth river goes out on the opposite side, and falls first of all into a wild and savage region, which is all of a dark blue colour, like lapis lazuli; and this is that river which is called the Stygian river, and falls into and forms the Lake Styx, and after falling into the lake and receiving strange powers in the waters, passes under the earth, winding round in the opposite direction, and comes near the Acherusian lake from the opposite side to Pyriphlegethon. And the water of this river too mingles with no other, but flows round in a circle and falls into Tartarus over against Pyriphlegethon; and the name of the river, as the poets say, is Cocytus.

The judgment of the dead.

Such is the nature of the other world; and when the dead arrive at the place to which the genius of each severally guides them, first of all, they have sentence passed upon them, as they have lived well and piously or not. And those who appear to have lived neither well nor ill, go to the river Acheron, and embarking in any vessels which they may find, are carried in them to the lake, and there they dwell and are purified of their evil deeds, and having suffered the penalty of the wrongs which they have done to others, they are absolved, and receive the rewards of their good deeds, each of them according to his deserts. But those who appear to be incurable by reason of the greatness of their crimes—who have committed many and terrible deeds of sacrilege, murders foul and violent, or the like—such are hurled into Tartarus which is their suitable destiny, and they never come out. Those again who have committed crimes, which, although great, are not irremediable—who in a moment of anger, for example, have done some violence to a father or a mother, and have repented for the remainder of their lives, or, who have taken 114the life of another under the like extenuating circumstances—these are plunged into Tartarus, the pains of which they are compelled to undergo for a year, but at the end of the year the wave casts them forth—mere homicides by way of Cocytus, parricides and matricides by Pyriphlegethon—and they are borne to the Acherusian lake, and there they lift up their voices and call upon the victims whom they have slain or wronged, to have pity on them, and to be kind to them, and let them come out into the lake. And if they prevail, then they come forth and cease from their troubles; but if not, they are carried back again into Tartarus and from thence into the rivers unceasingly, until they obtain mercy from those whom they have wronged: for that is the sentence inflicted upon them by their judges. Those too who have been pre-eminent for holiness of life are released from this earthly prison, and go to their pure home which is above, and dwell in the purer earth; and of these, such as have duly purified themselves with philosophy live henceforth altogether without the body, in mansions fairer still, which may not be described, and of which the time would fail me to tell.

Wherefore, Simmias, seeing all these things, what ought not we to do that we may obtain virtue and wisdom in this life? Fair is the prize, and the hope great!

These descriptions are not true to the letter, but something like them is true.Socrates, Crito.

A man of sense ought not to say, nor will I be very confident, that the description which I have given of the soul and her mansions is exactly true. But I do say that, inasmuch as the soul is shown to be immortal, he may venture to think, not improperly or unworthily, that something of the kind is true. The venture is a glorious one, and he ought to comfort himself with words like these, which is the reason why I lengthen out the tale. Wherefore, I say, let a man be of good cheer about his soul, who having cast away the pleasures and ornaments of the body as alien to him and working harm rather than good, has sought after the pleasures of knowledge; and has arrayed the soul, not in some foreign attire, but in her own proper jewels, temperance, and justice, and courage, and nobility, and truth—in these adorned she 115is ready to go on her journey to the world below, when her hour comes. You, Simmias and Cebes, and all other men, will depart at some time or other. Me already, as a tragic poet would say, the voice of fate calls. Soon I must drink the poison; and I think that I had better repair to the bath first, in order that the women may not have the trouble of washing my body after I am dead.

When he had done speaking, Crito said: And have you any commands for us, Socrates—anything to say about your children, or any other matter in which we can serve you?

Nothing particular, Crito, he replied: only, as I have always told you, take care of yourselves; that is a service which you may be ever rendering to me and mine and to all of us, whether you promise to do so or not. But if you have no thought for yourselves, and care not to walk according to the rule which I have prescribed for you, not now for the first time, however much you may profess or promise at the moment, it will be of no avail.

We will do our best, said Crito: And in what way shall we bury you?

The dead body which remains is not the true Socrates.Socrates, Crito, The Jailer.

In any way that you like; but you must get hold of me, and take care that I do not run away from you. Then he turned to us, and added with a smile:—I cannot make Crito believe that I am the same Socrates who have been talking and conducting the argument; he fancies that I am the other Socrates whom he will soon see, a dead body—and he asks, How shall he bury me? And though I have spoken many words in the endeavour to show that when I have drunk the poison I shall leave you and go to the joys of the blessed,—these words of mine, with which I was comforting you and myself, have had, as I perceive, no effect upon Crito. And therefore I want you to be surety for me to him now, as at the trial he was surety to the judges for me: but let the promise be of another sort; for he was surety for me to the judges that I would remain, and you must be my surety to him that I shall not remain, but go away and depart; and then he will suffer less at my death, and not be grieved when he sees my body being burned or buried. I would not have him sorrow at my hard lot, or say at the burial, Thus we lay out Socrates, or, Thus we follow him to the grave or bury him; for false words are not only evil in themselves, but they infect the soul with evil. Be of good cheer then, my dear Crito, and say that you are burying my body only, and do with that whatever is usual, and what you 116think best.

He takes leave of his family.

When he had spoken these words, he arose and went into a chamber to bathe; Crito followed him and told us to wait. So we remained behind, talking and thinking of the subject of discourse, and also of the greatness of our sorrow; he was like a father of whom we were being bereaved, and we were about to pass the rest of our lives as orphans. When he had taken the bath his children were brought to him—(he had two young sons and an elder one); and the women of his family also came, and he talked to them and gave them a few directions in the presence of Crito; then he dismissed them and returned to us.

The humanity of the jailer.

Now the hour of sunset was near, for a good deal of time had passed while he was within. When he came out, he sat down with us again after his bath, but not much was said. Soon the jailer, who was the servant of the Eleven, entered and stood by him, saying:—To you, Socrates, whom I know to be the noblest and gentlest and best of all who ever came to this place, I will not impute the angry feelings of other men, who rage and swear at me, when, in obedience to the authorities, I bid them drink the poison—indeed, I am sure that you will not be angry with me; for others, as you are aware, and not I, are to blame. And so fare you well, and try to bear lightly what must needs be—you know my errand. Then bursting into tears he turned away and went out.

Socrates looked at him and said: I return your good wishes, and will do as you bid. Then turning to us, he said, How charming the man is: since I have been in prison he has always been coming to see me, and at times he would talk to me, and was as good to me as could be, and now see how generously he sorrows on my account. We must do as he says, Crito; and therefore let the cup be brought, if the poison is prepared: if not, let the attendant prepare some.

Crito would detain Socrates a little while.

Yet, said Crito, the sun is still upon the hill-tops, and I know that many a one has taken the draught late, and after the announcement has been made to him, he has eaten and drunk, and enjoyed the society of his beloved; do not hurry—there is time enough.

Socrates thinks that there is nothing to be gained by delay.

Socrates said: Yes, Crito, and they of whom you speak are right in so acting, for they think that they will be gainers by the delay; but I am right in not following their example, for I do not think that I should gain anything by 117drinking the poison a little later; I should only be ridiculous in my own eyes for sparing and saving a life which is already forfeit. Please then to do as I say, and not to refuse me.

The poison is brought.He drinks the poison.The company of friends are unable to control themselves.Says Socrates, 'A man should die in peace.'Socrates, Crito, Phaedo.The debt to Asclepius.

Crito made a sign to the servant, who was standing by; and he went out, and having been absent for some time, returned with the jailer carrying the cup of poison. Socrates said: You, my good friend, who are experienced in these matters, shall give me directions how I am to proceed. The man answered: You have only to walk about until your legs are heavy, and then to lie down, and the poison will act. At the same time he handed the cup to Socrates, who in the easiest and gentlest manner, without the least fear or change of colour or feature, looking at the man with all his eyes, Echecrates, as his manner was, took the cup and said: What do you say about making a libation out of this cup to any god? May I, or not? The man answered: We only prepare, Socrates, just so much as we deem enough. I understand, he said: but I may and must ask the gods to prosper my journey from this to the other world—even so—and so be it according to my prayer. Then raising the cup to his lips, quite readily and cheerfully he drank off the poison. And hitherto most of us had been able to control our sorrow; but now when we saw him drinking, and saw too that he had finished the draught, we could no longer forbear, and in spite of myself my own tears were flowing fast; so that I covered my face and wept, not for him, but at the thought of my own calamity in having to part from such a friend. Nor was I the first; for Crito, when he found himself unable to restrain his tears, had got up, and I followed; and at that moment, Apollodorus, who had been weeping all the time, broke out in a loud and passionate cry which made cowards of us all. Socrates alone retained his calmness: What is this strange outcry? he said. I sent away the women mainly in order that they might not misbehave in this way, for I have been told that a man should die in peace. Be quiet then, and have patience. When we heard his words we were ashamed, and refrained our tears; and he walked about until, as he said, his legs began to fail, and then he lay on his back, according to the directions, and the man who gave him the poison now and then looked at his feet and legs; and after a while he pressed his foot hard, and asked him if he could feel; and he said, No; and then his leg, and so upwards and 118upwards, and showed us that he was cold and stiff. And he felt them himself, and said: When the poison reaches the heart, that will be the end. He was beginning to grow cold about the groin, when he uncovered his face, for he had covered himself up, and said—they were his last words—he said: Crito, I owe a cock to Asclepius; will you remember to pay the debt? The debt shall be paid, said Crito; is there anything else? There was no answer to this question; but in a minute or two a movement was heard, and the attendants uncovered him; his eyes were set, and Crito closed his eyes and mouth.

Such was the end, Echecrates, of our friend; concerning whom I may truly say, that of all the men of his time whom I have known, he was the wisest and justest and best.

INTRODUCTION TO GORGIAS.

Gorgias. Introduction.

In several of the dialogues of Plato, doubts have arisen among his interpreters as to which of the various subjects discussed in them is the main thesis. The speakers have the freedom of conversation; no severe rules of art restrict them, and sometimes we are inclined to think, with one of the dramatis personae in the Theaetetus (177 C), that the digressions have the greater interest. Yet in the most irregular of the dialogues there is also a certain natural growth or unity; the beginning is not forgotten at the end, and numerous allusions and references are interspersed, which form the loose connecting links of the whole. We must not neglect this unity, but neither must we attempt to confine the Platonic dialogue on the Procrustean bed of a single idea. (Cp. Introduction to the Phaedrus.)

Two tendencies seem to have best the interpreters of Plato in this matter. First, they have endeavoured to hang the dialogues upon one another by the slightest threads; and have thus been led to opposite and contradictory assertions respecting their order and sequence. The mantle of Schleiermacher has descended upon his successors, who have applied his method with the most various results. The value and use of the method has been hardly, if at all, examined either by him or them. Secondly, they have extended almost indefinitely the scope of each separate dialogue; in this way they think that they have escaped all difficulties, not seeing that what they have gained in generality they have lost in truth and distinctness. Metaphysical conceptions easily pass into one another; and the simpler notions of antiquity, which we can only realize by an effort, imperceptibly blend with the more familiar theories of modern philosophers. An eye for proportion is needed (his own art of measuring) in the study of Plato, as well as of other great artists. We may readily admit that the moral antithesis of good and pleasure, or the intellectual antithesis of knowledge and opinion, being and appearance, are never far off in a Platonic discussion. But because they are in the background, we should not bring them into the foreground, or expect to discern them equally in all the dialogues.

There may be some advantage in drawing out a little the main outlines of the building; but the use of this is limited, and may be easily exaggerated. We may give Plato too much system, and alter the natural form and connection of his thoughts. Under the idea that his dialogues are finished works of art, we may find a reason for everything, and lose the highest characteristic of art, which is simplicity. Most great works receive a new light from a new and original mind. But whether these new lights are true or only suggestive, will depend on their agreement with the spirit of Plato, and the amount of direct evidence which can be urged in support of them. When a theory is running away with us, criticism does a friendly office in counselling moderation, and recalling us to the indications of the text.

Like the Phaedrus, the Gorgias has puzzled students of Plato by the appearance of two or more subjects. Under the cover of rhetoric higher themes are introduced; the argument expands into a general view of the good and evil of man. After making an ineffectual attempt to obtain a sound definition of his art from Gorgias, Socrates assumes the existence of a universal art of flattery or simulation having several branches;—this is the genus of which rhetoric is only one, and not the highest species. To flattery is opposed the true and noble art of life which he who possesses seeks always to impart to others, and which at last triumphs, if not here, at any rate in another world. These two aspects of life and knowledge appear to be the two leading ideas of the dialogue. The true and the false in individuals and states, in the treatment of the soul as well as of the body, are conceived under the forms of true and false art. In the development of this opposition there arise various other questions, such as the two famous paradoxes of Socrates (paradoxes as they are to the world in general, ideals as they may be more worthily called): (1) that to do is worse than to suffer evil; and (2) that when a man has done evil he had better be punished than unpunished; to which may be added (3) a third Socratic paradox or ideal, that bad men do what they think best, but not what they desire, for the desire of all is towards the good. That pleasure is to be distinguished from good is proved by the simultaneousness of pleasure and pain, and by the possibility of the bad having in certain cases pleasures as great as those of the good, or even greater. Not merely rhetoricians, but poets, musicians, and other artists, the whole tribe of statesmen, past as well as present, are included in the class of flatterers. The true and false finally appear before the judgment-seat of the gods below.

The dialogue naturally falls into three divisions, to which the three characters of Gorgias, Polus, and Callicles respectively correspond; and the form and manner change with the stages of the argument. Socrates is deferential towards Gorgias, playful and yet cutting in dealing with the youthful Polus, ironical and sarcastic in his encounter with Callicles. In the first division the question is asked—What is rhetoric? To this there is no answer given, for Gorgias is soon made to contradict himself by Socrates, and the argument is transferred to the hands of his disciple Polus, who rushes to the defence of his master. The answer has at last to be given by Socrates himself, but before he can even explain his meaning to Polus, he must enlighten him upon the great subject of shams or flatteries. When Polus finds his favourite art reduced to the level of cookery, he replies that at any rate rhetoricians, like despots, have great power. Socrates denies that they have any real power, and hence arise the three paradoxes already mentioned. Although they are strange to him, Polus is at last convinced of their truth; at least, they seem to him to follow legitimately from the premises. Thus the second act of the dialogue closes. Then Callicles appears on the scene, at first maintaining that pleasure is good, and that might is right, and that law is nothing but the combination of the many weak against the few strong. When he is confuted he withdraws from the argument, and leaves Socrates to arrive at the conclusion by himself. The conclusion is that there are two kinds of statesmanship, a higher and a lower—that which makes the people better, and that which only flatters them, and he exhorts Callicles to choose the higher. The dialogue terminates with a mythus of a final judgment, in which there will be no more flattery or disguise, and no further use for the teaching of rhetoric.

The characters of the three interlocutors also correspond to the parts which are assigned to them. Gorgias is the great rhetorician, now advanced in years, who goes from city to city displaying his talents, and is celebrated throughout Greece. Like all the Sophists in the dialogues of Plato, he is vain and boastful, yet he has also a certain dignity, and is treated by Socrates with considerable respect. But he is no match for him in dialectics. Although he has been teaching rhetoric all his life, he is still incapable of defining his own art. When his ideas begin to clear up, he is unwilling to admit that rhetoric can be wholly separated from justice and injustice, and this lingering sentiment of morality, or regard for public opinion, enables Socrates to detect him in a contradiction. Like Protagoras, he is described as of a generous nature; he expresses his approbation of Socrates' manner of approaching a question; he is quite 'one of Socrates' sort, ready to be refuted as well as to refute,' and very eager that Callicles and Socrates should have the game out. He knows by experience that rhetoric exercises great influence over other men, but he is unable to explain the puzzle how rhetoric can teach everything and know nothing.

Polus is an impetuous youth, a runaway 'colt,' as Socrates describes him, who wanted originally to have taken the place of Gorgias under the pretext that the old man was tired, and now avails himself of the earliest opportunity to enter the lists. He is said to be the author of a work on rhetoric (462 C), and is again mentioned in the Phaedrus (267 B), as the inventor of balanced or double forms of speech (cp. Gorg. 448 C, 467 C; Symp. 185 C). At first he is violent and ill-mannered, and is angry at seeing his master overthrown. But in the judicious hands of Socrates he is soon restored to good-humour, and compelled to assent to the required conclusion. Like Gorgias, he is overthrown because he compromises; he is unwilling to say that to do is fairer or more honourable than to suffer injustice. Though he is fascinated by the power of rhetoric, and dazzled by the splendour of success, he is not insensible to higher arguments. Plato may have felt that there would be an incongruity in a youth maintaining the cause of injustice against the world. He has never heard the other side of the question, and he listens to the paradoxes, as they appear to him, of Socrates with evident astonishment. He can hardly understand the meaning of Archelaus being miserable, or of rhetoric being only useful in self-accusation. When the argument with him has fairly run out,

Callicles, in whose house they are assembled, is introduced on the stage: he is with difficulty convinced that Socrates is in earnest; for if these things are true, then, as he says with real emotion, the foundations of society are upside down. In him another type of character is represented; he is neither sophist nor philosopher, but man of the world, and an accomplished Athenian gentleman. He might be described in modern language as a cynic or materialist, a lover of power and also of pleasure, and unscrupulous in his means of attaining both. There is no desire on his part to offer any compromise in the interests of morality; nor is any concession made by him. Like Thrasymachus in the Republic, though he is not of the same weak and vulgar class, he consistently maintains that might is right. His great motive of action is political ambition; in this he is characteristically Greek. Like Anytus in the Meno, he is the enemy of the Sophists; but favours the new art of rhetoric, which he regards as an excellent weapon of attack and defence. He is a despiser of mankind as he is of philosophy, and sees in the laws of the state only a violation of the order of nature, which intended that the stronger should govern the weaker (cp. Rep. ii. 358–360). Like other men of the world who are of a speculative turn of mind, he generalizes the bad side of human nature, and has easily brought down his principles to his practice. Philosophy and poetry alike supply him with distinctions suited to his view of human life. He has a good will to Socrates, whose talents he evidently admires, while he censures the puerile use which he makes of them. He expresses a keen intellectual interest in the argument. Like Anytus, again, he has a sympathy with other men of the world; the Athenian statesmen of a former generation, who showed no weakness and made no mistakes, such as Miltiades, Themistocles, Pericles, are his favourites. His ideal of human character is a man of great passions and great powers, which he has developed to the utmost, and which he uses in his own enjoyment and in the government of others. Had Critias been the name instead of Callicles, about whom we know nothing from other sources, the opinions of the man would have seemed to reflect the history of his life.

And now the combat deepens. In Callicles, far more than in any sophist or rhetorician, is concentrated the spirit of evil against which Socrates is contending, the spirit of the world, the spirit of the many contending against the one wise man, of which the Sophists, as he describes them in the Republic, are the imitators rather than the authors, being themselves carried away by the great tide of public opinion. Socrates approaches his antagonist warily from a distance, with a sort of irony which touches with a light hand both his personal vices (probably in allusion to some scandal of the day) and his servility to the populace. At the same time, he is in most profound earnest, as Chaerephon remarks. Callicles soon loses his temper, but the more he is irritated, the more provoking and matter of fact does Socrates become. A repartee of his which appears to have been really made to the 'omniscient' Hippias, according to the testimony of Xenophon (Mem. iv. 4, 6, 10), is introduced (490 E). He is called by Callicles a popular declaimer, and certainly shows that he has the power, in the words of Gorgias, of being 'as long as he pleases,' or 'as short as he pleases' (cp. Protag. 336 D). Callicles exhibits great ability in defending himself and attacking Socrates, whom he accuses of trifling and word-splitting; he is scandalized (p. 494) that the legitimate consequences of his own argument should be stated in plain terms; after the manner of men of the world, he wishes to preserve the decencies of life. But he cannot consistently maintain the bad sense of words; and getting confused between the abstract notions of better, superior, stronger, he is easily turned round by Socrates, and only induced to continue the argument by the authority of Gorgias. Once, when Socrates is describing the manner in which the ambitious citizen has to identify himself with the people, he partially recognizes the truth of his words.

The Socrates of the Gorgias may be compared with the Socrates of the Protagoras and Meno. As in other dialogues, he is the enemy of the Sophists and rhetoricians; and also of the statesmen, whom he regards as another variety of the same species. His behaviour is governed by that of his opponents; the least forwardness or egotism on their part is met by a corresponding irony on the part of Socrates. He must speak, for philosophy will not allow him to be silent. He is indeed more ironical and provoking than in any other of Plato's writings: for he is 'fooled to the top of his bent' by the worldliness of Callicles. But he is also more deeply in earnest. He rises higher than even in the Phaedo and Crito: at first enveloping his moral convictions in a cloud of dust and dialectics, he ends by losing his method, his life, himself, in them. As in the Protagoras and Phaedrus, throwing aside the veil of irony, he makes a speech, but, true to his character, not until his adversary has refused to answer any more questions. The presentiment of his own fate is hanging over him. He is aware that Socrates, the single real teacher of politics, as he ventures to call himself, cannot safely go to war with the whole world, and that in the courts of earth he will be condemned. But he will be justified in the world below. Then the position of Socrates and Callicles will be reversed; all those things 'unfit for ears polite' which Callicles has prophesied as likely to happen to him in this life, the insulting language, the box on the ears, will recoil upon his assailant. (Compare Rep. x. 613, D, E, and the similar reversal of the position of the lawyer and the philosopher in the Theaetetus, 173–176.)

There is an interesting allusion to his own behaviour at the trial of the generals after the battle of Arginusae, which he ironically attributes to his ignorance of the manner in which a vote of the assembly should be taken (473 E). This is said to have happened 'last year' (b. c. 406), and therefore the assumed date of the dialogue has been fixed at 405 b. c., when Socrates would already have been an old man. The date is clearly marked, but is scarcely reconcilable with another indication of time, viz. the 'recent' usurpation of Archelaus, which occurred in the year 413 (470 D); and still less with the 'recent' death (503 B) of Pericles, who really died twenty-four years previously (429 b. c.) and is afterwards reckoned among the statesmen of a past age (cp. 517 A); or with the mention of Nicias, who died in 413, and is nevertheless spoken of as a living witness (472 A, B). But we shall hereafter have reason to observe, that although there is a general consistency of times and persons in the Dialogues of Plato, a precise dramatic date is an invention of his commentators (Preface to Republic, p. ix).

The conclusion of the Dialogue is remarkable, (1) for the truly characteristic declaration of Socrates (p. 509 A) that he is ignorant of the true nature and bearing of these things, while he affirms at the same time that no one can maintain any other view without being ridiculous. The profession of ignorance reminds us of the earlier and more exclusively Socratic Dialogues. But neither in them, nor in the Apology, nor in the Memorabilia of Xenophon, does Socrates express any doubt of the fundamental truths of morality. He evidently regards this 'among the multitude of questions' which agitate human life 'as the principle which alone remains unshaken' (527 B). He does not insist here, any more than in the Phaedo, on the literal truth of the myth, but only on the soundness of the doctrine which is contained in it, that doing wrong is worse than suffering, and that a man should be rather than seem; for the next best thing to a man's being just is that he should be corrected and become just; also that he should avoid all flattery, whether of himself or of others; and that rhetoric should be employed for the maintenance of the right only. The revelation of another life is a recapitulation of the argument in a figure.

(2) Socrates makes the singular remark, that he is himself the only true politician of his age. In other passages, especially in the Apology, he disclaims being a politician at all. There he is convinced that he or any other good man who attempted to resist the popular will would be put to death before he had done any good to himself or others. Here he anticipates such a fate for himself, from the fact that he is 'the only man of the present day who performs his public duties at all.' The two points of view are not really inconsistent, but the difference between them is worth noticing: Socrates is and is not a public man. Not in the ordinary sense, like Alcibiades or Pericles, but in a higher one; and this will sooner or later entail the same consequences on him. He cannot be a private man if he would; neither can he separate morals from politics. Nor is he unwilling to be a politician, although he foresees the dangers which await him; but he must first become a better and wiser man, for he as well as Callicles is in a state of perplexity and uncertainty (527 D, E). And yet there is an inconsistency: for should not Socrates too have taught the citizens better than to put him to death (519)?

And now, as he himself says (506 D), we will 'resume the argument from the beginning.'

Analysis.

Socrates, who is attended by his inseparable disciple, Chaerephon, 447meets Callicles in the streets of Athens. He is informed that he has just missed an exhibition of Gorgias, which he regrets, because he was desirous, not of hearing Gorgias display his rhetoric, but of interrogating him concerning the nature of his art. Callicles proposes that they shall go with him to his own house, where Gorgias is staying. There they find the great 448rhetorician and his younger friend and disciple Polus.

Soc. Put the question to him, Chaerephon. *Ch.* What question? *Soc.* Who is he?—such a question as would elicit from a man the answer, 'I am a cobbler.' Polus suggests that Gorgias may be tired, and desires to answer for him. 'Who is Gorgias?' asks Chaerephon, imitating the manner of his master Socrates. 'One of the best of men, and a proficient in the best and noblest of experimental arts,' etc., replies Polus, in rhetorical and balanced phrases. Socrates is dissatisfied at the length and unmeaningness of the answer; he tells the disconcerted volunteer that he has mistaken the quality for the nature of the art, and remarks to Gorgias, that Polus has learnt how to make a speech, but not how to answer a question. He wishes that Gorgias would answer him. Gorgias is willing enough, and replies to the question asked by Chaerephon,—that he is a rhetorician, and in Homeric language, 'boasts 449himself to be a good one.' At the request of Socrates he promises to be brief; for 'he can be as long as he pleases, and as short as he pleases.' Socrates would have him bestow his length on others, and proceeds to ask him a number of questions, which are answered by him to his own great satisfaction, and with a brevity which excites the admiration of Socrates. The result of the discussion may be summed up as follows:—

450Rhetoric treats of discourse; but music and medicine, and other particular arts, are also concerned with discourse; in what way then does rhetoric differ from them? Gorgias draws a distinction between the arts which deal with words, and the arts which have to do with external actions. Socrates extends this distinction further, and divides all productive arts into two classes: (1) arts which may be carried on in silence; and (2) arts which have to do with words, or in which words are coextensive with action, such as arithmetic, geometry, rhetoric. But still 451Gorgias could hardly have meant to say that arithmetic was the same as rhetoric. Even in the arts which are concerned with words there are differences. What then distinguishes rhetoric from the other arts which have to do with words? 'The words which rhetoric uses relate to the best and greatest of human things.' But tell me, Gorgias, what are the best? 'Health first, beauty next, wealth third,' in the words of the old song, or how would you rank them? The arts will come to you in a body, each 452claiming precedence and saying that her own good is superior to that of the rest—How will you choose between them? 'I should say, Socrates, that the art of persuasion, which gives freedom to all men, and to individuals power in the state, is the greatest 453good.' But what is the exact nature of this persuasion?—is the persevering retort: You could not describe Zeuxis as a painter, or even as a painter of figures, if there were other painters of figures; neither can you define rhetoric simply as an art of persuasion, because there are other arts which persuade, such as arithmetic, which is an art of persuasion about odd and even numbers. Gorgias is made to see the necessity of a further limitation, and he now defines rhetoric as the art of persuading in 454the law courts, and in the assembly, about the just and unjust. But still there are two sorts of persuasion: one which gives knowledge, and another which gives belief without knowledge; and knowledge is always true, but belief may be either true or 455false,—there is therefore a further question: which of the two sorts of persuasion does rhetoric effect in courts of law and assemblies? Plainly that which gives belief and not that which gives knowledge; for no one can impart a real knowledge of such matters to a crowd of persons in a few minutes. And there is another point to be considered:—when the assembly meets to advise about walls or docks or military expeditions, the rhetorician is not taken into counsel, but the architect, or the general. How would Gorgias explain this phenomenon? All who intend to become disciples, of whom there are several in the company, and not Socrates only, are eagerly asking:—About what then will rhetoric teach us to persuade or advise the state?

Gorgias illustrates the nature of rhetoric by adducing the example of Themistocles, who persuaded the Athenians to build their docks and walls, and of Pericles, whom Socrates himself has heard speaking about the middle wall of the Piraeus. He adds 456that he has exercised a similar power over the patients of his brother Herodicus. He could be chosen a physician by the assembly if he pleased, for no physician could compete with a rhetorician in popularity and influence. He could persuade the multitude of anything by the power of his rhetoric; not that the rhetorician ought to abuse this power any more than a boxer 457should abuse the art of self-defence. Rhetoric is a good thing, but, like all good things, may be unlawfully used. Neither is the teacher of the art to be deemed unjust because his pupils are unjust and make a bad use of the lessons which they have learned from him.

Socrates would like to know before he replies, whether Gorgias will quarrel with him if he points out a slight inconsistency into which he has fallen, or whether he, like himself, is one who loves 458to be refuted. Gorgias declares that he is quite one of his sort, but fears that the argument may be tedious to the company. The company cheer, and Chaerephon and Callicles exhort them to proceed. Socrates gently points out the supposed inconsistency into which Gorgias appears to have fallen, and which he is inclined to think may arise out of a misapprehension of his own. 459The rhetorician has been declared by Gorgias to be more persuasive to the ignorant than the physician, or any other expert. And he is said to be ignorant, and this ignorance of his is regarded by Gorgias as a happy condition, for he has escaped the trouble of learning. But is he as ignorant of just and unjust as he 460is of medicine or building? Gorgias is compelled to admit that if he did not know them previously he must learn them from his teacher as a part of the art of rhetoric. But he who has learned carpentry is a carpenter, and he who has learned music is a musician, and he who has learned justice is just. The rhetorician then must be a just man, and rhetoric is a just thing. But Gorgias has already admitted the opposite of this, viz. that rhetoric may be abused, and that the rhetorician may act unjustly. How is the 461inconsistency to be explained?

The fallacy of this argument is twofold; for in the first place, a man may know justice and not be just—here is the old confusion of the arts and the virtues;—nor can any teacher be expected to counteract wholly the bent of natural character; and secondly, a man may have a degree of justice, but not sufficient to prevent him from ever doing wrong. Polus is naturally exasperated at the sophism, which he is unable to detect; of course, he says, the rhetorician, like every one else, will admit that he knows justice (how can he do otherwise when pressed by the interrogations of Socrates?), but he thinks that great want of manners is shown in bringing the argument to such a pass. Socrates ironically replies, that when old men trip, the young set 462them on their legs again; and he is quite willing to retract, if he can be shown to be in error, but upon one condition, which is that Polus studies brevity. Polus is in great indignation at not being allowed to use as many words as he pleases in the free state of Athens. Socrates retorts, that yet harder will be his own case, if he is compelled to stay and listen to them. After some altercation they agree (cp. Protag. 338), that Polus shall ask and Socrates answer.

'What is the art of Rhetoric?' says Polus. Not an art at all, replies Socrates, but a thing which in your book you affirm to have created art. Polus asks, 'What thing?' and Socrates answers, An experience or routine of making a sort of delight or gratification. 'But is not rhetoric a fine thing?' I have not yet told you what rhetoric is. Will you ask me another question—What is cookery? 'What is cookery?' An experience or routine of making a sort of delight or gratification. Then they are the same, or rather fall under the same class, and rhetoric 463has still to be distinguished from cookery. 'What is rhetoric?' asks Polus once more. A part of a not very creditable whole, which may be termed flattery, is the reply. 'But what part?' A shadow of a part of politics. This, as might be expected, is wholly unintelligible, both to Gorgias and Polus; and, in order 464to explain his meaning to them, Socrates draws a distinction between shadows or appearances and realities; e.g. there is real health of body or soul, and the appearance of them; real arts and sciences, and the simulations of them. Now the soul and body have two arts waiting upon them, first the art of politics, which attends on the soul, having a legislative part and a judicial part; and another art attending on the body, which has no generic name, but may also be described as having two divisions, one of which is medicine and the other gymnastic. Corresponding with these four arts or sciences there are four shams or simulations of them, mere experiences, as they may be termed, because they give no reason of their own existence. The art of dressing up is the sham or simulation of gymnastic, the art of cookery, of medicine; 465rhetoric is the simulation of justice, and sophistic of legislation.

They may be summed up in an arithmetical formula:—

Tiring : gymnastic : : cookery : medicine : : sophistic : legislation.

And,

Cookery : medicine : : rhetoric : the art of justice.

And this is the true scheme of them, but when measured only by the gratification which they procure, they become jumbled together and return to their aboriginal chaos. Socrates apologizes for the 466length of his speech, which was necessary to the explanation of the subject, and begs Polus not unnecessarily to retaliate on him.

'Do you mean to say that the rhetoricians are esteemed flatterers?' They are not esteemed at all. 'Why, have they not 467great power, and can they not do whatever they desire?' They have no power, and they only do what they think best, and never what they desire; for they never attain the true object of desire, which is the good. 'As if you, Socrates, would not envy the possessor of despotic power, who can imprison, exile, kill any one whom he -469pleases.' But Socrates replies that he has no wish to put any one to death; he who kills another, even justly, is not to be envied, and he who kills him unjustly is to be pitied; it is better to suffer than to do injustice. He does not consider that going about with a dagger and putting men out of the way, or setting a house on 470fire, is real power. To this Polus assents, on the ground that such acts would be punished, but he is still of opinion that evildoers, if they are unpunished, may be happy enough. He instances Archelaus, son of Perdiccas, the usurper of Macedonia. 471Does not Socrates think him happy?—Socrates would like to know more about him; he cannot pronounce even the great king to be happy, unless he knows his mental and moral condition. Polus explains that Archelaus was a slave, being the son of a woman who was the slave of Alcetas, brother of Perdiccas king of Macedon—and he, by every species of crime, first murdering his uncle and then his cousin and half-brother, obtained the kingdom. This was very wicked, and yet all the world, including 472Socrates, would like to have his place. Socrates dismisses the appeal to numbers; Polus, if he will, may summon all the rich men of Athens, Nicias and his brothers, Aristocrates, the house of Pericles, or any other great family—this is the kind of evidence which is adduced in courts of justice, where truth depends upon numbers. But Socrates employs proof of another sort; his appeal is to one witness only,—that is to say, the person with whom he is speaking; him he will convict out of his own mouth. And he is prepared to show, after his manner, that Archelaus cannot be a wicked man and yet happy. 473

The evil-doer is deemed happy if he escapes, and miserable if he suffers punishment; but Socrates thinks him less miserable if he suffers than if he escapes. Polus is of opinion that such a paradox as this hardly deserves refutation, and is at any rate sufficiently refuted by the fact. Socrates has only to compare the lot of the successful tyrant who is the envy of the world, and of the wretch who, having been detected in a criminal attempt against the state, is crucified or burnt to death. Socrates replies, that if they are both criminal they are both miserable, but that the unpunished is the more miserable of the two. At this Polus laughs outright, which leads Socrates to remark that laughter is a new species of refutation. Polus replies, that he is already refuted; for if he will take the votes of the company, he will find that no one agrees with 474him. To this Socrates rejoins, that he is not a public man, and (referring to his own conduct at the trial of the generals after the battle of Arginusae) is unable to take the suffrages of any company, as he had shown on a recent occasion; he can only deal with one witness at a time, and that is the person with whom he is arguing. But he is certain that in the opinion of any man to do is worse than to suffer evil.

Polus, though he will not admit this, is ready to acknowledge that to do evil is considered the more foul or dishonourable of the two. But what is fair and what is foul; whether the terms are applied to bodies, colours, figures, laws, habits, studies, must they not be defined with reference to pleasure and utility? Polus 475assents to this latter doctrine, and is easily persuaded that the fouler of two things must exceed either in pain or in hurt. But the doing cannot exceed the suffering of evil in pain, and therefore must exceed in hurt. Thus doing is proved by the testimony of Polus himself to be worse or more hurtful than suffering.

There remains the other question: Is a guilty man better off 476when he is punished or when he is unpunished? Socrates replies, that what is done justly is suffered justly: if the act is just, the effect is just; if to punish is just, to be punished is just, and therefore fair, and therefore beneficent; and the benefit is that the soul 477is improved. There are three evils from which a man may suffer, and which affect him in estate, body, and soul;—these are, poverty, disease, injustice; and the foulest of these is injustice, the evil of the soul, because that brings the greatest hurt. And there are 478three arts which heal these evils—trading, medicine, justice—and the fairest of these is justice. Happy is he who has never committed 479injustice, and happy in the second degree he who has been healed by punishment. And therefore the criminal should himself 480go to the judge as he would to the physician, and purge away his crime. Rhetoric will enable him to display his guilt in proper colours, and to sustain himself and others in enduring the necessary 481penalty. And similarly if a man has an enemy, he will desire not to punish him, but that he shall go unpunished and become worse and worse, taking care only that he does no injury to himself. These are at least conceivable uses of the art, and no others have been discovered by us.

Here Callicles, who has been listening in silent amazement, asks Chaerephon whether Socrates is in earnest, and on receiving the assurance that he is, proceeds to ask the same question of Socrates himself. For if such doctrines are true, life must have been turned upside down, and all of us are doing the opposite of what we ought to be doing.

Socrates replies in a style of playful irony, that before men can understand one another they must have some common feeling. And such a community of feeling exists between himself and Callicles, for both of them are lovers, and they have both a pair of 482loves; the beloved of Callicles are the Athenian Demos and Demos the son of Pyrilampes; the beloved of Socrates are Alcibiades and philosophy. The peculiarity of Callicles is that he can never contradict his loves; he changes as his Demos changes in all his opinions; he watches the countenance of both his loves, and repeats their sentiments, and if any one is surprised at his sayings and doings, the explanation of them is, that he is not a free agent, but must always be imitating his two loves. And this is the explanation of Socrates' peculiarities also. He is always repeating what his mistress, Philosophy, is saying to him, who, unlike his other love, Alcibiades, is ever the same, ever true. Callicles must refute her, or he will never be at unity with himself; and discord in life is far worse than the discord of musical sounds.

Callicles answers, that Gorgias was overthrown because, as Polus said, in compliance with popular prejudice he had admitted that if his pupil did not know justice the rhetorician must teach him; and Polus has been similarly entangled, because his modesty led him to admit that to suffer is more honourable than to do injustice. By custom 'yes,' but not by nature, says Callicles. And Socrates is 483always playing between the two points of view, and putting one in the place of the other. In this very argument, what Polus only meant in a conventional sense has been affirmed by him to be a law of nature. For convention says that 'injustice is dishonourable,' but nature says that 'might is right.' And we are always taming down the nobler spirits among us to the conventional level. But sometimes a great man will rise up and reassert his original rights, trampling under foot all our formularies, and then the light 484of natural justice shines forth. Pindar says, 'Law, the king of all, does violence with high hand;' as is indeed proved by the example of Heracles, who drove off the oxen of Geryon and never paid for them.

This is the truth, Socrates, as you will be convinced, if you leave philosophy and pass on to the real business of life. A little philosophy is an excellent thing; too much is the ruin of a man. He who has not 'passed his metaphysics' before he has grown up to manhood will never know the world. Philosophers are ridiculous when they take to politics, and I dare say that politicians are equally ridiculous when they take to philosophy: 'Every man,' as Euripides says, 'is fondest of that in which he is best.' Philosophy 485is graceful in youth, like the lisp of infancy, and should be cultivated as a part of education; but when a grown-up man lisps or studies philosophy, I should like to beat him. None of those over-refined natures ever come to any good; they avoid the busy haunts of men, and skulk in corners, whispering to a few admiring youths, and never giving utterance to any noble sentiments.

For you, Socrates, I have a regard, and therefore I say to you, as Zethus says to Amphion in the play, that you have 'a noble soul 486disguised in a puerile exterior.' And I would have you consider the danger which you and other philosophers incur. For you would not know how to defend yourself if any one accused you in a law-court,—there you would stand, with gaping mouth and dizzy brain, and might be murdered, robbed, boxed on the ears with impunity. Take my advice, then, and get a little common sense; leave to others these frivolities; walk in the ways of the wealthy and be wise.

Socrates professes to have found in Callicles the philosopher's touchstone; and he is certain that any opinion in which they both agree must be the very truth. Callicles has all the three qualities 487which are needed in a critic—knowledge, good-will, frankness; Gorgias and Polus, although learned men, were too modest, and their modesty made them contradict themselves. But Callicles is well-educated; and he is not too modest to speak out (of this he has already given proof), and his good-will is shown both by his own profession and by his giving the same caution against philosophy to Socrates, which Socrates remembers hearing him give 488long ago to his own clique of friends. He will pledge himself to retract any error into which he may have fallen, and which Callicles may point out. But he would like to know first of all what he and Pindar mean by natural justice. Do they suppose that the rule of justice is the rule of the stronger or of the better? 'There is no difference.' Then are not the many superior to the one, and the opinions of the many better? And their opinion is that justice is equality, and that to do is more dishonourable than to suffer wrong. 489And as they are the superior or stronger, this opinion of theirs must be in accordance with natural as well as conventional justice. 'Why will you continue splitting words? Have I not told you that the superior is the better?' But what do you mean by the better? Tell me that, and please to be a little milder in your language, if 490you do not wish to drive me away. 'I mean the worthier, the wiser.' You mean to say that one man of sense ought to rule over ten thousand fools? 'Yes, that is my meaning.' Ought the physician then to have a larger share of meats and drinks? or the weaver to have more coats, or the cobbler larger shoes, or the 491farmer more seed? 'You are always saying the same things, Socrates.' Yes, and on the same subjects too; but you are never saying the same things. For, first, you defined the superior to be the stronger, and then the wiser, and now something else;—what *do* you mean? 'I mean men of political ability, who ought to govern and to have more than the governed.' Than themselves? 'What do you mean?' I mean to say that every man is his own governor. 'I see that you mean those dolts, the temperate. But my doctrine is, that a man should let his desires grow, and take the means of satisfying them. To the many this is impossible, 492and therefore they combine to prevent him. But if he is a king, and has power, how base would he be in submitting to them! To invite the common herd to be lord over him, when he might have the enjoyment of all things! For the truth is, Socrates, that luxury and self-indulgence are virtue and happiness; all the rest is mere talk.'

Socrates compliments Callicles on his frankness in saying what other men only think. According to his view, those who want nothing are not happy. 'Why,' says Callicles, 'if they were, stones and the dead would be happy.' Socrates in reply is led into a half-serious, half-comic vein of reflection. 'Who knows,' as Euripides says, 'whether life may not be death, and death life?' Nay, there are philosophers who maintain that even in life we are 493dead, and that the body (σωμα) is the tomb (σημα) of the soul. And some ingenious Sicilian has made an allegory, in which he represents fools as the uninitiated, who are supposed to be carrying water to a vessel, which is full of holes, in a similarly holey sieve, and this sieve is their own soul. The idea is fanciful, but nevertheless is a figure of a truth which I want to make you acknowledge, viz. that the life of contentment is better than the life of indulgence. Are you disposed to admit that? 'Far otherwise.' Then hear another parable. The life of self-contentment and self-indulgence may be represented respectively by two men, who are filling jars with streams of wine, honey, milk,—the jars of the one are sound, and the jars of the other leaky; the first fills his jars, and has no more trouble with them; the second is always filling 494them, and would suffer extreme misery if he desisted. Are you of the same opinion still? 'Yes, Socrates, and the figure expresses what I mean. For true pleasure is a perpetual stream, flowing in and flowing out. To be hungry and always eating, to be thirsty and always drinking, and to have all the other desires and to satisfy them, that, as I admit, is my idea of happiness.' And to be itching and always scratching? 'I do not deny that there may be happiness even in that.' And to indulge unnatural desires, if they are abundantly satisfied? Callicles is indignant at the introduction of such topics. But he is reminded by Socrates that they are 495introduced, not by him, but by the maintainer of the identity of pleasure and good. Will Callicles still maintain this? 'Yes, for the sake of consistency, he will.' The answer does not satisfy Socrates, who fears that he is losing his touchstone. A profession of seriousness on the part of Callicles reassures him, and they proceed with the argument. Pleasure and good are the same, but knowledge and courage are not the same either with pleasure or good, or with one another. Socrates disproves the first of these statements by showing that two opposites cannot coexist, but must 496alternate with one another—to be well and ill together is impossible. But pleasure and pain are simultaneous, and the cessation of them is simultaneous; e.g. in the case of drinking and thirsting, 497whereas good and evil are not simultaneous, and do not cease simultaneously, and therefore pleasure cannot be the same as good.

Callicles has already lost his temper, and can only be persuaded to go on by the interposition of Gorgias. Socrates, having already guarded against objections by distinguishing courage and knowledge from pleasure and good, proceeds:—The good are good by the presence of good, and the bad are bad by the presence of evil. 498And the brave and wise are good, and the cowardly and foolish are bad. And he who feels pleasure is good, and he who feels pain is bad, and both feel pleasure and pain in nearly the same degree, and sometimes the bad man or coward in a greater degree. 499Therefore the bad man or coward is as good as the brave or may be even better.

Callicles endeavours now to avert the inevitable absurdity by affirming that he and all mankind admitted some pleasures to be good and others bad. The good are the beneficial, and the bad are the hurtful, and we should choose the one and avoid the other. But this, as Socrates observes, is a return to the old doctrine of himself and Polus, that all things should be done for the sake of the good.

500Callicles assents to this, and Socrates, finding that they are agreed in distinguishing pleasure from good, returns to his old 501division of empirical habits, or shams, or flatteries, which study pleasure only, and the arts which are concerned with the higher interests of soul and body. Does Callicles agree to this division? Callicles will agree to anything, in order that he may get through the argument. Which of the arts then are flatteries? Flute-playing, harp-playing, choral exhibitions, the dithyrambics of Cinesias are all equally condemned on the ground that they give pleasure only; and Meles the harp-player, who was the father of 502Cinesias, failed even in that. The stately muse of Tragedy is bent upon pleasure, and not upon improvement. Poetry in general is only a rhetorical address to a mixed audience of men, women, and children. And the orators are very far from speaking with a view to what is best; their way is to humour the assembly as if they were children.

Callicles replies, that this is only true of some of them; others have a real regard for their fellow-citizens. Granted; then there are two species of oratory; the one a flattery, another which has a real regard for the citizens. But where are the orators among whom you find the latter? Callicles admits that there are none 503remaining, but there were such in the days when Themistocles, Cimon, Miltiades, and the great Pericles were still alive. Socrates replies that none of these were true artists, setting before themselves the duty of bringing order out of disorder. The good man 504and true orator has a settled design, running through his life, to which he conforms all his words and actions; he desires to implant justice and eradicate injustice, to implant all virtue and eradicate all vice in the minds of his citizens. He is the physician 505who will not allow the sick man to indulge his appetites with a variety of meats and drinks, but insists on his exercising self-restraint. And this is good for the soul, and better than the unrestrained indulgence which Callicles was recently approving.

Here Callicles, who had been with difficulty brought to this point, turns restive, and suggests that Socrates shall answer his own questions. 'Then,' says Socrates, 'one man must do for two;' and though he had hoped to have given Callicles an 'Amphion' in return for his 'Zethus,' he is willing to proceed; at the 506same time, he hopes that Callicles will correct him, if he falls into error. He recapitulates the advantages which he has already won:—

The pleasant is not the same as the good—Callicles and I are agreed about that,—but pleasure is to be pursued for the sake of the good, and the good is that of which the presence makes us good; we and all things good have acquired some virtue or other. And virtue, whether of body or soul, of things or persons, is not attained by accident, but is due to order and harmonious arrangement. 507And the soul which has order is better than the soul which is without order, and is therefore temperate and is therefore good, and the intemperate is bad. And he who is temperate is also just and brave and pious, and has attained the perfection of goodness and therefore of happiness, and the intemperate whom you approve is the opposite of all this and is wretched. He therefore who would be happy must pursue temperance and avoid intemperance, and if possible escape the necessity of punishment, but if he have done wrong he must endure punishment. In this 508way states and individuals should seek to attain harmony, which, as the wise tell us, is the bond of heaven and earth, of gods and men. Callicles has never discovered the power of geometrical proportion in both worlds; he would have men aim at disproportion and excess. But if he be wrong in this, and if self-control is the true secret of happiness, then the paradox is true that the only use of rhetoric is in self-accusation, and Polus was right in saying that to do wrong is worse than to suffer wrong, and Gorgias was right in saying that the rhetorician must be a just man. And you were wrong in taunting me with my defenceless condition, and in saying that I might be accused or put to death or boxed on the ears with impunity. For I may repeat once more, that to strike is 509worse than to be stricken—to do than to suffer. What I said then is now made fast in adamantine bonds. I myself know not the true nature of these things, but I know that no one can deny my words and not be ridiculous. To do wrong is the greatest of evils, 510and to suffer wrong is the next greatest evil. He who would avoid the last must be a ruler, or the friend of a ruler; and to be the friend he must be the equal of the ruler, and must also resemble him. Under his protection he will suffer no evil, but will he also do no evil? Nay, will he not rather do all the evil which 511he can and escape? And in this way the greatest of all evils will befall him. 'But this imitator of the tyrant,' rejoins Callicles, 'will kill any one who does not similarly imitate him.' Socrates replies that he is not deaf, and that he has heard that repeated many times, and can only reply, that a bad man will kill a good one. 'Yes, and that is the provoking thing.' Not provoking to a man of sense who is not studying the arts which will preserve him from danger; and this, as you say, is the use of rhetoric in courts of justice. But how many other arts are there which also save men from death, and are yet quite humble in their pretensions—such as the art of swimming, or the art of the pilot? Does not the pilot do men at least as much service as the rhetorician, and yet for the voyage from Aegina to Athens he does not charge more than two obols, and when he disembarks is quite unassuming in his demeanour? The reason is that he is not certain 512whether he has done his passengers any good in saving them from death, if one of them is diseased in body, and still more if he is diseased in mind—who can say? The engineer too will often save whole cities, and yet you despise him, and would not allow your son to marry his daughter, or his son to marry yours. But what reason is there in this? For if virtue only means the saving of life, whether your own or another's, you have no right to despise him or any practiser of saving arts. But is not virtue something different from saving and being saved? I would have 513you rather consider whether you ought not to disregard length of life, and think only how you can live best, leaving all besides to the will of Heaven. For you must not expect to have influence either with the Athenian Demos or with Demos the son of Pyrilampes, unless you become like them. What do you say to this?

'There is some truth in what you are saying, but I do not entirely believe you.'

That is because you are in love with Demos. But let us have a little more conversation. You remember the two processes—one which was directed to pleasure, the other which was directed to making men as good as possible. And those who have the care of the city should make the citizens as good as possible. But who 514would undertake a public building, if he had never had a teacher of the art of building, and had never constructed a building before? or who would undertake the duty of state-physician, if he had never cured either himself or any one else? Should we not examine him before we entrusted him with the office? And as Callicles is about to enter public life, should we not examine him? Whom has he made better? For we have already admitted that 515 this is the statesman's proper business. And we must ask the same question about Pericles, and Cimon, and Miltiades, and Themistocles. Whom did they make better? Nay, did not Pericles make the citizens worse? For he gave them pay, and at first he was very popular with them, but at last they condemned him to 516death. Yet surely he would be a bad tamer of animals who, having received them gentle, taught them to kick and butt, and man is an animal; and Pericles who had the charge of man only made him wilder, and more savage and unjust, and therefore he could not have been a good statesman. The same tale might be repeated about Cimon, Themistocles, Miltiades. But the 517chariLoteer who keeps his seat at first is not thrown out when he gains greater experience and skill. The inference is, that the statesman of a past age were no better than those of our own. They may have been cleverer constructors of docks and harbours, but they did not improve the character of the citizens. I have told you again and again (and I purposely use the same images) that the soul, like the body, may be treated in two ways—there is 518the meaner and the higher art. You seemed to understand what I said at the time, but when I ask you who were the really good statesmen, you answer—as if I asked you who were the good trainers, and you answered, Thearion, the baker, Mithoecus, the author of the Sicilian cookery-book, Sarambus, the vintner. And you would be affronted if I told you that these are a parcel of cooks who make men fat only to make them thin. And those whom they have fattened applaud them, instead of finding fault with them, and lay the blame of their subsequent disorders on their physicians. In this respect, Callicles, you are like them; you applaud the statesmen of old, who pandered to the vices of the citizens, and filled the city with docks and harbours, but neglected 519virtue and justice. And when the fit of illness comes, the citizens who in like manner applauded Themistocles, Pericles, and others, will lay hold of you and my friend Alcibiades, and you will suffer for the misdeeds of your predecessors. The old story is always being repeated—'after all his services, the ungrateful city banished him, or condemned him to death.' As if the statesman should not have taught the city better! He surely cannot blame the state for having unjustly used him, any more than the sophist or teacher 520can find fault with his pupils if they cheat him. And the sophist and orator are in the same case; although you admire rhetoric and despise sophistic, whereas sophistic is really the higher of the two. The teacher of the arts takes money, but the teacher of virtue or politics takes no money, because this is the only kind of service which makes the disciple desirous of requiting his teacher.

Socrates concludes by finally asking, to which of the two modes of serving the state Callicles invites him:—'to the inferior and ministerial one,' is the ingenuous reply. That is the only way of 521avoiding death, replies Socrates; and he has heard often enough, and would rather not hear again, that the bad man will kill the good. But he thinks that such a fate is very likely reserved for him, because he remarks that he is the only person who teaches the true art of politics. And very probably, as in the case which 522he described to Polus, he may be the physician who is tried by a jury of children. He cannot say that he has procured the citizens any pleasure, and if any one charges him with perplexing them, or with reviling their elders, he will not be able to make them understand that he has only been actuated by a desire for their good. And therefore there is no saying what his fate may be. 'And do you think that a man who is unable to help himself is in a good condition?' Yes, Callicles, if he have the true self-help, which is never to have said or done any wrong to himself or others. If I had not this kind of self-help, I should be ashamed; but if I die for want of your flattering rhetoric, I shall die in peace. For death is no evil, but to go to the world below laden with offences is the worst of evils. In proof of which I will tell you a tale:—

Under the rule of Cronos, men were judged on the day of their 523death, and when judgment had been given upon them they departed—the good to the islands of the blest, the bad to the house of vengeance. But as they were still living, and had their clothes on at the time when they were being judged, there was favouritism, and Zeus, when he came to the throne, was obliged to alter the mode of procedure, and try them after death, having first sent down Prometheus to take away from them the foreknowledge of death. Minos, Rhadamanthus, and Aeacus were appointed to be the 524judges; Rhadamanthus for Asia, Aeacus for Europe, and Minos was to hold the court of appeal. Now death is the separation of soul and body, but after death soul and body alike retain their characteristics; the fat man, the dandy, the branded slave, are all distinguishable. Some prince or potentate, perhaps even the great king himself, appears before Rhadamanthus, and he instantly 525detects him, though he knows not who he is; he sees the scars of perjury and iniquity, and sends him away to the house of torment.

For there are two classes of souls who undergo punishment—the curable and the incurable. The curable are those who are benefited by their punishment; the incurable are such as Archelaus, who benefit others by becoming a warning to them. The latter class are generally kings and potentates; meaner persons, happily for themselves, have not the same power of doing injustice. Sisyphus and Tityus, not Thersites, are supposed by Homer to be undergoing everlasting punishment. Not that there is anything to prevent a great man from being a good one, as is 526shown by the famous example of Aristeides, the son of Lysimachus. But to Rhadamanthus the souls are only known as good or bad; they are stripped of their dignities and preferments; he despatches the bad to Tartarus, labelled either as curable or incurable, and looks with love and admiration on the soul of some just one, whom he sends to the islands of the blest. Similar is the practice of Aeacus; and Minos overlooks them, holding a golden sceptre, as Odysseus in Homer saw him

'Wielding a sceptre of gold, and giving laws to the dead.'

My wish for myself and my fellow-men is, that we may present our souls undefiled to the judge in that day; my desire in life is to 527be able to meet death. And I exhort you, and retort upon you the reproach which you cast upon me,—that you will stand before the judge, gaping, and with dizzy brain, and any one may box you on the ear, and do you all manner of evil.

Perhaps you think that this is an old wives' fable. But you, who are the three wisest men in Hellas, have nothing better to say, and no one will ever show that to do is better than to suffer evil. A man should study to be, and not merely to seem. If he is bad, he should become good, and avoid all flattery, whether of the many or of the few.

Follow me, then; and if you are looked down upon, that will do you no harm. And when we have practised virtue, we will betake ourselves to politics, but not until we are delivered from the shameful state of ignorance and uncertainty in which we are at present. Let us follow in the way of virtue and justice, and not in the way to which you, Callicles, invite us; for that way is nothing worth.

Introduction.

We will now consider in order some of the principal points of the dialogue. Having regard (1) to the age of Plato and the ironical character of his writings, we may compare him with himself and with other great teachers, and we may note in passing the objections of his critics. And then (2) casting one eye upon him, we may cast another upon ourselves, and endeavour to draw out the great lessons which he teaches for all time, stripped of the accidental form in which they are enveloped.

(1) In the Gorgias, as in nearly all the other dialogues of Plato, we are made aware that formal logic has as yet no existence. The old difficulty of framing a definition recurs. The illusive analogy of the arts and the virtues also continues. The ambiguity of several words, such as nature, custom, the honourable, the good, is not cleared up. The Sophists are still floundering about the distinction of the real and seeming. Figures of speech are made the basis of arguments. The possibility of conceiving a universal art or science, which admits of application to a particular subject-matter, is a difficulty which remains unsolved, and has not altogether ceased to haunt the world at the present day (cp. Charmides, 166 ff.). The defect of clearness is also apparent in Socrates himself, unless we suppose him to be practising on the simplicity of his opponent, or rather perhaps trying an experiment in dialectics. Nothing can be more fallacious than the contradiction which he pretends to have discovered in the answers of Gorgias (see Analysis). The advantages which he gains over Polus are also due to a false antithesis of pleasure and good, and to an erroneous assertion that an agent and a patient may be described by similar predicates;—a mistake which Aristotle partly shares and partly corrects in the Nicomachean Ethics, V. i. 4; xi. 2. Traces of a 'robust sophistry' are likewise discernible in his argument with Callicles (pp. 490, 496, 516).

(2) Although Socrates professes to be convinced by reason only, yet the argument is often a sort of dialectical fiction, by which he conducts himself and others to his own ideal of life and action. And we may sometimes wish that we could have suggested answers to his antagonists, or pointed out to them the rocks which lay concealed under the ambiguous terms good, pleasure, and the like. But it would be as useless to examine his arguments by the requirements of modern logic, as to criticise this ideal from a merely utilitarian point of view. If we say that the ideal is generally regarded as unattainable, and that mankind will by no means agree in thinking that the criminal is happier when punished than when unpunished, any more than they would agree to the stoical paradox that a man may be happy on the rack, Plato has already admitted that the world is against him. Neither does he mean to say that Archelaus is tormented by the stings of conscience; or that the sensations of the impaled criminal are more agreeable than those of the tyrant drowned in luxurious enjoyment. Neither is he speaking, as in the Protagoras, of virtue as a calculation of pleasure, an opinion which he afterwards repudiates in the Phaedo. What then is his meaning? His meaning we shall be able to illustrate best by parallel notions, which, whether justifiable by logic or not, have always existed among mankind. We must remind the reader that Socrates himself implies that he will be understood or appreciated by very few.

He is speaking not of the consciousness of happiness, but of the idea of happiness. When a martyr dies in a good cause, when a soldier falls in battle, we do not suppose that death or wounds are without pain, or that their physical suffering is always compensated by a mental satisfaction. Still we regard them as happy, and we would a thousand times rather have their death than a shameful life. Nor is this only because we believe that they will obtain an immortality of fame, or that they will have crowns of glory in another world, when their enemies and persecutors will be proportionably tormented. Men are found in a few instances to do what is right, without reference to public opinion or to consequences. And we regard them as happy on this ground only, much as Socrates' friends in the opening of the Phaedo are described as regarding him; or as was said of another, 'they looked upon his face as upon the face of an angel.' We are not concerned to justify this idealism by the standard of utility or public opinion, but merely to point out the existence of such a sentiment in the better part of human nature.

The idealism of Plato is founded upon this sentiment. He would maintain that in some sense or other truth and right are alone to be sought, and that all other goods are only desirable as means towards these. He is thought to have erred in 'considering the agent only, and making no reference to the happiness of others, as affected by him.' But the happiness of others or of mankind, if regarded as an end, is really quite as ideal and almost as paradoxical to the common understanding as Plato's conception of happiness. For the greatest happiness of the greatest number may mean also the greatest pain of the individual which will procure the greatest pleasure of the greatest number. Ideas of utility, like those of duty and right, may be pushed to unpleasant consequences. Nor can Plato in the Gorgias be deemed purely self-regarding, considering that Socrates expressly mentions the duty of imparting the truth when discovered to others. Nor must we forget that the side of ethics which regards others is by the ancients merged in politics. Both in Plato and Aristotle, as well as in the Stoics, the social principle, though taking another form, is really far more prominent than in most modern treatises on ethics.

The idealizing of suffering is one of the conceptions which have exercised the greatest influence on mankind. Into the theological import of this, or into the consideration of the errors to which the idea may have given rise, we need not now enter. All will agree that the ideal of the Divine Sufferer, whose words the world would not receive, the man of sorrows of whom the Hebrew prophets spoke, has sunk deep into the heart of the human race. It is a similar picture of suffering goodness which Plato desires to pourtray, not without an allusion to the fate of his master Socrates. He is convinced that, somehow or other, such an one must be happy in life or after death. In the Republic, he endeavours to show that his happiness would be assured here in a well-ordered state. But in the actual condition of human things the wise and good are weak and miserable; such an one is like a man fallen among wild beasts, exposed to every sort of wrong and obloquy.

Plato, like other philosophers, is thus led on to the conclusion, that if 'the ways of God' to man are to be 'justified,' the hopes of another life must be included. If the question could have been put to him, whether a man dying in torments was happy still, even if, as he suggests in the Apology, 'death be only a long sleep,' we can hardly tell what would have been his answer. There have been a few, who, quite independently of rewards and punishments or of posthumous reputation, or any other influence of public opinion, have been willing to sacrifice their lives for the good of others. It is difficult to say how far in such cases an unconscious hope of a future life, or a general faith in the victory of good in the world, may have supported the sufferers. But this extreme idealism is not in accordance with the spirit of Plato. He supposes a day of retribution, in which the good are to be rewarded and the wicked punished (522 E). Though, as he says in the Phaedo, no man of sense will maintain that the details of the stories about another world are true, he will insist that something of the kind is true, and will frame his life with a view to this unknown future. Even in the Republic he introduces a future life as an afterthought, when the superior happiness of the just has been established on what is thought to be an immutable foundation. At the same time he makes a point of determining his main thesis independently of remoter consequences (x. 612 A).

(3) Plato's theory of punishment is partly vindictive, partly corrective. In the Gorgias, as well as in the Phaedo and Republic, a few great criminals, chiefly tyrants, are reserved as examples. But most men have never had the opportunity of attaining this pre-eminence of evil. They are not incurable, and their punishment is intended for their improvement. They are to suffer because they have sinned; like sick men, they must go to the physician and be healed. On this representation of Plato's the criticism has been made, that the analogy of disease and injustice is partial only, and that suffering, instead of improving men, may have just the opposite effect.

Like the general analogy of the arts and the virtues, the analogy of disease and injustice, or of medicine and justice, is certainly imperfect. But ideas must be given through something; the nature of the mind which is unseen can only be represented under figures derived from visible objects. If these figures are suggestive of some new aspect under which the mind may be considered, we cannot find fault with them for not exactly coinciding with the ideas represented. They partake of the imperfect nature of language, and must not be construed in too strict a manner. That Plato sometimes reasons from them as if they were not figures but realities, is due to the defective logical analysis of his age.

Nor does he distinguish between the suffering which improves and the suffering which only punishes and deters. He applies to the sphere of ethics a conception of punishment which is really derived from criminal law. He does not see that such punishment is only negative, and supplies no principle of moral growth or development. He is not far off the higher notion of an education of man to be begun in this world, and to be continued in other stages of existence, which is further developed in the Republic. And Christian thinkers, who have ventured out of the beaten track in their meditations on the 'last things,' have found a ray of light in his writings. But he has not explained how or in what way punishment is to contribute to the improvement of mankind. He has not followed out the principle which he affirms in the Republic, that 'God is the author of evil only with a view to good,' and that 'they were the better for being punished.' Still his doctrine of a future state of rewards and punishments may be compared favourably with that perversion of Christian doctrine which makes the everlasting punishment of human beings depend on a brief moment of time, or even on the accident of an accident. And he has escaped the difficulty which has often beset divines, respecting the future destiny of the meaner sort of men (Thersites and the like), who are neither very good nor very bad, by not counting them worthy of eternal damnation.

We do Plato violence in pressing his figures of speech or chains of argument; and not less so in asking questions which were beyond the horizon of his vision, or did not come within the scope of his design. The main purpose of the Gorgias is not to answer questions about a future world, but to place in antagonism the true and false life, and to contrast the judgments and opinions of men with judgment according to the truth. Plato may be accused of representing a superhuman or transcendental virtue in the description of the just man in the Gorgias, or in the companion portrait of the philosopher in the Theaetetus; and at the same time may be thought to be condemning a state of the world which always has existed and always will exist among men. But such ideals act powerfully on the imagination of mankind. And such condemnations are not mere paradoxes of philosophers, but the natural rebellion of the higher sense of right in man against the ordinary conditions of human life. The greatest statesmen have fallen very far short of the political ideal, and are therefore justly involved in the general condemnation.

Subordinate to the main purpose of the dialogue are some other questions, which may be briefly considered:—

a. The antithesis of good and pleasure, which as in other dialogues is supposed to consist in the permanent nature of the one compared with the transient and relative nature of the other. Good and pleasure, knowledge and sense, truth and opinion, essence and generation, virtue and pleasure, the real and the apparent, the infinite and finite, harmony or beauty and discord, dialectic and rhetoric or poetry, are so many pairs of opposites, which in Plato easily pass into one another, and are seldom kept perfectly distinct. And we must not forget that Plato's conception of pleasure is the Heracleitean flux transferred to the sphere of human conduct. There is some degree of unfairness in opposing the principle of good, which is objective, to the principle of pleasure, which is subjective. For the assertion of the permanence of good is only based on the assumption of its objective character. Had Plato fixed his mind, not on the ideal nature of good, but on the subjective consciousness of happiness, that would have been found to be as transient and precarious as pleasure.

b. The arts or sciences, when pursued without any view to truth, or the improvement of human life, are called flatteries. They are all alike dependent upon the opinion of mankind, from which they are derived. To Plato the whole world appears to be sunk in error, based on self-interest. To this is opposed the one wise man hardly professing to have found truth, yet strong in the conviction that a virtuous life is the only good, whether regarded with reference to this world or to another. Statesmen, Sophists, rhetoricians, poets, are alike brought up for judgment. They are the parodies of wise men, and their arts are the parodies of true arts and sciences. All that they call science is merely the result of that study of the tempers of the Great Beast, which he describes in the Republic.

c. Various other points of contact naturally suggest themselves between the Gorgias and other dialogues, especially the Republic, the Philebus, and the Protagoras. There are closer resemblances both of spirit and language in the Republic than in any other dialogue, the verbal similarity tending to show that they were written at the same period of Plato's life. For the Republic supplies that education and training of which the Gorgias suggests the necessity. The theory of the many weak combining against the few strong in the formation of society (which is indeed a partial truth), is similar in both of them, and is expressed in nearly the same language. The sufferings and fate of the just man, the powerlessness of evil, and the reversal of the situation in another life, are also points of similarity. The poets, like the rhetoricians, are condemned because they aim at pleasure only, as in the Republic they are expelled the State, because they are imitators, and minister to the weaker side of human nature. That poetry is akin to rhetoric may be compared with the analogous notion, which occurs in the Protagoras, that the ancient poets were the Sophists of their day. In some other respects the Protagoras rather offers a contrast than a parallel. The character of Protagoras may be compared with that of Gorgias, but the conception of happiness is different in the two dialogues; being described in the former, according to the old Socratic notion, as deferred or accumulated pleasure, while in the Gorgias, and in the Phaedo, pleasure and good are distinctly opposed.

This opposition is carried out from a speculative point of view in the Philebus. There neither pleasure nor wisdom are allowed to be the chief good, but pleasure and good are not so completely opposed as in the Gorgias. For innocent pleasures, and such as have no antecedent pains, are allowed to rank in the class of goods. The allusion to Gorgias' definition of rhetoric (Philebus, 58 A, B; cp. Gorg. 452 D, E), as the art of persuasion, of all arts the best, for to it all things submit, not by compulsion, but of their own free will—marks a close and perhaps designed connection between the two dialogues. In both the ideas of measure, order, harmony, are the connecting links between the beautiful and the good.

In general spirit and character, that is, in irony and antagonism to public opinion, the Gorgias most nearly resembles the Apology, Crito, and portions of the Republic, and like the Philebus, though from another point of view, may be thought to stand in the same relation to Plato's theory of morals which the Theaetetus bears to his theory of knowledge.

d. A few minor points still remain to be summed up: (1) The extravagant irony in the reason which is assigned for the pilot's modest charge (p. 512); and in the proposed use of rhetoric as an instrument of self-condemnation (p. 480); and in the mighty power of geometrical equality in both worlds (p. 508). (2) The reference of the mythus to the previous discussion should not be overlooked: the fate reserved for incurable criminals such as Archelaus (p. 525); the retaliation of the box on the ears (p. 527); the nakedness of the souls and of the judges who are stript of the clothes or disguises which rhetoric and public opinion have hitherto provided for them (p. 523; cp. Swift's notion that the universe is a suit of clothes, Tale of a Tub, section 2). The fiction seems to have involved Plato in the necessity of supposing that the soul retained a sort of corporeal likeness after death (p. 524). (3) The appeal to the authority of Homer, who says that Odysseus saw Minos in his court 'holding a golden sceptre,' which gives verisimilitude to the tale (p. 526).

It is scarcely necessary to repeat that Plato is playing 'both sides of the game,' and that in criticising the characters of Gorgias and Polus, we are not passing any judgment on historical individuals, but only attempting to analyze the 'dramatis personae' as they were conceived by him. Neither is it necessary to enlarge upon the obvious fact that Plato is a dramatic writer, whose real opinions cannot always be assumed to be those which he puts into the mouth of Socrates, or any other speaker who appears to have the best of the argument; or to repeat the observation that he is a poet as well as a philosopher; or to remark that he is not to be tried by a modern standard, but interpreted with reference to his place in the history of thought and the opinion of his time.

It has been said that the most characteristic feature of the Gorgias is the assertion of the right of dissent, or private judgment. But this mode of stating the question is really opposed both to the spirit of Plato and of ancient philosophy generally. For Plato is not asserting any abstract right or duty of toleration, or advantage to be derived from freedom of thought; indeed, in some other parts of his writings (e. g. Laws, x), he has fairly laid himself open to the charge of intolerance. No speculations had as yet arisen respecting the 'liberty of prophesying;' and Plato is not affirming any abstract right of this nature: but he is asserting the duty and right of the one wise and true man to dissent from the folly and falsehood of the many. At the same time he acknowledges the natural result, which he hardly seeks to avert, that he who speaks the truth to a multitude, regardless of consequences, will probably share the fate of Socrates.

The irony of Plato sometimes veils from us the height of idealism to which he soars. When declaring truths which the many will not receive, he puts on an armour which cannot be pierced by them. The weapons of ridicule are taken out of their hands and the laugh is turned against themselves. The disguises which Socrates assumes are like the parables of the New Testament, or the oracles of the Delphian God; they half conceal, half reveal, his meaning. The more he is in earnest, the more ironical he becomes; and he is never more in earnest or more ironical than in the Gorgias. He hardly troubles himself to answer seriously the objections of Gorgias and Polus, and therefore he sometimes appears to be careless of the ordinary requirements of logic. Yet in the highest sense he is always logical and consistent with himself. The form of the argument may be paradoxical; the substance is an appeal to the higher reason. He is uttering truths before they can be understood, as in all ages the words of philosophers, when they are first uttered, have found the world unprepared for them. A further misunderstanding arises out of the wildness of his humour; he is supposed not only by Callicles, but by the rest of mankind, to be jesting when he is profoundly serious. At length he makes even Polus (p. 468) in earnest. Finally, he drops the argument, and heedless any longer of the forms of dialectic, he loses himself in a sort of triumph, while at the same time he retaliates upon his adversaries. From this confusion of jest and earnest, we may now return to the ideal truth, and draw out in a simple form the main theses of the dialogue.

First Thesis:—

It is a greater evil to do than to suffer injustice.

Compare the New Testament—

'It is better to suffer for well doing than for evil doing.'— 1 Pet. iii. 17.

And the Sermon on the Mount—

'Blessed are they that are persecuted for righteousness' sake.'—Matt. v. 10.

The words of Socrates are more abstract than the words of Christ, but they equally imply that the only real evil is moral evil. The righteous may suffer or die, but they have their reward; and even if they had no reward, would be happier than the wicked. The world, represented by Polus, is ready, when they are asked, to acknowledge that injustice is dishonourable, and for their own sakes men are willing to punish the offender (cp. Rep. ii. 360 D). But they are not equally willing to acknowledge that injustice, even if successful, is essentially evil, and has the nature of disease and death. Especially when crimes are committed on the great scale—the crimes of tyrants, ancient or modern—after a while, seeing that they cannot be undone, and have become a part of history, mankind are disposed to forgive them, not from any magnanimity or charity, but because their feelings are blunted by time, and 'to forgive is convenient to them.' The tangle of good and evil can no longer be unravelled; and although they know that the end cannot justify the means, they feel also that good has often come out of evil. But Socrates would have us pass the same judgment on the tyrant now and always; though he is surrounded by his satellites, and has the applauses of Europe and Asia ringing in his ears; though he is the civilizer or liberator of half a continent, he is, and always will be, the most miserable of men. The greatest consequences for good or for evil cannot alter a hair's breadth the morality of actions which are right or wrong in themselves. This is the standard which Socrates holds up to us. Because politics, and perhaps human life generally, are of a mixed nature we must not allow our principles to sink to the level of our practice.

And so of private individuals—to them, too, the world occasionally speaks of the consequences of their actions:—if they are lovers of pleasure, they will ruin their health; if they are false or dishonest, they will lose their character. But Socrates would speak to them, not of what will be, but of what is—of the present consequence of lowering and degrading the soul. And all higher natures, or perhaps all men everywhere, if they were not tempted by interest or passion, would agree with him—they would rather be the victims than the perpetrators of an act of treachery or of tyranny. Reason tells them that death comes sooner or later to all, and is not so great an evil as an unworthy life, or rather, if rightly regarded, not an evil at all, but to a good man the greatest good. For in all of us there are slumbering ideals of truth and right, which may at any time awaken and develop a new life in us.

Second Thesis:—

It is better to suffer for wrong doing than not to suffer.

There might have been a condition of human life in which the penalty followed at once, and was proportioned to the offence. Moral evil would then be scarcely distinguishable from physical; mankind would avoid vice as they avoid pain or death. But nature, with a view of deepening and enlarging our characters, has for the most part hidden from us the consequences of our actions, and we can only foresee them by an effort of reflection. To awaken in us this habit of reflection is the business of early education, which is continued in maturer years by observation and experience. The spoilt child is in later life said to be unfortunate—he had better have suffered when he was young, and been saved from suffering afterwards. But is not the sovereign equally unfortunate whose education and manner of life are always concealing from him the consequences of his own actions, until at length they are revealed to him in some terrible downfall, which may, perhaps, have been caused not by his own fault? Another illustration is afforded by the pauper and criminal classes, who scarcely reflect at all, except on the means by which they can compass their immediate ends. We pity them, and make allowances for them; but we do not consider that the same principle applies to human actions generally. Not to have been found out in some dishonesty or folly, regarded from a moral or religious point of view, is the greatest of misfortunes. The success of our evil doings is a proof that the gods have ceased to strive with us, and have given us over to ourselves. There is nothing to remind us of our sins, and therefore nothing to correct them. Like our sorrows, they are healed by time;

- 'While rank corruption, mining all within,
- Infects unseen.'

The 'accustomed irony' of Socrates adds a corollary to the argument:—'Would you punish your enemy, you should allow him to escape unpunished'—this is the true retaliation. (Compare the obscure verse of Proverbs, xxv. 21, 22, 'Therefore if thine enemy hunger, feed him,' etc., quoted in Romans xii. 20.)

Men are not in the habit of dwelling upon the dark side of their own lives: they do not easily see themselves as others see them. They are very kind and very blind to their own faults; the rhetoric of self-love is always pleading with them on their own behalf. Adopting a similar figure of speech, Socrates would have them use rhetoric, not in defence but in accusation of themselves. As they are guided by feeling rather than by reason, to their feelings the appeal must be made. They must speak to themselves; they must argue with themselves; they must paint in eloquent words the character of their own evil deeds. To any suffering which they have deserved, they must persuade themselves to submit. Under the figure there lurks a real thought, which, expressed in another form, admits of an easy application to ourselves. For do not we too accuse as well as excuse ourselves? And we call to our aid the rhetoric of prayer and preaching, which the mind silently employs while the struggle between the better and the worse is going on within us. And sometimes we are too hard upon ourselves, because we want to restore the balance which self-love has overthrown or disturbed; and then again we may hear a voice as of a parent consoling us. In religious diaries a sort of drama is often enacted by the consciences of men 'accusing or else excusing them.' For all our life long we are talking with ourselves:—What is thought but speech? What is feeling but rhetoric? And if rhetoric is used on one side only we shall be always in danger of being deceived. And so the words of Socrates, which at first sounded paradoxical, come home to the experience of all of us.

Third Thesis:—

We do not what we will, but what we wish.

Socrates would teach us a lesson which we are slow to learn—that good intentions, and even benevolent actions, when they are not prompted by wisdom, are of no value. We believe something to be for our good which we afterwards find out not to be for our good. The consequences may be inevitable, for they may follow an invariable law, yet they may often be the very opposite of what is expected by us. When we increase pauperism by almsgiving; when we tie up property without regard to changes of circumstances; when we say hastily what we deliberately disapprove; when we do in a moment of passion what upon reflection we regret; when from any want of self-control we give another an advantage over us—we are doing not what we will, but what we wish. All actions of which the consequences are not weighed and foreseen, are of this impotent and paralytic sort; and the author of them has 'the least possible power' while seeming to have the greatest. For he is actually bringing about the reverse of what he intended. And yet the book of nature is open to him, in which he who runs may read if he will exercise ordinary attention; every day offers him experiences of his own and of other men's characters, and he passes them unheeded by. The contemplation of the consequences of actions, and the ignorance of men in regard to them, seems to have led Socrates to his famous thesis:—'Virtue is knowledge;' which is not so much an error or paradox as a half truth, seen first in the twilight of ethical philosophy, but also the half of the truth which is especially needed in the present age. For as the world has grown older men have been too apt to imagine a right and wrong apart from consequences; while a few, on the other hand, have sought to resolve them wholly into their consequences. But Socrates, or Plato for him, neither divides nor identifies them; though the time has not yet arrived either for utilitarian or transcendental systems of moral philosophy, he recognizes the two elements which seem to lie at the basis of morality .

Fourth Thesis:—

To be and not to seem is the end of life.

The Greek in the age of Plato admitted praise to be one of the chief incentives to moral virtue, and to most men the opinion of their fellows is a leading principle of action. Hence a certain element of seeming enters into all things; all or almost all desire to appear better than they are, that they may win the esteem or admiration of others. A man of ability can easily feign the language of piety or virtue; and there is an unconscious as well as a conscious hypocrisy which, according to Socrates, is the worst of the two. Again, there is the sophistry of classes and professions. There are the different opinions about themselves and one another which prevail in different ranks of society. There is the bias given to the mind by the study of one department of human knowledge to the exclusion of the rest; and stronger far the prejudice engendered by a pecuniary or party interest in certain tenets. There is the sophistry of law, the sophistry of medicine, the sophistry of politics, the sophistry of theology. All of these disguises wear the appearance of the truth; some of them are very ancient, and we do not easily disengage ourselves from them; for we have inherited them, and they have become a part of us. The sophistry of an ancient Greek sophist is nothing compared with the sophistry of a religious order, or of a church in which during many ages falsehood has been accumulating, and everything has been said on one side, and nothing on the other. The conventions and customs which we observe in conversation, and the opposition of our interests when we have dealings with one another ('the buyer saith, it is nought—it is nought,' etc.), are always obscuring our sense of truth and right. The sophistry of human nature is far more subtle than the deceit of any one man. Few persons speak freely from their own natures, and scarcely any one dares to think for himself: most of us imperceptibly fall into the opinions of those around us, which we partly help to make. A man who would shake himself loose from them, requires great force of mind; he hardly knows where to begin in the search after truth. On every side he is met by the world, which is not an abstraction of theologians, but the most real of all things, being another name for ourselves when regarded collectively and subjected to the influences of society.

Then comes Socrates, impressed as no other man ever was, with the unreality and untruthfulness of popular opinion, and tells mankind that they must be and not seem. How are they to be? At any rate they must have the spirit and desire to be. If they are ignorant, they must acknowledge their ignorance to themselves; if they are conscious of doing evil, they must learn to do well; if they are weak, and have nothing in them which they can call themselves, they must acquire firmness and consistency; if they are indifferent, they must begin to take an interest in the great questions which surround them. They must try to be what they would fain appear in the eyes of their fellow-men. A single individual cannot easily change public opinion; but he can be true and innocent, simple and independent; he can know what he does, and what he does not know; and though not without an effort, he can form a judgment of his own, at least in common matters. In his most secret actions he can show the same high principle (cp. Rep. viii. 554 D) which he shows when supported and watched by public opinion. And on some fitting occasion, on some question of humanity or truth or right, even an ordinary man, from the natural rectitude of his disposition, may be found to take up arms against a whole tribe of politicians and lawyers, and be too much for them.

Who is the true and who the false statesman?—

The true statesman is he who brings order out of disorder; who first organizes and then administers the government of his own country; and having made a nation, seeks to reconcile the national interests with those of Europe and of mankind. He is not a mere theorist, nor yet a dealer in expedients; the whole and the parts grow together in his mind; while the head is conceiving, the hand is executing. Although obliged to descend to the world, he is not of the world. His thoughts are fixed not on power or riches or extension of territory, but on an ideal state, in which all the citizens have an equal chance of health and life, and the highest education is within the reach of all, and the moral and intellectual qualities of every individual are freely developed, and 'the idea of good' is the animating principle of the whole. Not the attainment of freedom alone, or of order alone, but how to unite freedom with order is the problem which he has to solve.

The statesman who places before himself these lofty aims has undertaken a task which will call forth all his powers. He must control himself before he can control others; he must know mankind before he can manage them. He has no private likes or dislikes; he does not conceal personal enmity under the disguise of moral or political principle: such meannesses, into which men too often fall unintentionally, are absorbed in the consciousness of his mission, and in his love for his country and for mankind. He will sometimes ask himself what the next generation will say of him; not because he is careful of posthumous fame, but because he knows that the result of his life as a whole will then be more fairly judged. He will take time for the execution of his plans; not hurrying them on when the mind of a nation is unprepared for them; but like the Ruler of the Universe Himself, working in the appointed time, for he knows that human life, 'if not long in comparison with eternity' (Rep. vi. 498 D), is sufficient for the fulfilment of many great purposes. He knows, too, that the work will be still going on when he is no longer here; and he will sometimes, especially when his powers are failing, think of that other 'city of which the pattern is in heaven' (Rep. ix. 592 B).

The false politician is the serving-man of the state. In order to govern men he becomes like them; their 'minds are married in conjunction;' they 'bear themselves' like vulgar and tyrannical masters, and he is their obedient servant. The true politician, if he would rule men, must make them like himself; he must 'educate his party' until they cease to be a party; he must breathe into them the spirit which will hereafter give form to their institutions. Politics with him are not a mechanism for seeming what he is not, or for carrying out the will of the majority. Himself a representative man, he is the representative not of the lower but of the higher elements of the nation. There is a better (as well as a worse) public opinion of which he seeks to lay hold; as there is also a deeper current of human affairs in which he is borne up when the waves nearer the shore are threatening him. He acknowledges that he cannot take the world by force—two or three moves on the political chessboard are all that he can foresee—two or three weeks or months are granted to him in which he can provide against a coming struggle. But he knows also that there are permanent principles of politics which are always tending to the well-being of states—better administration, better education, the reconciliation of conflicting elements, increased security against external enemies. These are not 'of to-day or yesterday,' but are the same in all times, and under all forms of government. Then when the storm descends and the winds blow, though he knows not beforehand the hour of danger, the pilot, not like Plato's captain in the Republic, half-blind and deaf, but with penetrating eye and quick ear, is ready to take command of the ship and guide her into port.

The false politician asks not what is true, but what is the opinion of the world—not what is right, but what is expedient. The only measures of which he approves are the measures which will pass. He has no intention of fighting an uphill battle; he keeps the roadway of politics. He is unwilling to incur the persecution and enmity which political convictions would entail upon him. He begins with popularity, and in fair weather sails gallantly along. But unpopularity soon follows him. For men expect their leaders to be better and wiser than themselves: to be their guides in danger, their saviours in extremity; they do not really desire them to obey all the ignorant impulses of the popular mind; and if they fail them in a crisis they are disappointed. Then, as Socrates says, the cry of ingratitude is heard, which is most unreasonable; for the people, who have been taught no better, have done what might be expected of them, and their statesmen have received justice at their hands.

The true statesman is aware that he must adapt himself to times and circumstances. He must have allies if he is to fight against the world; he must enlighten public opinion; he must accustom his followers to act together. Although he is not the mere executor of the will of the majority, he must win over the majority to himself. He is their leader and not their follower, but in order to lead he must also follow. He will neither exaggerate nor undervalue the power of a statesman, neither adopting the 'laissez faire' nor the 'paternal government' principle; but he will, whether he is dealing with children in politics, or with full-grown men, seek to do for the people what the government can do for them, and what, from imperfect education or deficient powers of combination, they cannot do for themselves. He knows that if he does too much for them they will do nothing; and that if he does nothing for them they will in some states of society be utterly helpless. For the many cannot exist without the few; if the material force of a country is from below, wisdom and experience are from above. It is not a small part of human evils which kings and governments make or cure. The statesman is well aware that a great purpose carried out consistently during many years will at last be executed. He is playing for a stake which may be partly determined by some accident, and therefore he will allow largely for the unknown element of politics. But the game being one in which chance and skill are combined, if he plays long enough he is certain of victory. He will not be always consistent, for the world is changing; and though he depends upon the support of a party, he will remember that he is the minister of the whole. He lives not for the present, but for the future, and he is not at all sure that he will be appreciated either now or then. For he may have the existing order of society against him, and may not be remembered by a distant posterity.

There are always discontented idealists in politics who, like Socrates in the Gorgias, find fault with all statesmen past as well as present, not excepting the greatest names of history. Mankind have an uneasy feeling that they ought to be better governed than they are. Just as the actual philosopher falls short of the one wise man, so does the actual statesman fall short of the ideal. And so partly from vanity and egotism, but partly also from a true sense of the faults of eminent men, a temper of dissatisfaction and criticism springs up among those who are ready enough to acknowledge the inferiority of their own powers. No matter whether a statesman makes high professions or none at all—they are reduced sooner or later to the same level. And sometimes the more unscrupulous man is better esteemed than the more conscientious, because he has not equally deceived expectations. Such sentiments may be unjust, but they are widely spread; we constantly find them recurring in reviews and newspapers, and still oftener in private conversation.

We may further observe that the art of government, while in some respects tending to improve, has in others a tendency to degenerate, as institutions become more popular. Governing for the people cannot easily be combined with governing by the people: the interests of classes are too strong for the ideas of the statesman who takes a comprehensive view of the whole. According to Socrates the true governor will find ruin or death staring him in the face, and will only be induced to govern from the fear of being governed by a worse man than himself (Rep. i. 347 C). And in modern times, though the world has grown milder, and the terrible consequences which Plato foretells no longer await an English statesman, any one who is not actuated by a blind ambition will only undertake from a sense of duty a work in which he is most likely to fail; and even if he succeed, will rarely be rewarded by the gratitude of his own generation.

Socrates, who is not a politician at all, tells us that he is the only real politician of his time. Let us illustrate the meaning of his words by applying them to the history of our own country. He would have said that not Pitt or Fox, or Canning or Sir R. Peel, are the real politicians of their time, but Locke, Hume, Adam Smith, Bentham, Ricardo. These during the greater part of their lives occupied an inconsiderable space in the eyes of the public. They were private persons; nevertheless they sowed in the minds of men seeds which in the next generation have become an irresistible power. 'Herein is that saying true, One soweth and another reapeth.' We may imagine with Plato an ideal statesman in whom practice and speculation are perfectly harmonized; for there is no necessary opposition between them. But experience shows that they are commonly divorced—the ordinary politician is the interpreter or executor of the thoughts of others, and hardly ever brings to the birth a new political conception. One or two only in modern times, like the Italian statesman Cavour, have created the world in which they moved. The philosopher is naturally unfitted for political life; his great ideas are not understood by the many; he is a thousand miles away from the questions of the day. Yet perhaps the lives of thinkers, as they are stiller and deeper, are also happier than the lives of those who are more in the public eye. They have the promise of the future, though they are regarded as dreamers and visionaries by their own contemporaries. And when they are no longer here, those who would have been ashamed of them during their lives claim kindred with them, and are proud to be called by their names. (Cp. Thucyd. vi. 16.)

Who is the true poet?

Plato expels the poets from his Republic because they are allied to sense; because they stimulate the emotions; because they are thrice removed from the ideal truth. And in a similar spirit he declares in the Gorgias that the stately muse of tragedy is a votary of pleasure and not of truth. In modern times we almost ridicule the idea of poetry admitting of a moral. The poet and the prophet, or preacher, in primitive antiquity are one and the same; but in later ages they seem to fall apart. The great art of novel writing, that peculiar creation of our own and the last century, which, together with the sister art of review writing, threatens to absorb all literature, has even less of seriousness in her composition. Do we not often hear the novel writer censured for attempting to convey a lesson to the minds of his readers?

Yet the true office of a poet or writer of fiction is not merely to give amusement, or to be the expression of the feelings of mankind, good or bad, or even to increase our knowledge of human nature. There have been poets in modern times, such as Goethe or Wordsworth, who have not forgotten their high vocation of teachers; and the two greatest of the Greek dramatists owe their sublimity to their ethical character. The noblest truths, sung of in the purest and sweetest language, are still the proper material of poetry. The poet clothes them with beauty, and has a power of making them enter into the hearts and memories of men. He has not only to speak of themes above the level of ordinary life, but to speak of them in a deeper and tenderer way than they are ordinarily felt, so as to awaken the feeling of them in others. The old he makes young again; the familiar principle he invests with a new dignity; he finds a noble expression for the common-places of morality and politics. He uses the things of sense so as to indicate what is beyond; he raises us through earth to heaven. He expresses what the better part of us would fain say, and the half-conscious feeling is strengthened by the expression. He is his own critic, for the spirit of poetry and of criticism are not divided in him. His mission is not to disguise men from themselves, but to reveal to them their own nature, and make them better acquainted with the world around them. True poetry is the remembrance of youth, of love, the embodiment in words of the happiest and holiest moments of life, of the noblest thoughts of man, of the greatest deeds of the past. The poet of the future may return to his greater calling of the prophet or teacher; indeed, we hardly know what may not be effected for the human race by a better use of the poetical and imaginative faculty. The reconciliation of poetry, as of religion, with truth, may still be possible. Neither is the element of pleasure to be excluded. For when we substitute a higher pleasure for a lower we raise men in the scale of existence. Might not the novelist, too, make an ideal, or rather many ideals of social life, better than a thousand sermons? Plato, like the Puritans, is too much afraid of poetic and artistic influences. But he is not without a true sense of the noble purposes to which art may be applied (Rep. iii. 401).

Modern poetry is often a sort of plaything, or, in Plato's language, a flattery, a sophistry, or sham, in which, without any serious purpose, the poet lends wings to his fancy and exhibits his gifts of language and metre. Such an one seeks to gratify the taste of his readers; he has the '*savoir faire,*' or trick of writing, but he has not the higher spirit of poetry. He has no conception that true art should bring order out of disorder (504 A); that it should make provision for the soul's highest interest (501 C); that it should be pursued only with a view to 'the improvement of the citizens' (502, 503). He ministers to the weaker side of human nature (Rep. x. 603–605); he idealizes the sensual; he sings the strain of love in the latest fashion; instead of raising men above themselves he brings them back to the 'tyranny of the many masters,' from which all his life long a good man has been praying to be delivered. And often, forgetful of measure and order, he will express not that which is truest, but that which is strongest. Instead of a great and nobly-executed subject, perfect in every part, some fancy of a heated brain is worked out with the strangest incongruity. He is not the master of his words, but his words—perhaps borrowed from another—the faded reflection of some French or German or Italian writer, have the better of him. Though we are not going to banish the poets, how can we suppose that such utterances have any healing or life-giving influence on the minds of men?

'Let us hear the conclusion of the whole matter:' Art then must be true, and politics must be true, and the life of man must be true and not a seeming or sham. In all of them order has to be brought out of disorder, truth out of error and falsehood. This is what we mean by the greatest improvement of man. And so, having considered in what way 'we can best spend the appointed time, we leave the result with God' (512 E). Plato does not say that God will order all things for the best (cp. Phaedo, 97 C), but he indirectly implies that the evils of this life will be corrected in another. And as we are very far from the best imaginable world at present, Plato here, as in the Phaedo and Republic, supposes a purgatory or place of education for mankind in general, and for a very few a Tartarus or hell. The myth which terminates the dialogue is not the revelation, but rather, like all similar descriptions, whether in the Bible or Plato, the veil of another life. For no visible thing can reveal the invisible. Of this Plato, unlike some commentators on Scripture, is fully aware. Neither will he dogmatize about the manner in which we are 'born again' (Rep. vi. 498 D). Only he is prepared to maintain the ultimate triumph of truth and right, and declares that no one, not even the wisest of the Greeks, can affirm any other doctrine without being ridiculous.

There is a further paradox of ethics, in which pleasure and pain are held to be indifferent, and virtue at the time of action and without regard to consequences is happiness. From this elevation or exaggeration of feeling Plato seems to shrink: he leaves it to the Stoics in a later generation to maintain that when impaled or on the rack the philosopher may be happy (cp. Rep. ii. 361 ff.). It is observable that in the Republic he raises this question, but it is not really discussed; the veil of the ideal state, the shadow of another life, are allowed to descend upon it and it passes out of sight. The martyr or sufferer in the cause of right or truth is often supposed to die in raptures, having his eye fixed on a city which is in heaven. But if there were no future, might he not still be happy in the performance of an action which was attended only by a painful death? He himself may be ready to thank God that he was thought worthy to do Him the least service, without looking for a reward; the joys of another life may not have been present to his mind at all. Do we suppose that the mediaeval saint, St. Bernard, St. Francis, St. Catharine of Sienna, or the Catholic priest who lately devoted himself to death by a lingering disease that he might solace and help others, was thinking of the 'sweets' of heaven? No; the work was already heaven to him and enough. Much less will the dying patriot be dreaming of the praises of man or of an immortality of fame: the sense of duty, of right, and trust in God will be sufficient, and as far as the mind can reach, in that hour. If he were certain that there were no life to come, he would not have wished to speak or act otherwise than he did in the cause of truth or of humanity. Neither, on the other hand, will he suppose that God has forsaken him or that the future is to be a mere blank to him. The greatest act of faith, the only faith which cannot pass away, is his who has not known, but yet has believed. A very few among the sons of men have made themselves independent of circumstances, past, present, or to come. He who has attained to such a temper of mind has already present with him eternal life; he needs no arguments to convince him of immortality; he has in him already a principle stronger than death. He who serves man without the thought of reward is deemed to be a more faithful servant than he who works for hire. May not the service of God, which is the more disinterested, be in like manner the higher? And although only a very few in the course of the world's history—Christ himself being one of them—have attained to such a noble conception of God and of the human soul, yet the ideal of them may be present to us, and the remembrance of them be an example to us, and their lives may shed a light on many dark places both of philosophy and theology.

The Myths of Plato.

The myths of Plato are a phenomenon unique in literature. There are four longer ones: these occur in the Phaedrus (244–256), Phaedo (110–115), Gorgias (523–527), and Republic (x. 614–621). That in the Republic is the most elaborate and finished of them. Three of these greater myths, namely those contained in the Phaedo, the Gorgias and the Republic, relate to the destiny of human souls in a future life. The magnificent myth in the Phaedrus treats of the immortality, or rather the eternity of the soul, in which is included a former as well as a future state of existence. To these may be added, (1) the myth, or rather fable, occurring in the Statesman (268–274), in which the life of innocence is contrasted with the ordinary life of man and the consciousness of evil: (2) the legend of the Island of Atlantis, an imaginary history, which is a fragment only, commenced in the Timaeus (21–26) and continued in the Critias: (3) the much less artistic fiction of the foundation of the Cretan colony which is introduced in the preface to the Laws (iii. 702), but soon falls into the background: (4) the beautiful but rather artificial tale of Prometheus and Epimetheus narrated in his rhetorical manner by Protagoras in the dialogue called after him (320–328): (5) the speech at the beginning of the Phaedrus (231–234), which is a parody of the orator Lysias; the rival speech of Socrates and the recantation of it (237–241). To these may be added (6) the tale of the grasshoppers, and (7) the tale of Thamus and of Theuth, both in the Phaedrus (259 and 274–5): (8) the parable of the Cave (Rep. vii. *ad init.*), in which the previous argument is recapitulated, and the nature and degrees of knowledge having been previously set forth in the abstract are represented in a picture: (9) the fiction of the earthborn men (Rep. iii. 414; cp. Laws ii. 664), in which by the adaptation of an old tradition Plato makes a new beginning for his society: (10) the myth of Aristophanes respecting the division of the sexes, Sym. 189: (11) the parable of the noble captain, the pilot, and the mutinous sailors (Rep. vi. 488), in which is represented the relation of the better part of the world, and of the philosopher, to the mob of politicians: (12) the ironical tale of the pilot who plies between Athens and Aegina charging only a small payment for saving men from death, the reason being that he is uncertain whether to live or die is better for them (Gor. 511): (13) the treatment of freemen and citizens by physicians and of slaves by their apprentices,—a somewhat laboured figure of speech intended to illustrate the two different ways in which the laws speak to men (Laws iv. 720). There also occur in Plato continuous images; some of them extend over several pages, appearing and reappearing at intervals: such as the bees stinging and stingless (paupers and thieves) in the Eighth Book of the Republic (554), who are generated in the transition from timocracy to oligarchy: the sun, which is to the visible world what the idea of good is to the intellectual, in the Sixth Book of the Republic (508–9): the composite animal, having the form of a man, but containing under a human skin a lion and a many-headed monster (Rep. ix. 588–9): the great beast (vi. 493), i.e. the populace: and the wild beast within us, meaning the passions which are always liable to break out (ix. 571): the animated comparisons of the degradation of philosophy by the arts to the dishonoured maiden (vi. 495–6), and of the tyrant to the parricide, who 'beats his father, having first taken away his arms' (viii. 569): the dog, who is your only philosopher (ii. 376 B): the grotesque and rather paltry image of the argument wandering about without a head (Laws vi. 752), which is repeated, not improved, from the Gorgias (509 D): the argument personified as veiling her face (Rep. vi. 503 A), as engaged in a chase (iv. 427 C), as breaking upon us in a first, second and third wave (v. 457 C, 472 A, 473 C):—on these figures of speech the changes are rung many times over. It is observable that nearly all these parables or continuous images are found in the Republic; that which occurs in the Theaetetus (149 ff.), of the midwifery of Socrates, is perhaps the only exception. To make the list complete, the mathematical figure of the number of the state (Rep. viii. 546), or the numerical interval which separates king from tyrant (ix. 587–8), should not be forgotten.

The myth in the Gorgias is one of those descriptions of another life which, like the Sixth Aeneid of Virgil, appear to contain reminiscences of the mysteries. It is a vision of the rewards and punishments which await good and bad men after death. It supposes the body to continue and to be in another world what it has become in this. It includes a Paradiso, Purgatorio, and Inferno, like the sister myths of the Phaedo and the Republic. The Inferno is reserved for great criminals only. The argument of the dialogue is frequently referred to, and the meaning breaks through so as rather to destroy the liveliness and consistency of the picture. The structure of the fiction is very slight, the chief point or moral being that in the judgments of another world there is no possibility of concealment: Zeus has taken from men the power of foreseeing death, and brings together the souls both of them and their judges naked and undisguised at the judgment-seat. Both are exposed to view, stripped of the veils and clothes which might prevent them from seeing into or being seen by one another.

The myth of the Phaedo is of the same type, but it is more cosmological, and also more poetical. The beautiful and ingenious fancy occurs to Plato that the upper atmosphere is an earth and heaven in one, a glorified earth, fairer and purer than that in which we dwell. As the fishes live in the ocean, mankind are living in a lower sphere, out of which they put their heads for a moment or two and behold a world beyond. The earth which we inhabit is a sediment of the coarser particles which drop from the world above, and is to that heavenly earth what the desert and the shores of the ocean are to us. A part of the myth consists of description of the interior of the earth, which gives the opportunity of introducing several mythological names and of providing places of torment for the wicked. There is no clear distinction of soul and body; the spirits beneath the earth are spoken of as souls only, yet they retain a sort of shadowy form when they cry for mercy on the shores of the lake; and the philosopher alone is said to have got rid of the body. All the three myths in Plato which relate to the world below have a place for repentant sinners, as well as other homes or places for the very good and very bad. It is a natural reflection which is made by Plato elsewhere, that the two extremes of human character are rarely met with, and that the generality of mankind are between them. Hence a place must be found for them. In the myth of the Phaedo they are carried down the river Acheron to the Acherusian lake, where they dwell, and are purified of their evil deeds, and receive the rewards of their good. There are also incurable sinners, who are cast into Tartarus, there to remain as the penalty of atrocious crimes; these suffer everlastingly. And there is another class of hardly-curable sinners who are allowed from time to time to approach the shores of the Acherusian lake, where they cry to their victims for mercy; which if they obtain they come out into the lake and cease from their torments.

Neither this, nor any of the three greater myths of Plato, nor perhaps any allegory or parable relating to the unseen world, is consistent with itself. The language of philosophy mingles with that of mythology; abstract ideas are transformed into persons, figures of speech into realities. These myths may be compared with the Pilgrim's Progress of Bunyan, in which discussions of theology are mixed up with the incidents of travel, and mythological personages are associated with human beings: they are also garnished with names and phrases taken out of Homer, and with other fragments of Greek tradition.

The myth of the Republic is more subtle and also more consistent than either of the two others. It has a greater verisimilitude than they have, and is full of touches which recall the experiences of human life. It will be noticed by an attentive reader that the twelve days during which Er lay in a trance after he was slain coincide with the time passed by the spirits in their pilgrimage. It is a curious observation, not often made, that good men who have lived in a well-governed city (shall we say in a religious and respectable society?) are more likely to make mistakes in their choice of life than those who have had more experience of the world and of evil. It is a more familiar remark that we constantly blame others when we have only ourselves to blame; and the philosopher must acknowledge, however reluctantly, that there is an element of chance in human life with which it is sometimes impossible for man to cope. That men drink more of the waters of forgetfulness than is good for them is a poetical description of a familiar truth. We have many of us known men who, like Odysseus, have wearied of ambition and have only desired rest. We should like to know what became of the infants 'dying almost as soon as they were born,' but Plato only raises, without satisfying, our curiosity. The two companies of souls, ascending and descending at either chasm of heaven and earth, and conversing when they come out into the meadow, the majestic figures of the judges sitting in heaven, the voice heard by Ardiaeus, are features of the great allegory which have an indescribable grandeur and power. The remark already made respecting the inconsistency of the two other myths must be extended also to this: it is at once an orrery, or model of the heavens, and a picture of the Day of Judgment.

The three myths are unlike anything else in Plato. There is an Oriental, or rather an Egyptian element in them, and they have an affinity to the mysteries and to the Orphic modes of worship. To a certain extent they are un-Greek; at any rate there is hardly anything like them in other Greek writings which have a serious purpose; in spirit they are mediaeval. They are akin to what may be termed the underground religion in all ages and countries. They are presented in the most lively and graphic manner, but they are never insisted on as true; it is only affirmed that nothing better can be said about a future life. Plato seems to make use of them when he has reached the limits of human knowledge; or, to borrow an expression of his own, when he is standing on the outside of the intellectual world. They are very simple in style; a few touches bring the picture home to the mind, and make it present to us. They have also a kind of authority gained by the employment of sacred and familiar names, just as mere fragments of the words of Scripture, put together in any form and applied to any subject, have a power of their own. They are a substitute for poetry and mythology; and they are also a reform of mythology. The moral of them may be summed up in a word or two: After death the Judgment; and 'there is some better thing remaining for the good than for the evil.'

All literature gathers into itself many elements of the past: for example, the tale of the earth-born men in the Republic appears at first sight to be an extravagant fancy, but it is restored to propriety when we remember that it is based on a legendary belief. The art of making stories of ghosts and apparitions credible is said to consist in the manner of telling them. The effect is gained by many literary and conversational devices, such as the previous raising of curiosity, the mention of little circumstances, simplicity, picturesqueness, the naturalness of the occasion, and the like. This art is possessed by Plato in a degree which has never been equalled.

The myth in the Phaedrus is even greater than the myths which have been already described, but is of a different character. It treats of a former rather than of a future life. It represents the conflict of reason aided by passion or righteous indignation on the one hand, and of the animal lusts and instincts on the other. The soul of man has followed the company of some god, and seen truth in the form of the universal before it was born in this world. Our present life is the result of the struggle which was then carried on. This world is relative to a former world, as it is often projected into a future. We ask the question, Where were men before birth? as we likewise enquire, What will become of them after death? The first question is unfamiliar to us, and therefore seems to be unnatural; but if we survey the whole human race, it has been as influential and as widely spread as the other. In the Phaedrus it is really a figure of speech in which the 'spiritual combat' of this life is represented. The majesty and power of the whole passage—especially of what may be called the theme or proem (beginning 'The mind through all her being is immortal') can only be rendered very inadequately in another language.

The myth in the Statesman relates to a former cycle of existence, in which men were born of the earth, and by the reversal of the earth's motion had their lives reversed and were restored to youth and beauty: the dead came to life; the old grew middle-aged, and the middle-aged young; the youth became a child, the child an infant, the infant vanished into the earth. The connection between the reversal of the earth's motion and the reversal of human life is of course verbal only, yet Plato, like theologians in other ages, argues from the consistency of the tale to its truth. The new order of the world was immediately under the government of God; it was a state of innocence in which men had neither wants nor cares, in which the earth brought forth all things spontaneously, and God was to man what man now is to the animals. There were no great estates, or families, or private possessions, nor any traditions of the past, because men were all born out of the earth. This is what Plato calls the 'reign of Cronos;' and in like manner he connects the reversal of the earth's motion with some legend of which he himself was probably the inventor.

The question is then asked, under which of these two cycles of existence was man the happier,—under that of Cronos, which was a state of innocence, or that of Zeus, which is our ordinary life? For a while Plato balances the two sides of the serious controversy, which he has suggested in a figure. The answer depends on another question: What use did the children of Cronos make of their time? They had boundless leisure and the faculty of discoursing, not only with one another, but with the animals. Did they employ these advantages with a view to philosophy, gathering from every nature some addition to their store of knowledge? or, Did they pass their time in eating and drinking and telling stories to one another and to the beasts?—in either case there would be no difficulty in answering. But then, as Plato rather mischievously adds, 'Nobody knows what they did,' and therefore the doubt must remain undetermined.

To the first there succeeds a second epoch. After another natural convulsion, in which the order of the world and of human life is once more reversed, God withdraws his guiding hand, and man is left to the government of himself. The world begins again, and arts and laws are slowly and painfully invented. A secular age succeeds to a theocratical. In this fanciful tale Plato has dropped, or almost dropped, the garb of mythology. He suggests several curious and important thoughts, such as the possibility of a state of innocence, the existence of a world without traditions, and the difference between human and divine government. He has also carried a step further his speculations concerning the abolition of the family and of property, which he supposes to have no place among the children of Cronos any more than in the ideal state.

It is characteristic of Plato and of his age to pass from the abstract to the concrete, from poetry to reality. Language is the expression of the seen, and also of the unseen, and moves in a region between them. A great writer knows how to strike both these chords, sometimes remaining within the sphere of the visible, and then again comprehending a wider range and soaring to the abstract and universal. Even in the same sentence he may employ both modes of speech not improperly or inharmoniously. It is useless to criticise the broken metaphors of Plato, if the effect of the whole is to create a picture not such as can be painted on canvas, but which is full of life and meaning to the reader. A poem may be contained in a word or two, which may call up not one but many latent images; or half reveal to us by a sudden flash the thoughts of many hearts. Often the rapid transition from one image to another is pleasing to us: on the other hand, any single figure of speech if too often repeated, or worked out too much at length, becomes prosy and monotonous. In theology and philosophy we necessarily include both 'the moral law within and the starry heaven above,' and pass from one to the other (cp. for examples Psalm xviii. 1–

25, xix. 1–9, etc.). Whether such a use of language is puerile or noble depends upon the genius of the writer or speaker, and the familiarity of the associations employed.

In the myths and parables of Plato the ease and grace of conversation is not forgotten: they are spoken, not written words, stories which are told to a living audience, and so well told that we are more than half-inclined to believe them (cp. Phaedrus 274). As in conversation too, the striking image or figure of speech is not forgotten, but is quickly caught up, and alluded to again and again; as it would still be in our own day in a genial and sympathetic society. The descriptions of Plato have a greater life and reality than is to be found in any modern writing. This is due to their homeliness and simplicity. Plato can do with words just as he pleases; to him they are indeed 'more plastic than wax' (Rep. ix. 588 D). We are in the habit of opposing speech and writing, poetry and prose. But he has discovered a use of language in which they are united; which gives a fitting expression to the highest truths; and in which the trifles of courtesy and the familiarities of daily life are not overlooked.

GORGIAS.

PERSONS OF THE DIALOGUE.

Callicles.

Socrates.

Chaerephon.

Gorgias.

Polus.

Scene: The house of Callicles.

Callicles.

Gorgias. Socrates, Callicles. Chaerephon.

447 The wise man, as the proverb says, is late for a fray, but not for a feast.

Socrates.

And are we late for a feast?

Cal.

Yes, and a delightful feast; for Gorgias has just been exhibiting to us many fine things.

Soc.

It is not my fault, Callicles; our friend Chaerephon is to blame; for he would keep us loitering in the Agora.

Chaerephon.

Never mind, Socrates; the misfortune of which I have been the cause I will also repair; for Gorgias is a friend of mine, and I will make him give the exhibition again either now, or, if you prefer, at some other time.

Cal.

What is the matter, Chaerephon—does Socrates want to hear Gorgias?

Chaer.

Yes, that was our intention in coming.

Cal.

Come into my house, then; for Gorgias is staying with me, and he shall exhibit to you.

Soc.

Very good, Callicles; but will he answer our questions? for I want to hear from him what is the nature of his art, and what it is which he professes and teaches; he may, as you [Chaerephon] suggest, defer the exhibition to some other time.

Cal.

Socrates, Gorgias, Chaerephon, Polus.

There is nothing like asking him, Socrates; and indeed to answer questions is a part of his exhibition, for he was saying only just now, that any one in my house might put any question to him, and that he would answer.

Soc.

How fortunate! will you ask him, Chaerephon—?

Chaer.

What shall I ask him?

Soc.

Ask him who he is.

Chaer.

What do you mean?

Soc.

I mean such a question as would elicit from him, if he had been a maker of shoes, the answer that he is a cobbler. Do you understand?

Chaer.

I understand, and will ask him: Tell me, Gorgias, is our friend Callicles right in saying that you undertake to answer any questions which you are asked?

Gorgias.

Quite right, Chaerephon: I was saying as much only just now; and I may add, that many years have elapsed 448 since any one has asked me a new one.

Chaer.

Then you must be very ready, Gorgias.

Gor.

Of that, Chaerephon, you can make trial.

Polus.

Polus offers to take the place of Gorgias in the argument.

Yes, indeed, and if you like, Chaerephon, you may make trial of me too, for I think that Gorgias, who has been talking a long time, is tired.

Chaer.

And do you, Polus, think that you can answer better than Gorgias?

Pol.

What does that matter if I answer well enough for you?

Chaer.

Not at all:—and you shall answer if you like.

Pol.

Ask:—

Chaer.

My question is this: If Gorgias had the skill of his brother Herodicus, what ought we to call him? Ought he not to have the name which is given to his brother?

Pol.

Certainly.

Chaer.

Then we should be right in calling him a physician?

Pol.

Yes.

Chaer.

The question is asked, 'What is Gorgias?'

And if he had the skill of Aristophon the son of Aglaophon, or of his brother Polygnotus, what ought we to call him?

Pol.

Clearly, a painter.

Chaer.

But now what shall we call him—what is the art in which he is skilled?

Pol.

Socrates, Gorgias, Polus.Answer:—Gorgias is one of the best proficients in the noblest art.

O Chaerephon, there are many arts among mankind which are experimental, and have their origin in experience, for experience makes the days of men to proceed according to art, and inexperience according to chance, and different persons in different ways are proficient in different arts, and the best persons in the best arts. And our friend Gorgias is one of the best, and the art in which he is a proficient is the noblest.

Soc.

Polus has been taught how to make a capital speech, Gorgias; but he is not fulfilling the promise which he made to Chaerephon.

Gor.

What do you mean, Socrates?

Soc.

I mean that he has not exactly answered the question which he was asked.

Gor.

Then why not ask him yourself?

Soc.

But I would much rather ask you, if you are disposed to answer: for I see, from the few words which Polus has uttered, that he has attended more to the art which is called rhetoric than to dialectic.

Pol.

What makes you say so, Socrates?

Soc.

This is no answer.

Because, Polus, when Chaerephon asked you what was the art which Gorgias knows, you praised it as if you were answering some one who found fault with it, but you never said what the art was.

Pol.

Why, did I not say that it was the noblest of arts?

Soc.

Yes, indeed, but that was no answer to the question: nobody asked what was the quality, but what was the nature, of the art, and by what name we were to describe Gorgias. 449And I would still beg you briefly and clearly, as you answered Chaerephon when he asked you at first, to say what this art is, and what we ought to call Gorgias: Or rather, Gorgias, let me turn to you, and ask the same question,— what are we to call you, and what is the art which you profess?

Gor.

Better:—Gorgias is a rhetorician and a teacher of rhetoric.

Rhetoric, Socrates, is my art.

Soc.

Then I am to call you a rhetorician?

Gor.

Yes, Socrates, and a good one too, if you would call me that which, in Homeric language, 'I boast myself to be.'

Soc.

I should wish to do so.

Gor.

Then pray do.

Soc.

Socrates, Gorgias.

And are we to say that you are able to make other men rhetoricians?

Gor.

Yes, that is exactly what I profess to make them, not only at Athens, but in all places.

Soc.

And will you continue to ask and answer questions, Gorgias, as we are at present doing, and reserve for another occasion the longer mode of speech which Polus was attempting? Will you keep your promise, and answer shortly the questions which are asked of you?

Gor.

Some answers, Socrates, are of necessity longer; but I will do my best to make them as short as possible; for a part of my profession is that I can be as short as any one.

Soc.

That is what is wanted, Gorgias; exhibit the shorter method now, and the longer one at some other time.

Gor.

Well, I will; and you will certainly say, that you never heard a man use fewer words.

Soc.

Very good then; as you profess to be a rhetorician, and a maker of rhetoricians, let me ask you, with what is rhetoric concerned: I might ask with what is weaving concerned, and you would reply (would you not?), with the making of garments?

Gor.

Yes.

Soc.

And music is concerned with the composition of melodies?

Gor.

It is.

Soc.

By Herè, Gorgias, I admire the surpassing brevity of your answers.

Gor.

Yes, Socrates, I do think myself good at that.

Soc.

And rhetoric is concerned with discourse.

I am glad to hear it; answer me in like manner about rhetoric: with what is rhetoric concerned?

Gor.

With discourse.

Soc.

What sort of discourse, Gorgias?—such discourse as would teach the sick under what treatment they might get well?

Gor.

No.

Soc.

Then rhetoric does not treat of all kinds of discourse?

Gor.

Certainly not.

Soc.

And yet rhetoric makes men able to speak?

Gor.

Yes.

Soc.

And to understand that about which they speak?

Gor.

Of course.

Soc.

But does not the art of medicine, which we were just 450now mentioning, also make men able to understand and speak about the sick?

Gor.

Certainly.

Soc.

Then medicine also treats of discourse?

Gor.

Yes.

Soc.

Of discourse concerning diseases?

Gor.

Just so.

Soc.

And does not gymnastic also treat of discourse concerning the good or evil condition of the body?

Gor.

Very true.

Soc.

But so are all the other arts.

And the same, Gorgias, is true of the other arts:—all of them treat of discourse concerning the subjects with which they severally have to do.

Gor.

Clearly.

Soc.

Then why, if you call rhetoric the art which treats of discourse, and all the other arts treat of discourse, do you not call them arts of rhetoric?

Gor.

Because, Socrates, the knowledge of the other arts has only to do with some sort of external action, as of the hand; but there is no such action of the hand in rhetoric which works and takes effect only through the medium of discourse. And therefore I am justified in saying that rhetoric treats of discourse.

Soc.

I am not sure whether I entirely understand you, but I dare say I shall soon know better; please to answer me a question:—you would allow that there are arts?

Gor.

Yes.

Soc.

As to the arts generally, they are for the most part concerned with doing, and require little or no speaking; in painting, and statuary, and many other arts, the work may proceed in silence; and of such arts I suppose you would say that they do not come within the province of rhetoric.

Gor.

You perfectly conceive my meaning, Socrates.

Soc.

You mean to say that rhetoric belongs to that class of arts which is chiefly concerned with words.

But there are other arts which work wholly through the medium of language, and require either no action or very little, as, for example, the arts of arithmetic, of calculation, of geometry, and of playing draughts; in some of these speech is pretty nearly co-extensive with action, but in most of them the verbal element is greater—they depend wholly on words for their efficacy and power: and I take your meaning to be that rhetoric is an art of this latter sort?

Gor.

Exactly.

Soc.

And yet you would not call arithmetic rhetoric.

And yet I do not believe that you really mean to call any of these arts rhetoric; although the precise expression which you used was, that rhetoric is an art which works and takes effect only through the medium of discourse; and an adversary who wished to be captious might say, 'And so, Gorgias, you call arithmetic rhetoric.' But I do not think that you really call arithmetic rhetoric any more than geometry would be so called by you. 451

Gor.

You are quite right, Socrates, in your apprehension of my meaning.

Soc.

Illustrations.

Well, then, let me now have the rest of my answer:—seeing that rhetoric is one of those arts which works mainly by the use of words, and there are other arts which also use words, tell me what is that quality in words with which rhetoric is concerned:—Suppose that a person asks me about some of the arts which I was mentioning just now; he might say, 'Socrates, what is arithmetic?' and I should reply to him, as you replied to me, that arithmetic is one of those arts which take effect through words. And then he would proceed to ask: 'Words about what?' and I should reply, Words about odd and even numbers, and how many there are of each. And if he asked again: 'What is the art of calculation?' I should say, That also is one of the arts which is concerned wholly with words. And if he further said, 'Concerned with what?' I should say, like the clerks in the assembly, 'as aforesaid' of arithmetic, but with a difference, the difference being that the art of calculation considers not only the quantities of odd and even numbers, but also their numerical relations to themselves and to one another. And suppose, again, I were to say that astronomy is only words—he would ask, 'Words about what, Socrates?' and I should answer, that astronomy tells us about the motions of the stars and sun and moon, and their relative swiftness.

Gor.

You would be quite right, Socrates.

Soc.

And now let us have from you, Gorgias, the truth about rhetoric: which you would admit (would you not?) to be one of those arts which act always and fulfil all their ends through the medium of words?

Gor.

Rhetoric has to do with words: about the greatest and best of human things.

True.

Soc.

Words which do what? I should ask. To what class of things do the words which rhetoric uses relate?

Gor.

To the greatest, Socrates, and the best of human things.

Soc.

That again, Gorgias, is ambiguous; I am still in the dark: for which are the greatest and best of human things? I dare say that you have heard men singing at feasts the old drinking song, in which the singers enumerate the goods of life, first health, beauty next, thirdly, as the writer of the song says, wealth honestly obtained.

Gor.

452 Yes, I know the song; but what is your drift?

Soc.

But which are they?

I mean to say, that the producers of those things which the author of the song praises, that is to say, the physician, the trainer, the money-maker, will at once come to you, and first the physician will say: 'O Socrates, Gorgias is deceiving you, for my art is concerned with the greatest good of men and not his.' And when I ask, Who are you? he will reply, 'I am a physician.' What do you mean? I shall say. Do you mean that your art produces the greatest good? 'Certainly,' he will answer, 'for is not health the greatest good? What greater good can men have, Socrates?' And after him the trainer will come and say, 'I too, Socrates, shall be greatly surprised if Gorgias can show more good of his art than I can show of mine.' To him again I shall say, Who are you, honest friend, and what is your business? 'I am a trainer,' he will reply, 'and my business is to make men beautiful and strong in body.' When I have done with the trainer, there arrives the money-maker, and he, as I expect, will utterly despise them all. 'Consider, Socrates,' he will say, 'whether Gorgias or any one else can produce any greater good than wealth.' Well, you and I say to him, and are you a creator of wealth? 'Yes,' he replies. And who are you? 'A money-maker.' And do you consider wealth to be the greatest good of man? 'Of course,' will be his reply. And we shall rejoin: Yes; but our friend Gorgias contends that his art produces a greater good than yours. And then he will be sure to go on and ask, 'What good? Let Gorgias answer.' Now I want you, Gorgias, to imagine that this question is asked of you by them and by me; What is that which, as you say, is the greatest good of man, and of which you are the creator? Answer us.

Gor.

Freedom and power,

That good, Socrates, which is truly the greatest, being that which gives to men freedom in their own persons, and to individuals the power of ruling over others in their several states.

Soc.

And what would you consider this to be?

Gor.

and the word which gives them.

What is there greater than the word which persuades the judges in the courts, or the senators in the council, or the citizens in the assembly, or at any other political meeting?—if you have the power of uttering this word, you will have the physician your slave, and the trainer your slave, and the money-maker of whom you talk will be found to gather treasures, not for himself, but for you who are able to speak and to persuade the multitude.

Soc.

Now I think, Gorgias, that you have very accurately explained what you conceive to be the art of rhetoric; and you mean to say, if I am not mistaken, that rhetoric is the 453artificer of persuasion, having this and no other business, and that this is her crown and end. Do you know any other effect of rhetoric over and above that of producing persuasion?

Gor.

Rhetoric is the art of persuading, says Gorgias.

No: the definition seems to me very fair, Socrates; for persuasion is the chief end of rhetoric.

Soc.

Then hear me, Gorgias, for I am quite sure that if there ever was a man who entered on the discussion of a matter from a pure love of knowing the truth, I am such a one, and I should say the same of you.

Gor.

What is coming, Socrates?

Soc.

I will tell you: I am very well aware that I do not know what, according to you, is the exact nature, or what are the topics of that persuasion of which you speak, and which is given by rhetoric; although I have a suspicion about both the one and the other. And I am going to ask—what is this power of persuasion which is given by rhetoric, and about what? But why, if I have a suspicion, do I ask instead of telling you? Not for your sake, but in order that the argument may proceed in such a manner as is most likely to set forth the truth. And I would have you observe, that I am right in asking this further question: If I asked, 'What sort of a painter is Zeuxis?' and you said, 'The painter of figures,' should I not be right in asking, 'What kind of figures, and where do you find them?'

Gor.

Certainly.

Soc.

And the reason for asking this second question would be, that there are other painters besides, who paint many other figures?

Gor.

True.

Soc.

But if there had been no one but Zeuxis who painted them, then you would have answered very well?

Gor.

Quite so.

Soc.

But so is arithmetic, so is painting.

Now I want to know about rhetoric in the same way;—is rhetoric the only art which brings persuasion, or do other arts have the same effect? I mean to say—Does he who teaches anything persuade men of that which he teaches or not?

Gor.

He persuades, Socrates,—there can be no mistake about that.

Soc.

Again, if we take the arts of which we were just now speaking:—do not arithmetic and the arithmeticians teach us the properties of number?

Gor.

Certainly.

Soc.

And therefore persuade us of them?

Gor.

Yes.

Soc.

Then arithmetic as well as rhetoric is an artificer of persuasion?

Gor.

Clearly.

Soc.

And if any one asks us what sort of persuasion, and about what,—we shall answer, persuasion which teaches the quantity of odd and even; and we shall be able to show that 454all the other arts of which we were just now speaking are artificers of persuasion, and of what sort, and about what.

Gor.

Very true.

Soc.

Then rhetoric is not the only artificer of persuasion?

Gor.

True.

Soc.

Of what persuasion is rhetoric the artificer?

Seeing, then, that not only rhetoric works by persuasion, but that other arts do the same, as in the case of the painter, a question has arisen which is a very fair one: Of what persuasion is rhetoric the artificer, and about what?—is not that a fair way of putting the question?

Gor.

I think so.

Soc.

Then, if you approve the question, Gorgias, what is the answer?

Gor.

Of persuasion in the courts and assemblies about the just and unjust.

I answer, Socrates, that rhetoric is the art of persuasion in courts of law and other assemblies, as I was just now saying, and about the just and unjust.

Soc.

And that, Gorgias, was what I was suspecting to be your notion; yet I would not have you wonder if by-and-by I am found repeating a seemingly plain question; for I ask not in order to confute you, but as I was saying that the argument may proceed consecutively, and that we may not get the habit of anticipating and suspecting the meaning of one another's words; I would have you develop your own views in your own way, whatever may be your hypothesis.

Gor.

I think that you are quite right, Socrates.

Soc.

Then let me raise another question; there is such a thing as 'having learned'?

Gor.

Yes.

Soc.

And there is also 'having believed'?

Gor.

Yes.

Soc.

Knowledge and belief are not the same things; for there may be a false belief, but not a false knowledge.

And is the 'having learned' the same as 'having believed,' and are learning and belief the same things?

Gor.

In my judgment, Socrates, they are not the same.

Soc.

And your judgment is right, as you may ascertain in this way:—If a person were to say to you, 'Is there, Gorgias, a false belief as well as a true?'—you would reply, if I am not mistaken, that there is.

Gor.

Yes.

Soc.

Well, but is there a false knowledge as well as a true?

Gor.

No.

Soc.

No, indeed; and this again proves that knowledge and belief differ.

Gor.

Very true.

Soc.

And yet those who have learned as well as those who have believed are persuaded?

Gor.

Just so.

Soc.

Shall we then assume two sorts of persuasion,—one which is the source of belief without knowledge, as the other is of knowledge?

Gor.

By all means.

Soc.

And which sort of persuasion does rhetoric create in courts of law and other assemblies about the just and unjust, the sort of persuasion which gives belief without knowledge, or that which gives knowledge?

Gor.

455Clearly, Socrates, that which only gives belief.

Soc.

And rhetoric is only the creator of a belief, but gives no instruction.

Then rhetoric, as would appear, is the artificer of a persuasion which creates belief about the just and unjust, but gives no instruction about them?

Gor.

True.

Soc.

And the rhetorician does not instruct the courts of law or other assemblies about things just and unjust, but he creates belief about them; for no one can be supposed to instruct such a vast multitude about such high matters in a short time?

Gor.

Certainly not.

Soc.

Neither is the rhetorician taken into counsel when anything has to be done.

Come, then, and let us see what we really mean about rhetoric; for I do not know what my own meaning is as yet. When the assembly meets to elect a physician or a shipwright or any other craftsman, will the rhetorician be taken into counsel? Surely not. For at every election he ought to be chosen who is most skilled; and, again, when walls have to be built or harbours or docks to be constructed, not the rhetorician but the master workman will advise; or when generals have to be chosen and an order of battle arranged, or a position taken, then the military will advise and not the rhetoricians: what do you say, Gorgias? Since you profess to be a rhetorician and a maker of rhetoricians, I cannot do better than learn the nature of your art from you. And here let me assure you that I have your interest in view as well as my own. For likely enough some one or other of the young men present might desire to become your pupil, and in fact I see some, and a good many too, who have this wish, but they would be too modest to question you. And therefore when you are interrogated by me, I would have you imagine that you are interrogated by them. 'What is the use of coming to you, Gorgias?' they will say—'about what will you teach us to advise the state?—about the just and unjust only, or about those other things also which Socrates has just mentioned?' How will you answer them?

Gor.

But, says Gorgias, he will persuade people to do it.

I like your way of leading us on, Socrates, and I will endeavour to reveal to you the whole nature of rhetoric. You must have heard, I think, that the docks and the walls of the Athenians and the plan of the harbour were devised in accordance with the counsels, partly of Themistocles, and partly of Pericles, and not at the suggestion of the builders.

Soc.

Such is the tradition, Gorgias, about Themistocles; and I myself heard the speech of Pericles when he advised us about the middle wall.

Gor.

And you will observe, Socrates, that when a decision 456has to be given in such matters the rhetoricians are the advisers; they are the men who win their point.

Soc.

I had that in my admiring mind, Gorgias, when I asked what is the nature of rhetoric, which always appears to me, when I look at the matter in this way, to be a marvel of greatness.

Gor.

The rhetorician more than a match for a man of any other profession.His pupils may make a bad use of his instructions, but he is not to be blamed for this.

A marvel, indeed, Socrates, if you only knew how rhetoric comprehends and holds under her sway all the inferior arts. Let me offer you a striking example of this. On several occasions I have been with my brother Herodicus or some other physician to see one of his patients, who would not allow the physician to give him medicine, or apply the knife or hot iron to him; and I have persuaded him to do for me what he would not do for the physician just by the use of rhetoric. And I say that if a rhetorician and a physician were to go to any city, and had there to argue in the Ecclesia or any other assembly as to which of them should be elected state-physician, the physician would have no chance; but he who could speak would be chosen if he wished; and in a contest with a man of any other profession the rhetorician more than any one would have the power of getting himself chosen, for he can speak more persuasively to the multitude than any of them, and on any subject. Such is the nature and power of the art of rhetoric! And yet, Socrates, rhetoric should be used like any other competitive art, not against everybody,—the rhetorician ought not to abuse his strength any more than a pugilist or pancratiast or other master of fence;—because he has powers which are more than a match either for friend or enemy, he ought not therefore to strike, stab, or slay his friends. Suppose a man to have been trained in the palestra and to be a skilful boxer,—he in the fulness of his strength goes and strikes his father or mother or one of his familiars or friends; but that is no reason why the trainers or fencing-masters should be held in detestation or banished from the city;—surely not. For they taught their art for a good purpose, to be used against enemies and evil-doers, in self-defence not in aggression, and others have perverted 457their instructions, and turned to a bad use their own strength and skill. But not on this account are the teachers bad, neither is the art in fault, or bad in itself; I should rather say that those who make a bad use of the art are to blame. And the same argument holds good of rhetoric; for the rhetorician can speak against all men and upon any subject,—in short, he can persuade the multitude better than any other man of anything which he pleases, but he should not therefore seek to defraud the physician or any other artist of his reputation merely because he has the power; he ought to use rhetoric fairly, as he would also use his athletic powers. And if after having become a rhetorician he makes a bad use of his strength and skill, his instructor surely ought not on that account to be held in detestation or banished. For he was intended by his teacher to make a good use of his instructions, but he abuses them. And therefore he is the person who ought to be held in detestation, banished, and put to death, and not his instructor.

Soc.

If Gorgias, like Socrates, is one of those who rejoice in being refuted, he would like to cross-examine him; if not, not.Socrates, Gorgias, Chaerephon, Callicles.

You, Gorglas, like myself, have had great experience of disputations, and you must have observed, I think, that they do not always terminate in mutual edification, or in the definition by either party of the subjects which they are discussing; but disagreements are apt to arise—somebody says that another has not spoken truly or clearly; and then they get into a passion and begin to quarrel, both parties conceiving that their opponents are arguing from personal feeling only and jealousy of themselves, not from any interest in the question at issue. And sometimes they will go on abusing one another until the company at last are quite vexed at themselves for ever listening to such fellows. Why do I say this? Why, because I cannot help feeling that you are now saying what is not quite consistent or accordant with what you were saying at first about rhetoric. And I am afraid to point this out to you, lest you should think that I have some animosity against you, and that I speak, not for the sake of discovering the truth, but from jealousy of you. Now if you are one of my sort, I should like to cross-examine you, but if not I will let you alone. And what is my sort? 458you will ask. I am one of those who are very willing to be refuted if I say anything which is not true, and very willing to refute any one else who says what is not true, and quite as ready to be refuted as to refute; for I hold that this is the greater gain of the two, just as the gain is greater of being cured of a very great evil than of curing another. For I imagine that there is no evil which a man can endure so great as an erroneous opinion about the matters of which we are speaking; and if you claim to be one of my sort, let us have the discussion out, but if you would rather have done, no matter;—let us make an end of it.

Gor.

I should say, Socrates, that I am quite the man whom you indicate; but, perhaps, we ought to consider the audience, for, before you came, I had already given a long exhibition, and if we proceed the argument may run on to a great length. And therefore I think that we should consider whether we may not be detaining some part of the company when they are wanting to do something else.

Chaer.

Delight of the audience at the prospect of an argument.

You hear the audience cheering, Gorgias and Socrates, which shows their desire to listen to you; and for myself, Heaven forbid that I should have any business on hand which would take me away from a discussion so interesting and so ably maintained.

Cal.

By the gods, Chaerephon, although I have been present at many discussions, I doubt whether I was ever so much delighted before, and therefore if you go on discoursing all day I shall be the better pleased.

Soc.

I may truly say, Callicles, that I am willing, if Gorgias is.

Gor.

Socrates, Gorgias.

After all this, Socrates, I should be disgraced if I refused, especially as I have promised to answer all comers; in accordance with the wishes of the company, then, do you begin, and ask of me any question which you like.

Soc.

Let me tell you then, Gorgias, what surprises me in your words; though I dare say that you may be right, and I may have misunderstood your meaning. You say that you can make any man, who will learn of you, a rhetorician?

Gor.

Yes.

Soc.

Do you mean that you will teach him to gain the ears of the multitude on any subject, and this not by instruction 459but by persuasion?

Gor.

Quite so.

Soc.

The rhetorician has greater powers of persuasion with the mob than e. g. the physician.

You were saying, in fact, that the rhetorician will have greater powers of persuasion than the physician even in a matter of health?

Gor.

Yes, with the multitude,—that is.

Soc.

You mean to say, with the ignorant; for with those who know he cannot be supposed to have greater powers of persuasion.

Gor.

Very true.

Soc.

The more ignorant therefore will have more power than he who knows.

But if he is to have more power of persuasion than the physician, he will have greater power than he who knows?

Gor.

Certainly.

Soc.

Although he is not a physician:—is he?

Gor.

No.

Soc.

And he who is not a physician must, obviously, be ignorant of what the physician knows.

Gor.

Clearly.

Soc.

Then, when the rhetorician is more persuasive than the physician, the ignorant is more persuasive with the ignorant than he who has knowledge?—is not that the inference?

Gor.

In the case supposed:—yes.

Soc.

And the same holds of the relation of rhetoric to all the other arts; the rhetorician need not know the truth about things; he has only to discover some way of persuading the ignorant that he has more knowledge than those who know?

Gor.

Yes, Socrates, and is not this a great comfort?—not to have learned the other arts, but the art of rhetoric only, and yet to be in no way inferior to the professors of them?

Soc.

And is the rhetorician as ignorant of good and evil, just and unjust, as about special arts; or will Gorgias teach him these things first?

Whether the rhetorician is or is not inferior on this account is a question which we will hereafter examine if the enquiry is likely to be of any service to us; but I would rather begin by asking, whether he is or is not as ignorant of the just and unjust, base and honourable, good and evil, as he is of medicine and the other arts; I mean to say, does he really know anything of what is good and evil, base or honourable, just or unjust in them; or has he only a way with the ignorant of persuading them that he not knowing is to be esteemed to know more about these things than some one else who knows? Or must the pupil know these things and come to you knowing them before he can acquire the art of rhetoric? If he is ignorant, you who are the teacher of rhetoric will not teach him — it is not your business; but you will make him seem to the multitude to know them, when he does not know them; and seem to be a good man, when he is not. Or will you be unable to teach him rhetoric 460at all, unless he knows the truth of these things first? What is to be said about all this? By heaven, Gorgias, I wish that you would reveal to me the power of rhetoric, as you were saying that you would.

Gor.

He must be taught.

Well, Socrates, I suppose that if the pupil does chance not to know them, he will have to learn of me these things as well.

Soc.

Say no more, for there you are right; and so he whom you make a rhetorician must either know the nature of the just and unjust already, or he must be taught by you.

Gor.

Certainly.

Soc.

Well, and is not he who has learned carpentering a carpenter?

Gor.

Yes.

Soc.

And he who has learned music a musician?

Gor.

Yes.

Soc.

And he who has learned medicine is a physician, in like manner? He who has learned anything whatever is that which his knowledge makes him.

Gor.

Certainly.

Soc.

And in the same way, he who has learned what is just is just?

Gor.

To be sure.

Soc.

He who has learned what is just, is admitted to be just and to act justly. But if so, the rhetorician, having learned what is just, must act justly, and can never therefore make an ill use of rhetoric.

And he who is just may be supposed to do what is just?

Gor.

Yes.

Soc.

And must not the just man always desire to do what is just?

Gor.

That is clearly the inference.

Soc.

Surely, then, the just man will never consent to do injustice?

Gor.

Certainly not.

Soc.

And according to the argument the rhetorician must be a just man?

Gor.

Yes.

Soc.

And will therefore never be willing to do injustice?

Gor.

Clearly not.

Soc.

But do you remember saying just now that the trainer is not to be accused or banished if the pugilist makes a wrong use of his pugilistic art; and in like manner, if the rhetorician makes a bad and unjust use of his rhetoric, that is not to be laid to the charge of his teacher, who is not to be banished, but the wrong-doer himself who made a bad use of his rhetoric—he is to be banished—was not that said?

Gor.

Yes, it was.

Soc.

But now we are affirming that the aforesaid rhetorician will never have done injustice at all?

Gor.

True.

Soc.

And at the very outset, Gorgias, it was said that rhetoric treated of discourse, not [like arithmetic] about odd and even, but about just and unjust? Was not this said?

Gor.

Yes.

Soc.

Socrates, Polus.

I was thinking at the time, when I heard you saying so, that rhetoric, which is always discoursing about justice, could not possibly be an unjust thing. But when you added, shortly afterwards, that the rhetorician might make a bad use 461of rhetoric I noted with surprise the inconsistency into which you had fallen; and I said, that if you thought, as I did, that there was a gain in being refuted, there would be an advantage in going on with the question, but if not, I would leave off. And in the course of our investigations, as you will see yourself, the rhetorician has been acknowledged to be incapable of making an unjust use of rhetoric or of willingness to do injustice. By the dog, Gorgias, there will be a great deal of discussion, before we get at the truth of all this.

Polus.

The paradoxes of Socrates arouse the ire of Polus.

And do even you, Socrates, seriously believe what you are now saying about rhetoric? What! because Gorgias was ashamed to deny that the rhetorician knew the just and the honourable and the good, and admitted that to any one who came to him ignorant of them he could teach them, and then out of this admission there arose a contradiction—the thing which you so dearly love, and to which not he, but you, brought the argument by your captious questions—[do you seriously believe that there is any truth in all this?] For will any one ever acknowledge that he does not know, or cannot teach, the nature of justice? The truth is, that there is great want of manners in bringing the argument to such a pass.

Soc.

Socrates is willing enough to receive his correction, if he will only be brief.

Illustrious Polus, the reason why we provide ourselves with friends and children is, that when we get old and stumble, a younger generation may be at hand to set us on our legs again in our words and in our actions: and now, if I and Gorgias are stumbling, here are you who should raise us up; and I for my part engage to retract any error into which you may think that I have fallen—upon one condition:

Pol.

What condition?

Soc.

That you contract, Polus, the prolixity of speech in which you indulged at first.

Pol.

'Am I to be deprived of speech in a free state?'

What! do you mean that I may not use as many words as I please?

Soc.

'Am I to be compelled to listen?'

Only to think, my friend, that having come on a visit to Athens, which is the most free-spoken state in Hellas, you when you got there, and you alone, should be deprived of the power of speech—that would be hard indeed. But then consider my case:—shall not I be very hardly used, if, when you are making a long oration, and refusing to answer what you are asked, I am compelled to stay and listen to you, and may 462not go away? I say rather, if you have a real interest in the argument, or, to repeat my former expression, have any desire to set it on its legs, take back any statement which you please; and in your turn ask and answer, like myself and Gorgias—refute and be refuted: for I suppose that you would claim to know what Gorgias knows—would you not?

Pol.

Yes.

Soc.

And you, like him, invite any one to ask you about anything which he pleases, and you will know how to answer him?

Pol.

To be sure.

Soc.

And now, which will you do, ask or answer?

Pol.

I will ask; and do you answer me, Socrates, the same question which Gorgias, as you suppose, is unable to answer: What is rhetoric?

Soc.

Do you mean what sort of an art?

Pol.

Yes.

Soc.

Socrates in his answer contrives to give Polus a lesson.

To say the truth, Polus, it is not an art at all, in my opinion.

Pol.

Then what, in your opinion, is rhetoric?

Soc.

A thing which, as I was lately reading in a book of yours, you say that you have made an art.

Pol.

What thing?

Soc.

I should say a sort of experience.

Pol.

Does rhetoric seem to you to be an experience?

Soc.

That is my view, but you may be of another mind.

Pol.

An experience in what?

Soc.

An experience in producing a sort of delight and gratification.

Pol.

And if able to gratify others, must not rhetoric be a fine thing?

Soc.

What are you saying, Polus? Why do you ask me whether rhetoric is a fine thing or not, when I have not as yet told you what rhetoric is?

Pol.

Did I not hear you say that rhetoric was a sort of experience?

Soc.

Will you, who are so desirous to gratify others, afford a slight gratification to me?

Pol.

I will.

Soc.

Will you ask me, what sort of an art is cookery?

Pol.

What sort of an art is cookery?

Soc.

Not an art at all, Polus.

Pol.

Socrates, Polus, Gorgias.

What then?

Soc.

I should say an experience.

Pol.

He puts rhetoric and cookery in the same class;

In what? I wish that you would explain to me.

Soc.

An experience in producing a sort of delight and gratification, Polus.

Pol.

Then are cookery and rhetoric the same?

Soc.

No, they are only different parts of the same profession.

Pol.

Of what profession?

Soc.

I am afraid that the truth may seem discourteous; and I hesitate to answer, lest Gorgias should imagine that I am making fun of his own profession. For whether or no this is that art of rhetoric which Gorgias practises I 463really cannot tell:—from what he was just now saying, nothing appeared of what he thought of his art, but the rhetoric which I mean is a part of a not very creditable whole.

Gor.

A part of what, Socrates? Say what you mean, and never mind me.

Soc.

and that class is flattery.

In my opinion then, Gorgias, the whole of which rhetoric is a part is not an art at all, but the habit of a bold and ready wit, which knows how to manage mankind: this habit I sum up under the word 'flattery;' and it appears to me to have many other parts, one of which is cookery, which may seem to be an art, but, as I maintain, is only an experience or routine and not an art:—another part is rhetoric, and the art of attiring and sophistry are two others: thus there are four branches, and four different things answering to them. And Polus may ask, if he likes, for he has not as yet been informed, what part of flattery is rhetoric: he did not see that I had not yet answered him when he proceeded to ask a further question: Whether I do not think rhetoric a fine thing? But I shall not tell him whether rhetoric is a fine thing or not, until I have first answered, 'What is rhetoric?' For that would not be right, Polus; but I shall be happy to answer, if you will ask me, What part of flattery is rhetoric?

Pol.

I will ask, and do you answer? What part of flattery is rhetoric?

Soc.

Will you understand my answer? Rhetoric, according to my view, is the ghost or counterfeit of a part of politics.

Pol.

Rhetoric is the shadow of a part of politics.

And noble or ignoble?

Soc.

Ignoble, I should say, if I am compelled to answer, for I call what is bad ignoble:—though I doubt whether you understand what I was saying before.

Gor.

Indeed, Socrates, I cannot say that I understand myself.

Soc.

I do not wonder, Gorgias; for I have not as yet explained myself, and our friend Polus, colt by name and colt by nature, is apt to run away.

Gor.

'But what in the world does this mean?'

Never mind him, but explain to me what you mean by saying that rhetoric is the counterfeit of a part of politics.

Soc.

I will try, then, to explain my notion of rhetoric, and 464if I am mistaken, my friend Polus shall refute me. We may assume the existence of bodies and of souls?

Gor.

Of course.

Soc.

Returning to first principles, Socrates assumes the existence of souls and bodies which may or may not be in a good condition, real or apparent.

You would further admit that there is a good condition of either of them?

Gor.

Yes.

Soc.

Which condition may not be really good, but good only in appearance? I mean to say, that there are many persons who appear to be in good health, and whom only a physician or trainer will discern at first sight not to be in good health.

Gor.

True.

Soc.

And this applies not only to the body, but also to the soul: in either there may be that which gives the appearance of health and not the reality?

Gor.

Yes, certainly.

Soc.

To the soul corresponds the art of politics which has two parts, legislation and justice, and to the body corresponds another nameless art of training which has two parts, medicine and gymnastic; and these four have four shams corresponding to them.Socrates.

And now I will endeavour to explain to you more clearly what I mean: The soul and body being two, have two arts corresponding to them: there is the art of politics attending on the soul; and another art attending on the body, of which I know no single name, but which may be described as having two divisions, one of them gymnastic, and the other medicine. And in politics there is a legislative part, which answers to gymnastic, as justice does to medicine; and the two parts run into one another, justice having to do with the same subject as legislation, and medicine with the same subject as gymnastic, but with a difference. Now, seeing that there are these four arts, two attending on the body and two on the soul for their highest good; flattery knowing, or rather guessing their natures, has distributed herself into four shams or simulations of them; she puts on the likeness of some one or other of them, and pretends to be that which she simulates, and having no regard for men's highest interests, is ever making pleasure the bait of the unwary, and deceiving them into the belief that she is of the highest value to them. Cookery simulates the disguise of medicine, and pretends to know what food is the best for the body; and if the physician and the cook had to enter into a competition in which children were the judges, or men who had no more sense than children, as to which of them best understands the goodness or badness of food, the physician would be starved to death. A flattery I deem this to be and of an ignoble sort, Polus, for to you 465I am now addressing myself, because it aims at pleasure without any thought of the best. An art I do not call it, but only an experience, because it is unable to explain or to give a reason of the nature of its own applications. And I do not call any irrational thing an art; but if you dispute my words, I am prepared to argue in defence of them.

Cookery, then, I maintain to be a flattery which takes the form of medicine; and tiring, in like manner, is a flattery which takes the form of gymnastic, and is knavish, false, ignoble, illiberal, working deceitfully by the help of lines, and colours, and enamels, and garments, and making men affect a spurious beauty to the neglect of the true beauty which is given by gymnastic.

The shams are cooking, dressing up, sophistry, rhetoric.

I would rather not be tedious, and therefore I will only say, after the manner of the geometricians, (for I think that by this time you will be able to follow,)

as tiring : gymnastic : : cookery : medicine;

or rather,

as tiring : gymnastic : : sophistry : legislation;

and

Socrates, Polus.

as cookery : medicine : : rhetoric : justice.

Socrates excuses himself for the length at which he has spoken.

And this, I say, is the natural difference between the rhetorician and the sophist, but by reason of their near connection, they are apt to be jumbled up together; neither do they know what to make of themselves, nor do other men know what to make of them. For if the body presided over itself, and were not under the guidance of the soul, and the soul did not discern and discriminate between cookery and medicine, but the body was made the judge of them, and the rule of judgment was the bodily delight which was given by them, then the word of Anaxagoras, that word with which you, friend Polus, are so well acquainted, would prevail far and wide: 'Chaos' would come again, and cookery, health, and medicine would mingle in an indiscriminate mass. And now I have told you my notion of rhetoric, which is, in relation to the soul, what cookery is to the body. I may have been inconsistent in making a long speech, when I would not allow you to discourse at length. But I think that I may be excused, because you did not understand me, and could make no use of my answer when I spoke shortly, and therefore 466I had to enter into an explanation. And if I show an equal inability to make use of yours, I hope that you will speak at equal length; but if I am able to understand you, let me have the benefit of your brevity, as is only fair: And now you may do what you please with my answer.

Pol.

What do you mean? do you think that rhetoric is flattery?

Soc.

Nay, I said a part of flattery; if at your age, Polus, you cannot remember, what will you do by-and-by, when you get older?

Pol.

And are the good rhetoricians meanly regarded in states, under the idea that they are flatterers?

Soc.

Is that a question or the beginning of a speech?

Pol.

I am asking a question.

Soc.

Then my answer is, that they are not regarded at all.

Pol.

Polus cannot be made to understand that rhetoricians have no real power in a state, because they do not do what they ultimately will, but only what they think best.

How not regarded? Have they not very great power in states?

Soc.

Not if you mean to say that power is a good to the possessor.

Pol.

And that is what I do mean to say.

Soc.

Then, if so, I think that they have the least power of all the citizens.

Pol.

What! are they not like tyrants? They kill and despoil and exile any one whom they please.

Soc.

By the dog, Polus, I cannot make out at each deliverance of yours, whether you are giving an opinion of your own, or asking a question of me.

Pol.

I am asking a question of you.

Soc.

Yes, my friend, but you ask two questions at once.

Pol.

How two questions?

Soc.

Why, did you not say just now that the rhetoricians are like tyrants, and that they kill and despoil or exile any one whom they please?

Pol.

I did.

Soc.

Well then, I say to you that here are two questions in one, and I will answer both of them. And I tell you, Polus, that rhetoricians and tyrants have the least possible power in states, as I was just now saying; for they do literally nothing which they will, but only what they think best.

Pol.

And is not that a great power?

Soc.

Polus has already said the reverse.

Pol.

Said the reverse! nay, that is what I assert.

Soc.

No, by the great—what do you call him?—not you, for you say that great power is a good to him who has the power.

Pol.

I do.

Soc.

And would you maintain that if a fool does what he thinks best, this is a good, and would you call this great power?

Pol.

I should not.

Soc.

For a fool and a flatterer cannot know what is good.

Then you must prove that the rhetorician is not a fool, and that rhetoric is an art and not a flattery—and so 467you will have refuted me; but if you leave me unrefuted, why, the rhetoricians who do what they think best in states, and the tyrants, will have nothing upon which to congratulate themselves, if, as you say, power be indeed a good, admitting at the same time that what is done without sense is an evil.

Pol.

Yes: I admit that.

Soc.

How then can the rhetoricians or the tyrants have great power in states, unless Polus can refute Socrates, and prove to him that they do as they will?

Pol.

This fellow—

Soc.

I say that they do not do as they will;—now refute me.

Pol.

Why, have you not already said that they do as they think best?

Soc.

And I say so still.

Pol.

Then surely they do as they will?

Soc.

I deny it.

Pol.

But they do what they think best?

Soc.

Aye.

Pol.

That, Socrates, is monstrous and absurd.

Soc.

Good words, good Polus, as I may say in your own peculiar style; but if you have any questions to ask of me, either prove that I am in error or give the answer yourself.

Pol.

Very well, I am willing to answer that I may know what you mean.

Soc.

Do men appear to you to will that which they do, or to will that further end for the sake of which they do a thing? when they take medicine, for example, at the bidding of a physician, do they will the drinking of the medicine which is painful, or the health for the sake of which they drink?

Pol.

Clearly, the health.

Soc.

And when men go on a voyage or engage in business, they do not will that which they are doing at the time; for who would desire to take the risk of a voyage or the trouble of business?—But they will, to have the wealth for the sake of which they go on a voyage.

Pol.

Certainly.

Soc.

A man cannot will unless he knows the ultimate good for the sake of which he acts.

And is not this universally true? If a man does something for the sake of something else, he wills not that which he does, but that for the sake of which he does it.

Pol.

Yes.

Soc.

And are not all things either good or evil, or intermediate and indifferent?

Pol.

To be sure, Socrates.

Soc.

Wisdom and health and wealth and the like you would call goods, and their opposites evils?

Pol.

I should.

Soc.

And the things which are neither good nor evil, and 468which partake sometimes of the nature of good and at other times of evil, or of neither, are such as sitting, walking, running, sailing; or, again, wood, stones, and the like:—these are the things which you call neither good nor evil?

Pol.

Exactly so.

Soc.

Are these indifferent things done for the sake of the good, or the good for the sake of the indifferent?

Pol.

Clearly, the indifferent for the sake of the good.

Soc.

When we walk we walk for the sake of the good, and under the idea that it is better to walk, and when we stand we stand equally for the sake of the good?

Pol.

Yes.

Soc.

And when we kill a man we kill him or exile him or despoil him of his goods, because, as we think, it will conduce to our good?

Pol.

Certainly.

Soc.

Men who do any of these things do them for the sake of the good?

Pol.

Yes.

Soc.

And did we not admit that in doing something for the sake of something else, we do not will those things which we do, but that other thing for the sake of which we do them?

Pol.

Most true.

Soc.

Then we do not will simply to kill a man or to exile him or to despoil him of his goods, but we will to do that which conduces to our good, and if the act is not conducive to our good we do not will it; for we will, as you say, that which is our good, but that which is neither good nor evil, or simply evil, we do not will. Why are you silent, Polus? Am I not right?

Pol.

You are right.

Soc.

Hence we may infer, that if any one, whether he be a tyrant or a rhetorician, kills another or exiles another or deprives him of his property, under the idea that the act is for his own interests when really not for his own interests, he may be said to do what seems best to him?

Pol.

Yes.

Soc.

But does he do what he wills if he does what is evil? Why do you not answer?

Pol.

No man does what he wills who does what is evil.

Well, I suppose not.

Soc.

Then if great power is a good as you allow, will such a one have great power in a state?

Pol.

He will not.

Soc.

Then I was right in saying that a man may do what seems good to him in a state, and not have great power, and not do what he wills?

Pol.

As though you, Socrates, would not like to have the power of doing what seemed good to you in the state, rather than not; you would not be jealous when you saw any one killing or despoiling or imprisoning whom he pleased, Oh, no!

Soc.

469Justly or unjustly, do you mean?

Pol.

In either case is he not equally to be envied?

Soc.

Forbear, Polus!

Pol.

Why 'forbear'?

Soc.

Because you ought not to envy wretches who are not to be envied, but only to pity them.

Pol.

And are those of whom I spoke wretches?

Soc.

Yes, certainly they are.

Pol.

He who makes a bad use of power is not to be envied, but pitied.

And so you think that he who slays any one whom he pleases, and justly slays him, is pitiable and wretched?

Soc.

No, I do not say that of him: but neither do I think that he is to be envied.

Pol.

Were you not saying just now that he is wretched?

Soc.

Yes, my friend, if he killed another unjustly, in which case he is also to be pitied; and he is not to be envied if he killed him justly.

Pol.

At any rate you will allow that he who is unjustly put to death is wretched, and to be pitied?

Soc.

Not so much, Polus, as he who kills him, and not so much as he who is justly killed.

Pol.

How can that be, Socrates?

Soc.

That may very well be, inasmuch as doing injustice is the greatest of evils.

Pol.

But is it the greatest? Is not suffering injustice a greater evil?

Soc.

Certainly not.

Pol.

Then would you rather suffer than do injustice?

Soc.

Better to suffer than to do injustice.

I should not like either, but if I must choose between them, I would rather suffer than do.

Pol.

Then you would not wish to be a tyrant?

Soc.

Not if you mean by tyranny what I mean.

Pol.

I mean, as I said before, the power of doing whatever seems good to you in a state, killing, banishing, doing in all things as you like.

Soc.

A tyrant has no real power any more than a man who runs out into the Agora carrying a dagger.

Well then, illustrious friend, when I have said my say, do you reply to me. Suppose that I go into a crowded Agora, and take a dagger under my arm. Polus, I say to you, I have just acquired rare power, and become a tyrant; for if I think that any of these men whom you see ought to be put to death, the man whom I have a mind to kill is as good as dead; and if I am disposed to break his head or tear his garment, he will have his head broken or his garment torn in an instant. Such is my great power in this city. And if you do not believe me, and I show you the dagger, you would probably reply: Socrates, in that sort of way any one may have great power—he may burn any house which he pleases, and the docks and triremes of the Athenians, and all their other vessels, whether public or private—but can you believe that this mere doing as you think best is great power?

Pol.

Certainly not such doing as this.

Soc.

But can you tell me why you disapprove of such a 470power?

Pol.

I can.

Soc.

Why then?

Pol.

Why, because he who did as you say would be certain to be punished.

Soc.

And punishment is an evil?

Pol.

Certainly.

Soc.

And you would admit once more, my good sir, that great power is a benefit to a man if his actions turn out to his advantage, and that this is the meaning of great power; and if not, then his power is an evil and is no power. But let us look at the matter in another way:—do we not acknowledge that the things of which we were speaking, the infliction of death, and exile, and the deprivation of property are sometimes a good and sometimes not a good?

Pol.

Certainly.

Soc.

Even what we commonly call the evils of life may be goods in disguise.

About that you and I may be supposed to agree?

Pol.

Yes.

Soc.

Tell me, then, when do you say that they are good and when that they are evil—what principle do you lay down?

Pol.

I would rather, Socrates, that you should answer as well as ask that question.

Soc.

Well, Polus, since you would rather have the answer from me, I say that they are good when they are just, and evil when they are unjust.

Pol.

You are hard of refutation, Socrates, but might not a child refute that statement?

Soc.

Then I shall be very grateful to the child, and equally grateful to you if you will refute me and deliver me from my foolishness. And I hope that refute me you will, and not weary of doing good to a friend.

Pol.

Yes, Socrates, and I need not go far or appeal to antiquity; events which happened only a few days ago are enough to refute you, and to prove that many men who do wrong are happy.

Soc.

What events?

Pol.

You see, I presume, that Archelaus the son of Perdiccas is now the ruler of Macedonia?

Soc.

At any rate I hear that he is.

Pol.

And do you think that he is happy or miserable?

Soc.

I cannot say, Polus, for I have never had any acquaintance with him.

Pol.

And cannot you tell at once, and without having an acquaintance with him, whether a man is happy?

Soc.

Most certainly not.

Pol.

Is the great king happy?

Then clearly, Socrates, you would say that you did not even know whether the great king was a happy man?

Soc.

And I should speak the truth; for I do not know how he stands in the matter of education and justice.

Pol.

What! and does all happiness consist in this?

Soc.

Yes, indeed, Polus, that is my doctrine; the men and women who are gentle and good are also happy, as I maintain, and the unjust and evil are miserable.

Pol.

Then, according to your doctrine, the said Archelaus 471is miserable?

Soc.

Yes, my friend, if he is wicked.

Pol.

Polus attempts to prove the happiness of the unjust by the story of Archelaus, who has lately by many crimes gained the throne of Macedonia.

That he is wicked I cannot deny; for he had no title at all to the throne which he now occupies, he being only the son of a woman who was the slave of Alcetas the brother of Perdiccas; he himself therefore in strict right was the slave of Alcetas; and if he had meant to do rightly he would have remained his slave, and then, according to your doctrine, he would have been happy. But now he is unspeakably miserable, for he has been guilty of the greatest crimes: in the first place he invited his uncle and master, Alcetas, to come to him, under the pretence that he would restore to him the throne which Perdiccas had usurped, and after entertaining him and his son Alexander, who was his own cousin, and nearly of an age with him, and making them drunk, he threw them into a waggon and carried them off by night, and slew them, and got both of them out of the way; and when he had done all this wickedness he never discovered that he was the most miserable of all men, and was very far from repenting: shall I tell you how he showed his remorse? he had a younger brother, a child of seven years old, who was the legitimate son of Perdiccas, and to him of right the kingdom belonged; Archelaus, however, had no mind to bring him up as he ought and restore the kingdom to him; that was not his notion of happiness; but not long afterwards he threw him into a well and drowned him, and declared to his mother Cleopatra that he had fallen in while running after a goose, and had been killed. And now as he is the greatest criminal of all the Macedonians, he may be supposed to be the most miserable and not the happiest of them, and I dare say that there are many Athenians, and you would be at the head of them, who would rather be any other Macedonian than Archelaus!

Soc.

Socrates sees no force in such arguments.

I praised you at first, Polus, for being a rhetorician rather than a reasoner. And this, as I suppose, is the sort of argument with which you fancy that a child might refute me, and by which I stand refuted when I say that the unjust man is not happy. But, my good friend, where is the refutation? I cannot admit a word which you have been saying.

Pol.

That is because you will not; for you surely must think as I do.

Soc.

The multitude of witnesses are nothing to him. He must convince his opponent and himself by argument.

Not so, my simple friend, but because you will refute me after the manner which rhetoricians practise in courts of law. For there the one party think that they refute the other when they bring forward a number of witnesses of good repute in proof of their allegations, and their adversary 472has only a single one or none at all. But this kind of proof is of no value where truth is the aim; a man may often be sworn down by a multitude of false witnesses who have a great air of respectability. And in this argument nearly every one, Athenian and stranger alike, would be on your side, if you should bring witnesses in disproof of my statement;—you may, if you will, summon Nicias the son of Niceratus, and let his brothers, who gave the row of tripods which stand in the precincts of Dionysus, come with him; or you may summon Aristocrates, the son of Scellius, who is the giver of that famous offering which is at Delphi;

summon, if you will, the whole house of Pericles, or any other great Athenian family whom you choose;—they will all agree with you: I only am left alone and cannot agree, for you do not convince me; although you produce many false witnesses against me, in the hope of depriving me of my inheritance, which is the truth. But I consider that nothing worth speaking of will have been effected by me unless I make you the one witness of my words; nor by you, unless you make me the one witness of yours; no matter about the rest of the world. For there are two ways of refutation, one which is yours and that of the world in general; but mine is of another sort—let us compare them, and see in what they differ. For, indeed, we are at issue about matters which to know is honourable and not to know disgraceful; to know or not to know happiness and misery—that is the chief of them. And what knowledge can be nobler? or what ignorance more disgraceful than this? And therefore I will begin by asking you whether you do not think that a man who is unjust and doing injustice can be happy, seeing that you think Archelaus unjust, and yet happy? May I assume this to be your opinion?

Pol.

Certainly.

Soc.

According to Polus the unjust man may be happy if he is unpunished: Socrates maintains that he is more happy, or less unhappy, if he meets with retribution.

But I say that this is an impossibility—here is one point about which we are at issue:—very good. And do you mean to say also that if he meets with retribution and punishment he will still be happy?

Pol.

Certainly not; in that case he will be most miserable.

Soc.

On the other hand, if the unjust be not punished, then, according to you, he will be happy?

Pol.

Yes.

Soc.

But in my opinion, Polus, the unjust or doer of unjust actions is miserable in any case,—more miserable, however, if he be not punished and does not meet with retribution, and less miserable if he be punished and meets with retribution at the hands of gods and men. 473

Pol.

You are maintaining a strange doctrine, Socrates.

Soc.

I shall try to make you agree with me, O my friend, for as a friend I regard you. Then these are the points at issue between us—are they not? I was saying that to do is worse than to suffer injustice?

Pol.

Exactly so.

Soc.

And you said the opposite?

Pol.

Yes.

Soc.

I said also that the wicked are miserable, and you refuted me?

Pol.

By Zeus I did.

Soc.

In your own opinion, Polus.

Pol.

Yes, and I rather suspect that I was in the right.

Soc.

You further said that the wrong-doer is happy if he be unpunished?

Pol.

Certainly.

Soc.

And I affirm that he is most miserable, and that those who are punished are less miserable—are you going to refute this proposition also?

Pol.

A proposition which is harder of refutation than the other, Socrates.

Soc.

Say rather, Polus, impossible; for who can refute the truth?

Pol.

What nonsense! Do you mean that the man who expires among tortures is happier than the successful tyrant?

What do you mean? If a man is detected in an unjust attempt to make himself a tyrant, and when detected is racked, mutilated, has his eyes burned out, and after having had all sorts of great injuries inflicted on him, and having seen his wife and children suffer the like, is at last impaled or tarred and burned alive, will he be happier than if he escape and become a tyrant, and continue all through life doing what he likes and holding the reins of government, the envy and admiration both of citizens and strangers? Is that the paradox which, as you say, cannot be refuted?

Soc.

There again, noble Polus, you are raising hobgoblins instead of refuting me; just now you were calling witnesses against me. But please to refresh my memory a little; did you say—'in an unjust attempt to make himself a tyrant'?

Pol.

Yes, I did.

Soc.

Neither is to be called happy if both are wicked.

Then I say that neither of them will be happier than the other,—neither he who unjustly acquires a tyranny, nor he who suffers in the attempt, for of two miserables one cannot be the happier, but that he who escapes and becomes a tyrant is the more miserable of the two. Do you laugh, Polus? Well, this is a new kind of refutation,—when any one says anything, instead of refuting him to laugh at him.

Pol.

Why refute what nobody believes? Ask the company.

But do you not think, Socrates, that you have been sufficiently refuted, when you say that which no human being will allow? Ask the company.

Soc.

Socrates never could count heads. [This is his description of one of the noblest actions of his life.] Say rather, why affirm what every body knows?

O Polus, I am not a public man, and only last year, when my tribe were serving as Prytanes, and it became my duty as their president to take the votes, there was a laugh at 474me, because I was unable to take them. And as I failed then, you must not ask me to count the suffrages of the company now; but if, as I was saying, you have no better argument than numbers, let me have a turn, and do you make trial of the sort of proof which, as I think, is required; for I shall produce one witness only of the truth of my words, and he is the person with whom I am arguing; his suffrage I know how to take; but with the many I have nothing to do, and do not even address myself to them. May I ask then whether you will answer in turn and have your words put to the proof? For I certainly think that I and you and every man do really believe, that to do is a greater evil than to suffer injustice: and not to be punished than to be punished.

Pol.

And I should say neither I, nor any man: would you yourself, for example, suffer rather than do injustice?

Soc.

Yes, and you, too; I or any man would.

Pol.

Quite the reverse; neither you, nor I, nor any man.

Soc.

But will you answer?

Pol.

To be sure, I will; for I am curious to hear what you can have to say.

Soc.

Polus, while denying that to do injustice is worse than to suffer, acknowledges it to be more disgraceful. Hence the shipwreck of his argument.

Tell me, then, and you will know, and let us suppose that I am beginning at the beginning: which of the two, Polus, in your opinion, is the worst?—to do injustice or to suffer?

Pol.

I should say that suffering was worst.

Soc.

And which is the greater disgrace?—Answer.

Pol.

To do.

Soc.

And the greater disgrace is the greater evil?

Pol.

Certainly not.

Soc.

I understand you to say, if I am not mistaken, that the honourable is not the same as the good, or the disgraceful as the evil?

Pol.

Certainly not.

Soc.

Let me ask a question of you: When you speak of beautiful things, such as bodies, colours, figures, sounds, institutions, do you not call them beautiful in reference to some standard: bodies, for example, are beautiful in proportion as they are useful, or as the sight of them gives pleasure to the spectators; can you give any other account of personal beauty?

Pol.

I cannot.

Soc.

And you would say of figures or colours generally that they were beautiful, either by reason of the pleasure which they give, or of their use, or of both?

Pol.

Yes, I should.

Soc.

And you would call sounds and music beautiful for the same reason?

Pol.

I should.

Soc.

Laws and institutions also have no beauty in them except in so far as they are useful or pleasant or both?

Pol.

I think not. 475

Soc.

And may not the same be said of the beauty of knowledge?

Pol.

To be sure, Socrates; and I very much approve of your measuring beauty by the standard of pleasure and utility.

Soc.

All things may be measured by the standard of pleasure and utility or of pain and evil.

And deformity or disgrace may be equally measured by the opposite standard of pain and evil?

Pol.

Certainly.

Soc.

Then when of two beautiful things one exceeds in beauty, the measure of the excess is to be taken in one or both of these; that is to say, in pleasure or utility or both?

Pol.

Very true.

Soc.

And of two deformed things, that which exceeds in deformity or disgrace, exceeds either in pain or evil—must it not be so?

Pol.

Yes.

Soc.

But then again, what was the observation which you just now made, about doing and suffering wrong? Did you not say, that suffering wrong was more evil, and doing wrong more disgraceful?

Pol.

I did.

Soc.

If to do is, as Polus admits, more disgraceful than to endure wrong, it must also be more evil.

Then, if doing wrong is more disgraceful than suffering, the more disgraceful must be more painful and must exceed in pain or in evil or both: does not that also follow?

Pol.

Of course.

Soc.

First, then, let us consider whether the doing of injustice exceeds the suffering in the consequent pain: Do the injurers suffer more than the injured?

Pol.

No, Socrates; certainly not.

Soc.

Then they do not exceed in pain?

Pol.

No.

Soc.

But if not in pain, then not in both?

Pol.

Certainly not.

Soc.

Then they can only exceed in the other?

Pol.

Yes.

Soc.

That is to say, in evil?

Pol.

True.

Soc.

Then doing injustice will have an excess of evil, and will therefore be a greater evil than suffering injustice?

Pol.

Clearly.

Soc.

But have not you and the world already agreed that to do injustice is more disgraceful than to suffer?

Pol.

Yes.

Soc.

And that is now discovered to be more evil?

Pol.

True.

Soc.

And would you prefer a greater evil or a greater dishonour to a less one? Answer, Polus, and fear not; for you will come to no harm if you nobly resign yourself into the healing hand of the argument as to a physician without shrinking, and either say 'Yes' or 'No' to me.

Pol.

I should say 'No.'

Soc.

Would any other man prefer a greater to a less evil?

Pol.

No, not according to this way of putting the case, Socrates.

Soc.

Polus is refuted out of his own mouth.

Then I said truly, Polus, that neither you, nor I, nor any man, would rather do than suffer injustice; for to do injustice is the greater evil of the two.

Pol.

That is the conclusion.

Soc.

The next question: Is it better for the guilty to suffer or not to suffer punishment?

You see, Polus, when you compare the two kinds of refutations, how unlike they are. All men, with the exception of myself, are of your way of thinking; but your single assent and witness are enough for me,—I have no need of any 476other; I take your suffrage, and am regardless of the rest. Enough of this, and now let us proceed to the next question; which is, Whether the greatest of evils to a guilty man is to suffer punishment, as you supposed, or whether to escape punishment is not a greater evil, as I supposed. Consider:—You would say that to suffer punishment is another name for being justly corrected when you do wrong?

Pol.

I should.

Soc.

And would you not allow that all just things are honourable in so far as they are just? Please to reflect, and tell me your opinion.

Pol.

Yes, Socrates, I think that they are.

Soc.

Consider again:—Where there is an agent, must there not also be a patient?

Pol.

I should say so.

Soc.

And will not the patient suffer that which the agent does, and will not the suffering have the quality of the action? I mean, for example, that if a man strikes, there must be something which is stricken?

Pol.

Yes.

Soc.

And if the striker strikes violently or quickly, that which is struck will be struck violently or quickly?

Pol.

True.

Soc.

And the suffering to him who is stricken is of the same nature as the act of him who strikes?

Pol.

Yes.

Soc.

And if a man burns, there is something which is burned?

Pol.

Certainly.

Soc.

And if he burns in excess or so as to cause pain, the thing burned will be burned in the same way?

Pol.

Truly.

Soc.

And if he cuts, the same argument holds—there will be something cut?

Pol.

Yes.

Soc.

And if the cutting be great or deep or such as will cause pain, the cut will be of the same nature?

Pol.

That is evident.

Soc.

Since the affection of the patient answers to the act of the agent, it follows that he who is punished justly suffers justly, and therefore honourably,

Then you would agree generally to the universal proposition which I was just now asserting: that the affection of the patient answers to the act of the agent?

Pol.

I agree.

Soc.

Then, as this is admitted, let me ask whether being punished is suffering or acting?

Pol.

Suffering, Socrates; there can be no doubt of that.

Soc.

And suffering implies an agent?

Pol.

Certainly, Socrates; and he is the punisher.

Soc.

And he who punishes rightly, punishes justly?

Pol.

Yes.

Soc.

And therefore he acts justly?

Pol.

Justly.

Soc.

Then he who is punished and suffers retribution, suffers justly?

Pol.

That is evident.

Soc.

And that which is just has been admitted to be honourable?

Pol.

Certainly.

Soc.

Then the punisher does what is honourable, and the punished suffers what is honourable?

Pol.

True.

Soc.

And if what is honourable, then what is good, for the honourable is either pleasant or useful? 477

Pol.

Certainly.

Soc.

Then he who is punished suffers what is good?

Pol.

That is true.

Soc.

Then he is benefited?

Pol.

Yes.

Soc.

Do I understand you to mean what I mean by the term 'benefited'? I mean, that if he be justly punished his soul is improved.

Pol.

Surely.

Soc.

Then he who is punished is delivered from the evil of his soul?

Pol.

Yes.

Soc.

and is delivered from the greatest of all evils, the evil of the soul, which, being the most disgraceful, is also the most painful or hurtful.

And is he not then delivered from the greatest evil? Look at the matter in this way:—In respect of a man's estate, do you see any greater evil than poverty?

Pol.

There is no greater evil.

Soc.

Again, in a man's bodily frame, you would say that the evil is weakness and disease and deformity?

Pol.

I should.

Soc.

And do you not imagine that the soul likewise has some evil of her own?

Pol.

Of course.

Soc.

And this you would call injustice and ignorance and cowardice, and the like?

Pol.

Certainly.

Soc.

So then, in mind, body, and estate, which are three, you have pointed out three corresponding evils—injustice, disease, poverty?

Pol.

True.

Soc.

And which of the evils is the most disgraceful?—Is not the most disgraceful of them injustice, and in general the evil of the soul?

Pol.

By far the most.

Soc.

And if the most disgraceful, then also the worst?

Pol.

What do you mean, Socrates?

Soc.

I mean to say, that what is most disgraceful has been already admitted to be most painful or hurtful, or both.

Pol.

Certainly.

Soc.

And now injustice and all evil in the soul has been admitted by us to be most disgraceful?

Pol.

It has been admitted.

Soc.

And most disgraceful either because most painful and causing excessive pain, or most hurtful, or both?

Pol.

Certainly.

Soc.

And therefore to be unjust and intemperate, and cowardly and ignorant, is more painful than to be poor and sick?

Pol.

Polus stumbles at the notion which he has already admitted, that the evil of the soul is more painful than that of the body.

Nay, Socrates; the painfulness does not appear to me to follow from your premises.

Soc.

Then, if, as you would argue, not more painful, the evil of the soul is of all evils the most disgraceful; and the excess of disgrace must be caused by some preternatural greatness, or extraordinary hurtfulness of the evil.

Pol.

Clearly.

Soc.

And that which exceeds most in hurtfulness will be the greatest of evils?

Pol.

Yes.

Soc.

Then injustice and intemperance, and in general the depravity of the soul, are the greatest of evils?

Pol.

That is evident.

Soc.

Now, what art is there which delivers us from poverty? Does not the art of making money?

Pol.

Yes.

Soc.

And what art frees us from disease? Does not the art of medicine?

Pol.

Very true.

Soc.

478And what from vice and injustice? If you are not able to answer at once, ask yourself whither we go with the sick, and to whom we take them.

Pol.

To the physicians, Socrates.

Soc.

And to whom do we go with the unjust and intemperate?

Pol.

To the judges, you mean.

Soc.

—Who are to punish them?

Pol.

Yes.

Soc.

And do not those who rightly punish others, punish them in accordance with a certain rule of justice?

Pol.

Clearly.

Soc.

Then the art of money-making frees a man from poverty; medicine from disease; and justice from intemperance and injustice?

Pol.

That is evident.

Soc.

Which, then, is the best of these three?

Pol.

Will you enumerate them?

Soc.

Money-making, medicine, and justice.

Pol.

Justice, Socrates, far excels the two others.

Soc.

And justice, if the best, gives the greatest pleasure or advantage or both?

Pol.

Yes.

Soc.

But is the being healed a pleasant thing, and are those who are being healed pleased?

Pol.

I think not.

Soc.

A useful thing, then?

Pol.

Yes.

Soc.

Punishment is the deliverance from evil, and he who is punished, like him who is healed, is happier than he who is not punished or not healed.

Yes, because the patient is delivered from a great evil; and this is the advantage of enduring the pain—that you get well?

Pol.

Certainly.

Soc.

And would he be the happier man in his bodily condition, who is healed, or who never was out of health?

Pol.

Clearly he who was never out of health.

Soc.

Yes; for happiness surely does not consist in being delivered from evils, but in never having had them.

Pol.

True.

Soc.

And suppose the case of two persons who have some evil in their bodies, and that one of them is healed and delivered from evil, and another is not healed, but retains the evil—which of them is the most miserable?

Pol.

Clearly he who is not healed.

Soc.

And was not punishment said by us to be a deliverance from the greatest of evils, which is vice?

Pol.

True.

Soc.

And justice punishes us, and makes us more just, and is the medicine of our vice?

Pol.

True.

Soc.

Happiest of all is he who is just;

He, then, has the first place in the scale of happiness who has never had vice in his soul; for this has been shown to be the greatest of evils.

Pol.

Clearly.

Soc.

And he has the second place, who is delivered from vice?

Pol.

happy in the second degree he who is delivered from injustice by punishment, most deluded and most unhappy of all he who lives on, enjoying the fruit of his crimes.

True.

Soc.

That is to say, he who receives admonition and rebuke and punishment?

Pol.

Yes.

Soc.

Then he lives worst, who, having been unjust, has no deliverance from injustice?

Pol.

Certainly.

Soc.

479That is, he lives worst who commits the greatest crimes, and who, being the most unjust of men, succeeds in escaping rebuke or correction or punishment; and this, as you say, has been accomplished by Archelaus and other tyrants and rhetoricians and potentates ?

Pol.

True.

Soc.

May not their way of proceeding, my friend, be compared to the conduct of a person who is afflicted with the worst of diseases and yet contrives not to pay the penalty to the physician for his sins against his constitution, and will not be cured, because, like a child, he is afraid of the pain of being burned or cut:—Is not that a parallel case?

Pol.

Yes, truly.

Soc.

He would seem as if he did not know the nature of health and bodily vigour; and if we are right, Polus, in our previous conclusions, they are in a like case who strive to evade justice, which they see to be painful, but are blind to the advantage which ensues from it, not knowing how far more miserable a companion a diseased soul is than a diseased body; a soul, I say, which is corrupt and unrighteous and unholy. And hence they do all that they can to avoid punishment and to avoid being released from the greatest of evils; they provide themselves with money and friends, and cultivate to the utmost their powers of persuasion. But if we, Polus, are right, do you see what follows, or shall we draw out the consequences in form?

Pol.

If you please.

Soc.

Is it not a fact that injustice, and the doing of injustice, is the greatest of evils?

Pol.

That is quite clear.

Soc.

And further, that to suffer punishment is the way to be released from this evil?

Pol.

True.

Soc.

And not to suffer, is to perpetuate the evil?

Pol.

Yes.

Soc.

To do wrong, then, is second only in the scale of evils; but to do wrong and not to be punished, is first and greatest of all?

Pol.

That is true.

Soc.

Archelaus then is more miserable than his victims.

Well, and was not this the point in dispute, my friend? You deemed Archelaus happy, because he was a very great criminal and unpunished: I, on the other hand, maintained that he or any other who like him has done wrong and has not been punished, is, and ought to be, the most miserable of all men; and that the doer of injustice is more miserable than the sufferer; and he who escapes punishment, more miserable than he who suffers.—Was not that what I said?

Pol.

Yes.

Soc.

And it has been proved to be true?

Pol.

Certainly.

Soc.

Well, Polus, but if this is true, where is the great use 480of rhetoric? If we admit what has been just now said, every man ought in every way to guard himself against doing wrong, for he will thereby suffer great evil?

Pol.

True.

Soc.

Injustice, if not removed, will become the cancer of the soul.

And if he, or any one about whom he cares, does wrong, he ought of his own accord to go where he will be immediately punished; he will run to the judge, as he would to the physician, in order that the disease of injustice may not be rendered chronic and become the incurable cancer of the soul; must we not allow this consequence, Polus, if our former admissions are to stand:—is any other inference consistent with them?

Pol.

To that, Socrates, there can be but one answer.

Soc.

The only use of rhetoric is that it enables a man to Socrates, Polus, Callicles. expose his own injustice and to petition for speedy punishment.

Then rhetoric is of no use to us, Polus, in helping a man to excuse his own injustice, or that of his parents or friends, or children or country; but may be of use to any one who holds that instead of excusing he ought to accuse—himself above all, and in the next degree his family or any of his friends who may be doing wrong; he should bring to light the iniquity and not conceal it, that so the wrong-doer may suffer and be made whole; and he should even force himself and others not to shrink, but with closed eyes like brave men to let the physician operate with knife or searing iron, not regarding the pain, in the hope of attaining the good and the honourable; let him who has done things worthy of stripes, allow himself to be scourged, if of bonds, to be bound, if of a fine, to be fined, if of exile, to be exiled, if of death, to die, himself being the first to accuse himself and his own relations, and using rhetoric to this end, that his and their unjust actions may be made manifest, and that they themselves may be delivered from injustice, which is the greatest evil. Then, Polus, rhetoric would indeed be useful. Do you say 'Yes' or 'No' to that?

Pol.

To me, Socrates, what you are saying appears very strange, though probably in agreement with your premises.

Soc.

Is not this the conclusion, if the premises are not disproven?

Pol.

Yes; it certainly is.

Soc.

A slighter and secondary use of rhetoric in self-defence against an enemy, or in preventing the punishment of an enemy.

And from the opposite point of view, if indeed it be our duty to harm another, whether an enemy or not—I except the case of self-defence—then I have to be upon my 481guard—but if my enemy injures a third person, then in every sort of way, by word as well as deed, I should try to prevent his being punished, or appearing before the judge; and if he appears, I should contrive that he should escape, and not suffer punishment: if he has stolen a sum of money, let him keep what he has stolen and spend it on him and his, regardless of religion and justice; and if he have done things worthy of death, let him not die, but rather be immortal in his wickedness; or, if this is not possible, let him at any rate be allowed to live as long as he can. For such purposes, Polus, rhetoric may be useful, but is of small if of any use to him who is not intending to commit injustice; at least, there was no such use discovered by us in the previous discussion.

Cal.

Tell me, Chaerephon, is Socrates in earnest, or is he joking?

Chaer.

Socrates, Callias, Chaerephon.

I should say, Callicles, that he is in most profound earnest; but you may as well ask him.

Cal.

Callicles asks in amazement whether Socrates really means what he says.

By the gods, and I will. Tell me, Socrates, are you in earnest, or only in jest? For if you are in earnest, and what you say is true, is not the whole of human life turned upside down; and are we not doing, as would appear, in everything the opposite of what we ought to be doing?

Soc.

I am only repeating the words of philosophy, whose lover I am. For as you love the Athenian people and their namesake Demus, so I have two loves, philosophy and Alcibiades. The son of Cleinias is inconstant, but philosophy is ever the same: she it is whom you have to refute: I am only her mouthpiece. Socrates, Callicles.

O Callicles, if there were not some community of feelings among mankind, however varying in different persons—I mean to say, if every man's feelings were peculiar to himself and were not shared by the rest of his species—I do not see how we could ever communicate our impressions to one another. I make this remark because I perceive that you and I have a common feeling. For we are lovers both, and both of us have two loves apiece:—I am the lover of Alcibiades, the son of Cleinias, and of philosophy; and you of the Athenian Demus, and of Demus the son of Pyrilampes. Now, I observe that you, with all your cleverness, do not venture to contradict your favourite in any word or opinion of his; but as he changes you change, backwards and forwards. When the Athenian Demus denies anything that you are saying in the assembly, you go over to his opinion; and you do the same with Demus, the fair young son of Pyrilampes. For you have not the power to resist the words and ideas of your loves; and if a person were to express surprise at the strangeness of what you say from time to time when under their influence, you would probably reply to 482him, if you were honest, that you cannot help saying what your loves say unless they are prevented; and that you can only be silent when they are. Now you must understand that my words are an echo too, and therefore you need not wonder at me; but if you want to silence me, silence philosophy, who is my love, for she is always telling me what I am now telling you, my friend; neither is she capricious like my other love, for the son of Cleinias says one thing to-day and another thing to-morrow, but philosophy is always true. She is the teacher at whose words you are now wondering, and you have heard her yourself. Her you must refute, and either show, as I was saying, that to do injustice and to escape punishment is not the worst of all evils; or, if you leave her word unrefuted, by the dog the god of Egypt, I declare, O Callicles, that Callicles will never be at one with himself, but that his whole life will be a discord. And yet, my friend, I would rather that my lyre should be inharmonious, and that there should be no music in the chorus which I provided; aye, or that the whole world should be at odds with me, and oppose me, rather than that I myself should be at odds with myself, and contradict myself.

Cal.

Polus was vanquished because he refused to take a bold line.Callicles would return to the rule of nature in the lower sense of the term.Callicles.Convention was only introduced by the weak majority in order to protect themselves against the few strong.A man of courage would easily break down the guards of convention.

O Socrates, you are a regular declaimer, and seem to be running riot in the argument. And now you are declaiming in this way because Polus has fallen into the same error himself of which he accused Gorgias:—for he said that when Gorgias was asked by you, whether, if some one came to him who wanted to learn rhetoric, and did not know justice, he would teach him justice, Gorgias in his modesty replied that he would, because he thought that mankind in general would be displeased if he answered 'No;' and then in consequence of this admission, Gorgias was compelled to contradict himself, that being just the sort of thing in which you delight. Whereupon Polus laughed at you deservedly, as I think; but now he has himself fallen into the same trap. I cannot say very much for his wit when he conceded to you that to do is more dishonourable than to suffer injustice, for this was the admission which led to his being entangled by you; and because he was too modest to say what he thought, he had his mouth stopped. For the truth is, Socrates, that you, who pretend to be engaged in the pursuit of truth, are appealing now to the popular and vulgar notions of right, which are not natural, but only conventional. Convention and nature are generally at variance with one another: and hence, if a person is too 483modest to say what he thinks, he is compelled to contradict himself; and you, in your ingenuity perceiving the advantage to be thereby gained, slyly ask of him who is arguing conventionally a question which is to be determined by the rule of nature; and if he is talking of the rule of nature, you slip away to custom: as, for instance, you did in this very discussion about doing and suffering injustice. When Polus was speaking of the conventionally dishonourable, you assailed him from the point of view of nature; for by the rule of nature, to suffer injustice is the greater disgrace because the greater evil; but conventionally, to do evil is the more disgraceful. For the suffering of injustice is not the part of a man, but of a slave, who indeed had better die than live; since when he is wronged and trampled upon, he is unable to help himself, or any other about whom he cares. The reason, as I conceive, is that the makers of laws are the majority who are weak; and they make laws and distribute praises and censures with a view to themselves and to their own interests; and they terrify the stronger sort of men, and those who are able to get the better of them, in order that they may not get the better of them; and they say, that dishonesty is shameful and unjust; meaning, by the word injustice, the desire of a man to have more than his neighbours; for knowing their own inferiority, I suspect that they are too glad of equality. And therefore the endeavour to have more than the many, is conventionally said to be shameful and unjust, and is called injustice , whereas nature herself intimates that it is just for the better to have more than the worse, the more powerful than the weaker; and in many ways she shows, among men as well as among animals, and indeed among whole cities and races, that justice consists in the superior ruling over and having more than the inferior. For on what principle of justice did Xerxes invade Hellas, or his father the Scythians? (not to speak of numberless other examples). Nay, but these are the men who act according to nature; yes, by Heaven, and according to the law of nature: not, perhaps, according to that artificial law, which we invent and impose upon our fellows, of whom we take the best and strongest from their youth upwards, and tame them like young lions,—charming them with the sound 484of the voice, and saying to them, that with equality they must be content, and that the equal is the honourable and the just. But if there were a man who had sufficient force, he would shake off and break through, and escape from all this; he would trample under foot all our formulas and spells and charms, and all our laws which are against nature: the slave would rise in rebellion and be lord over us, and the light of natural justice would shine forth. And this I take to be the sentiment of Pindar, when he says in his poem, that

- Callicles.
- 'Law is the king of all, of mortals as well as of immortals;'

this, as he says,

Pindar.

'Makes might to be right, doing violence with highest hand; as I infer from the deeds of Heracles, for without buying them—'

A little philosophy not a bad thing in youth.

—I do not remember the exact words, but the meaning is, that without buying them, and without their being given to him, he carried off the oxen of Geryon, according to the law of natural right, and that the oxen and other possessions of the weaker and inferior properly belong to the stronger and superior. And this is true, as you may ascertain, if you will leave philosophy and go on to higher things: for philosophy, Socrates, if pursued in moderation and at the proper age, is an elegant accomplishment, but too much philosophy is the ruin of human life. Even if a man has good parts, still, if he carries philosophy into later life, he is necessarily ignorant of all those things which a gentleman and a person of honour ought to know; he is inexperienced in the laws of the State, and in the language which ought to be used in the dealings of man with man, whether private or public, and utterly ignorant of the pleasures and desires of mankind and of human character in general. And people of this sort, when they betake themselves to politics or business, are as ridiculous as I imagine the politicians to be, when they make their appearance in the arena of philosophy. For, as Euripides says,

Euripides.

'Every man shines in that and pursues that, and devotes the greatest portion of the day to that in which he most excels,'

Callicles. But the study should not be continued into later life.

485 but anything in which he is inferior, he avoids and depreciates, and praises the opposite from partiality to himself, and because he thinks that he will thus praise himself. The true principle is to unite them. Philosophy, as a part of education, is an excellent thing, and there is no disgrace to a man while he is young in pursuing such a study; but when he is more advanced in years, the thing becomes ridiculous, and I feel towards philosophers as I do towards those who lisp and imitate children. For I love to see a little child, who is not of an age to speak plainly, lisping at his play; there is an appearance of grace and freedom in his utterance, which is natural to his childish years. But when I hear some small creature carefully articulating its words, I am offended; the sound is disagreeable, and has to my ears the twang of slavery. So when I hear a man lisping, or see him playing like a child, his behaviour appears to me ridiculous and unmanly and worthy of stripes. And I have the same feeling about students of philosophy; when I see a youth thus engaged,—the study appears to me to be in character, and becoming a man of a liberal education, and him who neglects philosophy I regard as an inferior man, who will never aspire to anything great or noble. But if I see him continuing the study in later life, and not leaving off, I should like to beat him, Socrates; for, as I was saying, such a one, even though he have good natural parts, becomes effeminate. He flies from the busy centre and the market-place, in which, as the poet says, men become distinguished; he creeps into a corner for the rest of his life, and talks in a whisper with three or four admiring youths, but never speaks out like a freeman in a satisfactory manner. Now I, Socrates, am very well inclined towards you, and my feeling may be compared with that of Zethus towards Amphion, in the play of Euripides, whom I was mentioning just now: for I am disposed to say to you much what Zethus said to his brother, that you, Socrates, are careless about the things of which you ought to be careful; and that you

- 'Who have a soul so noble, are remarkable for a puerile exterior; 486
- Neither in a court of justice could you state a case, or give any reason or proof,
- Or offer valiant counsel on another's behalf.'

Socrates, Callicles.

And you must not be offended, my dear Socrates, for I am speaking out of good-will towards you, if I ask whether you are not ashamed of being thus defenceless; which I affirm to be the condition not of you only but of all those who will carry the study of philosophy too far. For suppose that some one were to take you, or any one of your sort, off to prison, declaring that you had done wrong when you had done no wrong, you must allow that you would not know what to do:—there you would stand giddy and gaping, and not having a word to say; and when you went up before the Court, even if the accuser were a poor creature and not good for much, you would die if he were disposed to claim the penalty of death. And yet, Socrates, what is the value of

- 'An art which converts a man of sense into a fool,'

who is helpless, and has no power to save either himself or others, when he is in the greatest danger and is going to be despoiled by his enemies of all his goods, and has to live, simply deprived of his rights of citizenship?—he being a man who, if I may use the expression, may be boxed on the ears with impunity. Then, my good friend, take my advice, and refute no more:

- 'Learn the philosophy of business, and acquire the reputation of wisdom.
- But leave to others these niceties,'

whether they are to be described as follies or absurdities:

- 'For they will only
- Give you poverty for the inmate of your dwelling.'

Cease, then, emulating these paltry splitters of words, and emulate only the man of substance and honour, who is well to do.

Soc.

Callicles the desired touchstone of Socrates.

If my soul, Callicles, were made of gold, should I not rejoice to discover one of those stones with which they test gold, and the very best possible one to which I might bring my soul; and if the stone and I agreed in approving of her training, then I should know that I was in a satisfactory state, and that no other test was needed by me.

Cal.

What is your meaning, Socrates?

Soc.

I will tell you; I think that I have found in you the desired touchstone.

Cal.

Why?

Soc.

Socrates.Other men have not the knowledge or frankness or good-will which is required; and they are too modest. His sincerity is shown by his consistency.Socrates, Callicles.But still he would ask, What Callicles means by the superior?

Because I am sure that if you agree with me in any of the opinions which my soul forms, I have at last found the truth indeed. For I consider that if a man is to make a 487complete trial of the good or evil of the soul, he ought to have three qualities—knowledge, good-will, outspokenness, which are all possessed by you. Many whom I meet are unable to make trial of me, because they are not wise as you are; others are wise, but they will not tell me the truth, because they have not the same interest in me which you have; and these two strangers, Gorgias and Polus, are undoubtedly wise men and my very good friends, but they are not outspoken enough, and they are too modest. Why, their modesty is so great that they are driven to contradict themselves, first one and then the other of them, in the face of a large company, on matters of the highest moment. But you have all the qualities in which these others are deficient, having received an excellent education; to this many Athenians can testify. And you are my friend. Shall I tell you why I think so? I know that you, Callicles, and Tisander of Aphidnae, and Andron the son of Androtion, and Nausicydes of the deme of Cholarges, studied together: there were four of you, and I once heard you advising with one another as to the extent to which the pursuit of philosophy should be carried, and, as I know, you came to the conclusion that the study should not be pushed too much into detail. You were cautioning one another not to be overwise; you were afraid that too much wisdom might unconsciously to yourselves be the ruin of you. And now when I hear you giving the same advice to me which you then gave to your most intimate friends, I have a sufficient evidence of your real good-will to me. And of the frankness of your nature and freedom from modesty I am assured by yourself, and the assurance is confirmed by your last speech. Well then, the inference in the present case clearly is, that if you agree with me in an argument about any point, that point will have been sufficiently tested by us, and will not require to be submitted to any further test. For you could not have agreed with me, either from lack of knowledge or from superfluity of modesty, nor yet from a desire to deceive me, for you are my friend, as you tell me yourself. And therefore when you and I are agreed, the result will be the attainment of perfect truth. Now there is no nobler enquiry, Callicles, than that which you censure me for making,—What ought the character of a man to be, and what his pursuits, and how far is he to go, both in maturer years and in youth? For be assured that if I err in my own conduct I do not err intentionally, 488but from ignorance. Do not then desist from advising me, now that you have begun, until I have learned clearly what this is which I am to practise, and how I may acquire it. And if you find me assenting to your words, and hereafter not doing that to which I assented, call me 'dolt,' and deem me unworthy of receiving further instruction. Once more, then, tell me what you and Pindar mean by natural justice: Do you not mean that the superior should take the property of the inferior by force; that the better should rule the worse, the noble have more than the mean? Am I not right in my recollection?

Cal.

Yes; that is what I was saying, and so I still aver.

Soc.

And do you mean by the better the same as the superior? for I could not make out what you were saying at the time—whether you meant by the superior the stronger, and that the weaker must obey the stronger, as you seemed to imply when you said that great cities attack small ones in accordance with natural right, because they are superior and stronger, as though the superior and stronger and better were the same; or whether the better may be also the inferior and weaker, and the superior the worse, or whether better is to be defined in the same way as superior:—this is the point which I want to have cleared up. Are the superior and better and stronger the same or different?

Cal.

I say unequivocally that they are the same.

Soc.

He means the better and stronger, and therefore the many who make the laws, which are noble because they are made by the better.

Then the many are by nature superior to the one, against whom, as you were saying, they make the laws?

Cal.

Certainly.

Soc.

Then the laws of the many are the laws of the superior?

Cal.

Very true.

Soc.

Then they are the laws of the better; for the superior class are far better, as you were saying?

Cal.

Yes.

Soc.

And since they are superior, the laws which are made by them are by nature good?

Cal.

Yes.

Soc.

And the many are also of opinion that to do is more disgraceful than to suffer injustice.Socrates, Callicles.

And are not the many of opinion, as you were lately 489saying, that justice is equality, and that to do is more disgraceful than to suffer injustice?—is that so or not? Answer, Callicles, and let no modesty be found to come in the way ; do the many think, or do they not think thus?—I must beg of you to answer, in order that if you agree with me I may fortify myself by the assent of so competent an authority.

Cal.

Yes; the opinion of the many is what you say.

Soc.

Then not only custom but nature also affirms that to do is more disgraceful than to suffer injustice, and that justice is equality; so that you seem to have been wrong in your former assertion, when accusing me you said that nature and custom are opposed, and that I, knowing this, was dishonestly playing between them, appealing to custom when the argument is about nature, and to nature when the argument is about custom?

Cal.

'Of course I don't mean the mob.'

This man will never cease talking nonsense. At your age, Socrates, are you not ashamed to be catching at words and chuckling over some verbal slip? do you not see—have I not told you already, that by superior I mean better: do you imagine me to say, that if a rabble of slaves and nondescripts, who are of no use except perhaps for their physical strength, get together, their ipsissima verba are laws?

Soc.

Ho! my philosopher, is that your line?

Cal.

Certainly.

Soc.

I was thinking, Callicles, that something of the kind must have been in your mind, and that is why I repeated the question,—What is the superior? I wanted to know clearly what you meant; for you surely do not think that two men are better than one, or that your slaves are better than you because they are stronger? Then please to begin again, and tell me who the better are, if they are not the stronger; and I will ask you, great Sir, to be a little milder in your instructions, or I shall have to run away from you.

Cal.

You are ironical.

Soc.

Then once more,—Who are the better?

No, by the hero Zethus, Callicles, by whose aid you were just now saying (486 A) many ironical things against me, I am not:—tell me, then, whom you mean by the better?

Cal.

I mean the more excellent.

Soc.

Do you not see that you are yourself using words which have no meaning and that you are explaining nothing?—will you tell me whether you mean by the better and superior the wiser, or if not, whom?

Cal.

490Most assuredly, I do mean the wiser.

Soc.

The wiser: the one wise among ten thousand fools,—he ought to rule.

Then according to you, one wise man may often be superior to ten thousand fools, and he ought to rule them, and they ought to be his subjects, and he ought to have more than they should. This is what I believe that you mean (and you must not suppose that I am word-catching), if you allow that the one is superior to the ten thousand?

Cal.

Yes; that is what I mean, and that is what I conceive to be natural justice—that the better and wiser should rule and have more than the inferior.

Soc.

But this is contrary to the analogy of the other arts.

Stop there, and let me ask you what you would say in this case: Let us suppose that we are all together as we are now; there are several of us, and we have a large common store of meats and drinks, and there are all sorts of persons in our company having various degrees of strength and weakness, and one of us, being a physician, is wiser in the matter of food than all the rest, and he is probably stronger than some and not so strong as others of us—will he not, being wiser, be also better than we are, and our superior in this matter of food?

Cal.

Certainly.

Soc.

Either, then, he will have a larger share of the meats and drinks, because he is better, or he will have the distribution of all of them by reason of his authority, but he will not expend or make use of a larger share of them on his own person, or if he does, he will be punished;—his share will exceed that of some, and be less than that of others, and if he be the weakest of all, he being the best of all will have the smallest share of all, Callicles:—am I not right, my friend?

Cal.

Callicles is disgusted at the commonplace parallels of Socrates.

You talk about meats and drinks and physicians and other nonsense; I am not speaking of them.

Soc.

Well, but do you admit that the wiser is the better? Answer 'Yes' or 'No.'

Cal.

Yes.

Soc.

And ought not the better to have a larger share?

Cal.

Not of meats and drinks.

Soc.

I understand: then, perhaps, of coats—the skilfullest weaver ought to have the largest coat, and the greatest number of them, and go about clothed in the best and finest of them?

Cal.

Fudge about coats!

Soc.

Then the skilfullest and best in making shoes ought to have the advantage in shoes; the shoemaker, clearly, should walk about in the largest shoes, and have the greatest number of them?

Cal.

Fudge about shoes! What nonsense are you talking?

Soc.

Or, if this is not your meaning, perhaps you would say that the wise and good and true husbandman should actually have a larger share of seeds, and have as much seed as possible for his own land?

Cal.

How you go on, always talking in the same way, Socrates!

Soc.

Yes, Callicles, and also about the same things. 491

Cal.

Yes, by the Gods, you are literally always talking of cobblers and fullers and cooks and doctors, as if this had to do with our argument.

Soc.

But why will you not tell me in what a man must be superior and wiser in order to claim a larger share; will you neither accept a suggestion, nor offer one?

Cal.

I have already told you. In the first place, I mean by superiors not cobblers or cooks, but wise politicians who understand the administration of a state, and who are not only wise, but also valiant and able to carry out their designs, and not the men to faint from want of soul.

Soc.

Socrates is accused of always saying the same things: he accuses Callicles of never saying the same about the same.

See now, most excellent Callicles, how different my charge against you is from that which you bring against me, for you reproach me with always saying the same; but I reproach you with never saying the same about the same things, for at one time you were defining the better and the superior to be the stronger, then again as the wiser, and now you bring forward a new notion; the superior and the better are now declared by you to be the more courageous: I wish, my good friend, that you would tell me, once for all, whom you affirm to be the better and superior, and in what they are better?

Cal.

I have already told you that I mean those who are wise and courageous in the administration of a state—they ought to be the rulers of their states, and justice consists in their having more than their subjects.

Soc.

But whether rulers or subjects will they or will they not have more than themselves, my friend?

Cal.

What do you mean?

Soc.

I mean that every man is his own ruler; but perhaps you think that there is no necessity for him to rule himself; he is only required to rule others?

Cal.

What do you mean by his 'ruling over himself'?

Soc.

A simple thing enough; just what is commonly said, that a man should be temperate and master of himself, and ruler of his own pleasures and passions.

Cal.

What innocence! you mean those fools,—the temperate?

Soc.

Certainly:—any one may know that to be my meaning.

Cal.

Callicles reasserts his doctrine that the esteem in which virtue and justice are held is due only to men's fear for themselves. No man who has the power to enjoy himself practises self-control.

Quite so, Socrates; and they are really fools, for how can a man be happy who is the servant of anything? On the contrary, I plainly assert, that he who would truly live ought to allow his desires to wax to the uttermost, and not to chastise them; but when they have grown to their greatest 492he should have courage and intelligence to minister to them and to satisfy all his longings. And this I affirm to be natural justice and nobility. To this however the many cannot attain; and they blame the strong man because they are ashamed of their own weakness, which they desire to conceal, and hence they say that intemperance is base. As I have remarked already, they enslave the nobler natures, and being unable to satisfy their pleasures, they praise temperance and justice out of their own cowardice. For if a man had been originally the son of a king, or had a nature capable of acquiring an empire or a tyranny or sovereignty, what could be more truly base or evil than temperance—to a man like him, I say, who might freely be enjoying every good, and has no one to stand in his way, and yet has admitted custom and reason and the opinion of other men to be lords over him?—must not he be in a miserable plight whom the reputation of justice and temperance hinders from giving more to his friends than to his enemies, even though he be a ruler in his city? Nay, Socrates, for you profess to be a votary of the truth, and the truth is this:—that luxury and intemperance and licence, if they be provided with means, are virtue and happiness—all the rest is a mere bauble, agreements contrary to nature, foolish talk of men, nothing worth .

Soc.

There is a noble freedom, Callicles, in your way of approaching the argument; for what you say is what the rest of the world think, but do not like to say. And I must beg of you to persevere, that the true rule of human life may become manifest. Tell me, then:—you say, do you not, that in the rightly-developed man the passions ought not to be controlled, but that we should let them grow to the utmost and somehow or other satisfy them, and that this is virtue?

Cal.

Yes; I do.

Soc.

Then those who want nothing are not truly said to be happy?

Cal.

To live without pleasure or passion is to be dead.

No indeed, for then stones and dead men would be the happiest of all.

Soc.

But surely life according to your view is an awful thing; and indeed I think that Euripides may have been right in saying,

- 'Who knows if life be not death and death life;'

No; the true death, as Pythagorean philosophy tells us, is to pour water out of a vessel full of holes into a colander full of holes.

and that we are very likely dead; I have heard a philosopher 493say that at this moment we are actually dead, and that the body (σωμα) is our tomb (σημα), and that the part of the soul which is the seat of the desires is liable to be tossed about by words and blown up and down; and some ingenious person, probably a Sicilian or an Italian, playing with the word, invented a tale in which he called the soul—because of its believing and make-believe nature—a vessel, and the ignorant he called the uninitiated or leaky, and the place in the souls of the uninitiated in which the desires are seated, being the intemperate and incontinent part, he compared to a vessel full of holes, because it can never be satisfied. He is not of your way of thinking, Callicles, for he declares, that of all the souls in Hades, meaning the invisible world (ἀειδες), these uninitiated or leaky persons are the most miserable, and that they pour water into a vessel which is full of holes out of a colander which is similarly perforated. The colander, as my informer assures me, is the soul, and the soul which he compares to a colander is the soul of the ignorant, which is likewise full of holes, and therefore incontinent, owing to a bad memory and want of faith. These notions are strange enough, but they show the principle which, if I can, I would fain prove to you; that you should change your mind, and, instead of the intemperate and insatiate life, choose that which is orderly and sufficient and has a due provision for daily needs. Do I make any impression on you, and are you coming over to the opinion that the orderly are happier than the intemperate? Or do I fail to persuade you, and, however many tales I rehearse to you, do you continue of the same opinion still?

Cal.

The latter, Socrates, is more like the truth.

Soc.

The temperate man is the sound, the intemperate the leaky vessel.

Well, I will tell you another image, which comes out of the same school:—Let me request you to consider how far you would accept this as an account of the two lives of the temperate and intemperate in a figure:—There are two men, both of whom have a number of casks; the one man has his casks sound and full, one of wine, another of honey, and a third of milk, besides others filled with other liquids, and the streams which fill them are few and scanty, and he can only obtain them with a great deal of toil and difficulty; but when his casks are once filled he has no need to feed them any more, and has no further trouble with them or care about them. The other, in like manner, can procure streams, though not without difficulty; but his vessels are leaky and unsound, and night and day he is compelled to be filling 494them, and if he pauses for a moment, he is in an agony of pain. Such are their respective lives:—And now would you say that the life of the intemperate is happier than that of the temperate? Do I not convince you that the opposite is the truth?

Cal.

The life of desire and pleasure is not to be compared to a full vessel, but to an ever-running stream.

You do not convince me, Socrates, for the one who has filled himself has no longer any pleasure left; and this, as I was just now saying, is the life of a stone: he has neither joy nor sorrow after he is once filled; but the pleasure depends on the superabundance of the influx.

Soc.

But the more you pour in, the greater the waste; and the holes must be large for the liquid to escape.

Cal.

Certainly.

Soc.

The life which you are now depicting is not that of a dead man, or of a stone, but of a cormorant; you mean that he is to be hungering and eating?

Cal.

Yes.

Soc.

And he is to be thirsting and drinking?

Cal.

Yes, that is what I mean; he is to have all his desires about him, and to be able to live happily in the gratification of them.

Soc.

Capital, excellent; go on as you have begun, and have no shame; I, too, must disencumber myself of shame: and first, will you tell me whether you include itching and scratching, provided you have enough of them and pass your life in scratching, in your notion of happiness?

Cal.

What a strange being you are, Socrates! a regular mob-orator.

Soc.

That was the reason, Callicles, why I scared Polus and Gorgias, until they were too modest to say what they thought; but you will not be too modest and will not be scared, for you are a brave man. And now, answer my question.

Cal.

I answer, that even the scratcher would live pleasantly.

Soc.

And if pleasantly, then also happily?

Cal.

To be sure.

Soc.

Callicles professes a virtuous indignation at the very mention of the consequences of his own doctrine.

But what if the itching is not confined to the head? Shall I pursue the question? And here, Callicles, I would have you consider how you would reply if consequences are pressed upon you, especially if in the last resort you are asked, whether the life of a catamite is not terrible, foul, miserable? Or would you venture to say, that they too are happy, if they only get enough of what they want?

Cal.

Are you not ashamed, Socrates, of introducing such topics into the argument?

Soc.

Well, my fine friend, but am I the introducer of these topics, or he who says without any qualification that all who feel pleasure in whatever manner are happy, and who admits of no distinction between good and bad pleasures? And I 495 would still ask, whether you say that pleasure and good are the same, or whether there is some pleasure which is not a good?

Cal.

Well, then, for the sake of consistency, I will say that they are the same.

Soc.

You are breaking the original agreement, Callicles, and will no longer be a satisfactory companion in the search after truth, if you say what is contrary to your real opinion.

Cal.

Why, that is what you are doing too, Socrates.

Soc.

Then we are both doing wrong. Still, my dear friend, I would ask you to consider whether pleasure, from whatever source derived, is the good; for, if this be true, then the disagreeable consequences which have been darkly intimated must follow, and many others.

Cal.

That, Socrates, is only your opinion.

Soc.

And do you, Callicles, seriously maintain what you are saying?

Cal.

Indeed I do.

Soc.

Then, as you are in earnest, shall we proceed with the argument?

Cal.

By all means .

Soc.

Callicles, having admitted that pleasure and good are the same, is led to make the further admission that pleasure and knowledge and courage are different.

Well, if you are willing to proceed, determine this question for me:—There is something, I presume, which you would call knowledge?

Cal.

There is.

Soc.

And were you not saying just now, that some courage implied knowledge?

Cal.

I was.

Soc.

And you were speaking of courage and knowledge as two things different from one another?

Cal.

Certainly I was.

Soc.

And would you say that pleasure and knowledge are the same, or not the same?

Cal.

Not the same, O man of wisdom.

Soc.

And would you say that courage differed from pleasure?

Cal.

Certainly.

Soc.

Well, then, let us remember that Callicles, the Acharnian, says that pleasure and good are the same; but that knowledge and courage are not the same, either with one another, or with the good.

Cal.

And what does our friend Socrates, of Foxton, say—does he assent to this, or not?

Soc.

He does not assent; neither will Callicles, when he sees himself truly. You will admit, I suppose, that good and evil fortune are opposed to each other?

Cal.

Yes.

Soc.

And if they are opposed to each other, then, like health and disease, they exclude one another; a man cannot have them both, or be without them both, at the same time?

Cal.

What do you mean?

Soc.

Take the case of any bodily affection:—a man may have the complaint in his eyes which is called ophthalmia?

Cal.

To be sure. 496

Soc.

But he surely cannot have the same eyes well and sound at the same time?

Cal.

Certainly not.

Soc.

And when he has got rid of his ophthalmia, has he got rid of the health of his eyes too? Is the final result, that he gets rid of them both together?

Cal.

Certainly not.

Soc.

That would surely be marvellous and absurd?

Cal.

Very.

Soc.

A man may have good and evil by turns, but not at the same time.

I suppose that he is affected by them, and gets rid of them in turns?

Cal.

Yes.

Soc.

And he may have strength and weakness in the same way, by fits?

Cal.

Yes.

Soc.

Or swiftness and slowness?

Cal.

Certainly.

Soc.

And does he have and not have good and happiness, and their opposites, evil and misery, in a similar alternation?

Cal.

Certainly he has.

Soc.

If then there be anything which a man has and has not at the same time, clearly that cannot be good and evil—do we agree? Please not to answer without consideration.

Cal.

I entirely agree.

Soc.

Go back now to our former admissions.—Did you say that to hunger, I mean the mere state of hunger, was pleasant or painful?

Cal.

I said painful, but that to eat when you are hungry is pleasant.

Soc.

I know; but still the actual hunger is painful: am I not right?

Cal.

Yes.

Soc.

And thirst, too, is painful?

Cal.

Yes, very.

Soc.

Need I adduce any more instances, or would you agree that all wants or desires are painful?

Cal.

I agree, and therefore you need not adduce any more instances.

Soc.

Very good. And you would admit that to drink, when you are thirsty, is pleasant?

Cal.

Yes.

Soc.

And in the sentence which you have just uttered, the word 'thirsty' implies pain?

Cal.

Yes.

Soc.

And the word 'drinking' is expressive of pleasure, and of the satisfaction of the want?

Cal.

Yes.

Soc.

There is pleasure in drinking?

Cal.

Certainly.

Soc.

When you are thirsty?

Cal.

Yes.

Soc.

And in pain?

Cal.

Yes.

Soc.

But he may have pleasure and pain at the same time.

Do you see the inference:—that pleasure and pain are simultaneous, when you say that being thirsty, you drink? For are they not simultaneous, and do they not affect at the same time the same part, whether of the soul or the body?—which of them is affected cannot be supposed to be of any consequence: Is not this true?

Cal.

It is.

Soc.

You said also, that no man could have good and evil fortune at the same time?

Cal.

Yes, I did.

Soc.

Socrates, Callicles, Gorgias.

But you admitted, that when in pain a man might also 497have pleasure?

Cal.

Clearly.

Soc.

Therefore pleasure and pain are not the same as good and evil.

Then pleasure is not the same as good fortune, or pain the same as evil fortune, and therefore the good is not the same as the pleasant?

Cal.

I wish I knew, Socrates, what your quibbling means.

Soc.

You know, Callicles, but you affect not to know.

Cal.

Well, get on, and don't keep fooling: then you will know what a wiseacre you are in your admonition of me.

Soc.

Does not a man cease from his thirst and from his pleasure in drinking at the same time?

Cal.

I do not understand what you are saying.

Gor.

Nay, Callicles, answer, if only for our sakes;—we should like to hear the argument out.

Cal.

Yes, Gorgias, but I must complain of the habitual trifling of Socrates; he is always arguing about little and unworthy questions.

Gor.

What matter? Your reputation, Callicles, is not at stake. Let Socrates argue in his own fashion.

Cal.

Well, then, Socrates, you shall ask these little peddling questions, since Gorgias wishes to have them.

Soc.

I envy you, Callicles, for having been initiated into the great mysteries before you were initiated into the lesser. I thought that this was not allowable. But to return to our argument:—Does not a man cease from thirsting and from the pleasure of drinking at the same moment?

Cal.

True.

Soc.

And if he is hungry, or has any other desire, does he not cease from the desire and the pleasure at the same moment?

Cal.

Very true.

Soc.

Then he ceases from pain and pleasure at the same moment?

Cal.

Yes.

Soc.

But he does not cease from good and evil at the same moment, as you have admitted:—do you still adhere to what you said?

Cal.

Yes, I do; but what is the inference?

Soc.

Socrates, Callicles. Another point of view.

Why, my friend, the inference is that the good is not the same as the pleasant, or the evil the same as the painful; there is a cessation of pleasure and pain at the same moment; but not of good and evil, for they are different. How then can pleasure be the same as good, or pain as evil? And I would have you look at the matter in another light, which could hardly, I think, have been considered by you when you identified them: Are not the good good because they have good present with them, as the beautiful are those who have beauty present with them?

Cal.

Yes.

Soc.

And do you call the fools and cowards good men? For you were saying just now that the courageous and the wise are the good—would you not say so?

Cal.

Certainly.

Soc.

And did you never see a foolish child rejoicing?

Cal.

Yes, I have.

Soc.

And a foolish man too?

Cal.

Yes, certainly; but what is your drift?

Soc.

498Nothing particular, if you will only answer.

Cal.

Yes, I have.

Soc.

And did you ever see a sensible man rejoicing or sorrowing?

Cal.

Yes.

Soc.

Which rejoice and sorrow most—the wise or the foolish?

Cal.

They are much upon a par, I think, in that respect.

Soc.

Enough: And did you ever see a coward in battle?

Cal.

To be sure.

Soc.

And which rejoiced most at the departure of the enemy, the coward or the brave?

Cal.

I should say 'most' of both; or at any rate, they rejoiced about equally.

Soc.

No matter; then the cowards, and not only the brave, rejoice?

Cal.

Greatly.

Soc.

And the foolish; so it would seem?

Cal.

Yes.

Soc.

And are only the cowards pained at the approach of their enemies, or are the brave also pained?

Cal.

Both are pained.

Soc.

And are they equally pained?

Cal.

I should imagine that the cowards are more pained.

Soc.

And are they not better pleased at the enemy's departure?

Cal.

I dare say.

Soc.

Good is in proportion to pleasure, and the bad are often as much or more pleased than the good.

Then are the foolish and the wise and the cowards and the brave all pleased and pained, as you were saying, in nearly equal degree; but are the cowards more pleased and pained than the brave?

Cal.

Yes.

Soc.

But surely the wise and brave are the good, and the foolish and the cowardly are the bad?

Cal.

Yes.

Soc.

Then the good and the bad are pleased and pained in a nearly equal degree?

Cal.

Yes.

Soc.

Then are the good and bad good and bad in a nearly equal degree, or have the bad the advantage both in good and evil? [i. e. in having more pleasure and more pain.]

Cal.

I really do not know what you mean.

Soc.

Why, do you not remember saying that the good were good because good was present with them, and the evil because evil; and that pleasures were goods and pains evils?

Cal.

Yes, I remember.

Soc.

And are not these pleasures or goods present to those who rejoice—if they do rejoice?

Cal.

Certainly.

Soc.

Then those who rejoice are good when goods are present with them?

Cal.

Yes.

Soc.

And those who are in pain have evil or sorrow present with them?

Cal.

Yes.

Soc.

And would you still say that the evil are evil by reason of the presence of evil?

Cal.

I should.

Soc.

Then those who rejoice are good, and those who are in pain evil?

Cal.

Yes.

Soc.

The degrees of good and evil vary with the degrees of pleasure and of pain?

Cal.

Yes.

Soc.

Have the wise man and the fool, the brave and the coward, joy and pain in nearly equal degrees? or would you say that the coward has more?

Cal.

I should say that he has.

Soc.

Help me then to draw out the conclusion which follows from our admissions; for it is good to repeat and 499review what is good twice and thrice over, as they say. Both the wise man and the brave man we allow to be good?

Cal.

Yes.

Soc.

And the foolish man and the coward to be evil?

Cal.

Certainly.

Soc.

And he who has joy is good?

Cal.

Yes.

Soc.

And he who is in pain is evil?

Cal.

Certainly.

Soc.

The good and evil both have joy and pain, but, perhaps, the evil has more of them?

Cal.

Yes.

Soc.

Therefore the bad man is as good as the good, or perhaps even better.

Then must we not infer, that the bad man is as good and bad as the good, or, perhaps, even better?—is not this a further inference which follows equally with the preceding from the assertion that the good and the pleasant are the same:—can this be denied, Callicles?

Cal.

I have been listening and making admissions to you, Socrates; and I remark that if a person grants you anything in play, you, like a child, want to keep hold and will not give it back. But do you really suppose that I or any other human being denies that some pleasures are good and others bad?

Soc.

Socrates begins again with some obvious truisms.

Alas, Callicles, how unfair you are! you certainly treat me as if I were a child, sometimes saying one thing, and then another, as if you were meaning to deceive me. And yet I thought at first that you were my friend, and would not have deceived me if you could have helped. But I see that I was mistaken; and now I suppose that I must make the best of a bad business, as they said of old, and take what I can get out of you.—Well, then, as I understand you to say, I may assume that some pleasures are good and others evil?

Cal.

Yes.

Soc.

The beneficial are good, and the hurtful are evil?

Cal.

To be sure.

Soc.

And the beneficial are those which do some good, and the hurtful are those which do some evil?

Cal.

Yes.

Soc.

Take, for example, the bodily pleasures of eating and drinking, which we were just now mentioning—you mean to say that those which promote health, or any other bodily excellence, are good, and their opposites evil?

Cal.

Certainly.

Soc.

And in the same way there are good pains and there are evil pains?

Cal.

To be sure.

Soc.

And ought we not to choose and use the good pleasures and pains?

Cal.

Certainly.

Soc.

But not the evil?

Cal.

Clearly.

Soc.

Because, if you remember, Polus and I have agreed that all our actions are to be done for the sake of the good;—and will you agree with us in saying, that the good is the end of all our actions, and that all our actions are to be done for the sake of the good, and not the good for the sake of 500them?—will you add a third vote to our two?

Cal.

I will.

Soc.

Then pleasure, like everything else, is to be sought for the sake of that which is good, and not that which is good for the sake of pleasure?

Cal.

To be sure.

Soc.

But can every man choose what pleasures are good and what are evil, or must he have art or knowledge of them in detail?

Cal.

He must have art.

Soc.

Let me now remind you of what I was saying to Gorgias and Polus; I was saying, as you will not have forgotten, that there were some processes which aim only at pleasure, and know nothing of a better and worse, and there are other processes which know good and evil. And I considered that cookery, which I do not call an art, but only an experience, was of the former class, which is concerned with pleasure, and that the art of medicine was of the class which is concerned with the good. And now, by the god of friendship, I must beg you, Callicles, not to jest, or to imagine that I am jesting with you; do not answer at random and contrary to your real opinion;—for you will observe that we are arguing about the way of human life; and to a man who has any sense at all, what question can be more serious than this?—whether he should follow after that way of life to which you exhort me, and act what you call the manly part of speaking in the assembly, and cultivating rhetoric, and engaging in public affairs, according to the principles now in vogue; or whether he should pursue the life of philosophy;—and in what the latter way differs from the former. But perhaps we had better first try to distinguish them, as I did before, and when we have come to an agreement that they are distinct, we may proceed to consider in what they differ from one another, and which of them we should choose. Perhaps, however, you do not even now understand what I mean?

Cal.

No, I do not.

Soc.

Then I will explain myself more clearly: seeing that you and I have agreed that there is such a thing as good, and that there is such a thing as pleasure, and that pleasure is not the same as good, and that the pursuit and process of acquisition of the one, that is pleasure, is different from the pursuit and process of acquisition of the other, which is good—I wish that you would tell me whether you agree with me thus far or not—do you agree?

Cal.

I do.

Soc.

Socrates repeats his distinction between true arts and flatteries or shams.

Then I will proceed, and ask whether you also agree 501with me, and whether you think that I spoke the truth when I further said to Gorgias and Polus that cookery in my opinion is only an experience, and not an art at all; and that whereas medicine is an art, and attends to the nature and constitution of the patient, and has principles of action and reason in each case, cookery in attending upon pleasure never regards either the nature or reason of that pleasure to which she devotes herself, but goes straight to her end, nor ever considers or calculates anything, but works by experience and routine, and just preserves the recollection of what she has usually done when producing pleasure. And first, I would have you consider whether I have proved what I was saying, and then whether there are not other similar processes which have to do with the soul—some of them processes of art, making a provision for the soul's highest interest—others despising the interest, and, as in the previous case, considering only the pleasure of the soul, and how this may be acquired, but not considering what pleasures are good or bad, and having no other aim but to afford gratification, whether good or bad. In my opinion, Callicles, there are such processes, and this is the sort of thing which I term flattery, whether concerned with the body or the soul, or whenever employed with a view to pleasure and without any consideration of good and evil. And now I wish that you would tell me whether you agree with us in this notion, or whether you differ.

Cal.

to which Callicles pretends to give assent.

I do not differ; on the contrary, I agree; for in that way I shall soonest bring the argument to an end, and shall oblige my friend Gorgias.

Soc.

And is this notion true of one soul, or of two or more?

Cal.

Equally true of two or more.

Soc.

Then a man may delight a whole assembly, and yet have no regard for their true interests?

Cal.

Yes.

Soc.

There are arts which delight mankind but which never consider the soul's higher interest.

Can you tell me the pursuits which delight mankind—or rather, if you would prefer, let me ask, and do you answer, which of them belong to the pleasurable class, and which of them not? In the first place, what say you of flute-playing? Does not that appear to be an art which seeks only pleasure, Callicles, and thinks of nothing else?

Cal.

I assent.

Soc.

And is not the same true of all similar arts, as, for example, the art of playing the lyre at festivals?

Cal.

Yes.

Soc.

And what do you say of the choral art and of dithyrambic poetry?—are not they of the same nature? Do you imagine that Cinesias the son of Meles cares about what 502will tend to the moral improvement of his hearers, or about what will give pleasure to the multitude?

Cal.

There can be no mistake about Cinesias, Socrates.

Soc.

And what do you say of his father, Meles the harp-player? Did he perform with any view to the good of his hearers? Could he be said to regard even their pleasure? For his singing was an infliction to his audience. And of harp-playing and dithyrambic poetry in general, what would you say? Have they not been invented wholly for the sake of pleasure?

Cal.

That is my notion of them.

Soc.

And as for the Muse of Tragedy, that solemn and august personage—what are her aspirations? Is all her aim and desire only to give pleasure to the spectators, or does she fight against them and refuse to speak of their pleasant vices, and willingly proclaim in word and song truths welcome and unwelcome?—which in your judgment is her character?

Cal.

There can be no doubt, Socrates, that Tragedy has her face turned towards pleasure and the gratification of the audience.

Soc.

And is not that the sort of thing, Callicles, which we were just now describing as flattery?

Cal.

Quite true.

Soc.

Well now, suppose that we strip all poetry of song and rhythm and metre, there will remain speech?

Cal.

To be sure.

Soc.

And this speech is addressed to a crowd of people?

Cal.

Yes.

Soc.

Then poetry is a sort of rhetoric?

Cal.

True.

Soc.

And do not the poets in the theatres seem to you to be rhetoricians?

Cal.

Yes.

Soc.

Poetry is of the nature of flattery.

Then now we have discovered a sort of rhetoric which is addressed to a crowd of men, women, and children, freemen and slaves. And this is not much to our taste, for we have described it as having the nature of flattery.

Cal.

Quite true.

Soc.

Oratory, too, as practised regards the interest of the speaker rather than the good of the people.

Very good. And what do you say of that other rhetoric which addresses the Athenian assembly and the assemblies of freemen in other states? Do the rhetoricians appear to you always to aim at what is best, and do they seek to improve the citizens by their speeches, or are they too, like the rest of mankind, bent upon giving them pleasure, forgetting the public good in the thought of their own interest, playing with the people as with children, and trying to amuse them, but never considering whether they are better or worse for this?

Cal.

I must distinguish. There are some who have a real 503care of the public in what they say, while others are such as you describe.

Soc.

There might be a higher style of oratory; and Callicles thinks that such really existed in the great days of old, the days of Miltiades and Themistocles and Pericles.

I am contented with the admission that rhetoric is of two sorts; one, which is mere flattery and disgraceful declamation; the other, which is noble and aims at the training and improvement of the souls of the citizens, and strives to say what is best, whether welcome or unwelcome, to the audience; but have you ever known such a rhetoric; or if you have, and can point out any rhetorician who is of this stamp, who is he?

Cal.

But, indeed, I am afraid that I cannot tell you of any such among the orators who are at present living.

Soc.

Well, then, can you mention any one of a former generation, who may be said to have improved the Athenians, who found them worse and made them better, from the day that he began to make speeches? for, indeed, I do not know of such a man.

Cal.

What! did you never hear that Themistocles was a good man, and Cimon and Miltiades and Pericles, who is just lately dead, and whom you heard yourself?

Soc.

Yet even these famous men had no ideal or standard.

Yes, Callicles, they were good men, if, as you said at first, true virtue consists only in the satisfaction of our own desires and those of others; but if not, and if, as we were afterwards compelled to acknowledge, the satisfaction of some desires makes us better, and of others, worse, and we ought to gratify the one and not the other, and there is an art in distinguishing them,—can you tell me of any of these statesmen who did distinguish them?

Cal.

No, indeed, I cannot.

Soc.

Some standard needed other than a man's interest.

Yet, surely, Callicles, if you look you will find such a one. Suppose that we just calmly consider whether any of these was such as I have described. Will not the good man, who says whatever he says with a view to the best, speak with a reference to some standard and not at random; just as all other artists, whether the painter, the builder, the shipwright, or any other look all of them to their own work, and do not select and apply at random what they apply, but strive to give a definite form to it? The artist disposes all 504things in order, and compels the one part to harmonize and accord with the other part, until he has constructed a regular and systematic whole; and this is true of all artists, and in the same way the trainers and physicians, of whom we spoke before, give order and regularity to the body: do you deny this?

Cal.

No; I am ready to admit it.

Soc.

Order is good, disorder evil, in a ship, in a human body, in a human soul.

Then the house in which order and regularity prevail is good; that in which there is disorder, evil?

Cal.

Yes.

Soc.

And the same is true of a ship?

Cal.

Yes.

Soc.

And the same may be said of the human body?

Cal.

Yes.

Soc.

And what would you say of the soul? Will the good soul be that in which disorder is prevalent, or that in which there is harmony and order?

Cal.

The latter follows from our previous admissions.

Soc.

What is the name which is given to the effect of harmony and order in the body?

Cal.

I suppose that you mean health and strength?

Soc.

Yes, I do; and what is the name which you would give to the effect of harmony and order in the soul? Try and discover a name for this as well as for the other.

Cal.

Why not give the name yourself, Socrates?

Soc.

Well, if you had rather that I should, I will; and you shall say whether you agree with me, and if not, you shall refute and answer me. 'Healthy,' as I conceive, is the name which is given to the regular order of the body, whence comes health and every other bodily excellence: is that true or not?

Cal.

True.

Soc.

From order and law spring temperance and justice.

And 'lawful' and 'law' are the names which are given to the regular order and action of the soul, and these make men lawful and orderly:—and so we have temperance and justice: have we not?

Cal.

Granted.

Soc.

The true rhetorician will seek to implant these virtues, to implant justice and take away injustice.

And will not the true rhetorician who is honest and understands his art have his eye fixed upon these, in all the words which he addresses to the souls of men, and in all his actions, both in what he gives and in what he takes away? Will not his aim be to implant justice in the souls of his citizens and take away injustice, to implant temperance and take away intemperance, to implant every virtue and take away every vice? Do you not agree?

Cal.

I agree.

Soc.

For what use is there, Callicles, in giving to the body of a sick man who is in a bad state of health a quantity of the most delightful food or drink or any other pleasant thing, which may be really as bad for him as if you gave him 505nothing, or even worse if rightly estimated. Is not that true?

Cal.

I will not say No to it.

Soc.

The body of the sick and the soul of the wicked must be chastised and improved.

For in my opinion there is no profit in a man's life if his body is in an evil plight—in that case his life also is evil: am I not right?

Cal.

Yes.

Soc.

When a man is in health the physicians will generally allow him to eat when he is hungry and drink when he is thirsty, and to satisfy his desires as he likes, but when he is sick they hardly suffer him to satisfy his desires at all: even you will admit that?

Cal.

Yes.

Soc.

And does not the same argument hold of the soul, my good sir? While she is in a bad state and is senseless and intemperate and unjust and unholy, her desires ought to be controlled, and she ought to be prevented from doing anything which does not tend to her own improvement.

Cal.

Yes.

Soc.

Such treatment will be better for the soul herself?

Cal.

To be sure.

Soc.

And to restrain her from her appetites is to chastise her?

Cal.

Yes.

Soc.

Then restraint or chastisement is better for the soul than intemperance or the absence of control, which you were just now preferring?

Cal.

I do not understand you, Socrates, and I wish that you would ask some one who does.

Soc.

Callicles does not wish to be improved.

Here is a gentleman who cannot endure to be improved or to subject himself to that very chastisement of which the argument speaks!

Cal.

I do not heed a word of what you are saying, and have only answered hitherto out of civility to Gorgias.

Soc.

What are we to do, then? Shall we break off in the middle?

Cal.

You shall judge for yourself.

Soc.

Well, but people say that 'a tale should have a head and not break off in the middle,' and I should not like to have the argument going about without a head; please then to go on a little longer, and put the head on.

Cal.

How tyrannical you are, Socrates! I wish that you and your argument would rest, or that you would get some one else to argue with you.

Soc.

But who else is willing?—I want to finish the argument.

Cal.

Cannot you finish without my help, either talking straight on, or questioning and answering yourself?

Soc.

Socrates, Gorgias, Callicles.

Must I then say with Epicharmus, 'Two men spoke before, but now one shall be enough'? I suppose that there is absolutely no help. And if I am to carry on the enquiry by myself, I will first of all remark that not only I but all of us should have an ambition to know what is true and what is false in this matter, for the discovery of the truth is a common good. And now I will proceed to argue according to 506my own notion. But if any of you think that I arrive at conclusions which are untrue you must interpose and refute me, for I do not speak from any knowledge of what I am saying; I am an enquirer like yourselves, and therefore, if my opponent says anything which is of force, I shall be the first to agree with him. I am speaking on the supposition that the argument ought to be completed; but if you think otherwise let us leave off and go our ways.

Gor.

I think, Socrates, that we should not go our ways until you have completed the argument; and this appears to me to be the wish of the rest of the company; I myself should very much like to hear what more you have to say.

Soc.

I too, Gorgias, should have liked to. continue the argument with Callicles, and then I might have given him an 'Amphion' in return for his 'Zethus' ; but since you, Callicles, are unwilling to continue, I hope that you will listen, and interrupt me if I seem to you to be in error. And if you refute me, I shall not be angry with you as you are with me, but I shall inscribe you as the greatest of benefactors on the tablets of my soul.

Cal.

My good fellow, never mind me, but get on.

Soc.

The pleasant not the same as the good, and is to be sought only for the sake of the good; and we are good when good is present in us, and good is the effect of order and truth and art.Socrates, Callicles.

Listen to me, then, while I recapitulate the argument:—Is the pleasant the same as the good? Not the same. Callicles and I are agreed about that. And is the pleasant to be pursued for the sake of the good? or the good for the sake of the pleasant? The pleasant is to be pursued for the sake of the good. And that is pleasant at the presence of which we are pleased, and that is good at the presence of which we are good? To be sure. And we are good, and all good things whatever are good when some virtue is present in us or them? That, Callicles, is my conviction. But the virtue of each thing, whether body or soul, instrument or creature, when given to them in the best way comes to them not by chance but as the result of the order and truth and art which are imparted to them: Am I not right? I maintain that I am. And is not the virtue of each thing dependent on order or arrangement? Yes, I say. And that which makes a thing good is the proper order inhering in each thing? Such is my view. And is not the soul which has an order of her own better than that which has no order? Certainly. And the soul which has order is orderly? Of course. And that which is orderly is temperate? Assuredly. And the 507 temperate soul is good? No other answer can I give, Callicles dear; have you any?

Cal.

Go on, my good fellow.

Soc.

Then I shall proceed to add, that if the temperate soul is the good soul, the soul which is in the opposite condition, that is, the foolish and intemperate, is the bad soul. Very true.

The temperate soul is the good soul, just in relation to men, and holy in relation to gods, and is therefore happy; and the intemperate is the reverse of all this.Socrates.If it be admitted that virtue is happiness and vice misery, then what Socrates said about the use of rhetoric in self-accusation turns out to be true.

And will not the temperate man do what is proper, both in relation to the gods and to men;—for he would not be temperate if he did not? Certainly he will do what is proper. In his relation to other men he will do what is just; and in his relation to the gods he will do what is holy; and he who does what is just and holy must be just and holy? Very true. And must he not be courageous? for the duty of a temperate man is not to follow or to avoid what he ought not, but what he ought, whether things or men or pleasures or pains, and patiently to endure when he ought; and therefore, Callicles, the temperate man, being, as we have described, also just and courageous and holy, cannot be other than a perfectly good man, nor can the good man do otherwise than well and perfectly whatever he does; and he who does well must of necessity be happy and blessed, and the evil man who does evil, miserable: now this latter is he whom you were applauding—the intemperate who is the opposite of the temperate. Such is my position, and these things I affirm to be true. And if they are true, then I further affirm that he who desires to be happy must pursue and practise temperance and run away from intemperance as fast as his legs will carry him: he had better order his life so as not to need punishment; but if either he or any of his friends, whether private individual or city, are in need of punishment, then justice must be done and he must suffer punishment, if he would be happy. This appears to me to be the aim which a man ought to have, and towards which he ought to direct all the energies both of himself and of the state, acting so that he may have temperance and justice present with him and be happy, not suffering his lusts to be unrestrained, and in the never-ending desire to satisfy them leading a robber's life. Such a one is the friend neither of God nor man, for he is incapable of communion, and he who is incapable of communion is also incapable of friendship. And philosophers tell us, Callicles, that communion and friendship and orderliness and temperance and justice bind together 508heaven and earth and gods and men, and that this universe is therefore called Cosmos or order, not disorder or misrule, my friend. But although you are a philosopher you seem to me never to have observed that geometrical equality is mighty, both among gods and men; you think that you ought to cultivate inequality or excess, and do not care about geometry.—Well, then, either the principle that the happy are made happy by the possession of justice and temperance, and the miserable miserable by the possession of vice, must be refuted, or, if it is granted, what will be the consequences? All the consequences which I drew before, Callicles, and about which you asked me whether I was in earnest when I said that a man ought to accuse himself and his son and his friend if he did anything wrong, and that to this end he should use his rhetoric—all those consequences are true. And that which you thought that Polus was led to admit out of modesty is true, viz. that, to do injustice, if more disgraceful than to suffer, is in that degree worse; and the other position, which, according to Polus, Gorgias admitted out of modesty, that he who would truly be a rhetorician ought to be just and have a knowledge of justice, has also turned out to be true.

Socrates, Callicles.The greatest evil to do injustice, but there is a greater still, not to be punished for doing injustice.

And now, these things being as we have said, let us proceed in the next place to consider whether you are right in throwing in my teeth that I am unable to help myself or any of my friends or kinsmen, or to save them in the extremity of danger, and that I am in the power of another like an outlaw to whom any one may do what he likes,—he may box my ears, which was a brave saying of yours; or take away my goods or banish me, or even do his worst and kill me; a condition which, as you say, is the height of disgrace. My answer to you is one which has been already often repeated, but may as well be repeated once more. I tell you, Callicles, that to be boxed on the ears wrongfully is not the worst evil which can befall a man, nor to have my purse or my body cut open, but that to smite and slay me and mine wrongfully is far more disgraceful and more evil; aye, and to despoil and enslave and pillage, or in any way at all to wrong me and mine, is far more disgraceful and evil to the doer of the wrong than to me who am the sufferer. 509These truths, which have been already set forth as I state them in the previous discussion, would seem now to have been fixed and riveted by us, if I may use an expression which is certainly bold, in words which are like bonds of iron and adamant; and unless you or some other still more enterprising hero shall break them, there is no possibility of denying what I say. For my position has always been, that I myself am ignorant how these things are, but that I have never met any one who could say otherwise, any more than you can, and not appear ridiculous. This is my position still, and if what I am saying is true, and injustice is the greatest of evils to the doer of injustice, and yet there is if possible a greater than this greatest of evils , in an unjust man not suffering retribution, what is that defence of which the want will make a man truly ridiculous? Must not the defence be one which will avert the greatest of human evils? And will not the worst of all defences be that with which a man is unable to defend himself or his family or his friends?—and next will come that which is unable to avert the next greatest evil; thirdly that which is unable to avert the third greatest evil; and so of other evils. As is the greatness of evil so is the honour of being able to avert them in their several degrees, and the disgrace of not being able to avert them. Am I not right, Callicles?

Cal.

Yes, quite right.

Soc.

Seeing then that there are these two evils, the doing injustice and the suffering injustice—and we affirm that to do injustice is a greater, and to suffer injustice a lesser evil—by what devices can a man succeed in obtaining the two advantages, the one of not doing and the other of not suffering injustice? must he have the power, or only the will to obtain them? I mean to ask whether a man will escape injustice if he has only the will to escape, or must he have provided himself with the power?

Cal.

He must have provided himself with the power; that is clear.

Soc.

And what do you say of doing injustice? Is the will only sufficient, and will that prevent him from doing injustice, or must he have provided himself with power and art; and if he have not studied and practised, will he be unjust still? Surely you might say, Callicles, whether you think that Polus and I were right in admitting the conclusion that no one does wrong voluntarily, but that all do wrong against their will?

Cal.

Granted, Socrates, if you will only have done. 510

Soc.

Then, as would appear, power and art have to be provided in order that we may do no injustice?

Cal.

Certainly.

Soc.

And what art will protect us from suffering injustice, if not wholly, yet as far as possible? I want to know whether you agree with me; for I think that such an art is the art of one who is either a ruler or even tyrant himself, or the equal and companion of the ruling power.

Cal.

Well said, Socrates; and please to observe how ready I am to praise you when you talk sense.

Soc.

Think and tell me whether you would approve of another view of mine: To me every man appears to be most the friend of him who is most like to him—like to like, as ancient sages say: Would you not agree to this?

Cal.

I should.

Soc.

The tyrant naturally hates both his superiors and inferiors: he likes only those who resemble him in character.

But when the tyrant is rude and uneducated, he may be expected to fear any one who is his superior in virtue, and will never be able to be perfectly friendly with him.

Cal.

That is true.

Soc.

Neither will he be the friend of any one who is greatly his inferior, for the tyrant will despise him, and will never seriously regard him as a friend.

Cal.

That again is true.

Soc.

Then the only friend worth mentioning, whom the tyrant can have, will be one who is of the same character, and has the same likes and dislikes, and is at the same time willing to be subject and subservient to him; he is the man who will have power in the state, and no one will injure him with impunity:—is not that so?

Cal.

Yes.

Soc.

And the way to be a great man and not to suffer injury is to become like him. And there can be no greater evil to him than this.

And if a young man begins to ask how he may become great and formidable, this would seem to be the way—he will accustom himself, from his youth upward, to feel sorrow and joy on the same occasions as his master, and will contrive to be as like him as possible?

Cal.

Yes.

Soc.

And in this way he will have accomplished, as you and your friends would say, the end of becoming a great man and not suffering injury?

Cal.

Very true.

Soc.

But will he also escape from doing injury? Must not the very opposite be true, if he is to be like the tyrant in his 511injustice, and to have influence with him? Will he not rather contrive to do as much wrong as possible, and not be punished?

Cal.

True.

Soc.

And by the imitation of his master and by the power which he thus acquires will not his soul become bad and corrupted, and will not this be the greatest evil to him?

Cal.

You always contrive somehow or other, Socrates, to invert everything: do you not know that he who imitates the tyrant will, if he has a mind, kill him who does not imitate him and take away his goods?

Soc.

But how provoking that the bad man should slay the good!

Excellent Callicles, I am not deaf, and I have heard that a great many times from you and from Polus and from nearly every man in the city, but I wish that you would hear me too. I dare say that he will kill him if he has a mind—the bad man will kill the good and true.

Cal.

And is not that just the provoking thing?

Soc.

Nay, but we should not always study the arts which save us from death;—the art of swimming, the art of the pilot, &c.

Nay, not to a man of sense, as the argument shows: do you think that all our cares should be directed to prolonging life to the uttermost, and to the study of those arts which secure us from danger always; like that art of rhetoric which saves men in courts of law, and which you advise me to cultivate?

Cal.

Yes, truly, and very good advice too.

Soc.

Well, my friend, but what do you think of swimming; is that an art of any great pretensions?

Cal.

No, indeed.

Soc.

Socrates.The pilot demands a very moderate payment as the fare of a passenger from Athens to Aegina, because he is not certain whether salvation from death be a good or an evil.

And yet surely swimming saves a man from death, and there are occasions on which he must know how to swim. And if you despise the swimmers, I will tell you of another and greater art, the art of the pilot, who not only saves the souls of men, but also their bodies and properties from the extremity of danger, just like rhetoric. Yet his art is modest and unpresuming: it has no airs or pretences of doing anything extraordinary, and, in return for the same salvation which is given by the pleader, demands only two obols, if he brings us from Aegina to Athens, or for the longer voyage from Pontus or Egypt, at the utmost two drachmae, when he has saved, as I was just now saying, the passenger and his wife and children and goods, and safely disembarked them at the Piraeus,—this is the payment which he asks in return for so great a boon; and he who is the master of the art, and has done all this, gets out and walks about on the sea-shore by his ship in an unassuming way. For he is able to reflect and is aware that he cannot tell which of his fellow-passengers he has benefited, and which of them he has injured in not allowing them to be drowned. He knows that they are just the same when he has disembarked them as when they embarked, 512and not a whit better either in their bodies or in their souls; and he considers that if a man who is afflicted by great and incurable bodily diseases is only to be pitied for having escaped, and is in no way benefited by him in having been saved from drowning, much less he who has great and incurable diseases, not of the body, but of the soul, which is the more valuable part of him; neither is life worth having nor of any profit to the bad man, whether he be delivered from the sea, or the law-courts, or any other devourer;—and so he reflects that such a one had better not live, for he cannot live well .

The engineer, too:—how much better than the pleader!Socrates, Callicles.He too is another of your saviours; but you despise him, whereas you ought to esteem him highly.I want you to consider whether you can possibly become great among the people unless you become like them.

And this is the reason why the pilot, although he is our saviour, is not usually conceited, any more than the engineer, who is not at all behind either the general, or the pilot, or any one else, in his saving power, for he sometimes saves whole cities. Is there any comparison between him and the pleader? And if he were to talk, Callicles, in your grandiose style, he would bury you under a mountain of words, declaring and insisting that we ought all of us to be engine-makers, and that no other profession is worth thinking about; he would have plenty to say. Nevertheless you despise him and his art, and sneeringly call him an engine-maker, and you will not allow your daughters to marry his son, or marry your son to his daughters. And yet, on your principle, what justice or reason is there in your refusal? What right have you to despise the engine-maker, and the others whom I was just now mentioning? I know that you will say, 'I am better, and better born.' But if the better is not what I say, and virtue consists only in a man saving himself and his, whatever may be his character, then your censure of the engine-maker, and of the physician, and of the other arts of salvation, is ridiculous. O my friend! I want you to see that the noble and the good may possibly be something different from saving and being saved:—May not he who is truly a man cease to care about living a certain time?—he knows, as women say, that no man can escape fate, and therefore he is not fond of life; he leaves all that with God, and considers in what way he can best spend his appointed term;— whether by assimilating himself to the constitution under which he 513lives, as you at this moment have to consider how you may become as like as possible to the Athenian people, if you mean to be in their good graces, and to have power in the state; whereas I want you to think and see whether this is for the interest of either of us;—I would not have us risk that which is dearest on the acquisition of this power, like the Thessalian enchantresses, who, as they say, bring down the moon from heaven at the risk of their own perdition. But if you suppose that any man will show you the art of becoming great in the city, and yet not conforming yourself to the ways of the city, whether for better or worse, then I can only say that you are mistaken, Callicles; for he who would deserve to be the true natural friend of the Athenian Demus, aye, or of Pyrilampes' darling who is called after them, must be by nature like them, and not an imitator only. He, then, who will make you most like them, will make you as you desire, a statesman and orator: for every man is pleased when he is spoken to in his own language and spirit, and dislikes any other. But perhaps you, sweet Callicles, may be of another mind. What do you say?

Cal.

Somehow or other your words, Socrates, always appear to me to be good words; and yet, like the rest of the world, I am not quite convinced by them .

Soc.

Callicles inclines for an instant to the Gospel of Socrates, but the love of the world and of popularity overcomes him.

The reason is, Callicles, that the love of Demus which abides in your soul is an adversary to me; but I dare say that if we recur to these same matters, and consider them more thoroughly, you may be convinced for all that. Please, then, to remember that there are two processes of training all things, including body and soul; in the one, as we said, we treat them with a view to pleasure, and in the other with a view to the highest good, and then we do not indulge but resist them: was not that the distinction which we drew?

Cal.

Two processes of training; one having a view to pleasure, the other to good.

Very true.

Soc.

And the one which had pleasure in view was just a vulgar flattery:—was not that another of our conclusions?

Cal.

Be it so, if you will have it.

Soc.

And the other had in view the greatest improvement of that which was ministered to, whether body or soul?

Cal.

Quite true.

Soc.

And we must train our citizens with a view to their good; and, as in other arts, we must show that we can be trusted to improve them.

And must we not have the same end in view in the treatment of our city and citizens? Must we not try and make them as good as possible? For we have already discovered that there is no use in imparting to them any other 514good, unless the mind of those who are to have the good, whether money, or office, or any other sort of power, be gentle and good. Shall we say that?

Cal.

Yes, certainly, if you like.

Soc.

Well, then, if you and I, Callicles, were intending to set about some public business, and were advising one another to undertake buildings, such as walls, docks or temples of the largest size, ought we not to examine ourselves, first, as to whether we know or do not know the art of building, and who taught us?—would not that be necessary, Callicles?

Cal.

True.

Soc.

In the second place, we should have to consider whether we had ever constructed any private house, either of our own or for our friends, and whether this building of ours was a success or not; and if upon consideration we found that we had had good and eminent masters, and had been successful in constructing many fine buildings, not only with their assistance, but without them, by our own unaided skill—in that case prudence would not dissuade us from proceeding to the construction of public works. But if we had no master to show, and only a number of worthless buildings or none at all, then, surely, it would be ridiculous in us to attempt public works, or to advise one another to undertake them. Is not this true?

Cal.

Certainly.

Soc.

And does not the same hold in all other cases? If you and I were physicians, and were advising one another that we were competent to practise as state-physicians, should I not ask about you, and would you not ask about me, Well, but how about Socrates himself, has he good health? and was any one else ever known to be cured by him, whether slave or freeman? And I should make the same enquiries about you. And if we arrived at the conclusion that no one, whether citizen or stranger, man or woman, had ever been any the better for the medical skill of either of us, then, by Heaven, Callicles, what an absurdity to think that we or any human being should be so silly as to set up as state-physicians and advise others like ourselves to do the same, without having first practised in private, whether successfully or not, and acquired experience of the art! Is not this, as they say, to begin with the big jar when you are learning the potter's art; which is a foolish thing?

Cal.

515True.

Soc.

And now, Callicles, what are you who are a public character doing for the improvement of the citizens?

And now, my friend, as you are already beginning to be a public character, and are admonishing and reproaching me for not being one, suppose that we ask a few questions of one another. Tell me, then, Callicles, how about making any of the citizens better? Was there ever a man who was once vicious, or unjust, or intemperate, or foolish, and became by the help of Callicles good and noble? Was there ever such a man, whether citizen or stranger, slave or freeman? Tell me, Callicles, if a person were to ask these questions of you, what would you answer? Whom would you say that you had improved by your conversation? There may have been good deeds of this sort which were done by you as a private person, before you came forward in public. Why will you not answer?

Cal.

You are contentious, Socrates.

Soc.

Callicles makes no answer.Or how did Pericles and the great of old benefit the citizens?

Nay, I ask you, not from a love of contention, but because I really want to know in what way you think that affairs should be administered among us—whether, when you come to the administration of them, you have any other aim but the improvement of the citizens? Have we not already admitted many times over that such is the duty of a public man? Nay, we have surely said so; for if you will not answer for yourself I must answer for you. But if this is what the good man ought to effect for the benefit of his own state, allow me to recall to you the names of those whom you were just now mentioning, Pericles, and Cimon, and Miltiades, and Themistocles, and ask whether you still think that they were good citizens.

Cal.

I do.

Soc.

But if they were good, then clearly each of them must have made the citizens better instead of worse?

Cal.

Yes.

Soc.

And, therefore, when Pericles first began to speak in the assembly, the Athenians were not so good as when he spoke last?

Cal.

Very likely.

Soc.

Nay, my friend, 'likely' is not the word; for if he was a good citizen, the inference is certain.

Cal.

And what difference does that make?

Soc.

Pericles corrupted them by giving them pay.

None; only I should like further to know whether the Athenians are supposed to have been made better by Pericles, or, on the contrary, to have been corrupted by him; for I hear that he was the first who gave the people pay, and made them idle and cowardly, and encouraged them in the love of talk and of money.

Cal.

You heard that, Socrates, from the laconising set who bruise their ears.

Soc.

He made them worse instead of better, for they all but put him to death.

But what I am going to tell you now is not mere hearsay, but well known both to you and me: that at first, Pericles was glorious and his character unimpeached by any verdict of the Athenians—this was during the time when they were not so good—yet afterwards, when they had been made good and gentle by him, at the very end of his life they convicted him of theft, and almost put him to death, clearly under the notion that he was a malefactor.

Cal.

Well, but how does that prove Pericles' badness?

Soc.

Why, surely, you would say that he was a bad manager of asses or horses or oxen, who had received them originally neither kicking nor butting nor biting him, and implanted in them all these savage tricks? Would he not be a bad manager of any animals who received them gentle, and made them fiercer than they were when he received them? What do you say?

Cal.

I will do you the favour of saying 'yes.'

Soc.

And will you also do me the favour of saying whether man is an animal?

Cal.

Certainly he is.

Soc.

And was not Pericles a shepherd of men?

Cal.

Yes.

Soc.

And if he was a good political shepherd, ought not the animals who were his subjects, as we were just now acknowledging, to have become more just, and not more unjust?

Cal.

Quite true.

Soc.

And are not just men gentle, as Homer says?—or are you of another mind?

Cal.

I agree.

Soc.

And yet he really did make them more savage than he received them, and their savageness was shown towards himself; which he must have been very far from desiring.

Cal.

Do you want me to agree with you?

Soc.

Yes, if I seem to you to speak the truth:

Cal.

Granted then.

Soc.

And if they were more savage, must they not have been more unjust and inferior?

Cal.

Granted again.

Soc.

Then upon this view, Pericles was not a good statesman?

Cal.

That is, upon your view.

Soc.

Cimon was ostracised; Themistocles was exiled; Miltiades was nearly thrown from the rock.

Nay, the view is yours, after what you have admitted. Take the case of Cimon again. Did not the very persons whom he was serving ostracize him, in order that they might not hear his voice for ten years? and they did just the same to Themistocles, adding the penalty of exile; and they voted that Miltiades, the hero of Marathon, should be thrown into the pit of death, and he was only saved by the Prytanis. And yet, if they had been really good men, as you say, these things would never have happened to them. For the good charioteers are not those who at first keep their place, and then, when they have broken-in their horses, and themselves become better charioteers, are thrown out—that is not the way either in charioteering or in any profession.—What do you think?

Cal.

I should think not.

Soc.

The older statesmen no better than the existing ones.

Well, but if so, the truth is as I have said already, 517that in the Athenian State no one has ever shown himself to be a good statesman—you admitted that this was true of our present statesmen, but not true of former ones, and you preferred them to the others; yet they have turned out to be no better than our present ones; and therefore, if they were rhetoricians, they did not use the true art of rhetoric or of flattery, or they would not have fallen out of favour.

Cal.

But surely, Socrates, no living man ever came near any one of them in his performances.

Soc.

The older statesmen not able really to elevate the state to a higher level, but more capable of gratifying its desires.Socrates.You might as well say that the cook or the baker is a good trainer as that they were great statesmen.Socrates.The statesman like the Sophist; neither has any right to accuse their followers of wronging them; they should have taught them better.Socrates, Callicles.

O, my dear friend, I say nothing against them regarded as the serving-men of the State; and I do think that they were certainly more serviceable than those who are living now, and better able to gratify the wishes of the State; but as to transforming those desires and not allowing them to have their way, and using the powers which they had, whether of persuasion or of force, in the improvement of their fellow-citizens, which is the prime object of the truly good citizen, I do not see that in these respects they were a whit superior to our present statesmen, although I do admit that they were more clever at providing ships and walls and docks, and all that. You and I have a ridiculous way, for during the whole time that we are arguing, we are always going round and round to the same point, and constantly misunderstanding one another. If I am not mistaken, you have admitted and acknowledged more than once, that there are two kinds of operations which have to do with the body, and two which have to do with the soul: one of the two is ministerial, and if our bodies are hungry provides food for them, and if they are thirsty gives them drink, or if they are cold supplies them with garments, blankets, shoes, and all that they crave. I use the same images as before intentionally, in order that you may understand me the better. The purveyor of the articles may provide them either wholesale or retail, or he may be the maker of any of them,—the baker, or the cook, or the weaver, or the shoemaker, or the currier; and in so doing, being such as he is, he is naturally supposed by himself and every one to minister to the body. For none of them know that there is another art—an art of gymnastic and medicine which is the true minister of the body, and ought to be the mistress of all the rest, and to use their results according to the knowledge which she has and they have not, of the real good or bad effects of meats 518and drinks on the body. All other arts which have to do with the body are servile and menial and illiberal; and gymnastic and medicine are, as they ought to be, their mistresses. Now, when I say that all this is equally true of the soul, you seem at first to know and understand and assent to my words, and then a little while afterwards you come repeating, Has not the State had good and noble citizens? and when I ask you who they are, you reply, seemingly quite in earnest, as if I had asked, Who are or have been good trainers?—and you had replied, Thearion, the baker, Mithoecus, who wrote the Sicilian cookery-book, Sarambus, the vintner: these are ministers of the body, first-rate in their art; for the first makes admirable loaves, the second excellent dishes, and the third capital wine;—to me these appear to be the exact parallel of the statesmen whom you mention. Now you would not be altogether pleased if I said to you, My friend, you know nothing of gymnastics; those of whom you are speaking to me are only the ministers and purveyors of luxury, who have no good or noble notions of their art, and may very likely be filling and fattening men's bodies and gaining their approval, although the result is that they lose their original flesh in the long run, and become thinner than they were before; and yet they, in their simplicity, will not attribute their diseases and loss of flesh to their entertainers; but when in after years the unhealthy surfeit brings the attendant penalty of disease, he who happens to be near them at the time, and offers them advice, is accused and blamed by them, and if they could they would do him some harm; while they proceed to eulogize the men who have been the real authors of the mischief. And that, Callicles, is just what you are now doing. You praise the men who feasted the citizens and satisfied their desires, and people say that they have made the city great, not seeing that the swollen and ulcerated condition of the State is to be attributed to these elder statesmen; for they have filled the city full of harbours and docks and walls and revenues and all that, and have left no room for justice and temperance. And when the crisis of the disorder comes, 519the people will blame the advisers of the hour, and applaud Themistocles and Cimon and Pericles, who are the real authors of their calamities; and if you are not careful they may assail you and my friend Alcibiades, when they are losing not only their new acquisitions, but also their original possessions; not that you are the authors of these misfortunes of theirs, although you may perhaps be accessories to them. A great piece of work is always being made, as I see and am told, now as of old, about our statesmen. When the State treats any of them as malefactors, I observe that there is a great uproar and indignation at the supposed wrong which is done to them; 'after all their many services to the State, that they should unjustly perish,'—so the tale runs. But the cry is all a lie; for no statesman ever could be unjustly put to death by the city of which he is the head. The case of the professed statesman is, I believe, very much like that of the professed sophist; for the sophists, although they are wise men, are nevertheless guilty of a strange piece of folly; professing to be teachers of virtue, they will often accuse their disciples of wronging them, and defrauding them of their pay, and showing no gratitude for their services. Yet what can be more absurd than that men who have become just and good, and whose injustice has been taken away from them, and who have had justice implanted in them by their teachers, should act unjustly by reason of the injustice which is not in them? Can anything be more irrational, my friend, than this? You, Callicles, compel me to be a mob-orator, because you will not answer.

Cal.

And you are the man who cannot speak unless there is some one to answer?

Soc.

I suppose that I can; just now, at any rate, the speeches which I am making are long enough because you refuse to answer me. But I adjure you by the god of friendship, my good sir, do tell me whether there does not appear to you to be a great inconsistency in saying that you have made a man good, and then blaming him for being bad?

Cal.

Yes, it appears so to me.

Soc.

520Do you never hear our professors of education speaking in this inconsistent manner?

Cal.

Yes, but why talk of men who are good for nothing?

Soc.

Sophistry is much superior to rhetoric.

I would rather say, why talk of men who profess to be rulers, and declare that they are devoted to the improvement of the city, and nevertheless upon occasion declaim against the utter vileness of the city:—do you think that there is any difference between one and the other? My good friend, the sophist and the rhetorician, as I was saying to Polus, are the same, or nearly the same; but you ignorantly fancy that rhetoric is a perfect thing, and sophistry a thing to be despised; whereas the truth is, that sophistry is as much superior to rhetoric as legislation is to the practice of law, or gymnastic to medicine. The orators and sophists, as I am inclined to think, are the only class who cannot complain of the mischief ensuing to themselves from that which they teach others, without in the same breath accusing themselves of having done no good to those whom they profess to benefit. Is not this a fact?

Cal.

Certainly it is.

Soc.

He who teaches honesty ought to teach his pupils to pay him for the lesson.

If they were right in saying that they make men better, then they are the only class who can afford to leave their remuneration to those who have been benefited by them. Whereas if a man has been benefited in any other way, if, for example, he has been taught to run by a trainer, he might possibly defraud him of his pay, if the trainer left the matter to him, and made no agreement with him that he should receive money as soon as he had given him the utmost speed; for not because of any deficiency of speed do men act unjustly, but by reason of injustice.

Cal.

Very true.

Soc.

And he who removes injustice can be in no danger of being treated unjustly: he alone can safely leave the honorarium to his pupils, if he be really able to make them good—am I not right?

Cal.

Yes.

Soc.

Then we have found the reason why there is no dishonour in a man receiving pay who is called in to advise about building or any other art?

Cal.

Yes, we have found the reason.

Soc.

But when the point is, how a man may become best himself, and best govern his family and state, then to say that you will give no advice gratis is held to be dishonourable?

Cal.

True.

Soc.

And why? Because only such benefits call forth a desire to requite them, and there is evidence that a benefit has been conferred when the benefactor receives a return; otherwise not. Is this true?

Cal.

It is.

Soc.

Callicles advises Socrates to be the servant of the state, and not run the risk of popular enmity.

Then to which service of the State do you invite me? determine for me. Am I to be the physician of the 521State who will strive and struggle to make the Athenians as good as possible; or am I to be the servant and flatterer of the State? Speak out, my good friend, freely and fairly as you did at first and ought to do again, and tell me your entire mind.

Cal.

I say then that you should be the servant of the State.

Soc.

The flatterer? well, sir, that is a noble invitation.

Cal.

The Mysian, Socrates, or what you please. For if you refuse, the consequences will be—

Soc.

Do not repeat the old story—that he who likes will kill me and get my money; for then I shall have to repeat the old answer, that he will be a bad man and will kill the good, and that the money will be of no use to him, but that he will wrongly use that which he wrongly took, and if wrongly, basely, and if basely, hurtfully.

Cal.

How confident you are, Socrates, that you will never come to harm! you seem to think that you are living in another country, and can never be brought into a court of justice, as you very likely may be brought by some miserable and mean person.

Soc.

Socrates has no fear of popular enmity, but is quite aware that he will incur it, because he is the only true politician of his time,

Then I must indeed be a fool, Callicles, if I do not know that in the Athenian State any man may suffer anything. And if I am brought to trial and incur the dangers of which you speak, he will be a villain who brings me to trial—of that I am very sure, for no good man would accuse the innocent. Nor shall I be surprised if I am put to death. Shall I tell you why I anticipate this?

Cal.

By all means.

Soc.

I think that I am the only or almost the only Athenian living who practises the true art of politics; I am the only politician of my time. Now, seeing that when I speak my words are not uttered with any view of gaining favour, and that I look to what is best and not to what is most pleasant, having no mind to use those arts and graces which you recommend, I shall have nothing to say in the justice court. And you might argue with me, as I was arguing with Polus:—I shall be tried just as a physician would be tried in a court of little boys at the indictment of the cook. What would he reply under such circumstances, if some one were to accuse him, saying, 'O my boys, many evil things has this man done to you: he is the death of you, especially of the younger ones among you, cutting and 522burning and starving and suffocating you, until you know not what to do; he gives you the bitterest potions, and compels you to hunger and thirst. How unlike the variety of meats and sweets on which I feasted you!' What do you suppose that the physician would be able to reply when he found himself in such a predicament? If he told the truth he could only say, 'All these evil things, my boys, I did for your health,' and then would there not just be a clamour among a jury like that? How they would cry out!

Cal.

I dare say.

Soc.

Would he not be utterly at a loss for a reply?

Cal.

He certainly would.

Soc.

and he has no defence against men such as his opponents:

And I too shall be treated in the same way, as I well know, if I am brought before the court. For I shall not be able to rehearse to the people the pleasures which I have procured for them, and which, although I am not disposed to envy either the procurers or enjoyers of them, are deemed by them to be benefits and advantages. And if any one says that I corrupt young men, and perplex their minds, or that I speak evil of old men, and use bitter words towards them, whether in private or public, it is useless for me to reply, as I truly might:—'All this I do for the sake of justice, and with a view to your interest, my judges, and to nothing else.' And therefore there is no saying what may happen to me.

Cal.

And do you think, socrates, that a man who is thus defenceless is in a good position?

Soc.

that is to say, he has the defence of truth, but not such a defence as men ordinarily produce.

Yes, Callicles, if he have that defence, which as you have often acknowledged he should have—if he be his own defence, and have never said or done anything wrong, either in respect of gods or men; and this has been repeatedly acknowledged by us to be the best sort of defence. And if any one could convict me of inability to defend myself or others after this sort, I should blush for shame, whether I was convicted before many, or before a few, or by myself alone; and if I died from want of ability to do so, that would indeed grieve me. But if I died because I have no powers of flattery or rhetoric, I am very sure that you would not find me repining at death. For no man who is not an utter fool and coward is afraid of death itself, but he is afraid of doing wrong. For to go to the world below having one's soul full of injustice is the last and worst of all evils. And in proof of what I say, if you have no objection, I should like to tell you a story.

Cal.

Very well, proceed; and then we shall have done.

Soc.

The philosopher has no reason to dread death, as Socrates will prove by a relation of what happens in the world below.Socrates.Before the days of Zeus, the judgments of another world too much resembled the judgments of this.Zeus takes measures for the correction and improvement of them.

Listen, then, as story-tellers say, to a very pretty 523tale, which I dare say that you may be disposed to regard as a fable only, but which, as I believe, is a true tale, for I mean to speak the truth. Homer tells us , how Zeus and Poseidon and Pluto divided the empire which they inherited from their father. Now in the days of Cronos there existed a law respecting the destiny of man, which has always been, and still continues to be in Heaven,—that he who has lived all his life in justice and holiness shall go, when he is dead, to the Islands of the Blessed, and dwell there in perfect happiness out of the reach of evil; but that he who has lived unjustly and impiously shall go to the house of vengeance and punishment, which is called Tartarus. And in the time of Cronos, and even quite lately in the reign of Zeus, the judgment was given on the very day on which the men were to die; the judges were alive, and the men were alive; and the consequence was that the judgments were not well given. The Pluto and the authorities from the Islands of the Blessed came to Zeus, and said that the souls found their way to the wrong places. Zeus said: 'I shall put a stop to this; the judgments are not well given, because the persons who are judged have their clothes on, for they are alive; and there are many who, having evil souls, are apparelled in fair bodies, or encased in wealth or rank, and, when the day of judgment arrives, numerous witnesses come forward and testify on their behalf that they have lived righteously. The judges are awed by them, and they themselves too have their clothes on when judging; their eyes and ears and their whole bodies are interposed as a veil before their own souls. All this is a hindrance to them; there are the clothes of the judges and the clothes of the judged.—What is to be done? I will tell you:—In the first place, I will deprive men of the foreknowledge of death, which they possess at present: this power which they have Prometheus has already received my orders to take from them: in the second place, they shall be entirely stripped before they are judged, for they shall be judged when they are dead; and the judge too shall be naked, that is to say, dead—he with his naked soul shall pierce into the other naked souls; and they shall die suddenly and be deprived of all their kindred, and leave their brave attire strewn upon the earth—conducted in this manner, the judgment will be just. I knew all about the matter before any of you, and therefore I have made my sons judges; two from Asia, Minos and Rhadamanthus, and one from Europe, 524Aeacus. And these, when they are dead, shall give judgment in the meadow at the parting of the ways, whence the two roads lead, one to the Islands of the Blessed, and the other to Tartarus. Rhadamanthus shall judge those who come from Asia, and Aeacus those who come from Europe. And to Minos I shall give the primacy, and he shall hold a court of appeal, in case either of the two others are in any doubt:—then the judgment respecting the last journey of men will be as just as possible.'

As the body is, so is the soul after death; they both retain the traces of what they were in life, and they are punished accordingly.

From this tale, Callicles, which I have heard and believe, I draw the following inferences:—Death, if I am right, is in the first place the separation from one another of two things, soul and body; nothing else. And after they are separated they retain their several natures, as in life; the body keeps the same habit, and the results of treatment or accident are distinctly visible in it: for example, he who by nature or training or both, was a tall man while he was alive, will remain as he was, after he is dead; and the fat man will remain fat; and so on; and the dead man, who in life had a fancy to have flowing hair, will have flowing hair. And if he was marked with the whip and had the prints of the scourge, or of wounds in him when he was alive, you might see the same in the dead body; and if his limbs were broken or misshapen when he was alive, the same appearance would be visible in the dead. And in a word, whatever was the habit of the body during life would be distinguishable after death, either perfectly, or in a great measure and for a certain time. And I should imagine that this is equally true of the soul, Callicles; when a man is stripped of the body, all the natural or acquired affections of the soul are laid open to view.—And when they come to the judge, as those from Asia come to Rhadamanthus, he places them near him and inspects them quite impartially, not knowing whose the soul is: perhaps he may lay hands on the soul of the great king, or of some other king or potentate, who has no soundness in him, but his soul is marked with the whip, and is full of the prints and scars of perjuries and crimes with which each action has stained him, and he is all crooked with falsehood and imposture, 525and has no straightness, because he has lived without truth. Him Rhadamanthus beholds, full of all deformity and disproportion, which is caused by licence and luxury and insolence and incontinence, and despatches him ignominiously to his prison, and there he undergoes the punishment which he deserves.

The proper office of punishment is either to improve or to deter. The meaner sort of men are incapable of great crimes. Great men have sometimes been good men but power is apt to corrupt them.

Now the proper office of punishment is twofold: he who is rightly punished ought either to become better and profit by it, or he ought to be made an example to his fellows, that they may see what he suffers, and fear and become better. Those who are improved when they are punished by gods and men, are those whose sins are curable; and they are improved, as in this world so also in another, by pain and suffering; for there is no other way in which they can be delivered from their evil. But they who have been guilty of the worst crimes, and are incurable by reason of their crimes, are made examples; for, as they are incurable, the time has passed at which they can receive any benefit. They get no good themselves, but others get good when they behold them enduring for ever the most terrible and painful and fearful sufferings as the penalty of their sins—there they are, hanging up as examples, in the prison-house of the world below, a spectacle and a warning to all unrighteous men who come thither. And among them, as I confidently affirm, will be found Archelaus, if Polus truly reports of him, and any other tyrant who is like him. Of these fearful examples, most, as I believe, are taken from the class of tyrants and kings and potentates and public men, for they are the authors of the greatest and most impious crimes, because they have the power. And Homer witnesses to the truth of this; for they are always kings and potentates whom he has described as suffering everlasting punishment in the world below: such were Tantalus and Sisyphus and Tityus. But no one ever described Thersites, or any private person who was a villain, as suffering everlasting punishment, or as incurable. For to commit the worst crimes, as I am inclined to think, was not in his power, and he was happier than those who had the power. No, Callicles, the very bad men come from the class of those who have power . And yet in that very class there may arise good men, and worthy of all admiration they are, for where there is great power to do wrong, to live and to die justly is a hard thing, and greatly to be praised, and few there are who attain to this. Such good and true men, however, there have been, and will be again, at Athens and in other states, who have fulfilled their trust righteously; and there is one who is quite famous all over Hellas, Aristeides, the son of Lysimachus. But, in general, great men are also bad, my friend.

The impartiality of the judges in another world.

As I was saying, Rhadamanthus, when he gets a soul of the bad kind, knows nothing about him, neither who he is, nor who his parents are; he knows only that he has got hold of a villain; and seeing this, he stamps him as curable or incurable, and sends him away to Tartarus, whither he goes and receives his proper recompense. Or, again, he looks with admiration on the soul of some just one who has lived in holiness and truth; he may have been a private man or not; and I should say, Callicles, that he is most likely to have been a philosopher who has done his own work, and not troubled himself with the doings of other men in his lifetime; him Rhadamanthus sends to the Islands of the Blessed. Aeacus does the same; and they both have sceptres, and judge;

but Minos alone has a golden sceptre and is seated looking on, as Odysseus in Homer declares that he saw him:

- 'Holding a sceptre of gold, and giving laws to the dead.'

Now I, Callicles, am persuaded of the truth of these things, and I consider how I shall present my soul whole and undefiled before the judge in that day. Renouncing the honours at which the world aims, I desire only to know the truth, and to live as well as I can, and, when I die, to die as well as I can. And, to the utmost of my power, I exhort all other men to do the same. And, in return for your exhortation of me, I exhort you also to take part in the great combat, which is the combat of life, and greater than every other earthly conflict. And I retort your reproach of me, and say, that you will not be able to help yourself when the day of trial and judgment, of which I was speaking, comes upon you; you will go before the judge, the son of Aegina, and, when he has got you in his grip and is carrying you off, you 527will gape and your head will swim round, just as mine would in the courts of this world, and very likely some one will shamefully box you on the ears, and put upon you any sort of insult.

Perhaps this may appear to you to be only an old wife's tale, which you will contemn. And there might be reason in your contemning such tales, if by searching we could find out anything better or truer: but now you see that you and Polus and Gorgias, who are the three wisest of the Greeks of our day, are not able to show that we ought to live any life which does not profit in another world as well as in this. And of all that has been said, nothing remains unshaken but the saying, that to do injustice is more to be avoided than to suffer injustice, and that the reality and not the appearance of virtue is to be followed above all things, as well in public as in private life; and that when any one has been wrong in anything, he is to be chastised, and that the next best thing to a man being just is that he should become just, and be chastised and punished; also that he should avoid all flattery of himself as well as of others, of the few or of the many: and rhetoric and any other art should be used by him, and all his actions should be done always, with a view to justice.

Follow me then, and I will lead you where you will be happy in life and after death, as the argument shows. And never mind if some one despises you as a fool, and insults you, if he has a mind; let him strike you, by Zeus, and do you be of good cheer, and do not mind the insulting blow, for you will never come to any harm in the practice of virtue, if you are a really good and true man. When we have practised virtue together, we will apply ourselves to politics, if that seems desirable, or we will advise about whatever else may seem good to us, for we shall be better able to judge then. In our present condition we ought not to give ourselves airs, for even on the most important subjects we are always changing our minds; so utterly stupid are we! Let us, then, take the argument as our guide, which has revealed to us that the best way of life is to practise justice and every virtue in life and death. This way let us go; and in this exhort all men to follow, not in the way to which you trust and in which you exhort me to follow you; for that way, Callicles, is nothing worth.

APPENDIX I.

Appendix I.

It seems impossible to separate by any exact line the genuine writings of Plato from the spurious. The only external evidence to them which is of much value is that of Aristotle; for the Alexandrian catalogues of a century later include manifest forgeries. Even the value of the Aristotelian authority is a good deal impaired by the uncertainty concerning the date and authorship of the writings which are ascribed to him. And several of the citations of Aristotle omit the name of Plato, and some of them omit the name of the dialogue from which they are taken. Prior, however, to the enquiry about the writings of a particular author, general considerations which equally affect all evidence to the genuineness of ancient writings are the following: Shorter works are more likely to have been forged, or to have received an erroneous designation, than longer ones; and some kinds of composition, such as epistles or panegyrical orations, are more liable to suspicion than others; those, again, which have a taste of sophistry in them, or the ring of a later age, or the slighter character of a rhetorical exercise, or in which a motive or some affinity to spurious writings can be detected, or which seem to have originated in a name or statement really occurring in some classical author, are also of doubtful credit; while there is no instance of any ancient writing proved to be a forgery, which combines excellence with length. A really great and original writer would have no object in fathering his works on Plato; and to the forger or imitator, the 'literary hack' of Alexandria and Athens, the Gods did not grant originality or genius. Further, in attempting to balance the evidence for and against a Platonic dialogue, we must not forget that the form of the Platonic writing was common to several of his contemporaries. Aeschines, Euclid, Phaedo, Antisthenes, and in the next generation Aristotle, are all said to have composed dialogues; and mistakes of names are very likely to have occurred. Greek literature in the third century before Christ was almost as voluminous as our own, and without the safeguards of regular publication, or printing, or binding, or even of distinct titles. An unknown writing was naturally attributed to a known writer whose works bore the same character; and the name once appended easily obtained authority. A tendency may also be observed to blend the works and opinions of the master with those of his scholars. To a later Platonist, the difference between Plato and his imitators was not so perceptible as to ourselves. The Memorabilia of Xenophon and the Dialogues of Plato are but a part of a considerable Socratic literature which has passed away. And we must consider how we should regard the question of the genuineness of a particular writing, if this lost literature had been preserved to us.

These considerations lead us to adopt the following criteria of genuineness: (1) That is most certainly Plato's which Aristotle attributes to him by name, which (2) is of considerable length, of (3) great excellence, and also (4) in harmony with the general spirit of the Platonic writings. But the testimony of Aristotle cannot always be distinguished from that of a later age (see above); and has various degrees of importance. Those writings which he cites without mentioning Plato, under their own names, e. g. the Hippias, the Funeral Oration, the Phaedo, etc., have an inferior degree of evidence in their favour. They may have been supposed by him to be the writings of another, although in the case of really great works, e. g. the Phaedo, this is not credible; those again which are quoted but not named, are still more defective in their external credentials. There may be also a possibility that Aristotle was mistaken, or may have confused the master and his scholars in the case of a short writing; but this is inconceivable about a more important work, e. g. the Laws, especially when we remember that he was living at Athens, and a frequenter of the groves of the Academy, during the last twenty years of Plato's life. Nor must we forget that in all his numerous citations from the Platonic writings he never attributes any passage found in the extant dialogues to any one but Plato. And lastly, we may remark that one or two great writings, such as the Parmenides and the Politicus, which are wholly devoid of Aristotelian (1) credentials may be fairly attributed to Plato, on the ground of (2) length, (3) excellence, and (4) accordance with the general spirit of his writings. Indeed the greater part of the evidence for the genuineness of ancient Greek authors may be summed up under two heads only: (1) excellence; and (2) uniformity of tradition—a kind of evidence, which though in many cases sufficient, is of inferior value.

Proceeding upon these principles we appear to arrive at the conclusion that nineteen-twentieths of all the writings which have ever been ascribed to Plato, are undoubtedly genuine. There is another portion of them, including the Epistles, the Epinomis, the dialogues rejected by the ancients themselves, namely, the Axiochus, De justo, De virtute, Demodocus, Sisyphus, Eryxias, which on grounds, both of internal and external evidence, we are able with equal certainty to reject. But there still remains a small portion of which we are unable to affirm either that they are genuine or spurious. They may have been written in youth, or possibly like the works of some painters, may be partly or wholly the compositions of pupils; or they may have been the writings of some contemporary transferred by accident to the more celebrated name of Plato, or of some Platonist in the next generation who aspired to imitate his master. Not that on grounds either of language or philosophy we should lightly reject them. Some difference of style, or inferiority of execution, or inconsistency of thought, can hardly be considered decisive of their spurious character. For who always does justice to himself, or who writes with equal care at all times? Certainly not Plato, who exhibits the greatest differences in dramatic power, in the formation of sentences, and in the use of words, if his earlier writings are compared with his later ones, say the Protagoras or Phaedrus with the Laws. Or who can be expected to think in the same manner during a period of authorship extending over above fifty years, in an age of great intellectual activity, as well as of political and literary transition? Certainly not Plato, whose earlier writings are separated from his later ones by as wide an interval of philosophical speculation as that which separates his later writings from Aristotle.

The dialogues which have been translated in the first Appendix, and which appear to have the next claim to genuineness among the Platonic writings, are the Lesser Hippias, the Menexenus or Funeral Oration, the First Alcibiades. Of these, the Lesser Hippias and the Funeral Oration are cited by Aristotle; the first in the Metaphysics, iv. 29, 5, the latter in the Rhetoric, iii. 14, 11. Neither of them are expressly attributed to Plato, but in his citation of both of them he seems to be referring to passages in the extant dialogues. From the mention of 'Hippias' in the singular by Aristotle, we may perhaps infer that he was unacquainted with a second dialogue bearing the same name. Moreover, the mere existence of a Greater and Lesser Hippias, and of a First and Second Alcibiades, does to a certain extent throw a doubt upon both of them. Though a very clever and ingenious work, the Lesser Hippias does not appear to contain anything beyond the power of an imitator, who was also a careful student of the earlier Platonic writings, to invent. The motive or leading thought of the dialogue may be detected in Xen. Mem. iv. 2, 21, and there is no similar instance of a 'motive' which is taken from Xenophon in an undoubted dialogue of Plato. On the other hand, the upholders of the genuineness of the dialogue will find in the Hippias a true Socratic spirit; they will compare the Ion as being akin both in subject and treatment; they will urge the authority of Aristotle; and they will detect in the treatment of the Sophist, in the satirical reasoning upon Homer, in the *reductio ad absurdum* of the doctrine that vice is ignorance, traces of a Platonic authorship. In reference to the last point we are doubtful, as in some of the other dialogues, whether the author is asserting or overthrowing the paradox of Socrates, or merely following the argument 'whither the wind blows.' That no conclusion is arrived at is also in accordance with the character of the earlier dialogues. The resemblances or imitations of the Gorgias, Protagoras, and Euthydemus, which have been observed in the Hippias, cannot with certainty be adduced on either side of the argument. On the whole, more may be said in favour of the genuineness of the Hippias than against it.

The Menexenus or Funeral Oration is cited by Aristotle, and is interesting as supplying an example of the manner in which the orators praised 'the Athenians among the Athenians,' falsifying persons and dates, and casting a veil over the gloomier events of Athenian history. It exhibits an acquaintance with the funeral oration of Thucydides, and was, perhaps, intended to rival that great work. If genuine, the proper place of the Menexenus would be at the end of the Phaedrus. The satirical opening and the concluding words bear a great resemblance to the earlier dialogues; the oration itself is professedly a mimetic work, like the speeches in the Phaedrus, and cannot therefore be tested by a comparison of the other writings of Plato. The funeral oration of Pericles is expressly mentioned in the Phaedrus, and this may have suggested the subject, in the same manner that the Cleitophon appears to be suggested by the slight mention of Cleitophon and his attachment to Thrasymachus in the Republic, cp. 465 A; and the Theages by the mention of Theages in the Apology and Republic; or as the Second Alcibiades seems to be founded upon the text of Xenophon, Mem. i. 3, 1. A similar taste for parody appears not only in the Phaedrus, but in the Protagoras, in the Symposium, and to a certain extent in the Parmenides.

To these two doubtful writings of Plato I have added the First Alcibiades, which, of all the disputed dialogues of Plato, has the greatest merit, and is somewhat longer than any other of them, though not verified by the testimony of Aristotle, and in many respects at variance with the Symposium in the description of the relations of Socrates and Alcibiades. Like the Lesser Hippias and the Menexenus, it is to be compared to the earlier writings of Plato. The motive of the piece may, perhaps, be found in that passage of the Symposium in which Alcibiades describes himself as self-convicted by the words of Socrates (216 B, C). For the disparaging manner in which Schleiermacher has spoken of this dialogue there seems to be no sufficient foundation. At the same time, the lesson imparted is simple, and the irony more transparent than in the undoubted dialogues of Plato. We know, too, that Alcibiades was a favourite thesis, and that at least five or six dialogues bearing this name passed current in antiquity, and are attributed to contemporaries of Socrates and Plato. (1) In the entire absence of real external evidence (for the catalogues of the Alexandrian librarians cannot be regarded as trustworthy); and (2) in the absence of the highest marks either of poetical or philosophical excellence; and (3) considering that we have express testimony to the existence of contemporary writings bearing the name of Alcibiades, we are compelled to suspend our judgment on the genuineness of the extant dialogue.

Neither at this point, nor at any other, do we propose to draw an absolute line of demarcation between genuine and spurious writings of Plato. They fade off imperceptibly from one class to another. There may have been degrees of genuineness in the dialogues themselves, as there are certainly degrees of evidence by which they are supported. The traditions of the oral discourses both of Socrates and Plato may have formed the basis of semi-Platonic writings; some of them may be of the same mixed character which is apparent in Aristotle and Hippocrates, although the form of them is different. But the writings of Plato, unlike the writings of Aristotle, seem never to have been confused with the writings of his disciples: this was probably due to their definite form, and to their inimitable excellence. The three dialogues which we have offered in the Appendix to the criticism of the reader may be partly spurious and partly genuine; they may be altogether spurious;—that is an alternative which must be frankly admitted. Nor can we maintain of some other dialogues, such as the Parmenides, and the Sophist, and Politicus, that no considerable objection can be urged against them, though greatly overbalanced by the weight (chiefly) of internal evidence in their favour. Nor, on the other hand, can we exclude a bare possibility that some dialogues which are usually rejected, such as the Greater Hippias and the Cleitophon, may be genuine. The nature and object of these semi-Platonic writings require more careful study and more comparison of them with one another, and with forged writings in general, than they have yet received, before we can finally decide on their character. We do not consider them all as genuine until they can be proved to be spurious, as is often maintained and still more often implied in this and similar discussions; but should say of some of them, that their genuineness is neither proven nor disproven until further evidence about them can be adduced. And we are as confident that the Epistles are spurious, as that the Republic, the Timaeus, and the Laws are genuine.

On the whole, not a twentieth part of the writings which pass under the name of Plato, if we exclude the works rejected by the ancients themselves and two or three other plausible inventions, can be fairly doubted by those who are willing to allow that a considerable change and growth may have taken place in his philosophy (see above). That twentieth debatable portion scarcely in any degree affects our judgment of Plato, either as a thinker or a writer, and though suggesting some interesting questions to the scholar and critic, is of little importance to the general reader.

INTRODUCTION TO LESSER HIPPIAS.

Lesser Hippias. Introduction.

The Lesser Hippias may be compared with the earlier dialogues of Plato, in which the contrast of Socrates and the Sophists is most strongly exhibited. Hippias, like Protagoras and Gorgias, though civil, is vain and boastful: he knows all things; he can make anything, including his own clothes; he is a manufacturer of poems and declamations, and also of seal-rings, shoes, strigils; his girdle, which he has woven himself, is of a finer than Persian quality. He is a vainer, lighter nature than the two great Sophists (cp. Protag. 314, 337), but of the same character with them, and equally impatient of the short cut-and-thrust method of Socrates, whom he endeavours to draw into a long oration. At last, he gets tired of being defeated at every point by Socrates, and is with difficulty induced to proceed (compare Thrasymachus, Protagoras, Callicles, and others, to whom the same reluctance is ascribed).

Analysis.

363Hippias like Protagoras has common sense on his side, when he argues, citing passages of the Iliad in support of his view, that Homer intended Achilles to be the bravest, Odysseus the wisest of the Greeks. But he is easily overthrown by the superior dialectics of Socrates, who pretends to show that Achilles is not -369true to his word, and that no similar inconsistency is to be found in Odysseus. Hippias replies that Achilles unintentionally, but 370Odysseus intentionally, speaks falsehood. But is it better to do wrong intentionally or unintentionally? Socrates, relying on the analogy of the arts, maintains the former, Hippias the latter of the -372two alternatives. . . . All this is quite conceived in the spirit of Plato, who is very far from making Socrates always argue on the side of truth. The over-reasoning on Homer, which is of course satirical, is also in the spirit of Plato. Poetry turned logic is even more ridiculous than 'rhetoric turned logic,' and equally fallacious. There were reasoners in ancient as well as in modern times, who could never receive the natural impression of Homer, or of any other book which they read. The argument of Socrates, in which he picks out the apparent inconsistencies and discrepancies in the speech and actions of Achilles, and the final paradox, 'that he who is true is also false,' remind us of the interpretation by Socrates of Simonides in the Protagoras, and of similar reasonings in the first book of the Republic. The discrepancies which Socrates discovers in the words of Achilles are perhaps as great as those discovered by some of the modern separatists of the Homeric poems. . . .

At last, Socrates having caught Hippias in the toils of the 376voluntary and involuntary, is obliged to confess that he is wandering about in the same labyrinth; he makes the reflection on himself which others would make upon him (cp. Protagoras, sub fin.). He does not wonder that he should be in a difficulty, but he wonders at Hippias, and he becomes sensible of the gravity of the situation, when ordinary men like himself can no longer go to the wise and be taught by them.

Introduction.

It may be remarked as bearing on the genuineness of this dialogue: (1) that the manners of the speakers are less subtle and refined than in the other dialogues of Plato; (2) that the sophistry of Socrates is more palpable and unblushing, and also more unmeaning; (3) that many turns of thought and style are found in it which appear also in the other dialogues:—whether resemblances of this kind tell in favour of or against the genuineness of an ancient writing, is an important question which will have to be answered differently in different cases. For that a writer may repeat himself is as true as that a forger may imitate; and Plato elsewhere, either of set purpose or from forgetfulness, is full of repetitions. The parallelisms of the Lesser Hippias, as already remarked, are not of the kind which necessarily imply that the dialogue is the work of a forger. The parallelisms of the Greater Hippias with the other dialogues, and the allusion to the Lesser 285, 286 A, B (where Hippias sketches the programme of his next lecture, and invites Socrates to attend and bring any friends with him who may be competent judges), are more than suspicious:—they are of a very poor sort, such as we cannot suppose to have been due to Plato himself. The Greater Hippias more resembles the Euthydemus than any other dialogue; but is immeasurably inferior to it. The Lesser Hippias seems to have more merit than the Greater, and to be more Platonic in spirit. The character of Hippias is the same in both dialogues, but his vanity and boasting are even more exaggerated in the Greater Hippias. His art of memory is specially mentioned in both. He is an inferior type of the same species as Hippodamus of Miletus (Arist. Pol. II. 8, § 1). Some passages in which the Lesser Hippias may be advantageously compared with the undoubtedly genuine dialogues of Plato are the following:—Less. Hipp. 369 B: cp. Rep. vi. 487 (Socrates' cunning in argument): ‖ ib. D, E: cp. Laches 188 (Socrates' feeling about arguments): ‖ 372 B, C: cp. Rep. i. 338 B (Socrates not unthankful): ‖ 373 B: cp. Rep. i. 340 D (Socrates dishonest in argument).

The Lesser Hippias, though inferior to the other dialogues, may be reasonably believed to have been written by Plato, on the ground (1) of considerable excellence; (2) of uniform tradition beginning with Aristotle and his school. That the dialogue falls below the standard of Plato's other works, or that he has attributed to Socrates an unmeaning paradox (perhaps with the view of showing that he could beat the Sophists at their own weapons; or that he could 'make the worse appear the better cause'; or merely as a dialectical experiment)—are not sufficient reasons for doubting the genuineness of the work.

LESSER HIPPIAS.

PERSONS OF THE DIALOGUE.

Eudicus, Socrates, Hippias.

Eudicus.

Socrates, Eudicus, Hippias.

363Why are you silent, Socrates, after the magnificent display which Hippias has been making? Why do you not either refute his words, if he seems to you to have been wrong in any point, or join with us in commending him? There is the more reason why you should speak, because we are now alone, and the audience is confined to those who may fairly claim to take part in a philosophical discussion.

Socrates.

The Iliad of Homer a finer work than the Odyssey, because Achilles, the hero of the poem, is greater than Odysseus.

I should greatly like, Eudicus, to ask Hippias the meaning of what he was saying just now about Homer. I have heard your father, Apemantus, declare that the Iliad of Homer is a finer poem than the Odyssey in the same degree that Achilles was a better man than Odysseus; Odysseus, he would say, is the central figure of the one poem and Achilles of the other. Now, I should like to know, if Hippias has no objection to tell me, what he thinks about these two heroes, and which of them he maintains to be the better; he has already told us in the course of his exhibition many things of various kinds about Homer and divers other poets.

Eud.

I am sure that Hippias will be delighted to answer anything which you would like to ask; tell me, Hippias, if Socrates asks you a question, will you answer him?

Hippias.

Socrates, Hippias.

Indeed, Eudicus, I should be strangely inconsistent if I refused to answer Socrates, when at each Olympic festival, as I went up from my house at Elis to the temple of Olympia, where all the Hellenes were assembled, I continually professed my willingness to perform any of the exhibitions which I had prepared, and to answer any questions which any one had to ask.

Soc.

Truly, Hippias, you are to be congratulated, if at 364every Olympic festival you have such an encouraging opinion of your own wisdom when you go up to the temple. I doubt whether any muscular hero would be so fearless and confident in offering his body to the combat at Olympia, as you are in offering your mind.

Hip.

And with good reason, Socrates; for since the day when I first entered the lists at Olympia I have never found any man who was my superior in anything.

Soc.

What an ornament, Hippias, will the reputation of your wisdom be to the city of Elis and to your parents! But to return: what say you of Odysseus and Achilles? Which is the better of the two? and in what particular does either surpass the other? For when you were exhibiting and there was company in the room, though I could not follow you, I did not like to ask what you meant, because a crowd of people were present, and I was afraid that the question might interrupt your exhibition. But now that there are not so many of us, and my friend Eudicus bids me ask, I wish you would tell me what you were saying about these two heroes, so that I may clearly understand; how did you distinguish them?

Hip.

Achilles the bravest, Nestor the wisest, and Odysseus the wiliest of the Greeks at Troy.

I shall have much pleasure, Socrates, in explaining to you more clearly than I could in public my views about these and also about other heroes. I say that Homer intended Achilles to be the bravest of the men who went to Troy, Nestor the wisest, and Odysseus the wiliest.

Soc.

O rare Hippias, will you be so good as not to laugh, if I find a difficulty in following you, and repeat my questions several times over? Please to answer me kindly and gently.

Hip.

I should be greatly ashamed of myself, Socrates, if I, who teach others and take money of them, could not, when I was asked by you, answer in a civil and agreeable manner.

Soc.

Thank you: the fact is, that I seemed to understand what you meant when you said that the poet intended Achilles to be the bravest of men, and also that he intended Nestor to be the wisest; but when you said that he meant Odysseus to be the wiliest, I must confess that I could not understand what you were saying. Will you tell me, and then I shall perhaps understand you better; has not Homer made Achilles wily?

Hip.

Certainly not, Socrates; he is the most straightforward of mankind, and when Homer introduces them talking with one another in the passage called the Prayers, Achilles is supposed by the poet to say to Odysseus:—

365'Son of Laertes, sprung from heaven, crafty Odysseus, I will speak out plainly the word which I intend to carry out in act, and which will, I believe, be accomplished. For I hate him like the gates of death who thinks one thing and says another. But I will speak that which shall be accomplished.'

Now, in these verses he clearly indicates the character of the two men; he shows Achilles to be true and simple, and Odysseus to be wily and false; for he supposes Achilles to be addressing Odysseus in these lines.

Soc.

Wily means false:

Now, Hippias, I think that I understand your meaning; when you say that Odysseus is wily, you clearly mean that he is false?

Hip.

Exactly so, Socrates; it is the character of Odysseus, as he is represented by Homer in many passages both of the Iliad and Odyssey.

Soc.

And Homer must be presumed to have meant that the true man is not the same as the false?

Hip.

Of course, Socrates.

Soc.

And is that your own opinion, Hippias?

Hip.

Certainly; how can I have any other?

Soc.

Well, then, as there is no possibility of asking Homer what he meant in these verses of his, let us leave him; but as you show a willingness to take up his cause, and your opinion agrees with what you declare to be his, will you answer on behalf of yourself and him?

Hip.

I will; ask shortly anything which you like.

Soc.

Do you say that the false, like the sick, have no power to do things, or that they have the power to do things?

Hip.

I should say that they have power to do many things, and in particular to deceive mankind.

Soc.

Then, according to you, they are both powerful and wily, are they not?

Hip.

And the false have the power of deceiving mankind; they are prudent and knowing and wise, and have the ability to speak falsely.

Yes.

Soc.

And are they wily, and do they deceive by reason of their simplicity and folly, or by reason of their cunning and a certain sort of prudence?

Hip.

By reason of their cunning and prudence, most certainly.

Soc.

Then they are prudent, I suppose?

Hip.

So they are—very.

Soc.

And if they are prudent, do they know or do they not know what they do?

Hip.

Of course, they know very well; and that is why they do mischief to others.

Soc.

And having this knowledge, are they ignorant, or are they wise?

Hip.

Wise, certainly; at least, in so far as they can deceive.

Soc.

Stop, and let us recall to mind what you are saying; 366are you not saying that the false are powerful and prudent and knowing and wise in those things about which they are false?

Hip.

To be sure.

Soc.

And the true differ from the false—the true and the false are the very opposite of each other?

Hip.

That is my view.

Soc.

Then, according to your view, it would seem that the false are to be ranked in the class of the powerful and wise?

Hip.

Assuredly.

Soc.

And when you say that the false are powerful and wise in so far as they are false, do you mean that they have or have not the power of uttering their falsehoods if they like?

Hip.

I mean to say that they have the power.

Soc.

In a word, then, the false are they who are wise and have the power to speak falsely?

Hip.

Yes.

Soc.

Then a man who has not the power of speaking falsely and is ignorant cannot be false?

Hip.

You are right.

Soc.

And every man has power who does that which he wishes at the time when he wishes. I am not speaking of any special case in which he is prevented by disease or something of that sort, but I am speaking generally, as I might say of you, that you are able to write my name when you like. Would you not call a man able who could do that?

Hip.

Yes.

Soc.

And tell me, Hippias, are you not a skilful calculator and arithmetician?

Hip.

Yes, Socrates, assuredly I am.

Soc.

And if some one were to ask you what is the sum of 3 multiplied by 700, you would tell him the true answer in a moment, if you pleased?

Hip.

Certainly I should.

Soc.

Is not that because you are the wisest and ablest of men in these matters?

Hip.

Yes.

Soc.

And being as you are the wisest and ablest of men in these matters of calculation, are you not also the best?

Hip.

To be sure, Socrates, I am the best.

Soc.

And therefore you would be the most able to tell the truth about these matters, would you not?

Hip.

Yes, I should.

Soc.

They must truly know that about which they falsely speak or they will fall into the error of speaking the truth by mistake.

And could you speak falsehoods about them equally well? I must beg, Hippias, that you will answer me with the same frankness and magnanimity which has hitherto characterized you. If a person were to ask you what is the sum of 3 multiplied by 700, would not you be the best and most consistent teller of a falsehood, having always the power of speaking falsely as you have of speaking truly, about these same matters, if you wanted to tell a falsehood, 367and not to answer truly? Would the ignorant man be better able to tell a falsehood in matters of calculation than you would be, if you chose? Might he not sometimes stumble upon the truth, when he wanted to tell a lie, because he did not know, whereas you who are the wise man, if you wanted to tell a lie would always and consistently lie?

Hip.

Yes; there you are quite right.

Soc.

Does the false man tell lies about other things, but not about number, or when he is making a calculation?

Hip.

To be sure; he would tell as many lies about number as about other things.

Soc.

Then may we further assume, Hippias, that there are men who are false about calculation and number?

Hip.

Yes.

Soc.

Who can they be? For you have already admitted that he who is false must have the ability to be false: you said, as you will remember, that he who is unable to be false will not be false?

Hip.

Yes, I remember; it was so said.

Soc.

And were you not yourself just now shown to be best able to speak falsely about calculation?

Hip.

Yes; that was another thing which was said.

Soc.

And are you not likewise said to speak truly about calculation?

Hip.

Certainly.

Soc.

Then the same person is able to speak both falsely and truly about calculation? And that person is he who is good at calculation—the arithmetician?

Hip.

Yes.

Soc.

Who, then, Hippias, is discovered to be false at calculation? Is he not the good man? For the good man is the able man, and he is the true man.

Hip.

That is evident.

Soc.

Therefore the same man must be true if he is to be truly false, in astronomy, in geometry, and in all the sciences.

Do you not see, then, that the same man is false and also true about the same matters? And the true man is not a whit better than the false; for indeed he is the same with him and not the very opposite, as you were just now imagining.

Hip.

Not in that instance, clearly.

Soc.

Shall we examine other instances?

Hip.

Certainly, if you are disposed.

Soc.

Are you not also skilled in geometry?

Hip.

I am.

Soc.

Well, and does not the same hold in that science also? Is not the same person best able to speak falsely or to speak truly about diagrams; and he is—the geometrician?

Hip.

Yes.

Soc.

He and no one else is good at it?

Hip.

Yes, he and no one else.

Soc.

Then the good and wise geometer has this double power in the highest degree; and if there be a man who is false about diagrams the good man will be he, for he is able to be false; whereas the bad is unable, and for this reason is not false, as has been admitted.

Hip.

True.

Soc.

Once more—let us examine a third case; that of the astronomer, in whose art, again, you, Hippias, profess to be a still greater proficient than in the preceding—do you not?

Hip.

368Yes, I am.

Soc.

And does not the same hold of astronomy?

Hip.

True, Socrates.

Soc.

And in astronomy, too, if any man be able to speak falsely he will be the good astronomer, but he who is not able will not speak falsely, for he has no knowledge.

Hip.

Clearly not.

Soc.

Then in astronomy also, the same man will be true and false?

Hip.

It would seem so.

Soc.

Socrates compliments Hippias on his skill in engraving gems, in making clothes and shoes and the finest fabrics, in writing poetry and prose of the most varied kind, and on the art of memory which he has invented.

And now, Hippias, consider the question at large about all the sciences, and see whether the same principle does not always hold. I know that in most arts you are the wisest of men, as I have heard you boasting in the agora at the tables of the money-changers, when you were setting forth the great and enviable stores of your wisdom; and you said that upon one occasion, when you went to the Olympic games, all that you had on your person was made by yourself. You began with your ring, which was of your own workmanship, and you said that you could engrave rings; and you had another seal which was also of your own workmanship, and a strigil and an oil flask, which you had made yourself; you said also that you had made the shoes which you had on your feet, and the cloak and the short tunic; but what appeared to us all most extraordinary and a proof of singular art, was the girdle of your tunic, which, you said, was as fine as the most costly Persian fabric, and of your own weaving; moreover, you told us that you had brought with you poems, epic, tragic, and dithyrambic, as well as prose writings of the most various kinds; and you said that your skill was also pre-eminent in the arts which I was just now mentioning, and in the true principles of rhythm and harmony and of orthography; and if I remember rightly, there were a great many other accomplishments in which you excelled. I have forgotten to mention your art of memory, which you regard as your special glory, and I dare say that I have forgotten many other things; but, as I was saying, only look to your own arts—and there are plenty of them—and to those of others; and tell me, having regard to the admissions which you and I have made, whether you discover any department of art or any description of wisdom or cunning, whichever name you use, in which the true and false are different and not the same: tell me, if you can, of any. But 369you cannot.

Hip.

Not without consideration, Socrates.

Soc.

Nor will consideration help you, Hippias, as I believe; but then if I am right, remember what the consequence will be.

Hip.

Yet he who knows and remembers all things can call to mind no instance in which the false is not also true, although he was saying just now that Achilles is true and Odysseus false.

I do not know what you mean, Socrates.

Soc.

I suppose that you are not using your art of memory, doubtless because you think that such an accomplishment is not needed on the present occasion. I will therefore remind you of what you were saying: were you not saying that Achilles was a true man, and Odysseus false and wily?

Hip.

I was.

Soc.

And now do you perceive that the same person has turned out to be false as well as true? If Odysseus is false he is also true, and if Achilles is true he is also false, and so the two men are not opposed to one another, but they are alike.

Hip.

O Socrates, you are always weaving the meshes of an argument, selecting the most difficult point, and fastening upon details instead of grappling with the matter in hand as a whole. Come now, and I will demonstrate to you, if you will allow me, by many satisfactory proofs, that Homer has made Achilles a better man than Odysseus, and a truthful man too; and that he has made the other crafty, and a teller of many untruths, and inferior to Achilles. And then, if you please, you shall make a speech on the other side, in order to prove that Odysseus is the better man; and this may be compared to mine, and then the company will know which of us is the better speaker.

Soc.

Socrates pays Hippias the compliment which he always pays to a wise man, of attending to him. He proves by example that Achilles, the true man, is always uttering falsehoods, Odysseus, the false man, never.

O Hippias, I do not doubt that you are wiser than I am. But I have a way, when anybody else says anything, of giving close attention to him, especially if the speaker appears to me to be a wise man. Having a desire to understand, I question him, and I examine and analyse and put together what he says, in order that I may understand; but if the speaker appears to me to be a poor hand, I do not interrogate him, or trouble myself about him, and you may know by this who they are whom I deem to be wise men, for you will see that when I am talking with a wise man, I am very attentive to what he says; and I ask questions of him, in order that I may learn, and be improved by him. And I could not help remarking while you were speaking, that when you recited the verses in which Achilles, as you argued, attacks Odysseus as a deceiver, that you must be strangely mistaken, because Odysseus, the man of wiles, is never found to tell a lie; but 370Achilles is found to be wily on your own showing. At any rate he speaks falsely; for first he utters these words, which you just now repeated,—

'He is hateful to me even as the gates of death who thinks one thing and says another:'—

And then he says, a little while afterwards, he will not be persuaded by Odysseus and Agamemnon, neither will he remain at Troy; but, says he,—

'To-morrow, when I have offered sacrifices to Zeus and all the Gods, having loaded my ships well, I will drag them down into the deep; and then you shall see, if you have a mind, and if such things are a care to you, early in the morning my ships sailing over the fishy Hellespont, and my men eagerly plying the oar; and, if the illustrious shaker of the earth gives me a good voyage, on the third day I shall reach the fertile Phthia.

And before that, when he was reviling Agamemnon, he said,—

'And now to Phthia I will go, since to return home in the beaked ships is far better, nor am I inclined to stay here in dishonour and amass wealth and riches for you.'

But although on that occasion, in the presence of the whole army, he spoke after this fashion, and on the other occasion to his companions, he appears never to have made any preparation or attempt to draw down the ships, as if he had the least intention of sailing home; so nobly regardless was he of the truth. Now I, Hippias, originally asked you the question, because I was in doubt as to which of the two heroes was intended by the poet to be the best, and because I thought that both of them were the best, and that it would be difficult to decide which was the better of them, not only in respect of truth and falsehood, but of virtue generally, for even in this matter of speaking the truth they are much upon a par.

Hip.

Aye, but the falsehood of Achilles is accidental; that of Odysseus intentional.

There you are wrong, Socrates; for in so far as Achilles speaks falsely, the falsehood is obviously unintentional. He is compelled against his will to remain and rescue the army in their misfortune. But when Odysseus speaks falsely he is voluntarily and intentionally false.

Soc.

You, sweet Hippias, like Odysseus, are a deceiver yourself.

Hip.

Certainly not, Socrates; what makes you say so? 371

Soc.

Because you say that Achilles does not speak falsely from design, when he is not only a deceiver, but besides being a braggart, in Homer's description of him is so cunning, and so far superior to Odysseus in lying and pretending, that he dares to contradict himself, and Odysseus does not find him out; at any rate he does not appear to say anything to him which would imply that he perceived his falsehood.

Hip.

What do you mean, Socrates?

Soc.

Did you not observe that afterwards, when he is speaking to Odysseus, he says that he will sail away with the early dawn; but to Ajax he tells quite a different story?

Hip.

Where is that?

Soc.

Where he says,—

'I will not think about bloody war until the son of warlike Priam, illustrious Hector, comes to the tents and ships of the Myrmidons, slaughtering the Argives, and burning the ships with fire; and about my tent and dark ship, I suspect that Hector, although eager for the battle, will nevertheless stay his hand.'

Now, do you really think, Hippias, that the son of Thetis, who had been the pupil of the sage Cheiron, had such a bad memory, or would have carried the art of lying to such an extent (when he had been assailing liars in the most violent terms only the instant before) as to say to Odysseus that he would sail away, and to Ajax that he would remain, and that he was not rather practising upon the simplicity of Odysseus, whom he regarded as an ancient, and thinking that he would get the better of him by his own cunning and falsehood?

Hip.

No, I do not agree with you, Socrates; but I believe that Achilles is induced to say one thing to Ajax, and another to Odysseus in the innocence of his heart, whereas Odysseus, whether he speaks falsely or truly, speaks always with a purpose.

Soc.

That proves Odysseus to be better than Achilles.

Then Odysseus would appear after all to be better than Achilles?

Hip.

Certainly not, Socrates.

Soc.

Why, were not the voluntary liars only just now shown to be better than the involuntary?

Hip.

And how, Socrates, can those who intentionally err, and voluntarily and designedly commit iniquities, be better 372than those who err and do wrong involuntarily? Surely there is a great excuse to be made for a man telling a falsehood, or doing an injury or any sort of harm to another in ignorance. And the laws are obviously far more severe on those who lie or do evil, voluntarily, than on those who do evil involuntarily.

Soc.

Socrates is convinced of his own ignorance because he never agrees with wise men. But he is willing to learn,Socrates, Hippias, Eudicus.and he desires to be cured by Hippias of his ignorance in as few words as possible.

You see, Hippias, as I have already told you, how pertinacious I am in asking questions of wise men. And I think that this is the only good point about me, for I am full of defects, and always getting wrong in some way or other. My deficiency is proved to me by the fact that when I meet one of you who are famous for wisdom, and to whose wisdom all the Hellenes are witnesses, I am found out to know nothing. For speaking generally, I hardly ever have the same opinion about anything which you have, and what proof of ignorance can be greater than to differ from wise men? But I have one singular good quality, which is my salvation; I am not ashamed to learn, and I ask and enquire, and am very grateful to those who answer me, and never fail to give them my grateful thanks; and when I learn a thing I never deny my teacher, or pretend that the lesson is a discovery of my own; but I praise his wisdom, and proclaim what I have learned from him. And now I cannot agree in what you are saying, but I strongly disagree. Well, I know that this is my own fault, and is a defect in my character, but I will not pretend to be more than I am; and my opinion, Hippias, is the very contrary of what you are saying. For I maintain that those who hurt or injure mankind, and speak falsely and deceive, and err voluntarily, are better far than those who do wrong involuntarily. Sometimes, however, I am of the opposite opinion; for I am all abroad in my ideas about this matter, a condition obviously occasioned by ignorance. And just now I happen to be in a crisis of my disorder at which those who err voluntarily appear to me better than those who err involuntarily. My present state of mind is due to our previous argument, which inclines me to believe that in general those who do wrong involuntarily are worse than those who do wrong voluntarily, and therefore I hope that you will be good to me, and not refuse to heal me; for you will do me a much greater benefit if you cure my soul of ignorance, than you would if you were to cure my body of disease. I must, however, tell you beforehand, that if you 373make a long oration to me you will not cure me, for I shall not be able to follow you; but if you will answer me, as you did just now, you will do me a great deal of good, and I do not think that you will be any the worse yourself. And I have some claim upon you also, O son of Apemantus, for you incited me to converse with Hippias; and now, if Hippias will not answer me, you must entreat him on my behalf.

Eud.

But I do not think, Socrates, that Hippias will require any entreaty of mine; for he has already said that he will refuse to answer no man.—Did you not say so, Hippias?

Hip.

Yes, I did; but then, Eudicus, Socrates is always troublesome in an argument, and appears to be dishonest .

Soc.

Excellent Hippias, I do not do so intentionally (if I did, it would show me to be a wise man and a master of wiles, as you would argue), but unintentionally, and therefore you must pardon me; for, as you say, he who is unintentionally dishonest should be pardoned.

Eud.

Yes, Hippias, do as he says; and for our sake, and also that you may not belie your profession, answer whatever Socrates asks you.

Hip.

I will answer, as you request me; and do you ask whatever you like.

Soc.

I am very desirous, Hippias, of examining this question, as to which are the better—those who err voluntarily or involuntarily? And if you will answer me, I think that I can put you in the way of approaching the subject: You would admit, would you not, that there are good runners?

Hip.

Socrates by citation of instances not 'in pari materia' proves that it is better to do evil intentionally;

Yes.

Soc.

And there are bad runners?

Hip.

Yes.

Soc.

And he who runs well is a good runner, and he who runs ill is a bad runner?

Hip.

Very true.

Soc.

And he who runs slowly runs ill, and he who runs quickly runs well?

Hip.

Yes.

Soc.

e. g. in running,

Then in a race, and in running, swiftness is a good, and slowness is an evil quality?

Hip.

To be sure.

Soc.

Which of the two then is a better runner? He who runs slowly voluntarily, or he who runs slowly involuntarily?

Hip.

He who runs slowly voluntarily.

Soc.

And is not running a species of doing?

Hip.

Certainly.

Soc.

And if a species of doing, a species of action?

Hip.

Yes.

Soc.

Then he who runs badly does a bad and dishonourable action in a race?

Hip.

Yes; a bad action, certainly.

Soc.

And he who runs slowly runs badly?

Hip.

Yes.

Soc.

Then the good runner does this bad and disgraceful action voluntarily, and the bad involuntarily?

Hip.

That is to be inferred.

Soc.

Then he who involuntarily does evil actions, is worse in a race than he who does them voluntarily?

Hip.

Yes, in a race.

Soc.

Well; but at a wrestling match—which is the better 374wrestler, he who falls voluntarily or involuntarily?

Hip.

Socrates, Hippias.

He who falls voluntarily, doubtless.

Soc.

in wrestling,

And is it worse or more dishonourable at a wrestling match, to fall, or to throw another?

Hip.

To fall.

Soc.

Then, at a wrestling match, he who voluntarily does base and dishonourable actions is a better wrestler than he who does them involuntarily?

Hip.

That appears to be the truth.

Soc.

And what would you say of any other bodily exercise—is not he who is better made able to do both that which is strong and that which is weak—that which is fair and that which is foul?—so that when he does bad actions with the body, he who is better made does them voluntarily, and he who is worse made does them involuntarily.

Hip.

Yes, that appears to be true about strength.

Soc.

in the action of the body,

And what do you say about grace, Hippias? Is not he who is better made able to assume evil and disgraceful figures and postures voluntarily, as he who is worse made assumes them involuntarily?

Hip.

True.

Soc.

Then voluntary ungracefulness comes from excellence of the bodily frame, and involuntary from the defect of the bodily frame?

Hip.

True.

Soc.

in singing,

And what would you say of an unmusical voice; would you prefer the voice which is voluntarily or involuntarily out of tune?

Hip.

That which is voluntarily out of tune.

Soc.

The involuntary is the worse of the two?

Hip.

Yes.

Soc.

And would you choose to possess goods or evils?

Hip.

Goods.

Soc.

in the use of the feet,

And would you rather have feet which are voluntarily or involuntarily lame?

Hip.

Feet which are voluntarily lame.

Soc.

But is not lameness a defect or deformity?

Hip.

Yes.

Soc.

And is not blinking a defect in the eyes?

Hip.

Yes.

Soc.

And would you rather always have eyes with which you might voluntarily blink and not see, or with which you might involuntarily blink?

Hip.

eyes,

I would rather have eyes which voluntarily blink.

Soc.

Then in your own case you deem that which voluntarily acts ill, better than that which involuntarily acts ill?

Hip.

Yes, certainly, in cases such as you mention.

Soc.

ears,

And does not the same hold of ears, nostrils, mouth, and of all the senses—those which involuntarily act ill are not to be desired, as being defective; and those which voluntarily act ill are to be desired as being good?

Hip.

I agree.

Soc.

of instruments.

And what would you say of instruments;—which are the better sort of instruments to have to do with?—those with which a man acts ill voluntarily or involuntarily? For example, had a man better have a rudder with which he will steer ill, voluntarily or involuntarily?

Hip.

He had better have a rudder with which he will steer ill voluntarily.

Soc.

And does not the same hold of the bow and the lyre, the flute and all other things?

Hip.

Very true.

Soc.

And would you rather have a horse of such a temper that you may ride him ill voluntarily or involuntarily?

Hip.

It is true also of animals,

375I would rather have a horse which I could ride ill voluntarily.

Soc.

That would be the better horse?

Hip.

Yes.

Soc.

Then with a horse of better temper, vicious actions would be produced voluntarily; and with a horse of bad temper involuntarily?

Hip.

Certainly.

Soc.

And that would be true of a dog, or of any other animal?

Hip.

Yes.

Soc.

in the practice of archery,

And is it better to possess the mind of an archer who voluntarily or involuntarily misses the mark?

Hip.

Of him who voluntarily misses.

Soc.

This would be the better mind for the purposes of archery?

Hip.

Yes.

Soc.

Then the mind which involuntarily errs is worse than the mind which errs voluntarily?

Hip.

Yes, certainly, in the use of the bow.

Soc.

of medicine,

And what would you say of the art of medicine;—has not the mind which voluntarily works harm to the body, more of the healing art?

Hip.

Yes.

Soc.

Then in the art of medicine the voluntary is better than the involuntary?

Hip.

Yes.

Soc.

Well, and in lute-playing and in flute-playing, and in all arts and sciences, is not that mind the better which voluntarily does what is evil and dishonourable, and goes wrong, and is not the worse that which does so involuntarily?

Hip.

That is evident.

Soc.

in the characters of slaves.

And what would you say of the characters of slaves? Should we not prefer to have those who voluntarily do wrong and make mistakes, and are they not better in their mistakes than those who commit them involuntarily?

Hip.

Yes.

Soc.

And should we not desire to have our own minds in the best state possible?

Hip.

Yes.

Soc.

And will our minds be better if they do wrong and make mistakes voluntarily or involuntarily?

Hip.

Hippias revolts at the conclusion.

O, Socrates, it would be a monstrous thing to say that those who do wrong voluntarily are better than those who do wrong involuntarily!

Soc.

And yet that appears to be the only inference.

Hip.

I do not think so.

Soc.

Socrates recapitulates the argument.

But I imagined, Hippias, that you did. Please to answer once more: Is not justice a power, or knowledge, or both? Must not justice, at all events, be one of these?

Hip.

Yes.

Soc.

But if justice is a power of the soul, then the soul which has the greater power is also the more just; for that which has the greater power, my good friend, has been proved by us to be the better.

Hip.

Yes, that has been proved.

Soc.

And if justice is knowledge, then the wiser will be the juster soul, and the more ignorant the more unjust?

Hip.

Yes.

Soc.

But if justice be power as well as knowledge—then will not the soul which has both knowledge and power be the more just, and that which is the more ignorant be the more unjust? Must it not be so?

Hip.

Clearly.

Soc.

And is not the soul which has the greater power and wisdom also better, and better able to do both good and evil in every action?

Hip.

Certainly.

Soc.

376The soul, then, which acts ill, acts voluntarily by power and art—and these either one or both of them are elements of justice?

Hip.

That seems to be true.

Soc.

And to do injustice is to do ill, and not to do injustice is to do well?

Hip.

Yes.

Soc.

And will not the better and abler soul when it does wrong, do wrong voluntarily, and the bad soul involuntarily?

Hip.

Clearly.

Soc.

And the good man is he who has the good soul, and the bad man is he who has the bad?

Hip.

Yes.

Soc.

Hippias, who has admitted the previous deductions, rebels at the final one. Socrates is himself dissatisfied. What remains if Socrates and a wiser than Socrates are alike in doubt?Socrates,

Then the good man will voluntarily do wrong, and the bad man involuntarily, if the good man is he who has the good soul?

Hip.

Which he certainly has.

Soc.

Then, Hippias, he who voluntarily does wrong and disgraceful things, if there be such a man, will be the good man?

Hip.

There I cannot agree with you.

Soc.

Nor can I agree with myself, Hippias; and yet that seems to be the conclusion which, as far as we can see at present, must follow from our argument. As I was saying before, I am all abroad, and being in perplexity am always changing my opinion. Now, that I or any ordinary man should wander in perplexity is not surprising; but if you wise men also wander, and we cannot come to you and rest from our wandering, the matter begins to be serious both to us and to you.

INTRODUCTION TO ALCIBIADES I.

Alcibiades I. Introduction.

The First Alcibiades is a conversation between Socrates and Alcibiades. Socrates is represented in the character which he attributes to himself in the Apology of a know-nothing who detects the conceit of knowledge in others. The two have met already in the Protagoras and in the Symposium; in the latter dialogue, as in this, the relation between them is that of a lover and his beloved. But the narrative of their loves is told differently in different places; for in the Symposium Alcibiades is depicted as the impassioned but rejected lover; here, as coldly receiving the advances of Socrates, who, for the best of purposes, lies in wait for the aspiring and ambitious youth.

Analysis.

103Alcibiades, who is described as a very young man, is about to enter on public life, having an inordinate opinion of himself, and an extravagant ambition. Socrates, 'who knows what is in man,' -106astonishes him by a revelation of his designs. But has he the knowledge which is necessary for carrying them out? He is 107going to persuade the Athenians—about what? Not about any particular art, but about politics—when to fight and when to make peace. Now, men should fight and make peace on just grounds, and therefore the question of justice and injustice must enter into -109peace and war; and he who advises the Athenians must know the difference between them. Does Alcibiades know? If he does, he must either have been taught by some master, or he must have discovered the nature of them himself. If he has had a master, Socrates would like to be informed who he is, that he 110may go and learn of him also. Alcibiades admits that he has never learned. Then has he enquired for himself? He may have, if he was ever aware of a time when he was ignorant. But he never was ignorant; for when he played with other boys at dice, he charged them with cheating, and this implied a knowledge of just and unjust. According to his own explanation, he had learned of the multitude. Why, he asks, should he not learn of them the nature of justice, as he has learned the Greek language of them? To this Socrates answers, that they can teach Greek, but they 111cannot teach justice; for they are agreed about the one, but they are not agreed about the other: and therefore Alcibiades, who 112has admitted that if he knows he must either have learned from a master or have discovered for himself the nature of justice, is convicted out of his own mouth. 113

Alcibiades rejoins, that the Athenians debate not about what is just, but about what is expedient; and he asserts that the two principles of justice and expediency are opposed. Socrates, by a 114series of questions, compels him to admit that the just and the expedient coincide. Alcibiades is thus reduced to the humiliating conclusion that he knows nothing of politics, even if, as he says, they are concerned with the expedient.

However, he is no worse than other Athenian statesmen; and he will not need training, for others are as ignorant as he is. He is reminded that he has to contend, not only with his own countrymen, but with their enemies—with the Spartan kings and with the great king of Persia; and he can only attain this higher aim of ambition by the assistance of Socrates. Not that Socrates himself professes to have attained the truth, but the questions which he asks bring others to a knowledge of themselves, and this is the first step in the practice of virtue.

The dialogue continues:—We wish to become as good as possible. But to be good in what? Alcibiades replies—'Good in transacting business.' But what business? 'The business of the most intelligent men at Athens.' The cobbler is intelligent in shoemaking, and is therefore good in that; he is not intelligent, and therefore not good, in weaving. Is he good in the sense which Alcibiades means, who is also bad? 'I mean,' replies Alcibiades, 'the man who is able to command in the city.' But to command what—horses or men? and if men, under what circumstances? 'I mean to say, that he is able to command men living in social and political relations.' And what is their aim? 'The better preservation of the city.' But when is a city better? 'When there is unanimity, such as exists between husband and wife.' Then, when husbands and wives perform their own special duties, there can be no unanimity between them; nor can a city be well ordered when each citizen does his own work only. Alcibiades, having stated first that goodness consists in the unanimity of the citizens, and then in each of them doing his own separate work, is brought to the required point of self-contradiction, leading him to confess his own ignorance.

But he is not too old to learn, and may still arrive at the truth, if he is willing to be cross-examined by Socrates. He must know himself; that is to say, not his body, or the things of the body, but his mind, or truer self. The physician knows the body, and the tradesman knows his own business, but they do not necessarily know themselves. Self-knowledge can be obtained only by looking into the mind and virtue of the soul, which is the diviner part of a man, as we see our own image in another's eye. And if we do not know ourselves, we cannot know what belongs to ourselves or belongs to others, and are unfit to take a part in political affairs. Both for the sake of the individual and of the state, we ought to aim at justice and temperance, not at wealth or power. The evil and unjust should have no power,—they should be the slaves of better men than themselves. None but the virtuous are deserving of freedom.

And are you, Alcibiades, a freeman? 'I feel that I am not; but I hope, Socrates, that by your aid I may become free, and from this day forward I will never leave you.'

Introduction.

The Alcibiades has several points of resemblance to the undoubted dialogues of Plato. The process of interrogation is of the same kind with that which Socrates practises upon the youthful Cleinias in the Euthydemus; and he characteristically attributes to Alcibiades the answers which he has elicited from him. The definition of good is narrowed by successive questions, and virtue is shown to be identical with knowledge. Here, as elsewhere, Socrates awakens the consciousness not of sin but of ignorance. Self-humiliation is the first step to knowledge, even of the commonest things. No man knows how ignorant he is, and no man can arrive at virtue and wisdom who has not once in his life, at least, been convicted of error. The process by which the soul is elevated is not unlike that which religious writers describe under the name of 'conversion,' if we substitute the sense of ignorance for the consciousness of sin.

In some respects the dialogue differs from any other Platonic composition. The aim is more directly ethical and hortatory; the process by which the antagonist is undermined is simpler than in other Platonic writings, and the conclusion more decided. There is a good deal of humour in the manner in which the pride of Alcibiades, and of the Greeks generally, is supposed to be taken down by the Spartan and Persian queens; and the dialogue has considerable dialectical merit. But we have a difficulty in supposing that the same writer, who has given so profound and complex a notion of the characters both of Alcibiades and Socrates in the Symposium, should have treated them in so thin and superficial a manner in the Alcibiades, or that he would have ascribed to the ironical Socrates the rather unmeaning boast that Alcibiades could not attain the objects of his ambition without his help (105 D foll.); or that he should have imagined that a mighty nature like his could have been reformed by a few not very conclusive words of Socrates. For the arguments by which Alcibiades is reformed are not convincing; the writer of the dialogue, whoever he was, arrives at his idealism by crooked and tortuous paths, in which many pitfalls are concealed. The anachronism of making Alcibiades about twenty years old during the life of his uncle, Pericles, may be noted; and the repetition of the favourite observation, which occurs also in the Laches and Protagoras, that great Athenian statesmen, like Pericles, failed in the education of their sons. There is none of the undoubted dialogues of Plato in which there is so little dramatic verisimilitude.

ALCIBIADES I.

PERSONS OF THE DIALOGUE.

Alcibiades, Socrates.

Socrates.

Alcibiades I. Socrates, Alcibiades. The pride of Alcibiades has been too much for his lovers.

103 I dare say that you may be surprised to find, O son of Cleinias, that I, who am your first lover, not having spoken to you for many years, when the rest of the world were wearying you with their attentions, am the last of your lovers who still speaks to you. The cause of my silence has been that I was hindered by a power more than human, of which I will some day explain to you the nature; this impediment has now been removed; I therefore here present myself before you, and I greatly hope that no similar hindrance will again occur. Meanwhile, I have observed that your pride has been too much for the pride of your admirers; they were numerous and high-spirited, but they have all run away, overpowered by your superior force of 104 character; not one of them remains. And I want you to understand the reason why you have been too much for them. You think that you have no need of them or of any other man, for you have great possessions and lack nothing, beginning with the body, and ending with the soul. In the first place, you say to yourself that you are the fairest and tallest of the citizens, and this every one who has eyes may see to be true; in the second place, that you are among the noblest of them, highly connected both on the father's and the mother's side, and sprung from one of the most distinguished families in your own state, which is the greatest in Hellas, and having many friends and kinsmen of the best sort, who can assist you when in need; and there is one potent relative, who is more to you than all the rest, Pericles the son of Xanthippus, whom your father left guardian of you, and of your brother, and who can do as he pleases not only in this city, but in all Hellas, and among many and mighty barbarous nations. Moreover, you are rich; but I must say that you value yourself least of all upon your possessions. And all these things have lifted you up; you have overcome your lovers, and they have acknowledged that you were too much for them. Have you not remarked their absence? And now I know that you wonder why I, unlike the rest of them, have not gone away, and what can be my motive in remaining.

Alcibiades.

Perhaps, Socrates, you are not aware that I was just going to ask you the very same question—What do you want? And what is your motive in annoying me, and always, wherever I am, making a point of coming ? I do really wonder what you mean, and should greatly like to know.

Soc.

Then if, as you say, you desire to know, I suppose that you will be willing to hear, and I may consider myself to be speaking to an auditor who will remain, and will not run away?

Al.

Certainly, let me hear.

Soc.

You had better be careful, for I may very likely be as unwilling to end as I have hitherto been to begin.

Al.

Proceed, my good man, and I will listen.

Soc.

Alcibiades a lover, not of pleasure, but of ambition; and he requires the help of Socrates for the accomplishment of his designs. And this is the reason why Socrates has clung to him; he is hoping when Alcibiades has become the ruler of Athens to rule over him.

I will proceed; and, although no lover likes to speak with one who has no feeling of love in him , I will make an effort, and tell you what I meant: My love, Alcibiades, which 105I hardly like to confess, would long ago have passed away, as I flatter myself, if I saw you loving your good things, or thinking that you ought to pass life in the enjoyment of them. But I shall reveal other thoughts of yours, which you keep to yourself; whereby you will know that I have always had my eye on you. Suppose that at this moment some God came to you and said: Alcibiades, will you live as you are, or die in an instant if you are forbidden to make any further acquisition?—I verily believe that you would choose death. And I will tell you the hope in which you are at present living: Before many days have elapsed, you think that you will come before the Athenian assembly, and will prove to them that you are more worthy of honour than Pericles, or any other man that ever lived, and having proved this, you will have the greatest power in the state. When you have gained the greatest power among us, you will go on to other Hellenic states, and not only to Hellenes, but to all the barbarians who inhabit the same continent with us. And if the God were then to say to you again: Here in Europe is to be your seat of empire, and you must not cross over into Asia or meddle with Asiatic affairs, I do not believe that you would choose to live upon these terms; but the world, as I may say, must be filled with your power and name—no man less than Cyrus and Xerxes is of any account with you. Such I know to be your hopes—I am not guessing only—and very likely you, who know that I am speaking the truth, will reply, Well, Socrates, but what have my hopes to do with the explanation which you promised of your unwillingness to leave me? And that is what I am now going to tell you, sweet son of Cleinias and Dinomachè. The explanation is, that all these designs of yours cannot be accomplished by you without my help; so great is the power which I believe myself to have over you and your concerns; and this I conceive to be the reason why the God has hitherto forbidden me to converse with you, and I have been long expecting his permission. For, as you hope to prove your own great value to the state, and having proved it, to attain at once to absolute power, so do I indulge a hope that I shall have the supreme power over you, if I am able to prove my own great value to you, and to show you that neither guardian, nor kinsman, nor any one is able to deliver into your hands the power which you desire, but I only, God being my helper. When you were young and your hopes were not yet matured, I should have wasted my time, and 106therefore, as I conceive, the God forbade me to converse with you; but now, having his permission, I will speak, for now you will listen to me.

Al.

Alcibiades does not deny the impeachment.

Your silence, Socrates, was always a surprise to me. I never could understand why you followed me about, and now that you have begun to speak again, I am still more amazed. Whether I think all this or not, is a matter about which you seem to have already made up your mind, and therefore my denial will have no effect upon you. But granting, if I must, that you have perfectly divined my purposes, why is your assistance necessary to the attainment of them? Can you tell me why?

Soc.

You want to know whether I can make a long speech, such as you are in the habit of hearing; but that is not my way. I think, however, that I can prove to you the truth of what I am saying, if you will grant me one little favour.

Al.

Yes, if the favour which you mean be not a troublesome one.

Soc.

Will you be troubled at having questions to answer?

Al.

Alcibiades is willing to answer questions.

Not at all.

Soc.

Then please to answer.

Al.

Ask me.

Soc.

Have you not the intention which I attribute to you?

Al.

I will grant anything you like, in the hope of hearing what more you have to say.

Soc.

You do, then, mean, as I was saying, to come forward in a little while in the character of an adviser of the Athenians? And suppose that when you are ascending the bema, I pull you by the sleeve and say, Alcibiades, you are getting up to advise the Athenians—do you know the matter about which they are going to deliberate, better than they?—How would you answer?

Al.

He is going to advise the Athenians about matters which he knows better than they.

I should reply, that I was going to advise them about a matter which I do know better than they.

Soc.

Then you are a good adviser about the things which you know?

Al.

Certainly.

Soc.

And do you know anything but what you have learned of others, or found out yourself?

Al.

That is all.

Soc.

And would you have ever learned or discovered anything, if you had not been willing either to learn of others or to examine yourself?

Al.

I should not.

Soc.

And would you have been willing to learn or to examine what you supposed that you knew?

Al.

Certainly not.

Soc.

Then there was a time when you thought that you did not know what you are now supposed to know?

Al.

Certainly.

Soc.

But when did he ever learn about these matters?

I think that I know tolerably well the extent of your acquirements; and you must tell me if I forget any of them: according to my recollection, you learned the arts of writing, of playing on the lyre, and of wrestling; the flute you never would learn; this is the sum of your accomplishments, unless there were some which you acquired in secret; and I think that secrecy was hardly possible, as you could not have come out of your door, either by day or night, without my seeing you.

Al.

Yes, that was the whole of my schooling.

Soc.

107And are you going to get up in the Athenian assembly, and give them advice about writing?

Al.

No, indeed.

Soc.

Or about the touch of the lyre?

Al.

Certainly not.

Soc.

And they are not in the habit of deliberating about wrestling, in the assembly?

Al.

Hardly.

Soc.

Then what are the deliberations in which you propose to advise them? Surely not about building?

Al.

No.

Soc.

For the builder will advise better than you will about that?

Al.

He will.

Soc.

Nor about divination?

Al.

No.

Soc.

About that again the diviner will advise better than you will?

Al.

True.

Soc.

Whether he be little or great, good or ill-looking, noble or ignoble—makes no difference.

Al.

Certainly not.

Soc.

A man is a good adviser about anything, not because he has riches, but because he has knowledge?

Al.

Assuredly.

Soc.

Whether their counsellor is rich or poor, is not a matter which will make any difference to the Athenians when they are deliberating about the health of the citizens; they only require that he should be a physician.

Al.

Of course.

Soc.

Then what will be the subject of deliberation about which you will be justified in getting up and advising them?

Al.

About their own concerns, Socrates.

Soc.

You mean about shipbuilding, for example, when the question is what sort of ships they ought to build?

Al.

No, I should not advise them about that.

Soc.

I suppose, because you do not understand shipbuilding:—is that the reason?

Al.

It is.

Soc.

Then about that concerns of theirs will you advise them?

Al.

He will advise them about war and peace, and with whom they had better go to war, and when and how long.

About war, Socrates, or about peace, or about any other concerns of the state.

Soc.

You mean, when they deliberate with whom they ought to make peace, and with whom they ought to go to war, and in what manner?

Al.

Yes.

Soc.

And they ought to go to war with those against whom it is better to go to war?

Al.

Yes.

Soc.

And when it is better?

Al.

Certainly.

Soc.

And for as long a time as is better?

Al.

Yes.

Soc.

But suppose the Athenians to deliberate with whom they ought to close in wrestling, and whom they should grasp by the hand, would you, or the master of gymnastics, be a better adviser of them?

Al.

Clearly, the master of gymnastics.

Soc.

And can you tell me on what grounds the master of gymnastics would decide, with whom they ought or ought not to close, and when and how? To take an instance: Would he not say that they should wrestle with those against whom it is best to wrestle?

Al.

Yes.

Soc.

108And as much as is best?

Al.

Certainly.

Soc.

And at such times as are best?

Al.

Yes.

Soc.

Again; you sometimes accompany the lyre with the song and dance?

Al.

Yes.

Soc.

When it is well to do so?

Al.

Yes.

Soc.

And as much as is well?

Al.

Just so.

Soc.

And as you speak of an excellence or art of the best in wrestling, and of an excellence in playing the lyre, I wish you would tell me what this latter is;—the excellence of wrestling I call gymnastic, and I want to know what you call the other.

Al.

I do not understand you.

Soc.

Then try to do as I do; for the answer which I gave is universally right, and when I say right, I mean according to rule.

Al.

Yes.

Soc.

And was not the art of which I spoke gymnastic?

Al.

Certainly.

Soc.

And I called the excellence in wrestling gymnastic?

Al.

You did.

Soc.

And I was right?

Al.

I think that you were.

Soc.

Alcibiades should learn to argue nicely.

Well, now,—for you should learn to argue prettily—let me ask you in return to tell me, first, what is that art of which playing and singing, and stepping properly in the dance, are parts,—what is the name of the whole? I think that by this time you must be able to tell.

Al.

Indeed I cannot.

Soc.

Then let me put the matter in another way: what do you call the Goddesses who are the patronesses of art?

Al.

The Muses do you mean, Socrates?

Soc.

Yes, I do; and what is the name of the art which is called after them?

Al.

I suppose that you mean music.

Soc.

What is the meaning of 'the better,' 'the more excellent.'

Yes, that is my meaning; and what is the excellence of the art of music, as I told you truly that the excellence of wrestling was gymnastic—what is the excellence of music—to be what?

Al.

To be musical, I suppose.

Soc.

Very good; and now please to tell me what is the excellence of war and peace; as the more musical was the more excellent, or the more gymnastical was the more excellent, tell me, what name do you give to the more excellent in war and peace?

Al.

But I really cannot tell you.

Soc.

The term better, when applied to food, means more wholesome.

But if you were offering advice to another and said to him—This food is better than that, at this time and in this quantity, and he said to you—What do you mean, Alcibiades, by the word 'better'? you would have no difficulty in replying that you meant 'more wholesome,' although you do not profess to be a physician: and when the subject is one of which you profess to have knowledge, and about which you are ready to get up and advise as if you knew, are you not ashamed, when you are asked, not to be able to answer the question? Is it not disgraceful? 109

Al.

Very.

Soc.

Well, then, consider and try to explain what is the meaning of 'better,' in the matter of making peace and going to war with those against whom you ought to go to war? To what does the word refer?

Al.

I am thinking, and I cannot tell.

Soc.

But you surely know what are the charges which we bring against one another, when we arrive at the point of making war, and what name we give them?

Al.

Yes, certainly; we say that deceit or violence has been employed, or that we have been defrauded.

Soc.

And how does this happen? Will you tell me how? For there may be a difference in the manner.

Al.

Do you mean by 'how,' Socrates, whether we suffered these things justly or unjustly?

Soc.

Exactly.

Al.

There can be no greater difference than between just and unjust.

Soc.

And would you advise the Athenians to go to war with the just or with the unjust?

Al.

That is an awkward question; for certainly, even if a person did intend to go to war with the just, he would not admit that they were just.

Soc.

He would not go to war, because it would be unlawful?

Al.

Neither lawful nor honourable.

Soc.

Then you, too, would address them on principles of justice?

Al.

Certainly.

Soc.

In going to war or not going to war, the better is the more just.

What, then, is justice but that better, of which I spoke, in going to war or not going to war with those against whom we ought or ought not, and when we ought or ought not to go to war?

Al.

Clearly.

Soc.

But how is this, friend Alcibiades? Have you forgotten that you do not know this, or have you been to the schoolmaster without my knowledge, and has he taught you to discern the just from the unjust? Who is he? I wish you would tell me, that I may go and learn of him—you shall introduce me.

Al.

You are mocking, Socrates.

Soc.

But where did Alcibiades acquire this notion of just and unjust?

No, indeed; I most solemnly declare to you by Zeus, who is the God of our common friendship, and whom I never will forswear, that I am not; tell me, then, who this instructor is, if he exists.

Al.

But, perhaps, he does not exist; may I not have acquired the knowledge of just and unjust in some other way?

Soc.

Yes; if you have discovered them.

Al.

But do you not think that I could discover them?

Soc.

I am sure that you might, if you enquired about them.

Al.

And do you not think that I would enquire?

Soc.

Yes; if you thought that you did not know them.

Al.

And was there not a time when I did so think?

Soc.

Very good; and can you tell me how long it is 110since you thought that you did not know the nature of the just and the unjust? What do you say to a year ago? Were you then in a state of conscious ignorance and enquiry? or did you think that you knew? And please to answer truly, that our discussion may not be in vain.

Al.

Well, I thought that I knew.

Soc.

And two years ago, and three years ago, and four years ago, you knew all the same?

Al.

I did.

Soc.

And more than four years ago you were a child—were you not?

Al.

Yes.

Soc.

And then I am quite sure that you thought you knew.

Al.

Why are you so sure?

Soc.

He always had them.

Because I often heard you when a child, in your teacher's house, or elsewhere, playing at dice or some other game with the boys, not hesitating at all about the nature of the just and unjust; but very confident—crying and shouting that one of the boys was a rogue and a cheat, and had been cheating. Is it not true?

Al.

But what was I to do, Socrates, when anybody cheated me?

Soc.

And how can you say, 'What was I to do'? if at the time you did not know whether you were wronged or not?

Al.

To be sure I knew; I was quite aware that I was being cheated.

Soc.

Then you suppose yourself even when a child to have known the nature of just and unjust?

Al.

Certainly; and I did know then.

Soc.

And when did you discover them—not, surely, at the time when you thought that you knew them?

Al.

Certainly not.

Soc.

And when did you think that you were ignorant—if you consider, you will find that there never was such a time?

Al.

Really, Socrates, I cannot say.

Soc.

Then you did not learn them by discovering them?

Al.

Clearly not.

Soc.

But just before you said that you did not know them by learning; now, if you have neither discovered nor learned them, how and whence do you come to know them?

Al.

I suppose that I was mistaken in saying that I knew them through my own discovery of them; whereas, in truth, I learned them in the same way that other people learn.

Soc.

So you said before, and I must again ask, of whom? Do tell me.

Al.

Of the many.

Soc.

He learned them of the many.

Do you take refuge in them? I cannot say much for your teachers.

Al.

Why, are they not able to teach?

Soc.

They could not teach you how to play at draughts, which you would acknowledge (would you not) to be a much smaller matter than justice?

Al.

Yes.

Soc.

And can they teach the better who are unable to teach the worse?

Al.

I think that they can; at any rate, they can teach many far better things than to play at draughts.

Soc.

111What things?

Al.

as he learned Greek;—of those who knew it.

Why, for example, I learned to speak Greek of them, and I cannot say who was my teacher, or to whom I am to attribute my knowledge of Greek, if not to those good-for-nothing teachers, as you call them.

Soc.

Why, yes, my friend; and the many are good enough teachers of Greek, and some of their instructions in that line may be justly praised.

Al.

Why is that?

Soc.

Why, because they have the qualities which good teachers ought to have.

Al.

What qualities?

Soc.

Why, you know that knowledge is the first qualification of any teacher?

Al.

Certainly.

Soc.

And if they know, they must agree together and not differ?

Al.

Yes.

Soc.

And would you say that they knew the things about which they differ?

Al.

No.

Soc.

Then how can they teach them?

Al.

They cannot.

Soc.

Yes: the many can teach things about which they are agreed.

Well, but do you imagine that the many would differ about the nature of wood and stone? are they not agreed if you ask them what they are? and do they not run to fetch the same thing, when they want a piece of wood or a stone? And so in similar cases, which I suspect to be pretty nearly all that you mean by speaking Greek.

Al.

True.

Soc.

These, as we were saying, are matters about which they are agreed with one another and with themselves; both individuals and states use the same words about them; they do not use some one word and some another.

Al.

They do not.

Soc.

Then they may be expected to be good teachers of these things?

Al.

Yes.

Soc.

And if we want to instruct any one in them, we shall be right in sending him to be taught by our friends the many?

Al.

Very true.

Soc.

But if we wanted further to know not only which are men and which are horses, but which men or horses have powers of running, would the many still be able to inform us?

Al.

Certainly not.

Soc.

And you have a sufficient proof that they do not know these things and are not the best teachers of them, inasmuch as they are never agreed about them?

Al.

Yes.

Soc.

But could the many teach things about which they are disagreed?

And suppose that we wanted to know not only what men are like, but what healthy or diseased men are like—would the many be able to teach us?

Al.

They would not.

Soc.

And you would have a proof that they were bad teachers of these matters, if you saw them at variance?

Al.

I should.

Soc.

And one of these things is justice.

Well, but are the many agreed with themselves, or with one another, about the justice or injustice of men and 112things?

Al.

Assuredly not, Socrates.

Soc.

There is no subject about which they are more at variance?

Al.

None.

Soc.

I do not suppose that you ever saw or heard of men quarrelling over the principles of health and disease to such an extent as to go to war and kill one another for the sake of them?

Al.

No, indeed.

Soc.

Did not a question of justice cause the war between the Trojans and Achaeans, and between the Athenians and Lacedaemonians?

But of the quarrels about justice and injustice, even if you have never seen them, you have certainly heard from many people, including Homer; for you have heard of the Iliad and Odyssey?

Al.

To be sure, Socrates.

Soc.

A difference of just and unjust is the argument of those poems?

Al.

True.

Soc.

Which difference caused all the wars and deaths of Trojans and Achaeans, and the deaths of the suitors of Penelope in their quarrel with Odysseus.

Al.

Very true.

Soc.

And when the Athenians and Lacedaemonians and Boeotians fell at Tanagra, and afterwards in the battle of Coronea, at which your father Cleinias met his end, the question was one of justice—this was the sole cause of the battles, and of their deaths.

Al.

Very true.

Soc.

And yet they did not know what they were fighting about?

But can they be said to understand that about which they are quarrelling to the death?

Al.

Clearly not.

Soc.

And yet those whom you thus allow to be ignorant are the teachers to whom you are appealing.

Al.

Very true.

Soc.

But how are you ever likely to know the nature of justice and injustice, about which you are so perplexed, if you have neither learned them of others nor discovered them yourself?

Al.

From what you say, I suppose not.

Soc.

See, again, how inaccurately you speak, Alcibiades!

Al.

In what respect?

Soc.

In saying that I say so.

Al.

Why, did you not say that I know nothing of the just and unjust?

Soc.

No; I did not.

Al.

Did I, then?

Soc.

Yes.

Al.

How was that?

Soc.

Let me explain. Suppose I were to ask you which is the greater number, two or one; you would reply 'two'?

Al.

I should.

Soc.

And by how much greater?

Al.

By one.

Soc.

Which of us now says that two is more than one?

Al.

I do.

Soc.

Did not I ask, and you answer the question?

Al.

Yes.

Soc.

Then who is speaking? I who put the question, or 113you who answer me?

Al.

I am.

Soc.

The answerer, not the questioner, has been drawing these inferences.

Or suppose that I ask and you tell me the letters which make up the name Socrates, which of us is the speaker?

Al.

I am.

Soc.

Now let us put the case generally: whenever there is a question and answer, who is the speaker,—the questioner or the answerer?

Al.

I should say, Socrates, that the answerer was the speaker.

Soc.

And have I not been the questioner all through?

Al.

Yes.

Soc.

And you the answerer?

Al.

Just so.

Soc.

Which of us, then, was the speaker?

Al.

The inference is, Socrates, that I was the speaker.

Soc.

Did not some one say that Alcibiades, the fair son of Cleinias, not understanding about just and unjust, but thinking that he did understand, was going to the assembly to advise the Athenians about what he did not know? Was not that said?

Al.

Very true.

Soc.

How can you teach what you do not know?

Then, Alcibiades, the result may be expressed in the language of Euripides. I think that you have heard all this 'from yourself, and not from me'; nor did I say this, which you erroneously attribute to me, but you yourself, and what you said was very true. For indeed, my dear fellow, the design which you meditate of teaching what you do not know, and have not taken any pains to learn, is downright insanity.

Al.

[*promotion of one's self interest*]

But the expedient, not the just, is the subject about which men commonly debate.

But, Socrates, I think that the Athenians and the rest of the Hellenes do not often advise as to the more just or unjust; for they see no difficulty in them, and therefore they leave them, and consider which course of action will be most expedient; for there is a difference between justice and expediency. Many persons have done great wrong and profited by their injustice; others have done rightly and come to no good.

Soc.

Well, but granting that the just and the expedient are ever so much opposed, you surely do not imagine that you know what is expedient for mankind, or why a thing is expedient?

Al.

Alcibiades insists that he will not have the old argument over again.

Why not, Socrates?—But I am not going to be asked again from whom I learned, or when I made the discovery.

Soc.

What a way you have! When you make a mistake which might be refuted by a previous argument, you insist on having a new and different refutation; the old argument is a worn out garment which you will no longer put on, but some 114one must produce another which is clean and new. Now I shall disregard this move of yours, and shall ask over again,—Where did you learn and how do you know the nature of the expedient, and who is your teacher? All this I comprehend in a single question, and now you will manifestly be in the old difficulty, and will not be able to show that you know the expedient, either because you learned or because you discovered it yourself. But, as I perceive that you are dainty, and dislike the taste of a stale argument, I will enquire no further into your knowledge of what is expedient or what is not expedient for the Athenian people, and simply request you to say why you do not explain whether justice and expediency are the same or different? And if you like you may examine me as I have examined you, or, if you would rather, you may carry on the discussion by yourself.

Al.

But I am not certain, Socrates, whether I shall be able to discuss the matter with you.

Soc.

Then imagine, my dear fellow, that I am the demus and the ecclesia; for in the ecclesia, too, you will have to persuade men individually.

Al.

Yes.

Soc.

And is not the same person able to persuade one individual singly and many individuals of the things which he knows? The grammarian, for example, can persuade one and he can persuade many about letters.

Al.

True.

Soc.

And about number, will not the same person persuade one and persuade many?

Al.

Yes.

Soc.

And this will be he who knows number, or the arithmetician?

Al.

Quite true.

Soc.

He who can persuade many can persuade one. Alcibiades should therefore be able to persuade Socrates.

And cannot you persuade one man about that of which you can persuade many?

Al.

I suppose so.

Soc.

And that of which you can persuade either is clearly what you know?

Al.

Yes.

Soc.

And the only difference between one who argues as we are doing, and the orator who is addressing an assembly, is that the one seeks to persuade a number, and the other an individual, of the same things.

Al.

I suppose so.

Soc.

Well, then, since the same person who can persuade a multitude can persuade individuals, try conclusions upon me, and prove to me that the just is not always expedient.

Al.

You take liberties, Socrates.

Soc.

I shall take the liberty of proving to you the opposite of that which you will not prove to me.

Al.

Proceed.

Soc.

Answer my questions—that is all.

Al.

Nay, I should like you to be the speaker.

Soc.

What, do you not wish to be persuaded?

Al.

Certainly I do.

Soc.

And can you be persuaded better than out of your own mouth?

Al.

I think not.

Soc.

Then you shall answer; and if you do not hear the words, that the just is the expedient, coming from your own lips, never believe another man again.

Al.

I won't; but answer I will, for I do not see how I can come to any harm.

Soc.

A man may do what is expedient and not just, but he cannot do what is honourable and not just and good.

115A true prophecy! Let me begin then by enquiring of you whether you allow that the just is sometimes expedient and sometimes not?

Al.

Yes.

Soc.

And sometimes honourable and sometimes not?

Al.

What do you mean?

Soc.

I am asking if you ever knew any one who did what was dishonourable and yet just?

Al.

Never.

Soc.

All just things are honourable?

Al.

Yes.

Soc.

And are honourable things sometimes good and sometimes not good, or are they always good?

Al.

I rather think, Socrates, that some honourable things are evil.

Soc.

And are some dishonourable things good?

Al.

Yes.

Soc.

You mean in such a case as the following:—In time of war, men have been wounded or have died in rescuing a companion or kinsman, when others who have neglected the duty of rescuing them have escaped in safety?

Al.

True.

Soc.

And to rescue another under such circumstances is honourable, in respect of the attempt to save those whom we ought to save; and this is courage?

Al.

True.

Soc.

But evil in respect of death and wounds?

Al.

Yes.

Soc.

And the courage which is shown in the rescue is one thing, and the death another?

Al.

Certainly.

Soc.

Then the rescue of one's friends is honourable in one point of view, but evil in another?

Al.

True.

Soc.

And if honourable, then also good: Will you consider now whether I may not be right, for you were acknowledging that the courage which is shown in the rescue is honourable? Now is this courage good or evil? Look at the matter thus: which would you rather choose, good or evil?

Al.

Good.

Soc.

And the greatest goods you would be most ready to choose, and would least like to be deprived of them?

Al.

Certainly.

Soc.

What would you say of courage? At what price would you be willing to be deprived of courage?

Al.

I would rather die than be a coward.

Soc.

Then you think that cowardice is the worst of evils?

Al.

I do.

Soc.

As bad as death, I suppose?

Al.

Yes.

Soc.

And life and courage are the extreme opposites of death and cowardice?

Al.

Yes.

Soc.

And they are what you would most desire to have, and their opposites you would least desire?

Al.

Yes.

Soc.

Is this because you think life and courage the best, and death and cowardice the worst?

Al.

Yes.

Soc.

And you would term the rescue of a friend in battle honourable, in as much as courage does a good work?

Al.

I should.

Soc.

But good may contain an element of evil. Good and evil are to be judged of by their consequences.

But evil because of the death which ensues?

Al.

Yes.

Soc.

Might we not describe their different effects as follows:—You may call either of them evil in respect of the evil which is the result, and good in respect of the good which is the result of either of them? 116

Al.

Yes.

Soc.

And they are honourable in so far as they are good, and dishonourable in so far as they are evil?

Al.

True.

Soc.

Then when you say that the rescue of a friend in battle is honourable and yet evil, that is equivalent to saying that the rescue is good and yet evil?

Al.

I believe that you are right, Socrates.

Soc.

Nothing honourable, regarded as honourable, is evil; nor anything base, regarded as base, good.

Al.

Clearly not.

Soc.

The honourable is identified with the good, and the good is the expedient,

Look at the matter yet once more in a further light: he who acts honourably acts well?

Al.

Yes.

Soc.

And he who acts well is happy?

Al.

Of course.

Soc.

And the happy are those who obtain good?

Al.

True.

Soc.

And they obtain good by acting well and honourably?

Al.

Yes.

Soc.

Then acting well is a good?

Al.

Certainly.

Soc.

And happiness is a good?

Al.

Yes.

Soc.

Then the good and the honourable are again identified.

Al.

Manifestly.

Soc.

Then, if the argument holds, what we find to be honourable we shall also find to be good?

Al.

Certainly.

Soc.

And is the good expedient or not?

Al.

Expedient.

Soc.

Do you remember our admissions about the just?

Al.

Yes; if I am not mistaken, we said that those who acted justly must also act honourably.

Soc.

And the honourable is the good?

Al.

Yes.

Soc.

And the good is expedient?

Al.

Yes.

Soc.

and therefore the just which is the honourable is also the expedient. All this has been proved by Alcibiades himself.

Then, Alcibiades, the just is expedient?

Al.

I should infer so.

Soc.

And all this I prove out of your own mouth, for I ask and you answer?

Al.

I must acknowledge it to be true.

Soc.

And having acknowledged that the just is the same as the expedient, are you not (let me ask) prepared to ridicule any one who, pretending to understand the principles of justice and injustice, gets up to advise the noble Athenians or the ignoble Peparethians, that the just may be the evil?

Al.

Yet he still finds himself in a perplexity,

I solemnly declare, Socrates, that I do not know what I am saying. Verily, I am in a strange state, for when you put questions to me I am of different minds in successive instants.

Soc.

And are you not aware of the nature of this perplexity, my friend?

Al.

Indeed I am not.

Soc.

Do you suppose that if some one were to ask you whether you have two eyes or three, or two hands or four, or anything of that sort, you would then be of different minds in successive instants?

Al.

I begin to distrust myself, but still I do not suppose 117that I should.

Soc.

You would feel no doubt; and for this reason—because you would know?

Al.

I suppose so.

Soc.

And the reason why you involuntarily contradict yourself is clearly that you are ignorant?

Al.

Very likely.

Soc.

and this is because he thinks that he knows, but if he knew that he were ignorant he would be in no perplexity.

And if you are perplexed in answering about just and unjust, honourable and dishonourable, good and evil, expedient and inexpedient, the reason is that you are ignorant of them, and therefore in perplexity. Is not that clear?

Al.

I agree.

Soc.

But is this always the case, and is a man necessarily perplexed about that of which he has no knowledge?

Al.

Certainly he is.

Soc.

And do you know how to ascend into heaven?

Al.

Certainly not.

Soc.

And in this case, too, is your judgment perplexed?

Al.

No.

Soc.

Do you see the reason why, or shall I tell you?

Al.

Tell me.

Soc.

The reason is, that you not only do not know, my friend, but you do not think that you know.

Al.

There again; what do you mean?

Soc.

Ask yourself; are you in any perplexity about things of which you are ignorant? You know, for example, that you know nothing about the preparation of food.

Al.

Very true.

Soc.

And do you think and perplex yourself about the preparation of food: or do you leave that to some one who understands the art?

Al.

The latter.

Soc.

Or if you were on a voyage, would you bewilder yourself by considering whether the rudder is to be drawn inwards or outwards, or do you leave that to the pilot, and do nothing?

Al.

It would be the concern of the pilot.

Soc.

Then you are not perplexed about what you do not know, if you know that you do not know it?

Al.

I imagine not.

Soc.

The people who make mistakes are neither those who know, nor those who do not know, but those who think that they know and do not know.

Do you not see, then, that mistakes in life and practice are likewise to be attributed to the ignorance which has conceit of knowledge?

Al.

Once more, what do you mean?

Soc.

I suppose that we begin to act when we think that we know what we are doing?

Al.

Yes.

Soc.

But when people think that they do not know, they entrust their business to others?

Al.

Yes.

Soc.

==And so there is a class of ignorant persons who do not make mistakes in life, because they trust others about things of which they are ignorant?== ☆

[margin note: Mentors, Masters]

Al.

True.

Soc.

Who, then, are the persons who make mistakes? They cannot, of course, be those who know?

Al.

Certainly not.

Soc.

But if neither those who know, nor those who know 118that they do not know, make mistakes, there remain those only who do not know and think that they know.

Al.

Yes, only those.

Soc.

Then this is ignorance of the disgraceful sort which is mischievous?

Al.

Yes.

Soc.

And most mischievous and most disgraceful when having to do with the greatest matters?

Al.

By far.

Soc.

And can there be any matters greater than the just, the honourable, the good, and the expedient?

Al.

There cannot be.

Soc.

And these, as you were saying, are what perplex you?

Al.

Yes.

Soc.

But if you are perplexed, then, as the previous argument has shown, you are not only ignorant of the greatest matters, but being ignorant you fancy that you know them?

Al.

I fear that you are right.

Soc.

And you, like other statesmen, rush into politics without being trained. Pericles, alone of them all, associated with the philosophers.

And now see what has happened to you, Alcibiades! I hardly like to speak of your evil case, but as we are alone I will: My good friend, you are wedded to ignorance of the most disgraceful kind, and of this you are convicted, not by me, but out of your own mouth and by your own argument; wherefore also you rush into politics before you are educated. Neither is your case to be deemed singular. For I might say the same of almost all our statesmen, with the exception, perhaps, of your guardian, Pericles.

Al.

Yes, Socrates; and Pericles is said not to have got his wisdom by the light of nature, but to have associated with several of the philosophers; with Pythocleides, for example, and with Anaxagoras, and now in advanced life with Damon, in the hope of gaining wisdom.

Soc.

Very good; but did you ever know a man wise in anything who was unable to impart his particular wisdom? For example, he who taught you letters was not only wise, but he made you and any others whom he liked wise.

Al.

Yes.

Soc.

And you, whom he taught, can do the same?

Al.

True.

Soc.

And in like manner the harper and gymnastic-master?

Al.

Certainly.

Soc.

When a person is enabled to impart knowledge to another, he thereby gives an excellent proof of his own understanding of any matter.

Al.

I agree.

Soc.

Well, and did Pericles make any one wise; did he begin by making his sons wise?

Al.

But, Socrates, if the two sons of Pericles were simpletons, what has that to do with the matter?

Soc.

And even he could not teach his own sons, or your brother Cleinias, nor did any one ever grow wiser in his society.

Well, but did he make your brother, Cleinias, wise?

Al.

Cleinias is a madman; there is no use in talking of him.

Soc.

But if Cleinias is a madman and the two sons of Pericles were simpletons, what reason can be given why he neglects you, and lets you be as you are?

Al.

I believe that I am to blame for not listening to him.

Soc.

But did you ever hear of any other Athenian or foreigner, bond or free, who was deemed to have grown wiser in the society of Pericles,—as I might cite Pythodorus, the son of Isolochus, and Callias, the son of Calliades, who have grown wiser in the society of Zeno, for which privilege they have each of them paid him the sum of a hundred minae to the increase of their wisdom and fame.

Al.

I certainly never did hear of any one.

Soc.

Well, and in reference to your own case, do you mean to remain as you are, or will you take some pains about yourself?

Al.

But if other statesmen are uneducated, what need has Alcibiades of education?

With your aid, Socrates, I will. And indeed, when I hear you speak, the truth of what you are saying strikes home to me, and I agree with you, for our statesmen, all but a few, do appear to be quite uneducated.

Soc.

What is the inference?

Al.

Why, that if they were educated they would be trained athletes, and he who means to rival them ought to have knowledge and experience when he attacks them; but now, as they have become politicians without any special training, why should I have the trouble of learning and practising? For I know well that by the light of nature I shall get the better of them.

Soc.

The lover is pained at hearing from the lips of Alcibiades so unworthy a sentiment. He should have a higher ambition than this.

My dear friend, what a sentiment! And how unworthy of your noble form and your high estate!

Al.

What do you mean, Socrates; why do you say so?

Soc.

I am grieved when I think of our mutual love.

Al.

At what?

Soc.

At your fancying that the contest on which you are entering is with people here.

Al.

Why, what others are there?

Soc.

Is that a question which a magnanimous soul should ask?

Al.

Do you mean to say that the contest is not with these?

Soc.

And suppose that you were going to steer a ship into action, would you only aim at being the best pilot on board? Would you not, while acknowledging that you must possess this degree of excellence, rather look to your antagonists, and not, as you are now doing, to your fellow combatants? You ought to be so far above these latter, that they will not even dare to be your rivals; and, being regarded by you as inferiors, will do battle for you against the enemy; this is the kind of superiority which you must establish over them, if you mean to accomplish any noble action really worthy of yourself and of the state.

Al.

That would certainly be my aim.

Soc.

Verily, then, you have good reason to be satisfied, if you are better than the soldiers; and you need not, when you are their superior and have your thoughts and actions fixed upon them, look away to the generals of the enemy.

Al.

Of whom are you speaking, Socrates?

Soc.

His rivals should be the Spartan and Persian kings, not any chance persons.

Why, you surely know that our city goes to war 120now and then with the Lacedaemonians and with the great king?

Al.

True enough.

Soc.

And if you meant to be the ruler of this city, would you not be right in considering that the Lacedaemonian and Persian king were your true rivals?

Al.

I believe that you are right.

Soc.

Oh no, my friend, I am quite wrong, and I think that you ought rather to turn your attention to Midias the quail-breeder and others like him, who manage our politics; in whom, as the women would remark, you may still see the slaves' cut of hair, cropping out in their minds as well as on their pates; and they come with their barbarous lingo to flatter us and not to rule us. To these, I say, you should look, and then you need not trouble yourself about your own fitness to contend in such a noble arena: there is no reason why you should either learn what has to be learned, or practise what has to be practised, and only when thoroughly prepared enter on a political career.

Al.

There, I think, Socrates, that you are right; I do not suppose, however, that the Spartan generals or the great king are really different from anybody else.

Soc.

But, my dear friend, do consider what you are saying.

Al.

What am I to consider?

Soc.

In the first place, will you be more likely to take care of yourself, if you are in a wholesome fear and dread of them, or if you are not?

Al.

Clearly, if I have such a fear of them.

Soc.

And do you think that you will sustain any injury if you take care of yourself?

Al.

No, I shall be greatly benefited.

Soc.

And this is one very important respect in which that notion of yours is bad.

Al.

True.

Soc.

In the next place, consider that what you say is probably false.

Al.

How so?

Soc.

Let me ask you whether better natures are likely to be found in noble races or not in noble races?

Al.

Clearly in noble races.

Soc.

Are not those who are well born and well bred most likely to be perfect in virtue?

Al.

Certainly.

Soc.

We too have our pride of birth, but how inferior are we to those who are descended from Zeus through a line of kings!

Then let us compare our antecedents with those of the Lacedaemonian and Persian kings; are they inferior to us in descent? Have we not heard that the former are sprung from Heracles, and the latter from Achaemenes, and that the race of Heracles and the race of Achaemenes go back to Perseus, son of Zeus?

Al.

121Why, so does mine go back to Eurysaces, and he to Zeus!

Soc.

The wealth and dignity of the Spartan kings is great, but it is as nothing compared with that of the Persians. The birth of the Persian princes is a world-famous event, and the utmost pains is taken with their education, which is entrusted to great and noble persons. When Alcibiades was born nobody knew or cared, and his education was handed over to a worn-out slave of his guardian's. The country called the 'queen's girdle,' the 'queen's veil,' and the like. The queen of Persia or of Sparta, if they heard that a youth of twenty, without resources and without education, was going to attack their son or husband, would deem him mad.

And mine, noble Alcibiades, to Daedalus, and he to Hephaestus, son of Zeus. But, for all that, we are far inferior to them. For they are descended 'from Zeus,' through a line of kings—either kings of Argos and Lacedaemon, or kings of Persia, a country which the descendants of Achaemenes have always possessed, besides being at various times sovereigns of Asia, as they now are; whereas, we and our fathers were but private persons. How ridiculous would you be thought if you were to make a display of your ancestors and of Salamis the island of Eurysaces, or of Aegina, the habitation of the still more ancient Aeacus, before Artaxerxes, son of Xerxes. You should consider how inferior we are to them both in the derivation of our birth and in other particulars. Did you never observe how great is the property of the Spartan kings? And their wives are under the guardianship of the Ephori, who are public officers and watch over them, in order to preserve as far as possible the purity of the Heracleid blood. Still greater is the difference among the Persians; for no one entertains a suspicion that the father of a prince of Persia can be any one but the king. Such is the awe which invests the person of the queen, that any other guard is needless. And when the heir of the kingdom is born, all the subjects of the king feast; and the day of his birth is for ever afterwards kept as a holiday and time of sacrifice by all Asia; whereas, when you and I were born, Alcibiades, as the comic poet says, the neighbours hardly knew of the important event. After the birth of the royal child, he is tended, not by a good-for-nothing woman-nurse, but by the best of the royal eunuchs, who are charged with the care of him, and especially with the fashioning and right formation of his limbs, in order that he may be as shapely as possible; which being their calling, they are held in great honour. And when the young prince is seven years old he is put upon a horse and taken to the riding-masters, and begins to go out hunting. And at fourteen years of age he is handed over to the royal schoolmasters, as they are termed: these are four chosen men, reputed to be the best among the Persians of a certain age; and one of them is the wisest, another the justest, a third the most temperate, and a fourth the most valiant. The first instructs him in the magianism of Zoroaster, the son of Oromasus, which is the worship of 122the Gods, and teaches him also the duties of his royal office; the second, who is the justest, teaches him always to speak the truth; the third, or most temperate, forbids him to allow any pleasure to be lord over him, that he may be accustomed to be a freeman and king indeed,—lord of himself first, and not a slave; the most valiant trains him to be bold and fearless, telling him that if he fears he is to deem himself a slave; whereas Pericles gave you, Alcibiades, for a tutor Zopyrus the Thracian, a slave of his who was past all other work. I might enlarge on the nurture and education of your rivals, but that would be tedious; and what I have said is a sufficient sample of what remains to be said. I have only to remark, by way of contrast, that no one cares about your birth or nurture or education, or, I may say, about that of any other Athenian, unless he has a lover who looks after him. And if you cast an eye on the wealth, the luxury, the garments with their flowing trains, the anointings with myrrh, the multitudes of attendants, and all the other bravery of the Persians, you will be ashamed when you discern your own inferiority; or if you look at the temperance and orderliness and ease and grace and magnanimity and courage and endurance and love of toil and desire of glory and ambition of the Lacedaemonians—in all these respects you will see that you are but a child in comparison of them. Even in the matter of wealth, if you value yourself upon that, I must reveal to you how you stand; for if you form an estimate of the wealth of the Lacedaemonians, you will see that our possessions fall far short of theirs. For no one here can compete with them either in the extent and fertility of their own and the Messenian territory, or in the number of their slaves, and especially of the Helots, or of their horses, or of the animals which feed on the Messenian pastures. But I have said enough of this: and as to gold and silver, there is more of them in Lacedaemon than in all the rest of Hellas, for during many generations gold has been always flowing in to them from the whole Hellenic world, and often from the barbarian also, and never going out, as in the fable of Aesop the fox said to the lion, 'The prints of the feet of those going in are distinct enough;' but who ever saw the trace of money going out of Lacedaemon? and therefore you may safely infer that the inhabitants are the richest of the Hellenes in gold and silver, and that their kings are the richest of them, for they have a larger share of these things, and they have also a tribute paid to them which is very considerable. Yet the Spartan wealth, though great in comparison of the wealth of the other Hellenes, is as nothing in comparison of that of the Persians and their kings. Why, I have been informed by a credible person who went up to the king [at Susa], that he passed through a large tract of excellent land, extending for nearly a day's journey, which the people of the country called the queen's girdle, and another, which they called her veil; and several other fair and fertile districts, which were reserved for the adornment of the queen, and are named after her several habiliments. Now, I cannot help thinking to myself, What if some one were to go to Amestris, the wife of Xerxes and mother of Artaxerxes, and say to her, There is a certain Dinomachè, whose whole wardrobe is not worth fifty minae—and that will be more than the value—and she has a son who is possessed of a three-hundred acre patch at Erchiae, and he has a mind to go to war with your son—would she not wonder to what this Alcibiades trusts for success in the conflict? 'He must rely,' she would say to herself, 'upon his training and wisdom—these are the things which Hellenes value.' And if she heard that this Alcibiades who is making the attempt is not as yet twenty years old, and is wholly uneducated, and when his lover tells him that he ought to get education and training first, and then go and fight the king, he refuses, and says that he is well enough as he is, would she not be amazed, and ask, 'On what, then, does the youth rely?' And if we replied: He relies on his beauty, and stature, and birth, and mental endowments, she would think that we were mad, Alcibiades, when she compared the advantages which you possess with those of her own people. And I believe that even Lampido, the daughter of Leotychides, the wife of Archidamus and mother of Agis, all of whom were kings, would have the same feeling; if, in your present uneducated state, you were to turn your thoughts against her son, she too would be equally astonished. But how disgraceful, that we should not have as high a notion of what is required in us as our enemies' wives and mothers have of the qualities which are required in their assailants! O my friend, be persuaded by me, and hear the Delphian inscription, 'Know thyself'—not the men whom you think, but these kings are our rivals, and we can only overcome them by pains and skill. And if you fail in the required qualities, you will fail also in becoming renowned among Hellenes and Barbarians, which you seem to desire more than any other man ever desired anything.

Al.

I entirely believe you; but what are the sort of pains which are required, Socrates,—can you tell me?

Soc.

I too need education; and God, who is my guardian, inspires me with the belief that I shall bring you to honour.

Yes, I can; but we must take counsel together concerning the manner in which both of us may be most improved. For what I am telling you of the necessity of education applies to myself as well as to you; and there is only one point in which I have an advantage over you.

Al.

What is that?

Soc.

I have a guardian who is better and wiser than your guardian, Pericles.

Al.

Who is he, Socrates?

Soc.

God, Alcibiades, who up to this day has not allowed me to converse with you; and he inspires in me the faith that I am especially designed to bring you to honour.

Al.

You are jesting, Socrates.

Soc.

Perhaps; at any rate, I am right in saying that all men greatly need pains and care, and you and I above all men.

Al.

You are not far wrong about me.

Soc.

And certainly not about myself.

Al.

But what can we do?

Soc.

There must be no hesitation or cowardice, my friend.

Al.

That would not become us, Socrates.

Soc.

We must take counsel together, (not about equestrian or naval affairs), but about the things which occupy the minds of wise men.

No, indeed, and we ought to take counsel together: for do we not wish to be as good as possible?

Al.

We do.

Soc.

In what sort of virtue?

Al.

Plainly, in the virtue of good men.

Soc.

Who are good in what?

Al.

Those, clearly, who are good in the management of affairs.

Soc.

What sort of affairs? Equestrian affairs?

Al.

Certainly not.

Soc.

You mean that about them we should have recourse to horsemen?

Al.

Yes.

Soc.

Well; naval affairs?

Al.

No.

Soc.

You mean that we should have recourse to sailors about them?

Al.

Yes.

Soc.

Then what affairs? And who do them?

Al.

The affairs which occupy Athenian gentlemen. 125

Soc.

And when you speak of gentlemen, do you mean the wise or the unwise?

Al.

The wise.

Soc.

And a man is good in respect of that in which he is wise?

Al.

Yes.

Soc.

And evil in respect of that in which he is unwise?

Al.

Certainly.

Soc.

The shoemaker, for example, is wise in respect of the making of shoes?

Al.

Yes.

Soc.

Then he is good in that?

Al.

He is.

Soc.

But in respect of the making of garments he is unwise?

Al.

Yes.

Soc.

Then in that he is bad?

Al.

Yes.

Soc.

Then upon this view of the matter the same man is good and also bad?

Al.

True.

Soc.

But would you say that the good are the same as the bad?

Al.

Certainly not.

Soc.

Then whom do you call the good?

Al.

And the wise are those who take counsel for the better order and improvement of the city.

I mean by the good those who are able to rule in the city.

Soc.

Not, surely, over horses?

Al.

Certainly not.

Soc.

But over men?

Al.

Yes.

Soc.

When they are sick?

Al.

No.

Soc.

Or on a voyage?

Al.

No.

Soc.

Or reaping the harvest?

Al.

No.

Soc.

When they are doing something or nothing?

Al.

When they are doing something, I should say.

Soc.

I wish that you would explain to me what this something is.

Al.

When they are having dealings with one another, and using one another's services, as we citizens do in our daily life.

Soc.

Illustrations.

Those of whom you speak are ruling over men who are using the services of other men?

Al.

Yes.

Soc.

Are they ruling over the signal-men who give the time to the rowers?

Al.

No; they are not.

Soc.

That would be the office of the pilot?

Al.

Yes.

Soc.

But, perhaps you mean that they rule over flute-players, who lead the singers and use the services of the dancers?

Al.

Certainly not.

Soc.

That would be the business of the teacher of the chorus?

Al.

Yes.

Soc.

Then what is the meaning of being able to rule over men who use other men?

Al.

I mean that they rule over men who have common rights of citizenship, and dealings with one another.

Soc.

And what sort of an art is this? Suppose that I ask you again, as I did just now, What art makes men know how to rule over their fellow-sailors,—how would you answer?

Al.

The art of the pilot.

Soc.

And, if I may recur to another old instance, what art enables them to rule over their fellow-singers?

Al.

The art of the teacher of the chorus, which you were just now mentioning.

Soc.

And what do you call the art of fellow-citizens?

Al.

I should say, good counsel, Socrates.

Soc.

And is the art of the pilot evil counsel?

Al.

No.

Soc.

But good counsel?

Al.

Yes, that is what I should say,—good counsel, of which 126the aim is the preservation of the voyagers.

Soc.

True. And what is the aim of that other good counsel of which you speak?

Al.

The aim is the better order and preservation of the city.

Soc.

And what is that of which the absence or presence improves and preserves the order of the city? Suppose you were to ask me, what is that of which the presence or absence improves or preserves the order of the body? I should reply, the presence of health and the absence of disease. You would say the same?

Al.

Yes.

Soc.

And if you were to ask me the same question about the eyes, I should reply in the same way, 'the presence of sight and the absence of blindness;' or about the ears, I should reply, that they were improved and were in better case, when deafness was absent, and hearing was present in them.

Al.

True.

Soc.

And this improvement is given by friendship and agreement,

And what would you say of a state? What is that by the presence or absence of which the state is improved and better managed and ordered?

Al.

I should say, Socrates:—the presence of friendship and the absence of hatred and division.

Soc.

And do you mean by friendship agreement or disagreement?

Al.

Agreement.

Soc.

What art makes cities agree about numbers?

Al.

Arithmetic.

Soc.

And private individuals?

Al.

The same.

Soc.

And what art makes each individual agree with himself?

Al.

The same.

Soc.

And what art makes each of us agree with himself about the comparative length of the span and of the cubit? Does not the art of measure?

Al.

Yes.

Soc.

Individuals are agreed with one another about this; and states, equally?

Al.

Yes.

Soc.

And the same holds of the balance?

Al.

True.

Soc.

But what is the other agreement of which you speak, and about what? what art can give that agreement? And does that which gives it to the state give it also to the individual, so as to make him consistent with himself and with another?

Al.

I should suppose so.

Soc.

But what is the nature of the agreement?—answer, and faint not.

Al.

such as exists between the members of a family, however they may differ in their qualities and accomplishments.

I mean to say that there should be such friendship and agreement as exists between an affectionate father and mother and their son, or between brothers, or between husband and wife.

Soc.

But can a man, Alcibiades, agree with a woman about the spinning of wool, which she understands and he does not?

Al.

No, truly.

Soc.

Nor has he any need, for spinning is a female accomplishment.

Al.

Yes.

Soc.

127And would a woman agree with a man about the science of arms, which she has never learned?

Al.

Certainly not.

Soc.

I suppose that the use of arms would be regarded by you as a male accomplishment?

Al.

It would.

Soc.

Then, upon your view, women and men have two sorts of knowledge?

Al.

Certainly.

Soc.

Then in their knowledge there is no agreement of women and men?

Al.

There is not.

Soc.

Nor can there be friendship, if friendship is agreement?

Al.

Plainly not.

Soc.

Then women are not loved by men when they do their own work?

Al.

I suppose not.

Soc.

Nor men by women when they do their own work?

Al.

No.

Soc.

If everybody is doing his own business, how can this promote friendship? And yet when individuals are doing each his own work, they are doing what is just.

Nor are states well administered, when individuals do their own work?

Al.

I should rather think, Socrates, that the reverse is the truth .

Soc.

What! do you mean to say that states are well administered when friendship is absent, the presence of which, as we were saying, alone secures their good order?

Al.

But I should say that there is friendship among them, for this very reason, that the two parties respectively do their own work.

Soc.

That was not what you were saying before; and what do you mean now by affirming that friendship exists when there is no agreement? How can there be agreement about matters which the one party knows, and of which the other is in ignorance?

Al.

Impossible.

Soc.

And when individuals are doing their own work, are they doing what is just or unjust?

Al.

What is just, certainly.

Soc.

And when individuals do what is just in the state, is there no friendship among them?

Al.

I suppose that there must be, Socrates.

Soc.

Then what do you mean by this friendship or agreement about which we must be wise and discreet in order that we may be good men? I cannot make out where it exists or among whom; according to you, the same persons may sometimes have it, and sometimes not.

Al.

But, indeed, Socrates, I do not know what I am saying; and I have long been, unconsciously to myself, in a most disgraceful state.

Soc.

Nevertheless, cheer up; at fifty, if you had discovered your deficiency, you would have been too old, and the time for taking care of yourself would have passed away, but yours is just the age at which the discovery should be made.

Al.

And what should he do, Socrates, who would make the discovery?

Soc.

The way to clear up difficulties is to answer questions. Alcibiades is willing to have recourse to this method of improvement.

Answer questions, Alcibiades; and that is a process which, by the grace of God, if I may put any faith in my oracle, will be very improving to both of us.

Al.

If I can be improved by answering, I will answer.

Soc.

128And first of all, that we may not peradventure be deceived by appearances, fancying, perhaps, that we are taking care of ourselves when we are not, what is the meaning of a man taking care of himself? and when does he take care? Does he take care of himself when he takes care of what belongs to him?

Al.

I should think so.

Soc.

When does a man take care of his feet? Does he not take care of them when he takes care of that which belongs to his feet?

Al.

I do not understand.

Soc.

Let me take the hand as an illustration; does not a ring belong to the finger, and to the finger only?

Al.

Yes.

Soc.

And the shoe in like manner to the foot?

Al.

Yes.

Soc.

And when we take care of our shoes, do we not take care of our feet?

Al.

I do not comprehend, Socrates.

Soc.

But you would admit, Alcibiades, that to take proper care of a thing is a correct expression?

Al.

Yes.

Soc.

And taking proper care means improving?

Al.

Yes.

Soc.

And what is the art which improves our shoes?

Al.

Shoemaking.

Soc.

Then by shoemaking we take care of our shoes?

Al.

Yes.

Soc.

And do we by shoemaking take care of our feet, or by some other art which improves the feet?

Al.

By some other art.

Soc.

And the same art improves the feet which improves the rest of the body?

Al.

Very true.

Soc.

Which is gymnastic?

Al.

Certainly.

Soc.

Then by gymnastic we take care of our feet, and by shoemaking of that which belongs to our feet?

Al.

Very true.

Soc.

And by gymnastic we take care of our hands, and by the art of graving rings of that which belongs to our hands?

Al.

Yes.

Soc.

And by gymnastic we take care of the body, and by the art of weaving and the other arts we take care of the things of the body?

Al.

Clearly.

Soc.

It has been shown by examples that a man does not take care of himself, when he only takes care of what belongs to him.

Then the art which takes care of each thing is different from that which takes care of the belongings of each thing?

Al.

True.

Soc.

Then in taking care of what belongs to you, you do not take care of yourself?

Al.

Certainly not.

Soc.

For the art which takes care of our belongings appears not to be the same as that which takes care of ourselves?

Al.

Clearly not.

Soc.

And now let me ask you what is the art with which we take care of ourselves?

Al.

I cannot say.

Soc.

At any rate, thus much has been admitted, that the art is not one which makes any of our possessions, but which makes ourselves better?

Al.

True.

Soc.

But should we ever have known what art makes a shoe better, if we did not know a shoe?

Al.

Impossible.

Soc.

Nor should we know what art makes a ring better, if we did not know a ring?

Al.

That is true.

Soc.

A man must know himself before he can improve himself or know what belongs to him.

And can we ever know what art makes a man better, 129if we do not know what we are ourselves?

Al.

Impossible.

Soc.

And is self-knowledge such an easy thing, and was he to be lightly esteemed who inscribed the text on the temple at Delphi? Or is self-knowledge a difficult thing, which few are able to attain?

Al.

At times I fancy, Socrates, that anybody can know himself; at other times the task appears to be very difficult.

Soc.

But whether easy or difficult, Alcibiades, still there is no other way; knowing what we are, we shall know how to take care of ourselves, and if we are ignorant we shall not know.

Al.

That is true.

Soc.

Well, then, let us see in what way the self-existent can be discovered by us; that will give us a chance of discovering our own existence, which otherwise we can never know.

Al.

You say truly.

Soc.

Come, now, I beseech you, tell me with whom you are conversing?—with whom but with me?

Al.

Yes.

Soc.

As I am, with you?

Al.

Yes.

Soc.

That is to say, I, Socrates, am talking?

Al.

Yes.

Soc.

And Alcibiades is my hearer?

Al.

Yes.

Soc.

And I in talking use words?

Al.

Certainly.

Soc.

And talking and using words have, I suppose, the same meaning?

Al.

To be sure.

Soc.

And the user is not the same as the thing which he uses?

Al.

What do you mean?

Soc.

I will explain; the shoemaker, for example, uses a square tool, and a circular tool, and other tools for cutting?

Al.

Yes.

Soc.

But the tool is not the same as the cutter and user of the tool?

Al.

Of course not.

Soc.

And in the same way the instrument of the harper is to be distinguished from the harper himself?

Al.

It is.

Soc.

Now the question which I asked was whether you conceive the user to be always different from that which he uses?

Al.

I do.

Soc.

Then what shall we say of the shoemaker? Does he cut with his tools only or with his hands?

Al.

With his hands as well.

Soc.

He uses his hands too?

Al.

Yes.

Soc.

And does he use his eyes in cutting leather?

Al.

He does.

Soc.

He is distinct from what he uses; and therefore distinct from his own body.

And we admit that the user is not the same with the things which he uses?

Al.

Yes.

Soc.

Then the shoemaker and the harper are to be distinguished from the hands and feet which they use?

Al.

Clearly.

Soc.

And does not a man use the whole body?

Al.

Certainly.

Soc.

And that which uses is different from that which is used?

Al.

True.

Soc.

Then a man is not the same as his own body?

Al.

That is the inference.

Soc.

What is he, then?

Al.

I cannot say.

Soc.

Nay, you can say that he is the user of the body.

Al.

Yes.

Soc.

And the user of the body is the soul? 130

Al.

Yes, the soul.

Soc.

And the soul rules?

Al.

Yes.

Soc.

Let me make an assertion which will, I think, be universally admitted.

Al.

But he must be one of three things:—

What is it?

Soc.

That man is one of three things.

Al.

What are they?

Soc.

Soul, body, or both together forming a whole.

Al.

Certainly.

Soc.

But did we not say that the actual ruling principle of the body is man?

Al.

Soul, body, or the union of the two. What is the ruling principle in him? Clearly the soul.

Yes, we did.

Soc.

And does the body rule over itself?

Al.

Certainly not.

Soc.

It is subject, as we were saying?

Al.

Yes.

Soc.

Then that is not the principle which we are seeking?

Al.

It would seem not.

Soc.

But may we say that the union of the two rules over the body, and consequently that this is man?

Al.

Very likely.

Soc.

The most unlikely of all things; for if one of the members is subject, the two united cannot possibly rule.

Al.

True.

Soc.

But since neither the body, nor the union of the two, is man, either man has no real existence, or the soul is man?

Al.

Just so.

Soc.

Is anything more required to prove that the soul is man?

Al.

Certainly not; the proof is, I think, quite sufficient.

Soc.

There remains a question of absolute existence, which has not been considered by us, or rather is being considered by us when we speak of the soul.

And if the proof, although not perfect, be sufficient, we shall be satisfied;—more precise proof will be supplied when we have discovered that which we were led to omit, from a fear that the enquiry would be too much protracted.

Al.

What was that?

Soc.

What I meant, when I said that absolute existence must be first considered; but now, instead of absolute existence, we have been considering the nature of individual existence, and this may, perhaps, be sufficient; for surely there is nothing which may be called more properly ourselves than the soul?

Al.

There is nothing.

Soc.

You and I are talking soul to soul.

Then we may truly conceive that you and I are conversing with one another, soul to soul?

Al.

Very true.

Soc.

And that is just what I was saying before—that I, Socrates, am not arguing or talking with the face of Alcibiades, but with the real Alcibiades; or in other words, with his soul.

Al.

True.

Soc.

Then he who bids a man know himself, would have him know his soul?

Al.

That appears to be true.

Soc.

But if the soul is the man, he who knows only the arts which concern man does not know himself.

He whose knowledge only extends to the body, 131knows the things of a man, and not the man himself?

Al.

That is true.

Soc.

Then neither the physician regarded as a physician, nor the trainer regarded as a trainer, knows himself?

Al.

He does not.

Soc.

The husbandmen and the other craftsmen are very far from knowing themselves, for they would seem not even to know their own belongings? When regarded in relation to the arts which they practise they are even further removed from self-knowledge, for they only know the belongings of the body, which minister to the body.

Al.

That is true.

Soc.

Then if temperance is the knowledge of self, in respect of his art none of them is temperate?

Al.

I agree.

Soc.

And this is the reason why their arts are accounted vulgar, and are not such as a good man would practise?

Al.

Quite true.

Soc.

Again, he who cherishes his body cherishes not himself, but what belongs to him?

Al.

That is true.

Soc.

But he who cherishes his money, cherishes neither himself nor his belongings, but is in a stage yet further removed from himself?

Al.

I agree.

Soc.

Then the money-maker has really ceased to be occupied with his own concerns?

Al.

True.

Soc.

The lover of the soul is the true lover.

And if any one has fallen in love with the person of Alcibiades, he loves not Alcibiades, but the belongings of Alcibiades?

Al.

True.

Soc.

But he who loves your soul is the true lover?

Al.

That is the necessary inference.

Soc.

The lover of the body goes away when the flower of youth fades?

Al.

True.

Soc.

He only remains and goes not away, so long as the soul of his beloved follows after virtue.

But he who loves the soul goes not away, as long as the soul follows after virtue?

Al.

Yes.

Soc.

And I am the lover who goes not away, but remains with you, when you are no longer young and the rest are gone?

Al.

Yes, Socrates; and therein you do well, and I hope that you will remain.

Soc.

Then you must try to look your best.

Al.

I will.

Soc.

The fact is, that there is only one lover of Alcibiades the son of Cleinias; there neither is nor ever has been seemingly any other; and he is his darling,—Socrates, the son of Sophroniscus and Phaenarete.

Al.

True.

Soc.

And did you not say, that if I had not spoken first, you were on the point of coming to me, and enquiring why I only remained?

Al.

That is true.

Soc.

And Socrates will never desert Alcibiades so long as he is not spoiled by the Athenian people.

The reason was that I loved you for your own sake, whereas other men love what belongs to you; and your 132beauty, which is not you, is fading away, just as your true self is beginning to bloom. And I will never desert you, if you are not spoiled and deformed by the Athenian people; for the danger which I most fear is that you will become a lover of the people and will be spoiled by them. Many a noble Athenian has been ruined in this way. For the demus of the great-hearted Erechtheus is of a fair countenance, but you should see him naked; wherefore observe the caution which I give you.

Al.

What caution?

Soc.

Practise yourself, sweet friend, in learning what you ought to know, before you enter on politics; and then you will have an antidote which will keep you out of harm's way.

Al.

Good advice, Socrates, but I wish that you would explain to me in what way I am to take care of myself.

Soc.

Have we not made an advance? for we are at any rate tolerably well agreed as to what we are, and there is no longer any danger, as we once feared, that we might be taking care not of ourselves, but of something which is not ourselves.

Al.

That is true.

Soc.

And the next step will be to take care of the soul, and look to that?

Al.

Certainly.

Soc.

Leaving the care of our bodies and of our properties to others?

Al.

Very good.

Soc.

He who would take care of himself must first of all know himself.

But how can we have a perfect knowledge of the things of the soul?—For if we know them, then I suppose we shall know ourselves. Can we really be ignorant of the excellent meaning of the Delphian inscription, of which we were just now speaking?

Al.

What have you in your thoughts, Socrates?

Soc.

I will tell you what I suspect to be the meaning and lesson of that inscription. Let me take an illustration from sight, which I imagine to be the only one suitable to my purpose.

Al.

What do you mean?

Soc.

The eye which would see itself must look into the pupil of another, which is the divinest part of the eye, and will then behold itself.

Consider; if some one were to say to the eye, 'See thyself,' as you might say to a man, 'Know thyself,' what is the nature and meaning of this precept? Would not his meaning be:—That the eye should look at that in which it would see itself?

Al.

Clearly.

Soc.

And what are the objects in looking at which we see ourselves?

Al.

Clearly, Socrates, in looking at mirrors and the like.

Soc.

Very true; and is there not something of the nature of a mirror in our own eyes?

Al.

Certainly.

Soc.

Did you ever observe that the face of the person looking into the eye of another is reflected as in a mirror; and in the visual organ which is over against him, and which 133is called the pupil, there is a sort of image of the person looking?

Al.

That is quite true.

Soc.

Then the eye, looking at another eye, and at that in the eye which is most perfect, and which is the instrument of vision, will there see itself?

Al.

That is evident.

Soc.

But looking at anything else either in man or in the world, and not to what resembles this, it will not see itself?

Al.

Very true.

Soc.

Then if the eye is to see itself, it must look at the eye, and at that part of the eye where sight which is the virtue of the eye resides?

Al.

True.

Soc.

And the soul which would know herself must look especially at that part of herself in which she resembles the divine.

And if the soul, my dear Alcibiades, is ever to know herself, must she not look at the soul; and especially at that part of the soul in which her virtue resides, and to any other which is like this?

Al.

I agree, Socrates.

Soc.

And do we know of any part of our souls more divine than that which has to do with wisdom and knowledge?

Al.

There is none.

Soc.

Then this is that part of the soul which resembles the divine; and he who looks at this and at the whole class of things divine, will be most likely to know himself?

Al.

Clearly.

Soc.

And self-knowledge we agree to be wisdom?

Al.

True.

Soc.

But if we have no self-knowledge and no wisdom, can we ever know our own good and evil?

Al.

How can we, Socrates?

Soc.

You mean, that if you did not know Alcibiades, there would be no possibility of your knowing that what belonged to Alcibiades was really his?

Al.

It would be quite impossible.

Soc.

He who knows not himself and his belongings, will not know others and their belongings, and therefore he will not know the affairs of states.

Nor should we know that we were the persons to whom anything belonged, if we did not know ourselves?

Al.

How could we?

Soc.

And if we did not know our own belongings, neither should we know the belongings of our belongings?

Al.

Clearly not.

Soc.

Then we were not altogether right in acknowledging just now that a man may know what belongs to him and yet not know himself; nay, rather he cannot even know the belongings of his belongings; for the discernment of the things of self, and of the things which belong to the things of self, appear all to be the business of the same man, and of the same art.

Al.

So much may be supposed.

Soc.

And he who knows not the things which belong to himself, will in like manner be ignorant of the things which belong to others?

Al.

Very true.

Soc.

And if he knows not the affairs of others, he will not know the affairs of states?

Al.

Certainly not.

Soc.

Then such a man can never be a statesman?

Al.

He cannot.

Soc.

Nor an economist?

Al.

He cannot.

Soc.

He will not know what he is doing? 134

Al.

He will not.

Soc.

And will not he who is ignorant fall into error?

Al.

Assuredly.

Soc.

And, if he knows not what he is doing, he will be miserable and will make others miserable.

And if he falls into error will he not fail both in his public and private capacity?

Al.

Yes, indeed.

Soc.

And failing, will he not be miserable?

Al.

Very.

Soc.

And what will become of those for whom he is acting?

Al.

They will be miserable also.

Soc.

Then he who is not wise and good cannot be happy?

Al.

He cannot.

Soc.

The bad, then, are miserable?

Al.

Yes, very.

Soc.

And if so, not he who has riches, but he who has wisdom, is delivered from his misery?

Al.

Clearly.

Soc.

Cities, then, if they are to be happy, do not want walls, or triremes, or docks, or numbers, or size, Alcibiades, without virtue?

Al.

Indeed they do not.

Soc.

And you must give the citizens virtue, if you mean to administer their affairs rightly or nobly?

Al.

Certainly.

Soc.

He must give the citizens wisdom and justice, and he cannot give what he has not got.

But can a man give that which he has not?

Al.

Impossible.

Soc.

Then you or any one who means to govern and superintend, not only himself and the things of himself, but the state and the things of the state, must in the first place acquire virtue.

Al.

That is true.

Soc.

You have not therefore to obtain power or authority, in order to enable you to do what you wish for yourself and the state, but justice and wisdom.

Al.

Clearly.

Soc.

If he acts wisely and justly he will act according to the will of God.

You and the state, if you act wisely and justly, will act according to the will of God?

Al.

Certainly.

Soc.

As I was saying before, you will look only at what is bright and divine, and act with a view to them?

Al.

Yes.

Soc.

In the mirror of the divine he will see his own good and will act rightly and be happy.

In that mirror you will see and know yourselves and your own good?

Al.

Yes.

Soc.

And so you will act rightly and well?

Al.

Yes.

Soc.

In which case, I will be security for your happiness.

Al.

I accept the security.

Soc.

But if you act unrighteously, your eye will turn to the dark and godless, and being in darkness and ignorance of yourselves, you will probably do deeds of darkness.

Al.

Very possibly.

Soc.

For if a man, my dear Alcibiades, has the power to do what he likes, but has no understanding, what is likely to 135be the result, either to him as an individual or to the state—for example, if he be sick and is able to do what he likes, not having the mind of a physician—having moreover tyrannical power, and no one daring to reprove him, what will happen to him? Will he not be likely to have his constitution ruined?

Al.

That is true.

Soc.

Or again, in a ship, if a man having the power to do what he likes, has no intelligence or skill in navigation, do you see what will happen to him and to his fellow-sailors?

Al.

Yes; I see that they will all perish.

Soc.

And in like manner, in a state, and where there is any power and authority which is wanting in virtue, will not misfortune, in like manner, ensue?

Al.

Certainly.

Soc.

Not power, but virtue, should be the aim both of individuals and of states: and he only is a freeman who has virtue.

Not tyrannical power, then, my good Alcibiades, should be the aim either of individuals or states, if they would be happy, but virtue.

Al.

That is true.

Soc.

And before they have virtue, to be commanded by a superior is better for men as well as for children?

Al.

That is evident.

Soc.

And that which is better is also nobler?

Al.

True.

Soc.

And what is nobler is more becoming?

Al.

Certainly.

Soc.

Then to the bad man slavery is more becoming, because better?

Al.

True.

Soc.

Then vice is only suited to a slave?

Al.

Yes.

Soc.

And virtue to a freeman?

Al.

Yes.

Soc.

And, O my friend, is not the condition of a slave to be avoided?

Al.

Certainly, Socrates.

Soc.

And are you now conscious of your own state? And do you know whether you are a freeman or not?

Al.

I think that I am very conscious indeed of my own state.

Soc.

And do you know how to escape out of a state which I do not even like to name to my beauty?

Al.

Yes, I do.

Soc.

How?

Al.

By your help, Socrates.

Soc.

That is not well said, Alcibiades.

Al.

What ought I to have said?

Soc.

By the help of God.

Al.

I agree; and I further say, that our relations are likely to be reversed. From this day forward, I must and will follow you as you have followed me; I will be the disciple, and you shall be my master.

Soc.

O that is rare! My love breeds another love: and so like the stork I shall be cherished by the bird whom I have hatched.

Al.

Strange, but true; and henceforward I shall begin to think about justice.

Soc.

And I hope that you will persist; although I have fears, not because I doubt you; but I see the power of the state, which may be too much for both of us.

INTRODUCTION TO MENEXENUS.

Menexenus. Introduction.

The Menexenus has more the character of a rhetorical exercise than any other of the Platonic works. The writer seems to have wished to emulate Thucydides, and the far slighter work of Lysias. In his rivalry with the latter, to whom in the Phaedrus Plato shows a strong antipathy, he is entirely successful, but he is not equal to Thucydides. The Menexenus, though not without real Hellenic interest, falls very far short of the rugged grandeur and political insight of the great historian. The fiction of the speech having been invented by Aspasia is well sustained, and is in the manner of Plato, notwithstanding the anachronism which puts into her mouth an allusion to the peace of Antalcidas, an event occurring forty years after the date of the supposed oration. But Plato, like Shakespeare, is careless of such anachronisms, which are not supposed to strike the mind of the reader. The effect produced by these grandiloquent orations on Socrates, who does not recover after having heard one of them for three days and more, is truly Platonic.

Such discourses, if we may form a judgment from the three which are extant (for the so-called Funeral Oration of Demosthenes is a bad and spurious imitation of Thucydides and Lysias), conformed to a regular type. They began with Gods and ancestors, and the legendary history of Athens, to which succeeded an almost equally fictitious account of later times. The Persian war usually formed the centre of the narrative; in the age of Isocrates and Demosthenes the Athenians were still living on the glories of Marathon and Salamis. The Menexenus veils in panegyric the weak places of Athenian history. The war of Athens and Boeotia is a war of liberation; the Athenians gave back the Spartans taken at Sphacteria out of kindness—indeed, the only fault of the city was too great kindness to their enemies, who were more honoured than the friends of others (cp. Thucyd. ii. 41, which seems to contain the germ of the idea); we democrats are the aristocracy of virtue, and the like. These are the platitudes and falsehoods in which history is disguised. The taking of Athens is hardly mentioned.

The author of the Menexenus, whether Plato or not, is evidently intending to ridicule the practice, and at the same time to show that he can beat the rhetoricians in their own line, as in the Phaedrus he may be supposed to offer an example of what Lysias might have said, and of how much better he might have written in his own style. The orators had recourse to their favourite *loci communes,* one of which, as we find in Lysias, was the shortness of the time allowed them for preparation. But Socrates points out that they had them always ready for delivery, and that there was no difficulty in improvising any number of such orations. To praise the Athenians among the Athenians was easy,—to praise them among the Lacedaemonians would have been a much more difficult task. Socrates himself has turned rhetorician, having learned of a woman, Aspasia, the mistress of Pericles; and any one whose teachers had been far inferior to his own—say, one who had learned from Antiphon the Rhamnusian—would be quite equal to the task of praising men to themselves. When we remember that Antiphon is described by Thucydides as the best pleader of his day, the satire on him and on the whole tribe of rhetoricians is transparent.

The ironical assumption of Socrates, that he must be a good orator because he had learnt of Aspasia, is not coarse, as Schleiermacher supposes, but is rather to be regarded as fanciful. Nor can we say that the offer of Socrates to dance naked out of love for Menexenus, is any more un-Platonic than the threat of physical force which Phaedrus uses towards Socrates (286 C). Nor is there any real vulgarity in the fear which Socrates expresses that he will get a beating from his mistress, Aspasia: this is the natural exaggeration of what might be expected from an imperious woman. Socrates is not to be taken seriously in all that he says, and Plato, both in the Symposium and elsewhere, is not slow to admit a sort of Aristophanic humour. How a great original genius like Plato might or might not have written, what was his conception of humour, or what limits he would have prescribed to himself, if any, in drawing the picture of the Silenus Socrates, are problems which no critical instinct can determine.

On the other hand, the dialogue has several Platonic traits, whether original or imitated may be uncertain. Socrates, when he departs from his character of a 'know nothing' and delivers a speech, generally pretends that what is speaking is not his own composition. Thus in the Cratylus he is run away with (410 E); in the Phaedrus he has heard somebody say something (235 C)—is inspired by the *genius loci* (238 D); in the Symposium he derives his wisdom from Diotima of Mantinea, and the like. But he does not impose on Menexenus by his dissimulation. Without violating the character of Socrates, Plato, who knows so well how to give a hint, or some one writing in his name, intimates clearly enough that the speech in the Menexenus like that in the Phaedrus is to be attributed to Socrates. The address of the dead to the living at the end of the oration may also be compared to the numerous addresses of the same kind which occur in Plato, in whom the dramatic element is always tending to prevail over the rhetorical. The remark has been often made, that in the Funeral Oration of Thucydides there is no allusion to the existence of the dead. But in the Menexenus a future state is clearly, although not strongly, asserted.

Whether the Menexenus is a genuine writing of Plato, or an imitation only, remains uncertain. In either case, the thoughts are partly borrowed from the Funeral Oration of Thucydides; and the fact that they are so, is not in favour of the genuineness of the work. Internal evidence seems to leave the question of authorship in doubt. There are merits and there are defects which might lead to either conclusion. The form of the greater part of the work makes the enquiry difficult; the introduction and the finale certainly wear the look either of Plato or of an extremely skilful imitator. The excellence of the forgery may be fairly adduced as an argument that it is not a forgery at all. In this uncertainty the express testimony of Aristotle, who quotes, in the Rhetoric , the well-known words, 'It is easy to praise the Athenians among the Athenians,' from the Funeral Oration, may perhaps turn the balance in its favour. It must be remembered also that the work was famous in antiquity, and is included in the Alexandrian catalogues of Platonic writings.

MENEXENUS.

PERSONS OF THE DIALOGUE.

Socrates and Menexenus.

Socrates.

*Menexenus.*Socrates, Menexenus.

234Whence come you, Menexenus? Are you from the Agora?

Menexenus.

Yes, Socrates; I have been at the Council.

Soc.

And what might you be doing at the Council? And yet I need hardly ask, for I see that you, believing yourself to have arrived at the end of education and of philosophy, and to have had enough of them, are mounting upwards to things higher still, and, though rather young for the post, are intending to govern us elder men, like the rest of your family, which has always provided some one who kindly took care of us.

Men.

Yes, Socrates, I shall be ready to hold office, if you allow and advise that I should, but not if you think otherwise. I went to the council chamber because I heard that the Council was about to choose some one who was to speak over the dead. For you know that there is to be a public funeral?

Soc.

Yes, I know. And whom did they choose?

Men.

No one; they delayed the election until to-morrow, but I believe that either Archinus or Dion will be chosen.

Soc.

The gain of dying in battle. The effect upon Socrates of panegyrical oratory.

O Menexenus! death in battle is certainly in many respects a noble thing. The dead man gets a fine and costly funeral, although he may have been poor, and an elaborate speech is made over him by a wise man who has long ago prepared what he has to say, although he who is praised may not have been good for much. The speakers praise him for what he has done and for what he has not done—that is the beauty of them—and they steal away our souls with their embellished words; in every conceivable form they praise 235the city; and they praise those who died in war, and all our ancestors who went before us; and they praise ourselves also who are still alive, until I feel quite elevated by their laudations, and I stand listening to their words, Menexenus, and become enchanted by them, and all in a moment I imagine myself to have become a greater and nobler and finer man than I was before. And if, as often happens, there are any foreigners who accompany me to the speech, I become suddenly conscious of having a sort of triumph over them, and they seem to experience a corresponding feeling of admiration at me, and at the greatness of the city, which appears to them, when they are under the influence of the speaker, more wonderful than ever. This consciousness of dignity lasts me more than three days, and not until the fourth or fifth day do I come to my senses and know where I am; in the meantime I have been living in the Islands of the Blest. Such is the art of our rhetoricians, and in such manner does the sound of their words keep ringing in my ears.

Men.

Socrates always making fun of the rhetoricians.

You are always making fun of the rhetoricians, Socrates; this time, however, I am inclined to think that the speaker who is chosen will not have much to say, for he has been called upon to speak at a moment's notice, and he will be compelled almost to improvise.

Soc.

But why, my friend, should he not have plenty to say? Every rhetorician has speeches ready made; nor is there any difficulty in improvising that sort of stuff. Had the orator to praise Athenians among Peloponnesians, or Peloponnesians among Athenians, he must be a good rhetorician who could succeed and gain credit. But there is no difficulty in a man's winning applause when he is contending for fame among the persons whom he is praising.

Men.

Do you think not, Socrates?

Soc.

Certainly 'not.'

Men.

Could Socrates himself make a funeral oration?

Do you think that you could speak yourself if there should be a necessity, and if the Council were to choose you?

Soc.

That I should be able to speak is no great wonder, Menexenus, considering that I have an excellent mistress in the art of rhetoric,—she who has made so many good speakers, and one who was the best among all the Hellenes—Pericles, the son of Xanthippus.

Men.

And who is she? I suppose that you mean Aspasia.

Soc.

Yes; for he is a pupil of Aspasia.

Yes, I do; and besides her I had Connus, the son of 236Metrobius, as a master, and he was my master in music, as she was in rhetoric. No wonder that a man who has received such an education should be a finished speaker; even the pupil of very inferior masters, say, for example, one who had learned music of Lamprus, and rhetoric of Antiphon the Rhamnusian, might make a figure if he were to praise the Athenians among the Athenians.

Men.

And what would you be able to say if you had to speak?

Soc.

The funeral oration composed by Aspasia.

Of my own wit, most likely nothing; but yesterday I heard Aspasia composing a funeral oration about these very dead. For she had been told, as you were saying, that the Athenians were going to choose a speaker, and she repeated to me the sort of speech which he should deliver, partly improvising and partly from previous thought, putting together fragments of the funeral oration which Pericles spoke, but which, as I believe, she composed.

Men.

And can you remember what Aspasia said?

Soc.

I ought to be able, for she taught me, and she was ready to strike me because I was always forgetting.

Men.

Then why will you not rehearse what she said?

Soc.

Because I am afraid that my mistress may be angry with me if I publish her speech.

Men.

Nay, Socrates, let us have the speech, whether Aspasia's or any one else's, no matter. I hope that you will oblige me.

Soc.

But I am afraid that you will laugh at me if I continue the games of youth in old age.

Men.

Far otherwise, Socrates; let us by all means have the speech.

Soc.

Truly I have such a disposition to oblige you, that if you bid me dance naked I should not like to refuse, since we are alone. Listen then: If I remember rightly, she began as follows, with the mention of the dead :—

Socrates.

There is a tribute of deeds and of words. The departed have already had the first, when going forth on their destined journey they were attended on their way by the state and by their friends; the tribute of words remains to be given to them, as is meet and by law ordained. For noble words are a memorial and a crown of noble actions, which are given to the doers of them by the hearers. A word is needed which will duly praise the dead and gently admonish the living, exhorting the brethren and descendants of the departed to imitate their virtue, and consoling their fathers and mothers and the survivors, if any, who may chance to be alive of the 237previous generation. What sort of a word will this be, and how shall we rightly begin the praises of these brave men? In their life they rejoiced their own friends with their valour, and their death they gave in exchange for the salvation of the living. And I think that we should praise them in the order in which nature made them good, for they were good because they were sprung from good fathers. Wherefore let us first of all praise the goodness of their birth; secondly, their nurture and education; and then let us set forth how noble their actions were, and how worthy of the education which they had received.

The departed were the children of the soil;

And first as to their birth. Their ancestors were not strangers, nor are these their descendants sojourners only, whose fathers have come from another country; but they are the children of the soil, dwelling and living in their own land. And the country which brought them up is not like other countries, a stepmother to her children, but their own true mother; she bore them and nourished them and received them, and in her bosom they now repose. It is meet and right, therefore, that we should begin by praising the land which is their mother, and that will be a way of praising their noble birth.

and their country is dear to the Gods, who contended for the possession of her. She first brought forth man, and proved her true motherhood by providing food for her own offspring. The Gods were the rulers of primitive men, and gave them arts.

The country is worthy to be praised, not only by us, but by all mankind; first, and above all, as being dear to the Gods. This is proved by the strife and contention of the Gods respecting her. And ought not the country which the Gods praise to be praised by all mankind? The second praise which may be fairly claimed by her, is that at the time when the whole earth was sending forth and creating diverse animals, tame and wild, she our mother was free and pure from savage monsters, and out of all animals selected and brought forth man, who is superior to the rest in understanding, and alone has justice and religion. And a great proof that she brought forth the common ancestors of us and of the departed, is that she provided the means of support for her offspring. For as a woman proves her motherhood by giving milk to her young ones (and she who has no fountain of milk is not a mother), so did this our land prove that she was the mother of men, for in those days she alone and first of all brought forth wheat and barley for human 238food, which is the best and noblest sustenance for man, whom she regarded as her true offspring. And these are truer proofs of motherhood in a country than in a woman, for the woman in her conception and generation is but the imitation of the earth, and not the earth of the woman. And of the fruit of the earth she gave a plenteous supply, not only to her own, but to others also; and afterwards she made the olive to spring up to be a boon to her children, and to help them in their toils. And when she had herself nursed them and brought them up to manhood, she gave them Gods to be their rulers and teachers, whose names are well known, and need not now be repeated. They are the Gods who first ordered our lives, and instructed us in the arts for the supply of our daily needs, and taught us the acquisition and use of arms for the defence of the country.

We have a good government, which is sometimes called a democracy, but is really an aristocracy, for the best rule with the consent of the many. The principle of our government is equality; the only superiority is that of virtue and wisdom.

Thus born into the world and thus educated, the ancestors of the departed lived and made themselves a government, which I ought briefly to commemorate. For government is the nurture of man, and the government of good men is good, and of bad men bad. And I must show that our ancestors were trained under a good government, and for this reason they were good, and our contemporaries are also good, among whom our departed friends are to be reckoned. Then as now, and indeed always, from that time to this, speaking generally, our government was an aristocracy—a form of government which receives various names, according to the fancies of men, and is sometimes called democracy, but is really an aristocracy or government of the best which has the approval of the many. For kings we have always had, first hereditary and then elected, and authority is mostly in the hands of the people, who dispense offices and power to those who appear to be most deserving of them. Neither is a man rejected from weakness or poverty or obscurity of origin, nor honoured by reason of the opposite, as in other states, but there is one principle—he who appears to be wise and good is a governor and ruler. The basis of this our government is equality of birth; for other states are made up of all sorts and unequal conditions of men, and therefore their governments are unequal; there are tyrannies and there are oligarchies, in which the one party are slaves and the others masters. But we and our citizens are brethren, the children all of one 239mother, and we do not think it right to be one another's masters or servants; but the natural equality of birth compels us to seek for legal equality, and to recognize no superiority except in the reputation of virtue and wisdom.

The greatness of Persia. Yet at Marathon the army of Darius was overcome by the Athenians almost single-handed. The men of Marathon should have the first place: those who followed in the war were their disciples, except the men who defeated the Persians at Salamis and first made proof of them at sea: these have the second place. And the third place is to be assigned to those who fought at Plataea.Eurymedon; Cyprus; Egypt.

And so their and our fathers, and these, too, our brethren, being nobly born and having been brought up in all freedom, did both in their public and private capacity many noble deeds famous over the whole world. They were the deeds of men who thought that they ought to fight both against Hellenes for the sake of Hellenes on behalf of freedom, and against barbarians in the common interest of Hellas. Time would fail me to tell of their defence of their country against the invasion of Eumolpus and the Amazons, or of their defence of the Argives against the Cadmeians, or of the Heracleids against the Argives; besides, the poets have already declared in song to all mankind their glory, and therefore any commemoration of their deeds in prose which we might attempt would hold a second place. They already have their reward, and I say no more of them; but there are other worthy deeds of which no poet has worthily sung, and which are still wooing the poet's muse. Of these I am bound to make honourable mention, and shall invoke others to sing of them also in lyric and other strains, in a manner becoming the actors. And first I will tell how the Persians, lords of Asia, were enslaving Europe, and how the children of this land, who were our fathers, held them back. Of these I will speak first, and praise their valour, as is meet and fitting. He who would rightly estimate them should place himself in thought at that time, when the whole of Asia was subject to the third king of Persia. The first king, Cyrus, by his valour freed the Persians, who were his countrymen, and subjected the Medes, who were their lords, and he ruled over the rest of Asia, as far as Egypt; and after him came his son, who ruled all the accessible part of Egypt and Libya; the third king was Darius, who extended the land boundaries of the empire to 240Scythia, and with his fleet held the sea and the islands. None presumed to be his equal; the minds of all men were enthralled by him—so many and mighty and warlike nations had the power of Persia subdued. Now Darius had a quarrel against us and the Eretrians, because, as he said, we had conspired against Sardis, and he sent 500,000 men in transports and vessels of war, and 300 ships, and Datis as commander, telling him to bring the Eretrians and Athenians to the king, if he wished to keep his head on his shoulders. He sailed against the Eretrians, who were reputed to be amongst the noblest and most warlike of the Hellenes of that day, and they were numerous, but he conquered them all in three days; and when he had conquered them, in order that no one might escape, he searched the whole country after this manner: his soldiers, coming to the borders of Eretria and spreading from sea to sea, joined hands and passed through the whole country, in order that they might be able to tell the king that no one had escaped them. And from Eretria they went to Marathon with a like intention, expecting to bind the Athenians in the same yoke of necessity in which they had bound the Eretrians. Having effected one-half of their purpose, they were in the act of attempting the other, and none of the Hellenes dared to assist either the Eretrians or the Athenians, except the Lacedaemonians, and they arrived a day too late for the battle; but the rest were panic-stricken and kept quiet, too happy in having escaped for a time. He who has present to his mind that conflict will know what manner of men they were who received the onset of the barbarians at Marathon, and chastened the pride of the whole of Asia, and by the victory which they gained over the barbarians first taught other men that the power of the Persians was not invincible, but that hosts of men and the multitude of riches alike yield to valour. And I assert that those men are the fathers not only of ourselves, but of our liberties and of the liberties of all who are on the continent, for that was the action to which the Hellenes looked back when they ventured to fight for their own safety in the battles which ensued: they became disciples of the men of Marathon. To them, therefore, I assign in my speech the first place, and the second to those 241who fought and conquered in the sea fights at Salamis and Artemisium; for of them, too, one might have many things to say—of the assaults which they endured by sea and land, and how they repelled them. I will mention only that act of theirs which appears to me to be the noblest, and which followed that of Marathon and came nearest to it; for the men of Marathon only showed the Hellenes that it was possible to ward off the barbarians by land, the many by the few; but there was no proof that they could be defeated by ships, and at sea the Persians retained the reputation of being invincible in numbers and wealth and skill and strength. This is the glory of the men who fought at sea, that they dispelled the second terror which had hitherto possessed the Hellenes, and so made the fear of numbers, whether of ships or men, to cease among them. And so the soldiers of Marathon and the sailors of Salamis became the schoolmasters of Hellas; the one teaching and habituating the Hellenes not to fear the barbarians at sea, and the others not to fear them by land. Third in order, for the number and valour of the combatants, and third in the salvation of Hellas, I place the battle of Plataea. And now the Lacedaemonians as well as the Athenians took part in the struggle; they were all united in this greatest and most terrible conflict of all; wherefore their virtues will be celebrated in times to come, as they are now celebrated by us. But at a later period many Hellenic tribes were still on the side of the barbarians, and there was a report that the great king was going to make a new attempt upon the Hellenes, and therefore justice requires that we should also make mention of those who crowned the previous work of our salvation, and drove and purged away all barbarians from the sea. These were the men who fought by sea at the river Eurymedon, and who went on the expedition to Cyprus, and who sailed to Egypt and divers other places; and they should be gratefully remembered by us, because they compelled the king in fear for himself to look to his own safety instead of plotting the destruction of Hellas.

Tanagra; Oenophyta.Sphacteria.The Sicilian expedition.Cyzicus.Hellas betrayed to the Persian.Arginusae.The taking of the city is obscurely intimated.The great reconciliation of kindred.Change in the relation of the Athenians (1) to the other Hellenes; (2) to the Persian king.

242And so the war against the barbarians was fought out to the end by the whole city on their own behalf, and on behalf of their countrymen. There was peace, and our city was held in honour; and then, as prosperity makes men jealous, there succeeded a jealousy of her, and jealousy begat envy, and so she became engaged against her will in a war with the Hellenes. On the breaking out of war, our citizens met the Lacedaemonians at Tanagra, and fought for the freedom of the Boeotians; the issue was doubtful, and was decided by the engagement which followed. For when the Lacedaemonians had gone on their way, leaving the Boeotians, whom they were aiding, on the third day after the battle of Tanagra, our countrymen conquered at Oenophyta, and righteously restored those who had been unrighteously exiled. And they were the first after the Persian war who fought on behalf of liberty in aid of Hellenes against Hellenes; they were brave men, and freed those whom they aided, and were the first too who were honourably interred in this sepulchre by the state. Afterwards there was a mighty war, in which all the Hellenes joined, and devastated our country, which was very ungrateful of them; and our countrymen, after defeating them in a naval engagement and taking their leaders, the Spartans, at Sphagia, when they might have destroyed them, spared their lives, and gave them back, and made peace, considering that they should war with their fellow-countrymen only until they gained a victory over them, and not because of the private anger of the state destroy the common interest of Hellas; but that with barbarians they should war to the death. Worthy of praise are they also who waged this war, and are here interred; for they proved, if any one doubted the superior prowess of the Athenians in the former war with the barbarians, that their doubts had no foundation—showing by their victory in the civil war with Hellas, in which they subdued the other chief state of the Hellenes, that they could conquer single-handed those with whom they had been allied in the war against the barbarians. After the peace there followed a third war, which was of a terrible and desperate nature, and in this many brave men who are here interred lost their lives—many of them had won victories in Sicily, whither they had gone over the seas 243to fight for the liberties of the Leontines, to whom they were bound by oaths; but, owing to the distance, the city was unable to help them, and they lost heart and came to misfortune, their very enemies and opponents winning more renown for valour and temperance than the friends of others. Many also fell in naval engagements at the Hellespont, after having in one day taken all the ships of the enemy, and defeated them in other naval engagements. And what I call the terrible and desperate nature of the war, is that the other Hellenes, in their extreme animosity towards the city, should have entered into negotiations with their bitterest enemy, the king of Persia, whom they, together with us, had expelled;—him, without us, they again brought back, barbarian against Hellenes, and all the hosts, both of Hellenes and barbarians, were united against Athens. And then shone forth the power and valour of our city. Her enemies had supposed that she was exhausted by the war, and our ships were blockaded at Mitylene. But the citizens themselves embarked, and came to the rescue with sixty other ships, and their valour was confessed of all men, for they conquered their enemies and delivered their friends. And yet by some evil fortune they were left to perish at sea, and therefore are not interred here. Ever to be remembered and honoured are they, for by their valour not only that sea-fight was won for us, but the entire war was decided by them, and through them the city gained the reputation of being invincible, even though attacked by all mankind. And that reputation was a true one, for the defeat which came upon us was our own doing. We were never conquered by others, and to this day we are still unconquered by them; but we were our own conquerors, and received defeat at our own hands. Afterwards there was quiet and peace abroad, but there sprang up war at home; and, if men are destined to have civil war, no one could have desired that his city should take the disorder in a milder form. How joyful and natural was the reconciliation of those who came from the Piraeus and those who came from the city; with what moderation did they order the war against the tyrants in Eleusis, and in a manner how unlike what the other 244Hellenes expected! And the reason of this gentleness was the veritable tie of blood, which created among them a friendship as of kinsmen, faithful not in word only, but in deed. And we ought also to remember those who then fell by one another's hands, and on such occasions as these to reconcile them with sacrifices and prayers, praying to those who have power over them, that they may be reconciled even as we are reconciled. For they did not attack one another out of malice or enmity, but they were unfortunate. And that such was the fact we ourselves are witnesses, who are of the same race with them, and have mutually received and granted forgiveness of what we have done and suffered. After this there was perfect peace, and the city had rest; and her feeling was that she forgave the barbarians, who had severely suffered at her hands and severely retaliated, but that she was indignant at the ingratitude of the Hellenes, when she remembered how they had received good from her and returned evil, having made common cause with the barbarians, depriving her of the ships which had once been their salvation, and dismantling our walls, which had preserved their own from falling. She thought that she would no longer defend the Hellenes, when enslaved either by one another or by the barbarians, and did accordingly. This was our feeling, while the Lacedaemonians were thinking that we who were the champions of liberty had fallen, and that their business was to subject the remaining Hellenes. And why should I say more? for the events of which I am speaking happened not long ago and we can all of us remember how the chief peoples of Hellas, Argives and Boeotians and Corinthians, came to feel the need of us, and, what is the greatest miracle of all, the Persian king himself was driven to such extremity as to come round to the opinion, that from this city, of which he was the destroyer, and from no other, his salvation would proceed.

And if a person desired to bring a deserved accusation against our city, he would find only one charge which he could justly urge—that she was too compassionate and too favourable to the weaker side. And in this instance she was not able to hold out or keep her resolution of refusing aid to 245her injurers when they were being enslaved, but she was softened, and did in fact send out aid, and delivered the Hellenes from slavery, and they were free until they afterwards enslaved themselves. Whereas, to the great king she refused to give the assistance of the state, for she could not forget the trophies of Marathon and Salamis and Plataea; but she allowed exiles and volunteers to assist him, and they were his salvation. And she herself, when she was compelled, entered into the war, and built walls and ships, and fought with the Lacedaemonians on behalf of the Parians. Now the king fearing this city and wanting to stand aloof, when he saw the Lacedaemonians growing weary of the war at sea, asked of us, as the price of his alliance with us and the other allies, to give up the Hellenes in Asia, whom the Lacedaemonians had previously handed over to him, he thinking that we should refuse, and that then he might have a pretence for withdrawing from us. About the other allies he was mistaken, for the Corinthians and Argives and Boeotians, and the other states, were quite willing to let them go, and swore and covenanted, that, if he would pay them money, they would make over to him the Hellenes of the continent, and we alone refused to give them up and swear. Such was the natural nobility of this city, so sound and healthy was the spirit of freedom among us, and the instinctive dislike of the barbarian, because we are pure Hellenes, having no admixture of barbarism in us. For we are not like many others, descendants of Pelops or Cadmus or Egyptus or Danaus, who are by nature barbarians, and yet pass for Hellenes, and dwell in the midst of us; but we are pure Hellenes, uncontaminated by any foreign element, and therefore the hatred of the foreigner has passed unadulterated into the life-blood of the city. And so, notwithstanding our noble sentiments, we were again isolated, because we were unwilling to be guilty of the base and unholy act of giving up Hellenes to barbarians. And we were in the same case as when we were subdued before; but, by the favour of Heaven, we managed better, for we ended the war without the loss of our ships or walls or colonies; the enemy was only too glad to be quit of us. Yet in this war we lost many brave men, such as were those who fell owing to the ruggedness of the ground at the battle of Corinth, or by treason at Lechaeum. Brave men, too; were those who delivered the Persian king, and drove the Lacedaemonians 246from the sea. I remind you of them, and you must celebrate them together with me, and do honour to their memories.

Such were the actions of the men who are here interred, and of others who have died on behalf of their country; many and glorious things I have spoken of them, and there are yet many more and more glorious things remaining to be told—many days and nights would not suffice to tell of them. Let them not be forgotten, and let every man remind their descendants that they also are soldiers who must not desert the ranks of their ancestors, or from cowardice fall behind. Even as I exhort you this day, and in all future time, whenever I meet with any of you, shall continue to remind and exhort you, O ye sons of heroes, that you strive to be the bravest of men. And I think that I ought now to repeat what your fathers desired to have said to you who are their survivors, when they went out to battle, in case anything happened to them. I will tell you what I heard them say, and what, if they had only speech, they would fain be saying, judging from what they then said. And you must imagine that you hear them saying what I now repeat to you:—

'Sons, the event proves that your fathers were brave men; for we might have lived dishonourably, but have preferred to die honourably rather than bring you and your children into disgrace, and rather than dishonour our own fathers and forefathers; considering that life is not life to one who is a dishonour to his race, and that to such a one neither men nor Gods are friendly, either while he is on the earth or after death in the world below. Remember our words, then, and whatever is your aim let virtue be the condition of the attainment of your aim, and know that without this all possessions and pursuits are dishonourable and evil. For neither does wealth bring honour to the owner, if he be a coward; of such a one the wealth belongs to another, and not to himself. Nor does beauty and strength of body, when dwelling in a base and cowardly man, appear comely, but the reverse of comely, making the possessor more conspicuous, and manifesting forth his cowardice. And all knowledge, when separated from justice and virtue, is seen to be cunning and not wisdom; wherefore make this your first and last and constant and all-absorbing aim, to exceed, 247if possible, not only us but all your ancestors in virtue; and know that to excel you in virtue only brings us shame, but that to be excelled by you is a source of happiness to us. And we shall most likely be defeated, and you will most likely be victors in the contest, if you learn so to order your lives as not to abuse or waste the reputation of your ancestors, knowing that to a man who has any self-respect, nothing is more dishonourable than to be honoured, not for his own sake, but on account of the reputation of his ancestors. The honour of parents is a fair and noble treasure to their posterity, but to have the use of a treasure of wealth and honour, and to leave none to your successors, because you have neither money nor reputation of your own, is alike base and dishonourable. And if you follow our precepts you will be received by us as friends, when the hour of destiny brings you hither; but if you neglect our words and are disgraced in your lives, no one will welcome or receive you. This is the message which is to be delivered to our children.

'Some of us have fathers and mothers still living, and we would urge them, if, as is likely, we shall die, to bear the calamity as lightly as possible, and not to condole with one another; for they have sorrows enough, and will not need any one to stir them up. While we gently heal their wounds, let us remind them that the Gods have heard the chief part of their prayers; for they prayed, not that their children might live for ever, but that they might be brave and renowned. And this, which is the greatest good, they have attained. A mortal man cannot expect to have everything in his own life turning out according to his will; and they, if they bear their misfortunes bravely, will be truly deemed brave fathers of the brave. But if they give way to their sorrows, either they will be suspected of not being our parents, or we of not being such as our panegyrists declare. Let not either of the two alternatives happen, but rather let them be our chief and true panegyrists, who show in their lives that they are true men, and had men for their sons. Of old the saying, "Nothing too much," appeared to be, and really was, well said. For he whose happiness rests with himself, if possible, wholly, and if not, as far as is possible,—who is not hanging in suspense on other men, or changing with the vicissitude of their fortune,—has his life ordered for the best. He is the temperate and valiant and wise; and when his riches come and go, when his children are given and taken away, he will remember the proverb—"Neither rejoicing overmuch nor grieving overmuch," for he relies upon himself. And such we would have our parents to be—that is our word and wish, and as such we now offer ourselves, neither lamenting overmuch, nor fearing overmuch, if we are to die at this time. And we entreat our fathers and mothers to retain these feelings throughout their future life, and to be assured that they will not please us by sorrowing and lamenting over us. But, if the dead have any knowledge of the living, they will displease us most by making themselves miserable and by taking their misfortunes too much to heart, and they will please us best if they bear their loss lightly and temperately. For our life will have the noblest end which is vouchsafed to man, and should be glorified rather than lamented. And if they will direct their minds to the care and nurture of our wives and children, they will soonest forget their misfortunes, and live in a better and nobler way, and be dearer to us.

'This is all that we have to say to our families: and to the state we would say—Take care of our parents and of our sons: let her worthily cherish the old age of our parents, and bring up our sons in the right way. But we know that she will of her own accord take care of them, and does not need any exhortation of ours.'

Socrates, Menexenus.

This, O ye children and parents of the dead, is the message which they bid us deliver to you, and which I do deliver with the utmost seriousness. And in their name I beseech you, the children, to imitate your fathers, and you, parents, to be of good cheer about yourselves; for we will nourish your age, and take care of you both publicly and privately in any place in which one of us may meet one of you who are the parents of the dead. And the care of you which the city shows, you know yourselves; for she has made provision by law concerning the parents and children of those who die in war; the highest authority is specially entrusted with the duty of watching over them above all other citizens, and they will see that your fathers and mothers have no wrong done to them. The city herself shares in the education of the children, desiring as far as it is possible that their orphanhood may not be felt by them; while they are children she is a parent to them, and when they have arrived at man's estate she sends them to their several duties, in full armour clad; and bringing freshly to their minds the ways of their fathers, she places in their hands the instruments of their fathers' virtues; for the sake of the omen, she would have them from the first begin to rule over their own houses arrayed in the strength and arms of their fathers. And as for the dead, she never ceases honouring them, celebrating in common for all rites which become the property of each; and in addition to this, holding gymnastic and equestrian contests, and musical festivals of every sort. She is to the dead in the place of a son and heir, and to their sons in the place of a father, and to their parents and elder kindred in the place of a guardian—ever and always caring for them. Considering this, you ought to bear your calamity the more gently; for thus you will be most endeared to the dead and to the living, and your sorrows will heal and be healed. And now do you and all, having lamented the dead in common according to the law, go your ways.

You have heard, Menexenus, the oration of Aspasia the Milesian.

Men.

This speech, Socrates, was not composed by Aspasia, but by yourself.

Truly, Socrates, I marvel that Aspasia, who is only a woman, should be able to compose such a speech; she must be a rare one.

Soc.

Well, if you are incredulous, you may come with me and hear her.

Men.

I have often met Aspasia, Socrates, and know what she is like.

Soc.

Well, and do you not admire her, and are you not grateful for her speech?

Men.

Yes, Socrates, I am very grateful to her or to him who told you, and still more to you who have told me.

Soc.

Very good. But you must take care not to tell of me, and then at some future time I will repeat to you many other excellent political speeches of hers.

Men.

Fear not; only let me hear them, and I will keep the secret.

Soc.

Then I will keep my promise.

APPENDIX II. ALCIBIADES II. ERYXIAS.

Appendix II.

The two dialogues which are translated in the second appendix are not mentioned by Aristotle, or by any early authority, and have no claim to be ascribed to Plato. They are examples of Platonic dialogues to be assigned probably to the second or third generation after Plato, when his writings were well known at Athens and Alexandria. They exhibit considerable originality, and are remarkable for containing several thoughts of the sort which we suppose to be modern rather than ancient, and which therefore have a peculiar interest for us. The Second Alcibiades shows that the difficulties about prayer which have perplexed Christian theologians were not unknown among the followers of Plato. The Eryxias was doubted by the ancients themselves: yet it may claim the distinction of being, among all Greek or Roman writings, the one which anticipates in the most striking manner the modern science of political economy and gives an abstract form to some of its principal doctrines.

For the translation of these two dialogues I am indebted to my friend and secretary, Mr. Knight.

That the Dialogue which goes by the name of the Second Alcibiades is a genuine writing of Plato will not be maintained by any modern critic, and was hardly believed by the ancients themselves. The dialectic is poor and weak. There is no power over language, or beauty of style; and there is a certain abruptness and ἀγροικία in the conversation, which is very un-Platonic. The best passage is probably that about the poets, p. 147:—the remark that the poet, who is of a reserved disposition, is uncommonly difficult to understand, and the ridiculous interpretation of Homer, are entirely in the spirit of Plato (cp. Protag. 339 foll.; Ion 534; Apol. 22 D). The characters are ill-drawn. Socrates assumes the 'superior person' and preaches too much, while Alcibiades is stupid and heavy-in-hand. There are traces of Stoic influence in the general tone and phraseology of the Dialogue (cp. 138 B, ὅπως μὴ λήσει τις ... κακά: 139 C, ὅτι πας ἄφρων μαίνεται): and the writer seems to have been acquainted with the 'Laws' of Plato (cp. Laws 3. 687, 688; 7. 801; 11. 931 B). An incident from the Symposium (213 E) is rather clumsily introduced (151 A), and two somewhat hackneyed quotations (Symp. 174 D, Gorg. 484 E) recur at 140 A and 146 A. The reference to the death of Archelaus as having occurred 'quite lately' (141 D) is only a fiction, probably suggested by the Gorgias, 470 D, where the story of Archelaus is told, and a similar phrase occurs,—τὰ γὰρ ἐχθες καὶ πρώην γεγονότα ταντα, κ.τ.λ. There are several passages which are either corrupt or extremely ill-expressed (see pp. 144, 145, 146, 147, 150). But there is a modern interest in the subject of the dialogue; and it is a good example of a short spurious work, which may be attributed to the second or third century before Christ.

INTRODUCTION TO ALCIBIADES II.

PERSONS OF THE DIALOGUE.

Socrates and Alcibiades.

Soc.

Alcibiades II.

138Are you going, Alcibiades, to offer prayer to Zeus?

Al.

Yes, Socrates, I am.

Soc.

Socrates, Alcibiades.

You seem to be troubled and to cast your eyes on the ground, as though you were thinking about something.

Al.

Of what do you suppose that I am thinking?

Soc.

Of the greatest of all things, as I believe. Tell me, do you not suppose that the Gods sometimes partly grant and partly reject the requests which we make in public and private, and favour some persons and not others?

Al.

Certainly.

Soc.

The danger of a prayer which is ill-advised.

Do you not imagine, then, that a man ought to be very careful, lest perchance without knowing it he implore great evils for himself, deeming that he is asking for good, especially if the Gods are in the mood to grant whatever he may request? There is the story of Oedipus, for instance, who prayed that his children might divide their inheritance between them by the sword: he did not, as he might have done, beg that his present evils might be averted, but called down new ones. And was not his prayer accomplished, and did not many and terrible evils thence arise, upon which I need not dilate?

Al.

Yes, Socrates, but you are speaking of a madman: surely you do not think that any one in his senses would venture to make such a prayer?

Soc.

Madness, then, you consider to be the opposite of discretion?

Al.

Of course.

Soc.

And some men seem to you to be discreet, and others the contrary?

Al.

They do.

Soc.

Well, then, let us discuss who these are. We acknowledge that some are discreet, some foolish, and that some are mad?

Al.

Yes.

Soc.

And again, there are some who are in health?

Al.

There are.

Soc.

While others are ailing?

Al.

Yes. 139

Soc.

And they are not the same?

Al.

Certainly not.

Soc.

Nor are there any who are in neither state?

Al.

No.

Soc.

A man must either be sick or be well?

Al.

That is my opinion.

Soc.

Alcibiades first desires and afterwards admits that differences of kind do not exclude differences of degree.

Very good: and do you think the same about discretion and want of discretion?

Al.

How do you mean?

Soc.

Do you believe that a man must be either in or out of his senses; or is there some third or intermediate condition, in which he is neither one nor the other?

Al.

Decidedly not.

Soc.

He must be either sane or insane?

Al.

So I suppose.

Soc.

Did you not acknowledge that madness was the opposite of discretion?

Al.

Yes.

Soc.

And that there is no third or middle term between discretion and indiscretion?

Al.

True.

Soc.

And there cannot be two opposites to one thing?

Al.

There cannot.

Soc.

Then madness and want of sense are the same?

Al.

That appears to be the case.

Soc.

We shall be in the right, therefore, Alcibiades, if we say that all who are senseless are mad. For example, if among persons of your own age or older than yourself there are some who are senseless,—as there certainly are,—they are mad. For tell me, by heaven, do you not think that in the city the wise are few, while the foolish, whom you call mad, are many?

Al.

I do.

Soc.

But how could we live in safety with so many crazy people? Should we not long since have paid the penalty at their hands, and have been struck and beaten and endured every other form of ill-usage which madmen are wont to inflict? Consider, my dear friend: may it not be quite otherwise?

Al.

Why, Socrates, how is that possible? I must have been mistaken.

Soc.

So it seems to me. But perhaps we may consider the matter thus:—

Al.

How?

Soc.

I will tell you. We think that some are sick; do we not?

Al.

Yes.

Soc.

The sick may have many kinds of sickness; so there are different kinds of want of sense.

And must every sick person either have the gout, or be in a fever, or suffer from ophthalmia? Or do you believe that a man may labour under some other disease, even although he has none of these complaints? Surely, they are not the only maladies which exist?

Al.

Certainly not.

Soc.

And is every kind of ophthalmia a disease?

Al.

Yes.

Soc.

And every disease ophthalmia?

Al.

Surely not. But I scarcely understand what I mean myself.

Soc.

140Perhaps, if you give me your best attention, 'two of us' looking together, we may find what we seek.

Al.

I am attending, Socrates, to the best of my power.

Soc.

We are agreed, then, that every form of ophthalmia is a disease, but not every disease ophthalmia?

Al.

We are.

Soc.

And so far we seem to be right. For every one who suffers from a fever is sick; but the sick, I conceive, do not all have fever or gout or ophthalmia, although each of these is a disease, which, according to those whom we call physicians, may require a different treatment. They are not all alike, nor do they produce the same result, but each has its own effect, and yet they are all diseases. May we not take an illustration from the artizans?

Al.

Certainly.

Soc.

There are cobblers and carpenters and sculptors and others of all sorts and kinds, whom we need not stop to enumerate. All have their distinct employments and all are workmen, although they are not all of them cobblers or carpenters or sculptors.

Al.

No, indeed.

Soc.

And in like manner men differ in regard to want of sense. Those who are most out of their wits we call 'madmen,' while we term those who are less far gone 'stupid' or 'idiotic,' or, if we prefer gentler language, describe them as 'romantic' or 'simple-minded,' or, again, as 'innocent' or 'inexperienced' or 'foolish.' You may even find other names, if you seek for them; but by all of them lack of sense is intended. They only differ as one art appeared to us to differ from another or one disease from another. Or what is your opinion?

Al.

I agree with you.

Soc.

Then let us return to the point at which we digressed. We said at first that we should have to consider who were the wise and who the foolish. For we acknowledged that there are these two classes? Did we not?

Al.

To be sure.

Soc.

And you regard those as sensible who know what ought to be done or said?

Al.

Yes.

Soc.

The senseless are those who do not know this?

Al.

True.

Soc.

The latter will say or do what they ought not without their own knowledge?

Al.

Exactly.

Soc.

Men often, like Oedipus, pray unadvisedly.

Oedipus, as I was saying, Alcibiades, was a person of 141this sort. And even now-a-days you will find many who [have offered inauspicious prayers], although, unlike him, they were not in anger nor thought that they were asking evil. He neither sought, nor supposed that he sought for good, but others have had quite the contrary notion. I believe that if the God whom you are about to consult should appear to you, and, in anticipation of your request, enquired whether you would be contented to become tyrant of Athens, and if this seemed in your eyes a small and mean thing, should add to it the dominion of all Hellas; and seeing that even then you would not be satisfied unless you were ruler of the whole of Europe, should promise, not only that, but, if you so desired, should proclaim to all mankind in one and the same day that Alcibiades, son of Cleinias, was tyrant:—in such a case, I imagine, you would depart full of joy, as one who had obtained the greatest of goods.

Al.

And not only I, Socrates, but any one else who should meet with such luck.

Soc.

Yet you would not accept the dominion and lordship of all the Hellenes and all the barbarians in exchange for your life?

Al.

Certainly not: for then what use could I make of them?

Soc.

And would you accept them if you were likely to use them to a bad and mischievous end?

Al.

I would not.

Soc.

Archelaus and his beloved.Men never refuse the goods of fortune, however great the evils which may attend them.

You see that it is not safe for a man either rashly to accept whatever is offered him, or himself to request a thing, if he is likely to suffer thereby or immediately to lose his life. And yet we could tell of many who, having long desired and diligently laboured to obtain a tyranny, thinking that thus they would procure an advantage, have nevertheless fallen victims to designing enemies. You must have heard of what happened only the other day, how Archelaus of Macedonia was slain by his beloved , whose love for the tyranny was not less than that of Archelaus for him. The tyrannicide expected by his crime to become tyrant and afterwards to have a happy life; but when he had held the tyranny three or four days, he was in his turn conspired against and slain. Or look at certain of our own citizens,—and of their actions we have been not hearers, but eyewitnesses,—who have desired to obtain military command: of 142those who have gained their object, some are even to this day exiles from the city, while others have lost their lives. And even they who seem to have fared best, have not only gone through many perils and terrors during their office, but after their return home they have been beset by informers worse than they once were by their foes, insomuch that several of them have wished that they had remained in a private station rather than have had the glories of command. If, indeed, such perils and terrors were of profit to the commonwealth, there would be reason in undergoing them; but the very contrary is the case. Again, you will find persons who have prayed for offspring, and when their prayers were heard, have fallen into the greatest pains and sufferings. For some have begotten children who were utterly bad, and have therefore passed all their days in misery, while the parents of good children have undergone the misfortune of losing them, and have been so little happier than the others that they would have preferred never to have had children rather than to have had them and lost them. And yet, although these and the like examples are manifest and known of all, it is rare to find any one who has refused what has been offered him, or, if he were likely to gain aught by prayer, has refrained from making his petition. The mass of mankind would not decline to accept a tyranny, or the command of an army, or any of the numerous things which cause more harm than good: but rather, if they had them not, would have prayed to obtain them. And often in a short space of time they change their tone, and wish their old prayers unsaid. Wherefore also I suspect that men are entirely wrong when they blame the gods as the authors of the ills which befall them : 'their own presumption,' or folly (whichever is the right word)—

'Has brought these unmeasured woes upon them .'

He must have been a wise poet, Alcibiades, who, seeing as I believe, his friends foolishly praying for and doing things which would not really profit them, offered up a common prayer in behalf of them all:—

- 'King Zeus, grant us good whether prayed for or unsought by us; 143
- But that which we ask amiss, do thou avert .'

In my opinion, I say, the poet spoke both well and prudently; but if you have anything to say in answer to him, speak out.

Al.

It is difficult, Socrates, to oppose what has been well said. And I perceive how many are the ills of which ignorance is the cause, since, as would appear, through ignorance we not only do, but what is worse, pray for the greatest evils. No man would imagine that he would do so; he would rather suppose that he was quite capable of praying for what was best: to call down evil seems more like a curse than a prayer.

Soc.

But perhaps, my good friend, some one who is wiser than either you or I will say that we have no right to blame ignorance thus rashly, unless we can add what ignorance we mean and of what, and also to whom and how it is respectively a good or an evil?

Al.

How do you mean? Can ignorance possibly be better than knowledge for any person in any conceivable case?

Soc.

So I believe:—you do not think so?

Al.

Certainly not.

Soc.

Orestes and Alcmaeon.

And yet surely I may not suppose that you would ever wish to act towards your mother as they say that Orestes and Alcmaeon and others have done towards their parent.

Al.

Good words, Socrates, prithee.

Soc.

Ignorance of the best is bad: ignorance of the bad good.

You ought not to bid him use auspicious words, who says that you would not be willing to commit so horrible a deed, but rather him who affirms the contrary, if the act appear to you unfit even to be mentioned. Or do you think that Orestes, had he been in his senses and knew what was best for him to do, would ever have dared to venture on such a crime?

Al.

Certainly not.

Soc.

Nor would any one else, I fancy?

Al.

No.

Soc.

That ignorance is bad then, it would appear, which is of the best and does not know what is best?

Al.

So I think, at least.

Soc.

And both to the person who is ignorant and everybody else?

Al.

Yes.

Soc.

Let us take another case. Suppose that you were suddenly to get into your head that it would be a good thing 144to kill Pericles, your kinsman and guardian, and were to seize a sword and, going to the doors of his house, were to enquire if he were at home, meaning to slay only him and no one else:—the servants reply, 'Yes': (Mind, I do not mean that you would really do such a thing; but there is nothing, you think, to prevent a man who is ignorant of the best, having occasionally the whim that what is worst is best?

Al.

No.)

Soc.

A man might be prevented from committing murder by ignorance of the person whom he was going to murder.

—If, then, you went indoors, and seeing him, did not know him, but thought that he was some one else, would you venture to slay him?

Al.

Most decidedly not [it seems to me].

Soc.

For you designed to kill, not the first who offered, but Pericles himself?

Al.

Certainly.

Soc.

And if you made many attempts, and each time failed to recognize Pericles, you would never attack him?

Al.

Never.

Soc.

Well, but if Orestes in like manner had not known his mother, do you think that he would ever have laid hands upon her?

Al.

No.

Soc.

He did not intend to slay the first woman he came across, nor any one else's mother, but only his own?

Al.

True.

Soc.

Ignorance, then, is better for those who are in such a frame of mind, and have such ideas?

Al.

Obviously.

Soc.

You acknowledge that for some persons in certain cases the ignorance of some things is a good and not an evil, as you formerly supposed?

Al.

I do.

Soc.

And there is still another case which will also perhaps appear strange to you, if you will consider it?

Al.

What is that, Socrates?

Soc.

All knowledge if unaccompanied by a knowledge of the best is hurtful.

It may be, in short, that the possession of all the sciences, if unaccompanied by the knowledge of the best, will more often than not injure the possessor. Consider the matter thus:—Must we not, when we intend either to do or say anything, suppose that we know or ought to know that which we propose so confidently to do or say?

Al.

Yes, in my opinion.

Soc.

We may take the orators for an example, who from 145time to time advise us about war and peace, or the building of walls and the construction of harbours, whether they understand the business in hand, or only think that they do. Whatever the city, in a word, does to another city, or in the management of her own affairs, all happens by the counsel of the orators.

Al.

True.

Soc.

But now see what follows, if I can [make it clear to you] . You would distinguish the wise from the foolish?

Al.

Yes.

Soc.

The many are foolish, the few wise?

Al.

Certainly.

Soc.

And you use both the terms, 'wise' and 'foolish,' in reference to something?

Al.

I do.

Soc.

Examples.

Would you call a person wise who can give advice, but does not know whether or when it is better to carry out the advice?

Al.

Decidedly not.

Soc.

Nor again, I suppose, a person who knows the art of war, but does not know whether it is better to go to war or for how long?

Al.

No.

Soc.

Nor, once more, a person who knows how to kill another or to take away his property or to drive him from his native land, but not when it is better to do so or for whom it is better?

Al.

Certainly not.

Soc.

But he who understands anything of the kind and has at the same time the knowledge of the best course of action:—and the best and the useful are surely the same?—

Al.

Yes.

Soc.

—Such an one, I say, we should call wise and a useful adviser both of himself and of the city. What do you think?

Al.

I agree.

Soc.

And if any one knows how to ride or to shoot with the bow or to box or to wrestle, or to engage in any other sort of contest or to do anything whatever which is in the nature of an art,—what do you call him who knows what is best according to that art? Do you not speak of one who knows what is best in riding as a good rider?

Al.

Yes.

Soc.

And in a similar way you speak of a good boxer or a good flute-player or a good performer in any other art?

Al.

True.

Soc.

But is it necessary that the man who is clever in any of these arts should be wise also in general? Or is there a difference between the clever artist and the wise man?

Al.

All the difference in the world.

Soc.

A state would be bad which was composed only of skilful artists and clever politicians, but where no one had the knowledge of the best.

And what sort of a state do you think that would be which was composed of good archers and flute-players and athletes and masters in other arts, and besides them of those others about whom we spoke, who knew how to go to war and how to kill, as well as of orators puffed up with political pride, but in which not one of them all had this knowledge of the best, and there was no one who could tell when it was better to apply any of these arts or in regard to 146whom?

Al.

I should call such a state bad, Socrates.

Soc.

You certainly would when you saw each of them rivalling the other and esteeming that of the greatest importance in the state,

'Wherein he himself most excelled .'

—I mean that which was best in any art, while he was entirely ignorant of what was best for himself and for the state, because, as I think, he trusts to opinion which is devoid of intelligence. In such a case should we not be right if we said that the state would be full of anarchy and lawlessness?

Al.

Decidedly.

Soc.

But ought we not then, think you, either to fancy that we know or really to know, what we confidently propose to do or say?

Al.

Yes.

Soc.

And if a person does that which he knows or supposes that he knows, and the result is beneficial, he will act advantageously both for himself and for the state?

Al.

True.

Soc.

And if he do the contrary, both he and the state will suffer?

Al.

Yes.

Soc.

Well, and are you of the same mind, as before?

Al.

I am.

Soc.

But were you not saying that you would call the many unwise and the few wise?

Al.

I was.

Soc.

And have we not come back to our old assertion that the many fail to obtain the best because they trust to opinion which is devoid of intelligence?

Al.

That is the case.

Soc.

It is good, then, for the many, if they particularly desire to do that which they know or suppose that they know, neither to know nor to suppose that they know, in cases where if they carry out their ideas in action they will be losers rather than gainers?

Al.

What you say is very true.

Soc.

Do you not see that I was really speaking the truth when I affirmed that the possession of any other kind of knowledge was more likely to injure than to benefit the possessor, unless he had also the knowledge of the best?

Al.

I do now, if I did not before, Socrates.

Soc.

The soul requires this knowledge of the best before she sets sail on the voyage of life.

The state or the soul, therefore, which wishes to have a right existence must hold firmly to this knowledge, just as the sick man clings to the physician, or the passenger 147depends for safety on the pilot. And if the soul does not set sail until she have obtained this she will be all the safer in the voyage through life. But when she rushes  in pursuit of wealth or bodily strength or anything else, not having the knowledge of the best, so much the more is she likely to meet with misfortune. And he who has the love of learning , and is skilful in many arts, and does not possess the knowledge of the best, but is under some other guidance, will make, as he deserves, a sorry voyage:—he will, I believe, hurry through the brief space of human life, pilotless in mid-ocean, and the words will apply to him in which the poet blamed his enemy:—

- '. . . . . Full many a thing he knew;
- But knew them all badly .'

Al.

How in the world, Socrates, do the words of the poet apply to him? They seem to me to have no bearing on the point whatever.

Soc.

The poets spoke in riddles a hidden truth.

Quite the contrary, my sweet friend: only the poet is talking in riddles after the fashion of his tribe. For all poetry has by nature an enigmatical character, and it is by no means everybody who can interpret it. And if, moreover, the spirit of poetry happen to seize on a man who is of a begrudging temper and does not care to manifest his wisdom but keeps it to himself as far as he can, it does indeed require an almost superhuman wisdom to discover what the poet would be at. You surely do not suppose that Homer, the wisest and most divine of poets, was unaware of the impossibility of knowing a thing badly: for it was no less a person than he who said of Margites that 'he knew many things, but knew them all badly.' The solution of the riddle is this, I imagine:—By 'badly' Homer meant 'bad' and 'knew' stands for 'to know.' Put the words together;—the metre will suffer, but the poet's meaning is clear;—'Margites knew all these things, but it was bad for him to know so many things, he must have been a good-for-nothing, unless the argument has played us false.

Al.

But I do not think that it has, Socrates: at least, if the argument is fallacious, it would be difficult for me to find another which I could trust.

Soc.

And you are right in thinking so.

Al.

Well, that is my opinion.

Soc.

Alcibiades is too unstable to be able to trust his own prayers.

But tell me, by Heaven:—you must see now the nature and greatness of the difficulty in which you, like others, have your part. For you change about in all directions, and never come to rest anywhere: what you once most strongly inclined to suppose, you put aside again and 148quite alter your mind. If the God to whose shrine you are going should appear at this moment, and ask before you made your prayer, 'Whether you would desire to have one of the things which we mentioned at first, or whether he should leave you to make your own request:'—what in either case, think you, would be the best way to take advantage of the opportunity?

Al.

Indeed, Socrates, I could not answer you without consideration. It seems to me to be a wild thing to make such a request; a man must be very careful lest he pray for evil under the idea that he is asking for good, when shortly after he may have to recall his prayer, and, as you were saying, demand the opposite of what he at first requested.

Soc.

And was not the poet whose words I originally quoted wiser than we are, when he bade us [pray God] to defend us from evil even though we asked for it?

Al.

I believe that you are right.

Soc.

The Lacedaemonians, too, whether from admiration of the poet or because they have discovered the idea for themselves, are wont to offer the prayer alike in public and private, that the Gods will give unto them the beautiful as well as the good:—no one is likely to hear them make any further petition. And yet up to the present time they have not been less fortunate than other men; or if they have sometimes met with misfortune, the fault has not been due to their prayer. For surely, as I conceive, the Gods have power either to grant our requests, or to send us the contrary of what we ask.

Socrates. The silent prayer of the Lacedaemonians better than all the offerings of the other Hellenes.

And now I will relate to you a story which I have heard from certain of our elders. It chanced that when the Athenians and Lacedaemonians were at war, our city lost every battle by land and sea and never gained a victory. The Athenians being annoyed and perplexed how to find a remedy for their troubles, decided to send and enquire at the shrine of Ammon. Their envoys were also to ask, 'Why the Gods always granted the victory to the Lacedaemonians?' 'We,' (they were to say,) 'offer them more and finer sacrifices than any other Hellenic state, and adorn their temples with gifts, as nobody else does; moreover, we make the most solemn and costly processions to them every year, and spend more money in their service than all the rest of the Hellenes put together. But the Lacedaemonians take no thought of such matters, and pay so little respect to the Gods that they have a habit of sacrificing blemished animals to them, and in various ways are less zealous than we are, although their wealth is quite equal to ours.' When they had thus spoken, and had made their request to know what remedy they could find against the evils which troubled them, the prophet made no direct answer,—clearly because he was not allowed by the God to do so;—but he summoned them to him and said: 'Thus saith Ammon to the Athenians: "The silent worship of the Lacedaemonians pleaseth me better than all the offerings of the other Hellenes." ' Such were the words of the God, and nothing more. He seems to have meant by 'silent worship' the prayer of the Lacedaemonians, which is indeed widely different from the usual requests of the Hellenes. For they either bring to the altar bulls with gilded horns or make offerings to the Gods, and beg at random for what they need, good or bad. When, therefore, the Gods hear them using words of ill omen they reject these costly processions and sacrifices of theirs. And we ought, I think, to be very careful and consider well what we should say and what leave unsaid. Homer, too, will furnish us with similar stories. For he tells us how the Trojans in making their encampment,

'Offered up whole hecatombs to the immortals,'

Socrates, Alcibiades.

and how the 'sweet savour' was borne 'to the heavens by the winds;

- 'But the blessed Gods were averse and received it not.
- For exceedingly did they hate the holy Ilium,
- Both Priam and the people of the spear-skilled king.'

So that it was in vain for them to sacrifice and offer gifts, seeing that they were hateful to the Gods, who are not, like vile usurers, to be gained over by bribes. And it is foolish for us to boast that we are superior to the Lacedaemonians by reason of our much worship. The idea is inconceivable 150that the Gods have regard, not to the justice and purity of our souls, but to costly processions and sacrifices, which men may celebrate year after year, although they have committed innumerable crimes against the Gods or against their fellowmen or the state. For the Gods, as Ammon and his prophet declare, are no receivers of gifts, and they scorn such unworthy service. Wherefore also it would seem that wisdom and justice are especially honoured both by the Gods and by men of sense; and they are the wisest and most just who know how to speak and act towards Gods and men. But I should like to hear what your opinion is about these matters.

Al.

I agree, Socrates, with you and with the God, whom, indeed, it would be unbecoming for me to oppose.

Soc.

Do you not remember saying that you were in great perplexity, lest perchance you should ask for evil, supposing that you were asking for good?

Al.

I do.

Soc.

Alcibiades cannot tell whether he is asking for good or evil. 'Therefore let his words be few.'

You see, then, that there is a risk in your approaching the God in prayer, lest haply he should refuse your sacrifice when he hears the blasphemy which you utter, and make you partake of other evils as well. The wisest plan, therefore, seems to me that you should keep silence; for your 'highmindedness'—to use the mildest term which men apply to folly—will most likely prevent you from using the prayer of the Lacedaemonians. You had better wait until we find out how we should behave towards the Gods and towards men.

Al.

And how long must I wait, Socrates, and who will be my teacher? I should be very glad to see the man.

Soc.

It is he who takes an especial interest in you. But first of all, I think, the darkness must be taken away in which your soul is now enveloped, just as Athene in Homer removes the mist from the eyes of Diomede that

'He may distinguish between God and mortal man.'

Afterwards the means may be given to you whereby you may distinguish between good and evil. At present, I fear, this is beyond your power.

Al.

Only let my instructor take away the impediment, whether it pleases him to call it mist or anything else! I care not who he is; but I am resolved to disobey none of his commands, if I am likely to be the better for them.

Soc.

And surely he has a wondrous care for you. 151

Al.

It seems to be altogether advisable to put off the sacrifice until he is found.

Soc.

You are right: that will be safer than running such a tremendous risk.

Al.

But how shall we manage, Socrates?—At any rate I will set this crown of mine upon your head, as you have given me such excellent advice, and to the Gods we will offer crowns and perform the other customary rites when I see that day approaching: nor will it be long hence, if they so will.

Soc.

I accept your gift, and shall be ready and willing to receive whatever else you may proffer. Euripides makes Creon say in the play, when he beholds Teiresias with his crown and hears that he has gained it by his skill as the first-fruits of the spoil:—

- 'An auspicious omen I deem thy victor's wreath:
- For well thou knowest that wave and storm oppress us.'

And so I count your gift to be a token of good-fortune; for I am in no less stress than Creon, and would fain carry off the victory over your lovers.

INTRODUCTION TO ERYXIAS.

Eryxias. Introduction.

Much cannot be said in praise of the style or conception of the Eryxias. It is frequently obscure; like the exercise of a student, it is full of small imitations of Plato:—Phaeax returning from an expedition to Sicily (cp. Socrates in the Charmides from the army at Potidaea), the figure of the game at draughts, 395 B, borrowed from Rep. vi. 487, etc. It has also in many passages the ring of sophistry. On the other hand, the rather unhandsome treatment which is exhibited towards Prodicus is quite unlike the urbanity of Plato.

Yet there are some points in the argument which are deserving of attention. (1) That wealth depends upon the need of it or demand for it, is the first anticipation in an abstract form of one of the great principles of modern political economy, and the nearest approach to it to be found in an ancient writer. (2) The resolution of wealth into its simplest implements going on to infinity is a subtle and refined thought. (3) That wealth is relative to circumstances is a sound conception. (4) That the arts and sciences which receive payment are likewise to be comprehended under the notion of wealth, also touches a question of modern political economy. (5) The distinction of *post hoc* and *propter hoc,* often lost sight of in modern as well as in ancient times. These metaphysical conceptions and distinctions show considerable power of thought in the writer, whatever we may think of his merits as an imitator of Plato.

ERYXIAS.

PERSONS OF THE DIALOGUE.

Socrates.

Eryxias.

Erasistratus.

Critias.

Scene:—The portico of a temple of Zeus.

*Eryxias.*Socrates, Erasistratus.

392It happened by chance that Eryxias the Steirian was walking with me in the Portico of Zeus the Deliverer, when there came up to us Critias and Erasistratus, the latter the son of Phaeax, who was the nephew of Erasistratus. Now Erasistratus had just arrived from Sicily and that part of the world. As they approached, he said, Hail, Socrates!

Soc.

The same to you, I said; have you any good news from Sicily to tell us?

Eras.

Most excellent. But if you please, let us first sit down; for I am tired with my yesterday's journey from Megara.

Soc.

Gladly, if that is your desire.

Eras.

The troublesome Sicilians.Socrates, Erasistratus.

What would you wish to hear first? he said. What the Sicilians are doing, or how they are disposed towards our city? To my mind, they are very like wasps: so long as you only cause them a little annoyance they are quite unmanageable; you must destroy their nests if you wish to get the better of them. And in a similar way, the Syracusans, unless we set to work in earnest, and go against them with a great expedition, will never submit to our rule. The petty injuries which we at present inflict merely irritate them enough to make them utterly intractable. And now they have sent ambassadors to Athens, and intend, I suspect, to play us some trick.—While we were talking, the Syracusan envoys chanced to go by, and Erasistratus, pointing to one of them, said to me, That, Socrates, is the richest man in all Italy and Sicily. For who has larger estates or more land at his disposal to cultivate if he please? And they are of a quality, too, finer than any other land in Hellas. Moreover, he has all the things which go to make up wealth, slaves and horses innumerable, gold and silver without end.

I saw that he was inclined to expatiate on the riches of the man; so I asked him, Well, Erasistratus, and what sort of character does he bear in Sicily?

Eras.

The wicked millionaire.

He is esteemed to be, and really is, the wickedest of all the Sicilians and Italians, and even more wicked than he is rich; indeed, if you were to ask any Sicilian whom he thought to be the worst and the richest of mankind, you would never hear any one else named.

I reflected that we were speaking, not of trivial matters, but about wealth and virtue, which are deemed to be of the greatest moment, and I asked Erasistratus whom he considered the wealthier,—he who was the possessor of a talent of silver or he who had a field worth two talents?

Eras.

The owner of the field.

Soc.

And on the same principle he who had robes and bedding and such things which are of greater value to him than to a stranger would be richer than the stranger?

Eras.

True.

Soc.

And if any one gave you a choice, which of these would you prefer?

Eras.

That which was most valuable.

Soc.

Wealth consists of things which are valuable.

In which way do you think you would be the richer?

Eras.

By choosing as I said.

Soc.

And he appears to you to be the richest who has goods of the greatest value?

Eras.

He does.

Soc.

Socrates, Erasistratus, Eryxias.

And are not the healthy richer than the sick, since health is a possession more valuable than riches to the sick? Surely there is no one who would not prefer to be poor and well, rather than to have all the King of Persia's wealth and to be ill. And this proves that men set health above wealth, else they would never choose the one in preference to the other.

Eras.

True.

Soc.

And if anything appeared to be more valuable than health, he would be the richest who possessed it?

Eras.

He would.

Soc.

Suppose that some one came to us at this moment and were to ask, Well, Socrates and Eryxias and Erasistratus, can you tell me what is of the greatest value to men? Is it not that of which the possession will best enable a man to advise how his own and his friends' affairs should be administered?—What will be our reply?

Eras.

I should say, Socrates, that happiness was the most precious of human possessions.

Soc.

Not a bad answer. But do we not deem those men who are most prosperous to be the happiest?

Eras.

That is my opinion.

Soc.

And are they not most prosperous who commit the fewest errors in respect either of themselves or of other men?

Eras.

Certainly.

Soc.

And they who know what is evil and what is good; what should be done and what should be left undone;—these 394behave the most wisely and make the fewest mistakes?

Erasistratus agreed to this.

Soc.

Then the wisest and those who do best and the most fortunate and the richest would appear to be all one and the same, if wisdom is really the most valuable of our possessions?

Of what use would wisdom be, if a man had not the necessaries of life?

Yes, said Eryxias, interposing, but what use would it be if a man had the wisdom of Nestor and wanted the necessaries of life, food and drink and clothes and the like? Where would be the advantage of wisdom then? Or how could he be the richest of men who might even have to go begging, because he had not wherewithal to live?

Socrates, Eryxias.

I thought that what Eryxias was saying had some weight, and I replied, Would the wise man really suffer in this way, if he were so ill-provided; whereas if he had the house of Polytion, and the house were full of gold and silver, he would lack nothing?

Eryx.

Yes; for then he might dispose of his property and obtain in exchange what he needed, or he might sell it for money with which he could supply his wants and in a moment procure abundance of everything.

Soc.

The wisdom of Nestor better and even more saleable than the house of Polytion. And in the arts is not wisdom better than riches?

True, if he could find some one who preferred such a house to the wisdom of Nestor. But if there are persons who set great store by wisdom like Nestor's and the advantages accruing from it, to sell these, if he were so disposed, would be easier still. Or is a house a most useful and necessary possession, and does it make a great difference in the comfort of life to have a mansion like Polytion's instead of living in a shabby little cottage, whereas wisdom is of small use and it is of no importance whether a man is wise or ignorant about the highest matters? Or is wisdom despised of men and can find no buyers, although cypress wood and marble of Pentelicus are eagerly bought by numerous purchasers? Surely the prudent pilot or the skilful physician, or the artist of any kind who is proficient in his art, is more worth than the things which are especially reckoned among riches; and he who can advise well and prudently for himself and others is able also to sell the product of his art, if he so desire.

Eryxias looked askance, as if he had received some unfair 395treatment, and said, I believe, Socrates, that if you were forced to speak the truth, you would declare that you were richer than Callias the son of Hipponicus. And yet, although you claimed to be wiser about things of real importance, you would not any the more be richer than he.

Eryxias is supposed to reply that arguments can prove anything and convince no one.Socrates, Eryxias, Critias.

I dare say, Eryxias, I said, that you may regard these arguments of ours as a kind of game; you think that they have no relation to facts, but are like the pieces in the game of draughts which the player can move in such a way that his opponents are unable to make any countermove . And perhaps, too, as regards riches you are of opinion that while facts remain the same, there are arguments, no matter whether true or false, which enable the user of them to prove that the wisest and the richest are one and the same, although he is in the wrong and his opponents are in the right. There would be nothing strange in this; it would be as if two persons were to dispute about letters, one declaring that the word Socrates began with an S, the other that it began with an A, and the latter could gain the victory over the former.

Eryxias disclaims the answer which is attributed to him.

Eryxias glanced at the audience, laughing and blushing at once, as if he had had nothing to do with what had just been said, and replied,—No, indeed, Socrates, I never supposed that our arguments should be of a kind which would never convince any one of those here present or be of advantage to them. For what man of sense could ever be persuaded that the wisest and the richest are the same? The truth is that we are discussing the subject of riches, and my notion is that we should argue respecting the honest and dishonest means of acquiring them, and, generally, whether they are a good thing or a bad.

The argument is renewed from a fresh point of view. Eryxias declares riches to be a good; Critias maintains that they are sometimes an evil.

Very good, I said, and I am obliged to you for the hint: in future we will be more careful. But why do not you yourself, as you introduced the argument, and do not think that the former discussion touched the point at issue, tell us whether you consider riches to be a good or an evil?

I am of opinion, he said, that they are a good. He was about to add something more, when Critias interrupted him:—Do you really suppose so, Eryxias?

Certainly, replied Eryxias; I should be mad if I did not: and I do not fancy that you would find any one else of a contrary opinion.

And I, retorted Critias, should say that there is no one whom I could not compel to admit that riches are bad for some men. But surely, if they were a good, they could not appear bad for any one?

Socrates encourages the two disputants to follow up the argument.

Here I interposed and said to them: If you two were having an argument about equitation and what was the best way of riding, supposing that I knew the art myself, I should try to bring you to an agreement. For I should be ashamed if I were present and did not do what I could to prevent your difference. And I should do the same if you were quarrelling about any other art and were likely, unless you agreed on the point in dispute, to part as enemies instead of as friends. But now, when we are contending about a thing of which the usefulness continues during the whole of life, and it makes an enormous difference whether we are to regard it as beneficial or not,—a thing, too, which is esteemed of the highest importance by the Hellenes:— (for parents, as soon as their children are, as they think, come to years of discretion, urge them to consider how wealth may be acquired, since by riches the value of a man is judged):—When, I say, we are thus in earnest, and you, who agree in other respects, fall to disputing about a matter of such moment, that is, about wealth, and not merely whether it is black or white, light or heavy, but whether it is a good or an evil, whereby, although you are now the dearest of friends and kinsmen, the most bitter hatred may arise betwixt you, I must hinder your dissension to the best of my power. If I could, I would tell you the truth, and so put an end to the dispute; but as I cannot do this, and each of you supposes that you can bring the other to an agreement, I am prepared, as far as my capacity admits, to help you in solving the question. Please, therefore, Critias, try to make us accept the doctrines which you yourself entertain.

Crit.

I should like to follow up the argument, and will ask Eryxias whether he thinks that there are just and unjust men?

Eryx.

Most decidedly.

Crit.

And does injustice seem to you an evil or a good?

Eryx.

An evil.

Crit.

Do you consider that he who bribes his neighbour's wife and commits adultery with her, acts justly or unjustly, and this although both the state and the laws forbid?

Eryx.

Unjustly.

Crit.

Wealth may furnish the opportunity of crime.

And if the wicked man has wealth and is willing to 39/spend it, he will carry out his evil purposes? whereas he who is short of means cannot do what he fain would, and therefore does not sin? In such a case, surely, it is better that a person should not be wealthy, if his poverty prevents the accomplishment of his desires, and his desires are evil? Or, again, should you call sickness a good or an evil?

Eryx.

An evil.

Crit.

Well, and do you think that some men are intemperate?

Eryx.

Yes.

Crit.

Socrates, Eryxias, Critias, Erasistratus.

Then, if it is better for his health that the intemperate man should refrain from meat and drink and other pleasant things, but he cannot owing to his intemperance, will it not also be better that he should be too poor to gratify his lust rather than that he should have a superabundance of means? For thus he will not be able to sin, although he desire never so much.

Eryxias takes offence at Critias, whose argument, as Socrates pretends, is only the repetition of one which had been used by Prodicus of Ceos on the day before,

Critias appeared to be arguing so admirably that Eryxias, if he had not been ashamed of the bystanders, would probably have got up and struck him. For he thought that he had been robbed of a great possession when it became obvious to him that he had been wrong in his former opinion about wealth. I observed his vexation, and feared that they would proceed to abuse and quarrelling: so I said,—I heard that very argument used in the Lyceum yesterday by a wise man, Prodicus of Ceos; but the audience thought that he was talking mere nonsense, and no one could be persuaded that he was speaking the truth. And when at last a certain talkative young gentleman came in, and, taking his seat, began to laugh and jeer at Prodicus, tormenting him and demanding an explanation of his argument, he gained the ear of the audience far more than Prodicus.

Can you repeat the discourse to us? said Erasistratus.

Soc.

If I can only remember it, I will. The youth began by asking Prodicus, In what way did he think that riches were a good and in what an evil? Prodicus answered, as you did just now, that they were a good to good men and to those who knew in what way they should be employed, while to the bad and the ignorant they were an evil. The same is true, he went on to say, of all other things; men make them to be what they are themselves. The saying of Archilochus is true:—

'Men's thoughts correspond to the things which they meet with.'

and had been refuted by an impertinent youth.Socrates.

398Well, then, replied the youth, if any one makes me wise in that wisdom whereby good men become wise, he must also make everything else good to me. Not that he concerns himself at all with these other things, but he has converted my ignorance into wisdom. If, for example, a person teach me grammar or music, he will at the same time teach me all that relates to grammar or music, and so when he makes me good, he makes things good to me.

Prodicus did not altogether agree: still he consented to what was said.

And do you think, said the youth, that doing good things is like building a house,—the work of human agency; or do things remain what they were at first, good or bad, for all time?

Prodicus began to suspect, I fancy, the direction which the argument was likely to take, and did not wish to be put down by a mere stripling before all those present:—(if they two had been alone, he would not have minded):—so he answered, cleverly enough: I think that doing good things is a work of human agency.

And is virtue in your opinion, Prodicus, innate or acquired by instruction?

The latter, said Prodicus.

Then you would consider him a simpleton who supposed that he could obtain by praying to the Gods the knowledge of grammar or music or any other art, which he must either learn from another or find out for himself?

Prodicus agreed to this also.

And when you pray to the Gods that you may do well and receive good, you mean by your prayer nothing else than that you desire to become good and wise:—if, at least, things are good to the good and wise and evil to the evil. But in that case, if virtue is acquired by instruction, it would appear that you only pray to be taught what you do not know.

Hereupon I said to Prodicus that it was no misfortune to him if he had been proved to be in error in supposing that the Gods immediately granted to us whatever we asked:—if, I added, whenever you go up to the Acropolis you earnestly entreat the Gods to grant you good things, although you know not whether they can yield your request, it is as though you went to the doors of the grammarian and begged him, although you had never made a study of the art, to give you a knowledge of grammar which would enable you forthwith to do the business of a grammarian.

Socrates, Erasistratus.Prodicus is desired to leave the gymnasium because he is disturbing the minds of youth.

While I was speaking, Prodicus was preparing to retaliate 399 upon his youthful assailant, intending to employ the argument of which you have just made use; for he was annoyed to have it supposed that he offered a vain prayer to the Gods. But the master of the gymnasium came to him and begged him to leave because he was teaching the youths doctrines which were unsuited to them, and therefore bad for them.

I have told you this because I want you to understand how men are circumstanced in regard to philosophy. Had Prodicus been present and said what you have said, the audience would have thought him raving, and he would have been ejected from the gymnasium. But you have argued so excellently well that you have not only persuaded your hearers, but have brought your opponent to an agreement. For just as in the law courts, if two witnesses testify to the same fact, one of whom seems to be an honest fellow and the other a rogue, the testimony of the rogue often has the contrary effect on the judges' minds to what he intended, while the same evidence if given by the honest man at once strikes them as perfectly true. And probably the audience have something of the same feeling about yourself and Prodicus; they think him a Sophist and a braggart, and regard you as a gentleman of courtesy and worth. For they do not pay attention to the argument so much as to the character of the speaker.

Socrates jesting professes to be in earnest.

But truly, Socrates, said Erasistratus, though you may be joking, Critias does seem to me to be saying something which is of weight.

Soc.

I am in profound earnest, I assure you. But why, as you have begun your argument so prettily, do you not go on with the rest? There is still something lacking, now you have agreed that [wealth] is a good to some and an evil to others. It remains to enquire what constitutes wealth; for unless you know this, you cannot possibly come to an understanding as to whether it is a good or an evil. I am ready to assist you in the enquiry to the utmost of my power: but first let him who affirms that riches are a good, tell us what, in his opinion, is wealth.

Eras.

Indeed, Socrates, I have no notion about wealth beyond that which men commonly have. I suppose that wealth is a quantity of money; and this, I imagine, would also be Critias' definition.

Soc.

What is money? It is observed that different kinds of money pass current in different countries,—Carthage, Lacedaemon, Ethiopia, Scythia.

Then now we have to consider, What is money? Or else later on we shall be found to differ about the question. For instance, the Carthaginians use money of this sort. Something which is about the size of a stater is tied up in a 400small piece of leather: what it is, no one knows but the makers. A seal is next set upon the leather, which then passes into circulation, and he who has the largest number of such pieces is esteemed the richest and best off. And yet if any one among us had a mass of such coins he would be no wealthier than if he had so many pebbles from the mountain. At Lacedaemon, again, they use iron by weight which has been rendered useless: and he who has the greatest mass of such iron is thought to be the richest, although elsewhere it has no value. In Ethiopia engraved stones are employed, of which a Lacedaemonian could make no use. Once more, among the Nomad Scythians a man who owned the house of Polytion would not be thought richer than one who possessed Mount Lycabettus among ourselves. And clearly those things cannot all be regarded as possessions; for in some cases the possessors would appear none the richer thereby: but, as I was saying, some one of them is thought in one place to be money, and the possessors of it are the wealthy, whereas in some other place it is not money, and the ownership of it does not confer wealth; just as the standard of morals varies, and what is honourable to some men is dishonourable to others. And if we wish to enquire why a house is valuable to us but not to the Scythians, or why the Carthaginians value leather which is worthless to us, or the Lacedaemonians find wealth in iron and we do not, can we not get an answer in some such way as this: Would an Athenian, who had a thousand talents weight of the stones which lie about in the Agora and which we do not employ for any purpose, be thought to be any the richer?

Eras.

He certainly would not appear so to me.

Soc.

But if he possessed a thousand talents weight of some precious stone, we should say that he was very rich?

Eras.

Of course.

Soc.

The reason is that the one is useless and the other useful?

Eras.

Yes.

Soc.

And in the same way among the Scythians a house has no value because they have no use for a house, nor would a Scythian set so much store on the finest house in the world as on a leather coat, because he could use the one and not the other. Or again, the Carthaginian coinage is not wealth in our eyes, for we could not employ it, as we can silver, to procure what we need, and therefore it is of no use to us.

Eras.

True.

Soc.

Wealth is useful, but other things are useful besides wealth.

What is useful to us, then, is wealth, and what is useless to us is not wealth?

But how do you mean, Socrates? said Eryxias, interrupting. 401Do we not employ in our intercourse with one another speech and violence (?) and various other things? These are useful and yet they are not wealth.

Soc.

Clearly we have not yet answered the question, What is wealth? That wealth must be useful, to be wealth at all,—thus much is acknowledged by every one. But what particular thing is wealth, if not all things? Let us pursue the argument in another way; and then we may perhaps find what we are seeking. What is the use of wealth, and for what purpose has the possession of riches been invented,—in the sense, I mean, in which drugs have been discovered for the cure of disease? Perhaps in this way we may throw some light on the question. It appears to be clear that whatever constitutes wealth must be useful, and that wealth is one class of useful things; and now we have to enquire, What is the use of those useful things which constitute wealth? For all things probably may be said to be useful which we use in production, just as all things which have life are animals, but there is a special kind of animal which we call 'man.' Now if any one were to ask us, What is that of which, if we were rid, we should not want medicine and the instruments of medicine, we might reply that this would be the case if disease were absent from our bodies and either never came to them at all or went away again as soon as it appeared; and we may therefore conclude that medicine is the science which is useful for getting rid of disease. But if we are further asked, What is that from which, if we were free, we should have no need of wealth? can we give an answer? If we have none, suppose that we restate the question thus:—If a man could live without food or drink, and yet suffer neither hunger nor thirst, would he want either money or anything else in order to supply his needs?

Eryx.

He would not.

Soc.

If the body had no wants or feelings there would be no need of money.

And does not this apply in other cases? If we did not want for the service of the body the things of which we now stand in need, and heat and cold and the other bodily sensations were unperceived by us, there would be no use in this so-called wealth, if no one, that is, had any necessity for those things which now make us wish for wealth in order that we may satisfy the desires and needs of the body in respect of our various wants. And therefore if the possession of wealth is useful in ministering to our bodily wants, and bodily wants were unknown to us, we should not need wealth, and possibly there would be no such thing as wealth.

Eryx.

Clearly not.

Soc.

Then our conclusion is, as would appear, that wealth is what is useful to this end?

Eryxias once more gave his assent, but the small argument considerably troubled him.

Soc.

And what is your opinion about another question:—Would 402you say that the same thing can be at one time useful and at another useless for the production of the same result?

Eryx.

I cannot say more than that if we require the same thing to produce the same result, then it seems to me to be useful; if not, not.

Soc.

Then if without the aid of fire we could make a brazen statue, we should not want fire for that purpose; and if we did not want it, it would be useless to us? And the argument applies equally in other cases.

Eryx.

Clearly.

Soc.

And therefore conditions which are not required for the existence of a thing are not useful for the production of it?

Eryx.

Of course not.

Soc.

And if without gold or silver or anything else which we do not use directly for the body in the way that we do food and drink and bedding and houses,—if without these we could satisfy the wants of the body, they would be of no use to us for that purpose?

Eryx.

They would not.

Soc.

They would no longer be regarded as wealth, because they are useless, whereas that would be wealth which enabled us to obtain what was useful to us?

Eryx.

O Socrates, you will never be able to persuade me that gold and silver and similar things are not wealth. But I am very strongly of opinion that things which are useless to us are not wealth, and that the money which is useful for this purpose is of the greatest use; not that these things are not useful towards life, if by them we can procure wealth.

Soc.

The arts too are wealth, for by them the needs of life are satisfied.

And how would you answer another question? There are persons, are there not, who teach music and grammar and other arts for pay, and thus procure those things of which they stand in need?

Eryx.

There are.

Soc.

And these men by the arts which they profess, and in exchange for them, obtain the necessities of life just as we do by means of gold and silver?

Eryx.

True.

Soc.

Then if they procure by this means what they want for the purposes of life, that art will be useful towards life? For do we not say that silver is useful because it enables us to supply our bodily needs?

Eryx.

We do.

Soc.

Then if these arts are reckoned among things useful, the arts are wealth for the same reason as gold and silver are, for, clearly, the possession of them gives wealth. Yet a little while ago we found it difficult to accept the argument which proved that the wisest are the wealthiest. But now there seems no escape from this conclusion. Suppose that we are asked, 'Is a horse useful to everybody?' will not our reply be, 'No, but only to those who know how to use a horse?'

Eryx.

Certainly.

Soc.

And so, too, physic is not useful to every one, but only to him who knows how to use it?

Eryx.

Socrates, Eryxias, Critias.

True.

Soc.

And the same is the case with everything else?

Eryx.

Yes.

Soc.

Then gold and silver and all the other elements which are supposed to make up wealth are only useful to the person who knows how to use them?

Eryx.

Exactly.

Soc.

And were we not saying before that it was the business of a good man and a gentleman to know where and how anything should be used?

Eryx.

Yes.

Soc.

The good only know how to use things.

The good and gentle, therefore, will alone have profit from these things, supposing at least that they know how to use them. But if so, to them only will they seem to be wealth. It appears, however, that where a person is ignorant of riding, and has horses which are useless to him, if some one teaches him that art, he makes him also richer, for what was before useless has now become useful to him, and in giving him knowledge he has also conferred riches upon him.

Eryx.

That is the case.

Soc.

Yet I dare be sworn that Critias will not be moved a whit by the argument.

Crit.

No, by heaven, I should be a madman if I were. But why do you not finish the argument which proves that gold and silver and other things which seem to be wealth are not real wealth? For I have been exceedingly delighted to hear the discourses which you have just been holding.

Soc.

My argument, Critias (I said), appears to have given you the same kind of pleasure which you might have derived from some rhapsode's recitation of Homer; for you do not believe a word of what has been said. But come now, give me an answer to this question. Are not certain things useful to the builder when he is building a house?

Crit.

They are.

Soc.

Socrates, Critias.

And would you say that those things are useful which are employed in house building,—stones and bricks and beams and the like, and also the instruments with which the builder built the house, the beams and stones which they provided, and again the instruments by which these were obtained?

Crit.

It seems to me that they are all useful for building.

Soc.

And is it not true of every art, that not only the materials but the instruments by which we procure them and without which the work could not go on, are useful for that art?

Crit.

Certainly.

Soc.

And further, the instruments by which the instruments 404are procured, and so on, going back from stage to stage *ad infinitum,*—are not all these, in your opinion, necessary in order to carry out the work?

Crit.

We may fairly suppose such to be the case.

Soc.

A sophism. Gold and silver would be useless if they were not needed to obtain food; and things cannot be at one time useless, at another time useful, in the same actions.

And if a man has food and drink and clothes and the other things which are useful to the body, would he need gold or silver or any other means by which he could procure that which he now has?

Crit.

I do not think so.

Soc.

Then you consider that a man never wants any of these things for the use of the body?

Crit.

Certainly not.

Soc.

And if they appear useless to this end, ought they not always to appear useless? For we have already laid down the principle that things cannot be at one time useful and at another time not, in the same process.

Crit.

But in that respect your argument and mine are the same. For you maintain if they are useful to a certain end, they can never become useless; whereas I say that in order to accomplish some results bad things are needed, and good for others.

Soc.

But can a bad thing be used to carry out a good purpose?

Crit.

I should say not.

Soc.

And we call those actions good which a man does for the sake of virtue?

Crit.

Yes.

Soc.

But can a man learn any kind of knowledge which is imparted by word of mouth if he is wholly deprived of the sense of hearing?

Crit.

Certainly not, I think.

Soc.

And will not hearing be useful for virtue, if virtue is taught by hearing and we use the sense of hearing in giving instruction?

Crit.

Yes.

Soc.

There are indirect means towards ends.

And since medicine frees the sick man from his disease, that art too may sometimes appear useful in the acquisition of virtue, e. g. when hearing is procured by the aid of medicine.

Crit.

Very likely.

Soc.

But if, again, we obtain by wealth the aid of medicine, shall we not regard wealth as useful for virtue?

Crit.

True.

Soc.

And also the instruments by which wealth is procured?

Crit.

Certainly.

Soc.

Wealth may be gained discreditably, but spent in the acquisition of virtue.

Then you think that a man may gain wealth by bad and disgraceful means, and, having obtained the aid of medicine which enables him to acquire the power of hearing, may use that very faculty for the acquisition of virtue?

Crit.

Yes, I do.

Soc.

But can that which is evil be useful for virtue?

Crit.

No.

Soc.

It is not therefore necessary that the means by which we obtain what is useful for a certain object should always be useful for the same object: for it seems that bad actions may sometimes serve good purposes? The matter will be still plainer if we look at it in this way:—If things are useful towards the several ends for which they exist, which ends would not come into existence without them, how would you regard them? Can ignorance, for instance, be useful for knowledge, or disease for health, or vice for virtue?

Crit.

Never.

Soc.

And yet we have already agreed—have we not?—that there can be no knowledge where there has not previously been ignorance, nor health where there has not been disease, nor virtue where there has not been vice?

Crit.

Difference between causes and antecedents.

I think that we have.

Soc.

But then it would seem that the antecedents without which a thing cannot exist are not necessarily useful to it. Otherwise ignorance would appear useful for knowledge, disease for health, and vice for virtue.

Critias still showed great reluctance to accept any argument which went to prove that all these things were useless. I saw that it was as difficult to persuade him as (according to the proverb) it is to boil a stone, so I said: Let us bid 'good-bye' to the discussion, since we cannot agree whether these things are useful and a part of wealth or not. But what shall we say to another question: Which is the happier and better man,—he who requires the greatest quantity of necessaries for body and diet, or he who requires only the fewest and least? The answer will perhaps become more obvious if we suppose some one, comparing the man himself at different times, to consider whether his condition is better when he is sick or when he is well?

Crit.

That is not a question which needs much consideration.

Soc.

Health is a better condition than disease; and it needs less.

Probably, I said, every one can understand that health is a better condition than disease. But when have we the greatest and the most various needs, when we are sick or when we are well?

Crit.

When we are sick.

Soc.

And when we are in the worst state we have the greatest and most especial need and desire of bodily pleasures?

Crit.

True.

Soc.

So he is best off who has fewest desires.

And seeing that a man is best off when he is least in need of such things, does not the same reasoning apply to the case of any two persons, of whom one has many and great wants and desires, and the other few and moderate? For instance, some men are gamblers, some drunkards, and some gluttons: and gambling and the love of drink and greediness are all desires?

Crit.

Certainly.

Soc.

But desires are only the lack of something: and those who have the greatest desires are in a worse condition than those who have none or very slight ones?

Crit.

406Certainly I consider that those who have such wants are bad, and that the greater their wants the worse they are.

Soc.

And do we think it possible that a thing should be useful for a purpose unless we have need of it for that purpose?

Crit.

No.

Soc.

Then if these things are useful for supplying the needs of the body, we must want them for that purpose?

Crit.

That is my opinion.

Soc.

And he to whom the greatest number of things are useful for his purpose, will also want the greatest number of means of accomplishing it, supposing that we necessarily feel the want of all useful things?

Crit.

It seems so.

Soc.

The argument proves then that he who has great riches has likewise need of many things for the supply of the wants of the body; for wealth appears useful towards that end. And the richest must be in the worst condition, since they seem to be most in want of such things.

The Dialogues of Plato

The Dialogues of Plato

Made in the USA
San Bernardino, CA
23 January 2014